FOURTH EDITION

URBAN SOCIOLOGY

Images and Structure

William G. Flanagan
Coe College

Allyn and Bacon
Boston • London • Toronto • Sydney • Tokyo • Singapore

Series Editor: Jeff Lasser
Editor in Chief, Social Sciences: Karen Hanson
Editorial Assistant: Andrea Christie
Marketing Manager: Judeth Hall
Editorial-Production Administrator: Annette Joseph
Editorial-Production Service: Holly Crawford
Composition Buyer: Linda Cox
Electronic Composition: Graphic World Inc.
Manufacturing Buyer: Suzanne Lareau
Cover Administrator: Kristina Mose-Libon
Cover Designer: Joel Gendron

Copyright © 2002, 1999, 1995, 1990 by Allyn & Bacon
A Pearson Education Company
75 Arlington St., Ste. 300
Boston, MA 02116

Internet: www.ablongman.com

Between the time Website information is gathered and then published, it is not unusual for some sites to have closed. Also, the transcription of URLs can result in unintended typographical errors. The publisher would appreciate notification where these occur so that they may be corrected in subsequent editions. Thank you.

Library of Congress Cataloging-in-Publication Data

Flanagan, William G.
    Urban sociology : images and structure / William G. Flanagan.—4th ed.
       p. cm.
    Includes bibliographical references and index.
    ISBN 0-205-33532-2
      1. Sociology, Urban. 2. Sociology, Urban—United States. I. Title.

HT151.F53 2001
307.76—dc21   2001022108

Printed in the United States of America

10 9 8 7 6 5 4 3 2   06 05 04 03 02

Photo Credits: p. 67 by Amelia Ann Cranson; p. 192 by Allen P. Fisher; pp. 89, 325, 355, and 366 by Greg Garbers; pp. 5, 9, and 26 by Lynda L. Laughlin; pp. 95, 269, and 353 by Scott Mathers; pp. 20, 36, 44, 80, 114, 169, 236, 237, 344, and 348 by Elizabeth Rose; p. 3 by Christopher Smith; and pp. 22, 58, and 111 by Nelson Trombley.

See page 427 for a continuation of the copyright page.

CONTENTS

PREFACE TO THE FOURTH EDITION

If your subject matter is the city, it is not difficult to find plenty to write about in each new edition of your textbook. Texts are tools of the teacher's trade, easier to do the job with than without. But after you have used a text for a few years, some of the things that are in it begin to bother you, as well as some of what has been left out. The situation is no different if the text is your own, and I am always happy to have another chance to work with the editorial staff at Allyn and Bacon to see if we can't make the book more useful to faculty and students. Once again, I have not changed the original conceptual framework of *Urban Sociology: Images and Structure*. I still focus on that which is essentially *of* the city, shaped by it, rather than simply listing the things that happen in it—something that always bothered me about some other urban sociology texts and what originally moved me to write this one.

There are three major changes in this edition of the text. But first let me restate the emphasis that emerged with the Third Edition and remains a key feature of the Fourth Edition. This edition continues the effort to assess the intersection of the forces of globalization and the social importance of local space, as represented by cities and spatial communities.

Just as the city provided theorists trying to predict the social future at the close of the nineteenth century with a major theme, political, economic, and cultural globalization provides the major puzzle today for those who are trying to understand what the new spatial dimensions of society will be in the twenty-first century. Despite this shift to a wider analytic arena, the broad outlines of issues and debates in urban sociology remain in place. An introduction to the field of urban sociology can no more dispense with the classical themes of Durkheim, Marx, and Weber now than in the past. In the time of Robert Park, the city was the great experimental laboratory; in the present era, the single worldwide web of resources and market opportunities is the great experimental context. In Durkheim's time, at the turn of the last century, the question was, What does the city portend for the future? Today the question is, What does the economically restructured future hold for the cities of tomorrow? Yet there is a danger in overemphasizing the potential that the current economic and communications revolutions have for obliterating the importance of limited spatial arenas like cities. People still live lives confined physically to a particular locality; the consequences of shifting global enterprises are still experienced locally in the creation or loss of opportunity; and the local impact of global change is multiplied according to the number of people who occupy that space. The connection between urban conditions and the long waves of worldwide change is not something new, but there is a new immediacy to their mutual influence that must be addressed by a text treating the topic of urban sociology at this time. Here I have tried to establish a balance between my respect for the urban traditions in sociology and the urgency of the new agenda presented by an urban future that has already arrived—a balance between old questions of locality and new global concerns. It is my belief that a dynamic urban sociology continues to have a vital role to play within the general field of sociology, as it represents the subdiscipline concerned with all forms of spatial phenomena. This is the sociology that talks about what it means to connect the dots on a global field, as well as engaging in the old-fashioned questions of how cities make people think, feel, and treat each other.

Those familiar with this text will note three major changes. There is a new first chapter, "An Invitation to Urban Studies." While urban histories and prehistories, the subject matters of the first chapter in previous editions, are an important part of the study of urban sociology, they may lack intuitive appeal for students. The new Chapter 1 introduces a new dimension in this text, a more subjective, constructionist dimension, which I have found interests students and at the same time illustrates the fact that urban environments have a real impact on the way people organize and experience their lives. Instructors will recognize the importance of incorporating the work of Lofland, Lynch, Zukin, and others here. A second change is the refocusing of the policy discussion and the collapsing of what were Chapters 9 and 10 in earlier editions into a single chapter, Chapter 10, in this edition. While I believe policy and planning are very important concerns for urban sociologists, I believe that emphasizing the issue of housing provides a more vigorous topical focus that will sustain interest in this area. Finally, a third substantial change is the introduction of textual "boxes" that break up the reading and provide complementary foci for the ongoing discussion. These are designed to connect with students' interests and to provoke recognition of the practical significance of the ideas discussed in the text. They may help generate discussion.

An Instructor's Manual is available to faculty considering the text for adoption. The IM contains an outline of chapter objectives, suggested supplemental reading, objective and essay questions, suggestions for discussion, and video and other resources. I hope you will find it useful.

I would be very happy to hear from readers. Please send comments or suggestions to me at wflanaga@coe.edu.

I want to extend my thanks to Karen Hanson, Sarah Kelbaugh, Jeff Lasser, and Tom Jefferies at Allyn and Bacon, for the chance to revise once again my effort to say what urban sociology is. Thanks again to students and colleagues who have commented on earlier editions. This edition has benefited from the comments of various reviewers. I would like to thank Victor Agadjanian, Arizona State University; Dick De Lung, Wayland Baptist University; and Robert E.

Parker, University of Nevada. I would also like to thank Josef Gugler and Lynda Laughlin for reading and commenting on the text, and Dave Berri for his helpful suggestions. Sonya Luse, Lori Matthews, and Amanda Moutrie assisted with the research. I am very grateful to Randall Roeder, Susan Wagner-Hecht, and Betty Rogers of Coe College Library for rescuing me with last minute updated data. Thanks also to Annette Joseph for her production assistance at Allyn and Bacon and to Holly Crawford for copyediting and shepherding the book through production. I would also like to acknowledge the Stead Family who have supported my research of the last three years through their generous support of Coe College.

I want especially to thank my wife, Elizabeth Rose, who has provided cheerful support and encouragement through four editions, giving up at least that many summers, and putting up with a husband who becomes a pretty one-dimensional appendage of his textbook. Liz has been invaluable in helping me to work out ideas, has been an unflinching critic of my writing, has an unerring instinct for detecting unfinished thinking, and has provided many creative ideas for this and other projects. She is a good friend, fellow traveler, exacting photographer, and adventurer. I appreciate her patience. Together we are proving that a practicing psychologist and an academic sociologist *can* live together in harmony.

PREFACE TO THE FIRST EDITION

The purpose of this book is to establish a framework for the study of urban sociology. The time has come for those who practice urban sociology to identify what sets this subfield of sociology apart from other subfields. How does it make sense, in advanced industrial societies where the vast majority of the population lives in cities and their immediate surroundings, to continue to pursue a separate area of investigation labeled "urban sociology"? Hasn't the study of life in the urban landscape, for the most part, simply become the study of society?

This book deals systematically with the question of how we may establish the proper domain of urban sociology. It gives explicit recognition to the fact that there are currently two distinct orientations among urban sociologists; in fact, one could argue that there are two distinct urban sociologies.

The heirs of Tönnies and Durkheim, of Weber and Simmel, and of Park and Wirth treat the urban arena as an independent variable, *sui generis*. This is the orientation that has been labeled the "urban tradition" here. Its practitioners are concerned with the phenomena that comprise *urbanism*, a characteristically urban way of thinking, relating, and behaving. They are *culturalists* in that they see the city giving rise to an analytically distinguishable way of life.

Largely independent of this tradition, a vigorous *political economy* of cities has emerged, which argues that urban places are the manifestation of wider patterns of power and wealth. This *structuralist* argument holds that the ultimate causes of the patterns of thought, behavior, and organization that are characteristic of urban places lie beyond the urban environment. The cities themselves are not the cause: They are merely secondary causal factors. Events that take place in the urban arena require a perspective that is international in scope, that extends its analysis to worldwide issues of policy and economic trends.

In reality, the culturalist and structuralist orientations vary a great deal within themselves. Recently a modest mutual exploration of ideas between the two camps has begun, especially as a few ecologists have begun to consider the possibility of incorporating elements of political economic thought in their work. Major obstacles remain, however, to inhibit any attempt to synthesize the disparate approaches. In this book the areas of disagreement among culturalists and structuralists, ecologists and neo-Marxists, and modernization and dependency theorists are spelled out systematically. It is an effort to update textbook urban sociology, which has lagged behind the developments that have taken place in the field in the past fifteen years. I have tried to accomplish this in a language and style that is accessible to the average reader. There is no effort here to oversimplify the issues that are being debated today by urban scientists. In fact, every effort has been made to clearly explain these debates.

I have tried to do justice to both the culturalist and the structuralist arguments in this book. It will be apparent to the professional reader and the discerning student that I am persuaded by the structuralist point of view. I remain fascinated by life and social action as it is produced within the urban arena, however, and am content to identify myself as an urban sociologist.

Acknowledgments

This text is the result of a long-term writing project. I am grateful to have had the opportunity to devote the hours needed for reading and writing and simply thinking about a set of ideas that are an important part of me. A project such as this represents something of a self-indulgence. I have taken a lot of time from the people who are important to me to produce this work. I want to acknowledge their patience, generosity, and support.

The project has benefited from the critical attention of a number of colleagues. Josef Gugler, Bruce London, and Isaac W. Eberstein have had the patience to read the entire text. I am also grateful to Harold Abramson, Lewis Coser, James Randall, Kent Schwirian, Robert Marrs, Peter Marris, Karen E. Campbell, and Thomas J. Keil for their comments on the manuscript. The text has also benefited from the comments of a number of anonymous readers in its first review. Glenn Janus, Allen P. Fisher, and Lee Carl Binhammer have offered useful comments on additional sources of research materials.

Coe College has been generous in its material support of the project. It has demonstrated that a private liberal arts institution that emphasizes service to its students can also support the professional activities of its faculty. The college has also provided me with good students who have helped me to develop the framework of ideas contained in this text. I am especially grateful to Peggy Knott, a word-processing whiz in the broadest sense.

INTRODUCTION

This book has been conceived with two purposes in mind. The first purpose is to provide the student of urban sociology with a text that incorporates certain unifying themes, tying together the various subject matters that are treated by urban sociologists. The second purpose, very much related to the first, is to indicate that there *is* a distinct area of sociological enquiry, having to do with cities and their wider effects, that calls for a separate, specialized division within the social sciences. That is, there is a need for urban sociology as a specialized area of study, one with its own particular subject matter and perspectives. However, to be viable, urban sociology must be peculiarly adaptive, because the pattern of human settlement is constantly changing. It is increasingly evident that large and small population centers are interwoven culturally, politically, and economically in a common spatial system. The field of study traditionally known as urban sociology must adapt its analytical schemes to accommodate this new pattern of integrated space and to become *more than strictly urban* in its focus. It is a fascinating conceptual challenge that now faces the students of urban studies.

The conceptual challenge offered by urban sociology is to identify a discrete subject matter that is different from the subject matter studied by sociologists in other subdisciplines (e.g., political or economic sociology, social stratification, minority and ethnic studies). A fundamental (and reasonable) requirement of any science is that we must be able to say precisely what it is we are studying: what it is that sets our particular perspective on the world apart from the work of other social scientists with interests similar to our own.

Consider the subject *urban*. What is and what is not considered urban? Where do cities and their various influences begin and where do they end? For example, consider the circumstances of a midwestern farmer in contrast with the situation of a resident of a run-down apartment building in Boston, Massachusetts. The farmer may be regularly counted among the big-city residents of the United States by the Census Bureau if the farmstead happens to fall within one of the bureau's Metropolitan Statistical Areas, as many farmsteads do. The farmer's economic future will be determined in boardrooms and legislatures located in big cities where decisions are made about farm commodity prices, international trade, credit availability and interest rates, and other matters of vital interest to agricultural businesspeople. These elements can be seen as important *urban* dimensions of the farmer's circumstances. At the same time, research done in Boston has demonstrated that some urban residents, whose social worlds are encapsulated in intense networks of ethnicity and kinship, may be better understood as villagers than as urbanites (Gans [1962] 1982). The point is that even though we may have a fairly clear image in mind when we think of the "city," its margins or the limits of its influences are difficult to establish, so the urban concept remains problematic. Hence the difficulty of the question: What is (and what isn't) the appropriate subject matter of an urban sociology?

The problem of establishing a concrete and distinct subject matter and designating a separate sociology to deal with urban phenomena flows from the fluid nature of the subject. To say that we are engaged in a *sociological* study means that we are proceeding from the assumption that human experience and action are shaped in fundamental and important ways by the social arena in which they take place. This is to say that particular features of social organization influence the ways in which we understand or think about things, and the ways in which we act, react, and interact. To designate an area of enquiry as "urban sociology" is to assume that the city and its influences make a difference in shaping experience, behavior, and social relationships. If a discrete subfield of sociology is justified, then it has to demonstrate that *urban* exerts an identifiable, independent effect. There are several problems in establishing the legitimacy of such a domain of study.

The basic problems of definition cannot be ignored, such as What is a city? or the more difficult question, What is urban? We will examine a number of attempts to answer these questions and find that all fall short of a comprehensive cross-cultural model. Some of the difficulty stems from the fact that what we are trying to identify is in part a place, the city, and in part a social process, with radiating influences that originate in but carry far beyond these central and densely peopled spaces. Urban influences are organizational (growth in social complexity), cultural (ways of thinking and behaving), and political (relationships of power and control).

In the following chapters, we will attempt to disentangle the multiple kinds of social phenomena that are associated with the urban form. In the end, we will not have a comprehensive theoretical definition to offer, but we will have a clearer idea of the various dimensions and the complexity of urban influences. Urban sociology overlaps and shares the subject matters of a number of other sociological subfields and traditions. Urban sociologists address themselves to issues in social stratification, small groups, formal organization, the family, modernization and economic development, and political and even rural sociology. Our discussion will review and draw upon the various theoretical traditions in sociology, as well as borrow from scholarship in anthropology, economics, geography, history, political science, and political economy. In working with any of these areas, the questions will always be the same: What aspect of the behavior or relationship in question is the outcome of urban influences? Can an independent urban effect or contributing urban cause be established? The test is this: Apart from behaviors or relationships that take place *within* cities, is there a range of behaviors, processes, or relationships generated or influenced *by* the urban arena? That is, we are not necessarily interested here in things that happen in cities but in things that are of the city, whether or not they take place in cities. This is what is taken to be the legitimate domain of urban sociology in this text. At times we will find it necessary in this urban sociology to speak of farmers as well as urban villagers. Often we will step beyond the urban arena to address the global origins of many urban phenomena. City space is continuous with all aspects of global space: Economic, political, cultural, and environmental concerns draw our attention away from the city to global events and back again as we struggle to identify those aspects of a changing world that belong to the domain of urban science.

The Division of Urban Sociology: Culturalist and Structuralist Approaches

One characteristic of urban sociology that will become evident in the following chapters is the variety of approaches taken by its various students. These can, however, be divided into two major orientations: those that explore the cultural, organizational, and social psychological consequences of urban life, and those that are concerned with the wider economic and political impact of the city. The first orientation deals with people's experiences in cities, while the second asks how cities figure in the distribution of wealth and power in society. The terms that have been chosen to express the distinction between the two general approaches are reflected in the title of this text: *Urban Sociology: Images and Structure.* Social scientists who are part of the tradition that explores the impact of the urban form on experience are concerned with formulating appropriately complex *images* of the city: These urban sociologists are often referred to as *culturalists* because of their emphasis on the experiential aspect of life in cities. In any society, the urban arena generates values and styles of its own that vary from the values and styles evident in nonurban settings. Culturalists address how urban life feels, how people react to living in the urban arena, and how the city organizes personal lives. In contrast, those who investigate the interplay between political and economic forces, and the growth, decline, and changing spatial organization of urban space are concerned primarily with urban *structure.* These sociologists are appropriately referred to as *structuralists.* They see cities as the physical embodiment of political and economic relationships: Their argument is that the city itself is an effect of more fundamental forces, that cities are shaped by social powers that affect all aspects of human existence. In the structuralist view, an accurate assessment of the effects of urban life on people needs to begin with the understanding that the urban environment is a product of a set of more fundamental causal factors.

Any comprehensive discussion of urban sociology must address both the images of the cultural emphasis and the structural models. The order in which topics are presented in the text reflects the general division between the two approaches. Chapters 1, 3, and 4 deal largely with life in cities and the efforts of social scientists and others to understand that mode of existence. In these chapters, the questions of what has become of people's sense of community, whether life in the city or the rural area is richer socially, and how urban life modifies the experience of immigrant and minority populations are discussed. Chapters 6 through 10 generally focus on the interplay between urban and wider political and economic patterns. The relationship between urbanization and economic underdevelopment in the Third World, urban patterns that reinforce the conditions of poverty, and the question of who has the power to plan effectively are studied.

The culturalist and structuralist distinction is carried out within a number of chapters as well. Chapter 5 focuses on ethnic and minority groups in the city. The break in emphasis from cultural to structural factors in group formation comes in the transition from the discussion of ethnicity to that of minority groups. Here it is argued that ethnicity is an essentially cultural group phenomenon, while the minority/majority division is an essentially structural group phenomenon. In Chapters 6, 8, and 9 the cultural-structural distinction is between schools of thought, diametrically opposed explanations of the same phenomenon. Chapter 6 contrasts the modernization (cultural) and political economy (structural) approaches to the problem of underdevelopment. Chapter 8 distinguishes the traditional ecological and more recent Marxist interpretations of how urban space is ordered and reordered. Chapter 9 compares the culturalist and structuralist analyses of poverty and power in the city.

The Order of Topics

Chapter 1 emphasizes the ways urban space alters experience. Chapter 2 presents a history of the emergence, growth, and transformation of the urban form. It introduces the various dimensions of the process of urbanization and concludes with an introduction to the urban dimensions of the process of globalization. In Chapter 3, we explore a rich theoretical tradition in urban sociology that attempts to describe the impact of an increasingly urbanized world on the quality of social life. Chapter 4 describes processes of social conflict and cohesion as they are influenced by the urban environment. Here we find that the differences that separate us from each other also propel us into organizations and coalitions with those who share similar interests and objectives. Chapter 5 considers the place of ethnic and minority studies within urban sociology. The fact that distinct ethnic identities and minority groups are present and highly visible in cities is not enough to warrant special attention in an urban sociology course or textbook. According to the way we have defined the relevant subject matter, the emergence of ethnic and minority groups *must in some way be affected by urban forces*—either generated or altered by them—in order for these group processes to gain consideration. Chapter 5 demonstrates this kind of connection.

Chapters 6 through 10 provide an analysis of the economic and political forces associated with urban growth and change. As an economic and political force, the city constitutes a paradox. In Chapter 6, it emerges as a dominant agent in the processes of economic underdevelopment and development; as a magnet for wealth and power, too often a greedy giant; and as a center of comfort and privilege for a few in the Third World, where poverty and hunger remain the by-products of uneven patterns of economic growth. By contrast, as Chapter 7 progresses, many of the great urban centers of the United States will be seen to wither as they are transformed from the central arenas of the industrial age into deindustrialized and depopulated shells, relics of a bygone era, often only to regenerate, in a modified form, once again. Chapter 8 will then describe the ways in which cities *still* dominate the economic landscape as centers of regional or metropolitan community. The chapter presents the fundamental theoretical division that separates the ecological and Marxist interpretations of urban growth and change. The issues raised in Chapters 7 and 8 lead to the conclusion that the scope of study for understanding the major processes of urban growth, change, and decline needs to be expanded. The increasing rationalization of productive factors over the surface of the globe requires us to cast our spatial analysis at the regional, national, and international levels.

Chapters 9 and 10 survey the attitudes and policies of the state toward its cities. Questions of national policy form an integral part of the study of urban growth and change, since policy reflects the level at which these processes are understood, as well as which aspects of change are popularly or officially defined as problems (poverty and justice, housing, the consequences of further growth or decline, and so forth). These chapters review society's effectiveness or lack of effectiveness in dealing with officially recognized problems. Chapter 9 outlines the dimensions of poverty, political power, and crime as major policy issues. Chapter 10 presents a historical overview of urban policy and planning strategies, from early days when planners thought in terms of visions of the ideal future and the grand scheme through the disillusionment with U.S. programs in the 1960s and 1970s. It concludes with an update of policy in the United States and contrasts it with policy in selected countries outside the United States.

The concluding chapter considers the current state of the field of urban sociology. Up until the present time, the division between the culturalists and structuralists has in some ways been productive. They ask very different questions about the nature and consequences of urban life, and their work has offered two distinctive lines of insight into urban phenomena. Today the challenge is to find a way to integrate the findings of the different approaches. Chapter 11 offers one scheme and makes modest proposals for additional areas to which urbanologists might productively turn their attention.

1

AN INVITATION TO URBAN STUDIES

Cities have a mind-altering quality. They speed you up, they lower inhibitions, space has a different energy, images jump. Not all urban spaces are equally like this, but certain large public arenas in the centers of large metropolises full of people—truly urban spaces—are. The anonymity of public spaces teeming with strangers invites people to play identity games, to pass themselves off as something they are not, to try on altered identities. They offer the opportunity for the adventure of dropping your routine guard against interacting with strangers and to experiment instead with chance encounters. Cities allow you—require you—to make your way among a broad range of others, as they provide the context that offers up the richest array of diversity and freedoms available (Lofland 1985, 163–171). But this is no neutral territory; it may present its own unexpected adventure to the unwary wanderer, so you have to be ready for the potential "rough adventure of the street" (Charyn 1987), a tense confrontation, an aggressive intrusion on your personal space: This is a prospect that attracts some modern-day adventurers and repels others who want to keep their urban experience under control and at a distance.

For tens of millions of poor people in the wealthy nations, the city is a different kind of adventure: a lifelong struggle to get an adequate diet, shelter, education, and medical attention in overcrowded public clinics and to get by in built-for-profit environments featuring the highest costs of living in the world. For hundreds of millions of people in the poorest countries of the world, cities promise hope and deliver on the promise in every shade of good and ill fortune imaginable, from lavish comfort to a daily bitter struggle for the barest existence. For more than five thousand years, the city is the place where the greatest intensity of human experience, the biggest stories of change, and the most significant events of history have been anchored. This is our subject matter.

Conceptual Challenges in Understanding Urban Space

Sociologists study the structural elements of society. Structural elements include the class system that determines the ways that some people are advantaged while others are disadvantaged, the political system that has to do with who holds power and what they do with it, and ongoing institutional arrangements, such as the form that the family takes in a given era. In the field of sociology, we are interested in the ways that these structural elements come into being and change. Ultimately, we are interested in the consequences of structural arrangements for the way people think and behave.

Our study in this volume is *urban* sociology, one of the many subdivisions of the broad field of sociology. In urban sociology, we focus on just one aspect of society, a certain kind of physical environment, how it is produced, and the social consequences that result. The premise of urban sociology is that urban environments have identifiable consequences regarding the ways that people experience themselves and others, the way they interact, and the way their lives are organized. To identify a subfield of sociology as urban sociology, we are thereby proposing a hypothesis: Something called *urban* is a sociological variable that affects people in systematic and identifiable ways. Urban sociology is the field of scientific study that seeks to discover those systematic causes and effects.

The study of cities involves many conceptual challenges, but it is an exciting and worthwhile intellectual enterprise. What we are setting out to discover—the city and its influence—is all around and therefore difficult to see. It is part of who we are, just as we are part of it. We subscribe to urban styles and ideas; we are its models and agents, spreading its influences as we act and speak. It may be difficult to see this at first, but that is because, unlike previous generations, we in Western society have little that is nonurban with which to contrast it.

One of the key features of any science is an almost obsessive attention to terms and definitions, and in urban sociology we immediately run into a problem. It may surprise you to learn that urban sociology has some difficulty defining what is meant by *urban*. In part, the difficulty has to do with the complexity of the structure we are trying to define; in part, it has to do with the emotional response of people to the idea of the city. First, regarding complexity, keep in mind that when we say we are going to study *the city*, we are referring to a matrix of structures and activities that comprise one of the largest and most complex forms of social organization. Unlike other complex structures, the city has no formally defined central organizational structure. We make a distinction here between two kinds of organization in order to make this point. One kind of organization is *enacted*; the other kind comes into being through a *crescive* process (Warren [1963] 1972).

An example of an enacted organization would be a large automobile manufacturing and sales corporation. We say it is enacted because it is planned as a unit from the beginning, and while its organizational structure may expand and become more complex over time, these changes are deliberate and planned out. No matter how large and varied the work of the company becomes, there will be a formal organizational chart and a company handbook that traces the specified relationship between bureaucratic positions from executive board members down through production line workers. The body of rules and regulations gives overall coherence to such disparate activities as research and development, marketing and advertising, sales and financing, worldwide manufacturing operations and subcontracting, quality control, and dealing with lawsuits resulting from product

Times Square: How many elements in this narrow glimpse identify this as urban space? What force has crowded these elements into this confined space? Who is in charge; who is in control?

failures. Whatever new directions it may take, the company remains a formal organization with clearly defined lines of communication and command.

Now think of how the organization of the city differs from that of the corporation. Is there an organizational chart that identifies the status and set of relationships of every individual involved in some way with a particular city? Such a chart exists for city government with its many agencies and branches, but this is not the unit we are trying to understand. When we say that cities come into being crescively, we are saying that their elements emerge gradually, over time, and that the interrelationships among their many parts are not due to formal deliberation so much as to spontaneous accommodations among the different parts and individuals. That is, if we take the sum total of activities carried out and lives lived in the city, what we have is an arena of action where no one is totally aware and no authorities are totally in charge of how the whole thing operates or even how it holds together. In reaching for a way to express this kind of organization of space and human activity, Long (1958) offered the image of "an ecology of games." Games are the things that people do—for a living, for recreation, for gaining and maintaining shelter, in generally going about their business. *Ecology,* an important concept in urban sociology that we will discuss from time to time in this text, is used here similarly to the way biologists use it. It refers to a natural order that has been worked out over time among various organisms, a process that allows a variety of life-forms to use the same environment in mutually beneficial ways.

This is a useful metaphor in thinking about how people use the urban environment and how that environment is ordered, so long as we remember not to overemphasize harmony and balance to the exclusion of conflict and exploitation: In an ecology, big ones eat little ones, and the powerful grow sleek off the weak (eventually microorganisms gobble up all else, but here we reach the limits of our analogy). Urban environments harbor long-standing conflicts, sudden confrontations, distractions, and discontinuities. The city is an arena, a place in which the balance of elements often involves a standoff among antagonists. Law enforcement and crime, political protest and routine acts of government, fundamentalist religious practices and pornography mills, the industrial production of environmental toxins and community discussions of environmental goals: These are all "games," very serious games, that take place side by side in an arena that makes room for all of them and holds them in tension with one another.

Related to the challenge of understanding the informal structure of cities is the fact that the urban arena lacks physical or spatial closure. The nature of the city is such that it has no natural boundaries or limits; it is peculiarly open-ended. Standing at the center of a large city, an individual can easily see the physical evidence of the city and perceive the life around as characteristically urban in quality. That is not the challenge in establishing the unit of space that makes up the subject of study here. The challenge comes because the sociological consequences of the city reach far beyond the space that we identify as characteristically urban. Although the heights of buildings and density of structures typically diminish as we move away from central cities, through their suburbs and into the open countryside, we have not reached the limits of urban influence when we can no longer see the city skyline on the horizon. Electronic media, city newspapers, urban lifestyle, and political and economic domination emanate from the built-up population centers. Culturally, politically, and economically, the city has no geographic limits in a rapidly urbanizing world.

A further difficulty in conceptualizing the urban form is the fact that cities and the nature of urban life vary among societies. Also, urban places look and operate differently within the same society at different points in history. As we think about how to define the city and urban life, we need to remember to make the definition broad enough to encompass the ancient cities of prehistory, the walled cities of the Renaissance, the cities of the Industrial Revolution, the cities of less-developed countries, and the sprawling modern metropolitan centers of economic activity. Not surprisingly, it has proven difficult to formulate a single definition of the urban form that applies with equal validity cross-culturally and historically to all those places in the world that we would like to recognize as having urban qualities.

There is one final difficulty in defining what we mean by urban, and this has to do with the kinds of effects the city has on people. The public reacts emotionally to cities, and this colors what they think the social consequence of urban life is.

As we move away from the city center, "urban" influences diminish, but at no point do we encounter a clear demarcation between urban and nonurban.

Maybe we think that urban life is faster, colder, cooler, socially richer, morally corrupting, spiritually uplifting, and more exciting and therefore either more attractive or more off-putting than life in nonurban places. What we understand as *urban qualities* means different things to different people. People tend to feel strongly, emotionally, about cities, about certain areas of cities, and about their own versus other cities or neighborhoods. The way we feel about cities influences what we "know" about cities, and we may believe so strongly in our emotionally stoked vision that we resist learning other things. This is not the ideal condition under which to conduct science, where differing, strongly held opinions vie with evidence, but it makes for interesting arguments. Is life in the city cold and heartless? Yes. Is it warm and richly human? Yes. Is it a place where people become lost, isolated, or are alone? Yes. Is it a great place to build a wonderful social life? Yes. Is it the dominant pulsating engine of the international economy that gathers in enormous wealth? Yes. Is it subject to unanticipated changes in global arrangements that can destroy the core of its local economy? Yes. The contradictions imbedded in these observations are not resolvable by research-based "facts." The evidence tells us that all of these statements are true. The city is a big place, where 2,850,000,000 people lived in the year 2000. It is big enough to contain many contradictions.

In the remainder of the chapter, we set out to discover in an informal way some examples of how cities influence human experience and shape our thinking and behavior in subtle and not so subtle ways.

Experiencing Urban Space

In 1998 the American Psychological Association devoted most of the June issue of the journal *American Psychologist* to the theme *urban life*. This followed five years of study by a task force set up by the association to study the effects of living in the city on people's mental health. Although it was recognized that urban life might have some beneficial effects, the impetus for the study was clearly a concern with the negative consequences of living in cities, including "alienation, demoralization, helplessness, hostility, substance abuse, distrust, isolation, apathy, marginalization and powerlessness" (Marsella, Wandersman, and Cantor 1998, 621). An extensive review of the international literature on the mental health consequences of life in urban and nonurban settings led to the conclusion that the beneficial effects of urban living, such as "intellectual and cultural growth and development, tolerance for diversity, and opportunity for social mobility" needed to be appreciated as well as the potential negative effects (Marsella 1998, 632). What interests us here is the operating assumption by professional psychologists that the urban environment produces a real and important impact on experience and the way people define reality. Cities probably affect us in an infinite number of ways. Here we consider a few.

Public Spaces and Human Behavior

When we think about the effects of cities on experience and behavior, we are most likely thinking in terms of the public spaces that characterize urban life. What marks these territories is the fact that, except for the occasional chance meeting of acquaintances, they are peopled by strangers. These are spaces where a certain social tension is inherent and where the successful negotiation of the environment depends on employing knowledge about how to conduct yourself and how to strategically move about in public (Lofland 1998, 28). As a competent participant, you need to be able to reach back into a half-articulated store of knowledge—of public- or street-lore—about how to move through crowds, what seat to choose in a bar or on a bus, how not to draw unwanted attention, the proper way to conduct yourself while standing in line waiting, how to react to someone who appears to need assistance, and how to recognize immediately threats to personal safety and what to do about them. Urban public space affects what we think and do. To the extent thought and behavior reflect who we are—our self-image, how we see ourselves in relationship to others—we are talking about an environment that is arguably of considerable importance for understanding ourselves.

Cities as Culture

If we step back to see what we are saying about cities, it is that cities, in producing their own cues for behavior and their own rules, are altering the cultural world in which we live. The effects of urban ways of life on personal styles, tastes, and attitude are not confined to cities. Given the prominent place of the urban environment in our imagination and the attention it draws to itself as the center of multiple fascinations, we see that the high-profile cultural influences present in the city are quickly communicated to the rest of society. The influences take many shapes and speak in many voices. Zukin (1995) identified some of these. "The cultures of cities certainly include ethnicities, lifestyles, and images—if we take into account the concentration of all kinds of minority groups in urban populations, the availability and variety of consumer goods, the diffusion through the mass media of style. Cities are the sites of culture industries, where artists, designers, and performers produce and sell their creative work" (264). In fact, cities represent a multifaceted environment where different messages about the basic nature of urban culture—the symbolic significance of The City—compete with one another.

What do cities symbolize? According to Zukin, there is the message of danger, in part a product of the popular media image of the city as a dangerous place, but reinforced in everyday urban experience by such symbols as the presence of armed security guards employed to set aside "safe" spaces. How do we interpret places outside the perimeter set up for the safety of shoppers and strollers, the "other" city? Concerns about security permeate the consciousness and conversations of urban residents and visitors alike. The high visibility of minority and immigrant groups within urban populations has given another symbolic element to the meaning of the city. Cities are the place of beginnings, of cultural transitions, where generations of immigrant cultural others struggle to make peace with the host culture. And cities are places where cultural differences often do not melt down, where assimilation is blocked, where disadvantage becomes in some measure permanent, where prejudice and discrimination against some categories of outsider become chronic, and minority groups settle into pockets of social exclusion. Some of the messages broadcast from the city to the wider society reflect elements of inner-city minority cultures, which grow rich as expressive traditions of art and music with themes that grow out of poverty and economic isolation. Cities and their mainstream institutes of high culture, such as museums and performance centers, find themselves arguing publicly that *they* represent the true cultural expression of the city, not the life of the streets and alternative cultures that occasionally gain a strong and audible voice, such as that expressed through the popularity of hip hop. At the same time, the rising number of immigrants from new origins—from Africa, the Middle East, and the Caribbean—transform the neighborhoods and streets of wealthy European and U.S. cities by setting up new market areas evocative of Third World themes. These exotic images compete with other urban themes for a place in shaping the meaning of the city, influencing the self-portrait that the city presents to the world in general, a world that invariably looks to the city to learn what is on the cutting edge of cultural change. Meanwhile, the wealth of the corporation has come to play a more visible role in what we experience as urban culture, making the corporation's presence felt through promotions and advertising even in formerly public space. Public places—parks, squares, and other gathering places—have symbolically gone private, bear the logos and slogans of corporate sponsors, and at times are renamed in honor of their corporate benefactors (Zukin 1995, 265–267).

The combination of all of these elements and many more play a part in informing our image of what the city means, and images of urban life exert an atmospheric influence on contemporary popular culture in general. Think of the streaming images of action and change that play through the channels of entertainment and information media, that play up the themes of style, of edginess, of sensuous experience, lavish lifestyle, the blurred edge of legitimacy and hustle. Can there be any question of whether these images are urban in origin? In any world region, for at least the past five thousand years, the cultural future of the next generation was always taking shape in the cities. Cities influence our thinking and behavior in profound ways, whether or not we actually live within the city.

Structuring Personal Experience

For those who do live within the city, we can identify a number of ways that the built environment of urban space itself structures experience and behavior. Lynch's (1960) classic work systematically explained for the first time how cities manage the experience of their residents and visitors. In sum, the significance of Lynch's work is his identification and description of structural elements in the urban environment that channel both perception and movement. He identified five categories of physical elements: paths, edges, districts, nodes, and landmarks. Paths are the channels people travel in moving about the city. They are important determinants of how individuals experience the city. Long-term residents will know several alternatives in going from place to place, leading through different neighborhoods and districts and opening to different experiences. Newcomers' experiences of the city will be more narrowly channeled, more restricted. Edges are barriers, usually linear, that hem in movement. Bodies of water, including rivers like the Charles in Boston, which can only be crossed at a limited number of points, tend to corral experience, holding it in on one side. Highways cutting through cities with limited over- or underpasses can work the same way. Districts are relatively large areas that have a somewhat cohesive quality, a theme or a characteristic feel. Boston's ethnic North End with its narrow streets or fashionable Beacon Hill are each experienced as having a unified texture. The Chinatowns in lower Manhattan and San Francisco are particularly well defined districts. The perception of the unity of some less well defined districts may be made clearer by well-defined edges. Nodes are smaller public places that may best be thought of in terms of junctions or turning points, such as traffic circles, squares, or major mass transit exchange or transfer points. They may also be points at which people concentrate. The clearest examples are both points of exchange and places where people congregate. One might find no better example than the *piazzas* of Italian cities, where people returning home from work or classes in the evening engage in the *passeggiata,* a slow, stylized amble, ideally accompanied by a well-dressed other or at least an engaged cell phone. The plaza, with streets radiating outward from it, is a place of many crossings, a place to linger, to see and be seen, to savor city life. Nodes are distinguished from Lynch's last element of physical structure, the landmark. The landmark is an outstanding feature of the visual cityscape, a marker that helps anchor the individual's mental map of the city. More prominent than the Italian *piazza* is likely to be the dome of the cathedral or public building that stands at the edge of the broad public space, commanding the local scene. Los Angeles has its Civic Center, Boston the Old North Church and Faneuil Hall, New York the Empire State Building and the World Trade Center. What distinguishes landmarks is that most people usually pass them by rather than entering them, experiencing them as external markers.

Lynch's approach to understanding urban space has interesting implications. One is that each of us carries a somewhat different image of the city around inside of us, even though the broad outlines are shared among many. The newcomer lives in a different city from that of the long-time resident, in this sense, because of the fragmentary experience of the city. It follows that even among long-term residents, different perceptions of the city are bound to exist because people who live in different sections will travel different paths framed by different edges through different nodes past different landmarks and will become familiar with different districts. Thus, they carry a different image of the whole of the city in their heads. Also,

One of the bridges crossing the Delaware River from Philadelphia to New Jersey. The pedestrian and the motorist acquire a particular image of the city as they depart or approach this urban edge via this pathway through this district.

Lynch made the point that cities have different degrees of *imageability*, the degree to which they lend themselves to being captured in the mind's eye. He compared three cities—Boston, Jersey City, and Los Angeles—and found that people had the easiest time embracing Boston as a whole, due to its multiple identifiable districts, landmarks, and nodes. The residents of Jersey City emphasized the sameness of their different streets and neighborhoods, while Angelinos tried to hang onto the anchoring influence of the old city center as their city sprawled beyond the capacity of their imagination to contain it.

The Micro Order

Cities by their nature are large and complex structures. But some sociologists have oriented their study to smaller units of space within the urban environment. William H. Whyte is prominent among them. Whyte (1988) is an observer of incidental public behaviors, and so he became familiar with the kinds of public space that people were comfortable in and the kinds of spaces that thwarted sociable mingling. His careful and systematic observations of behavior yielded surprising results. Although people who work and live in the city might talk about longing for a break from the crowds, about getting away from it all, Whyte observed that people on their lunch hours and other breaks appeared to be drawn to other people, to crowded spaces. His work reveals that for people who are a part of them every day, crowds are stimulating in the sense that they are a desirable and congenial medium in which to pass time. When acquaintances meet on crowded sidewalks, contrary to what we might expect, they stop in their tracks and carry on extended conversations in the streams of highest pedestrian traffic. And, also contrary to expectations, the obstructed pedestrians squeezing past knots of conversation are polite and unruffled for the most part (10).

Whyte's work led him to consider what types of spaces, besides crowded ones, people found most congenial for passing leisure time and for accommodating *schmoozing*, a Yiddish term that translates roughly as "nothing talk," gossip, small talk (11). The crowded sidewalk is the schmoozer's natural habitat in the large metropolis, but Whyte found that the engineering of microenvironments was very important in determining whether a particular space was welcoming or off-putting as a site for spending little snatches of leisure. Setting aside space in the city is not enough to ensure people will use it. Whyte observed that many set-aside spaces were nearly empty, while others were jammed. A number of factors appeared to determine which spaces would be most well used. Pedestrians will not go far to relax, and when they get there, they want to sit down. Whyte was surprised and dismayed by the number of instances where low ledges along buildings and walls adjacent to walkways actually seemed to be designed to discourage sitting, being too narrow or fitted with hostile pointed surfaces, apparently intended to keep people moving, to prevent them from becoming knots of obstruction. Food will draw people, the sound of falling water and rustling leaves overhead will soothe them, low ledges and alcoved seating will get them to linger, shade in summer and sunlight in winter will comfort them. Long blank walls, en-

Some urban spaces announce that the passerby is welcome to linger, especially if there are surfaces suitable for sitting and greenery close to areas of foot traffic.

closed and elevated walkways, the nearby rush of traffic will keep them moving, reduce chance streetcorner meetings, discourage lingering, and all but eliminate the natural tendency of urbanites to schmooze. For our interest, Whyte's work is a reminder that even the most incidental aspects of the structuring of the urban environment have real consequences for the quality of experience and patterns of behavior. Urban environments shape social life.

Personal Management of the Public Experience

While Whyte is interested in engineering social space to make it more accommodating to human needs, Lyn Lofland (1985) is interested in the ways that private individuals and small groups take matters into their own hands by taking over public spaces and making them their own. She observed that through the regular and routine use of a particular restaurant, plaza, or section of park, individuals and small groups of individuals may gain a sense of priority over the space, a kind of informal ownership or stewardship. Through regular use, the individual passes from the status of regular "customer" (who has the general lay of things clearly in mind) through that of "patron" (who has some familiarity with other regulars and whatever official staff or attendants may be present) to that of "resident," the culmination of cultivating a sense of place. "The resident, who, by dint of not only using the locale regularly but using it on most occasions for long period of time, acquires . . . an intimate knowledge of all that there is to know and a set of privileges that goes with such mastery" (122). This person, connected to this public space as a matter of choice, having dedicated weeks and months to establishing a familiar presence in that place, having become a recognized fixture in the minds of other users, has effectively *colonized* the territory. It becomes a home away from home, a semi-privatized realm in the resident's mind. The resident may be surrounded by strangers, but these simply become part of a moving backdrop, just another familiar element of the local scene. As part of the moving curtain of strangers yourself, you can identify the residents by their body language and their demeanor: They are relaxed, informal, sprawling, presiding over their domain. They are at home in a world of strangers who are temporarily moving through their space.

All of these writers, from the American Psychological Association through those like Whyte and Lofland who take a microview, show us many ways to think about how cities shape experience. The urban environment is more than a backdrop; it actively intervenes in the social process. It is created by our collective attitudes and actions, and in turn it impacts who we are by becoming part of our consciousness and influencing our culture. You may love what the city is, you may hate it, but whether or not you live in one, the city is here. Its influence is all around you, you are a part of it and it is part of you—and not just because you have been assigned to read this textbook, but that, too.

Our Love/Hate Relationship with the City

In Chapter 3, we will see how important attitudes of Western culture toward cities have been historically in shaping urban theory in sociology. Here we look briefly at how people feel about cities today.

There is a long history of city bashing in the United States; it is somewhat less pronounced in Europe. Moralists and anxious politicians have been concerned with the effects of teeming urban centers on the human soul and on the political future of the state, respectively. Each succeeding era finds something new about the city to be put off by. In the United States, this has meant shifting concern away from Eastern European immigrants and Catholics at the beginning of the twentieth century to Third World immigrants and racial purity at the beginning of the twenty-first, away from infectious epidemics of influenza and tuberculosis to HIV, from gangsters to gangsta. Lofland (1998, 113) said that when she asks her students on the first day of her urban sociology class for impressions that come to mind when she says the word "city," she gets back "frenetic, crowded, loud, smelly, dangerous, indifferent, anonymous, dirty, filled with hostile strangers, and littered with the unsightly homeless and the unsightly poor." Others who find themselves living in cities by choice or default have made peace with it and find it downright appealing. We are divided in our society between *cityphobes* and *cityphiles*—those who hate and those who love the city. Many may respond to this distinction by recognizing a little or a lot of both within themselves.

Cityphiles have learned to use the city to suit their needs and their tastes. They are at home in cities in general or in love with their own city in particular. If they are not living in a city, or a large enough, exciting enough, or varied enough city, they will let everyone around them know of the shortcomings of their compromised life situation. Once one is used to the smorgasbord of elective diversions that prevail in the pace of life, the politics, art, and culinary variety of the world city, it is hard to be happy anywhere else. Box 1-1 invades a chat room hosted by the official Austin, Texas, website. Within Texas and the Southwest region, Austin generally has a reputation as an appealing and highly livable university town. However, the first speaker is disappointed that Austin falls short of expectations acquired from living in other cities. Note that the argument is about the virtues of particular cities of different sizes and characteristics: These speakers are emotionally tied to their favorite city, not necessarily the city in which they live or the city in general.

BOX 1-1 My City Can Beat Your City

One of the things we have learned about the Internet is that people tend to speak plainly about what is on their minds, dispensing with normal rules of civil interaction, their true identities buffered by their online alter egos. In this e-mail exchange, the first speaker derides Austin, Texas, in a chat room peopled largely by other Austin residents. "Austin is way over-rated . . . following the hype of Austin, I moved from San Jose. . . . The tech industry is not what I thought. Little pay $$ and the Austin base economy is very small. . . . It's still very much a college town, which is ok if you are going to school. However, the pay sucks and the traffic is worst than S.J. Stay in New York with a real job with real pay. I plan to move to Dallas, where the pay is 5 times better and the industry is highly diverse. . . . It's no wonder . . . high tech industries always choose a city like Dallas (a real city with real money and a real Airport!, not a college town) over Austin. Move to Dallas!!!"

The response from Austin defenders is equally direct: "Spoken like a true Californian—GO HOME THEN. We don't really want people here who don't get what Austin is about anyway. Austin is NOT Dallas and I can only pray to God that IT NEVER WILL BE!!! Dallas is filled with plastic attitudes polluting the quality of life (just like California)—Austinites have always taken great pride in the fact that we ARE NOT Dallas or Houston. . . . You should go—hurry—and a take a few of your buddies with you because 150 people move here every day due to the fact that it is such a desirable place to live. . . . BYE BYE—we really don't need you congesting our roads, polluting our air, depleting our springs, destroying our parks, or infecting our children with such shallow, superficial principles." Others agree, including this resident of San Francisco: "If you don't get it . . . leave. Austin is heaven. San Jose has F—'ed their city up by letting the techs do as they want. I live in SF and work in 'the valley of death' (AKA silicon valley) and I spend as little time there under that cloud of brown 'prosperity' as possible." And a third defender steps out of the my city/your city box: "As for Dallas, it has its pluses I'm sure, but my impression is it's a big flat sprawled out city. It matters what you are wanting out of a city and if where you are doesn't fulfill it, then everyone has the option of moving elsewhere. It doesn't mean that where you left isn't the perfect place for someone else, now does it?"

The last speaker really does seem to "get it."

There is a lot at stake in the argument in Box 1-1. People need to feel good about the city in which they live or about the wisdom of choosing to live elsewhere. Technology has reduced geographic distance, and electronic data gathering and communication have allowed people to compare the quality of life among different cities using objective criteria. In effect, you can now shop around for the city that suits you, aided by such reference works as *America's Top Rated Cities* (1999), *50 Fabulous Places to Raise Your Family* (1997), the *Gale City and Metro Rankings Reporter* (1994), *The 100 Best Small Towns in America* (1995), *Great Gay and Lesbian Places to Live* (1995), *Rating Guide to Environmentally Healthy Metro Areas* (1997), *Funky Towns USA* (1995), or *The 100 Best Small Art Towns In America* (1998). These sources are probably not going to resolve arguments about whether one town is better than another, but they do supply data on selected criteria that will help people make informed choices about where to live. Such lists also generate their own heated disagreements in the quality-of-life rivalry when some cities are left out or placed lower on the list than other cities.

The criteria employed to make selections for the best-cities lists vary somewhat, although all attempt to measure both economic vigor and quality-of-life variables. *America's Top Rated Cities* (1999) offers information on state and municipal finances, population, employment and earnings, taxes, transportation and commercial real estate prices, as well as cost of living, housing, education, health care, public safety, climate, and water quality. In selecting the *50 Fabulous Places to Raise Your Family* (1997, 8–9), the author stressed the importance of a diversified housing market, ample recreation, cultural and "family fun" opportunities, progressive environmental policies, ethnic diversity (a positive value), scenic beauty, and a welcoming attitude toward newcomers. The *100 Best Small Towns in America* list (1995, 6–8) adds the city's annual growth rate, the proportion of residents between 25 and 34 years old, the number of physicians, the percentage of people with at least a bachelor's degree, whether it has its own newspaper, whether there is a plan in place to train residents to assume positions of community responsibility, and whether there is a program to assist low-income people to acquire their own housing. Clearly, the developers of this set of criteria have a particular vision in mind for selecting their best-places list. At the other extreme, the *Gale City and Metro Rankings Reporter* (1994) simply presents raw data on hundreds of wide-ranging variables including occupational categories, poverty rates, weather extremes, measures of environmental quality, and categories of criminal offense. Although the resource needs updating, readers who know what is important to themselves in choosing a city will quickly have their questions answered by this index. Aspiring actors and directors probably don't need to be told that they have the best chance of landing work in Los Angeles or New York City. However, other people planning to relocate to Fort Pierce, Florida, may find it useful to think about the implications of the city's distinction of having the highest per capita proportion of domestic cooks in the United States. Those with their sights set on Utica, New York, will probably find the fact that it has the highest per capita employment of correctional officers worthwhile information. For the actors and directors headed for Los Angeles and New York City, it might be useful to know that those cities ranked first and fifth in the nation in the levels of air pollution.

How does Austin, Texas, rank among U.S. cities according to the various indexes? It made the *America's Top Rated Cities* list, reflecting its favorable ranking in a number of national and international best-city lists based on favorable business prospects, livability, accommodation to women's issues and interests, favorable ratings by business travelers, and as one of the top electronically networked cities in the United States (1999, 22). It was one of the 50 best family-rearing places to live (Dallas didn't make this list), cited for its liberal atmosphere, recreational features, cost of living, employment opportunities, and entertainment (Giovagnoli 1997, 295). It was also included in *Great Gay and Lesbian Places to Live,* based on its liberal and accepting atmosphere, its compassion for people with HIV and AIDS, its relatively unbiased media, and several welcoming churches (Dills and West 1995, 260). However, according to the data reported in the *Gale City and Metro Rankings Reporter,* Austin also had a poverty rate that placed it just behind Dallas, giving it the twentieth highest rate in the nation (1994, 684).

Those of us who have lived in different cities are bound to feel that there is something suspect in any attempt to sum up any city's qualities in a set of standardized comparisons. Indeed, we can assume that the compilers of these city comparisons offer them only as the roughest guides to the would-be intercity migrant. Different people are going to be emotionally caught up in their love or hate reactions to the San Francisco Bay area, San Jose, Dallas, and Austin. Even where we employ handy standardized criteria, we end up allowing the last speaker in Box 1-1 to have the final word.

The True Cityphile and the Idealization of Urban Space

Some of us are tied emotionally to the city in general, the very idea of the city, a specific kind of city that embodies what we feel to be the fulfillment of the true urban promise of enriched living. Oldenberg (1989) wrote about the array of "great good places" harbored by the great cities—the pubs, cafés, and coffeehouses that are welcoming to the stranger. Oldenberg agreed that much about cities is potentially off-putting, and believed that the city has the capacity to divide human beings and isolate them (48). But that is the beauty of the welcoming public place, which provides a haven. The German or transplanted German American beer garden is a place of festivity waiting to happen, the English "pub" combines the contradiction of the public place (from which its name is contracted) with the private familiarity of long and intimate associations among neighbors, and the French café or bistro is a democratizing force where all classes rub shoulders during prolonged and very regular visits. Oldenberg took Lyn Lofland's observation, that regulars colonize space and make it their own, a step further. He suggested that even strangers are welcomed by certain urban public spaces.

Oldenberg wrote about spaces more characteristic of the old-fashioned convivial urban environments of the city center, and we may wonder whether the changing North American metropolis, with its sprawling suburbs, will continue to provide such convivial public environments. He warned that "Where urban growth proceeds with no indigenous version of a public gathering place proliferated along the way and integral in the lives of the people, the promise of the city is denied" (Oldenberg 1989, *xv*). In this vein, Janusz Mucha (1993, 22), a sociologist visiting the United States from Poland in the 1990s, found that outside of three American cities—New Orleans, New York, and San Francisco—"The idea of the 'city,' as I conceive it, hardly exists in America." He means that there is a dearth of public squares where people safely meet, talk, or buy flowers. It is hard to find a decent coffee shop or café. There is no theater culture in the downtown; everyone has gone to the "movies" at the sprawling suburban mall. Mucha is passionate about cities, particularly familiar cities, cities that are the cultural heart and life blood of a society, *his* cities. Those of us who love the city are apt to be passionate, to have allegiance to a certain form of urban environment, and to feel robbed by its absence. Oldenberg and Mucha wanted cities that gather people in their leisure to the center and gently hold them there through the lure of welcoming public space.

But are these writers talking about a real or a romanticized city? How do the spaces they are speaking of square with the prevailing image of the inner city in the United States? The city is not for everyone, not for the cityphobic. Suburbs are testimony to the way many Americans who find themselves tied by work to the large metropolis feel about the city. Suburbanites are willing to commute long hours from home to work each week so that they do not have to sleep where they work. As we see in Chapter 7, many corporate headquarters, other offices, and even manufacturing complexes have followed the commuter out of the city. And people employed in the suburbs respond by pushing the edge of the metropolis still further into surrounding plains, hillsides, and deserts, creating the *exurbs* from which they commute back to jobs in the suburbs created a decade or so earlier. Some urban exiles have gone still farther, leaving behind the sprawling metropolis in favor of small town life. The Midwest has become home in recent years to a number of metropolitan refugees fleeing the East and West coastal regions. William E. Pike (2000) tells his story in Box 1-2.

People *are* leaving the city. Not only Washington, D.C., but also North American cities in general have lost population in the past few decades. Most of those leaving the city aren't going far, not as far as Pierre. As we will see in Chapter 7, there is something of a contradiction in the general pattern of urban population loss. While Washington's population slipped by almost 14 percent, from 606,900 in 1990 to 523,000 in 1996, the greater Washington metropolitan area, extending into western Maryland and northern Virginia, increased by over 19 percent, from under 4 million to well over 4.5 million in the same period. People leave the city proper, but most remain within the sprawling urban regions, and newcomers arrive daily. Also, while many of the older urban cores are losing population, they are taking on new functions and a new character. Washington, of course, retains its old federal architectural quality and government function as the national capital, with its 2.8 million government employees. But another important economic feature of the capital is tourism: Washington, D.C. is host to millions of tourists each year, 20 million in 1997 alone. In city after city, governments and promoters of local economic growth are going after tourism and convention business more competitively. The downtown area of the capital city in the middle to late 1990s

---

BOX 1-2   Choosing Pierre, South Dakota, over Washington, D.C.

William Pike (2000) made a choice. He moved from the nation's capital to the capital of South Dakota, population 13,000. He wrote, "After four years at Harvard and another year and a half in Washington, urban life was wearing me down. I was not meant to tread along exhaust-choked streets, ride on subways, and stand in lines for everything. Nor was I willing to put up with a cynical culture, continuous late nights at work, a constant striving for material gain, and an empty view of life as a chore, not a privilege. I had seen one too many jaundiced, suit-clad, vacant-eyed paper pushers riding the metro, 30 years older than me and not a day wiser. I knew I must escape before I too fell into this trap called The City and suffered under its slow death sentence." Pike visited Pierre and found a job with the state legislature and an apartment, loaded the rent-a-truck, and never looked back. He reversed the logic of the old German saying, "City air makes men free,"

and enjoys new freedoms in Pierre, like not having to lock the car doors, being able to walk anywhere at any hour of the night, eating lunch at home if he wants to, and leaving the office at five o'clock each evening. These are freedoms that many residents of the coastal metropolises may long for. But his description of the open prairie surrounding Pierre, the lack of neighboring towns, and the peace of the countryside is not going to appeal to the city-phile. Phrases that would leap to their lips might include "boondocks" and "the middle of nowhere." Pike acknowledged that where he lives is not paradise, but when locals ask him why he moved there, he asks back, "Have you ever lived in D.C.?" In response, they smile and nod knowingly. It is interesting to think about vacationers from one of these places, Pierre or D.C., visiting the other, and what they would miss, if anything, when they returned home.

---

acquired a new look, with new retail development, a new convention center, and a $100 million sports arena (*America's Top-Rated Cities* 1999, 332–333).

As metropolitan regions sprawl around them, older urban cores are threatened with losing their old importance, even symbolically, as the heart of their region. The most dynamic growth takes place on the region's periphery, where the affluent middle class resides. If the welcoming public spaces that attract Oldenberg and Mucha are to survive, they must learn to live here in the suburb. Suburbanites and inner-city residents have many issues that divide them, in terms of economics, culture, and politics. Under what circumstances can we still talk about urban regions as representing a meaningful sociocultural unit generating among all the elements of the population a common sense of identity—an identity attached to the broad physical space they share? Of the little we have said about the District of Columbia, the new sports arena may provide the most valuable hint.

We're Number One

As we have seen, place of residence generates a sense of allegiance for many people. This is especially so in the case of hometowns, the place of birth. For people who were born in large cities, the "hometown" may be the whole city, or a neighborhood or named area within it (the South End, the West Side, and so forth). For those born in metropolitan regions, the question of what is "local" is problematic.

People in the Boston metro region—a large, but by no means the largest, example we might have chosen—may live in and identify themselves as being from Brookline, Dedham, Quincy, Newton, Chelsea, or a dozen other possibilities. Is Greater Boston a "real" place to its residents? Let us acknowledge that the following observations are not based so much on careful scientific data gathering as they are on a set of truths that become immediately recognizable as fact once they are expressed. We enter the dangerous realm of common observation.

To highlight the dimension of the urban experience having to do with the way people identify the spatial unit in which they live, we turn our attention to a particular aspect of popular culture that has very wide appeal. When this cultural force comes into play, geographic allegiance comes to extend to the city as a whole, to cut across all demographic categories, to unite all social classes, to extend even through the suburban metropolitan region joining all in a single solidarity based on shared space and glory. This powerful force is not warfare or mortal threat, at least not in the literal sense. This force exists, by advancing degrees, where there is a local professional team competing in a major sport, when that team is having a winning season, when that team makes the playoffs, when that team is champion. This is the one force to unite the cityphile and cityphobe in celebration or mutual despair. It is a phenomenon similar to the patriotic experience that attends the playing of the gold medal winner's national anthem at the Olympics. In the case of professional sports in North America, the rivalry is not so often international as it is intercity.

Red Sox and Yankee fans root not for a team representing the Northeast, but for a team from their metro region, and when the two teams play each other, the rivalry is at its height. The pitch of local identification and rivalry is repeated in city after city. The *Cleveland Plain Dealer*, during the 1999 National Football League season, sponsored a web site where Cleveland Browns fans could trade insults with Pittsburgh Steelers fans, soon provoking a similar site sponsored by a Pittsburgh-region newspaper. The sponsors of both sites had some trouble keeping the exchanges limited to "good clean fun" (Williams, 1999).

Anthropologically, team rivalry is thought to represent a new form of tribalism. Psychologists talk about the degree to which fans identify with their team, experiencing a surging sense of well-being when the home team wins and a deflated sense of self with each loss. On-site studies show that male fans, during important games, undergo a physiological transformation expressed in substantial increases in testosterone levels, which only lasts beyond the duration of the game if their team is victorious. When teams win an important championship, hometown fans are apt to rampage through the streets, as in Los Angeles when the Lakers won the NBA title in 2000, in Denver in 1998 and 1999 in response to their team's Superbowl victories, and in Detroit in 1984 when the Tigers won the World Series (*New York Times*, August 11, 2000, A-1, C-24).

One disreputable element among the ranks of European soccer fans is notorious for inflicting damage and injury. The phenomenon, known as *football hooliganism*, is especially associated with international matches, but opposing fans and the city hosting a domestic intercity contest often come in for rough treatment as well. British sportswriter and fan Hunter Davies (1999) once attended an international soccer match between his own country's badly outmatched Arsenal team and Spain's Barcelona at Wembley Stadium. At halftime, with their team behind by two goals, disgruntled Arsenal fans roughed him up because they suspected he was a Tottenham (another British team) fan, even though, as far as he could tell, he showed no outward sign of that secret allegiance. There simply were no Barcelona fans available, and a fan of an urban rival was a worthy substitute.

The phenomenon of sport interests us here because of its unifying power. This power is tied to location, and at least while the winning streak, championship game, or playoff series is underway, we have a glimpse of the power of place, of allegiance to a particular city, to transcend the important sociological differences that otherwise separate populations on a daily basis. Professional sports is one of the most powerful forces for getting people to use the term *we* inclusively, with reference to all of the people in an urban region, and mean it. Of course, the "we" don't all have to be living in the city of the home team, but we can be sure that the most ardent body of fans are there—the highest per capita ratio of fan to inhabitant. When the Yankees and the Red Sox are battling each other for the pennant, it is possible to find Yankee fans from Boston and Red Sox fans from New York in the stadium, but there won't be many, and they may not admit it.

It would be highly desirable to harness the unifying power of sport, to generalize and apply it to the cause of social unity on a routine basis, and to preserve the spirit of fellowship that it generates among metropolitan populations. So far no one has thought of a way to do it (short of actually going to war with neighboring city-states), and any lingering sense of solidarity and common cause probably does not extend beyond the stadium parking lot. Still, it gives us another glimpse of the sociological importance of space.

The Urban Arena: Playground and Politics

The ancient city of Athens, in 400 B.C., provides insight into one very important feature of all cities: Cities are arenas or stages that naturally lend themselves to spectacle. The daily business of Athens took place in the open, in the central marketplace where goods from all over the known world were sold, all trades plied, and all services provided. This was also the site in the early years for entertainments, athletic games, and equestrian displays (Hall 1998, 38). Although the population of Athens was modest by current urban standards (at its peak, having no more than 300,000 inhabitants), by the standards of the age Athens provided a spectacular pageant even as it went about its daily business. One of the ways that cities are different today is that most business and entertainment are somewhat less likely to be carried out in the open. But there is still much activity that spills out into the streets and plazas, and cities remain natural arenas for festival and dramatization because of the sheer numbers of people they contain.

People find cities attractive playgrounds, and local authorities and organizers, aware of this fact, sponsor festivals to remind residents and visitors to have a good time—and spend some money. The International Festival and Events Association estimates that there are 32,000 urban festivals each year in the United States (Ward 2000b). The authoritative New York City street festival web site (jimsdeli.com/guide/events.htm) listed 275 festivals for the 2000 season, most of them clustered from April through October (June is the big month with 57). These include *La Gran Parada Dominicana,* Feasts of Our Lady of Mount Carmel (two, one in Manhattan and another in the Bronx), the Israeli Education Fund Street Fair, the United Ireland Foundation Festival, the East Side Rezoning Alliance Street Fair, and the Fulton Street Food Festival. Organizers in smaller cities may make do with just one street festival a year in an effort to put their city on the map: Gilroy, California's Garlic Festival each July, and Moriarity, New Mexico's Pinto Bean Fiesta in October.

One of the most popular festival themes combines ethnic celebration and food. Some cities host multiethnic food fairs, like St. Petersburg's Ethnic Food Festival or, with more emphasis on food than ethnicity, Chicago's Taste of Chicago. Mexicans, Germans, Greeks, Chinese—many traditions know how to party in the streets, but none seem so dedicated or naturally adept at it as Italians in the United States. There are no fewer than 33 major Italian American street festivals in the United States each year, from Sacramento's *Festa Italiano* to Saint Anthony's Feast

City festivals bring people into the city and city people into the streets. The annual Taste of Chicago is one of the most well established. People come for the variety of foods that reflect the city's diversity and for the free music.

in Boston. Probably none of them is larger or better known than New York's San Gennaro Festival held each September in the Little Italy neighborhood. Like many Italian American festivals, it combines a good time with observation and celebration of a saint's feast day, in this case San Gennaro, Patron Saint of Naples. The continuation of the festival is important to the long-time residents of Manhattan's Little Italy, which is today roughly a six-block area on the Lower East Side, bounded by Mulberry, Canal, and Prince Streets. Formerly, the area known as Little Italy was much larger, but it has shrunk from generation to generation, and the third and fourth generation Italian community is being succeeded by Chinese, Vietnamese, and Spanish populations. The language in which Mass is now said in formerly Italian Catholic churches is that of more recently arrived ethnic groups. The street festival gives the remaining 11,000 people of Italian immigrant descent a few days each September when they symbolically reclaim the streets, although most of the locals who watch the parade and other festivities are of Asian birth or descent (Leyden, 1999).

Another symbolically important feature of the festival lies in its organization and sponsorship. An annual event since its beginning in 1927, it is alleged for much of its existence to have been run by sponsors with ties to organized crime, and the proceeds, which were raised for charity, are thought to have been skimmed by major New York crime figures. In 1996, after a two-year investigation, the City of New York barred the former sponsors from organizing the festival, and neighborhood interests immediately founded a nonprofit organization to take over the festival's operation (Leyden, 1999). The potentially damaging publicity, made-to-order to fit negative stereotypes attached to successful Italian American enterprise, was quickly defused. In 1999, the president of the new community-based organization said, "It all started here for our families, the roots are here. Why should we end this? The neighborhood is smaller, but the tradition, the heritage—it's a big thing. People come back. . . . The point is Little Italy is a very big part of people's lives" (Leyden, 1999, A3). Between one and three million people, according to various estimates, are attracted to the food and games every year, and lend weight to the Italian American claim that they still own a couple of blocks on Mulberry Street for a few days each September.

Cities for Fun and Profit

Urban street festivals are a public expression of the identity and solidarity of a community. A particular festival may express the ethnic identity of an urban subculture, like the San Gennaro festival; it may support a particular neighborhood cause, like New York's East Side Rezoning Alliance's Street Fair; or it may celebrate something about the city as a whole, like Moriarity, New Mexico's annual Pinto Bean Fiesta. Whatever their theme, festivals reframe public space for a time, maximize its potential to be experienced as warm and welcoming, and invite visitors to join with locals in a time and place that's "just for fun."

But a lot of work by neighbors, volunteers, or members of religious organizations is required to bring off a successful public event, and because at least a share of the proceeds is typically marked for charity or for community improvement, an important measure of success is the bottom line—how well the event worked as a money raiser. The increasing popularity of the street fair or citywide festival has created a growth industry for private consulting companies that specialize in engineering financially successful festivals. Behind the expressions of solidarity, tradition, and people having a good time is a set of promoters doing business.

The urban festival's potential to generate profit has not been lost on the entertainment industry and other promotional entrepreneurs. If a neighborhood can generate substantial profits in a few days of organized nostalgia each year, why not create year-round festival zones in the heart of large urban centers featuring proven crowd-pleasing, money-making attractions—minus the for-charity motive? Some believe that this realization is producing important changes in the city and the urban experience. Cities or large districts within cities, taking a cue from Las Vegas and Disney World, are being repackaged and turned into entertainment zones, into "Fantasy Cities."

Hannigan (1998) used the term *Fantasy City* to describe the "urban entertainment destination" (UED) projects that were being contemplated or actively developed by nearly every major entertainment company and several large real estate developers by the late 1990s. The phenomenon being described here combines elements of old-fashioned entertainment districts that have developed *crescively*, with the *enacted* form of environment characteristic of the theme park. (These terms were introduced at the beginning of this chapter.) Some districts may be

Public space has always been used for diversion and spectacle. Every local promoter understands the importance of selling the idea that cities are fun.

wholly designed and managed by a single concern. Others involve many developers, designing their projects independently, but all united in the recognition that a particular urban area is taking shape as a UED; they scramble to position their restaurant, theme bar, multi-screen theater, or retail complex strategically within it. The idea is to create a public space that appeals to the tourist and consumer mass market, a secure environment that has something for everyone, and where the attraction is fun. It is typically a day-and-night operation in the spirit of the Las Vegas casino, and visitors carry away with them prestige logo-embossed souvenirs—maybe the best example is the Hard Rock Café T-shirt—bearing the imprint of the UED, one of its many attractions, or the logo of such an area's corporate sponsor, attesting to the fact that they had been to the site.

> *Fantasy City . . . is constructed around technologies of simulation, virtual reality, and the thrill of the spectacle. Without a doubt, a major inspiration has been the Disney model, not only because it has been widely imitated but also because a number of the Disney "imagineers" (designers) have migrated to other entertainment and real estate companies and projects where they bring their "Magic Kingdom" sensibility. Increasingly, as motion picture and amusement park technologies merge to produce a new generation of attractions, the space between authenticity and illusion recedes, creating the condition of "hyperreality." (Hannigan 1998, 4)*

Hannigan's examples include as many actual theme parks as sanitized and revised downtown sites, but some of the prominent illustrations of the concept include the desexualized revision of Times Square, the South Street Seaport (also in Manhattan), Faneuil Hall Marketplace in Boston, Harbor Place in Baltimore, the Metreon entertainment complex in San Francisco, Madchester and Gay City in the old industrial city of Manchester, England, and several urban or urban-adjacent entertainment complexes in Japan, South Korea, and Hong Kong. Areas in other cities undergoing change show symptoms, if not the full-blown Fantasy City condition. In a brief essay that describes the contemporary experience of Chicago's Michigan Avenue, Ehrenhalt (1999, 7) wrote that, at 9 P.M. on a warm Saturday, the avenue is "bursting with life. People are eating ice cream cones, pushing strollers, holding hands, carrying shopping bags, waiting in bistro lines, staring at window displays, staring at tall buildings, staring at each other . . ." He noted, however, that critics find something suspect about the Michigan Avenue scene. It does not belong specifically to Chicago. The stores drawing the crowds are the same upscale chains that are found in other cities, selling hyper-marketed image items in such super outlet operations as Niketown, Disney Quest, and the new American Girl Place. Michigan Avenue feels more like a theme park than it does an integral part of Chicago. In this public space, minorities are dramatically underrepresented among the shopping crowds, and the poor have no reason to be there. Ehrenhalt concluded that, although these are serious criticisms of the changed and changing Michigan Avenue district, the slick and segregated environment is succeeding on its own terms and that is worth something in an era when many downtowns are struggling economically. His response to critics of the new *shoppertainment* environment is summed up, "No matter how much you might wish to deny it, most of the people strolling down Michigan Avenue on a Saturday night are enjoying themselves. If they're suckers, they're happy suckers. It's a little presumptuous to second-guess their contentment."

It is the *synergy*, the combined effects of the various elements of these urban fun zones, that interests us in this chapter. Here, we are trying to see how urban space and different kinds of urban space impact the perceptions, the mood, and the behavior of people who occupy them. The developers of the urban fun zones—the Fantasy Cities—realize that urban space can be engineered to produce a particular kind of experience. In effect, they are doing urban sociology, a kind of applied sociology or human engineering—deliberately attempting to modify urban environments to produce particular perceptions and behaviors that are compatible with the profit motive. They are providing cues that are widely recognizable to people who have absorbed and been absorbed by urban culture to induce the "here's where we begin to have fun and spend some money" reaction. We may define this neutrally as facilitating recreational behavior or more critically as shaking down the suckers, but whatever our interpretation, we are operating within the assumption that urban space alters behavior and that by altering the space itself, a particular behavioral tendency can be created.

One final and especially curious form of the imagineered urban experience is the re-creation of historic, exotic, or even current urban environments somewhere else—in a theme park or a foreign UED. A small but perhaps familiar example is the transplanted-brick-by-brick Irish pub. On a somewhat larger scale, you can experience New York in Las Vegas in the New York New York casino, which reproduces New York environments for Las Vegas tourists—many of whom are visiting from New York. The casino's operators lifted a selection of Manhattan's street performers in 1997 to put on a 90-minute "authentic" expression of New York street culture, "MADhattan," backdropped on stage by a graffitied street scene (Hannigan 1998, 74). Universal Studios takes the quest for authenticity to a new level in its recreation of New York City, combining the resources of the world's fantasy capitals, Hollywood (the movie capital) and Orlando (the Disney capital). In the Universal Orlando theme park, a New York experience richer than the experience of New York itself is afforded the visitor. In Orlando, you can walk through the booming South Street waterfront district—not Manhattan's South Street Seaport fun zone of today, but the "real" South Street waterfront of the 1920s. As you make your way through the theme park's Little Italy and walk up Fifth Avenue, you will pass through the Great Depression and finally come to a "cleaner, more upscale locale that represents contemporary metropolitan New York." The dizzying quality of your time travel experience will be enhanced if you follow Universal's instructions to "keep your chin up" and "your eyes on the ground" in order to get the full benefit of the attention to detail—from rust stains on pipes to cobwebs and sidewalk bubble gum to the patina left by the "dust kicked up by thousands of feet" (www.uescape.com). The newest of three Universal theme parks opened in Osaka, Japan, in 2001. It recreates authentic urban experiences from cities in the United States. These include an Irish pub, not from Dublin but from Brooklyn, a Chinese fast food restaurant from San Francisco, and yes, a re-created authentic Japanese restaurant—from Manhattan's Soho district.

The line between what is real and what is fantasy is blurred by the near-miraculous capacity of rapidly advancing technology to create illusion. In Fantasy City, it has been combined with unprecedented levels of modern corporate wealth to build physical environments that mimic Hollywood's capacity to create two-dimensional illusions on the movie screen. It seems both ironic and natural that it is the movie set that has taken fantasized urban environments to their logical extreme: fantasy in the round. But there is the possibility of a further step here, that the fantasy cityscape will escape from the theme park and reenter the everyday, lived-in urban environment and transform it to conform with the fantasized, re-created, sanitized, and perfected theme park city scenes. Zukin (1995, 65–69) believes that is just what has happened. The Disney formula for simplifying and stylistically coordinating the appearance of spaces that people use, so that their themed message can be easily understood and digested—what has been called the sanitization of experience—is at work in such diverse projects as the wholly planned community of Seaside, Florida, and the cleanup and redesign of New York City's Times Square. The Disney Company during the 1980s was commissioned to redesign Seattle Center by that city, but concerns over whether the center would be turned into a theme park where those needing access would be charged an admission fee, the company's reported unwillingness to incorporate input from the city or its citizens, and cost overruns caused the city to look elsewhere for design ideas. In order to apply theme park criteria to actual urban space, "Its charming surface and smooth-running infrastructure would only be achieved through planning practices that are unacceptably authoritarian in the real world" (Warren, 1994). To the extent the imagineer's sense of visual and social order prevails in reshaping the public environments of future cities, making them safe and predictable, the urban features that draw many of us to the study and the experience of the city will have been lost. Toontown may be safe, it may be fun, but it lacks intrigue, chance events, surprises. It lacks many of the features that delight the urban sociologist and the cityphile alike.

Cities and Political Expression

Just as cities provide an arena for festival, they offer a natural setting for dramatic political expression. For one thing, they provide large numbers of people that can be mobilized by those in power for political rallies in support of government and its policies and for mass expressions of solidarity on national political holidays. But they also provide the critical mass of like-minded dissenters who can take to the streets to express dissatisfaction, mistrust, and opposition to a government or its unpopular policies. Historically, the city provided a natural arena where political demonstrations were communicated effectively and immediately to the largest audience possible simply by the noise and spectacle of mass gatherings themselves. In recent centuries, communication of urban demonstrations has been insured by the concentration in cities of the news-gathering resources of the print

Cities provide a natural stage for political expression and an effective communication medium. These marchers in Philadelphia sought to distract some of the attention from the Republican National Convention in summer 2000.

and electronic news media. The objective of most political demonstrations is expressive, designed to communicate a message of dissent and a call for change. Major cities provide a showcase, a setting that lends weight to the cause, a setting where large numbers of people in the streets are optimally disruptive, where the consequences of massed opposition have the greatest effect. Cities also draw political demonstrations because the targets of the demonstrators reside there: congresses and parliaments, presidents and prime ministers, corporate headquarters and other influential institutions. Cities have also been the natural setting for demonstrations because they contain the most substantial numbers of the poor and minorities. As people in the United States know from the experience of recent decades, confrontations between agents of law and order and members of minority communities regularly invite the perception of injustice and the use of excessive force. These can quickly generate massive rioting.

Cities appear to continue to be a necessary component in political causes that employ public demonstrations as a means to gain the attention of policymakers. Whether the mode of operation is a candlelight prayer vigil or an act of terrorism, if it takes place in the heart of a world city or capital, it will be a more effective means of communicating the cause. Farmers seeking a change in policies that affect their livelihood bring their tractors to the capital; they don't demonstrate in rural areas. Revolutionaries, anarchists, and other activists may come together on the Internet to refine their positions and strategize activities, but if they live only in cyberspace, few of us will take note of their activity unless we deliberately take the trouble to look for them. Cities are a different type of communication medium. Here the world is forced to take note. In June 2000, Third World immigrants to Italy, appealing for the right to become permanent residents, might have demonstrated in their residential neighborhoods and hoped to attract news media attention. Instead, they selected St. Peter's Square in Vatican City in Rome, during an outdoor mass said by the Pope, as the site of their demonstration. They drew the immediate attention of thousands, and that evening their cause was repeatedly broadcast on televised evening news programs.

For those who feel pushed aside by economic globalization itself, where better to address the remote and faceless process than the streets of Seattle, London, and Washington, D.C., as the executives of the World Trade Organization (WTO) come together to meet? Symbolizing both the shrunken globe and the continued relevance of local space, 50,000 demonstrators who had gathered from throughout the world blocked the streets in Seattle in 1999 and prevented the United Nations Secretary General from addressing the assembled WTO delegates in person. Tens of thousands of protesters, gathered to shout their defiance of the remote and faceless engines of global economic change, may not be a sufficient force to reverse the process. They may accomplish little more than to inconvenience the executive agents of the organization convened to set the terms of global change. But the people in the streets are a highly visible force that effectively draws the attention of the watching world to what the demonstrators see as the dark side of the most recent economic revolution. The streets and public squares of the city are more than a backdrop to the drama: They provide the setting for the massing of human energies, the infectious excitement of being a part of a huge crowd that shares what they see as a set of noble goals. Each protester's voice is amplified into a thunder of collected voices and together the protesters enjoy the empowering experience of standing against lines of police, the coverage of hundreds of television cameras and news reporters from around the world, and the validating sense of the crowd that they are up to something worthy of note on the broadest possible scale. This new worldwide movement was sustained in demonstrations outside the meetings of the WTO in London, Washington, D.C., and Prague and again in the streets of Philadelphia and San Francisco for the National Republican and Democratic Party Conventions.

In many ways the political use of the street is the ultimate expression of people taking control of public space, making it their own, and feeling perfectly welcome and at home there, at least while the demonstration lasts. At the same time, they are in the company of thousands of strangers. At this moment, the city, by virtue of providing the conditions that invite collective political expression, is having a profound impact on each of the people gathered there, on their sense of who they are, on the way they perceive others, on the way they perceive the world, and on the way they organize their lives.

We conclude this chapter in Box 1-3 with an examination of events that are both festivals and episodes of collective political expression: the urban tradition known as the gay rights march.

BOX 1-3   From Stonewall to Rome

On June 8, 1969, the patrons of a Manhattan bar, the Stonewall Inn, took to the streets in defiance of public homophobia and in direct response to a police raid on the drinking establishment where they had carved out a safe place—an establishment that catered primarily to gays—in a hostile environment. "Stonewall" became a rallying symbol of defiance against the suppressed right of affectional choice, and a powerful political movement emerged. During the next three decades, the gay pride march became a familiar fixture in many cities. Chicago, San Francisco, Boston, and New York regularly host celebrations of gay, lesbian, bisexual, and transgendered identities. The marches, which in the beginning were political demonstrations of solidarity akin to those of the Civil Rights movement in the 1960s, had by the 1990s become parades surrounded by a festival atmosphere. While the marchers are still subject to counterdemonstrations, threats of violence, and hecklers, they are now regularly joined by family members, community leaders, celebrities, and political figures.

The annual New York City Gay Games, a gay olympics, draws thousands of athletes and estimated hundreds of thousands of spectators. The May 2000 gay pride celebration at the National Mall in Washington, D.C., included a six-block street fair and featured such prominent corporate sponsors as United Airlines, America OnLine, and the Miller Brewing Company. Comedian Ellen Degeneris wore a Mickey Mouse T-shirt and publicly thanked the ABC television network, owned by the Disney Company, for airing her weekly show. Martina Navritalova, former tennis champion, appeared as spokesperson for both Subaru and the VISA Rainbow Card. The event demonstrated how far the Gay Rights movement had come from the days of the Stonewall march. Members of the movement had found a broad base of public support, and many enjoyed a level of economic success that made them an important market that could not be ignored (Wildman 2000, 14).

In Rome, Italy, 2000 was also the year of the World Pride celebration. Rights demonstrators had organized parades and rallies in many countries in recent years, from Ireland to Mexico to Australia, and it was time to bring the cause to the world's attention in a focused and highly publicized event in the Eternal City. The weeklong event in early July drew between 200,000 and 300,000 participants. It occurred during the summer of the Vatican's Jubilee Year, a year that combined celebration and solemn purpose, and attracted hundreds of thousands of pilgrims from around the world. The juxtaposition of these celebrations generated expected controversies, which highlighted the political purpose of the World Pride event. Some organizers had favored the more gay-friendly cities of Amsterdam or London for the international celebration, but Rome was chosen due to the Church's opposition to homosexuality. In the weeks leading up to July, the Vatican openly criticized the movement's plans, the mayor of Rome withdrew the city's welcome, Catholics held public vigils in opposition to the World Pride gathering, and neo-fascist organizations marched through the streets and threatened violence.

In the end, the World Pride celebration took place peacefully, as scheduled, with conferences, fashion shows, a parade, theater events, and concerts. The parade was broadcast live on Italian television. The atmosphere was festive, but the undercurrent of hostility was a reminder that gay rights is still fundamentally a political cause with far to go toward the goal of universal acceptance. As one of the organizers said of Rome, "This is turning into another Stonewall" (New York Times, July 9, 2000).

The celebration and the controversy surrounding it highlight the fact that the city is an arena, a showcase for the culture and politics of the times. Social movements must still come to the city to achieve their political and social ends. International social movements select spectacular arenas of expression, and Rome, the ancient and Eternal City, the former seat of empire, is hard to beat as a stage from which to address the world.

2

FROM ANCIENT CITIES TO AN URBAN WORLD

In order to appreciate the way cities shape social life, it is necessary to begin by tracing the advent and development of the urban form—to study the origins of cities and how they have changed over time. In this chapter, we begin with what we think were the first cities—located in the Middle East—and also look at the earliest cities in other regions of the world—China and Mesoamerica. We then turn to the urbanization of Europe and assess the impact of the Industrial Revolution. In both the ancient period and the period of rapid industrialization, there are three distinguishable categories of social change: the impact of the city on culture and experience; the scale and nature of social organization, specifically social stratification; and the process of political and economic centralization. In both the ancient and industrial eras, the magnitude of the change associated with new urban centers was truly revolutionary in terms of the conditions under which people would live their lives and experience the world. These eras laid the groundwork for the urbanization of the world, a process that continues today. The chapter concludes with a discussion of current patterns of urbanization as the focus of urban growth has shifted to the southern hemisphere and the pace of urbanization accelerates.

The Emergence of the Urban Form

The city as a type of human organization and settlement, measured against the record of human existence and settlement, is a relatively recent innovation. Our modern ancestor, Homo sapiens, emerged 40,000–50,000 years ago. The last ice age ended 10,000 years ago. Permanent human settlement is commonly thought to have begun shortly thereafter, as scattered human populations could turn from hunting to agriculture and the domestication of livestock. The earliest human settlements that would seem to qualify as cities come into the archeological picture in about 3500 B.C. in Mesopotamia and about the same time or shortly thereafter (3300 B.C.) in the Indus River Valley.

Although the city has emerged only recently as an artifact of human existence, its emergence still came some time before there was a written language to record its history. This means that whatever we learn of the origins of urban life must be pieced together from archeological remains. As Mumford (1961, 55) wrote in *The City in History*, "This inquiry into the origin of the city would read more clearly were it not for the fact that perhaps most of the critical changes took place before the historical era opens. By the time the city comes clearly into view it is already old."

In Search of the First City: The Middle East

The first cities probably were built in what is today southern Iraq, in the area between the Tigris and Euphrates rivers, and these were followed within two hundred years by the development of cities in the Indus River Valley in contemporary Pakistan, and later in Egypt. The emergence of cities in these regions came only after a long preurban period of permanent human settlement and technological advancement, the development of a dependable agriculture, and an increase in population. Gradually, the nature of the settlements in question underwent a qualitative change, a transition from a locally focused, isolated, economically and socially self-contained, and basically agricultural community to a form of settlement that demanded recognition as distinctly urban. Even if we had a perfectly clear account of the entire era of transition from preurban to urban society, it would still be impossible to establish at what point the transition took place. We can imagine that the change came about by degrees. The nature of that difference is reflected in the following passage from Childe:

> By 3000 B.C. the archeologist's picture of Egypt, Mesopotamia, and the Indus Valley no longer focuses attention on communities of simple farmers, but on States embracing various professions and classes. The foreground is occupied by priests, princes, scribes, and officials, and an army of specialized craftsmen, professional soldiers, and miscellaneous laborers, all withdrawn from the primary task of food-production. The most striking objects now unearthed are no longer the tools of agriculture and the chase, and other products of domestic industry, but temple furniture, weapons, wheel-made pots, jewelry, and other manufactures turned-out on a large scale by skilled artisans. As monuments we have instead of huts and farmhouses monumental tombs, temples, palaces and workshops. And in these we find all manner of exotic substances, not as rarities, but regularly imported and used in everyday life. (Childe 1951, 115–116)

Figure 2-1 shows the location of many of the earliest and most important cities in the ancient Middle East and the Indus River Valley. At the ancient site of Erech, an early Mesopotamian city, excavation revealed a mound of debris (a *tell*) fifty feet high. It consisted mostly of the ruins of mud and reed huts, layer upon layer, the result of centuries of continuous occupation. Over time the village grew in size

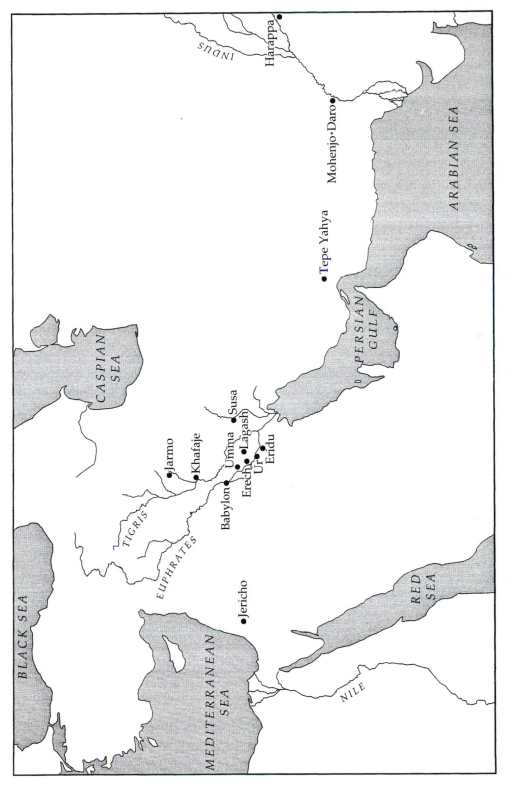

FIGURE 2-1   Ancient Middle East and Indus River Valley

31

and wealth, but it remained a village. Above the older ruins, however, was evidence of a monumental structure, an artificial mountain of clay, carefully modeled and decorated, thirty-five feet high and a thousand yards square at the top. Its religious purpose was revealed by a small shrine built atop the structure, raised closer to heaven by the mound. Larger temples were built at the base of the sloping sides of the earthwork (Childe 1951, 117).

The decorated mound of clay at Erech reveals something about the material and spiritual culture that produced it, but does it mark a transition from preurban to urban society? It does so as a symbol, albeit an early and modest one, of three dimensions of social change that are associated with the rise of the urban form: the nature and scale of social organization, the transformation of culture and experience, and the rise of empire or the state, expressed in the growing political-economic power of city-based leaders to command and control.

Change in the Scale of Social Organization

The earliest cities were not very large, either in terms of population or in the area of land that they covered. Sjoberg (1960, 36–37), upon viewing the evidence, put the population of the larger Mesopotamian centers at between five and ten thousand late in the fourth millennium. After 3000 B.C. the estimates for specific sites are somewhat higher, ranging from 12,000 (Khafaje) to 24,000 (Ur), but Sjoberg suspected that these figures are inflated. This raises the question of how big a population center has to be before it can be recognized as a city or a truly "urban" place.

There are perhaps three ways of handling this question. The first is to avoid the issue as unresolvable. A second is to attempt to establish an acceptable base figure, such as 2,500, 5,000, 10,000, or 20,000—all of which are currently employed by various census bureaus or worldwide data-gathering agencies. The problem is that to some extent these figures are all arbitrary and that a case may be made for setting any of them, or some other figure, as a standard. The third approach is to admit that we have no numerical answer to the question, How big is a city? or What is the scale of urban life? and to establish the question of size in a different way. Instead of attempting to posit a critical number of inhabitants, we look for the effects of increasing population size on the number and nature of different roles and relationships that occur among densely concentrated populations. This is essentially what the theorists Emile Durkheim ([1893] 1993) and Louis Wirth (1938), whose contributions to urban sociology are discussed in the next chapter, were attempting to establish in their work: A concentration of population leads to the specialization of the workforce. At some point, the density of sizeable populations generates the demand for specialists who are thus freed partially or altogether from agricultural production—assuming that the remaining agriculturalists can be induced to produce sufficient surplus food to support those withdrawn from production.

This is the specialization referred to by Childe in the emergence of "the army of specialized craftsmen, scribes, soldiers and miscellaneous laborers." But in the same passage, Childe notes that the archaelogical record discloses something else about the changes in social organization that were taking place. Where specialization created interdependence among the population, it also produced scarcity, in that access to the most highly valued goods and services was restricted to the few. Wealth was required for their acquisition, and some mechanism of distribution was needed to decide who would have access. The emerging urban social differentiation produced a more elaborate system of social stratification than had previously existed. Consequently, that hierarchical division of society into groups having greater and lesser access to wealth and life chances became more complex and the differences more extreme. Unprecedented positions of wealth and power were found at the peak of the elaborated hierarchy of statuses in the new, complex urban society.

Although we can understand the systemic relationship between the size and density of populations, and how these give rise to diversity and stratification, it is more difficult to reconstruct the reasons that these populations were drawn together in the first place. Childe (1951, 88–90) offered the hypothesis that in the case of the very oldest cities, massive drainage and irrigation works were required to turn swampland into productive agricultural lands. This, in turn, required the coordination of very large workforces. He reasoned that the administrative demands of coordinating this large labor force required a complex social structure, including a system of command. The logic here is that the cooperation and coordination demanded by the environment led to the permanent settlement of relatively large populations of individuals who were mutually dependent on their collective efforts.

More recent consideration suggests that the elaborate hydraulic works that Childe referred to are likely to have evolved gradually from earlier, simpler ones that required neither a large labor force nor an extensive administration in their earlier stages (McNairn 1980, 102). Even if we could resolve the question of what social and environmental forces gave rise to the first Mesopotamian city, it is unlikely that the reasons that urban societies came about in other places would have been the same. The conditions that have called forth human organization on a larger scale are likely to have varied and at different times may have involved the gradual growth of protective agricultural communities. In other cases, urban settlement may have resulted from the continuous occupation of permanent military encampments; it may have been called forth by the wealth and administrative necessity generated by trade; or it may have been related to the requirements of religious practice—as in the building of monuments requiring large-scale coordination.

To summarize, when we speak of the emergence of an urban form of *social organization*, we have the following transition in mind: As society became more urbanized, it became more socially differentiated, more specialized. This specialization, in turn, created an interdependence among the various members of society who were no longer individually capable of providing for all of their own material needs. At the same time, the variety of fine works, luxuries, and comforts magnified and elaborated the difference between the rich and poor.

These emerging cities were clearly different from the large agrarian centers that preceded them. It is important, however, not to equate the relative richness and variety that these cities contained with that of cities familiar to today's urbanite. The level of comfort enjoyed by the very few four or five thousand years ago would seem modest by current standards of affluence. Famine and invasion were recurrent threats. Luxury, restricted to the elite, was purchased at the price of the slavery or poverty of the many, whose labor supported the standards of the rich and powerful. For most of the city's existence, most urbanites lived in huts of mud or clay.

The Urban Form as Culture and the Transformation of Experience

As the dimensions of the social order became enlarged and as the division of labor produced skilled specialists and a more stratified and heterogeneous society, more elaborate and sophisticated cultures evolved that mirrored these social complexities. Early records show that trade routes covering considerable distances brought diverse cultures face to face in orderly exchange. The interminglings of societies were also generated by war and conquest. Although the average urbanite might live in a hut as a laborer or slave, the experience of the soldiers and the stories of traders and other travelers would filter to all quarters of the city. The order of the universe and the relation of heaven and earth were now interpreted by high priests, and the margins of the known world were pushed beyond the horizons that had limited experience in the long stages of prehistory. Life took place on a new scale and with a new variety. As Mumford's colorful vision states:

> In the city, godlike kings, winged bulls, hawk headed men, lionlike women, hugely magnified, erupted in clay, stone, brass, and gold. It is not merely in the theater that the spectator feels that the actors are larger than their actual life size. This is a characteristic illusion produced by the city, because the urban center is in fact a theater. . . . Thus the old active participant in the village ritual became the passive chorus, the spectators and commentators in the new urban drama. Once upon a time in the old village these lookers-on had a full share in what went on, and could perform successfully all the roles, by turn actor and spectator. Now, in the city they were diminished to supernumeraries. Perhaps not the least mission of urban monumental art was the reduction of the common man. (Mumford 1961, 70)

Although the individual's influence in shaping the new order may have diminished proportionately to the growth of social scale, Mumford (1961, 66–67) suggested further that a sense of participation and identification with a particular city may have compensated at the same time. "If the inhabitant of the city exulted in his powerful gods, he was no less proudly conscious of the circling and all containing wall: to contemporaries it seemed the great gods had fashioned the city and its temple—'the house descending from heaven'—and above all 'its great wall touching the clouds.'"

Life meanings were transformed, mystified, and raised up in the emerging urban culture, so that at its highest point heaven and earth seemed to be touching; the city provided the vehicle that brought these two planes together. Ultimately, death carried the worthy citizen across to the other side. In ancient Sumer, the wealth and position of one's temporal existence was not left behind. Wenke (1980, 415–416) noted that through 3800 B.C., at even the largest settlements, grave sites evidenced little social differentiation. By 3000 B.C., however, there was a striking difference in mortuary practice. At Ur, excavators working in the 1920s uncovered a burial pit that eventually revealed tombs of three distinct social strata: simple graves that presumably contained the remains of the common people, the more elaborate graves of the well-to-do, and a total of 16 royal tombs. In one of these tombs were the remains of a queen, found partially hidden under a mass of gold beads and precious stones. She was surrounded by sacrificial attendants and guards whose duty it apparently was to assist her in her journey, for which the party was equipped with a jeweled chariot and similarly decorated wagons. Lying nearby was a gold- and jewel-encrusted harp, across which were strewn the bones of a gold-crowned harpist.

Even though it may not be possible to pinpoint the dates at which the first urban cultures emerged, we are still able to sense something of the differences embodied in the change. At some stage, people were clearly living in a different, wider, richer world, where specialists could devote more time to contemplating the metaphysical mysteries and debating their answers. The city transformed the human experience for those living within and around its walls. But its influence did not end there.

The Rise of the State and the Growth of Political-Economic Power

Any discussion of the advent and growth of cities would be incomplete if it focused exclusively on events that occurred within and around the walls of the early city. As the urban form took shape and grew in size, the territory that came under its influence grew as well. Whatever the other requirements of urban existence, the one undeniable condition that must be met is that of a sufficiently productive agricultural base. To the extent that all early urbanites were not self-sustaining peasants or farmers, and we have observed that many were not food producers, farmers had to be induced to produce a surplus of staple food crops. As Sjoberg (1960, 68) observed, "Peasant farmers . . . rarely produce and relinquish a surplus willingly in feudal societies; thus tribute, taxation and the like must be exacted if cities are going to gain the wherewithal to support their populations." As the city emerges, therefore, we witness simultaneously the creation of a hinterland, an area containing a population that is not urbanite but subject to urban rule. They are a people whose lives have been transformed by the city, an example of the expanding dimensions of the power associated with the new form of organization. Whether it is through the teachings of the priest or the sword of the soldier, they learn that they owe their allegiance and the first share of their productive efforts to the city.

The rise of the ancient city coincides with the rise of the state, a territory under its control. The ancient city of Rome, its ruins pictured here, was the seat of a vast empire. By the Roman era, the urban form was already 3,000 years old.

If the territories under the control of the early population centers of Mesopotamia were limited to a radius of a few miles in 3500 B.C., as Hawley (1981, 22) concluded, it is not likely that this remained the case for long. Shortages of the best agricultural land are likely to have made the maintenance of territorial borders a source of constant concern and conflict (Adams 1966, 157). A growing population with the need to secure additional supplies of food, or a stable population given the uncertainties of nature, would have provided sufficient motive for territorial expansion. Sjoberg (1960, 69) observed the general rule for cities of this type: The cities that prosper most have ever-widening hinterlands. These cities must command territories that are characterized by strength, stability, and open trade routes, in addition to a dependable tributary population of agriculturalists. This is a principle that these early societies had centuries to observe and came to understand well. The city had come to represent the seat of *imperial power.*

There is evidence that the rulers of the early Mesopotamian cities were eager to extend their control beyond the area necessary for subsistence and to develop agricultural surpluses useful in military campaigns. A common feature of the early dynastic period of Sumer was the attempt by the rulers of some cities to establish hegemony over others. Regarding one of the entombments at the burial pit at Ur, Hammond (1972, 42–43) concluded that the magnitude of the riches displayed indicates that the ruler must have had military might sufficient to acquire such great wealth: "Presumably a monarch interred so elaborately ruled not only Ur but other cities as well." Adams (1966, 162) suggested that rivalry between cities periodically generated the need for military leadership and that the rise of this kind of secular ruler led to predatory expansionism among the fledgling states. In any event, written records indicate that by the latter part of this era a distinction emerged in the title of address between the rulers of dominant cities and the governors of dependent cities.

The ancient cities of the Indus River Valley, in what is today Pakistan, were in many ways typical of cities in other ancient regions of the Middle East, but in at least one important way, they were different. Harappa and Moenjo-daro were two of the major population centers in the region. Harappa probably got its start as a farming village in 3300 B.C. and by 2200 B.C. had grown to a population of 80,000, about the same size as the city of Ur in Mesopotamia. Like other ancient cities, it commanded long-distance trade. Merchants came from what today are Baluchistan and northern Afghanistan to supply copper, tin, and lapis lazuli. Sea shells, which provided the medium for local carvers, were brought from the southern seacoast. The lower slopes of the Himalayas supplied timber; semiprecious stones came from Gujarat; silver and gold arrived from as far away as Central Asia. Just as the city was influenced by distant cultures, its own culture influenced other settlements in the Indus Valley, and it exported its products to Mesopotamia, Iran, and Central Asia. Goods entering and leaving the city passed through a narrow gate in the wall that completely surrounded the settlement, and the city raised revenue from taxes on goods going in and out.

The nature of this wall and other archeological evidence has led to speculation that Harappa and the other cities of the Indus Valley may have had a different kind of history than that of other Middle Eastern cities. The straight wall, without strategic angles that would have made it a more effective device if the city were under siege, was apparently not built for military defense, but to prevent the smuggling of goods and the evasion of the tax collectors. The archeological remains of Harappa and the other major population centers in the Indus Valley bear no evidence of warfare. While Indus Valley society was clearly an economically powerful force in the ancient world—covering a territory twice the size of Mesopotamia—it was apparently not a battleground in which city-states fought to dominate one another. Current speculation is that after 700 years of stability, the end of this social order came as a result of ecological and climatic changes, not conquest (Kenoyer 1998; Menon 1998).

Once the urban form emerged in the ancient world, it exerted a central organizing influence on surrounding territories—with or without military force—developing a set of territorial relationships in which the major urban center, as political and economic nucleus, played the dominant role. In his classic work on the development of metropolitan economies, Gras (1922) focused on patterns of economic domination and subordination among settlements of different sizes. He observed that any village could contain a marketplace, but a marketplace of small traders or craftspeople did not make a city. Once those marketplaces attracted a class of trading specialists who controlled large stores of goods, however, then the settlement was more properly called a city rather than a village. Furthermore, when that city came to dominate others, becoming a center for far-flung trade, reducing other cities in the region to the status of daughter cities subordinate to its central influence, then that city had become a metropolitan center, providing a focus for a regional economy and extending its influence far beyond its immediate vicinity. In Gras's time, the evidence yielded by the ancient sites was less detailed, but he thought that perhaps some of these centers were on their way to developing true metropolitan economic influence. Today, the emerging evidence allows us to conclude more confidently that ancient centers like Harappa were indeed dominant forces that began the process of knitting distant resources into a single network of markets; these metropolitan economies were taking the first steps in organizing the exchange of the resources of the known world, what we refer to today as *globalization*.

The Development of Cities in China and Mesoamerica

Although the Middle East may have produced the earliest cities, two other regions evolved ancient urban-based societies, China and Mesoamerica. The parallels between these and early Middle Eastern societies suggest that the broad principles of urban-related social, cultural, and political changes we have described for the Middle East are generalizable. In fact, there has been some controversy, historically, about whether cities evolved independently in China, or whether the urban form was somehow transported from the Middle East in the period before written history. Today the weight of evidence supports the argument that China's historical traditions are rooted in a long prehistory of evolving local settlements and indigenous traditions (Huang 1988, 5).

There had long been speculation that China's first dynasty, the Xia dynasty, had generated the earliest urban settlements in China, but archaeologists were not able to produce a clear record of the nature of the Xia population centers until very recently. In 1990, Chinese archaeologists announced that a site that had been under excavation for several decades in coastal Shandong Province was indeed an ancient city, dating from 1900 B.C. At the same time, the group announced that an even older settlement had been discovered in the area, dating to 2600 B.C. While the older site was associated with tools made of stone and bone, it also contained a distinct style of black pottery of "exquisite craftsmanship," which indicated that pottery-making had become a specialized occupation by that time. The society that occupied the older site is known as the Longshan Culture and is identified by the distinctive pottery industry found there and elsewhere in China. The thick walls at this site enclosed a rectangular area that measured about one-fourth by one-third of a mile. Remains indicate that the site was apparently thickly populated. The substantial area covered within walls, and the probability that its population included a number of specialized artisans (indicating also the probability of a status hierarchy), favor its classification as a true city, the status attributed to it by the archeologists working at the site. The later, Xia dynasty city is more than eight times as large as the earlier site, and fills the prehistorical gap between the Longshan Culture and the more clearly documented Shang dynasty, which lasted from the sixteenth to the eleventh century B.C. (*Beijing Review*, October 1, 1990, 45–46).

Rich archeological evidence is associated with the earliest cities of the Shang dynasty, which date to 1600 B.C. The 500-year history of the dynasty, where rule was passed from brother to brother or father to son, has been preserved in writing on tens of thousands of bone fragments, the famous "oracle bones" (Huang 1988, 6–7). The record reveals, for example, that the last Shang king sent a military expedition to subdue an enemy, that the expedition took a total of 260 days, and that 2,656 enemy soldiers were killed. This may seem like a trivial piece of history to us, but we may assume that it was important news at the time and was duly recorded in 78 entries in the oracle records (Cheng 1982, 18–19). It reveals the kind of detail that a written history can provide, how much clearer the record of urban-based cultures can be where written records survive.

Between 1600 B.C. and 1100 B.C., the Shang dynasty moved its capital at least a half-dozen times. Excavations at three of these sites have brought forth massive amounts of architectural remains and other materials showing that the cities were not only administrative centers but also centers of industry. The populations were highly stratified and consisted of royal families and nobles, officials, warriors, merchants, artisans, commoners, and slaves. One of the capitals, the city of Ao (in Henan Province today), comprised an area of just under four square kilometers within the wall, and the large number of house and workship foundations located outside the wall indicate that the city had outgrown its original boundaries. By contrast, the Great City Shang, further to the north, covered an area of between 30 and 40 square kilometers and consisted of three recognizable sectors. In one of these three are 53 buildings, believed to include the palace, ancestral hall, and ceremonial compound of the Shang royal house, all apparently laid out according to a preconceived plan. The buildings are surrounded by the sacrificial burials of humans and horse chariots. Storage pits containing the valuable oracle bones were found here. Not far away is a royal cemetery where the graves of the kings are lavishly furnished and include human sacrificial remains. The dwellings of the common people and their cemeteries were separated by some distance, but all were part of the single Great City Shang (Cheng 1982, 19–20).

By the time of the Shang dynasty, the city is clearly established in China. As elsewhere, however, the date of China's very first cities is clouded by the imperfect light that can be shed by archeology. Excavation of archeological sites has been underway in China since the beginning of the twentieth century, but the interpretation of the evidence was at first hampered by the belief that city building was most likely an imported technology from the West. As Chinese antiquarians, through new discoveries, push back the record of permanent settlement and cultural advance to ever earlier dates, they thereby establish the continuity of local development, and the indigenization of Chinese urban culture is increasingly assured.

The precursors of urban civilization now appear to have been established in China as long ago as 5000 B.C. The Yi people of present-day Yunnan, Sichuan, and Guizhou provinces had by then devised a solar calendar. They built three-story, pyramid-shaped tombs that were systematically oriented with respect to solar movements and stellar formations, and served as observatories as well as grave sites. The culture of the builders bears a few striking resemblances to the Mayan culture of the New World. The Maya also had a solar calendar, and like the Yi people they adopted the tiger as their totem; they also developed similar hieroglyphic conventions and built three-tiered pyramidal platforms surprisingly similar to those of the Yi culture (*Beijing Review,* March 20, 1989, 46). There has been at least some speculation that Mesoamerican city building was inspired in the prehistoric period by Chinese cultures (Meggers 1975).

Mesoamerican cities developed much later than in Mesopotamia or China. Settled, agricultural life in Mexico apparently dates only from about 4000 B.C.: The first evidence of any human habitation goes back only to 10,000 B.C. The first long-distance traders and the earliest culture to leave monumental architectural and stone-sculptured remains were the Olmecs, whose oldest monumental artifacts appear on the southern coast of Mexico in about 1200 B.C.

The Olmecs are important because they unified a large area of southern Mexico with territories as far south as Costa Rica. Their trade items, including objects made by artists and artisans, evolved into important symbols of prestige in many areas and were available from no other source. As the artifacts produced by the Olmecs became incorporated into many of the cultures in the region, the trade provided an overall unity and order to the region. Olmec trading activity fostered a series of market sites and manufacturing sites or "towns," and it laid the commercial groundwork for the development of a succession of regional empires based in large population centers (Litvak-King 1985, 16–36). The unifying force of long-distance trade integrated much of modern-day Mexico with Guatemala, Belize, and parts of Honduras and Ecuador, creating a cultural unity referred to by anthropologists as a *culture area,* which provides a basis for the concept *Mesoamerica* (Sabloff 1989, 19). The period from 1200 B.C. through the period following the European invasion and conquest in the sixteenth century is seen most appropriately as a single complex era of cultural and political development, with exceptional periods of achievement, such as those characterized by Maya and Aztec hegemony.

The first cities in the Americas apparently were built not by the Olmecs but by their successors, including the Maya. There is probably more heated academic argument here than anywhere else over whether the early population centers of ancient Mexico were "true" cities. Two main features distinguish early Mesoamerican population centers from ancient centers elsewhere in the world: First, they have traditionally been seen as ceremonial rather than commercial centers. Their main architectural features are religious monuments that are positioned to address one another in a highly formalized, almost sculpted overall plan. Second, while these ancient sites served as the foci for large regional populations, these populations were not housed within city walls. Instead, populations were spread out over large areas. For example, Tikal, located in modern-day Guatemala, grew into a major Mayan city between 300 B.C. and 800 A.D. At its peak, it had between 30,000 and 40,000 people, but this population was scattered over about 120 square kilometers (Sabloff 1989, 83). This amounts to an average of about 290 people per square kilometer, or a little more than one person per acre. Are we prepared to see this as an urban site? Recent scholarship emphasizes the differences between Mesoamerican sites, observing that some of the larger centers fit the Western concept of "urban" places better than others (Sanders and Webster 1988). Others argue that smaller and less densely populated places served similar functions to other ancient cities, and therefore deserve to be recognized as such (Smith 1989).

Keeping this debate in mind, it appears that most regional scholars are of the opinion that the first Mesoamerican cities appeared in about 500 B.C. In quick succession, large religious and administrative centers arose in the Valley of Oaxaca; at Teotihuacan in Central Mexico (300 B.C.); and at various Mayan sites in Belize, Guatemala, and Yucatan (300 B.C.). The first of these, today called Monte Alban, grew to a population of 15,000 by the third century B.C. A century later the population of a rival city, Teotihuacan, was probably 40,000; it continued to grow during the next six centuries to between 120,000 and 200,000 people.

The Classic Period of Mayan civilization, dating from 300 B.C. to 800 A.D., featured familiar patterns associated with the growth of ancient cities elsewhere. These included increasing populations, increasing nucleation of the population, craft specialization, the growth of wealth and power of the urban elite, expanding bureaucracy, increased social stratification, and an increase in the competition between cities. The Mayan age lasted long enough that it was characterized by many fluctuations in political and economic fortunes, and many regional shifts, as some urban sites declined and others rose to prominence. The archeological record does not indicate clearly why particular sites declined when they did, and speculation centers on many factors that may have contributed to their decline (political infighting, ecological collapse following extended occupation of a site, or changes in relationships with other population centers) (Sabloff 1989, 92–93).

The Aztecs came to dominate the other people of Mexico late in the period leading up to the Spanish invasion in 1521. Beginning in 1325, they built up the site for the city of Tenochtitlan from swampy islands at the edge of Lake Texcoco. Over the course of the fifteenth century, the Aztecs came to rule a large empire in central Mexico from their capital city. They collected tribute from subject peoples throughout the region. At its height, early in the sixteenth century, it is estimated that the population of Tenochtitlan was between 200,000 and 300,000 people. The Spaniards wrote that they were amazed, could not believe their eyes, at the scale of the conquered city. But the conquest and European diseases brought complete destruction. "The complex, civilized world of ancient Mexico, which had produced such marvels as . . . Tenochtitlan over a 3,000-year-long period, came to an abrupt, catastrophic end" (Sabloff 1989, 130). Archaeologists continue to explore the ancient settlement, hampered by the fact that today the largest city in the world, Mexico City, grows on the site.

The Significance of Early Urbanization

Changes in the scale of social organization, the transformation of culture, and the rise of the state led V. Gordon Childe to designate the ancient era as the era of *the* Urban Revolution (1951, Chapter 7). Among its revolutionary achievements, he included the growth of technology, especially in architecture and the smelting of metals, and the long-distance trade among urbanizing cultures that led to the diffusion of ideas and skills, in addition to goods. Once the city had emerged as a social invention, it proliferated and persisted. Although particular urban societies came and went, the city remained the heart of empire, technology, and civilization. The ancient city reached its fullest development in Greek and Roman cultures. Athens may have had 120,000 to 180,000 inhabitants at its peak in the fifth century B.C. (Davis 1955, 432). Estimates of the population of the city of Rome range from a few hundred thousand upwards to nearly two million. Mumford's (1961, 231, 236) sources indicate that in Rome as many as 200,000 poor received regular rations of bread issued from public storehouses. An inventory dating from early in the fourth century A.D. indicates that there were 46,602 "lodging houses" in the city. In addition to the great city itself, the Roman Empire fostered a number of provincial capitals. Although the decline of Rome may have ushered in a dark age for much of Europe, as the empire's urban outposts withered until they contained mere fractions of their former populations, other urban cultures were flourishing. The seventh century marked the beginning of the rapid expansion of Islamic cities that would continue throughout the medieval period. Udovitch (1977, 143) observed that "urbanism is a characteristic feature of the entire [medieval Islamic] period and all its parts. . . . The spiritual, material, and political culture of medieval Islam was an almost exclusively urban creation."

By the medieval era, China, where the city had come into existence by 2000 B.C., had become a network of administrative cities organized in a hierarchy, each one typically planned to symbolically reflect the relationship between humanity and nature by its spatial arrangement (Williams 1983, 413–417). Between A.D. 900 and 1200, it is possible that four or five of the largest Chinese cities were not far short of a million inhabitants (Elvin 1978, 79). From their earliest beginnings, the number of people who lived within the cities of the great societies, or whose lives were subject to urban-based rule, was gradually increasing.

Yet Kingsley Davis (1955, 429-432) believed that the influence of urbanization in any era before the late eighteenth century was too limited to qualify as an "urban revolution." While he conceded that the advent of the urban form represents a fundamental change in the pattern of social life, he argued that this change touched the lives of relatively few people living in earlier times. Observing that it must have taken the work of fifty to ninety farmers to support a single urbanite, he concluded that the urban proportion of a given population must have been limited to 1 or 2 percent. Furthermore, he was critical of elevating some of the earlier and smaller places that we have discussed to the status of "city," noting what he felt is the inclination of researchers to call any unearthed settlement a city if it had "a few streets and a public building or two." Although Davis allowed that by 3000 B.C. "true" cities had emerged, he reserved the designation of "true urban revolution" for the era of explosive growth that accompanied the Industrial Revolution. Not until this point in history were large proportions of the population of a major world region gathered into cities.

The Urbanization of Europe

When the Roman Empire disintegrated, it left its urban outposts isolated, and in Europe they fell prey to the formerly conquered and subjected societies of the region. Many of these cities disappeared, while others shrank into towns and villages. The achievements of urban culture, such as those in medicine and astronomy, were maintained in these smaller centers or kept alive in monasteries or other cloisters. However, by the tenth century, Venice and other independent Italian cities had been called to new life by Mediterranean trade with the cities of the Eastern Roman Empire, which had continued under Byzantine rule (Sjoberg [1965] 1973, 25–26).

Elsewhere in Europe, towns gradually grew again in response to trade, the opportunity for which was created by the stirrings and movements of the repeated crusades to the Holy Land. The medieval cities that profited and grew were in some ways similar to and in other ways different from the ancient cities. The cities were still walled for protection, and their growing numbers of inhabitants were squeezed within these walls, making them vulnerable to repeated epidemics of disease, such as the plague. As was the case in ancient times, staple grains were stockpiled against years when crops failed or warfare threatened (Rorig [1955] 1967, 113–114). Among the differences that set medieval cities apart from ancient cities were the nature of government and the locus of power within the population. From the eleventh through the thirteenth centuries, among the German states, power slipped away from the religious leaders and the nobility where it had traditionally resided. They were replaced by the richest burghers and the long-distance traders, who embodied the new urban theme that had given the medieval city its reason for being—the marketplace (Rorig [1955] 1967, 22–29).

German traders set out deliberately to found a string of urban "colonies" reaching north into the Baltic Sea, a trading network that developed into a monopoly of regional trade from the middle of the twelfth until well into the thirteenth century. For the first time, German merchants thus united northern Europe into an important economic entity. Although these towns were modest in size, seldom exceeding 20,000 in population, it would be a mistake to attempt to assess their importance by comparing them to population units of similar size today. These compact settlements would have "fulfilled a political, economic, and cultural function [of] which many a present-day town of several hundred thousand would be envious," according to Rorig. In his estimation, "the medieval town [was] one of the most important impulses in world history" (Rorig [1955] 1967, 111, 113).

By 1300, urban growth on a larger scale was once again occurring in Europe. London had grown on the site of the old Roman outpost to a population of 45,000; Paris was much larger, perhaps containing 228,000 people by that date (Chandler 1987). In Italy, several of the urban centers that lent their names to the city-states they ruled had grown through three centuries of sustained economic and population expansion. But before the Renaissance would regenerate urban growth in the fifteenth century, the Black Plague of 1348 and subsequent years of epidemic diseases reduced the population of Italian cities, as they did the populations of other European centers, by 35 to 65 percent. Milan had 150,000 inhabitants in 1300, but a century after the plaque had rebounded only to fewer than 90,000. The populations of other Italian cities—Venice, Florence, Genoa, Bologna, Siena, Pisa, Padua—smaller than Milan before the epidemics, were similarly reduced. This makes the achievements of the Renaissance era that were sponsored by these centers all the more remarkable. Box 2-1 briefly describes Florence, where the population was at least halved (from 95,000 to perhaps 40,000) between 1300 and the early 1400s (Martines 1979, 168).

BOX 2-1   Renaissance Florence

We associate the Renaissance, the rebirth of artistic and other high cultural achievement in Europe, with the great Italian city-states of the 1400s. Among the most prominent of the Italian Renaissance cities was Florence. Within the space of a few decades, Brunelleschi created the dome of the great cathedral, Ghiberti sculpted the astonishing North Doors of the Baptistery, Fra Angelico executed the frescoes of the convent San Marco, Massaccio painted his *Trinity* for the cathedral Santa Maria Novella, Donatello sculpted *The Maddelina*, and others, including Fra Filippo Lippi, Domenico Veneziano, Andrea del Castagno, and Uccello, were at work adding to the storm of creative energy that brought every public space, facade, and interior to life. Peter Hall (1998, 69–70) made two observations that help us appreciate the extraordinary nature of Florentine accomplishment. First, Hall noted that Renaissance Florence had

The Ponte Vecchio, the old bridge over the Arno, served as a private covered walkway for the wealthy Medici family as they traveled daily from palace to business in Renaissance Florence. Today, it is lined with the shops of jewelers, and by night, immigrant African street traders offer bargain designer copies.

BOX 2-1 *Continued*

at most 95,000 people (probably far fewer), roughly equivalent to the present-day population of a "smallish English country town," or Bakersfield, California. The Florence that produced the great volume of art in the fifteenth century was by no means a large city by today's standards. Second, the creative burst of energies was no accident or coincidence: Civic leaders consciously promoted the ascendancy of Florence over other Renaissance cities in accordance with what they believed was the city's destiny. As Hall put it, "these works were the conscious creations of the entire collectivity, they were not simply expressions of individual creativity or genius, but the result of long deliberations in committees and rigorous, indeed contentious and bitter, competition among artists of huge talent—and frequently—egos to match" (65). Florence was a self-contained state that waged wars with similar states, where the Medici, Pitti, and Rucellai families created empires of wealth and, along with the Church, became patrons of architecture, sculpture, and painting. It was a place where the populace believed that "By its ugliness an old building may be a disgrace to the town, while a new one should redound to its honor and ornament" (Burkhardt 1985, 4). The wealth of achievements in art and architecture that has survived the ages and draws us to Florence today was created within an atmosphere of inspiration that was not simply artistic, but also combined a particular mix of political and economic factors and local civic loyalties. Taking nothing away from the talents or genius of the individuals who produced the works themselves, we may ask to what extent it is appropriate to argue that the city, rather than its artists, produced Florence's contribution to the Renaissance. Or, if we stand before the great Florentine works that are included in the city's Uffizi Gallery, what are we seeing? What are we missing by not knowing at least a little of the history of the city that provided a time and place for their creation?

In the next three or four centuries, European exploration and colonization fueled the growth of the continental capitals and other cities. Lisbon had a population of more than 100,000 by 1600, and grew to more than 200,000 by the mid-1700s. The population of Madrid is estimated to have reached 80,000 in 1600, and 110,000 in 1750. By 1700, the populations of London and Paris surpassed the half-million mark (Chandler 1987, 474–484).

By the early 1700s, the landscape of Europe became increasingly dotted with an assortment of manufacturing and market towns, provincial centers, and cities of various sizes, in addition to the growing metropolises. The world was about to enter a period of revolutionary change in which the city once more would play an important role.

The Industrial Revolution

For some time historians have been refocusing the image of the Industrial Revolution until it is no longer viewed as a relatively sudden transformation, but as the culmination of a gradual economic process that took place over several centuries. By the early sixteenth century, there was already some evidence of local industrial specialization in England. Coventry specialized in textiles and metals, Northampton and Leicester in leather trades, and Birmingham in metals (Musson 1978, 17).

Although the populations of industrial cities would grow explosively from the 1760s through the mid-1800s—the period generally considered as the Industrial Revolution—the population of Liverpool had already multiplied by ten times from 1680 to 1760, and the population of Manchester by five times from 1717 to 1773. Moreover, a full-fledged textile factory had been in operation at Derby since 1719 (George 1931, 144–147).

> *There was no sharp division between the medieval and early modern economy and society. Towns had been growing, trade and industry had been expanding, a monetary economy and a system of mercantile credit had been developing over earlier centuries and as markets expanded . . . industrial specialization and the division of labor had been increasing, tending to produce distinctions between agriculture and industry, between town and country. (Musson 1978, 21)*

Therefore, it is important to recognize that the roots of the Industrial Revolution began deep in the medieval period, and that it is more accurately viewed as a gradual process rather than an abrupt change occurring at some point around the date of 1760. However, the cumulation of changes that occurred after this approximate date is dramatic.

The Industrial Revolution is considered to be comprised of improvements in industrial machinery, especially textiles, of improvements in the steam engine and its utilization as a source of power in manufacturing, and of the use of coal in iron smelting. However, a number of other changes, having no direct relationship to industrial or manufacturing technology, were occurring at the same time, each seemingly amplifying the effect of the others. Between 1750 and 1800, the European population grew as death rates declined. This decline in death rates is attributed to improvements in agricultural productivity, which included the introduction of artificial manures, new methods of crop rotation, and the development of heavier, more efficient livestock through planned breeding techniques. Fluctuations in yearly harvests were reduced, and except for Ireland (1845–1850), famine had largely disappeared from western Europe. Medical practice and the understanding of disease improved, although plague, typhus, smallpox, cholera, malaria, and tuberculosis still took a terrible toll (Armengaud [1970] 1976, 38–43).

England, which led the way in industrialization, was in the process of establishing a colonial empire and took measures to control or eliminate competition in trade; thus the city retained the imperial function it had acquired in ancient times. This trade, which provided the basis for a large shipbuilding industry, was carried on in part with Africa, India, and the Americas, giving rise to industries that processed tropical raw materials and providing markets for the export of textiles, metals, and other manufactures. Trade was necessary to maintain the rapid growth of industry and, thereby, the growth of European cities. It was the dimensions of this growth that led Davis (1955, 433) to conclude that "the transformation thus achieved in the nineteenth century was the true urban revolution, for it meant not only the rise of a few scattered towns and cities, but the appearance of genuine urbanization in the sense that a substantial proportion of the population lived in towns and cities."

At this stage of the history of urban growth it became more possible to speak in terms of the important concept of *urbanization*. As Davis pointed out, this is the growth of the proportion or percent of a given (for example, national) population living in urban areas. In the early nineteenth century, reliable comparative data became available from national census records, and we can compare rates of urbanization country by country, at least for Europe. This makes it possible to begin to evaluate Davis's claim that the nineteenth century marked a truly revolutionary era measured in terms of urbanization rates.

The urbanization of the populations of selected European nations is reflected in Table 2-1. That portion of the British Isles that includes England, Scotland, and Wales most clearly embodies the revolutionary change referred to by Davis. The island was transformed from a predominantly rural society to a predominantly urban society within the span of the nineteenth century. However, the experience of the other European nations, as well as Russia and the United States, falls into one of two general patterns. For the Netherlands, Spain, and Portugal, the urbanization curve is rather flat. In these countries, urban growth was sponsored in an earlier era by imperial trade rather than by industrial growth. The pattern is different, however, for another group of countries that includes Belgium, Prussia, the United States, France, Switzerland, Austria, and Russia. In the most urbanized of these countries, only about one-fourth of the population was living in cities of 20,000 or more by the end of the century. The impact of the Industrial Revolution

TABLE 2-1   The Urbanizing World in the Nineteenth Century: Percentage of Populations Living in Cities of 20,000 or More

	1800	1850	1890
England and Wales	16.9 (1801)	35.0 (1851)	53.6 (1891)
Scotland	13.9 (1801)	27.7 (1851)	42.4 (1891)
Belgium	8.7 (1800-1810)	16.6 (1846)	26.1 (1890)
Netherlands	24.5 (1795)	21.7 (1849)	31.3 (1889)
Prussia	6.0 (1816)	7.8 (1849)	23.0 (1890)
United States	3.8 (1800)	9.8 (1850)	23.8 (1890)
France	6.7 (1801)	10.6 (1851)	21.1 (1891)
Spain	9.8 (1820 ca.)	9.6 (1857)	18.0 (1887)
Ireland	6.6 (1800 ca.)	8.7 (1851)	15.3 (1891)
Switzerland	1.3 (1822)	5.2 (1850)	13.2 (1888)
Austria	3.6 (1800 ca.)	4.2 (1843)	12.0 (1890)
Portugal	10.3 (1801)	10.7 (1857)	9.2 (1890)
Russia	2.4 (1820)	3.5 (1856)	7.2 (1885)

Source: Adna F. Weber [1899] 1965, 144–145. *The Growth of Cities in the Nineteenth Century: A Study in Statistics.* Ithaca, NY: Cornell University Press.
Note: Figures have been rounded to nearest tenth.

came more gradually and later to these countries. So when referring to the Industrial Revolution in Europe, we need to keep these variations in mind. Finally, Ireland has been included as a special case: The population of this country was rapidly urbanizing during the nineteenth century, although the trend is not apparent from the data presented in the table. This is because the "urbanization" of the Irish population was taking place through emigration in England, the United States, Canada, and Australia.

Also hidden in the growth rates, and adding to their significance, is the fact that the overall population of Europe, rural as well as urban, was growing. Due to mortality rates that remained high throughout the century, urban populations did not experience a natural increase (i.e., an increase caused by having a birthrate higher than the prevailing death rate). Urban growth is attributable to the fact that the cities continued to draw a large portion of their labor force through migration from rural areas. Even so, the growth of the rural population kept pace with the growth of the urban population through the late 1700s (Armengaud [1970] 1976, 32). During the 1800s, as the *proportion* of rural population began to decrease in relation to the growing urban population, the *absolute number* of people employed in the agricultural labor force remained steady, supported by the increasing food demand of the growing urban population (Bergier [1971] 1976, 423–424).

The increase in urban population reflects both the growth in the number of urban places and the growth in the size of individual cities. For example, in 1800 six cities within the states of Italy were above 100,000 in population; just over a century later (1910), thirteen cities were above this figure in population. In 1800 only St. Petersburg and Moscow in Russia could count over 100,000 inhabitants, but by 1910 twelve cities were in this category in Russia, with Moscow having 1.5 million inhabitants and St. Petersburg nearly 2 million (Armengaud [1970] 1976, 34–35). Table 2-2 traces the growth of individual capitals during the nineteenth century. By 1891 London, with over 4 million people, had grown to nearly five times its size at the turn of the century. And in ninety years, Paris, with almost 2.5 million, had grown to four and one-half times its former size. The most rapid urban growth, however, was taking place not in these old centers but in a new urban form, the industrial city. Although London continued to grow at the remarkable rate of 16 to 20 percent per decade throughout the century, much greater rates of growth were being recorded in the rapidly industrializing north at Liverpool, Birmingham, Leeds, Sheffield, and Manchester, each of which had grown by more than 40 percent in just ten years between 1821 and 1831. In addition, Bradford had grown by 65 percent (Sheppard 1971, xv–xviii).

These cities presented an alteration of the urban form, a new city whose reason for being sprang from the technology and economics of factory production, where it became practical to collect large numbers of workers in proximity to the power source—the great steam engine. The industrial focus of the new cities affected all dimensions of life for those who were gathered to work and live in them. But many of the old established centers were also deeply changed by the process of industrialization. Despite the rapid growth of the industrial cities of Lancashire

TABLE 2-2 The Growth of Major Cities during the Nineteenth Century

	1800	1820	1840	1860	1880	1890
London	864,845 (1801)	1,224,694 (1821)	1,873,676 (1841)	2,803,989 (1861)	2,823,354 (1881)	4,232,118 (1891)
Paris	547,756 (1801)	713,966 (1821)	935,261 (1841)	1,696,741 (1861)	2,269,023 (1881)	2,447,957 (1891)
Berlin	—	201,138 (1819)	283,727 (1837)	547,571 (1861)	1,122,330 (1880)	1,578,794 (1890)
Vienna	232,000 (1800)	260,224 (1821)	356,869 (1840)	476,222 (1857)	705,402 (1880)	798,719 (1890)
Glasgow	81,048 (1801)	147,043 (1821)	274,533 (1841)	436,432 (1861)	674,095 (1881)	782,445 (1891)
Budapest	61,000 (1800)	85,000 (1820)	156,506 (1850)	186,945 (1857)	360,551 (1880)	491,938 (1890)
Madrid	156,670 (1805 ca.)	167,607 (1820 ca.)	—	281,170 (1857)	—	470,283 (1887)
Lisbon	350,000 (1801)	—	—	275,286 (1857)	246,343 (1878)	370,661 (1890)

Source: Adna F. Weber [1899] 1965, 46, 60, 73, 84, 95, 101, 119, 120. *The Growth of Cities in the Nineteenth Century: A Study in Statistics.* Ithaca, NY: Cornell University Press.

and Yorkshire, London became and remained the leading manufacturing center of the country (Sheppard 1971, 158). During the 1800s,

> *The view from Westminster Bridge (and from many other places in London too) had changed greatly. The air had become laden with smoke of steam vessels, gas-works, and the furnaces of a host of industrial establishments, and the snort and hiss of railway locomotives at the new terminus at Waterloo Station could constantly be heard. Downstream, the noble prospect towards the City and the dome of St. Paul's had been ruthlessly sundered by the brick and iron of Charing Cross Railway Bridge. Beneath Westminster Bridge itself still flowed the perennial river, no longer gliding "at its own sweet will," but controlled and restricted by the great granite wall of Victoria Embankment, along which clattered an endless procession of carriages, buses, cabs and carts, and beneath which there now extended an underground railway and two giant tunnels, one for gas and water pipes and telegraph wires, and the other for sewage. Upstream, too, the change was as great—to the left a vast new hospital, to the right a new palace of Westminster, more embankments, more bridges. Nothing within sight "lay open to the fields," and even the sooty parapet of Westminster Bridge itself was new—iron in place of stone. London had been transformed. (Sheppard 1971, xv–xvi)*

The Dimensions of Urbanization in the Industrial Revolution

The industrialization of cities meant much more than their rapid growth and change in appearance. The discussion of the earliest cities explored three major dimensions of their existence: a change in social organization, an enriched human experience, and the advent of the urban form creating the territorial city/hinterland relationship. The Industrial Revolution held its own powerful consequence for the ways in which the city influenced society and affected experience. In the following discussion, these three dimensions, which denote the consequences of urbanization, are considered for the industrial era.

Social Organization

Along with the rise of industrial urbanization in England, a conservative, reformist criticism of the ways in which common people spent their leisure time emerged among the guardians of the social conscience. In addition to football, cricket, and other team sports, other pastimes popular with townspeople in the 1700s were bearbaiting and bullbaiting, cockfighting, wrestling, cudgel playing (dueling with poles), dancing, and parish feasts and fairs. According to Malcolmson (1973, 170–171), these traditional recreations were rooted in a society that was still predominantly agrarian and parochial. Those concerned with public order did not see these pastimes as being compatible with a society that was increasingly contractual and individualistic, and that accommodated first and foremost to the requirements of industrial production and factory discipline. Whereas such popular recreations may have had their place in a medieval setting, in 1743 *Gentleman's Magazine* warned that "the Diversion of Cricket might be proper in Holiday-Time in the Country, but upon Days when men might be busy, and in the Neighborhood of a great City, it is not only improper but mischievous in a high Degree" (Malcolmson 1973, 161).

In the industrial villages, the textile centers, and the industrializing metropolis concern for the discipline of the growing workforce was most pronounced and problems of social control were most closely studied. By the end of the eighteenth century, opposition to traditional recreations was the ascendant voice, and by the second quarter of the nineteenth century, the very limited supply of alternative, attractive sources of recreation was marked by the overwhelming importance of the public house (Malcolmson 1973, 171). Urban life, to the extent that it had now become industrial life, demanded a new level of discipline or at least the docile compliance of its workforce.

The largest proportion of the growing urban population was made up of industrial workers. Most of them had no real property and owned no share in the productive machinery at which they worked—they were a proletariat. The proletariat had existed before the Industrial Revolution, living in the towns, overcrowded and overworked; "a state of affairs that industry could generalize and prolong, but hardly worsen" (Bergier [1971] 1976, 419–420). Understanding these people's story is essential to understanding life in the cities of this era. However, the changes in organization that occurred in this period went beyond the expansion of a great laboring class. The impact of industrial urbanization on social organization was nearly as sweeping as that of the revolutionary changes in social life brought about by the advent of the first cities. The requirements of industrial technology called forth an increasing number of specialists to design, finance, build, sell, provide services for, and administer this complex apparatus and its products. The division of labor became extremely rationalized, breaking the production process down into its least, irreducible tasks and coordinating the integration of the many productive functions. This was the era of the rise and formalization of bureaucracy, again a rational system of social organization devoted to the accomplishment of complex tasks, such as the construction of a steamship or the administration of the city itself. Bureaucracy mimicked the efficient machinery of the industrial age within the realm of social organization.

The industrial city contained a large number of statuses and occupations. In early nineteenth-century Germany, differentiation within the ranks of the industrial workers themselves is reflected in the fact that some male workers received eight to twelve times as much as the lowest paid child, and four to five times as much as the lowest paid adult male worker (Sagarra 1977, 363). Beyond industry, we find further differentiation among the urban populations. The distribution of occupations in London in 1851 is presented in Table 2-3. London may not have been the typical industrial city, but it did remain the foremost manufacturing center in Britain throughout the period. Although Table 2-3 does not distinguish

TABLE 2-3   Distribution of Occupations in London, 1851

Occupational Category	Percentage of Workforce
Skilled labor	39.2
Semiskilled labor	23.6
Unskilled labor	10.5
Shopkeepers	9.5
Subprofessionals	7.0
Professionals (including owners and managers)	4.3
Employees and clerks	1.9
Agricultural	.5
Others, unknown	3.5

Source: Recalculated from "Statistical Appendix" in Sheppard (1971, 389). Data compiled by Lees (1969).

industrial work from other work, industry's share of the labor force is included in the three categories of labor, totaling nearly three-fourths (73.3 percent) of all occupations. Shopkeepers (large and small), along with professionals (including owners) and subprofessionals, make up a large proportion of the remainder of the workforce. The figures also conceal the large number of domestic workers (servants), which, for Britain as a whole, numbered more than 1 million in 1851, and 1.8 million by 1881.

Another important category is comprised of those outside of the labor force, accounting for nearly half the population of the city. This segment of the population can be divided into those who could afford not to work and those who could not find work. Many of the latter were forced to turn to the streets for their livelihood. In Box 2-2, Sheppard provides a reconstruction of street life in London, which shows both its color and the desperation of some of those who had to make their living from it.

The enormous congregation of population in the cities of the nineteenth century was a huge, spontaneous experiment. It caused many to wonder whether society could continue, what form it would take, and how the massing populations would be controlled. What would be the consequences of the urbanization of the world? We will postpone consideration of the speculation that was offered in response to these kinds of questions until Chapter 3.

The Urban Experience in the Industrialized City

For most of the inhabitants of the new city, the conditions of life were dominated by the conditions of work. These have become more or less well known. It is necessary to understand, however, that a workday comprised of long, hard hours was not something new in itself: Artisans and farmers had always worked similarly long hours. What was new was the monotony of the work and the strict and constant supervision under which it was carried out. It may have been because the repetitive work was so dulling and dehumanizing—in addition to the fact that through the practice of child labor, adults had become socialized to accept their

---

BOX 2-2   Petty Trades and Street Life in Nineteenth
Century London

Besides those who worked for a wage there were thousands of others who worked in equally various ways on their own account. For such people the public streets were the cheapest places to work in, for there were no rents or rates to pay, nor heating or lighting, and in many trades the equipment required could be bought for a shilling or two. The streets of mid-nineteenth century London bustled and rang with a quasi-nomadic economic life which has now almost completely disappeared. There were some 30,000 coster mongers alone, dealing in fruit, vegetables, or fish, either going their rounds with their barrows, or congregating at the street markets, particularly on Saturday nights and Sunday mornings when the poor did their shopping. But almost any article of food could be bought in the streets, delicacies such as hot eels, pickled whelks, and sheep's trotters being included in the daily menu alongside such more commonplace items as bread, milk, cat's meat, and even water. Many small manufactured articles were always on offer

from itinerant salesmen-fusees, flypapers, cutlery, old clothes, rat poison, toys, and spectacles, for instance; there were dog-sellers, bird-sellers, goldfish-sellers, blind sellers of matches or needles, and in the poorer districts a living could be made (or at any rate attempted) by the writing of begging letters to individual customer's requirements. But the street was more than a place of business; the acrobats, jugglers, conjurers, singers, pavement artists, strong men, hurdy-gurdy men, and Punch-and-Judy men made it a place of entertainment as well. Shoe-blacking or cross-sweeping often provided children with a cheap mode of entry into the great world of street trade, and if all else failed, the destitute could resort to the collection of the very ordure of the streets—cigar ends, the droppings of horses and even dogs, the last being sold by the pail-full to the tanneries. . . . Destitution, in fact, led many women to prostitution and many children to crime. (Sheppard 1971, 365-367)

---

condition—that workers had neither the energy nor the will to successfully resist the imposition (Bergier [1971] 1976, 430–431).

In Germany in the mid-nineteenth century, the average number of hours worked per day was 15 or 16, often without a break for meals. Work could begin at four or five in the morning and finish at eight or nine at night. Child labor reforms, prohibiting the employment of children under nine and limiting the workday to 10 hours for children fourteen or younger, were not effectively enforced until the 1860s in Prussia, Bavaria, and Baden (Sagarra 1977, 364), Still, this made cities there among the earliest examples of effective child labor laws in the industrializing nations.

Although industrial wages were low for most workers, in many cases they were higher than those received by agricultural workers. However, industrial work could be intermittent, as a result of fluctuations in the demand for manufactured products or the increasing ability of industrial production technology to outstrip existing levels of demand. In contrast with those living and working in rural areas, or in the towns of an earlier era, "in the crowded industrial towns, the urban worker had no garden in which to grow his vegetables, or common on which to keep his pig or poultry, no wood from which to gather kindling or game to trap or poach" (Minchinton [1973] 1976, 112). The urbanite had become a hybrid,

The streets of the cities of the Industrial Revolution were filled by people attempting to earn a living by street trades. Here Gustave Doré's drawing of London's Bishopsgate Street in the 1870s preserves a glimpse of that street life.

wholly dependent upon external conditions of supply and demand over which the individual had no control.

The Industrial Revolution that called the people of Europe to its cities did not automatically foster enlightened and effective government planning and housing policies. The lessons of how to accommodate and care for the health and welfare of the huge and rapidly growing populations of the urban poor were learned slowly, through trial and error, and not in time to benefit those who took part in the earlier phases of the revolution. At first, industrialization led to desperate conditions of crowding throughout Europe. Every available inch of residential space was exploited, and new housing was built within the shadows of factories, as in the case of the back-to-back row houses of English cities that allowed no air or light into the back rooms where families crowded. Although the conditions of housing were bad by any standard, it is necessary to recall, for the purpose of drawing appropriate comparisons, the conditions of the housing that was being left behind by migrants from rural areas. Typically their housing consisted of rough huts of timber, sod, or stone, with earth floors and small holes for windows (not always glazed); the huts were often smoke filled and chimneyless, overcrowded and cold (Minchinton [1973] 1976, 144–145). Nevertheless, the concentration of the poor in cities led to conditions difficult to imagine. We have vivid descriptions of those conditions from the fiction of Charles Dickens and the accounts of Alexis de Tocqueville, but none more grim than the passage in Box 2-3 from Friedrich Engels, who conducts us on a stroll through certain sections of Manchester, England, in 1844. The city had grown from 70,000 in 1801 to 240,000 in 1841. At the end of the passage, Engels tells us that his description is not an exaggeration.

The conditions of crowding and poverty were, of course, not only restricted to rapidly growing English cities but also existed elsewhere in Europe and the United States. In Germany the conditions may have been made more serious by the fact that, until the second half of the nineteenth century, many cities, including Frankfurt and Hamburg, were walled and their gates closed at night. In Barmen in 1847, an inspector on an inspection tour for that city's rehousing commission found "in a room like a broken down stable some twelve feet long, seven feet wide, and six feet high were ten people of both sexes in one bed covered with rags; in another, right under the roof, six feet long, seven feet wide, and five feet high were four people; in a cellar ten feet long, eight feet wide, and six feet high were six more" (Sagarra 1977, 393). In the United States, industrial growth spread out from the cities' centers into residential areas, where the existing housing was modified to accommodate the families of the working poor into single rooms and makeshift dwellings erected in backyards. Some of these were multistoried. Alternatively, existing structures would be demolished, and more efficient but equally overcrowded tenements erected in their place. Breweries, outhouses, and warehouses were also converted for rental to the poor. A final alternative, chosen by many, was to become an illegal squatter on vacant land. As many as three-fifths of the recipients of private and public charity in New York City in 1860 were shack-dwelling squatters (Klebanow, Jonas, and Leonard 1977, 82–83).

BOX 2-3   Friedrich Engels's Manchester, 1844

Going from Old Church to Long Millgate, the stroller has at once a row of old-fashioned houses to the right, of which not one has kept its original level; these are remnants of the old pre-manufacturing Manchester. . . . But all this is nothing compared to the courts and lanes which lie behind, to which passage can be gained only through covered passages, in which no two human beings can pass at the same time. Of the irregular cramming together of dwellings in ways which defy all rational plan, of the tangle in which they are crowded literally one upon the other, it is impossible to convey an idea. . . .

The south bank of the [River] Irk here is very steep and between fifteen and thirty feet high. On this declivitous hillside there are planted three rows of houses, of which the lowest rises directly out of the river . . . a narrow coal black foul-smelling stream, full of debris and refuse, which it deposits on the shallower right bank. In dry weather, a long string of the most disgusting, blackish-green slime pools are left standing on the bank, from the depths of which bubbles of miasmatic gas constantly arise and give forth a stench unendurable even on the bridge forty or fifty feet above the surface of the stream. But besides this, the stream is checked every few paces by high weirs, behind which slime and refuse accumulate and rot in thick masses.

Above the bridge are tanneries, bone-mills, and gas-works, from which all drains and refuse find their way into the Irk, which receives further the contents of all the neighbouring sewers and privies. It may be easily imagined, therefore, what sort of residue the stream deposits. Below the bridge you look upon the piles of debris, the refuse, filth, and offal from the courts on the steep left bank; here each house is packed close behind its neighbor and a piece of each is visible, all black, smoky, crumbling, ancient, with broken panes and window frames. The background is furnished by old barrack-like factory buildings. . . .

Such is the old town of Manchester, and on re-reading my description, I am forced to admit that instead of being exaggerated, it is far from black enough to convey a true impression of the filth, ruin, and uninhabitableness, the defiance of all considerations of cleanliness, ventilation, and health which characterize the construction of this single district, containing at least twenty to thirty thousand inhabitants. . . . True, this is the Old Town . . . but what does that prove? Everything which here rouses horror and indignation is of recent origin, belongs to the industrial epoch *(Engels 1970 [1936] 27–32).*

As these descriptions suggest, cities remained unhealthy places in which to live and work. Besides the desperate residential and work conditions suffered by urban residents, the general environment of the city was filthy. There was, in many places, a chronic difficulty in keeping sewage out of the water supply, and everywhere the practice was to dispose of all forms of garbage and waste in the street. Here the waste would await the rummaging of dogs or swine or, when the public roads became truly impassable, the irregular removal efforts sponsored by the city governments. Despite the advances in nutrition and medicine mentioned earlier, mortality rates in urban areas remained higher and life expectancy lower than regional or national norms. Crude statistics gathered in the late 1800s revealed that the average person in Massachusetts could expect to live 41.5 years, while the average native Bostonian could anticipate only 34.9 years. Comparable figures for France and for Paris are 42.2 and 28.1 years, respectively; and 38.1 and 30.3 years, respectively, for the Netherlands and its urban population (Weber [1899] 1965, 346). Urban mortality rates were correlated further with the density of population in particular districts. In the London district of St. Giles in the Fields, where densities remained at around 220 per acre for the period in question, annual mortality rose from 26 per thousand in the 1840s to 28 per thousand in the 1850s and 29 per thousand in the 1860s. In Church Lane, in an area referred to as the "Irish rookery," 310 of each 1,000 children born in the 1840s died before reaching age one; of the remainder, 457 of each 1,000 died before age two (Sheppard 1971, 17).

The conditions of employment were dangerous for early industrial and other workers, and an injury such as a broken leg could mean permanent disability to a wage earner and pauperism to his family. Women and children worked in the new industries of early nineteenth century America and Europe. Women earned lower wages than men and were segregated into a few types of manufacturing, which added to the competition for positions and thus drove down their wages. In New York, the labor market was oversupplied with female job seekers, which often allowed wages to fall below subsistence: A woman could expect to be unemployed periodically and overworked when she found a job. Before 1850 a system of "outwork" prevailed in which women were badly exploited in their homes for piecework wages. The growth of the factory system after 1850 was actually an improvement in work conditions and wages, though we remember this as the advent of the sweatshop today. The gathering of women (as also with men) into factories did provide for a growth of camaraderie that in turn provided the basis for the development of labor organizations (Stansell 1986).

Crime posed another danger for the eighteenth- and nineteenth-century urbanite. The lack of employment and opportunity left many with no legal alternative but pauperism. In the United States and Europe, gangs controlled particular streets and neighborhoods, and remained outside the control of police. In London, where police protection was loosely organized and inadequate, gangs of up to several hundred in number periodically terrorized shopkeepers and other citizens. One of their modes of operation involved stampeding stolen cattle through the streets of the city in order to create mayhem, then preying on their victims in the ensuing confusion (Sheppard 1971, 32).

It is difficult for the present-day urbanite to imagine the life experience of the typical resident of a large nineteenth-century city. Most of the day was consumed by the long hours of hard work under unhealthy and often dangerous conditions. Home was not a comfortable retreat but a cramped refuge for meals and sleep; the streets and other public places were a source of entertainment but also of danger, and, for some, livelihood. Childhood was shorter than we have made it today; it was a risky stage of life punctuated and threatened by illness. There was but a brief time to learn the rules of city life and to prepare for a career of work. This is not all there was to life, and certainly not the fate of the affluent, but it is the big story of the urban experience for most of its participants.

City and Hinterland

One final consideration of urbanization in the industrializing era is that of how the city related to the wider world. Was it the engine of conquest and empire that the early city had been? The eighteenth and nineteenth centuries were clearly a period

*Many European cities still contain a good stock of nine-
teenth century housing. We can assume that the current occupants of these refurbished row houses, however modest
their means by contemporary standards, live more comfortable lives than earlier tenants.*

of European expansion, colonialism, and struggle to maintain or expand domination or control of far-flung territories, culminating at the end of the nineteenth century in the partitioning of Africa by the European nations. The question of the role
of the *city* in this era of conquest and competition is a difficult one. It would be difficult to argue that European, or American, expansion took place due to some inherent requirement of the growing cities alone. True, part of the reason for the
rapid industrialization and, therefore, of urban growth had to do with the flood of

cheaply obtainable raw materials that fed the growth of the manufacturing centers. It seems more accurate, however, to conclude that rapid urbanization was in part a by-product of the complementary processes of colonialism and industrialization, rather than to conclude that the cities exerted some independent, causal influence on the process as a whole.

Instead of attributing an independent role to the city as an agent of empire in this era, we need to distinguish between what the cities did and what actors and agents (governments, industrialists, banks, trading companies, speculators) located within the cities did. In some abstract sense, cities such as London, Paris, New York, Boston, and Madrid may be said to have dominated world trade or have been the seat of empire during all or part of this era. It is also appropriate to recognize vast and distant areas of the world as their hinterlands. But the city itself did not require these territories in the same way that the early city needed to expand and dominate its suppliers of necessities in order to survive. It can be argued at least hypothetically that large urban populations can be sustained through amiable and balanced trading arrangements rather than through world conquest or the domination of the terms of trade by the stronger nations. The true agents of expansion were the business interests and policymakers seeking to serve not the city but either profitability or the "national interest" or both. Nevertheless, the dramatic growth cities did undergo in this era was a direct offshoot of conquest, empire, and, in the case of the United States, the economic consolidation of territorial expansion.

Urbanization did exert a more direct territorial influence locally and nationally. It demanded the development of transportation technology to carry more and more passengers and goods cheaply and quickly. First in Europe and later in the United States, the need was met by the omnibus, the tramway, and, of course, the development of the intermetropolitan railway system.

Large urban centers came to dominate smaller ones politically and economically. Fashion and style typically radiated from the city and came to shape national and international trends and tastes; where this influence stopped marked the boundary that set ruralites and small-town types apart as objects of ridicule by sophisticated society. The influence of the cities became that much stronger through the changes in transportation and communication that had their inception during the Industrial Revolution.

As difficult as it is to mark the beginning of the Industrial Revolution and the urban growth associated with it, there is no question that a revolutionary upheaval was in full swing by the middle of the nineteenth century. The pattern of glacial advance, retreat, and advance of urbanization characteristic of earlier ages was over as the city erupted everywhere, eventually absorbing the majority of the population in one industrializing nation after another—although in most cases this would not be accomplished until well into the twentieth century. In its early stages, the conditions urbanization produced for the vast majority of urbanites were dreary and harsh. But these conditions improved gradually as the masses of the poor demanded and eventually received the attention of the reformers and, finally, the government.

Urban Change in the Present Era

Changes that took place in the twentieth century can be considered comparable in scope to the dimensions of change in those earlier eras that have come to be recognized as revolutionary. It is difficult to identify discrete periods in human history that deserve to be set off by the revolutionary designation, and it is especially dangerous to promote the period in which we happen to be living in this way because we are too close to judge impartially the enduring significance of the way we are changing the world. The work of identifying truly significant periods of change has to be left to historians. Nevertheless, for anyone with a special interest in the evolution of cities, it is difficult to escape the sense that the implications of the changes occurring today rival earlier upheavals in their potential for affecting people's lives and in their impact on patterns of human settlement.

Two seemingly opposite patterns mark global urban trends at the moment. Closer examination reveals them to be part of the same globalization process that was discussed in the first chapter. In some parts of the globe, urbanization may have reached its practical limits. In the countries where cities grew most rapidly during the Industrial Revolution, current economic and technological changes appear to indicate less need for populations to be concentrated in cities. We may be looking at the early stages of a general *decentralization* of population, manifest today in urban sprawl and the fact that the most rapid growth is occurring on the edge of metropolitan regions. At the same time, we find urban populations growing at historically unprecedented rates: This accelerated urbanization is occurring largely in the former colonial territories of the industrialized nations, in the poorer and less developed nations. Both trends, decentralization and continued urbanization, are part of a single wider process. The forces of industrialization that gave rise to population concentration in the nineteenth century are now obsolete, as the economies of these nations deindustrialize. At the same time, the shift in the location of industry to poorer nations holds up at least the promise of more manufacturing jobs in the cities of the less developed regions. Yet, prosperity eludes the vast majority of people in the most rapidly growing cities of the world, and their rapid growth cannot be explained in terms of the demand for industrial labor.

The Shifting Center of Urban Growth in the Twentieth Century

During the twentieth century, urban growth became more generalized around the globe, and by the latter half of the century the most dynamic growth shifted to the Southern hemisphere, to the less developed countries. In the richer more industrialized nations, the increase in the proportion of people living in cities slowed, as the level of urbanization for the more developed nations taken together slightly exceeded 75 percent (Table 2-4). No one knows the urban saturation point for a given population. At the end of the century, the population of Hong Kong was 94 percent urbanized, that of Kuwait 96 percent. The question of urban saturation

TABLE 2-4 Distribution of Population in More and Less Developed World Regions, 1975–2015

Economic Region	Settlement Size	Population (millions)			Percentage			NET URBAN INCREASE	
		1975	2000	2015	1975	2000	2015	1975–2000 Percent / Number (millions)	2000–2015 Percent / Number (millions)
More Developed	5+ million	98	112	120	9.3	9.5	9.9		
	1–5 million	145	219	250	13.9	18.5	20.6	6.1	3.7
	<1 million	491	571	598	46.8	48.1	49.3		
	(Total urban)	(734)	(902)	(968)	(70.0)	(76.1)	(79.8)	168	66
	Rural	315	285	246	30.0	24.0	20.3		
	Total population	1,048	1,188	1,214	100	100	100		
Less Developed	5+ million	97	305	503	3.2	6.3	8.5		
	1–5 million	182	485	756	6.0	10.0	12.7	13.2	8.0
	<1 million	531	1,152	1,591	17.6	23.7	26.8		
	(Total urban)	(810)	(1,942)	(2,850)	(26.8)	(40.0)	(48.0)	1,132	908
	Rural	2,217	2,925	3,091	73.2	60.1	52.0		
	Total population	3,026	4,867	5,940	100	100	100		
World	(Total urban)	(1,544)	(2,844)	(3,818)	(37.9)	(47.0)	(53.4)	9.1	6.4
	Total population	4,075	6,055	7,154	100	100	100	1,300	974

Source: Adapted from United Nations Population Division (1999, 5), Table 3.

can no longer be answered in terms of the proportion of agriculturalists it would take to sustain the nonfarming population. While the formula may have helped us to think about limits on the urbanization of local populations in ancient times, in today's global marketplace food flows across national borders and around the world to reach those with the income to pay for it. Theoretically, a nation's population may be 100 percent urbanized and include not so much as a single rooftop vegetable garden (Box 2-4).

Table 2-4 presents the record of urban growth for the last quarter of the twentieth century and projected urban growth through the year 2015. The table is divided to show the differences in trends between the more developed and less developed regions, and it arranges the urban population according to cities of different size. The highlighted area presents a summary of just how much the urban populations of each region and of the world as a whole have increased. Note that both the number and the percentage of each population category are given. As we have said, *urbanization* is the measure of the proportion or percent of people living in cities relative to the total population of a nation: This is an important piece of the picture of urban growth. However, *wherever the total population of the nation or region in question is increasing,* changes in the level of urbanization, taken alone, will fail to convey an adequate impression of just how much city populations are growing. In that case, we also want to look at the increase in the *number* of people living in cities. In order to understand this point, consider the hypothetical case of a nation where the total population doubles in size over the course

---

BOX 2-4   Urban Gardens for Fun and Profit

There was a period in the early stages of industrialization when factories of modest size developed along fast flowing streams in Northern Europe, and in New England as well. Along with them grew towns of modest size, and very often the whole populace of the town was dependent for livelihood on one or two local mill industries. People kept gardens and small livestock to supplement their income and to tide them over in hard times. Immigrants to the United States in the late nineteenth and early twentieth centuries also kept vegetable plots and chickens in the cities they came to in order to supplement their income and maintain rural food traditions from the Old Country. Today, there are many urban vegetable gardeners in the large cities of Europe and the United States who tend their plants in recaptured vacant lots, on terraces, in rented plots in areas set aside by the city for community gardening, and on rooftops. In 1999, there were 741 Parks Department–supported community garden projects in New York City, and countless other gardeners grew fruits and vegetables on private plots of "land." Zabar's, a world famous upscale delicatessen and restaurant in Manhattan, maintains one of the city's rooftop gardens. By supplying some of its own vegetables, the business's rooftop garden is a small gesture that defies the general dependency of urban populations on remote rural producers. The irony here is that Zabar's is known throughout the culinary world for its stock of fresh and processed exotic food imports from all over. With access to Zabar's, Manhattan's West Siders sit at the head of the global table, with some of the ingredients for the restaurant's dishes coming from just upstairs.

of 40 years (at present the estimated doubling time of populations in less developed regions is only 33 years). If 50 percent of the people were living in cities at both the beginning and end of this 40-year period, we would say that nation had experienced an urbanization rate of zero. Yet its urban population—the number of people living in cities—would have doubled in size. Two real-world examples help to make the point of the importance of considering both urbanization and urban population figures. Between the early 1970s and the mid-1990s the urban population of the East African nation of Tanzania increased *six times*, giving the country 4.5 million more people living in cities and a dizzying rate of urbanization. During the same period, India, the second most populous nation in the world after China, experienced an increase of only *six percentage points* in its urban population, as the proportion of people living in cities grew from 20 percent to 26 percent. But with its much larger population base, this meant that India, in just two decades, added *118 million* more people to its urban population. The importance of regarding size as well as proportion in thinking about just how dramatically the urban population of the world is growing at present is made quite forcefully by the figures in Table 2-4. The table is derived from data gathered by the Population Information Network (POPIN), a cooperative association of various institutions concerned about world population change, the efforts of which are coordinated by the United Nations Population Division (United Nations Population Division 1999).

During the last quarter of the twentieth century, the urban population of the world increased from 37.9 percent to 47 percent, a change of 9 percentage points. In that period, the world added half again as many people to its total population as there were in 1975, growing from just over four billion to just over six billion people. Most of those two billion new people, 1.3 billion of them, were living in cities in 2000. So a mere change of 9 percentage points in the level of urbanization, in a world with a rapidly growing population, means 1,300,000,000 more people lived in cities in the year 2000 than in 1975. The vast majority of these new additions to the world's urban population, 1.1 billion of them, lived in the less developed nations.

Table 2-4 also projects population trends into the future, to the year 2015. In these projections, the most notable trends of the past 25 years continue, with the vast majority of increase occurring in cities—and in cities of the less developed nations. Some further points to note with regard to Table 2-4:

- The most rapidly growing segment of the world's urban population is not the largest cities, but cities under a million in population: This holds true for both the more developed and less developed regions.
- The population of cities with more than 5 million people has grown and will continue to grow rapidly, but this is especially the case in poorer countries, where between the years 1975 and 2000 the number of people living in cities larger than 5 million increased threefold; in these poorer nations in the year 2015, there will be five times more people in cities with populations above 5 million than there were in 1975.

- The population of rural areas in the more developed countries continues to shrink in number and proportion, while the rural population of poorer nations will continue to grow or stabilize, representing a reservoir of potential urban migrants that promises to swell the number of people living in cities for decades beyond the year 2015.
- The highlighted, right portion of the table reveals just how much more rapidly the urban population of the less developed category is growing in comparison to the urban population of more developed nations. In the last 25 years of the twentieth century, over a billion people were added to the population of cities in the poorer nations, and in the first 15 years of the twenty-first century, nearly a billion more will be added. In contrast, the net urban population growth of the more developed nations will slow appreciably between the two periods, adding only 66 million in the latter period.

The shift in rapid urban growth from North to South is highlighted by the growth of the world's largest cities. In 1975, there were five cities worldwide with 10 million or more people: Tokyo, New York, Shanghai, Mexico City, and Sao Paulo. By 2000, there were 19, and 16 were in the less developed regions. The projected number for 2015 is 23, with all of the newcomers in the less developed nations (United Nations Population Division 1999, 8). While the proportion of the world population living in such large cities is relatively small (7 percent), these cities mark an important new phase in the urbanization of the world. They draw our attention because they are located in regions of the world where 80 percent of the world's population lives, where total populations are growing more rapidly, and where there are currently 3 billion people living in rural areas, some unknown number of them poised to migrate to the cities.

A revealing exercise is to consider the kind of urban growth taking place today in the light of Kingsley Davis's (1955) argument (reviewed earlier) that the true urban revolution coincided with the Industrial Revolution. If we employ his criteria—dramatic change in the size and proportion of populations living in cities in the nineteenth century—we may decide that the current era represents something of an urban revolution. In the nineteenth century, an outstanding example of urban growth was Birmingham, England. The city grew in just six decades from a population of 72,000 (1800) to 400,000, and then to 1.25 million in the next four decades (1900). With comparable growth taking place in other English cities, as well as elsewhere in Northern Europe and at a couple of points in the United States (New York and Philadelphia), we can appreciate the revolutionary impact of these changes on human experience and social organization. But compare the dimensions of nineteenth century urban growth to what is happening to cities in the present era. In 1975, Mexico City already had 11 million people. Twenty-five years later, it had at least 18 million—no one knows for sure: Such measures are difficult in the poorer nations. Between 1975 and 2000, the population of Bombay grew from 7 to 18 million, São Paulo from 10 to 18 million, and Lagos, Nigeria, from a mere 3 to 13.5 million. These cities are projected to reach from near 20 million (Mexico City) to 26 million people (Bombay) within the first 15 years of the twenty-first century. In 1900, at the end of the century of the Industrial Revolution, there were between one and two billion people in the world, and less than a tenth of them lived in cities. Sometime between 2000 and 2015, as the world population grows from 6 to 7 billion people, the urbanization of the population will have progressed beyond 50 percent. By 2030 the world population will add 2 billion people, and virtually all of that growth will be in cities (United Nations Population Division 1999). If we are going to recognize an urban revolution in any period of history, we cannot omit consideration of the present era.

Globalization and the Place of the City

If we consider the earlier phases of city-hinterland development that have been reviewed in this chapter, the world may be seen as evolving through a series of stages, with each involving an increasing degree of economic rationalization or management of the far-flung economic resources of the globe. Ancient cities were relatively modest in size, but they began the process of organizing distant resources into a common network of trade by providing populous markets, a degree of private wealth, and points of exchange. The cities of the Industrial Revolution were built upon still larger empires that included distant colonies and a diverse international trade, setting in place the framework of a single word economy. The present era represents yet another step in the consolidation and rational management of that single world economy, in the organization of the productive capacity of the globe into a single marketplace. In this latter phase, it becomes more difficult to talk about the city's role as being at the center of change. The requirements of the Industrial Revolution were served by the large-scale gathering of workers into industrial cities. The spatial implications of today's sweeping changes are different. As the globalization of the economy and changes in communication and transportation technology reach their logical extreme, city and hinterland will become one: the globe. That is, with routine and instantaneous communication about market-relevant information, the geographic space in which individuals live and act is everywhere at the same time. In effect, all points of the globe are localized, at least with respect to certain strategic decision-making dimensions of economic existence.

In our discussions of the ancient and industrial urban revolutions, we considered three dimensions of change: changes in the scale of social organization, in culture and experience, and in the political organization of society. We return briefly to these criteria to indicate some of the present implications of change.

Social Organization
In the global era, there are notable changes in organization. During earlier urban revolutions, new statuses were created, as individuals were thrust into the roles of priest or industrialist. In the new economic order, there is a new mover, the global manager, who feels little attachment or allegiance to anything but the best interests of his or her business. Reich described how these managers coordinate investment and technological services from around the globe, targeting international markets with the same natural ease that creative managers of earlier eras

coordinated such resources within a particular city or national region. Global enterprise represents a new form of capitalism that is more purely economically rational "having shed the old affiliations with people and place. Today corporate decisions about production and location are driven by the dictates of global competition, not by national allegiance" (Reich 1995, 161).

Another dimension of organization we have considered in connection with past periods of revolutionary change had to do with social stratification. In the past, social stratification was measured with reference to the degrees of inequality that existed within a society, between priest and peasant, industrialist and laborer, householder and servant. In a world economy, stratification must be reckoned according to the inequalities that exist within this single, international economic system. It becomes more clearly relevant to talk about the standard of living enjoyed by affluent populations in Europe and the United States in contrast to that of rural laborers in Latin America or Asia who toil at the margins of existence in the production of cheap agricultural exports consumed at bargain prices in the affluent nations. Similarly, it is relevant to examine the living conditions of children who labor for meager wages manufacturing products sold in the markets of wealthy nations. The scale of comparison of the conditions of the rich and poor in a global economy has reached its maximum dimension.

Culture

Human experience in a globalized culture represents converging styles and tastes, for better or worse. At its furthest reaches, globalization touches the most remote peoples. Wireless electronic communication reaches every part of the globe; corporations learn that billions of poor people with little disposable income when taken as a whole still constitute an enormous mass market; and we are amused by tales of salespeople in canoes peddling expensive cosmetics "door to door" in the most isolated territories of the Amazon or of equally inaccessible indigenous peoples being organized to supply natural rainforest products to upscale ice cream and cosmetics manufacturers in Europe and the United States. These more extreme examples serve to illustrate that cultural homogenization is taking place on a global scale and that the people who are less remote are more influenced, but no one is immune. We can still argue that the global culture is an urban culture, because what are popularly considered to be the attractive products and ideas that are disseminated through the global web still emanate for the most part from urban-based enterprises, styles, and art forms.

West African filmmaker, Gaston Kabore, has complained that West African audiences, especially young audiences, prefer films made in the United States dealing with a fantasy world designed to sell theater tickets. These audiences will not support the development of films made by African filmmakers dealing with African topics that speak with an African voice. Does it make more sense to say he is describing an essentially urban cultural influence or a Western influence? When we speak of the globalization of culture, we are speaking primarily of its Westernization, and it is difficult to extract exactly what the urban component of that is, in abstract terms, especially when what is being communicated through film, as well as through advertising, is a fantasy world that exists nowhere.

Political Order

The political dimension of global reorganization is well known. It is expressed in the many regional trade agreements that have emerged within the past decade. These agreements are designed to facilitate trade by lowering or eliminating tariffs and creating free trade zones for manufacturing. The North American Free Trade Agreement (NAFTA), the Treaty on the European Union——creating the European Union (EU), which integrates the economies of the 12 member European states—and the Association of Southeast Asian Nations (ASEAN) are all examples of such agreements. In every area such agreements create controversy because they are seen by some as eliminating the trade protections that support domestic employment, especially in manufacturing. There is by now a widespread if guarded commitment on the part of governments to facilitate open trade across borders—the belief being that a failure to do so would in the near future hamper businesses that operate partly within their borders and damage national economic interests that are thought to be served by full participation in the growing global economy. There is still a role to be played by local municipal governments in the new world order. Local governments engage in promoting the assets of their cities internationally as mayors and other local officials make periodic visits abroad (Fry 1995, 25). Common regional interests at times overlap international borders, such as in Seattle, Washington, and Vancouver, British Columbia, in the Pacific Northwest. In the case of this important region on the northern edge of the international trade-oriented Pacific Rim, city and regional governments have undertaken joint efforts at promotion and preservation (Artibise 1995; Cohn and Smith 1995).

In the enthusiastic atmosphere surrounding the promotion of globalism, the greatest political obstacle is often maintaining domestic harmony. Workers are

In a globalizing world, is locality as important as it once was? Jerusalem symbolizes, in the extreme, the potential for "place" to provide such a focus for passionate attachments that they often threaten to destabilize the international order.

most often distrustful of new arrangements that threaten their livelihood and hard-won standard of living. In South Korea, a decision to eliminate job security led to demonstrations by workers. It is often a difficult lesson for workers to learn that when their jobs are more unstable, everyone, including themselves, is better off in the long term. Yet, according to the conservative *Economist,* this is the lesson of the new age, and the problem is that governments have so far done an inept job of educating their citizens about the need to accept the proposition that unleashing the global economy will inevitably raise everyone's standard of living (1997). In fact, accepting the doctrine of faith in the power of capitalism to serve the greatest good can in itself put some governments in a difficult position. The People's Republic of China, committed to socialist principles of even development that serves equally the interests of all of its people, finds itself confronted with the need to jump onto the bandwagon of globalism or be left behind. The Chinese economy now has one of the most impressive records of private investment and accumulation of private fortunes ever seen anywhere. It struggles to reconcile this reality with a socialist philosophy, and the struggle produces ideological tensions within government and between government and its citizens. Everyone has been touched by Western political and popular culture flowing through the open windows of global influence. At the same time, however, people are understandably troubled when the industries that they work for fail and the government must explain that their hardship is part of the new reality of the marketplace.

It is possible to say much about how the world is changing today—to talk about what appear to be revolutionary changes in organization, culture, and politics—without drawing cities into the discussion in a central way. This is something new, to be able to speak about an important era of change without talking much about the city, which has been the historical engine of change. This reflects the declining position of place, the emergence of placelessness in the way lives are lived—at least in the affluent reaches of the world where the globalization process is most advanced.

What is left to say about the sociological significance of the city? In a physical sense, the process of spatial decentralization is still in its infancy—decentralization is such a big story because it represents a break with the long historical pattern of the centralization of populations. By and large, the world population continues the long-term trend described in this chapter toward concentrating in cities and metropolitan regions. Predictions that the old centralizing influences of clustered industries and downtown corporate headquarters that provided the economic impetus that brought people to the cities may soon be things of the past (Reich 1995, 165–167) appear sound. Yet, we are caught in a time when the city persists, and persists forcefully, as a major social presence.

We still look to major metropolitan regions to discover new trends in how technology is changing work. We still find manufacturing and industrial processing plants, old and new, in the centers and on the edges of cities of all sizes and in all world regions. Cities remain the laboratories where experiments of living and working together are worked out by the most culturally diversified elements of population. The drama of urban life, excitement, opportunity, and risk still draw the popular imagination and the ambitious, the talented, and the daring among us. Sassen (1996) reminds us that there is still much for the sociologist to study and understand about urban places where work is changing, about the ways that changes are affecting people's lives, especially those lives made more difficult as the result of change. In addition to changes in wage and salaried employment patterns, small neighborhood entrepreneurs increasingly face competition from international chains that open franchised retail outlets on their blocks, selling mass-marketed goods that may have been manufactured by people working at subsistence wages in sweatshops in a distant, huge, and growing Third World city. The global and the local are not opposites, but are intimately interrelated. All sorts of firms that enjoy high profits derived from the global economy can have the effect of superheating local urban economies as they, their high-wage employees, and upscale services and other businesses that cater to them drive up the cost for space, affecting the ability of other businesses and residents to afford urban rents. At the same time, the extreme level of inequality that exists between international urban centers drives immigration from poorer nations to the cities of the more developed nations, where the new immigrants, used to less, compete for jobs and customers. In a fairly common pattern, recent

The global and the local are not opposites, but are intimately related. This sidewalk bazaar, reminiscent of many Third World street scenes, is repeated daily in lower Manhattan.

immigrants pool the modest material resources of family members, along with their combined labor, to open businesses that survive on the margins of local economies, adding a further dimension to the localized manifestation of the global marketplace and enriching the cultural diversity of the urban experience. By 1990, European nations were host to 25 million immigrants, and North America had 24 million (United Nations 1997a). Immigration further alters receiving cities, the favored destination of newcomers. Immigrants revitalize old residential neighborhoods, introduce new forms of economic activity, and change the appearance, language, and urban cultural style where they settle. Cities of a globalizing world contain many of the economically and politically displaced: In addition to immigrants and refugees, we count here minority populations of the wealthy nations and the masses of poor people crowding into the cities of the less developed regions of the world. Cities, therefore, continue to demand our attention as sociologists, just as they have done since the emergence of the discipline.

Globalization is a little understood, shadowy presence in the contemporary world. Sassen (1996) speculates that in rich nations some of the urban tensions and violence evidenced by young people may relate to a feeling of frustration and anger at the remoteness of the source of the change that is affecting their lives. She suggests that their aggressive behavior is in some manner an unarticulated political statement. More clearly articulated political resistance to the remote forces of profit-led globalization comes in the form of the increasingly visible mass political movements that took to the streets of Seattle, London, Washington, D.C., and Philadelphia in 1999 and 2000. Demonstrators sought to challenge the legitimacy of the World Trade Organization and to challenge the position of political candidates suspected of placing the interests of global corporations above the interests of people in rich and poor economic regions. The city affords demonstrators a dramatic stage for the presentation of their grievances, and insures coverage and broadcast of their message.

Although we stand on the threshold of new decentralizing tendencies that are sure to profoundly alter cities and patterns of human settlement in the future, we stand within a society and a history that remain the product of a thoroughly urbanized past and a present in which the city continues to be a stubbornly persistent magnet for migration, human imagination, and major change. The city is still a very big story of human history and a useful focus for understanding the social world.

3

THE URBAN TRADITION IN SOCIOLOGY

The same physical environment can be experienced in a number of different ways. That is, reality has a subjective side; we attach our own personal meaning to our experience of the world. The city has a different symbolic and emotional impact on different people. For example, people who have spent all of their years in the modern cities of London or New York will experience large cities in a different way from people from a small town or village. As cities grew rapidly in the nineteenth century and continued their unprecedented expansion in the next century, people, both the average person and the professional social observer, struggled to make sense of the new environment—this new experiment in living that gathered millions onto a single patch of land. Because urban growth of this sort was new and seemed to have infinite potential for continued expansion, many observers were awed and even fearful of the city's capacity for social disruption.

Urban sociology was produced by a sense of urgency, the recognition that cities were changing social life, and the desire to understand or predict the nature of those changes. Most early theoretical interpretations reflected that popular sense of urgency and tended to focus on the negative or disorganizing aspects of city living. In this chapter, we will examine the cumulation of a particular image of the city, a subjective interpretation that continued to dominate urban sociology for the first half or more of the twentieth century. This image has now come to be widely criticized for emphasizing the negative, for being too one-sided, too "anti-urban." However, criticisms notwithstanding, the body of theory that we refer to here as the "urban tradition" has something important to tell us about the burgeoning urban form and its impact on social organization and experience. The following passage from Louis Wirth, the most influential of the urban tradition theorists, is representative of that point of view.

> *The close living together and working together of individuals who have no sentimental ties fosters a spirit of competition, aggrandizement, and mutual exploitation. Formal controls are instituted to counteract irresponsibility and potential disorder. Without rigid adherence to predictable routines a large compact society*

would scarcely be able to maintain itself. The clock and the traffic signal are symbolic of the basis of our social order in the urban world. Frequent close physical contact, coupled with great social distance, accentuates the reserve of unattached individuals toward one another and, unless compensated for by other opportunities for response, gives rise to loneliness. The necessary frequent movement of great numbers of individuals in a congested habitat causes friction and irritation. Nervous tensions that derive from such personal frustrations are increased by the rapid tempo and the complicated technology under which life in dense areas must be lived. (Wirth 1938, 15–16)

This passage is remarkable for several reasons. The first is the vivid imagery it presents. We can see and feel the alienation experienced in the bustling crowds of anonymous and diverse strangers rushing past one another in their hectic yet routine quest to meet the demands of punctuality. This portrait of the city appeals to intuition. It is almost a caricature in that it draws out and emphasizes certain prominent characteristics, making the urban experience immediately recognizable to members of a wide audience who share these impressions of city life. Wirth's passage is also remarkable because he has managed, in so few words, to capture so many of the themes developed by earlier sociologists and other prominent students of the city. The essay from which the quotation is taken, "Urbanism as a Way of Life," is an eclectic work, drawing broadly from within the mainstream of sociological thought. In it Wirth managed to integrate almost every major sociological observation that had been made about the city up until the time that he wrote. His work also reflects the fact that although many of these early theorists were ambivalent about the conditions of urban life, most were distrustful of the urban future, and many brooded over its prospect. It was no accident that Wirth's work reflected the considerable sense of foreboding that attended the urban tradition in sociology, and he was bound by this tradition to end up composing a bleak portrait of urbanism. In the following sections, we will consider the evolution of ideas that Wirth eventually combined into his image of the city. Figure 3-1 (page 88) provides a brief summary of the people and ideas contributing to Wirth's understanding.

The Changing Scale and the Social Order

The rapid urbanization of Western societies raised interesting questions for those who found themselves caught up in it. Aside from the fact that people would increasingly become concentrated in cities, what would be the other social consequences of the great transformation? How would life be organized in an urban society? How would social order be maintained? How would it differ in principle from the preurban order?

These questions were first squarely addressed by three writers, Ferdinand Tönnies, Henry Maine, and Emile Durkheim, each considering a somewhat different feature of social organization, but all three intent on saying how the old and new ways of living were different from each other. Each of them saw the old social order and the new in terms of opposites, that is, the old and new orders could not be more different from one another. And although these contrasts were meant to apply to societies in general, the old order always described life in small villages and rural settings, and we therefore take the descriptions of the new social order to apply in particular to life in cities. These are *proto-urban sociologies;* they provided the groundwork for the urban tradition.

Ferdinand Tönnies adapted the terms *Gemeinschaft* and *Gesellschaft* from his native German language to express the distinction between life in small-scale rural societies and life in the growing urban order. By *Gemeinschaft,* Tönnies ([1887] 1940, 37–39) was referring to "any arrangements that involved intimate, private and exclusive living together" in a single community. The term was intended to convey a particular intensity of social integration. In a *Gemeinschaft,* the individual is socially immersed as a segment of a social unity, a component of the whole—with that whole being the group. "In *Gemeinschaft* . . . with one's family, one lives from birth on, bound to it in weal and woe" (Tönnies [1887] 1940). Tönnies referred also to "the *Gemeinschaft* of property between husband and wife," and that "likewise, each member of a bridal couple knows that he or she goes into marriage as a complete *Gemeinschaft*" ([1887] 1940, 38). If forced to choose a single word in the English language to express the idea, translators invariably choose "community," although it is clear that in doing so the more intense connotations are lost. The term *Gesellschaft* can be translated (also inadequately) as "society"; it was intended to signify "public life—it is the world itself," or the wider social world without intimate ties. "One goes into *Gesellschaft* . . . as one goes into a strange country. . . . A young man is warned about bad *Gesellschaft,* but the expression bad *Gemeinschaft* violates the meaning of the word" (Tönnies [1887] 1940, 37–39).

The distinction was not, strictly speaking, devised to contrast rural social life and urban social life. However, the *association* of *Gemeinschaft* with rural society and *Gesellschaft* with urban society was explicit. "All praise of rural life has pointed out that the *Gemeinschaft* among people is stronger there and more alive; it is the lasting and genuine form of living together. . . . In contrast, *Gesellschaft* is transitory and superficial" (Tönnies [1887] 1940, 39). Furthermore, Tönnies observed a direct tension between *Gemeinschaft* and the city. The rural village was compatible with the feeling of unity; it was stable, and small-scale, and the web of relationships within it was seasoned with age. But the city introduced division by social class, created tensions between the interests of capital and labor, was characterized by hostility, and had no natural need or place for family.

> *The city is typical of* Gesellschaft *in general. It is essentially a commercial town and, in so far as commerce dominates its productive labor, a factory town. Its wealth is capital wealth which, in the form of trade, usury, or industrial capital, is used and multiplies. Capital is the means for the appropriation of products of labor or for the exploitation of workers. The city is also the center of science and culture, which always go hand in hand with commerce and industry. Here the arts must make a living; they are exploited in a capitalistic way. Thoughts spread and change with astonishing rapidity. (Tönnies [1887] 1940, 266)*

Generally stated, there is a difference between the countryside and the city in the forces that draw and hold people together. In the rural sphere, the actions of individuals are derived from the will and spirit of unity—the family and community to which one is bound and which will bear the consequences of one's actions. In the city, actions are coordinated simply by their calculated exchange values. The *Gesellschaft* gives the appearance of many living together peacefully, but in fact "everybody is by himself and isolated, and there exists a condition of tension against all others" (Tönnies [1887] 1940, 74).

Tönnies argued that a gradual change had occurred in the law and in the relationship between the individual and the state that had accompanied the social transition from *Gemeinschaft* to *Gesellschaft*. Here he relied heavily on Henry Maine and his influential work, *Ancient Law* (Tönnies [1887] 1940, 211ff.). In it, Maine traced the replacement of a system of laws based on what he referred to as *status* with an ever-emerging legal arrangement that he called *contract* ([1861] 1917, 98–100). Under the older system, the state and its laws addressed only the head of the household, the parent, who was responsible for and essentially ruled over the

---

BOX 3-1   Understanding *Gemeinschaft*

It is easier for contemporary students of the social order to understand intuitively the concept *Gesellschaft* than to fully comprehend *Gemeinschaft*. Individualism is an idea consistent with the system of rewards that makes up our era; when we interpret or explain ourselves to others, the emphasis is most likely to be on our personal achievements and goals; the "I" stands out in each personal narrative. On the other hand, the components of the self that we define in terms of group membership—the portion of our identity that we take from being a *member* of our particular family, having meaningful ties of memory to the neighborhood in which we grew up, and enjoying the friendships and play and work groups that contribute importantly to our sense of who we are—these are *Gemeinschaft*-like elements of experience. But it is rare in contemporary Western societies to find pure examples of *Gemeinschaft*. In large part, this is because Tönnies was defining polar opposites, and so he imagined extreme conditions that no real-world example, past or present, would fully fit. Every era has elements of each polar extreme. We can assume that there

were more good examples, more lives that were lived closer to the model of *Gemeinschaft*, prior to Tönnies's time than there are today. It may be a useful exercise, in order to test your understanding of these ideas, to think about the balance in your own self-image between individual and group elements of your identity. How much of your identity is submerged within your single closest affiliation (extended family, religious community, sports team, and so on)? Would you lose your sense of place in the world if you lost that affiliation? Would it be difficult to see or define yourself? How much does success in achieving your goals depend on the group's continued existence and your continued membership in good standing within it? How much of the way the outside world sees you is tied to your membership? Is your membership and the meaning it imparts to your identity lifelong? These are the *Gemeinschaft* questions. What are the *Gesellschaft* questions? What is the balance between *Gemeinschaft* and *Gesellschaft* components of your identity? How does/how would the city affect the balance?

family and servants. Tönnies viewed this arrangement as characteristic of the collective nature and the unity of *Gemeinschaft*. Increasingly this arrangement was being undermined by the growing legal apparatus of the state and its government. The idea of *individual* obligations and liability was laid down in contract terms or the common rules (laws) of the state.

> *The movement of the progressive societies has been uniform in one respect. Through all its course it has been distinguished by the gradual dissolution of Family dependency and the growth of individual obligation in its place. The individual is steadily substituted for the Family, as the unit of which the civil laws take account. . . . Nor is it difficult to see what is the tie between man and man which replaces by degrees those forms of reciprocity in rights and duties which have their origin in the Family. It is Contract. Starting as from one terminus of history, from a condition of society in which all the relations of Persons are summed up in the relations of Family, we seem to have moved steadily towards a phase of social order in which all these relations arise from the free agreement of Individuals. . . . We may say that the movement of the progressive societies has hitherto been a movement* from Status to Contract. *(Maine [1861] 1917, p. 99)*

There was no specific reference in Maine's account to the corresponding urbanization of society with the transition from status to contract. It was Tönnies who formally associated status relations with *Gemeinschaft* and contract relations with *Gesellschaft*. In the former, social control of individual behavior is stipulated by the nature of the individual's attachment to the group. In *Gesellschaft*, where the individual is cut free from group constraints, social control must be ensured by an external factor—a code of laws and punishments, a contract that demands predictable behavior.

Tönnies's work emphasized the fragility and, in his view, the "artificiality" of the emerging urban society. He had found in Maine's account some basis for regulating the tensions aroused by the self-interest on which relations in urban society were founded. On the other hand, the French sociologist Emile Durkheim believed that the basis for understanding the more complex order of an urban society was to be found in the principles of natural ecology. Durkheim ([1893] 1933) contrasted the type of society governed by what he called *mechanical solidarity* with that characterized by *organic solidarity*. Mechanical solidarity was the principal mechanism of social integration in small-scale, agrarian societies, where the division of labor or specialization was negligible and especially where a strong, common religious belief persisted. In such societies social cohesion was provided by the homogeneous experience of all of the society's members, and "religion pervade[d] the whole of social life, . . . because social life [was] made up almost exclusively of common beliefs and common practices which derive[d] from unanimous adhesion to a very particular intensity" (Durkheim [1893] 1933, 178). Common, mutually reinforcing experience and religious themes in small-scale, socially homogeneous societies resulted in a collective consciousness, a common way of seeing and a common identity that held the society together. Here Durkheim pointed out what costs are involved in the closely circumscribed worlds of *Gemeinschaft*:

> *Solidarity that comes from likenesses is at its maximum when the collective con-science completely envelopes the whole conscience and coincides in all points with it. But at that moment our individuality is nil. It can be born only if the commu-nity takes a smaller toll of us. (Durkheim [1893] 1933, 130)*

It is clear that the basis of this mechanical solidarity is being undermined wherever differences in experience and ideas can be found among a given popu-lation. However, these differences are the natural product of the growth and con-centration of populations, conditions that lead in turn to a division of labor. It is here that Durkheim turned to natural ecology and the observations of Charles Darwin to explain what he saw as the natural progression of society toward more complex forms.

> *Darwin justly observed that the struggle between two organisms is as active as they are analogous. Having the same needs and pursuing the same objects, they are in rivalry everywhere. As long as they have more resources than they need, they can live side by side, but if their number increases to such proportions that all appetites can no longer be sufficiently satisfied, war breaks out. . . . It is quite different if the coexisting individuals are of different species or varieties. As they do not feed in the same manner, and do not lead the same kind of life, they do not disturb each other. . . . Men submit to the same law. In the same city different oc-cupations can coexist without being obliged mutually to destroy one another, for they pursue different objects. . . . The oculist does not struggle with the psychia-trist, nor the shoemaker with the hatter. . . . Since they perform different services, they can perform them parallely. (Durkheim [1893] 1933, 265–266)*

Durkheim emphasized that he did not mean to say that the growth and con-densation of the population *permitted* a greater division of labor, but that these con-ditions *demanded* it and that the city was a prime arena in which to observe this process ([1893] 1933, 258, 262). He termed the resultant form of solidarity *organic,* because under an elaborated division of labor, each of the specialized divisions of society was *interdependent,* which was analogous to the interdependence of the var-ious organs of the human body. This interdependence of each part upon the whole, or *organic solidarity,* replaced the unity of conscience, or *mechanical solidarity,* as the major unifying social force. This specialization and interdependence among indi-viduals was repeated again in society in the division of labor that emerged among different regions and among different cities. The process through which the divi-sion of labor evolved was the same at all levels: It involved competition and the elimination of rivals as "the small employer [became] a foreman, the small mer-chant [became] an employee" (Durkheim [1893] 1933, 369). Likewise, some cities were in a better position to provide certain functions to society, and came to domi-nate or monopolize them; for example, a particular manufacture, center of govern-ment, shipping, or higher education (Durkheim [1893] 1933, 188). As societies evolved, the division of labor became more complex and the interdependence of the parts, the organic nature of social integration, became more complete.

The overall result is social progress, although Durkheim was concerned that the division of labor, as it was actually taking place in his time, was characterized by certain liabilities. Among these were the results of unregulated competition, class conflict, and the feeling of meaninglessness generated by routinized industrial work—this last liability being a direct result of the division of labor. But he felt that these social and psychological consequences were abnormal and temporary by-products of the rapid rate at which industrialization had taken place, and that appropriate economic controls and norms of industrial relations would emerge in time to remedy them (Lukes 1972, 174). Likewise, Durkheim believed that tendencies toward moral confusion or *anomie* were largely the result of the rapid and incomplete transition from the old moral order to a society governed by organic solidarity that, when mature, would be characterized by social justice and equality of opportunity. In this, it may be seen that Durkheim favored the emergence of the city as an advancement of the human condition; unlike many of his colleagues, Durkheim was pro-urban.

Taken together, the impressions of urbanizing society compiled by Tönnies, Maine, and Durkheim include the following elements: the erosion of an intimate community and the rise of conflictual relations in the city, the decline of family authority and the rise of contractual relations, and the replacement of solidarity based upon common experience and identity with solidarity based upon the differentiation of individuals and their consequent functional interdependence. One more important contribution is offered by this trio of social observers: They present a common methodology for considering social change—the construction of polar opposites. At each pole is posited an abstract model, an ideal that is not an actual society or situation, but an image of a type of society. Actual societies, examples from the "real world," will conform to these models to a greater or lesser extent, insofar as they can provide a good or bad example of what the model is supposed to describe. A continuum is implied in any construction of polar opposites, where all real-world examples can be arranged according to how well or how poorly they manifest one or another of the opposed qualities. That is, any society fits somewhere on the *Gemeinschaft*-status-mechanical solidarity / *Gesellschaft*-contract-organic solidarity continuum. This use of opposites, whether explicit or implied, has been a favorite device for dealing with the difficult problem of characterizing urban society. The strategy consists of establishing the characteristics of urban society in contrast to what we suppose are the characteristics of nonurban or preurban society. Max Weber, a contemporary of Tönnies and Durkheim, took a different approach. He developed the methodology of *ideal type* by constructing his model of the city from the observable historical characteristics of the cities themselves.

The Urban Sociology of Max Weber, Georg Simmel, and Oswald Spengler

Urban social theory has been heavily influenced by a few German writers whose work followed that of Tönnies and built upon his major themes. Most prominent among these theorists is Max Weber, who, in his wide-ranging and monumental achievements in sociology, included an attempt to formally define the city. His objective was to devise a comprehensive and concise model, an ideal type, that would identify the essential elements that make up the city. After considering a variety of characteristics that he found associated with cities historically, he arrived at the following formula:

> *To constitute a full urban community a settlement must display a relative predominance of trade-commercial relations with the settlement as a whole displaying the following features: 1. a fortification; 2. a market; 3. a court of its own and at least partially autonomous law; 4. a related form of association; 5. at least partial autonomy and autocephally, thus also an administration by authorities in the election of which the burghers participated. (Weber [1905] 1958, 80–81)*

While some of these criteria, such as the existence of a market and of municipal regulation, seem perfectly appropriate in the construction of a general model, the criterion of fortification seems anachronistic. When Weber's work appeared in 1905, the walled city was, for the most part, a thing of the past; industrialization had taken and reshaped the city, as Weber himself pointed out in the same essay ([1905] 1958, 75). But this did not affect the model that he constructed.

Weber was not interested in describing cities but in modeling *The City*. Each of his core criteria had to qualify as a necessary component of the model. The predominance of trade-commercial relations was the most basic of these criteria. "The 'city' is a marketplace," he wrote; but of course he did not intend to elevate every marketplace to the status of "city." To qualify, the market or the "practiced trades" that made up and served the market had to demonstrate a certain "versatility," or diversity. In addition, he wrote, "We wish to speak of a city only in cases where the local inhabitants satisfy an economically substantial part of their daily wants in the local market. It is only in this sense that the city is a 'market settlement'" (Weber [1905] 1958, 66–67).

In his model, Weber made the city a fusion of fortress and marketplace, systematically interwoven components of the full urban community. The *full* urban citizen was bound to perform certain military duties—to build or maintain the fortification and to guard or to defend the settlement—as an expression of membership in and allegiance to the community. It was in accordance with this reasoning and in this sense that Weber incorporated the idea of a fortification in his model. The town center could serve alternately as marketplace or drill field. In Weber's own words, "The politically oriented castle and economically oriented market . . . often stand in plastic dualism beside one another" ([1905] 1958, 78).

It follows that a settlement so constituted be self-aware, and that it, to some extent, determine and regulate its own policies and laws. It is because of this connection that Weber included the third criterion ("a court of its own and at least partially autonomous law") and the fifth criterion (at least partial political self-direction) in his list. In the area of setting policy or managing receipts and expenditures, as well as the regulation of conditions under which production and exchange in the market are carried out, the agents of the city constitute the commonly recognized "urban authority," of which any concept of the city must take account. Weber made a simple but critically important point for establishing a clear understanding of the nature of the city here: "The economic concept previously discussed must be entirely separated from the political administrative concept of the city. Only in the latter sense may a special area belong to a city" ([1905] 1958, 74). That is, by distinguishing the city's economic features from its political features, it is possible to see that the city consists of a finite, formally orchestrated political arena, which exists within the economic field; the influence of the economic field extends outward indefinitely.

The remaining criterion to be considered, that of "a related form of association," is connected to the other components of Weber's definition. What he was looking for here were elements of social organization peculiar to the city, which helped to distinguish the urban from the nonurban. He believed that the emergence of a large *burgher* class or "estate," a politically powerful and privileged citizen-merchant-soldier strata of the population that was able to perceive its interests and take action, was an earmark of the true urban community. The formation of traders and artisans into "urban corporations," such as guilds, is one example of this characteristically urban form of association (Weber [1905] 1958, 81–89).

In sum, the model that Weber constructed is of a diversified market economy upon which the largest number of inhabitants are regularly and primarily dependent. Furthermore, it is a self-aware and somewhat autonomous unit, within which special forms of social unity arise, which are responsible in part for the settlement's defense. This is *The City*. It is intended as a model against which any city from any time period may be measured. That is, ancient cities, contemporary cities, and all of the variations between may be held up to this single model to see how well they would fit as "full urban communities." While any city will reflect certain qualities of this model, the medieval town most closely approximates this model. As the translator of Weber's essay comment, this suggests an interesting conclusion regarding the urban era (Martindale 1958, 62). Although we can continue to observe the increase in the size of urban populations, we should not "confuse physical aggregation with the growth of the city in the sociological sense." The city no longer defends itself militarily, its legal and political autonomy was subordinated long ago to the authority of the state; in addition, individual interests and loyalties are fragmented and drawn in many directions beyond those of a local, civic nature. Martindale concluded, "The modern city is losing its external and formal structure. Internally it is in a state of decay while the new community represented by the nation everywhere grows at its expense. The age of the city seems to be at an end" (Martindale 1958, 67). It is only in the context of Weber's model, and what he intended by it, that we can understand such a conclusion. For Weber, the urban age had reached a peak. The city at the beginning of the twentieth century was becoming reorganized. New relationships based on models of efficiency, namely, bureaucracy, had come to characterize the new age: The city no longer held out the promise that *The City* had once offered.

The work of examining the *experience* of urban life in the new age was undertaken by Weber's colleague, Georg Simmel. Whereas Weber was interested in identifying the broadest features of the urban question, Simmel, in his essay "The Metropolis and Mental Life" ([1905] 1950, 409–424), sought to understand what the urban experience did to the way people thought and behaved. He believed that there were two important features of urban life that conditioned how urban-ites thought and acted: the intensity of nervous stimuli or sensation in the city, and the pervasiveness of the market's effect on urban relations. Simmel observed that urbanities had no choice but to become insensitive to the events and people around them. He reasoned:

> *the rapid crowding of changing images, the sharp discontinuity in the grasp of a single glance, and the unexpectedness of onrushing impressions. These are the psychological conditions which the metropolis creates. With each crossing of the street, with the tempo and multiplicity of economic, occupational, and social life, the city sets up a deep contrast with small town and rural life with reference to the sensory foundations of psychic life. (Simmel [1905] 1950, 410)*

True urbanites must develop a special capacity to avoid emotional involve-ment in all that takes place around them. This capacity resides in the "intellect" and its careful cultivation and development, and displays itself in the "blasé" attitude, "so unconditionally reserved for the metropolis." In contrast to those who reside in small towns and villages, who have the capacity to embrace each

Georg Simmel thought that cash was an overriding concern for city-dwellers, reducing most interactions to the question, "How much?"

other in more deeply felt and emotional relationships, metropolitan beings must hold themselves apart. Of his "metropolitan type of man," Simmel said, "he reacts with his head instead of his heart" ([1905] 1950, 410, 412–413).

The tendency toward reserve, brought about by the intensity of experience, is reinforced by the economic basis of life in the city. Where Weber observed the city as a marketplace, Simmel asked what life in a marketplace would do to social relations. His answer was that it drew people into relationships characterized by tension and calculation.

> *The metropolis has always been the seat of the money economy. . . . Money economy and the dominance of the intellect are intrinsically connected. They share a matter of fact attitude in dealing with men and things; and in this attitude a formal justice is often coupled with an inconsiderate hardness. The intellectually sophisticated person is indifferent to all genuine individuality. . . . Money is concerned only with what is common to all: it asks for the exchange value, it reduces all quality and individuality to the question: How much? All intimate emotional relations between persons are founded in this individuality, whereas in rational relations man is reckoned with like a number, like an element which is in itself indifferent. (Simmel [1905] 1950, 411)*

In the metropolitan milieu, the modern mind with its predominant qualities of punctuality and exactness becomes ever more calculating. Simmel suspected that if we dared to examine more closely the reserve characteristic of urbanites, we would find that it merely cloaks the aversion, even mutual repulsion, with which people regard one another in the city. This stems from the sheer impossibility of becoming socially involved with everyone in the metropolis and also from "the right to distrust. . . . in the face of the touch and go elements of metropolitan life" (Simmel [1905] 1950, 415).

Having alienated and isolated metropolitans from one another in this manner, one might expect that Simmel would have despaired at the urban condition. That was not the case, however. If individuals were socially isolated in the metropolis, this meant that they were also set free from one another. Simmel ([1905] 1950, 416–417) observed that the small, tightly knit social circles that characterized non-metropolitan social conditions bound individuals to a narrow set of expectations and allowed little individualism or autonomy. In the metropolis, the division of labor provided the opportunity for the development of differences among individuals. And, as the size of any "group" grew, its inner unity loosened and individual freedom increased. "The smaller the circle which forms our milieu . . . the more anxiously the circle guards the achievements, the conduct of life, and the outlook of the individual, and the more readily . . . specialization would break up the framework of the whole little circle" (Simmel [1905] 1950, 417). In this view, the transition from *Gemeinschaft* to *Gesellschaft* was a liberation.

One further reference to German influence, which comes from outside the field of sociology, must be made before turning to the urban sociological tradition in the United States. Oswald Spengler believed that history revealed that the city was a central actor in the story of every great civilization. His greatest impact was realized through his work *The Decline of the West* ([1922] 1928), which was widely read by both popular and scholarly audiences. Readers were drawn by the power and elegance of his writing, while they were compelled by his apocalyptic vision.

Spengler ([1922] 1928, 90–95) hinged his thesis on the observation that all great cultures had been urban cultures and that the city was the engine of "civilization" (a term he used broadly with reference to the industrialized West). The quality that set the city apart was the emergence of a "soul"—an embodiment of the urban culture as the city (its population) became aware of itself as a special entity. The city was regarded, or in this sense regarded itself, as apart from and superior to its environs, its hinterland. The soul of the city spoke a new language; urban architecture denied any relationship to organic or natural forms; and urban art, religion, and science became progressively alien to the land and were beyond the understanding of the peasant.

> *It is the Late City that first defies the land, contradicts Nature in the lines of its silhouette, denies all nature. It wants to be something different from and higher than Nature. These high-pitched gables, these Baroque cupolas, spires and pinnacles, neither are, nor desire to be, related with anything in Nature. And then begins the gigantic megalopolis, the city-as-world, which suffers nothing beside itself and sets about annihilating the country picture. . . . In the village the thatched roof is still hill-like and the street is of the same nature as the baulk of earth between the fields. But here the picture is of deep, long gorges between high, stony houses filled with colored dust and strange uproar, and men dwell in these houses, the like of which no nature being has ever conceived. Costumes, even faces, are adjusted to a background of stone. By day there is a street traffic of strange colors and tones, and by night a new light that outshines the moon. And the yokel stands helpless on the pavement, understanding nothing and understood by nobody, tolerated as a useful type in farce and provider of this world's daily bread. (Spengler [1922] 1928, 93)*

Echoing Simmel's concerns over the leveling effects of the preoccupation with money and the rise of intellect on the quality of human relationships, Spengler projected no such compensatory consequences as a gain in individual freedoms. According to Spengler, the growth of the city, for all of its promise, was a terminal condition for society. In the end, "the giant city sucks the country dry, insatiably and incessantly demanding and devouring fresh streams of men, till it wearies and dies in the midst of an almost uninhabited waste of country" (Spengler [1922] 1928, 102). In the end, no one would want to live in the country. In the end, the city, which was the product of human thought and effort, would turn and seize its makers; each of us would be "made its creature, its executive organ, and finally its victim. This stony mass [was] the *absolute* city" (Spengler [1922] 1928, 99).

Spengler held out no hope that the process could be reversed. The history of civilization, given the emergence of the city, was an inevitable rise and fall. As he put it elsewhere, "Only dreamers believe that there is a way out. Optimism is cowardice" (Spengler 1932, 103). Today this rigid interpretation of history and projection of social change is without adherents or followers. It is easy to see, however, the shadows of Spengler's gloomy musings cast across the pages of early urban sociology in the United States.

The Urban Tradition Comes to the United States

The foundation of urban sociology in the United States is credited to Robert Park. Park was a newspaper reporter who came to sociology late in his career, after becoming convinced that a more scientific approach was required in order to write the "big story" of the city. In 1899 he went to Berlin, where he studied with Georg Simmel. After returning to the United States, he spent several years serving as a secretary and assistant to Booker T. Washington at Tuskegee, where he met the sociologist W. I. Thomas. Thomas encouraged him to accept a teaching position at the University of Chicago (Faris 1967, 28–29). Thus, Chicago became both a laboratory and a classroom for Park and his students.

Besides echoing in his sociology many of the earlier themes that have been examined here, Park developed his own ideas about the ways in which spatial features of the environment influence organization and experience. There are two nested themes in Park's work and, because of his pivotal position as a founder of urban sociology in the United States, each of these themes has had an enormous influence on the developing field. First, Park was interested in the evolving structure of the city itself, the physical form of the city and the way different land uses and neighborhoods became oriented toward one another. This interest laid the foundations for the school of urban sociology that came to be known as urban ecology. Second, Park was fascinated by the different patterns of human adjustment in the city, the "ways of life" of urbanites. He urged his students to get into the streets and investigate firsthand the ways that modern city dwellers acted, thought, and felt. This emphasis gave rise to the study of urban culture, or "urbanism." He saw both of these elements, ecology and urbanism, as naturally intertwined, and combined them in his own work. The ecological order was the dominant factor: The urban arena was a self-contained universe upon which a science could be based. The physical arena provided a natural order, an urban ecology, that gave rise to distinctive behaviors. In this thinking, he borrowed from Durkheim's division of labor thesis and combined elements of field biology, producing a very distinctive realm of study for urban sociology.

The Ecology of Urban Life

The major elements of the urban arena, the different kinds of land use, and the varied urban populations that occupied the city were sorted or sorted themselves into distinguishable areas. These "neighborhoods" (Park 1915, 580) or "natural areas" (Park [1929] 1952, 196) had particular affinities or aversions to one another, resulting overall in an urban ecology—a spatial division of the city that corresponds to the functional division of labor occurring within it. Some common examples of such specialized areas include the central business district, exclusive residential areas, areas of heavy or light industry, slums, ghettos, immigrant communities, bohemias, and "hobohemias." These are *natural* areas, Park believed, because they are the products of ecological forces that work to distribute the city's populations and functions in an orderly fashion, with respect to one another. Those who can afford to do so, sort themselves away from functions or elements of the population that they regard as distasteful or dirty. Those without the economic means are relegated to the residual areas, perhaps those neighborhoods popularly regarded as containing criminal or "abnormal" types (Park 1915, 612). Each area, whatever its qualities, is characterized by its own "moral code," which corresponds to the interests and tastes of those who use it and what they use it for—residential or recreational purposes, for example. Each district is its own moral region, and in this sense each is segregated from the others. "The processes of segregation make the city a mosaic of little worlds that touch, but do not interpenetrate." Park saw the modern urbanite of his time passing quickly among these worlds, from one moral milieu to the next, "a fascinating but dangerous experiment in living at the same time in several different contiguous, perhaps, but widely separated worlds." In his view, it is this segmentation and transience that generates the superficial quality of urban life, or urbanism (Park 1915, 608). Although the city provides its inhabitants with these little localized, more manageable social orders (the city is, in fact carved up into these social worlds *by* its inhabitants), the areas do not provide *stability* because urbanites don't live in any one of them. Instead, every individual lives among many of them, playing roles that are only partial to one's entire self. For Park, neighborhood or community offered little in the way of refuge from the impersonality of the city, and urbanites remained loosely integrated, and even emotionally unstable in the urban environment.

Robert Park's influence on sociology in the United States has been broad and enduring. He presided over the work of what has been described as "an army of students of cities and city life" (Hughes 1952, 6). His students, working in the great open laboratory of Chicago, produced doctoral dissertations with titles such as "The Hobo," "The Gang," "The Gold Coast and the Slum," and "The Ghetto." The last of these was completed in 1927 by Louis Wirth, who a decade later published an essay that became one of the most influential documents in modern sociology, certainly in the field of urban sociology. This is the essay, "Urbanism as a Way of Life" (Wirth 1938), which was quoted at the opening of the present chapter.

Urbanism as a Way of Life

Although Wirth's essay has drawn its share of criticism, it remains important more than half a century later because his observations represent the capstone of the classical urban tradition. In his essay, the major themes of that tradition have been woven into a single, conceptual cloth. His essay was intended as nothing less than a comprehensive, theoretical definition of the city and urban life. In this endeavor, Wirth acknowledged the efforts of Max Weber and Robert Park but argued that prior to his attempt, these approximations to a systematic theory of the city fell short of providing a complete framework. In his construction, Wirth linked the definition of the urban form to its consequences for social organization and the nature of individual experience. He identified the quality that he was attempting to capture as "urbanism." It was a quality that characterized life at one end of a continuum, while life at the opposite end of the continuum was occupied by rural or "folk" society. Wirth identified three key criteria that directly determined the degree of urbanism found in a given society: size, density, and heterogeneity of the population. He was unwilling to recognize any quantitative threshold that might be attached to these criteria in order to distinguish urban society from rural society. For example, Wirth demonstrated that any attempts to establish an absolute criteria of urban size would produce an arbitrary and, therefore, useless set of numbers. Wirth was not prepared to answer the question, "How large is an urban population?" The question he was prepared to deal with, however, was "How urban is this place?" because the answer had to do with the size, density, and heterogeneity of that population. Consistent with his continuum approach, the answer was expressed in terms of more or less.

The following paragraphs describe Wirth's observations with respect to the effect of each of his key variables—size, density, and heterogeneity—on social life in the city. Note the numerous points of continuity with earlier concepts.

Size
The greater the size of a given population, the greater the likelihood that different kinds (races, statuses) of people make it up. This, in turn, tends to give rise to spatial segregation within the population. Without a common tradition or experience, there can be no common identity, and "competition and formal control mechanisms furnish the substitute for the bonds of solidarity that are relied upon to hold a folk society together" (Wirth 1938, 11). Wirth referred directly to Weber's and Simmel's observations that typical social relations must be more shallow in the city, due to the sheer numbers involved. Human relationships are highly segmented or specialized, and contact as full personalities is impossible. The city is thus characterized by secondary rather than primary relationships. Many of these relationships remain face-to-face, but they are impersonal, superficial, and transitory. According to Wirth, the reserve, indifference, and blasé outlook that he believed typify the urban type are really the urbanites' "devices for immunizing themselves against the personal claims and expectations of others." The relationships in the city that we do take the trouble to maintain are instrumental in nature, and we regard them merely as a means for the achievement of our own ends, not for the value of the relationship itself.

Wirth allowed that individuals in urban life gain some element of freedom from the control of the intimate group, but that they also lose the reassurance that comes from life in a more emotionally integrated society. Along with freedom comes a social void and sense of anomie. Although the division of labor and the growth of specialization (even among cities themselves) lead to the social solidarity of interdependence, the pure market motives that bring us together, the "pecuniary nexus," lead to relationships of a predominantly predatory nature. Finally, in the vast numbers of the city, the individual counts for little politically.

Density

When numbers increase and area is held constant, specialization must occur among the population of organisms occupying the space. With this, Wirth indicated his basic agreement with both Darwin and Durkheim. The general effect of density is to reinforce that of size; thus it would appear that many of Wirth's observations regarding density also could have been made under the heading of size.

One consequence of having numerous but superficial and anonymous contacts is that people come to look for cues or symbols of who the other is and how they may be expected to act. Wirth cited Simmel's reference to the importance of the "uniform" that identifies the role of the particular functionary, while the personality remains hidden behind it. Wirth believed that as urbanites we have become attuned to the world of artifacts and are "progressively further removed from the world of nature."

The effect of density is also evident in the spatial configuration of the city. Its surface is divided into different uses, and the urban population is distributed into more or less distinct settlements, which become segregated to the degree that their requirements and mode of life are incompatible with one another. The inhabitants of the city travel among these settlements, "a mosaic of social worlds in which the transition from one to the other is abrupt" and where the result is that the participant traveler develops a relativistic perspective and a greater tolerance of differences. But the dominant spirit that emerges from the close aggregation of divergent types is that of competition and mutual exploitation in an urban world where the clock and the traffic signal are the symbolic basis of the social order.

Heterogeneity

By the time Wirth came to this third criterion, he had already discussed its effects in relation to both size (in that the city draws to it a diverse population) and density (which creates a division of labor and, thus, a diverse population). The particular consequence of this variable is that every individual in the city is in regular contact with a wide diversity of other individuals, which presents the opportunity for the development of a variety of interests, orientations, memberships, and allegiances for each individual. What sets apart the urbanite is that she or he has no undivided allegiances to any particular group. It is in this consideration of the significance of urban heterogeneity that Wirth's concern for the massing of human society emerges. Instead of enriching individual's lives, socially or culturally, these multiple memberships become transitory and relatively unimportant. Rather than anchoring individuals in a stable social life, these multiple and shifting memberships pull them in conflicting and changing directions. Instead of providing modes of individual expression, "the cultural institutions, such as the schools, the movies, the radio, and the newspapers by virtue of their mass clientele, . . . operate as leveling influences. . . . If the individual would participate at all in the social, political, and economic life of the city, he must subordinate some of his individuality to the demands of the larger community, and in that measure immerse himself in mass movements" (Wirth 1938, 16–18).

In the end, the image of the urban condition that Wirth leaves with us is one where individuals are alienated, alone, and adrift in a sea of competing norms and values. Increasing size, density, and heterogeneity leave people socially uprooted and politically powerless, conditions that are lessened only to the extent that urbanites are willing to submerge their identity in mass movements. Community is obliterated and in its place rises the "mass society"—a society of undifferentiated humanity, in which individuals are reduced to a common condition. The leveling of individuality in urban society is completed by the mass messages and faceless ministrations of its massive bureaucratic institutions.

The Image of the City in the Urban Tradition and in American Culture

Wirth's conclusions are clearly a product of the sociological tradition within which he worked. Some of the themes of this urban sociology, especially as they were expressed by Simmel, Park, and Wirth, also mirrored certain Western European and North American cultural attitudes toward the growing and spreading cities in the nineteenth and early twentieth centuries. Popular attitudes, supported by contemporary religious writers and literary themes, were characterized largely by a mistrust of the city. White and White (1962) made a strong case that there has been an antiurban intellectual tradition in the United States, from the time of Thomas Jefferson through Frank Lloyd Wright. On the other hand, Glaab and Brown (1983, 52) took issue with this interpretation, arguing that it would be a mistake to characterize either intellectual themes or popular thought as single-mindedly antiurban. North Americans have not wholeheartedly loved their cities, they argue, but they have been fascinated by them, especially as symbols of progress. Those nineteenth century critics, like Henry David Thoreau, who questioned the proposition that material growth meant social progress, were in the minority:

> The rationale that developed in defense and explanation of American capitalist expansion had the city as one of its principal elements. We read Thoreau today and are moved by his prophetic remonstration against American materialism, against the city, the machine and the factory. Yet in his own time people were more likely to read the poetic tributes to the telegraph, the iron horse, or the country's magnificent thriving cities to be found in their commercial magazines or local newspapers. Although the anti-urban philosophers and novelists of the nineteenth century intrigue the contemporary mind, the defenders and prophets of the material city perhaps reflect more exactly the early popular view of the city. (Glaab and Brown 1983, 66–67)

Nevertheless, a strong current of popular criticism directed at the city did exist in the late nineteenth century and into the twentieth century. In its simplest

FIGURE 3-1   Keeping Track of Who's Who in the "Urban Tradition"

Three Protourban Contrasts

Ferdinand Tönnies	*Gemeinschaft* Communal plight	*Gesellschaft* Commercial individualism
Henry Maine	Status Family honor	Contract Formalized individual responsibility
Emile Durkheim	Mechanical solidarity Common experience and collective consciousness	Organic solidarity Division of labor and functional interdependence

Three German Perspectives

Max Weber	The ideal type, city as marketplace, fortress, at least limited political autonomy, and related forms of association
Georg Simmel	The mental life of the metropolis is conditioned by overstimulation and the exchange of cash
Oswald Spengler	The city has a soul, which means that its human subjects feel superior to rural types The denial of nature ultimately contributes to urban demise

The Urban Tradition in the United States

Robert Park	The city as an ecology of natural areas each of which generates its own moral code
Louis Wirth	"Urbanism as a Way of Life" essay integrates the major elements of all previous writers in the urban tradition as Wirth examines the combined effects of size, density, and heterogeneity

form, this criticism was inspired by the fear of unpredictable urban masses, which was supported in turn by the xenophobic reaction in the United States to large-scale European immigration. In its more sophisticated form, the popular view of the city shared the concern so common among urban sociologists—of life reduced to its most commercial and calculating dimensions.

In 1872 Charles Loring Brace, a clergyman who worked among the destitute of New York City, published *The Dangerous Classes of New York*. In his book, he urged the keepers of the law to watch closely over the homeless and hungry, or someday they may find that city suddenly reduced "to ashes and blood" (Glaab and Brown 1983, 231). Similarly, the Reverend Josiah Strong ([1885] 1968, 128) wrote of his concern over the growing concentration of European immigrants in the cities of the United States, where the juxtaposition of poverty and wealth in their most extreme forms chafed on the public conscience. He warned that socialism bred in the city: "Here is heaped the social dynamite; her roughs, gamblers, thieves, robbers, desperate men of all sorts congregate; men who are ready on any pretext to raise riots for the purpose of destruction and plunder; here gather foreigners and wage workers; here skepticism and irreligion abound" (Strong [1885] 1968, 128).

According to the classical view within urban sociology, individuals tend to be isolated and withdrawn in the urban arena.

Lincoln Steffens (1904), in *The Shame of the Cities,* focused America's attention on the corruption of urban governments. He criticized the common tendency of the times to blame the "foreign element" for the moral failure of urban government as "one of the hypocritical lies that save us from the clear sight of ourselves." Instead, what was wrong with politics, he argued, was the same thing that was wrong with "everything"—art, literature, religion, journalism, law, medicine— they were all *businesses.* The motives of urban politicians were based upon commercial principles. "The commercial spirit is the spirit of profit, not patriotism; of credit, not honor; or individual gain, not national prosperity; of trade and dickering, not principle." Self-interest and personal gain were not motives peculiar to politicians, however; these people were simply in a position to make bigger deals and turn a larger profit than the average citizen (Steffens 1904, 5–7). In the popular mind, the typical urbanite was thoroughly distracted by concern with money and profit. In this vein, Rudyard Kipling was inspired by a post-turn-of-the-century visit to Chicago to write:

> *I spent ten hours in that huge wilderness, wandering through scores of miles of these terrible streets, and jostling some few hundred thousand of these terrible people who talked money through their noses. The cabman [his guide] left me: but after a while I picked up another man who was full of figures, and into my ears*

he poured them as occasion required or the big blank factories suggested. Here they turned out so many hundred thousand dollars worth of such and such an article; there so many million other things; this house is worth so many million dollars; that one so many million more or less. It was like listening to a child babbling of its hoard of shells. It was like watching a fool play with buttons. But I was expected to do more than listen or watch. He demanded that I should admire. (Kipling [1913] 1968, 42)

It is a familiar story. We cannot know what proportion of Kipling's audience was sympathetic to his view, willing or perhaps even eager to accept his caricature of the typical urbanite. We can, however, observe that social science had produced little in its formulations of the nature of urban life that would contradict Kipling's image.

Many early twentieth-century American writers were drawn to the urban milieu in their work. In addition to the concern for materialism in modern urban life, their popular writings contained a number of familiar sociological themes, which included isolation and alienation, the collapse of community and the breakdown of tradition, and the weakening of ties of affection and religion. As Gelfant (1954, 21–22) wrote at midcentury, "The comprehensive theme of city fiction is personal dissociation: the prototype for the hero is the self-divided man . . . the community has failed to provide a cohesive tradition that can guide the individual in his choice of goals and moral alternatives."

The American novelist Theodore Dreiser was one of the throng of small-town migrants to the big city. By his own account, he was transformed by his urban experience: His small-town idealism was soon undone. He is another who was struck by the extremes of wealth and poverty that stood side by side in the city, and eventually he came to adopt the view of his hardened newspaper-reporting colleagues: Life is a fierce, grim struggle where one expects others to lie, cheat, and lay traps in order to achieve their ends (Gelfant 1954, 50). As a seasoned urbanite, he wrote, "For myself, I accept now no creeds. I do not know what the truth is, what beauty is, what love is, what hope is. I do not believe anyone absolutely and I do not doubt anyone absolutely" (Dreiser 1913, 4). In effect, this was a self-portrait of the figure evoked by the classical tradition of urban sociology. It echoed, in the first person, the theme of the anomic individual, alone in a sea of changing and conflicting ideas and values. There were other, more positive, popular reflections of the city that dated from the same era, as well as evidence that there was some resistance to the unremitting criticisms of contemporary life like those found in Dreiser (Glaab and Brown 1983, 248–250; Doctorow 1982, vii–ix). It is evident, however, that early in this century, sociologists were not alone in their suspicions and criticisms of the city. Many of the critical themes of the Chicago sociologists were part of the popular vocabulary.

Evaluating the Urban Tradition in Sociology

Just as it would be inaccurate to regard the popular attitudes of the times as uniformly antiurban, so it would be to fail to recognize the ambivalent feelings of the classical urban sociologists in this regard. However, each of the theorists reviewed in this chapter dwelt to a greater or lesser extent upon the loss of solidarity, security, and confidence in life lived in a world of primary ties. With the exception of the work of Emile Durkheim and Max Weber, it is the negative qualities of urbanism that become the most important features in identifying the urban condition. Finally, in Wirth's "Urbanism as a Way of Life," we have urban life stripped of all virtue. Does the emphasis on predatory relationships and human isolation in the crowd accurately describe the experience of the city dweller? Critics have argued that it is instead a poor, biased account.

It is important to recall what Wirth's purpose and method were, and not misinterpret his effort to model the urban experience. First, he was not trying to describe the experience of the average urbanite or life in the average city; instead he was constructing an ideal. Second, his method involved positing characteristics of one extreme (urban) in contrast to its assumed opposite (rural or folk society). The product of such reasoning, the ultimate model, may be expected to describe only the most extreme or "pure" elements of urban experience. It is not a description of all the lives lived in cities, but an effort to identify what it is about these lives that is characteristically urban. The way to employ such a model is not to hold it up to experience in order to evaluate it, but rather the other way around. That is, by taking a given situation, identifying its basic features, and comparing these features to the characteristics of Wirth's concept ("urbanism"), one may determine the degree to which that situation (experience) can be characterized by his ideal quality. In assessing the usefulness of the model, it is necessary to bear in mind that the nature of Wirth's method caused him to emphasize the most extreme attributes of urban life in contrast to what he felt were the most characteristic features of rural society. In this way his formulation remains useful.

There is no question that Wirth's emphasis on aversion and suspicion exaggerates the experience of most urbanites most of the time; but *situationally*, from time to time, we may recall having seen these factors at work or having felt them shape our own behavior. For example, consider the norms for interaction among strangers, even for looking at other people, on a crowded city bus or subway car, or even the driver of the car in the next lane in traffic. Do we engage or avoid each other? How should one react to a friendly approach by a perfect stranger on a crowded street in a large city? on an empty street?

For some, Wirth's portrayal may amount to an understatement, and Simmel's prescription for ignoring surrounding persons and events may be taken as bad advice. Anxiety and outright fear dominate their orientation to urban life in general, and public behavior in particular. The following is advice reportedly given by a seasoned veteran to her newly arrived friend in Manhattan:

> *You have to know your territory, she said. You have to be on the alert constantly, to sense when somebody nearby is out of place, waiting, looking, ready to pounce. You have to clutch your handbag up close, ready to fight for it should that become necessary. You have to put three locks on your door, plus a burglarproof chain. You have to avoid the subways, night or day, and don't smile at strangers on the bus. You have to leave your gold chains at home, and any*

other jewelry that might tempt a thief. You have to stick with your class, your
group. (Lewis 1981, 8)

Of course, this is only another glimpse of life in the city—a particular city—
seen through the eyes of a single person. For all of those who feel this way, there
are as many others who are at home and at ease in the city. But there is an important point here that is too easy for many of us to miss. The speaker in the quoted
passage is a woman. If we raise the question of whether the city is a hostile and
alienating environment, whether public places have the capacity to provoke anxiety, from a woman's perspective, does that affect the answer?

Gender and Public Space

We began this chapter with the observation that reality is to some extent subjective, that people with different backgrounds experience the world differently. The
point was made in order to provide a context for the discussion of theories that
came from a different period when the modern world was taking shape, when the
massive industrial city was just coming into being. It is also useful to keep this
subjective element of experience in mind if we are going to gain a full appreciation of contemporary urban life. As Wirth pointed out, urban populations are heterogeneous, and part of what this means is that they represent many perspectives.
One of the features of heterogeneous populations is that the individuals who
make them up have different amounts of power. Differences in power are present
in all social contexts, whether we are talking about families, classrooms, work-
places, or international organizations. It is also true of cities, and here we will pay
particular attention to public space, where the actors involved are all anonymous
strangers. The existence of differing amounts of power in such places will have
consequences for the way individuals experience those places, whether they experience them with a sense of proprietorship or vulnerability, whether their surroundings and the people in them make them feel secure or out of place. Categories of people who may be more prone to feeling out of place and vulnerable in
public space could include minorities, the elderly, gays and lesbians, and women.

A dimension of diversity that was particularly neglected by early theorists
was gender. Today there is an increasing awareness that men and women "strategize" public arenas differently (Gardner 1995, 200), which means that experience
has conditioned them to move through anonymous territories full of strangers
with different kinds of awareness, deliberation, and intent.

Nineteenth and twentieth century cities emerged as the seats of manufacturing and commerce, and public spaces within them emerged as the arteries and retreats that serviced the business and leisure needs of the men who conducted the
world's important business. The observation is trite but true nevertheless that the
modern city emerged at a time when the ordinary arena of activity for the gentle-
woman was her father's or husband's home. As Ryan (1990, 4–6) put it, "To search
for women in public is to subvert a longstanding tenet of the modern Western gender system, the presumption that social space is divided between the public and
the private, and that men claim the former while women are confined to the lat-

ter." She asserted that the role of the male planner, in creating order, is in part to exclude (genteel and domesticated) women along with other out-of-place and disruptive elements who threaten to spoil the male domain. Certainly poor women, as ragged scavengers and prostitutes, were fixtures of the street life of cities. But their presence, off-putting to the sensibilities of comfortable business folk, was no argument that urban public space was women's domain (Stansell 1986). Today, as the urban arena and other male domains have become contested ground in the battle for social equality, it is still possible to argue that men remain more at home and in control in anonymous public space than women do, and there are ways that members of a more powerful social majority remind the others that they are out of place.

BOX 3-2   Women Out of Place in the Nineteenth Century City

Richard Sennett's (1977) *The Fall of Public Man* is widely referenced, both within and outside sociology, as containing important insights into the degree to which women faced barriers to entering the public realm in the nineteenth century. Sennett emphasized the desire on the part of both sexes to be inconspicuous in public. Men looked to minute details of conformity in attire, while a woman could do little to avoid the possibility of "being read wrong or maliciously" when in public. There was both an expert and popular belief that it was possible to "read" a person's inner state from unconscious or unintended outward signs available to the properly trained eye. Sennett asked, "Is it any wonder that women would be afraid of showing themselves in public . . . ?"

Annabelle Cone (1996) explored fictional accounts in nineteenth century French novels of what became of young women who defied the prohibition on exploring urban public space on their own. Affluent women did have a recognized role in public as mass transportation and the renovation of Paris provided reasonably safe corridors of access to the center and as retail merchandising came to rival the purely industrial nature of the urban economy. But women were free only to extend their domestic role to shopping in the new department stores, not to wander the city, either alone or at night.

Griselda Pollock (1988) gave graphic expression to the public restrictions on nineteenth century women as she described the effects of restricted urban access on the work of painters who were women. Pollock drew attention to the works of Berthe Morisot and Mary Cassatt, indicating the disproportionate representations of domestic interiors and private gardens—rather than public spaces—in their works. When wider urban vistas are portrayed, the foreground is cropped by doorway or window or some other detail that places the viewer's vantage point within a domestic or other private setting. Restricted access is given voice by another artist, a contemporary of Morisot and Cassatt, Marie Bashkirtseff: "What I long for is the freedom of going out alone, of coming and going, of sitting in the seats of Tuileries, and especially in the Luxembourg, of stopping and looking at the artistic shops, of entering churches and museums, of walking about old streets at night; that's what I long for, and that's the freedom without which one cannot become a real artist" (Pollock 1988, 70).

Source: Adapted from Ellen Bradburn and William G. Flanagan, "Sex and the City: The Gender of Urban and Rural Spaces. A Research Agenda," presented at the American Sociological Association Annual Conference, Chicago, August 1999.

Women continued to occupy the status of the *urban other* through the middle of the twentieth century, a status that was an odd mixture of domestic forager, guest worker, and involuntary performer in the city's continuous erotic sideshow. Women were reminded of their status daily—an instance is offered by Davis and Lorenzowski's (1998) account of mass transit crowding during World War II in Canadian cities. Gasoline rationing and other shortages meant that the overtaxed bus and rail trolley system became even more crowded, especially at morning and evening rush hours. That these mass transit systems were a male province was symbolized by boarding steps that were clearly not designed for women wearing skirts or dresses and by the smoking sections present in each car that were *de facto* restricted to male riders. Male riders, it was assumed, were on their way to and from work, an activity that assumed a symbolic patriotic legitimacy during wartime. Two categories of women rode the passenger lines: workers and shoppers, the latter set apart by the bags and packages that made up their public uniform. It was this latter category of person, traveling during peak hours, who was the focus of widely aired complaints by men. The lines of conflict were drawn between the smokers and the *tardy shoppers* (so labeled because they chose to ride outside of the recommended hours of travel for nonworkers), which is to say the lines were drawn between men who claimed privileged access to the public domain and women who entered the public arena in an extension of their domestic role—whose claim thereby was of a lower order of legitimacy. Wartime did not create the distinctions in legitimate claim to space, but only accentuated them.

Gardner (1995) provided a useful insight into the processes of male public domination and control in her monograph, *Passing By: Gender and Public Harassment.* Her observations reflect the fact that women's public behavior is much more controlled by widely understood norms that apply specifically to women. These rules of public "etiquette," which have long been applied specifically to women, are lingering evidence that a woman alone in public is still an exceptional category, an "incomplete participation unit" as Goffman (1971) termed the condition. Old-fashioned norms that imposed limits on women's freedom of movement in public may seem laughably archaic to most people today, yet they continue to apply, making women in public a more restricted urban participant. The city is for women a more hostile and threatening environment. For women, being "street smart" includes additional considerations.

For example, women in public are still advised not to draw attention to themselves, either by manner or dress. They should take care to conceal their tracks, to keep separate their anonymous public presence and the locus of their personal life to avoid being followed back to their private sphere, for safety's sake. Women have to take special care in their necessary or casual interactions with strangers, so as not to transmit the wrong idea by an overly pleasant demeanor, to not seem to invite interest. And, in the event that public harassment occurs, the traditional advice to women is to avoid direct confrontation with their assailant in order to discreetly avert further assault. These extraordinary precautions that women are advised to observe, precautions that control their presence and make them a passive and wary presence in public, clearly identify urban space as not only a gen-

Some will see this as a public sidewalk full of people. Some will see it as a sidewalk full of men.

dered but also an "eroticized" environment (Young 1990), tinged with the excitement of the possibility of adventuresome encounters among strangers. As historically and presently constituted, such adventure carries sexualized overtones of threat for many women who negotiate these spaces.

Seen in this light—the anonymity of urban public life stressed by Wirth and his predecessors—the idea that there is a calculated and predatory aspect to city life takes on a new dimension. While people in general may express a concern for their safety on city streets, the concern of women is heightened by frequent reminders that they are at risk. These reminders take the form of what may be referred to generically as *public harassment*—whistles, comments, calls, solicitations, lewd looks, and physical contacts that create, overall, a threatening atmosphere

(Gardner 1995). Anonymity emboldens and provides cover for would-be casual assailants to engage in what *they* may consider minimally or playfully aggressive sexual behavior—a suggestive comment or a look. The cumulative experience of these breaches of civility condition the people subjected to these behaviors, making them wary and defensive.

When women present accounts of harassment, the normative structures or expectations that surround feminine public behavior reemerge as criteria for evaluating such complaints. In addition to questions about whether the event was really all that serious, the audience may raise questions about whether the victim of the assault was out of place or exercising inappropriate judgment under the circumstances: That is, any claim by a woman that an act of gross public incivility has occurred raises questions about *her* behavior. It is not hard to understand that for some women, dealing with even the intermittent prospect of harassment in public places can be exhausting and as alienating as any of the descriptions of urban life we have reviewed in this chapter. To the extent that it promotes a withdrawal from public space for any individual, it might be said that to that degree it has had an "atomizing" effect, to use Wirth's term.

While the actual incidence of physical sexual assault may be statistically rare, women who are daily reminded of the predatory nature of the urban environment are especially concerned about crime. A summary of research (Ferraro 1996) on the topic shows that women's fear of sexual assault is generalized to all categories of assaultive crimes: That is, a sense of vulnerability to sexual attack makes women more generally fearful of criminal confrontation. Although women are in fact less frequently victims of all forms of assault, with the exception of sexual assaults, than are men, they report a higher fear of being victimized by all varieties of crime than do men. This is apparently the result of the "shadow effect" of the fear of becoming a victim of a sexual crime, the fear that any form of criminal confrontation (for instance, robbery) might include rape. This generalized fear is especially high among women under 35, and personal safety is a daily concern that conditions the lives of many urban women (Ferraro 1996). A study of one British city (Bradford) discovered that 68 percent of women did not go out alone after dark, and in another (Nottingham) a small percentage of women were afraid to venture into the city in daylight, especially on weekends. That study, which covered nine cities, found that the availability of public transportation and taxis did not solve the problem of fear of public places, because women felt vulnerable to harassment or attack while waiting for a bus or subway or while riding the subway, and did not feel safe being transported alone by a male cabbie (Trench and Jones 1995).

As important as it is to recognize the subjective differences in the way men and women experience cities, it is also important not to engage in a kind of "victim feminism," which advocates for women's interests in terms of their perceived helplessness. A potential political liability is attached to the claim that cities are particularly hostile environments for women. The observation might invite the conclusion that, since the great centers are a naturally more threatening environment for women, women are naturally and permanently disadvantaged in their attempts to become full and equal participants in the political and economic life of cities. Elizabeth Wilson (1991) attempted to take this argument that women are less fit to survive in the urban jungle and stand it on its head. In *The Sphinx in the City*, she described what she understands as the implicit symbolism of the past two centuries of male-dominated Western urban culture. She built on the notion that the city is an especially sexual arena. "The sophisticated urban consciousness, which . . . reached a high point in Central Europe in the early twentieth century, was an especially male consciousness. Sexual unease and the pursuit of sexuality outside the constraints of the family were one of its major preoccupations" (5). The city was and remains today the arena of the forbidden in the male imagination— "what is most feared and desired"—and the women there are offhandedly classified according to categories of sexual desirability and accessibility.

At the same time, the urban arena offers a paradox to women. Because of its carnivalesque atmosphere, and despite its other, business face, the city offers a woman a kind of freedom, in contrast to the rural, suburban, and domestic isolation that are her other options. Despite the uncontestable fact that men own urban space, it may be that women are more at ease there because they do not experience the Euromasculine need to control and rationalize space. True, the city remains a dangerous place for women, with respect to their integrity as well as their physical well-being. To be in the city is almost to accept the sexualized connotation, the game woman, the prostitute. The resolution of the problem lies not in retreat: Instead, perceptions and the symbolic meaning of cities need to change in order to realize the freeing potential of the urban arena for women. "We must cease to perceive the city as a dangerous and disorderly zone from which women and others must be excluded for their own protection." Wilson said it is especially a mistake for feminists to focus on safety, welfare, and protection when addressing the urban environment because this plays into the hands of the paternalistic tradition of planners and protectors who know what is best for women. Safety is an issue, but it is necessary also to emphasize the other side of the argument, "to insist on women's right to the carnival, intensity, and even the risks of the city." She argued that it must be possible to be both pro-women and pro-city, to argue in the end that urban life, "however fraught with difficulty, has emancipated women more than rural life or suburban domesticity" (Wilson 1991, 8–10). Wilson was aware that in the carnival of urban life, women are disproportionately impoverished and vulnerable to violence. But, these facts "should not blind us to the pernicious effect of the ideology that has sought to banish *all* women from urban space, and to lock them into an often stifling domestic privacy" (119).

Wilson's ideas deserve careful consideration, especially if they at first seem to be describing a different time, before women had become as free to claim and use the urban environment as men. The point is that women are not as free. During any week of the year in any large city, one will find meetings where women are organizing to "take back the night," issuing mace and police whistles, attending self-defense classes, and training in the peer counseling of rape victims. Gay male and lesbian organizations will also be gathering to discuss and work to reduce victimization.

These are not the only groups who must struggle to make a place for themselves in public. Many categories of people are subject to abuse in public places and experience the city as a particularly hostile and alienating environment (Gardner

1995, 16). The study of women's safety in British cities referred to earlier recognized a number of groups who had particular concerns about safety (Trench and Jones 1995, 12). These included the elderly, blacks, ethnic minorities, and people with special physical needs. All of these groups were recognized as especially vulnerable to harassment and attack. One significant feature of this study is that it was part of the national government's "Action for Cities Initiative" that resulted in the establishment of special transportation programs designed to shelter some categories of people as they traveled through hostile urban environments. While the program represents a positive step in recognizing and treating the symptoms of the uncivil urban space, it perpetuates the notion that women and others must operate under some kind of curfew, and it protects them by removing them from the general stream of public life. It acquiesces to the popular image that the urban world is becoming an even more dangerous place in which some people must exercise special care in order to be safe. "Nevertheless, in the context of existing behavior patterns and crime rates, planning to minimize actual and perceived threats to the safety of women [and others] merits high priority" (Trench and Jones 1995, 13–14).

The urban environment resists efforts to transform it into a more secure and convivial space. Yet it was produced by deliberate actions, individual and communal, selfish and socially responsible, and it will continue to be modified by these forces. As diverse categories of social actors become more central to the shaping of urban space, demand more of it, and require it to serve equally the needs of a pluralistic population, the conviviality of the urban arena may be enhanced.

Updating the Urban Tradition

Certainly the city is a different place than was described by those who struggled to define urban life in the nineteenth and early twentieth century—Durkheim, Simmel, and Wirth—and yet certain features of the city are the same as when they wrote. One way to see the similarities and differences is to examine the stories that we tell about the city, and here a certain shift is detectable. On the one hand, we still talk about the future of cities and how they continue to impact the way we experience the world and organize our lives. But, the social impact of sheer urban *growth* is no longer the major "urban story" theme in Western culture, although it will remain so for decades to come in the poorer regions of the world.

Today the emphasis in the dramatic tale of city life has shifted from the issue of growth to that of social division: divisions between gendered identities, center and suburb, poverty and affluence, ethnic and racial classifications, renegade youth and solid citizen. It is heterogeneity itself that attracts and excites the popular imagination. Themes having to do with morality and the city still appear, applied mostly to political corruption and questions about poor people's behavior, such as their dependence on public assistance and their childbearing and marriage patterns. These turn-of-the-century issues are the same old stories of the previous turn of the century.

There may have been a period fifty years ago, at midcentury, when the city had become a mere dramatic backdrop in popular fiction, not the kind of social force that it had been to early reformers and sociologists. By midcentury, writers and readers were less awed by the city than they had been. They had simply got used to it; they themselves were products of the urban environment (Weimer 1966, 144–145). In the postmodern era, the meaning of *city* merges with themes related to the influence of the mass media and the operation of international capital, with some concern over the unique experiences of the rapidly growing "overpopulated" cities of poor nations. The image of the city "becomes more abstract and 'unreal,' as power operates from hidden sources." Those familiar with the perspective will immediately realize the consequence of the postmodern interpretation of the city: The city can only be known from within, an interpretation that takes on a meaning that is created and interpreted by each individual (Lehan 1998, 287–288). However, although it may be more difficult to tell stories about cities independent from themes of the global market and mass culture today than it was a hundred years ago, cities continue to emanate their own excitement, to magnify the scale of human action, and to showcase action.

Cities focus the racism that erupts into violence, headquarter the machinations of power brokers who orchestrate world resources, provide mass markets for large and petty drug dealers, represent the territorial frameworks that provide the incentive for gang fighters, and showcase the efforts of terrorists to attract the attention of the world. Not the least element in the drama of the city is the overwhelming spectacle of millions of poor people facing the threat of permanent economic obsolescence.

The wild city at the beginning of the twenty-first century, the lived-in city and the city of the imagination, is the setting for shadowy intrigues of young gun-slinging desperados, places where inhabitants don't need to have the term *street-smart* defined for them. Here the working-class and service populations hustle between formal and informal economic strategies to make ends meet. The working poor live on the margins of decaying housing supplies. Many of the poor—including some with regular jobs—find themselves living on the streets. In some ways these are not the cities that Louis Wirth wrote about in the 1930s, and in some ways they are. Certainly in the 1930s, there was poverty, crime, and disorder. We are missing something obvious and important if we conclude that today's city does not provoke alienation, suspicion, and outright fear, perhaps to an even greater extent than in Wirth's time.

If we consider the city from all the perspectives that reflect the diversity of the people who live there, we can still sense some of the awe and dread that drew the attention and concern of the early sociologists. It would be a mistake, however, to focus exclusively on the more sensational aspects of urban life. The city is simultaneously the place where many people live reasonably predictable and mundane lives, are at home, choose this above all other settings, and value the differences, the carnival, the excitement. We turn to the perspective of those who are at home with the city in the next chapter.

4

COMMUNITY AND THE CITY

In the preceding chapter, we reviewed the classical tradition of sociological reasoning, which, in the end, nearly despaired at the human condition in the modern world. Since the publication of Wirth's "Urbanism as a Way of Life" (1938), urban sociology has been preoccupied with reconciling this negative image with research that has revealed a very different picture of the quality of urban social life. In classical urban theory, mass society and utilitarian relationships dominate social experience: Individuals are largely powerless, alienated, and alone. This is the model of thoroughly urban existence, but this is not what research has revealed about life in the city. Instead, researchers have discovered repeatedly a strong sense of local community and involvement among neighbors, friends, kin, and others who share common interests. Preurban forms of sociability survive in the city, and the urban arena also makes possible new forms of community and solidarity, which is most important in an *urban* sociology because it addresses *the* urban question. While the survival of the forms of community usually associated with smaller types of settlements is interesting, the question for the urban sociologist is, How does the city modify this survival? And most importantly, What unique forms of community are caused by urban life?

In this chapter, we will consider a number of different forms of social cohesion in the city. We begin with an examination of the ways in which the concept of community has been used with reference to urban spaces and social groupings, and how that concept has been modified to make it more useful. For example, "community" has been modified by removing the locational connotations typically attached to the term. The point is that community, a form of social integration that fosters a sense of belonging, may or may not be synonymous with "neighborhood." The focus of community in urban sociology has shifted from the designation of a physical space to that of a social grouping or "social network." The forms of social organization discussed in this chapter portray the city as a rich social mosaic of interpenetrating worlds, giving individuals a sense of social attachment. While certain structural features of the urban environment create a tendency toward aversion among individuals, there are also multiple opportunities for the development of sustained and enriched social ties. Just as Wirth was able to make a case for the atomizing effects of the urban arena, we can make a case for the reinforcement of social ties in the urban arena. Indeed, the city may possess a peculiar capacity for fostering novel groupings of individuals with mutual interests.

It may be observed in the following discussion that social unity, whether expressed as community or in some other way, is often generated by opposition between competing groups. The heterogeneity that characterizes urban populations also increases the potential for strain, competition, or confrontation. Where we find unity in a city, we will often find conflict among its social units.

Urban Community Studies

A clear understanding of the nature of urban social life has been obscured on the one hand by the different and even contrary orientations of the classical urban theorists and on the other hand by the particular style of urban research. The development of urban *theory* was closely associated with the idea of the rise of the *mass society*. Conversely, urban *research* has developed an empirical tradition with a focus on *community study*. This method involves the close observation of a relatively small segment of the wider urban arena. The majority of these studies have focused on a combination of the working-class, ethnic, and minority populations.

Where a concern with the effects of mass society led the theorists to posit isolation and alienation as the predominant features of urban life, an orientation among the researchers toward a community approach predisposed them to uncover bonds of friendship, kinship, and neighborliness in urban life. This evidence of community in the city led, at least initially, to the belief that Wirth's interpretation of urbanism, as well as the theoretical tradition upon which his conclusions were based, had been proved wrong. However, since early in his career, Wirth had been fully aware of communities of close ties and supportive relations in the city. In fact, he had carefully documented these ties in his own research in Chicago's Jewish ghetto (Wirth 1928). These features of social life simply had found no place in his effort to construct an ideal urbanism. The accumulation of community-oriented research, however, clearly indicated that Wirth's classical model did not address the common experience of large categories of urbanites.

One of the earliest studies to challenge the theme of the undifferentiated mass and individual anomie was conducted in the North End of Boston. William Foote Whyte's *Street Corner Society* (1943) examined the nature of social organization in a poor working-class district of the city. The study showed fundamental differences in what insiders and outsiders saw when they looked at the same area. Whyte managed to gain the perspective of the "Cornerville" insiders. He did not romanticize the area and its residents; he carefully focused on the members of street corner gangs and the operation of racketeers and their payoffs to local police. He did not, however, see any of these elements as symptomatic of community breakdown or social disorganization.

What might have appeared as elements of disorganization or moral decay from the outside were interpreted as integrative and stabilizing influences within the community. For example, the notoriety enjoyed by a leader of street corner boys could provide useful visibility if he later chose to run for local political office. His leadership qualities could be put to good use by outside agents, such as social workers, to gain the cooperation of young people in the area for a city-sponsored recreation program that might otherwise be ignored by area youth. Or the abundance of illegal activities in a neighborhood could provide an alternative structure of opportunities whereby bright young people with few other options would work their way up the social and economic ladders. That all members of the community did not suffer a sense of indignation because there were artful lawbreakers in their midst was not due to any breakdown of moral order. Instead, the area studied by Whyte may be better understood in terms of Robert Park's "moral worlds," an urban area that embodies its own particular sense of right and order. For example, it was simply natural for a mother who sent her young daughter to the grocer for a bottle of milk to tell her to "put the change on a number" (i.e., play the illegal rackets-run lottery with the few cents left over). Whyte's study reflected that the residents of the area had a clear sense of what constituted order and honorable behavior; they paid close attention to community political affairs as well as kept an eye on what was going on in the street.

Since Whyte's study appeared in the 1940s, close on the heels of the publication of Wirth's essay, "hordes of scholars" have carefully researched and published studies that show "that urbanites still neighbor, still have a sense of local community, and still use neighborhood ties for sociability and support" (Wellman and Leighton 1979, 373). By the 1960s the survival of community in the city was a commonly recognized sociological fact. Among the most outstanding examples of this research was that done by Young and Willmott (1957), which focused in part on a poor working-class borough in London. They documented the central importance of kinship in the daily round of life and in times of need. The social worlds of the subjects in this study, especially the women, were intensely localized.

In Washington, D.C., Elliot Liebow (1967) studied the failed nuclear-family lives of black street corner men. Their families had been direct victims of racism and economic discrimination. Urban conditions, independent of the economic consequences of racial discrimination, were not responsible for the disintegration of family life. The street corner simply offered these men a refuge, a place to be with others who understood their frustration and a place where they could maintain their self-esteem. Although they had failed to achieve the kind of success that was most important to them—success as heads of their families and as dependable providers—they still had the sociability of the street. The street corner provided an alternate set of goals and opportunities. The wider society neither understood nor approved of these alternate goals, but it was society that had first set the conditions of failure.

Ulf Hannerz (1969), who studied the same city and strata of society during the same era (the mid-1960s), placed street life in the context of the wider community, and concurred with Liebow's interpretation. He emphasized that men who hung around street corners were often seen as troublesome from the perspective of other members of their community, but that not all their neighbors were willing to judge the behavior of those who sought the camaraderie of their street corner peers or to see personal failure on the part of others down on their luck. This is because unemployment and the difficulties of maintaining a stable family life that go with it were familiar to the many presently able to maintain those standards. The inability to maintain standards had to do with economic factors external to the ghetto. Hannerz warned that it is a mistake to think about similar communities of that era as divided between respectable and unrespectable residents, between family-oriented and street-oriented people. All understood the ideals of family and the vacillation of individual fortunes. They were all too familiar with the difficulty of approaching and maintaining the ideal. As was the case of the people studied by Liebow, however, Hannerz reflected the familiar image: The struggle to maintain family life in the absence of economic stability falls routinely to women (Hannerz 1969, 36–37, 96–99).

Gerald Suttles (1968) produced a remarkable study of a poor multiethnic area of Chicago, where he found an intricately organized social order based upon strong territorial identification. In what Suttles called the "Addams Area," Italians were slowly being replaced by growing numbers of blacks, Mexicans, and Puerto Ricans. Within the area, each ethnic segment remained socially independent and kept largely to itself. However, a sense of identification with the physical community that contained their residences and livelihoods was shared among all the ethnic groups. There was also a certain level of intergroup apprehension, but confrontation and conflict was avoided since the groups were tied to the same limited space. Suttles reported that open conflicts were limited to confrontations with groups from outside their local community. These conflicts usually began as fights between adolescents of the same ethnic origin. These disputes could linger and escalate into serious antagonisms—for example, between local and outside Italians—eventually involving older boys as well as adults. At this stage, according to Suttles, the lines of adversity could come to encircle all Addams Area residents on the one side and a similar community of outsiders on the other. Consequently, Suttles (1968, 32–33) argued that territorial identity was sufficiently strong to supercede ethnic and racial differences, and create a solidarity based upon common residence. The tendency toward territorial coalition was reinforced by the mutual suspicion among potential adversaries that opponents could be expected to unite in the same way, leaving them no choice but to bury their local differences. Suttles (1972, 21–35) called this type of community the "defended neighborhood" and wrote that "like the family, the neighborhood is largely an ascribed grouping and its members are joined in a common plight whether or not they like it."

Such a sense of community could arise in response to a wide variety of perceived threats and manifest itself in different forms. These might include locally organized vigilante citizens' groups, restrictive housing covenants designed to prevent certain groups from moving into an area, or groups of citizens organized to protest certain demolition and/or construction projects targeted for their area.

The idea is that the community is called into existence and becomes a recognized entity and source of group identification through the common perception of an outside threat. The defended neighborhood may or may not be a formally named community or one with official recognition. It may vary greatly in size, but it is typically large enough to include the full complement of establishments (businesses, playgrounds, places of religious assembly, etc.) whose goods and services are required by its members in their normal round of activities (Hunter and Suttles 1972, 58). Accordingly, this type of community may be defined as a spatial unit that serves the day-to-day living requirements of its members, who have developed some degree of collective self-awareness in response to a threatening outside force. The defended neighborhood provides us with one example of how conflict and cohesion occur as simultaneous outcomes of the same social process.

The defended neighborhood is just one of many forms of social unity found in cities. Hunter and Suttles (1972) offered in contrast to the defended neighborhood the "face block," the "community of limited liability," and the "expanding community of limited liability." The *face block* refers to people connected by mutual recognition, the familiar faces encountered in the routine of activities occurring close to home. As the name suggests, often this familiarity is limited to a single city block where, for example, parents may confine their children's play. In some instances the face block could be a defended neighborhood, but usually it is not large enough to supply all the routine needs of its members. Whereas the face block depends on the perceptions of its individual members for its existence, the *community of limited liability* is an area designated as a community by outsiders who have some political or commercial interest in its existence. Hallman (1984, 56) pointed out that many outside interests tend to see city spaces in this way. For example, realtors and mortgage lenders group properties of similar type and sales value, municipal administrators see service areas, school officials perceive school districts, politicians count voting precincts, and sociologists seek class or ethnic homogeneity. Politicians may encourage the development of a community identity among residents who potentially represent a constituency. Others perceive a consumer market whose loyalty to local merchants can be courted in advertising campaigns.

Given the fact that there are likely to be competing, overlapping appeals to a population's sense of belonging, especially in large cities, Suttles and Hunter noted that individuals may come to feel more or less a part of many such "communities"—hence the designation, community of limited liability. The *expanding community of limited liability* once again involves the designation of community status by some outside agent; for example, the reference in news reporting (or in urban sociology) to entire areas of a city as the "West Side" or the "South End." Hunter and Suttles believed that this enlargement of community corresponded to the increasing scale of government and business, as larger and larger units of jurisdiction and administration have been carved out. The designation of these larger units as communities can, in turn, call forth community self-perception, and community organization on this larger scale. While these large-scale organizations, which may claim to speak for tens of thousands of residents, may be more effective in getting the attention of city hall, the expanding community of limited liability is far removed from such units of sociability as the face block or the defended neighborhood.

It is necessary to bear in mind that the term *community* may refer to any of these varieties of social organization. Additional facets of the concept remain to be explored.

Case Studies

Neighborhood and community studies are case studies. The method involves the immersion of the researcher into the life of a particular neighborhood, an attempt to become part of the locality, and in the process bring it to life for the reader. The goal is to become a participant observer, to approximate the authentic experience of the insider. Usually, the term of research lasts a year or more, enough time to allow the fascination of the tourist to wear off, to allow the day-to-day rhythms of the place to set in, and to let the locals get used to your presence, enough so that they let down their guard and act in a normal manner. It is not an easy research strategy to accomplish. One never knows just what one is supposed to be looking for, especially at first. And once you have found something to write about, you can't be sure how representative either your particular field setting (neighborhood, in this case) or your particular interpretation is of places like this. The value of the case study is that we get to know a particular setting more intimately, that we get a feel for it.

Herbert Gans ([1962] 1982) produced what is perhaps the most widely referred to of all North American urban community studies, *The Urban Villagers*. Gans conducted his research in the late 1950s in the West End of Boston. During the period that he lived there, the residents' sense of the area as a community was reinforced and expanded by the threat of demolition, as the area became slated for urban renewal. The West End became, in effect, a defended neighborhood, but its defense was unsuccessful. Before the residents' efforts to fight city hall and to "Save the West End" had failed, Gans was able to chronicle a form of life in the city that led him to refer to the subjects of his study as "urban villagers."

Gans's subjects were largely working-class, second-generation Italian Americans, whose neighborhood was considered a slum by outsiders. The West Enders found the low rents compatible with their economic priorities and their limited incomes. Their social relationships consisted mainly of intense involvements with kin, mostly adult brothers and sisters and their families, and friends, all of whom lived close to one another. Sociability took the form of routine gatherings several times a week by these members of what Gans called a "peer group society." Gans placed great emphasis on these gatherings, noting that they were the ends for which other everyday activities were the means (Gans [1962] 1982, 74). The gatherings provided the chance to express oneself, exchange gossip, offer advice, and entertain and be entertained. The West Enders were truly themselves and fully alive only as members of this group.

This peer group society was based on a strong sense of equality. Although much of the group interaction was based on a competition among members, as in behavior calculated to draw the group members' attention and approval, there were strict limits to the amount of attention that one could demand. One could only expect a fair share. There was a general distaste for, and suspicion of, anyone who seemed to covet a leadership position. This is important to understand because it affected social involvement at a different level in the West End.

Whereas the peer group society was characterized by strong loyalties, people outside this group—even neighbors—were regarded with suspicion. This fact, coupled with the egalitarian norms of the peer group society, prevented the effective political mobilization of the West End. When it came time to defend the area against demolition by the city, the peer group orientation translated poorly into community-wide action. The group, as an end in itself, could not be used as a means to an end. Gans wrote,

> *The members are less interested in activities that require working together than in impressing each other. Moreover, if group tasks, especially those of a novel nature, are suggested, people become fearful that they will be used as pawns by an individual who will gain most by an activity. Consequently, the inability to participate in joint activities does inhibit community organization, even when it concerns the very survival of the group, as did the clearance of the West End. (Gans [1962] 1982, 89)*

In other words, that which made the West Enders ideal peers made them poor defenders. The community to which they were tied individually, the one which they identified with and cared about, was their narrow urban village, which consisted of only a few people, their own street, the stores they used, their church and parochial school, and, in some cases, a few organizational ties. It was only the impending destruction of the whole area that caused them to perceive the area as a whole (Gans [1962] 1982, 104); but by then it was too late, and they were still unable or unwilling to act together to save it. With the destruction of the West End, the West Enders were displaced to other parts of the city and the suburbs. A survey conducted two years after their relocation found many of them still grieving for their lost neighborhood and the close social relationships that had been lost with it (Fried 1963). In a 1982 postscript to the updated and expanded edition of his book, Gans commented that he did not believe that any conceivable effort by the community could have overcome the local and regional interests intent on clearing and redeveloping the area ([1962] 1982, 279).

Case studies can be compared in order to offer insight into how communities differ as well as share certain characteristics. Boxes 4-1 and 4-2 present brief accounts of community studies, one located a few miles from the West End and the other, half a world away.

BOX 4-1   Dorchester, Roxbury, and Mattapan: The Next
Generation Moves Up and Out

An interesting comparison with Gans's study is offered by the work of Levine and Harmon (1992) in the case of the decline of the Jewish-American community located in the Dorchester-Roxbury-Mattapan area of Boston. It is an account covering the history (1950–1970) of an ethnic community in which many of the members had become socially mobile and which suffered from an increasing division along the lines of social class. During this period, in which the United States was trading its working-class identity for a middle-class identity, many of this community's members had middle-class and suburban aspirations. The urban areas in which Jews were concentrated in Boston, as in many other U.S. cities, were part of the crumbling urban-American landscape. Yet many members of Dorchester and the related areas had strong ties to these places, to the familiar spaces over which they felt a sense of collective ownership and a strong sense of belonging. Levine and Harmon (13) offered openly nostalgic accounts of Blue Hill Avenue and the G&G delicatessen where an ethnically mixed crowd of regulars gathered in an atmosphere of sociability.

But these dilapidated areas did not suit the younger, university-educated generation who did not have the same strong sense of place as did the older generation. During the 1950s, after prolonged debate and division, a centrally important synagogue was moved to the suburbs. This removed an important symbol of the ties within the community. It also removed the most active and vocal spokespersons. In this case, the death of the community came not from city hall and not from a lack of willingness and ability to lead within the community. The leaders led the way to the suburbs, and they created a momentum that caused an enormous reduction in the number of Jews in the old communities.

Their place was taken by African Americans as that population was rapidly urbanizing. That this study details a process of ethnic and racial transformation that is generally widespread, whereby African American or Latino minorities succeed exiting European ethnic groups in inner-city neighborhoods (Alba, Logan, and Crowder 1997), lends added importance to it. The fact that the abandonment of the inner-city community was voluntary may have helped to cushion the experience of displacement, in contrast to the forced exodus of the West End that Gans wrote about. Nevertheless, it is clear that the abandonment of the familiar homeplace caused a sharp sense of loss that resulted in decades of grieving for a time when living in Boston meant a clearer and richer pattern of association for Jews.

The Reconciliation of Urbanism and Community

The findings of the various studies reviewed so far reflect a variety of forms of social unity in the city; for example, Liebow's study focused on the solidarity of the street corner, Young and Willmott on urban kinship, and Gans on the peer group. These studies have one common feature: Their findings do not bear much resemblance to the model of urbanism that was developed in Chapter 3. On the basis of his research and the research of others, Gans developed a formal criticism of Wirth's thesis (Gans 1962). He argued that Wirth's model of life in the city must be questioned on at least three counts. First, it seemed to have been constructed

---

**BOX 4-2   A Tokyo Community Study: Belonging in
Miyamoto-Cho**

Bestor (1989) studied the neighborhood of Miyamoto-cho in Tokyo during the 1980s. The population of Tokyo and the surrounding urbanized area reached 12 million by the end of the 1980s. The small area studied by Bestor is fully incorporated by the city, and the neighborhood conforms to the grey and dingy appearance for which Japanese urban places have acquired a reputation. Buildings are low, seldom above two stories, and crowded together. The more recent architecture is utilitarian and not fancy; the older buildings dating from the 1920s are dilapidated. This is an extremely crowded space. Shops are interspersed with residences, and the area is very busy during peak shopping hours (between four and six) when women, who must shop for the family meal every day, buy fresh meat, fish, and vegetables. On business streets, the parts of the neighborhood that contain bars, sushi counters, noodle stalls, restaurants, and karaoke establishments remain lively until late at night. Men go on a regular basis to the same bars and shops where they can expect to find their friends late in the evenings.

There is a deliberate effort by residents to support a neighborly and harmonious community life. Miyamoto-cho's residents are linked by ties of friendship, mutual aid, and social control, and appear to enjoy knowing and being known by other members of their community. The usual web of connections that one would assume to be part of a closely integrated neighborhood are found here. People gossip, help each other, attempt to chase away unsavory influences. Beyond friendship, members of each household are linked to the community through the neighborhood association to which they pay monthly dues, through an active women's auxiliary association that coordinates community-wide activities, and through the old-people's association. The neighborhood unit generates strong norms of universal participation, reciprocity, and mutual obligation. People do not seem to suffer from an overload of pressures for local sociability. Rather they seem quite happy to indulge in locally based friendships far beyond the call of loyalty.

The neighborhood is a main source of friendship, and people spend a great deal of their leisure with their neighborhood friends. In fact, when a family plans an excursion outside of the neighborhood, they very often take their friends with them. Bestor said that he was reasonably confident that the neighborhood he chose to study is not unusual in this regard.

---

only with reference to the inner city, the conditions of which cannot be generalized to all sections of the city—particularly the outer city and the suburbs. Second, evidence was lacking that ways of life, even in the inner city, resembled those described as urbanism: There was reason to doubt whether size, density, and heterogeneity produced the conditions attributed to urbanism. Third, even if it could be shown that the city produced such conditions, it had also been demonstrated that sizeable proportions of the urban population were insulated from the negative consequences of urbanism (Gans 1962, 628–629, 639). In summary, Gans was not convinced by the evidence available that Wirth's urbanism thesis could be supported, and if it could, it surely did not apply very widely to all segments of the urban population. Instead, Gans saw five major categories of adaptation to urban life (Gans 1962, 629–630):

1. The cosmopolites, who included students, artists, writers, musicians, entertainers and other intellectuals, and professionals choosing to live in the city to be close to its cultural amenities.
2. The unmarried or childless, who remained in the inner city to be close to work and entertainment.
3. The ethnic villagers, whom we have already met in Boston's West End. Their social life was rich in primary group ties; they were insulated from life outside of their immediate surroundings; and they were suspicious of anyone and anything outside of their neighborhood.
4. The deprived, who were the poor, emotionally disturbed, or otherwise seriously handicapped members of broken families, and people of color. They were relegated to the poorest housing.
5. The trapped and downwardly mobile, who were the people caught in transitions; for example, when the area in which they were living had deteriorated but they could not afford to escape, or when, as in the case of many elderly people, their standard of living had declined with the purchasing power of their small, fixed income.

Gans's general point was that there is not one style of urbanism in the inner city, but at least five, each sufficiently distinctive. It is hard to see how size, density, and heterogeneity could exert a common influence on their existence. The urban or ethnic villagers are insulated by their culture and social ties. The cosmopolites and the unmarried or childless have chosen the city for its convenience and cultural amenities. The remaining groups—the deprived and the trapped, and downwardly mobile—*are* affected by the conditions of transience and heterogeneity that generate the kind of segmental roles and superficial interaction that Wirth described: Anonymity, impersonality, and superficiality characterize many of their relationships. However, Gans (1962, 632) concluded that these conditions were most directly functions of poverty and discrimination, and that they were not generated by the nature of the city itself. He then asked the broader question of whether city/non-city differences (termed *settlement* or *ecological variables*) were useful for explaining ways of life. To this, he answered that his own suburban research led him to conclude that his subjects' move from city to suburb involved no significant behavior changes. Gans concluded that assumptions about urbanism and suburbanism as modes of life were misguided and that other factors, such as social class and stage of life, were more basic in explaining important, observable differences in behavior. In this view, the structural factors of size, density, and heterogeneity are simply not very interesting because they are not very consequential.

If this conclusion is correct, then it could be argued that urban sociology would be largely without an object of study. It is possible, however, to move beyond both Wirth's argument that urbanism had a disintegrative effect on social life and Gans's argument that the existence of a variety of lifestyles meant that the urban arena exerted no influence. Claude Fischer (1975; 1984) proposed that the question of the effect of the urban arena be cast in terms of what are the forces at work in the urban environment that contribute to characteristically urban forms of association. He believed that both Wirth's and Gans's approaches to this question were worthwhile, but he differed sharply in his conclusions about how the urban arena altered social life.

Fischer (1984, 28–29) found Wirth useful as the leading proponent of what he called the *determinist* school of urban thought—"determinist" because Wirth and those who took a similar view believed that the urban environment itself directly influenced or determined the way people thought and acted. Likewise, Fischer (1984, 32–33) found it necessary to retain Gans as most representative of the *compositional* school—"compositional" because it viewed the city population as being made up of a variety of styles and classes that were not leveled by a common urban experience.

Fischer developed his own synthesis of the determinist and compositional schools of thought, which he labeled the "subcultural" theory of urbanism. In this view the urban arena provides a supportive environment for the growth, differentiation, and interaction among groups of people who share common interests and orientations. Examples would include members of ethnic groups, people with particular cultural interests (e.g., music, theater, dance), and political movements: The more narrow the appeal of a particular interest or movement, the more vital is the size of the urban population to its success. The individuals involved would be unable or less able to find support for and express their interest in nonurban settings. For Fischer, population size was the central factor in determining urbanism. The urban area must be able to provide the *critical mass* necessary to permit people of the same interests to become a vital, active "subculture." Critical mass sustains interaction among like-minded individuals, allowing them to reaffirm their mutual identity and strengthen their subcultural identification.

The size of an urban area ensures the existence of a diversity of subcultures in two ways. First, there is the determinist explanation that the concentration of an urban population produces specialization, or the structural differentiation of inhabitants into different occupations and interests. Alternately, there is the compositional explanation that the larger the city, the wider will be the territories from which it draws its migrants, creating a more diverse population (Fischer 1984, 36–38). According to Fischer, these are complementary, not rival explanations of urban diversity. The heterogeneity produced by the processes of differentiation and migration is seen as a source of richness in the urban experience, as it increases the potential for the development of social ties by providing potential companions for a diversity of interests.

Although Fischer's subcultural view may be a synthesis owing to the traditions of both Wirth and Gans, it is important to recognize just how different his conclusions were from the earlier views:

> *Urbanism does shape social life—not, however, by destroying social groups as determinism suggests, but instead by strengthening them. The most significant social effect of community size is to promote diverse subcultures. . . . Like compositional theory, subcultural theory maintains that intimate social circles persist*

Fischer's subcultural theory argues that the city encourages diverse forms of association based on common interest.

> *in the urban environment. But, like determinism, it maintains that ecology significantly changes communities, precisely by supporting the emergence and vitality of subcultures. (Fischer 1984, 35–36)*

Unlike the determinists of the urban tradition, Fischer no longer interpreted urbanism as the leveling influence of mass society. And, opposite to the compositionalists who found little of interest in the urban variable, Fischer believed it had the power to enrich social experience by directly providing the conditions for a multiplication of diverse social worlds or, to use his term, subcultures. The more urban a place, the greater its subcultural variety. The larger the population, the more intense the subcultural experience. This is due to the capacity of a larger population to provide more complete support for cultural expression and activities, and the tendencies in certain cases for intergroup conflict to deepen loyalties within a group. At the same time, large cities provide opportunities for forms of contact among subcultures that allow for the diffusion of cultural elements or traits among the various groups. Thus, while a subculture is intensifying, it may be changing at the same time through the incorporation of traits borrowed from other groups. The theory also proposes that the more urban a place is (the greater its size), the higher will be the rates of deviance among its population. This proposition is based on the same principle of critical mass, which observes that larger cities provide unconventional subpopulations—thieves, counterculture experimenters, avant-garde intellectuals—with a community of like-minded individuals to support their particular values, beliefs, and practices (Fischer 1975, 1324–1329; Fischer 1984, 37–38).

The emphasis in subcultural theory is on the integrative quality of urbanism. It is the antithesis of the avoidance and anomic view. However, Fischer (1982, 233–235) pointed out that although some may feel that the negative determinist or Wirthian view had become outmoded, there was still considerable evidence to support it. Psychological research has suggested that city dwellers are less forthcoming to strangers and more estranged from and aggressive toward one another than people who live in smaller social arenas. Fischer proposed avoiding the sweeping psychological theories of chronic social withdrawal in order to explain the characteristic urban styles of disengagement and aversion. These styles may be accounted for instead through subcultural theory. The subcultural heterogeneity of the city regularly leads to contact among people who are not only strangers to each other, but also are culturally strange, perhaps even threatening, to one another. It is natural, therefore, as a consequence of urban life, for people to recoil from one another in public places. The more public the place, the more visible the strain. Cities generate a variety of cultural communities: in public encounters their members experience a mutual aversion. Urban sociologists have been mistaken in misinterpreting this public (and therefore highly visible) behavior as a central characteristic of the urban personality, or as reflective of the quality of private life (Fischer 1984, 214–215). This is an important point.

Fischer contributed to a clearer understanding of urban social processes. The subcultural theory of urbanism recognizes the energies generated by the urban environment to create both cohesive social units and conflicts among dissimilar social groupings. At the same time that Fischer's work is a departure from earlier theories, it stands within the tradition of urban sociology and does not reject altogether the older perspectives. Rather, it is a reinterpretation. The urban arena remains a mosaic of social worlds, as it was for Robert Park and Lewis Wirth, but living among these is no longer a hazardous social experiment. Instead, in subcultural theory, urbanism has become a rich and promising way of life.

Distinguishing between Social Spaces and Social Relationships

In this chapter, we have discussed a wide range of social relationships. Although these relationships have varied from friendships on the street corner to family ties to the expanding community of limited liability, each has come to be filed under the same general heading in sociology, as evidence of "community." In the course of such a general application, the meaning of the term has become increasingly broad and inclusive. Community has come to be applied to a number of social units, large and small, including entire cities and integrated systems of cities and towns (see the discussion of metropolitan community in Chapter 7). Now it is necessary to acknowledge one more important way that the meaning of community has been extended and complicated.

The preceding discussion of social relationships began with groupings tied physically or spatially to certain areas of the city (for example, the street corner or the neighborhood) and ended with groups formed on the basis of common interest without physical or spatial reference (for example, urban subcultures). The changing emphasis in our discussion mirrors a change in the understanding of community in urban sociology. According to Wellman and Leighton (1979, 369–374), urban sociology traditionally was preoccupied with divisions of space in the city and tended to consider group life only in the context of residential neighborhoods. Discussion of community was limited largely to the question of what had become of neighborhood ties. Early theorists, like Simmel and Wirth, who emphasized the breakdown of social ties in the city, are represented by Wellman and Leighton as the "community lost" school of thought. Urban neighborhood research, on the other hand, overwhelmingly supported the "community saved" school of thought, exhaustively documenting the survival of neighborhood ties and support. One of the outcomes of the neighborhood-research emphasis was that the concepts of neighborhood and community became entangled and confused due to the emphasis on place of residence. Wellman and Leighton (1979, 366) believed that this *a priori* emphasis on the organizing power of residential space caused social science to ignore other major spheres of daily action and sociability. They pointed out, with reference to neighborhood, that "residents tend to disappear from view in the morning and mysteriously reappear at dusk." What do we miss by ignoring their social affiliations beyond their area of residence?

Wellman and Leighton proposed to break this emphasis on neighborhood—and on any physical reference point—by rethinking the community concept. They referred to their social unit as "community liberated," meaning "liberated from constraints of space." This view recognizes a propensity among urbanites to form a number of primary relationships that go beyond and may not even include neighborhood ties (Wellman and Leighton 1979, 376–379). The liberated communities that they described were comparable to Fischer's subcultural groupings. Like Fischer, they emphasized that individuals were free to engage simultaneously in a number of social relationships. An individual's social relationships could be contained almost entirely within a neighborhood area, but most people had social ties to a number of different sets of relationships outside their area of residence. Wellman and Leighton (1979, 381–383) speculated that people whose social ties were concentrated within the neighborhood—in other words, those with ties corresponding most closely to the community-saved school—were likely to be people of limited economic and social resources, with limited ability to make contacts outside their residential area. On the other hand, Wellman and Leighton proposed that the

Patterns of association in the metropolis are not necessarily tied to residence. Here people are attracted to the rapid-fire timed chess matches on the sidewalks of midtown Manhattan because that is where the competition is. No one lives in this "neighborhood."

community-liberated pattern—where individuals formed ties to a number of friendship and resource pools not restricted to their residential area—was likely characteristic of more affluent segments of the urban population. The research conducted by Claude Fischer (1982, 251–252) seems to support this. He found, in a survey of northern California communities, that higher levels of education and income were associated with relationships that were more broadly based geographically and contained a lower proportion of kin.

Wellman and Leighton added to the complexity of the picture of urban social relationships by proposing the concept of social network to describe the pattern of these relationships. If it is inappropriate to see the community within which most urbanites live their lives as a neighborhood, then how are we to visualize it? The answer is that people's lives are contained in social networks. To describe the social worlds of individuals in this way presents a challenging set of conceptual and methodological issues.

Social Networks

The social network approach employed by Wellman and Leighton provides a useful framework for picturing the sets of interlocking relationships that make up the complex and diffuse organizational fields like those found in cities. The social network perspective stresses that people live their daily lives among a number of groups, organizations, and sets of friendship and kinship relations. Each one of these social contexts contains only a fragment of the total of a person's roles and relationships; therefore, each can be expected to yield only a fragmentary understanding of the social basis of an individual's behavior. Social network analysis traces social relationships across group boundaries. The following passage depicts the social network image as it was first described by J. A. Barnes.

> *Each person is, as it were, in touch with a number of other people, some of whom are directly in touch with each other, and some of whom are not. Similarly, each person has a number of friends, and these friends have their own friends; some of any one person's friends know each other, others do not. I find it convenient to talk of a social field of this kind as a* network. *The image I have is of a set of points, some of which are joined by lines. The points of the image are people, or sometimes groups, and the lines indicate which people interact with each other. . . . A network of this kind has no external boundary, nor has it any clear cut internal divisions, for each person sees himself at the centre of a collection of friends. (Barnes 1954, 43–44)*

Barnes makes a number of points in this definition that are worth emphasizing. First, the social network concept describes a web of relationships within which interaction is channeled. Second, not all of the members of a social unit are in contact or direct communication with each other, making the social unit in question a network and not a group. Thus, social networks not only consist of a person's contacts, but also contacts of contacts (for example, friends of friends), and so on. Third, there is no way to establish the boundary of such a network because relationships continue to radiate outward from every new member. Fourth, social networks are *egocentric;* that is, every network is anchored in the perception of a particular person, and it can be mapped and described only from that point of view.

The members of an individual's network include anyone whose actions or ideas personally affect the behavior of the person in question. However, a network is more than a reference group or communication channel, although it can also serve these functions. Networks have been interpreted, in part, as systems of interpersonal exchanges. In one view, the viability of a set of relationships is "governed by the principle that value gained from the interaction must be equal to or greater than the cost" (Boissevain 1974, 25). Seen in this way, an individual's net-work contains that person's "social capital" (Eames and Goode 1977, 130). Re-search has revealed, for example, that people's networks play a critical role in de-termining how successfully they cope with stressful events or personal crises (Gottlieb 1981, 36). Hirsch (1981, 160–162) found that networks help anchor and confirm the individual's social identity during times of stress and traumatic life transitions. However, if an individual's network contains every important rela-tionship of that person, then the network is not comprised entirely of mutually beneficial relationships. What is social capital for one member may very well be social liability for another, who, for whatever reason, is unwilling or unable to dis-engage from the network. People may feel far more socially hindered than so-cially supported in many of their relationships (Fischer 1982, 3). In addition to binding people together in mutual benefit or obligation, networks also consist of negative or antagonistic relationships that influence behavior. As Laumann (1973, 3–4) put it, "One individual may love another who reciprocates with hatred, but in any case they are mutually oriented to each other and take each other into ac-count in their own behavior." Therefore, each remains part of the other's social network. In fact, Boissevain (1974) emphasized the important role of conflict and competition between individuals in the formation and activation of strategic so-cial networks.

The network approach has been applied widely in urban studies. It has proved effective in describing the pattern of social relationships of urban, largely migrant populations in sub-Saharan Africa (Mitchell 1969), and has been widely adapted in urban social analysis elsewhere (Boissevain and Mitchell 1973; Laumann 1973). The network approach reveals a general difference in the struc-ture of social relationships between rural settings and urban settings. This differ-ence is diagrammed in a highly simplified fashion in Figure 4-1. Less urban set-

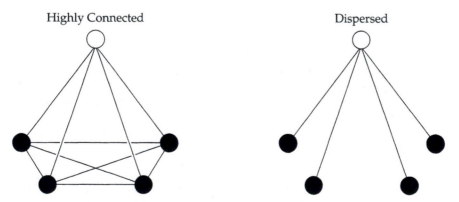

Highly Connected   Dispersed

FIGURE 4-1   Comparison of rural and urban network structures. Both
                    network fragments contain the same number of individuals,
                    but they stand at opposite extremes with regard to the
                    degree of connectedness among network members.

tings tend to be characterized by a higher proportion of mutual acquaintances and face-to-face interaction among the members of a given social network. In the urban arena, it is less common for a person's friends and other significant contacts to know and regularly meet one another. Within smaller populations, networks are denser, closely knit, and highly connected, while the urban network is open, loosely knit, and dispersed.

Frankenberg (1966) employed network density in this way to determine the degree to which a particular population could be characterized as rural or urban. In his review of community studies, which ranged from a small, relatively isolated Irish farming village (Arensberg 1939; Arensberg and Kimball 1940) to large urban housing developments (Young and Willmott 1957), he observed that greater network connectedness translates as greater social "transparency," while the loosely knit network associated with more urban settings "insulates" social actors. In the city, the individual is insulated because the many roles he or she plays are visible only to a portion of that individual's total network; therefore, only a segment of the individual's behavior is visible to each part of his or her network. In the densely knit network of a rural village, where each individual tends to know and communicate with all others, the scrutiny of the individual's behavior by the entire network is unrelenting due to the transparency among the various roles a person plays. It is a well-known principle that "news travels fast in a small town." This is because the communication network is so highly connected that a piece of gossip is quickly exchanged throughout the system. Insulation prevents this in the sparsely connected networks of the large city.

Frankenberg (1966, 241) also pointed to another way that network density could affect behavior. Although the greater social visibility of rural networks means that conflicts will lie closer to the surface and be more difficult to cover up, it also means that people will have to learn to live with and resolve conflicts amicably on a routine basis. Urban living does not demand such accommodation and, therefore, does not give rise to such skills. A broken or damaged personal relationship will resonate far less within an individual's more dispersed and divided urban network.

There are liabilities to life in the high-density networks characteristic of small rural settlements: Those who are not used to it would likely feel uncomfortable under the high social visibility associated with the densely connected network (where everyone knows more about everyone else's business). However, some research has pointed to what may be considered positive features in this type of social structure. Bott ([1957] 1971, 213) argued that individuals whose networks were characterized by more overlapping, interconnected ties were better able to derive clear-cut norms from them, in contrast with less closely integrated, socially mixed networks that transmitted mixed normative messages. Consistent with this view, Kadushin (1982), in a survey of battle-stressed Vietnam veterans living in northeastern cities in the United States, found that denser, more closely knit networks were generally related to low levels of mental distress. However, the evidence on network structure and stress adjustment is mixed. Other findings indicate that, under certain circumstances, a more dispersed network structure is advantageous. *Low* network density is associated with the successful adjustment of women who have become widowed (Hirsch 1981, 159) as well as those who have divorced (Wilcox 1981, 107–109). Hirsch speculated that, in general, the diversity of points of view in more open networks may offer a more adaptive orientation, while Wilcox added, with regard to divorce, that the lower proportion of family members in more highly dispersed networks may provide a more supportive and accepting base for this particular transition.

In addition to providing insight into the way that individuals' relationships are structured in the city, the social network approach has afforded some interesting ways of visualizing the overall structure of urban social relations. One way is that the social structure of each city can be seen as a network of networks (Craven and Wellman 1973; Wellman and Leighton 1979, 379). Such a view is readily derived from Boissevain's (1974) conceptualization of network structure. He divided each individual's network very broadly into first and second order zones. The first order zone, pictured in Figure 4-2, consists of persons with whom the individual in question (ego) maintains direct contact; the second order zone is comprised of people whom ego does not know directly, but who are known to his or her first order contacts; that is, they are friends of friends. As Figure 4-2 shows, the first order zone is broken down into six degrees of intimacy. The first three zones (I–III) include all those to whom ego is tied by intimacy and affection. The next three zones (IV–VI) consist of people with whom ego maintains a relationship simply because they, or the people they know, may be useful at some point. Each person maintains a series of these instrumental relationships. Consider that each person in ego's first and second order zones maintains the same sort of network, composed of intimate and strategic relationships as well as potential (second order) relationships, as does each person to whom he or she is connected, and so on. In this way not only is each individual potentially connected to every other individual in the city—or in society, as Boissevain (1974, 3) put it—but each city (or society) can be seen as a network of overlapping personal networks.

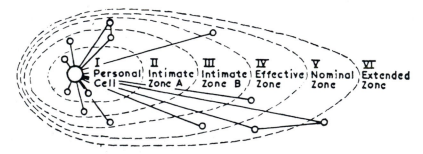

FIGURE 4-2   Subdivisions of the First Order Zone of a
             Social Network

Another useful description of urban social structure that has emerged from network-related analysis divides the city conceptually into two components: a social arena and its social fields (Kapferer 1972, 122–124, adapted from Swartz 1969). The social arena may be taken to include the sum of the various resources, conditions (economic, political, and cultural), organizations, and actors that comprise the urban environment. Within this arena various social fields emerge. The elements of the social arena are organized by the social fields and the various individuals who operate within them. Some of these fields are formally organized (e.g., political parties and unions), and others are social networks. The image of the city as an arena containing multiple social fields is useful in that it assigns no overall organizational unity to the city. In this way, the city can be seen as a place, a facility comprised of aggregated conditions, or a complex stage set for multiple scenarios of varying scale that are played out simultaneously, facilitating, hindering, or having no effect on one another. The term *urban arena* often seems to offer the most appropriate inference when referring to an urban place, and thus has been widely employed in this text.

The "network of networks" or "arena of social fields" metaphors of urban social relations present suitably complex images of the social morphology of the city. The picture of overall social organization of a city is difficult to imagine. It is equally difficult for the researcher to empirically establish this kind of structure. Barnes (1972, 3) noted that it was quite impractical for a single investigator to trace more than a small segment of the relationships within a network of any great size. We may speak of the network of networks, but it is an overwhelming task to measure or map such a structure in any detail. Laumann (1973, 7) acknowledged the practical difficulties involved in researching large networks but believed that the identification of certain network features could be successfully charted in populations numbering up to several million people. The effort to address larger networks has caused researchers to move increasingly in the direction of survey methods. This has altered considerably the nature of the work being done using the network approach, in contrast to earlier research in which the methodological emphasis was more qualitative.

For urban sociology, the question remains of whether a comprehensive picture of the urban whole can be constructed by piecing together information on such interpersonal linkages. The network approach adds clarity to the picture of urban relationships but in the end must be seen as only one of several perspectives required to describe the complex structure of the city.

The Persistence of Family Ties

Earlier we saw that in an important early study of urban community, Young and Willmott (1957) found that family ties were at the heart of neighborhood social life in postwar East London (Bethnal Green). There are, in fact, a number of studies that show the extended family, or kinship, is a very important focus of social life for some groups in the city. These studies challenge the long-standing assumption that urbanization caused the destruction of extended family ties. That assumption was based on the argument that eighteenth and nineteenth century industrialization involving widespread rural to urban migration, the frequent relocation of urban migrants, and the relatively restrictive nature of urban housing caused the extended family, which was associated with rural agricultural life, to break up into nuclear family units more appropriate to the shifting demands of urban living (Parsons [1949] 1959, 260ff; 1955 3ff). There are two problems with this well-known "isolated nuclear family hypothesis." The first is that historical research questions whether the extended family, consisting of more than one adult generation working and living together, was ever the norm in rural Europe, the historical context addressed by the hypothesis (Greenfield 1961). Second, a number of studies, including two of those we have already discussed (Young and Willmott 1957; Gans [1962] 1982), challenge the idea that extended family relations are no longer important in cities. Ties of kinship among adults have been shown to be generally important sources of sociability and support (Caplow et al. 1982, 195–223); Litwak 1960a, 1960b; Litwak and Szelenyi 1969), and urban-based studies have shown them to be especially crucial for poor and working-class people.

Active involvement with extended kin reflects the fact that even in cultures that emphasize individual adult responsibility, kin represent a pool of resources that people may fall back on in hard times. The poor and near poor may find more need to call on kin for assistance. Despite the fact that the resources poor relatives possess are relatively meager, people who are often in need themselves will find it difficult to refuse requests for aid from those who may have helped them in the past, or whose help they may need in the future. Anderson (1971), who pieced together a picture of kinship support in an English industrial town in the mid-nineteenth century, made this point. He found that personal crises were common in the lives of industrial workers, who struggled at low wages and were buffeted by the economic fluctuations of the textile industry. New arrivals sought the aid of family in finding work and housing: Their adult kin were anxious to assist them because the new workers widened the pool of potential mutual assistance in the future. Studies of rural French Canadian migrants to industrial New England showed a similar conscious pooling of extended family resources (Hareven 1976, 1978; Hareven and Langenbach 1978). In Young and Willmott's study (1957), it was the housing shortage in London that made women of the older generation—with their intimate knowledge of the neighborhood and their connections to rental agents—a key resource for the families of their adult daughters. Stack's (1974) fieldwork with a poor black population revealed a much more routine day-by-day exchange of assistance. Her work showed that the persistent and multifaceted needs of the poor were met by frequent small exchanges among relatives as a means of coping with such conditions as chronically inadequate income, loss of income, illness, evictions, childcare needs, and broken relationships. A norm of reciprocity, a willingness to help as well as be helped, was reflected in this study. It is interesting to recall in this connection that it was precisely a wariness of becoming obligated that made Gans's urban villagers reluctant to enter into exchanges of aid or gifts except within the closest family circles and that exchanges were kept carefully balanced to avoid losing status within the group.

BOX 4-3   The Ultimate Liberation of Community

In 1995, Claude Fischer took the opportunity of the twentieth anniversary of the first publication of his *subcultural theory* of urbanism argument (discussed earlier in this chapter) to reexamine his idea that cities provide a rich environment in which people with similar interests can come together to form subcultures. His perspective is consistent with the one that liberates community from local residential space, the idea that people associate on the basis of interest rather than neighborhood. It is also consistent with the imagery of the social network: A particular interest may provide just one of the many foundations for any individual's social interactions. Paraphrasing him, we can say that the larger a given city, the greater the number of networks based on mutual interest it will support; the larger the city, the greater the intensity of these interest-based liberated communities; the larger the city, the greater will be the subcultural reinforcement for unconventional thinking and behavior. Fischer wrote that after two decades of research and critical thought, he believed his theory still provided a promising alternative to Wirth's (1938) argument that urbanism produced personal isolation. But Fischer thought that his own work needed some rethinking and qualification. His most fascinating qualification is contained in the following: "As modern technologies allow interaction without proximity . . . subcultural processes are revealed to be fundamentally about *intragroup accessibility*. Spatial agglomeration is only one way group members gain access to one another. In the end, subcultural theory is ultimately about the ability of subculture members to communicate . . . and it is not necessarily about *cities* per se" (Fischer 1995, 549, italics in original). While he doesn't elaborate much on this observation—and despite a brief comment that he believes space continues to matter and urban-rural distinctions in particular remain relevant, Fischer has struck upon a profoundly important point. The ultimate domain within which communities of interest may come together is not the metropolis or even the nation: It is the international Web. Here, we may apply the central concept of Fischer's subcultural theory—critical mass, the idea that the city provides like-minded people with mutual access for building community—with maximum effectiveness. On the Web, we have the greatest number and potential intensity of subcultures of interest providing support for the greatest variety of unconventional thought and behavior. Genius can flourish, potential mass murderers can receive support and bomb-making advice, collectors of esoterica can bond, and experimenters on the sexual fringe can find each other. What is the impact of the Internet regarding observed differences between urban and rural social structure? Does life online negate or transcend the entire set of distinctions between rural networks (greater ease of communication among all members) and urban networks (more diffuse and restricted communication)? Fischer's (1995) tentative appraisal, "Perhaps these technologies are not as pervasive or as effective as imagined; perhaps people still need to meet face to face," has almost an old-fashioned appeal less than a decade later. Paraphrasing him once again, we might say, "You can get sex on the Web but you can't really have sex on the Web." However, you can give and take ideas on the Web, and develop those ideas and exchange them with new partners at any distance. It provides a forum for social intercourse that is not physical, that is safe by virtue of remoteness, contact that is superficial, where one's persona is shielded by anonymity, perhaps promoting a sense of daring that might become inconvenient if uttered or practiced within a local community, that provokes others to be more experimental in their mode of self-expression than they would otherwise be, and so forth. It would appear that on many levels we have reached a new plateau in the liberation of community that will require us to think critically about the ways we talk about rural-urban distinctions and cause us to question the assumptions of our urban sociology.

Evidence that extended family provides one important focus of social involvement for urban populations is widespread and not confined to the poor and the working class. The findings of observational and survey research show that it is important to consider the routine role of kinship in order to understand how people achieve and maintain their social and economic standing (Litwak 1960a, 1960b); that parents and adult offspring accept the mutual responsibility of looking after and caring for each other's needs (Caplow et al. 1982, 195–223); that family members are widely understood to bear the responsibility of looking after relatives in serious and long-term crises (Litwak and Szelenyi 1969, 473–475); and that extended kinship continues to play an important role for migrants attempting to gain an economic foothold in cities around the world (Wilkening et al. 1968; Kemper 1975; Gonzalez 1975; Philpott 1968; Caldwell 1965; Moock 1973; Oppong 1974; Aronson 1979; Brandes 1975). Most people living in cities may not live within extended family households, but it appears that most would not need to be reminded that family members beyond the household are part of their network of sociability and support.

Summary

Our review of the nature of social cohesion in the city reveals that the early efforts to develop an ideal model of urbanism paid little attention to the possibility of survival for traditional forms of sociability. Also neglected was the potential of the urban arena to give rise to new forms of community. The lost community was found, or saved, but the saved community turned out to confuse community with neighborhood. Community was defended, expanded, became limited, and finally identified as subcultural and liberated from spatial considerations. Once it is defined as a matter of mutual interests rather than as a residential area, community is a phenomenon potentially global in its reach—if we are willing to accept that electronic communication is a sufficient minimal criteria for its existence. This stretches the concept of community to its limits as a useful sociological term, and we will probably continue to argue about this extension of meaning for the next decade in the broader discussion of the transformative significance of the Internet for society in general. The various interpretations of community are indeed complementary, and help us to think about the diverse ways in which individuals are bonded to and communicate with each other. Each of us probably feels that we live within all of the types of community discussed here, from neighborhood to global network.

5

ETHNICITY AND MINORITY/MAJORITY RELATIONS IN URBAN STUDIES

Ethnic and minority/majority group studies have long been an important part of urban sociology. Cities are the showcases of colorful ethnic contrasts, as well as the arenas of intergroup conflict. An urban sociology must assume that cities provide more than a backdrop for these events. In this chapter, we are interested in how the urban arena influences the shaping of ethnic and minority groups. Following the same principle employed in the preceding chapters, this chapter focuses only on those features of ethnic and minority processes that are in some degree a product of the urban environment. Although the historical references that follow primarily regard the case of the United States, the discussion of the principles of intergroup relations can be applied to all societies where similar distinctions and conflicts persist among urban populations.

The manner in which the population of the United States reached its current—if ever-shifting—composition makes the study of ethnic and minority relations a central concern to the sociology of its cities. During the 1800s, the area covered by the continental United States reached its present boundaries and engulfed millions of native and Spanish-speaking people in its westward advance; cities grew rapidly from coast to coast; massive waves of millions of immigrants transformed the meaning of America. Late in the century, many of the freed and displaced descendants of slaves found their way to the cities of the North and South, beginning a migration trend that would accelerate in the following century. The 1800s were a period when the country underwent a transition from a predominantly agricultural economy to an industrial economy. By the early decades of the following century, the need for industrial labor and workers to construct everything from railroads to cities themselves had drawn nearly 50 million immigrants. These were accompanied by some unknown millions more of unrecorded arrivals. Immigration was slowed by restrictive legislation from 1921 through midcentury, but increased steadily thereafter: In the 10 years 1981 to 1990, nearly 7.5 million legal immigrants were admitted. Of the 25.8 million foreign-born people counted in the Census Bureau's March 1997 Current Population Survey, 24.3 million lived in metropolitan areas. Both historically and at the present time, the story of America's cities is the story of its diversity, and vice versa.

Since the earliest days of independence, there has been concern with the long-term effect of the influx of foreigners. A "gangplank" mentality has persisted: Once established, each newly arrived group would prefer to pull up the ramp that led them from ship to shore, ostensibly in order to preserve the existing population stock and national culture, but also to limit competition from other newly arriving groups offering cheap labor. There was always concern over whether each new wave could fit in, blend, and become indistinguishably American. In service to this concern, a "melting pot" theory emerged. The theory was as much an ideology of national unity, arguing that all the differences that set groups apart from one another could be melted down and made cohesive in a new cultural form that was identifiably American. The unspoken part of this creed was the understanding that what would melt away would be the Old World characteristics, except for those colorful traits of taste and tradition that could be unobtrusively incorporated in an Americanized product.

The melting pot thesis was based too much on the hope that people's cultural memories would not span generations, on the hope that the U.S. culture and its institutions would not be changed too much by the foreigners who came to participate in and interpret it, to adopt it and adapt it, and on the hope that the foreigners would stop coming. As the decades of the twentieth century passed, it became increasingly clear that ethnicity had a persistent quality, and beginning in the 1960s, there was a resurgence in people's interest in their cultural rootedness in other parts of the world. Moreover, ethnic identity was not a distant memory of generations past for many people in the United States. As in Europe and elsewhere in the world, fresh immigration in the last quarter of the twentieth century, often from new cultural and geographic sources, added new diversities of cultural richness to nations around the world. What some people experience as cultural richness others fear—fear that the most recent newcomers are too different for the new differences ever to melt out. Ethnic diversity often presents the danger that the cultural other will come to be vilified and scapegoated; that interethnic tensions will develop; and that new minorities will be forged by the heat of diversity and by the power of some groups to restrict the freedoms and rights of others, the less powerful, the newcomer. Urban settings constitute the laboratories where ethnic interactions are magnified and certain majority/minority conflicts are incubated.

Ethnicity and Minority

The primary goal of this chapter is to understand how the urban arena affects intergroup relations and the dynamics of group experience. In order to avoid confusion, it is necessary to distinguish among discrete concepts that unfortunately are often run together in practice. Of central concern are the concepts of ethnicity, ethnic group, and minority group. Stated simply, *ethnicity* refers to a quality of *experience* based on attachment to a *culturally* distinguishable group (ethnic group) that is contained along with other groups within a particular society. An ethnic group's members share the sense of a distinctive origin and experience. The term *minority group* identifies a group whose members share a subordinate *political* position marked by some disadvantage and degree of powerlessness, as well as some conscious conception of themselves as a distinct group. A minority group may or may not be an ethnic group (the Jews in Nazi Germany and the Basques in Spain are examples of ethnic minorities; women, handicapped persons, and homosexuals are minorities, but are not generally considered ethnic groups). Thus, it may not be assumed that an ethnic group is typically a minority group. In fact, some ethnic groups are majority groups, but the important point is that ethnicity is a concept altogether independent (at least in the analytic sense) of intergroup conflict or power relationships. The following discussion should make these distinctions clearer.

Although large numbers of immigrants were political refugees or those seeking relief from religious restriction or persecution, the decision to emigrate was usually an economic one for the vast majority of those who came to the United States in the great waves of the late nineteenth and early twentieth centuries. For those seeking to escape from poverty, it was a rational choice among a limited number of options. Those who left behind less desperate circumstances also expected to improve their living standards. Some were recruited directly by hiring agents sent overseas by industry, the railroads, or domestic employment services in the United States, while others were recruited indirectly by the news of opportunity passed on by those who had already left. Many, in fact, were sent for by relatives who had arrived earlier. Although a few might have been lured by visions of gold lying in the streets, most came with a good idea of the conditions awaiting them (Steinberg 1981, 37).

The demand for immigrant labor ensured that most of those who were strong and healthy could meet their basic needs, but the typical immigrant still lived close to the margins of viability in the crowded, makeshift slum of a large northern city. As the nineteenth century drew on, the crowded tenement slums and shantytowns grew and became more conspicuous. At the same time, the proportion of migrants from northern and western Europe dwindled, as the proportion of newcomers from southern and eastern Europe grew. These newcomers were more rural in their origins, and their language and appearance more "foreign" than that of the earlier immigrants. The sheer number of immigrants was growing as well, with nearly nine million arriving between 1901 and 1910. All of this contributed to increasing fears and suspicions among the established segments of the population, including many who were the offspring of earlier immigrants.

Foreigners were suspected of carrying disease, harboring radical political ideas, and undermining the existing American culture. They were blamed for the conditions of poverty in which they found themselves, and were perceived as both culturally and "racially" inferior. By 1921 increasingly restrictive legislation, limiting the total number of immigrants and imposing national quotas, had brought the era of large-scale immigration to a close. In the meantime, confrontation and conflict among the various groups had crystallized ethnic identities, giving the population of the United States and in particular its cities a fragmented, mosaic quality.

It is only partially correct to say that ethnic identity was something that immigrants brought with them from their places of origin. Ethnicity cannot exist in isolation (Jaffe, Cullen, and Boswell 1980, 10–11; Cohen 1974, ix–xi; Cohen 1981, 317–118). That is, this form of group self-awareness comes about as a result of *contact* between two or more groups, and the term *ethnicity* is usually reserved for instances in which the groups interact within the borders of a common society. For example, "the difference between the Chinese and the Indians, considered within their own respective countries, are national, not ethnic differences. But when groups of Chinese and Indian immigrants interact in a foreign land as Chinese and Indians they can be referred to as ethnic groups" (Cohen 1974, xi). In this sense, ethnicity is not something one carries from home to a strange place, but something one finds in a place where one is culturally different. Ethnicity is thus a product of migration.

The content of the ethnic experience is multifaceted and rooted in recollections and expressions of a common culture. Shared values and beliefs, norms of behavior and taste, a feeling of membership involving shared group memories and loyalties, and a tendency toward endogamy may be among the features of this common culture. All ethnic groups do not share in these characteristics to an equal degree: Intensity or orthodoxy of belief and practice vary from group to group, and within a particular group under different circumstances (Schermerhorn 1978, xiv–xv). The degree of intensity in feelings of attachment also varies among ethnic groups. Or as Cohen (1974, xiv) put it, "There is ethnicity and ethnicity." He suggested, by way of illustration, that we consider the members of a group that get together annually to perform a dance or take part in a ceremonial to commemorate their cultural ties, and contrast this with what one might imagine to be the intensity of ethnic sentiment among some Catholics (or Protestants) in the Irish North. One further note on the intensity of experience: Just as the degree of ethnic experience varies among and within different ethnic groups over time, it will vary among individuals within those groups at a given time as well.

In order to fully understand the ethnic phenomenon, it is useful to consider it from two different perspectives: the objective and the subjective (Ross 1980, 5). The content of ethnic culture and group membership may be established objectively. This "objectivist" approach is appropriate for discovering ethnic boundaries and describing component institutions—that is, for the study and understanding of the structure of the *ethnic group*. It cannot, however, yield an understanding of *ethnicity*—which requires a "subjectivist" approach in addressing the nature of the experience of ethnic membership. This is because ethnicity is neither a common culture nor a particular history, but, once again, the *experience* and *interpretation* of a particular culture and history. Ethnicity refers to the quality of bondedness among individuals. Milton Gordon (1964, 23–24) endowed this experience with clarity and simplicity. He referred to it as "a shared feeling of peoplehood." In this light, ethnicity may be most usefully seen as a social construction, the meaning of which is subject to an ongoing process of definition within the group as well as individual interpretation. This is not to say that individuals may make of their ethnic experience whatever they wish.

> *What we must realize is that the patterns of behavior that we call ethnicity are not the products of the idiosyncracies of individuals, but the collective representations of a group. They are certainly rooted in psychic processes . . . that are subjectively experienced. But the symbolic formations in which they are expressed . . . are social constructions which are impressed on the minds of members through continuous socialization . . . once they are externalized and adopted by a group they become collective and objective, assume an existence of their own, so to speak, and confront the individual from the outside. (Cohen 1981, 322)*

In this way, ethnicity first confronts individuals as an external, ongoing fact. But it is important to add that this particular social form is susceptible to reinterpretation and redefinition by members of the group. That is, ethnicity remains peculiarly open to modification so that its relevance and usefulness, or merely its ability to survive, can be continuously revised. As will be seen, both the content of ethnicity and the membership of ethnic groups change over time, adding or dropping particular traits or categories of membership in response to changing circumstances. For example, European ways of life suited to agricultural activity and the village scale could not be transplanted intact to the industrial cities of North America. Once transplanted, a newly emergent ethnic culture is born and endures as an adaptation. The cultural content of ethnic life is produced from its members' *selective* recollections of life as it was lived at home. Once removed to a foreign place, ethnic culture evolves separately from that of the homeland, as each new generation further modifies its heritage according to what is useful or adaptable from the old beliefs, styles, and customs.

There is disagreement over the long-term consequences of the tendency for each generation to revise the content of its ethnic identity. Some see the continuous adaptation as an inherent feature of the ethnic phenomenon (Ross 1980, 6–7; Cohen 1974, xiv). Others interpret the kinds of ethnic modification observed in the United States, at least with regard to the descendants of the early immigrant waves from Europe, as a gradual weakening of ethnicity. Stein and Hill (1977, 22–23) contrasted the ethnicity associated with the descendants of European immigrants with earlier forms of ethnic solidarity attributable to the immigrant generation itself. They characterized the contemporary version of ethnicity, where people may selectively retain what they like of the old country's culture and discard the rest, as "dime-store ethnicity." Steinberg (1981, 45, 58, 63) wrote similarly of cultural recollections that have grown thin with the passing of older generations and without the infusion of new life that would require continued, substantial immigration. In addition to facing this crisis of authenticity, there is little left of ethnic institutions or organization. Over time, members of ethnic groups *do* very little together. Steinberg believed that the symbolic value of ethnicity was not enough to ensure its continuation. In this view, the melting pot thesis is not incorrect, but its anticipation premature, waiting to be borne out at some time in the future.

Steinberg's (1981, 254–257) conclusion was based in part on his belief that the tradition of ethnic pluralism in America was built on systematic inequalities that existed in the past among the various immigrant groups. The argument that a viable ethnicity depends on sustained intergroup inequality and conflict needs close examination. Although intergroup strife is an effective mechanism for reenforcing intragroup cohesiveness, the argument that inequality and conflict are necessary for sustaining ethnic identity and group cohesion is overly restrictive. Ethnic and minority/majority group processes need to be kept analytically distinct, as cultural and political categories, respectively. If a group has suffered from discrimination in the past but since has become fully assimilated, then it has left behind its minority status. What has happened to the ethnic identity of its membership, on the other hand, remains an open question. The theme of having suffered together through injustice at some point in the past has proven to be one of the most cohesive themes in preserving strong feelings of ethnicity in subsequent generations. Much of an ethnic group's vitality may lie in its past political struggles, but the expression of its ethnicity is a cultural celebration of such themes—which, in fact, may grow in symbolic importance over generations of retelling.

There is no identifiable point at which an ethnic minority becomes—or is no longer—a minority. Membership in a particular group may take on minority characteristics if the group becomes stigmatized or is made a scapegoat for some social ill that has befallen society. Many immigrant groups entered the United States to find that they were the objects of prejudice and discrimination, if not at first, then as their numbers became conspicuous.

Wirth (1945, 347) devised a definition of the minority group that is still widely employed today: "We may define a minority as a group of people, who, because of their physical or cultural characteristics, are singled out from the others in the society in which they live for differential and unequal treatment, and who therefore regard themselves as objects of collective discrimination." The classification is said to be *political* because it focuses on the *power* of one group or category, the majority, to discriminate systematically against members of another group who have been ascribed a subordinate status. This discrimination involves limiting the access of minority members to rewards and opportunities (life chances) that are more freely accessible to nonminority members of a society.

Discrimination is justified by a widespread belief in the inferiority and unworthiness of minority members. Members are perceived more or less to possess certain characteristics, such as laziness, craftiness, dishonesty, or disloyalty, which justify the inferior position and treatment of each person; that is, majority/minority relations are characterized by prejudice, which provides the justification for discrimination. Prejudice is the ideological support that legitimates the maltreatment of minorities. Often in the history of immigration and intergroup relations in the United States, the majority has distinguished itself from an emerging minority by employing the idea that the newcomers were from a separate race;

for example, the Irish, Jews, and Italians were all in their turn mislabeled as "races," just as Asians and blacks still are today. This particular form of prejudice, and its consequences for the treatment of minorities, is *racism.*

The distinction between ethnic group as a *cultural* category and minority group as a *political* one is important and simple to see in the abstract. Actual immigrant groups, however, tend not to hold still for easy and final classification. Many ethnic groups of European origin in the United States, while they can hardly be regarded today as true minorities, are still the subject of stereotypes and ethnic jokes that reveal in varying measure the existence of prejudicial thinking. In a number of cities, movements have emerged to counter the defamation of particular ethnic groups and to bolster ethnic pride. Such movements, designed to improve the status of the group, are essentially political responses. Many groups that largely escaped the assignment of minority status nevertheless formed ethnic political organizations to advance the solidarity of their memberships. While ethnicity is essentially a cultural phenomenon, ethnic group members have often been political actors.

The Urban Dimensions of Immigration, Ethnic Persistence, and Assimilation

The study of ethnic groups and the study of the city in North America are bound together in two ways. First, immigration was largely to the cities. Second, the formation of ethnic identity was mediated to a large extent by the fact that it took place in large, heterogeneous centers of population. So, in addition to the fact that the ethnic experience manifested itself primarily *in* the city, that experience was altered in many ways by the urban arena, making ethnicity a process *of* the city as well.

During the nineteenth century, there was a pronounced tendency for immigrant groups to cluster around northeastern seaport cities. For those who ventured inland, it was most typically via chain migration directly to the large industrial cities of the Midwest, where work was known to be available (Cafferty et al. 1983, 68). By 1870, although immigration had added less than 15 percent to the size of the U.S. population, the foreign-born population of the 50 largest cities was 34 percent (Klebanow, Jonas, and Leonard 1977, 76). The foreign-born population of St. Louis was 60 percent, of Chicago 50 percent, of New York 48 percent, and of Boston 36 percent (Still 1974, 118–119). By the end of the first decade of the twentieth century, immigrant settlement had established a "great urban triangle" stretching from Boston to St. Louis to Washington, D.C., within which 80 percent of those who had emigrated from southern and eastern Europe lived (Cafferty et al. 1983, 47).

Life in the city helped to shape the nature of the ethnic experience. Ethnicity is, of course, not confined to the city, but the diversity of an urban population makes it particularly evident there. In the United States, just as the ethnic experience was molded by the city, the particular social qualities of the cities were molded by the large number of immigrants who had come together in them. "Vast armies of clergymen, policemen, sanitation workers, teachers and social reformers were recruited to serve the immigrant neighborhoods bursting at the seams with people and problems. The size and complexity of government increased, especially at the municipal and county levels, as the crush of population propelled government into new roles and redefined old ones. Public servants became stewards of the American way as they frantically tried to force newcomers to adjust themselves to America rather than vice versa" (Kraut 1982, 180).

For most immigrants, the primary problem of adjustment was the transition from a rural to an urban way of life, rather than from a European to an American culture. Rural Italians, for example, would have faced similar problems of adjustment whether moving to a large city in the United States or in Italy (Nelli 1970, 20). The condition in which the immigrants found themselves was what Handlin ([1951] 1973) characterized as having been "uprooted" from a familiar social and cultural environment and thrust into an uncertain and precarious struggle for survival without the familiar support of the old community. Under these circumstances, the solidarity of ethnicity was a refuge against having to face the enormous uncertainties of a new life alone far from home. Common ethnic membership provided such modest practical advantages as favored access to particular lines of work (not lucrative occupations for the most part, but work, nevertheless), a dependable clientele of co-ethnics for small entrepreneurs, or a reciprocal system of support and patronage for local political figures and their constituents (Hannerz 1974, 48–57). Competitive, face-to-face interaction among the members of different ethnic groups in the city typically had the effect of crystallizing ethnic identities and elevating group awareness (McRoberts 1980, 243–248).

That the urban environment proved to be a mechanism of solidarity should not be surprising if we recall Fischer's (1975, 1984) subcultural theory of urbanism discussed in Chapter 4. He made an extensive case that this theory was especially applicable to ethnic cohesiveness in the city. First of all, critical mass ensures that a large enough pool of co-ethnics exists to support a full range of common cultural institutions—churches, newspapers, stores, clubs, political organizations—which, in turn, sustain the ethnic identity. In addition, the larger the city, the more likely that friction will occur between ethnic groups. These groups will be more in number, well supported, and therefore mutually visible; and this will result in a stronger identification within each group. In short, we expect to find built-in supports for ethnicity in the urban arena. At the same time, however, the arena contains certain agents devoted to the reduction of cultural differences. In the city, as elsewhere, a tension exists between the forces of acculturation and the forces of ethnic cohesion.

The Elastic Qualities of Ethnicity

Ethnicity emerges and endures because people find it a useful or meaningful category of membership. In the culturally alien and heterogeneous U.S. city of the 1800s and early 1900s, immigrants naturally came to identify with others with whom they felt special ties of origin. In the process it was necessary to unlearn common identities that had circumscribed group ties in the Old World and had proved unworkably narrow under the changed circumstances of immigration, urbanization, and a world of redrawn geopolitical boundaries. Handlin ([1951] 1973, 8) wrote that at first immigrants began stories of themselves with the village from which they had come. It was a concrete place that could be remembered in each of its social and physical details, a place one could belong to. It was the village, county, or province of origin upon which a common sense of belonging was first founded. For example, in addition to distinguishing themselves as northerners and southerners, Italians initially distinguished themselves more precisely as *paesani*, people who came from a common village or locality. This was their allegiance and the bounds of their ethnicity that had to be unlearned in America.

> [When Tuscan immigrant Charles Fornesi was told] about the opportunities which were available for an industrious man in Seneca Falls, New York, he made up his mind to go there to seek his fortune. Fornesi became a pioneer, the first Italian to settle in Seneca Falls. To succeed, however, Fornesi needed help from his fellow Tuscans. He wrote to his relatives and friends in Licciana Nardi [his homeplace] and its nearby villages, inviting them to join him. Many came. Fornesi prospered by opening a bank and a grocery store which served his Tuscan neighbors.
>
> Sometime later, Benny Colella, an immigrant from Naples, came by mistake to Seneca Falls. Impressed with the possibilities he saw there, he urged his friends to join him. Immigrants from five or six towns near Naples established the community of Rumseyville in Seneca Falls, a neighborhood which for years remained isolated from the Tuscans living on the South Side. Colella and Fornesi established Neapolitan and Tuscan colonies, groupings of men and women who in their wildest dreams would never have imagined that, by early twentieth century, they would identify themselves primarily as Italian-Americans. (Iorizzo and Mondello 1980, 101)

In this sense, ethnic boundaries come to enclose "discovered identities, . . . the discovery by a group of people that they constitute a category in the minds of others that has not previously existed in their own system of classification of groups in society, or that they have not previously recognized as including themselves" (Cornell 2000, 98). In other words, the receiving or host culture has a powerful role in determining who one's co-ethnics are, and this is usually a broader category of membership than immigrants are used to.

The ethnic categories so recognizable today in the United States were largely created after the immigrants had arrived. As Handlin ([1951] 1973, 166–167) pointed out, these ethnic categories referred to national states not yet created or just coming to be at the time of immigration. It was only "much later, in deceptive retrospect, a man might tell his son, 'Why, we were Poles and we stayed that way'— or Italians, or Irish or German or Czechoslovaks." The need for broadened ethnic referents emerged in the New World where local and regional differences shrank into insignificance when confronted with the vast otherness of the whole urban immigrant population. Handlin related one instance which, although it referred to a town only in its infancy, illustrated the demand for expanded categories of ethnic membership.

> *In 1837 there was a falling-out among the men planting a new settlement in Illinois. One faction wished the name of the new township to be Westphalia, another, Hanover, each for its own native land. The compromise was significant—Germantown; the language took them all in. (Handlin [1951] 1973, 167)*

National origin and common language were new ethnic categories that identified a much broader sense of belonging than had existed in the homeplace of the immigrants.

This expansion of ethnic membership, mediated by the perception of outsiders, had the capacity to create categories of inclusion even broader than nation of origin. "Panethnic" identities emerge when previously distinctive membership groups, gathered together on distant shores, are effectively given a common label—such as African, Asian, Hispanic, or Scandinavian—that refers to an entire region of the globe comprised of more than a single nation (Cornell 1999, 99; Skardal 1974, 4). The existence of panethnic designations underlines the importance of outsiders in the negotiation of the content and scope of ethnic peoplehood. A people might protest the assignment of a broader category of membership—the members experiencing themselves as more authentically Korean or Korean American rather than Asian American, for example. However, the perceptions and sentiments of the host society toward the panethnic category are also strongly felt, and in this situation the identity in question becomes a source of struggle between insider and outsider.

Interethnic Hostility

Upon arrival in America, each of these ethnic groups was subject, in its turn, to prejudice and discrimination. German and Irish Catholics were the objects of ridicule and violence in the 1830s and 1840s. Anti-Catholicism smoldered until the 1880s when it flared anew with the influx of greater numbers of eastern and southern Europeans. (The eastern European influx generated a similar increase in anti-Semitism.) During the 1880s, Italian immigrants were commonly subject to especially harsh treatment by major newspapers that attacked them for suspected radical political and criminal tendencies, as well as blamed them for their impoverished condition. The Italian-language press fought back with a single voice, creating a focus for Italian-American pride and identity (Nelli 1970, 11–12; Iorizzo and Mondello 1980, 79–80).

Dinnerston, Nichols, and Raimers (1979, 236) suggested that under such conditions of prejudice and discrimination it could be expected that a forging of an interethnic solidarity might have taken place among the different groups facing a common plight; but, as these authors pointed out, such a coalition did not result.

Instead, each newly arrived group tended to displace the previous newly arrived group at the bottom of a hierarchy of interethnic domination. For example, in the late nineteenth century in Lowell, Massachusetts, the Irish continued to struggle against anti-Irish, anti-Catholic sentiment, and were only gradually establishing for themselves a position of relative economic security. Their eventual modest ascent within the working class was assisted by the arrival in number of French Canadians, who were treated by the Irish in the manner to which the Irish, themselves, had grown accustomed. The French Canadians, in turn, reportedly transferred their position to the more recently arrived Italians. The bottom of the ladder in Lowell by the 1970s was occupied by Latinos (Cubans, Puerto Ricans, and other Latin Americans) who endured the position reserved for the newcomer (Kolack 1980, 341–343).

Interethnic hostility was the dominant feature of intergroup relations. In some cases, it was brought about by economic or occupational competition among ethnic groups. In other cases, antagonisms had been carried with the immigrants from the Old World, or hostility simply may have resulted from the venting of frustrations by groups low in the social hierarchy on the only other groups socially available to receive them (Dinnerston, Nichols, and Raimers 1979, 236–238). The lines of conflict were drawn among Hungarians, Swedes, Italians, Irish, Greeks, Turks, Slavs, Finns, French, Germans, Poles, Syrians, Czechs, and Jews.

Vestiges of these rivalries, which found their most violent expression in the large cities, have remained a part of the ethnic legacy. Some analysts of ethnicity claim that there is an inherent chauvinism and social divisiveness in this form of group solidarity (Patterson 1977). Undoubtedly, the initial usefulness of ethnicity as a shield and a weapon for protecting or gaining a favorable position at the cost of other groups has left its mark on the ethnic experience and interethnic relationships.

Ethnic Culture: Survival or Hybrid?

However, the ethnic participation of the descendants of European immigrants today is not a response to ethnic conflict so much as it is a desire to preserve or recapture ties to cultural traditions perceived as worthwhile in their own right. These long-preserved or recaptured ethnicities tend to be cultures distinct unto themselves, likely to reflect, in the former case, a historical anachronism, and in the latter case, something that would likely prove only vaguely familiar to the original, immigrant generation. In the case of *preserved* ethnicity, what we have is an idealization and romanticism, handed down from generation to generation from an early era of widespread immigration. Thus, when a group of Scottish Americans traveled to Scotland for the International Gathering of the Clans in 1977, they were met with ridicule by the Scots for creating a spectacle with their bagpipes and kilts, and also for associating with descendants of wealthy clan chiefs whose ancestors had driven the ancestors of the visitors from Scotland (Steinberg 1981, 62).

In another instance, the arrival of a large number of displaced Polish immigrants under special legislation after World War II led to a similar disillusionment among Polish Americans. The newcomers, who reflected the changes that had taken place in Poland during the decades since the first wave of Poles had arrived in the United States, saw surviving members of the earlier immigration and their descendants as ignorant of Polish culture and history, and criticized their archaic, Americanized language (Lopata 1976, 26–27). Similarly, Tsai (1980, 329–337) described an enduring split among Chinese Americans, who were divided into the descendants of the early Chinese immigrants living mainly in the Chinatowns of large cities and those more recently arrived (since World War II) who are disproportionately better educated, more affluent, and whose settlement in the United States is widely scattered and suburban. The latter group have little social contact with the former, although they find Chinatown convenient for shopping and services. The recent immigrants look down on those who live there, however, as knowing little of genuine Chinese culture and as being "backward." This simple division of Chinese American ethnicity is now bound to undergo complication in New York City and very likely in other cities as well. Britain's agreement to turn Hong Kong over to the Chinese in 1997 led to the exodus of people and capital, with New York City's Chinatown district a favorite destination. The most recent Chinese immigrants now choose, primarily for business reasons, to live in the old ethnic enclaves. Will these become the *new* loci of authentic Chinese culture? While the impact on the overall configuration of Chinese ethnicity in the United States remains to be determined, the impact on the city district has been a tremendous pressure on space, especially commercial space; a dramatic increase in rents; and the rapid spread of the ethnic enclave beyond its old boundaries (*New York Times,* December 25, 1986, 1).

Each of these examples—Scottish, Polish, and Chinese—reveals something important about the qualities of preserved ethnicity. First, it is a cultural form in relative isolation where, by definition, emphasis is on the conservation of the old ways. The culture upon which it was originally based will have continued to change. The transplanted ethnic version will continue its adaptation, imperceptible to its participants, in its foreign surroundings. In this sense, preserved ethnicity becomes increasingly anachronistic. Second, a lengthy interruption (a matter of decades) in the flow of immigration, causing nominal co-ethnics to arrive in two or more distinct waves, will probably result in a disparity in the cultural content of ethnicity among the different waves. This is likely to be reflected in some strain between the groups regarding claims of authenticity of cultural practices.

It is the case, then, that what appears to be a straightforward and homogeneous cultural grouping from the outside is often seen by insiders as containing serious divisions. Another source of division occurs when some members reject accepted cultural definitions and styles and adopt new ones in their place—an attempt to *recapture* the relevance of ethnic identity.

Hamill ([1972] 1977, 290–299) presented an insider's account in which he distinguished between the content of "old" Irish and "new" Irish ethnicity. It was an account by one deeply alienated from sentimental and ritualistic Saint

Patrick's Day expressions of Irish American identity. In the 1970s, the conflict in Northern Ireland provoked, among many younger Irish Americans, a new interest in history, politics, and culture that had little in common with the carefully preserved *old* Irish ethnicity, proud of its hard-won rise to economic security and social acceptance. According to Hamill, the *new* Irish gained their sense of belonging from an intellectual tradition rooted in urban America, in universities and literatures sensitive to political and historical themes. The new Irish ethnicity is a product of the city. It was "New York . . . which was the native place, the place of beginnings, the place that served for us the same function that Ireland served for our parents" (Hamill [1972] 1977, 296). In this case it was particularly evident that the content of ethnic experience was not simply a survival: The new Irish ethnicity was an urban hybrid, the result of the demand that ethnic experience be relevant as well as authentic. Hamill reworked the meaning of his ethnicity until he was able, as he put it, to once again march in the Saint Patrick's Day Parade without embarrassment. He knew that many of those marching alongside him were not marching with him. Of course, this made their experience neither less genuine nor less authentic.

Urban Ethnic Enclaves

The ethnic heterogeneity of the growing U.S. city was accentuated by the formation of residential enclaves of people from the same ethnic group who gathered in particular areas of the city. These concentrations first arose in part as a matter of choice. Necessity dictated that immigrants sought out the lowest cost of housing in areas of the city where their particular group was not barred or discouraged from locating. In practice, there was a subtle interplay between voluntary and proscriptive factors. The dramatic increase in the immigration of Jews from eastern Europe in the 1880s resulted in the establishment of ghettoes in major cities. These may be seen as "voluntary ghettoes," efforts by people largely from rural backgrounds to reproduce the familiar *shtetl* (community) of the Old Country (Plesur 1982, 4–5). At the same time, it has been said of these immigrant settlements that "the American ghetto was from its inception a combined product of communal assistance and societal denial" (Rose 1969, 5). That is, the "choice" was reenforced by the perceived hostility of other groups that accompanied the expansion of the American Jewish population. The residential enclave offered refuge from more than the uncertainties of the strange urban way of life (Rose 1969, 5–6).

Each ethnic group's membership sorted itself roughly into distinct neighborhoods; sometimes the divisions were by individual tenements. While these ethnic enclaves allowed the immigrants and their children to exist in a capsule of familiar (though not unchanged) culture, the ethnic neighborhoods also provided a comforting home base for a more gradual adaptation to American society.

In his neighborhood, the immigrant found those who understood his native tongue and, perhaps, even his dialect. There he could purchase familiar foods, prepared in traditional fashion, from merchants who might even haggle over the price or sell the merchandise in amounts small enough to fit every budget. In the neighborhood of an American city, an immigrant might find that group taboos and traditional codes of personal behavior derived from old world experience and wisdom all continued to have relevance. (Kraut 1982, 117–118)

In this way the immigrant appears to be enveloped in a protective cultural co-coon, able almost completely to avoid contact with the outside. If the group were large and the opportunities offered within it ample enough, it would be possible to avoid the social and economic barriers imposed by not knowing English. The immigrant's native tongue could be employed both at work and after.

Interaction across ethnic boundaries can be hazardous, and it is easy to imagine people from different cultural backgrounds engaging in behaviors that are perceived as inappropriate, leading to confusion and animosity between parties. Rules and expectations vary. An expected small commission may be regarded as bribery; family loyalty carried out as a matter of obligation is nepotism; and expectations regarding assertiveness and extroversion vary across cultures, just as they do with regard to what constitutes being on time. Expectations also vary with regard to the giving and accepting of gifts and the etiquette of business transactions, including how close interacting persons may stand, what they should do with their eyes during interaction, and if and how they may touch one another. All of these expectations indicate important norms that often vary dramatically from one culture to another (Argyle 1982, 64–72). For example, gestures that one communicator may assume convey a message of goodwill, like a hand raised in greeting or the thumbs-up sign, may be taken with great offense by another (Collett 1982, 85).

In addition to unintended insults that pass between ethnic groups, the intended ones are also a means of maintaining group boundaries. Allen (1983, 15), in his study of the language of ethnic conflict, observed that one means of maintaining ethnic solidarity against the pressures of assimilation was through ethnic name-calling, making pejorative or invidious distinctions between one's own group and all others. Ethnic slurs are "labels for negative reference groups; they are a device by which people know who they are not and thereby who they are." The cultural mix of the urban setting provides ample opportunity for misunderstanding and abuse, and the ethnic enclave provides a safe and familiar haven from them.

This cultural encapsulation of immigrants and even subsequent generations might be promoted by particular agents within the ethnic community. There are those whose stake in the observance of group loyalties goes beyond the comfort of maintaining a shared cultural tradition. These include the politicians and entrepreneurs who appeal directly to co-ethnics for support. Dahya (1974, 91–94) presented the case of Pakistani businessmen in Britain whose livelihood was tied to the economic well-being, cohesion, and loyal patronage of the Pakistani community. Together, these shopkeepers and providers of services formed a network that reticulated within each city and between cities, carrying news of employment opportunities, which was passed on to customers and clients. Also, the business-men were active caretakers of culture (e.g., intervening with school boards on matters of policy regarding requirements of female dress in physical education classes), trying to ensure that their co-ethnics didn't lose their "Pakistanihood." From the customer's point of view, ethnic shops and services remained attractive because here transactions were carried on in one's own language, and news of home and topics of common interest were likely to be discussed. Dahya presented a set of relationships that systematically reenforced one another.

> *By taking hold of the immigrant's allegiance, the ethnic institutions bring about their relative incapsulation and reduce the potentiality for interpersonal relations across ethnic boundaries. The immigrants' support for ethnic and their avoid-ance of native institutions is not simply a matter of voluntary decision on their part; rather it is an obligation. ("If we do not patronize our own people, who else will?") Indeed it is an expression of one's loyalty to the homeland. (Dahya 1974, 94)*

If ethnic neighborhoods were important and useful during the immigrant phase of settlement, what happens to them in the future, after generations of settlement? Recent research in the New York metropolitan region (Alba, Logan, and Crowder 1997) demonstrates that (1) some inner-city ethnic neighborhoods are transformed as new waves of immigrants take over older neighborhoods and

---

BOX 5-1   New Immigrant Enclaves in New York

New York was receiving 110,000 new immi-grants a year in the 1990s. While the new sources of immigration transformed the city, the neighborhoods in which the immigrants settled were changed even more dramatically by the continued tendency for immigrants to form res-idential clusters. In the early 1990s, New York was absorbing an average of 22,000 people from the Dominican Republic per year, the largest of all immigrant streams to the city. Most Domini-cans gravitated to Upper Manhattan or the West Bronx. In the same period, the city was becom-ing home to 13,000 Ukrainians and Russians per year, with most settling in south Brooklyn. The 12,000 new Chinese immigrants each year could never be absorbed by Manhattan's Chinatown, even as it encroached on Little Italy, and neigh-borhoods throughout the city have come to take on a transplanted Chinese cultural quality. The fourth and fifth largest sources of new immi-grants to New York in this period were from Jamaica and Guyana, together totaling nearly 13,000 newcomers per year. Thirty percent of the residents in Brooklyn's Flatbush section were from Jamaica or Guyana (Edmondson 1997). The new immigrants provide an inter-esting perspective on ethnic enclaves. As the intensity of residential clustering of immigrant waves from early in the twentieth century sub-sides—as the cultural stamp of German, Irish, Polish and Italian neighborhoods fades—there emerges a new set of residential enclaves—often the same old neighborhoods with new cultural identities. For as long as immigration continues to be an important source of new life in old U.S. cities, ethnic neighborhoods will con-tinue to be a clearly identifiable feature con-tributing to the attractiveness of urban life.

give them a new ethnic identity (as Levine and Harmon [1992] found in the Dorchester/Roxbury/Mattapan area of Boston, discussed in Chapter 4); (2) some older ethnic neighborhoods maintain their ethnic heritage, including the daily use of the mother tongue, for generations beyond the immigrant one; and (3) ethnic concentrations, somewhat culturally diluted, may move to the suburbs with the upwardly mobile descendants of immigrant groups. In a comparison of ethnic persistence among three European American cultures, it was found that Italians were most likely to maintain patterns of clustered residences and ethnic culture, both in the old urban and new suburban locations, the Germans least likely, and the Irish somewhere in-between. While each step away from the old inner-city neighborhood is associated with a weakening of ethnic clustering and cultural affinity, "Nevertheless, it seems beyond question that white ethnic neighborhoods, especially Italian ones, will continue to be prominent in the region for the foreseeable future" (908). However, in favor of the assimilationist view of the potential *weakening* of ethnic identity, the authors add that a continued thinning out of the availability of co-ethnics in the region can only lead to a decline of ethnic identity and culture, as Italians (especially) and other relatively concentrated groups disperse to other areas of the country. "This point underscores the critical function of ethnic neighborhoods in maintaining forms of ethnicity that are more than private, beyond what can be transmitted by the family alone, and points up the larger significance of spatial assimilation in a region where ethnicity has flourished to a degree unsurpassed in the nation" (909).

Institutions in the Rivalry for Peoplehood

One of the great secondary themes in the history of immigration to North America involves the struggle between immigrants' loyalties to their native practices and values and the insistence that they adapt to their host culture. The major instruments in this battle for their loyalty and sense of belonging—their peoplehood—have been the institutions that ethnic groups have managed to erect as a means of preserving aspects of their own culture, arrayed against those of the host culture bent upon the Americanization of the foreigner. The major institutional supports erected by the immigrants and their descendants have included mutual assistance societies, religious institutions and parochial schools, and the native-language press. Similarly, the host society's efforts to acculturate the immigrants have been exerted through agencies that provided relief services, public schools, the influence of a religious hierarchy and attempts to control the foreign-language press.

As would be expected, the most complete set of ethnic institutions can be found in the larger population centers where there are sufficient numbers of co-ethnics to support them. Among the earliest of these institutions to emerge was the mutual assistance society. Handlin ([1951] 1973, 155–156) suggested that these societies grew naturally out of the common practice of "passing the hat" among neighbors and friends for contributions whenever some grave misfortune befell an immigrant family. Personal disasters were so frequent and terrible that the need for a formalized system of mutual insurance became evident, and the mutual assistance society, with membership usually determined by ethnic affiliation, was born. The services supplied by the societies expanded quickly—covering the needs of members from "cradle to grave"—and included orphanages, lobbying efforts on behalf of the ethnic group and the homeland, and savings and loan services. Ethnic groups addressed their particular problems through these societies. For example, Polish miners, whose work was considered too risky for them to be sold life insurance, were offered coverage through their society; Jews, treated unfairly by employment service practices, set up their own employment agency and vocational school; and Polish printers and German bakers also developed specialized employment services (Cafferty et al. 1983, 69–70). Beyond the immigrants' material needs, mutual assistance societies also provided moral support, giving advice on the practical problems of living in the United States and helping to combat feelings of loneliness and alienation. One especially important service offered to immigrants was peace of mind in the knowledge that when they died they would be laid to rest with the observation of the rites required by their religion. For both Roman Catholics and Orthodox Jews, correct practice included burial in consecrated ground. But whatever the immigrant's religious belief, no one wanted to be relegated to an unmarked grave (Kraut 1982, 132).

Mutual assistance societies lent structure to ethnic identity, providing for the concrete expression of a group's social cohesiveness. Religious institutions added a further, spiritual dimension to these separate identities. Among Roman Catholics, each language group preferred its own clergy to conduct mass and serve congregants in the familiar manner of their native communities. In the 1870s Italians in North Boston, feeling that they could no longer share a church that had come to be controlled by the Portuguese, founded their own church and parish one block away. Anxieties mounted in the new location because, although the Portuguese stayed away, increasing numbers of Irish and Southern Italians threatened the homogeneity of the parish—the founders of which were mainly Genoese (DeMarco 1981, 48–49). The Greeks built their communities with the goal of sending for their own priest and erecting their own church (Kraut 1982, 121–122). These ethnic religious institutions were strong vehicles of cohesion and identity.

During the late nineteenth and early twentieth centuries, the foreign-born were besieged by Americanization agents and programs. The general antipathy toward foreigners grew into anger and fear as their numbers and visibility in the city grew. Both religious and secular movements to assist the urban poor aimed at their cultural adaptation as well. The Catholic hierarchy, generally unsympathetic to the ethnic divisions at the parish level, often provided assistance to parishes contingent upon local policies of Americanization (Kraut 1982, 121). However, the apparent fragmentation of the Catholic church into several independent ethnic units, an illusion that in some quarters had given rise to concern over the ultimate unity of the church, actually worked as a safety valve (Dolan 1975, 93). It did so by avoiding the confrontation of antagonistic groups over the issue of religious practice, thereby preventing the splintering of religious factions and preserving the integrity of the church. The ethnic churches also acted as socializing and stabilizing influences on Catholic immigrants, providing them with a continuity of familiar beliefs and values. Through its charities, the church provided some relief from the conditions of poverty and cushioned the immigrants' adaptation to life in a new country. In the long run, as Henry Steele Commager recognized, "the Catholic Church was, during this period, one of the most effective of all agencies for . . . Americanization" (Ellis [1956] 1969, 104–105). Like the residential enclave of which it was a part, the ethnic Catholic parish was, through its cushioning and stabilizing influence, actually a subtle agent of adaptation and, ultimately, of acculturation.

Religious and other private organizations increasingly competed directly with the mutual assistance societies in the provision of aid to the immigrant poor. The settlement house movement, founded by social reformers like Jane Addams, who chartered Hull House in Chicago, demonstrated an appreciation of the immigrant's customs and skills, and recognized the need for assimilation to proceed at a pace that was not destructive to family and social life (Gordon 1964, 137–138). Yet the goal of the movement was to prepare immigrants for improving their condition, and this meant assimilation. Many "lineage societies," like the Daughters of the American Revolution and the Society of Colonial Dames, designed educational programs for the Americanization of immigrants (Gordon 1964, 99, 137–138). The Protestant Social Gospel movement's motive for seeing that immigrants passed as smoothly as possible through the initial material crises of settlement was to ensure that the process of Americanization would not be arrested (Kraut 1982, 127).

Another urban institution that devoted a good deal of effort to immigrant adaptation was the party political machine. These were permanent political organizations that coordinated the nomination and election of government officials through the systematic distribution of patronage in exchange for support at election time. An outstanding example was the protracted domination of Tammany Hall over New York City politics, and most prominent in its long succession of leaders was Boss (William Marcy) Tweed, who, in the tradition of political machine bosses, became rich through illegal dealings. The machine's interest in the immigrants lay in the immigrants' desperate condition and the potential votes they represented: for small gifts of material aid, legal help, or a note of introduction to an employer, an immigrant's gratitude could be drawn on at the polls for years to come. Control over voter registration procedures meant that immigrants would be made "into voting citizens so fast that their heads whirled" (Moscow 1971, 24). Although the machine did undeniable harm in subverting the electoral process and corrupting political leadership, it had its positive aspects from the immigrants' point of view.

The boss system took the immigrant . . . and made him an American citizen. It found him a place to live, kissed his babies, entertained his whole family on the district club's annual boat ride, picnic, or clambake, which was the event of the year in a lower-class society of limited pleasures. . . . The boss system made money for the boss and for the party organization, but it also made life more bearable for a lot of little people who had no access otherwise to government, who knew of its operations only through their contacts with the machine. (Moscow 1971, 10)

The machine eventually fell victim to restricted immigration (as well as political reforms that made it more difficult to control elections and distribute patronage), which dried up its compliant constituency. As the immigrants became more independent and secure economically and as they were replaced by their more educated and affluent offspring, the machine lost its political leverage, its power to control votes.

By the beginning of World War I, various agencies of the federal government turned their attention toward Americanizing the foreign-born urban population in response to hysterical popular concerns over national loyalty: "100% Americanism" had become the cry of the hour. In 1915, Woodrow Wilson declared to a gathering of naturalized citizens in Philadelphia that "a man who thinks of himself as belonging to a particular national group in America has not yet become an American" (Gordon 1964, 100–101). The gradual increase in government public assistance programs, unemployment insurance, and social security meant that mutual assistance societies had served their purpose and were becoming redundant. Ethnic associations functioned more and more as vehicles for simple sociability and symbolism among European immigrants and their descendants.

In the public schools, foreign culture and history were largely neglected in favor of American studies. Concerned parents and grandparents worked in both city and rural communities to preserve instruction in the native tongue, either through permission to employ it as the primary medium of instruction in the public schools or to teach it in the parochial schools. Yet the culturally leveling effect of language and the cultural and historical emphasis of the curriculum was an irresistible Americanizing force.

The general condemnation of foreign habits and culture was influenced by the American press, which missed no opportunity to cater to the prejudices of its readership through stereotypes and caricatures. More surprising was the fact that the foreign-language press eventually joined in, criticizing what it saw as maladaptive traits and endorsing the goals of Americanization. Originally the Italian American papers focused on local news stories from various immigrant points of origin in Italy; but by early in the twentieth century, these papers featured American as well as Italian news, ran articles on American historic and patriotic themes, and had become enthusiastic supporters of American culture and Americanization (Iorizzo and Mondello 1980, 116–117). Furthermore, Italian-language papers urged immigrants to adopt habits that would not make them conspicuously foreign to others (Nelli 1970, 168).

Thus, the foreign-language press, which could have continued as a formidable agent in the preservation of ethnic culture, was instead an ambivalent force. While it spoke to its readers in their native language, its message was of acculturation. There is evidence, however, that editorial policy may have been coerced in many instances. In his work on the rise of advertising and consumerism in America, Stuart Ewen (1976, 63–64) asserted that the directors of the American Association of Foreign Language Newspapers, through their control over the advertising patronage of large companies, could manipulate the editorial messages of the economically struggling foreign-language papers. Robert Park, who was a close student of the foreign-language press, commented that the director of the association had the power to "make or break" a publisher. The avowed goal of the association was the Americanization of immigrants; its strategy was to require the publication of editorials and news stories that it supplied. Its philosophy, in the words of one of its directors, was:

> *National advertising is the great Americanizer.*
>
> *American ideals and institutions, law, order and prosperity have not yet been sold to all of our immigrants.*
>
> *American products and standards of living have not yet been bought by the foreign born in America. . . .*
>
> *If Americans want to combine business and patriotism, they should advertise products, industry, and American institutions in the American Foreign Language press. (Ewen 1976, 64)*

The question of the outcome of the tug-of-war between the forces of Americanization and those supporting old-country ethnicities can never be answered with any finality: the answer is always unfolding as people's sense of peoplehood changes. Events around the world, in Poland or Northern Ireland, for example, continue to stir a sense of identity among long-settled groups. Other events generate new emigrations from such places as Afghanistan, Central America, and Southeast Asia. The more settled segments of the population of the United States still harbor, at various levels, old European, Asian, and other ties. Some, like Steinberg, expect these ties to continue to fade, to wash out in the massive movement to middle-class status and the suburbs. Others worry about the "meltability" of new immigrant ethnic groups. Such a concern has generated the current xenophobic and nativistic sympathies at state and national levels for the passage of laws making English the official language. These concerns seem timely and insightful only to those who fail to recognize that they represent a long tradition of fear of outsiders in the great melting pot.

Everyone an Ethnic

So far we have treated ethnicity in a conventional manner, focusing on the question of the survival of old-country (primarily European) cultural ties. Whenever the "survival of ethnicity" is discussed, ancestral origin is the inevitable frame of reference. This is a static and limiting perspective, however. Given this approach, some people are ethnics and some are not. Alternatively, it may be argued that given the appropriate circumstances, we are all ethnics; and perhaps these hidden or latent group identities have nothing to do with ties to a foreign culture.

In the preceding section, the struggle being discussed was not one between ethnic identity and no identity, but between competing peoplehoods. In this struggle, the less one remained culturally tied to the homeland, the more one became culturally tied to the new land. In this light, it is inappropriate to speak of one who is a product of generations that have grown progressively remote from a foreign ancestral home as having lost ethnic identity. Abramson (1973, 9) put it somewhat differently when he said, "The idea of ethnicity as a deviant to Anglo-American norms leads to a confusion that everybody is 'ethnic' in the United States except those with Anglo Saxon Protestant background. This of course is absurd. . . . White Americans, with Anglo Saxon Protestant background have their own national and regional ethnicity."

In order to see this point, it is necessary to abandon the view that ethnicity is restricted to people who come from a foreign country. Americans who travel and live abroad are regularly confronted with their "Americanness" and experience the awakening of a feeling of belonging—an American ethnicity. People who move regionally within the United States (for example, from the Northeast to the Sunbelt) commonly share a sense of special ties to other people that they meet from their "home" region. In large Sunbelt cities like Houston, there are social clubs formed by northerners based on home-state origins. Sunbelt natives themselves are less likely to be so particular in assigning "ethnic" memberships and may react to all newcomers categorically as "Yankees." Migrants from rural Appalachia to northern industrial cities face stereotypes and prejudices keyed to their area of origin, and it has been suggested that it may be useful sociologically to consider them an ethnic group (Obermiller 1981; Philliber 1981, 11–20). Everyone is prepared to fill in the blanks when it comes to stereotyping the midwesterner or southerner, or still more narrowly the San Franciscan or New Yorker. We are reluctant to label the facts and fictions of regional differences as "ethnic" because of a century of melting pot ideology and because ethnicity is a sense of belonging that we associate with international differences. However, we know that ethnicity is a matter of being confronted with one's own special sense of cultural attachment to a group. In Albany, a New Yorker is likely to be a New Yorker; in Houston, a Yankee; and in London, an American—of course, in all instances the person in question also may be, in varying degrees, a Polish Catholic.

The Urban Arena and the Formation of Minority Groups

For as long as the United States and its cities have been the target of immigration, observers have never exhausted the capacity to agonize over the assimilability of the most recent arrivals. Always, there have been the New Immigrants, assumed to be culturally and racially more distant than the by-then familiar Old Immigrants. After immigration restrictions stemmed the flow of Europeans, New and Old, the New-New Immigrants to the city came to include rural blacks migrating from the South; Latinos from Mexico, Puerto Rico, Cuba, and elsewhere in Latin America; Native Americans abandoning reservation life in search of greater economic opportunity in the cities; and recent Asian migrants. The most common feature of all immigrants, New and Old, is that they found themselves in the cities of the United States as a result of rational economic choice. What sets the various groups apart is the degree to which their initial displacement involved an element of political coercion. Those who arrived in the United States as political refugees represent the extreme instance.

Strictly speaking, African Americans and Native American do not fit neatly within a discussion of immigration because they came to the city as migrants (from domestic points of origin) rather than as immigrants (from outside of the national borders). The same applies to citizens who pass freely between Puerto Rico and the mainland. Nevertheless, since our interest here is in intergroup processes in the city, rather than the technical definition of immigration, we discuss them all in common, with reference to their point of destination as urban immigrants.

Population Trends and Minorities

According to the 2000 census, the population of the United States had reached 281.4 million. Official growth estimates expected it to add another hundred million by 2050, which would amount to a 50 percent increase in the total population in the six decades between 1990 and 2050. By projecting current trends, we can anticipate that an increasing proportion of the growing population will be made up of people of color. Between 1990 and 1999, the white (non-Hispanic) census category grew by 7.3 percent. During the same period, the African American population grew by 13.8 percent. The most rapid growth within large subsets of the population was for the Asian and Pacific Islander category, which increased by 43 percent, reaching 10.8 million, and the Bureau's "Hispanic, non-white" category, which grew by 38.8 percent, reaching a total of 31.3 million; a large proportion of the growth for these two groups came from immigration. Native Americans increased by 15.5 percent to 2.3 million in 1999. Census Bureau projections are for Latino growth to continue at substantially higher rates than those for other sub-populations, and that the Hispanic, nonwhite category will become the largest nonwhite group sometime in 2002 or 2003. By midyear 2010, when the total population reaches about 300 million, white non-Hispanics will make up just over two-thirds of the total (census.gov/population/projections/nation/summary).

The last census breakdown available at this writing (1990) showed that the proportion of people of color in metropolitan areas ranged from 8.7 percent in Minneapolis/St. Paul (Minnesota), to 52.2 percent in Miami (Frey 1993, 3-19–3-21). Most of the large metropolitan populations that included one-fourth or more blacks were in the South, while a majority of the largest metropolitan areas with one-fourth or more Latinos were in the West, especially in Texas and California. Asian, Pacific Islander, and Native American populations are too small to constitute a very large share of any metropolitan area (except in Honolulu), but some cities have large and visible concentrations of these groups. Asian and Pacific Islander concentrations are especially large in Los Angeles, San Francisco, New York, and Chicago. Cities with relatively large numbers of Native Americans include Los Angeles, Tulsa (Oklahoma), New York, Oklahoma City, Phoenix, Seattle, Minneapolis/St. Paul, Tucson (Arizona), and San Diego (U.S. Bureau of the Census 1992a, 33).

An increasingly important ethnic minority, especially in East Coast cities, and most especially in New York where its members numbered about 300,000 by 1990, is made up of people from the non-Spanish-speaking Caribbean. The category includes Haitians and Jamaicans, people who struggle to assert and maintain their distinctive Afro-Caribbean ethnic identities in a land that categorizes them as a part of the larger black minority (Kasinitz 1992).

Although the experience of each of these groups is unique, each has faced the risk of becoming a minority or of intensifying its minority status in the course of its urban resettlement. The degree to which newly immigrant groups are able to avoid minority status appears to be inversely related to their size and visibility in the urban arena. As a general rule, intergroup antagonism and discriminatory treatment are at least partly a product of the relative visibility of the group and the degree to which it is perceived to threaten the living standards of members of the majority. New urban immigrants are especially vulnerable to scapegoating—being blamed for society's problems—in periods of economic recession. The urbanization of African Americans illustrates the urban aspect of minority group formation.

African American Urbanization

During the twentieth century, the African American population of the United States underwent a rapid transformation from predominantly rural to predominantly urban. The 1890s saw a gradual increase in the rate of migration of southern blacks to the industrial cities of the North. During the next 70 to 80 years, Illinois, New York, Pennsylvania, New Jersey, Indiana, Michigan, and other northern and mid-Atlantic states, as well as the major cities of California, drew millions of black migrants from the South. World War I marked the beginning of what later came to be called the Great Migration, a response to the dwindling supply of European immigrant labor, the efforts of labor-recruiting agents who had been sent to the South as early as 1915, as well as the technological transformation of agriculture in the South. During the 1920s, the urban black population of the United States increased by 46 percent (compared to an increase of 24 percent in the urban white population). In the austerity of the depression that followed, rural blacks—typically without title to lands they worked and with a dwindling demand for labor in the rural South—continued with little option to gravitate to the cities. World War II saw the new recruitment of blacks into industry and added impetus to the northward movement. By 1950, almost the same proportion of the black population (62 percent) and the white population (64 percent) was urban, and the greatest concentrations and net gains from migration were in the larger central cities. In the early 1950s, a net out-migration of white population from major central cities began. (This trend is discussed in Chapter 7.) By 1970 about three-fourths of the black population of the United States lived in metropolitan areas, with 58 percent in central cities (Johnson and Campbell 1981). Since about 1970, however, there has been a modest reverse migration to the South and a cessation of the trend of increasing urban concentration. Still, 56 percent of the black population lived in central cities in 1991.

The factors that provided the impetus for the Great Migration are familiar. The imbalance in life chances between the rural South and the urban North provided more than adequate incentive for people to move, but southern racism and the repressive atmosphere it created must also be credited as motivating factors. Contributing to this atmosphere were collective acts of terrorism, including lynchings, and the mistreatment of blacks by law authorities in the South, especially toward the early part of the era. Whatever hardships they might contain, northern areas on the whole had a somewhat better reputation in the area of civil rights reform, reforms that generated white antagonisms in the South. Black women, who served as critical links in the migration chains that linked the regions, were driven as well by the fear of rape by whites in the South, and also by the oppressive conditions and fears of abuse within their own poor, rural communities (Hine 1996).

History reflects that northern cities were not altogether welcoming social environments for the new immigrants from the South. From the beginning, northern populations often proved hostile, especially in cities where there was substantial black population growth. Beginning with the eruption of violence against blacks in 1908 in Springfield, Illinois, and continuing periodically thereafter, in city after city, migrants faced resistance to their growing presence in the North (Zunz 1982, 373). Chicago, where the black population had grown from 15,000 in 1890 to 50,000 in 1915, was the scene of 13 days of violence in 1919 that left 28 people dead. While industries demanded more workers during World War II, city administrations failed to consider the pressures that would be brought by the growing numbers of migrants, and, as a result, violence occurred in Harlem, Los Angeles, and Detroit (Johnson and Campbell 1981).

Black migrants to northern cities faced similar problems and prejudices to those encountered by the European immigrant several decades earlier. However, although the experiences were similar, they were hardly equivalent; blacks faced greater obstacles to mobility and assimilation. Over time, residential segregation in the city became more pronounced, and blacks and whites, increasingly isolated from one another, traveled in segregated social worlds. In the South especially before 1954, the separation of races was mandated by laws that provided for segregated facilities for blacks and whites. In the North, segregation was the result of illegal but effective efforts on the part of the dominant majority to physically isolate the growing black minority.

Although many European groups were subject to discrimination, they were able to shake off, after a generation or two, the stigma of "race" that originally had distinguished them. Of course, this may have been in part because would-be discriminators were unable to effectively identify physical characteristics that would allow them to separate minority members among the various European groups. Lieberson (1980, 365) pointed out that this argument does not hold up for the Chinese and Japanese Americans who were able to modify substantially their minority status after their rocky beginnings in the United States. Lieberson raised the question of what it is that caused black Americans to continue in that status. He believed the answer has to do with numbers and, in the case of blacks, urbanization.

He observed (Lieberson 1980, 368) that the Chinese and Japanese were subject to savage treatment in the areas where they were concentrated early in the history of their immigration. However, in response to the prevailing negative dispositions toward them, their immigration was quickly brought to an end through modifications in immigration law. Gradually, Asian workers lost their attraction as a political issue and target of attack, and their numbers remained sufficiently low to enable them to find specialized occupational niches. In the case of black migrants, however, the flow and concentration of workers in the larger cities continued nonstop until recently. According to Lieberson, the most important effect that an unabated influx of an immigrant minority can have is to "raise the level of ethnic and/or racial consciousness on the part of others in the city; . . . from the point of view of the dominant outsiders, the newcomers may reenforce stereotypes and negative dispositions that affect all members of the group" (Lieberson 1980, 380).

Lieberson perceived the conflict between blacks and whites and the enduring minority status of blacks as the result of urban dynamics involving competition and containment. Blacks most certainly faced prejudice and discrimination in northern cities before the period of widespread migration. Curry (1981, 81–95), in his study of free blacks in urban America between 1800 and 1850, described the prevalence of the most blatant forms of racism and discriminatory practice. Even then, the most common concern among whites was that the tiny numbers of blacks in their city would increase. Lieberson's point was that, given relatively small numbers, race would have faded over time as a divisive factor. In this view protracted racism and discrimination are the outcome of the urban properties of population size and density.

Zunz's (1982, 6, 354) history of intergroup relations in Detroit from 1880 to 1920 lends indirect support to Lieberson's argument. Zunz wrote that blacks experienced a settlement process radically different from that of the earlier European groups.

> *Compared with white ethnic groups, Blacks lived history in reverse: while foreign immigrants ultimately became assimilated into a unified structure dominated by the native white American world and based on rank and social status within it, Blacks were increasingly segregated from whites on the basis of race and irrespective of their social status. (Zunz 1982)*

Although social class had come to challenge ethnicity as a basis for residential clustering among white groups by 1920, this was not the case for African

Americans. For this group, race rather than class standing remained the major criterion of classification, and segregation was entrenched.

Contributing to the intensification of segregation patterns was a large-scale white exodus to the suburbs beginning in the 1950s. Also, restrictive covenants excluded categories of "undesirables" from certain neighborhoods (until such agreements were declared unconstitutional in 1948), and these were followed by other informal practices by realtors and homeowners' organizations that kept even affluent celebrity members of minorities out of certain housing districts through the 1950s (Kusmer 1996, 324).

By the 1970s the Great Migration had ended, and there was even some return migration to the South and some dispersal of the urban African American populations to western and smaller cities. By that time, however, blacks comprised a third of the population of Chicago and Philadelphia, approximately 40 percent of the population of Cleveland, St. Louis, and Detroit, and were the numerical majority in Newark, Gary, and Washington, D.C. (Kusmer 1996, 323). Their presence in large numbers in the largest cities and subsequent tensions over employment, housing, and public education issues insured that the problem of racism in the United States was cast in terms of black and white differences. The city showcased African American and European American racial tension and kept it fresh in the popular mind.

At the end of the 1970s, William Julius Wilson (1978) advanced a controversial thesis: He said that the significance of race was declining and would continue to do so in the United States. The thrust of his argument, which we will consider in Chapter 9, was that restricted employment opportunities in a changing economy would hurt all people with marginal skills, not just people of color. True, a disproportionate number of people in that category were African Americans, but their disadvantage was a product of technological change, especially the deindustrialization of the economy, rather than overt racism. From the vantage point of the end of the 1970s, what was arguably the end of the United States' last liberal era (to date), Wilson believed that racial prejudice was on the wane, and he thought that the end of the Great Migration would hurry its decline, at least with respect to African Americans (Wilson 1983, 82). In light of Lieberson's (1980) argument regarding the importance of migration in sustaining minority status, Wilson hypothesized that a decline in the significance of race should coincide with the end of the recent history of African American migration patterns. Perhaps less controversial was his prediction that prejudice and discrimination against Latinos would grow with their increasing urban visibility.

Contemporary Immigration and the Making of Minorities

During the 1980s and 1990s, immigration became one of the most emotional political issues in the United States and other target nations. Among established populations there was a growing sense of limitation regarding the growth potential of national economies in a globalizing environment; this was reflected in a resentment directed toward the outside world over deindustrialization and the loss of jobs. There was a nationalist resentment over people entering traditionally affluent but economically beleaguered nations from poor and often politically turbulent regions of the world. Today, many of the places that immigrant people come from are locations in the underdeveloped regions of the world. "The popular complaint of the day . . . is that America has an 'immigration problem,' coded language for the arrival of too many brown-skinned people" (Maharidge 1996, 8).

In the United States, public opinion has been especially sensitive and vulnerable to manipulation over the issue of illegal entry from the south, from Mexico, from the Caribbean, and from Central and South America. Conservative spokespersons, including two-time presidential candidate Patrick Buchanan and former California governor Pete Wilson, exploited fears associated with images of the consequences of nonwhite immigration. Their statements echoed themes of the European far right, whose anti-immigrant rhetoric was gaining it some political success there (Muller 1993, 11). The more subtle racist positions taken by actors in the realm of legitimate politics are especially damaging if they can be seen as lending support to right-wing white supremacists in the United States, who use economic and racial invasion concerns to inflame xenophobic impulses. The easy exploitability of economic issues is reflected in the following crude leaflet distributed on the streets of San Diego in the 1970s by the National Socialist White Peoples Party (Bustamante 1980, 142–143).

> *STOP ILLEGAL ALIENS! Every month thousands of illegal aliens pour into San Diego County. TAKING YOUR JOBS! SPENDING YOUR TAX DOLLARS! USING YOUR PUBLIC SERVICES! SENDING THOUSANDS OF DOLLARS BACK INTO MEXICO! IF YOU KNOW WHERE THEY WORK IT IS YOUR DUTY TO REPORT IT TO THE IMMIGRATION DEPARTMENT OR BORDER PATROL. IF YOU WANT TO WORK FOR WHITE AMERICA, JOIN US!*

While most U.S. citizens are more measured in their concerns about undocumented workers, public opinion supports legislation to reduce immigration and to reduce or eliminate services to the undocumented and their offspring. California's voters in 1994 approved Proposition 187, which sought to deny public services such as hospitals and education and benefits to undocumented workers and their children. In addition, a provision in the national welfare reform legislation that became law in 1996 initially denied federal benefits to legal noncitizen residents of the country. What some see as a rising backlash of mean-spiritedness against all immigrants obviously had support not only among voters and lawmakers but also among conservative intellectuals. In *The Case Against Immigration*, an editor of *The Social Contract* magazine (Beck 1996) made the case that immigration should be reduced drastically. He believed immigration seriously aggravates a number of problems, including lowered wage levels, depressed economic conditions of African Americans, urban sprawl and white flight from cities, degradation of the environment and depletion of natural resources, reduced quality of education, increased disadvantage of previously arrived immigrants, and threatened domestic tranquility in general. In California, Barbara Coe, a leading spokesperson for the "Save Our State" campaign, which eventually gained material expression as Proposition 187, reportedly believed that the continued influx of Mexicans would provoke a massive out-migration of Anglo Californians and might be linked to a planned Mexican political takeover of the state (Maharidge 1996, 170–171).

Inflammatory denunciations of the economic impact of illegal aliens spill over and apply to legal immigrants as well as to people born in the United States who physically or linguistically fit the general image associated with points of origin of undocumented workers. Immigration becomes a problem in the public mind as all immigrants are assumed to be part of an unskilled, uneducated, and minimally employable mass, their poverty-level wages destining them to become a burden on the state. This is the traditional concern that transforms new immigrants into stigmatized minorities in the United States and elsewhere. The burden of proof remains as always with those who argue that the latest group, among all of the generations of urban immigrants, is the one that is truly different. However, today there are two differences that give new impetus to the argument of unmeltability. The first is the underlying and usually unstated concern referred to by Maharidge: This is the "racial" issue (although in the old days Europeans from one nation would have described people from another European country as being of a different race). Many of the new immigrants are brown-skinned and from the Third World, raising, as Maharidge put it in the title of his book, the prospect of *The Coming White Minority*. The second difference that lends impetus to the unmeltability argument is the point that today the structure of employment opportunity makes prospects more questionable than in the past for those lacking specific training and skills. However, there is a dynamic relationship between immigration and economic opportunity that must be appreciated.

Since the nineteenth century, the foreign-born population has sustained high rates of employment. People came to the United States (from Canada, Europe, and so forth) then, as now, in search of economic opportunity. In 1890, labor participation rates (the proportion of a population defined as being in the labor force) were higher for both male and female immigrants than for people born in the United States, and they have generally remained higher. Today, as always, immigrants gravitate to the inner cities and create ethnic employment niches. They have added to the economic vitality of the "gateway cities" that are the targets of many immigrants: Los Angeles, New York, Miami, San Francisco, Washington, and Chicago. Latino immigrants, especially Cubans, have vitalized the economy of Miami. For the last decade or so, illegal workers from Ireland have been reputed to be a key element in the construction trades of eastern metropolitan areas, especially in New York. For decades, illegal as well as documented agricultural workers have subsidized the low cost of farm produce with their bargain wages, and others have allowed clothing manufacturers in U.S. cities to compete with their Third World counterparts by replicating overseas sweatshop conditions and wages, particularly in the Los Angeles area (Box 5-2).

BOX 5-2   Sweatshops in the United States

Sweatshop is a highly descriptive term that was applied to working conditions in the garment industry early in twentieth century America. At the time, it alluded to the conditions under which a largely immigrant female workforce worked long hours for little pay in a poorly regulated industry. In recent decades, the term has been revived to describe exactly the same abuses in the same industry producing clothing for major fashion labels and retail chains, some of it overseas, some of it here in the United States. Los Angeles is home to countless sewing operations—most of them with fewer than 50 workers—that together employ thousands of illegal immigrants and others. The presence of the shops is no secret, and many of them operate in the downtown garment district near the Convention Center. Jo-Ann Mort presented the case histories of two of the workers employed in the district. She reported that Aracely works twelve hours a day, seven days a week, with no holidays. As a presser, with burn scars on her hands from the industrial iron she stands at all day, she was earning $80 a week in 1996. Minimum wage regulations, which have little relevance to the invisible illegal workforce at any rate, are easily circumvented. In Aracely's husband's case—he is also a sweatshop worker—the employer did not allow employees to punch-in until two hours after they started work. Leticia, a documented Mexican immigrant who is paid by the piece for what she sews, reports that her employer routinely rejects worker's production reports, claiming " 'I already paid for this work,' or 'This isn't finished' or 'It's not done well.' " Leticia says that at times when she has worked 35 or 40 hours, she will be paid for only 20 because of her supervisor's rejections. She makes up for the lost income by taking work home, finishing at ten or eleven at night, after her evening English language classes. These two workers reported that they labored under primitive conditions, with filthy toilet facilities, leaking roofs, and rats in the workplace. Undocumented Aracely says, "Every day I get up at four o'clock in the morning. At six thirty, I'm dropping off my kids at school. I pay someone to pick them up in the afternoon. . . . My worst nightmare is when a teacher wants to talk to me or I have to be at school. . . . Sometimes, I get very, very desperate but I know I have to keep up the struggle because I have children. We suffer a lot in this country, too much." Mort's sources indicated that the Southern California clothing industry in which Aracely, Leticia, and thousands of others worked was contributing $13.3 billion to the national economy in the mid-1990s (Mort 1996).

Everywhere, recent immigrants are seen in fast food and other retail work, taking the minimum wage jobs that are rejected by the native-born workforce.

Research on the impact of immigrants on the local economy and employment market reveals a complex reality. In Los Angeles, New York, San Francisco, and other cities, immigrant workers were shown to enhance the competitiveness of local industries (as in the case of the garment industry) through their relatively lower wages. This research showed that recent immigrants were a replacement labor force supporting upward mobility rather than causing job loss for native workers, including local minorities (Muller 1993, 142–148). However, a comparative study of immigrant workers in New York and London (Model and Ladipo 1996; Model 1997) showed that immigrants had at least the potential to take better jobs than those held by local minorities. Black immigrant males from Africa and the West Indies took jobs with higher average prestige rankings than existing minority males in New York, while in London immigrant males from similar origins tended to come into the labor market nearer the bottom. The study suggests that immigrants do not necessarily push long-standing minorities into better jobs, at least not in the United States.

Research on immigrants from different Caribbean island nations indicates a complex interaction among many factors in determining how competitive immigrants will be in finding work. In New York City, those who arrived with educational advantages from English-speaking cultures tended to take better jobs, and women from islands where there was a tradition of high female labor force participation were better able to make their way independently. Jamaicans, Cubans from families of higher socioeconomic backgrounds in Cuba, and Haitians were more competitive and economically successful than Puerto Rican, Dominican, and more recently arrived Cuban immigrants who came without the educational or material resources of the earlier Cuban generation (Grasmuck and Grosfoguel 1997). Taken together, these studies indicate, not surprisingly, that at least in the United States, immigrants of color who arrive with modest levels of training are likely to join the ranks of the urban working poor, while those with higher levels of training and skill will leap ahead of existing minorities.

Another impact of immigration on the local economy is through the creation of opportunities by immigrant entrepreneurs. There are essentially three reasons for recent immigrants to choose self-employment over hired work. Self-employment for new arrivals may be a default option in labor markets in which an oversupply of local labor produces lower wages, perhaps mixed with some level of outright discrimination against the immigrant group. Or self-employment is an obvious option created by the personal resources of the immigrant, as in the case of Filipino or Indian medical doctors who enter private practice. Or self-employment may be attractive because networks of previously arrived co-ethnics have carved out a business niche in the local economy. Ethnic concentration in particular small businesses is often a well-recognized pattern, especially in modest-sized cities. In addition to the Chinese restaurant phenomenon that is the most evident example, in smaller metropolitan areas Koreans are found in laundry services and the grocery business; North Africans, Arabs, and Palestinians are also grocers; Iranians run bars, restaurants, and other retail establishments; Mexicans are in the construction trades and small gardening and landscaping businesses. In larger metropolitan areas with diversified economic opportunities, immigrant entrepreneurs follow the Cuban Miami model: In that metropolitan region, Cuban immigrants have entered into a broad spectrum of businesses, supported both by a large community of Latino immigrants and the general market for goods and services. Still, the association between particular immigrant groups and particular businesses even in some large cities is evident: In 1990, a third of the Israeli Arab and Palestinian entrepreneurs in New York ran grocery stores, as did 43.5 percent of those in San Francisco, and 60 percent (when combined with liquor retailers) in the D.C. area (Razin and Light 1998, 350–352).

Where negative incentives, such as the lack of labor demand or discrimination, are the cause of going into business for oneself, earnings may be lower than what employed workers with similar skill-levels enjoy. Many self-employed Mexicans in the building and gardening trades are not occupied full-time and have low incomes, especially in smaller cities. However, in larger cities with larger Mexican populations, self-employed Mexican tradespeople tend to earn more, perhaps due to the larger co-ethnic clientele or because more work is funneled to them through a larger network of Mexican American contractors (Spener and Bean 1999).

An article in *Mortgage Banking* (Lachman and Brett 1997) weighed in on the positive side of the debate over the impact of immigration on local markets. In this account, immigrants are described as ready and willing workers who are making up an increasing share of the labor market, business people who are revitalizing declining neighborhoods, retail shoppers who contribute significantly to sales, experienced hoteliers infusing the hotel and motel business with new life through their investments, and home buyers who have proven to be a boon to the real estate market (immigrants owned over a half a million homes in Los Angeles in 1990). The article pointed out that while many immigrants have low incomes, in due time they become upscale consumers and investors and eventually make the move to the suburbs.

In fact, the immigrant stream is economically diverse, and the image of new immigrants waiting a generation or two to make it to the suburbs is as outmoded as the picture of old U.S. cities with heavy industrial cores. Since the sustained economic prosperity of the mid-1990s, U.S. businesses requiring employees with high-tech training are going directly to international labor pools to recruit them. The new recruits often go directly to the suburbs. Montgomery and Fairfax Counties outside Washington, D.C., make the point. The greater D.C. area in 1999 was home to 3,300 high-technology firms employing a quarter of a million workers. Since 1980, the area had attracted between 400,000 and 500,000 legal immigrants and perhaps half that number of illegal entries. The numbers indicate another side to the immigrant suburban trend taking place in such cities as Boston, Charlotte, and San Francisco. While many of the new immigrant suburbanites fit the profile of the affluent suburban resident, a large number of others, who accept jobs in simple light industrial assembly and custodial or day-care services, do not. The class polarization that divides the inner-city workers into wealthy and working-poor social strata applies as well as to the immigrant suburbanite population (Suro 1999).

Herbert Gans (1992) cautioned that even successful first-generation immigrants, particularly people of color, may not see their favorable social position translate into security or acceptance in subsequent generations. A downturn in the economy can revive the receiving society's penchant for turning new immigrants into minorities. A contracting employment market historically has spawned resentment toward newcomers who are then seen as taking good jobs and business opportunities from mainstream groups who see themselves as having established a prior claim to economic advantage by virtue of generations of citizenship. Even during the relative prosperity of the 1990s, citizen's movements in many states mounted campaigns to declare English the state's official language, an act symbolizing the age-old American demand for the cultural assimilation of immigrants.

By the end of the century, official-language legislative movements were under way or had already succeeded in 35 states.

The case of California is instructive because its large Third World immigrant population and the visibility of brown-skinned people in the major cities have made it a flashpoint of the fears and reactiveness of the U.S. majority to the perceived hazards of immigration. The interplay of racial and economic concerns is underlined by the fact that the question of what will become of immigrants once they get here is heard less often regarding Irish housepainters in Boston and New York than it is regarding Cubans, Dominicans, Mexicans, Puerto Ricans, Laotians, Vietnamese, Cambodians, and Filipinos wherever they achieve the critical mass that draws the concerned attention of the white non-immigrant generations that surround them with suspicion.

La Ciudad Latina

Of the 22.3 million people in the United States in 1991 with ties of identity (however distant) to New World Spanish colonial territories, 52 percent lived in central cities and 93 percent in metropolitan areas. This complex reference may leave some question as to precisely what group is being described here. We are describing no group precisely. The reference is not to a specific nation of origin. The category applies to people from the Spanish-speaking Caribbean—especially Puerto Rico and Cuba—Mexico, Central America, and South America. It also includes people who have been living in the United States all of their lives, and people descended from families that were living in territories in the Southwest, which only became part of the United States long after their families had settled in those territories. Conventionally referred to as Hispanic, because of assumptions of shared language, many designees have rejected that term because its reference is to a European language of conquest, which negates the Pre-Columbian dimensions of their culture. Many proudly prefer instead to be called Mexican, for example, or to be allowed to choose a more politically focused designation for themselves, such as "Chicano."

Nevertheless, the outside world experiences the influence of these cultures collectively and, in the tradition of blending all into one for the purpose of discussion, adopts the conventional term *Latino,* more acceptable than Hispanic, but retaining some of the problems of European rootedness as well as containing a gendered suffix (*Latino* is masculine, *Latina* feminine). (Similar problems of the inadequacy of terms of collective designation apply to the term *Asian American* in the next section of the chapter, and so we acknowledge here being able to find no way out and use that collective term self-consciously, trusting that it makes some sense to refer to the general case.)

The number of Latinos grew by more than 60 percent between 1990 and 2000 to 35.3 million, surpassing the number of African Americans somewhat earlier than had been predicted. Latinos are a visible and growing urban presence, especially in the cities of the Southwest, but also in other large metro areas, such as Chicago, Miami, and New York. Their visibility has caused many non-Latinos to jump to conclusions about illegal immigration. While estimates of the number of undocumented immigrants vary considerably, there is no question that the vast majority of Latinos are native to the United States or have immigrated legally. The evidence is that not only are Latinos heterogeneous in their places of origin, but also that they are sharply stratified. While some have experienced mobility, large numbers are absorbed into the ranks of the urban poor. They continue to face prejudice and discrimination.

For Latinos, as for African Americans, a substantial improvement in the life chances of a fraction tends to obscure the fact that conditions have not measurably improved for most. A lead article in the market-oriented *American Demographics* shouts "Vivan Los Suburbios!" According to the 1990 U.S. Census about 43 percent of Latinos lived in metropolitan suburbs, and they made up 23 percent of the 15.3 million people added to the suburban population in the 1980s (Frey and O'Hare 1993, 32). However, the United States Department of Housing and Urban Development (HUD) reported (1979b) that in comparison to the general population, nearly twice the proportion of Latinos are inadequately housed. Findings by HUD also show that Latinos in major cities with large Latino populations, such as Dallas and Denver, were routinely discriminated against by rental agents and real estate brokers in the 1980s (Newburger 1984, 8–12).

As was the case with earlier immigrant groups, cities have quickly come to reflect the cultural influence of the new immigrants. The life of some large cities of the United States, and large sections of many others, has been transformed and enriched by the Latino cultural presence. Los Angeles is proclaimed by some to be the capital of Mexican America (Steiner 1974, 141). New York reflects the culture of its large Puerto Rican population and other Latin and Caribbean influences. However, it is the city of Miami, conceded by the president of Ecuador in 1979 to be "the capital of Latin America," that has undergone the greatest transformation. Entrepreneurs who left Cuba in the wake of Fidel Castro's revolution settled in the Miami area and provided the impetus for the growth of a heterogeneous Latino economic and cultural community there. In addition to recent Cuban refugees, the Miami area has now attracted Latinos of all national origins. "The one-time winter vacation destination of the East Coast is now the nexus of trade that extends through all of Central and South America and much of the Caribbean." In the 1970s, it became the site of the annual Trade Fair of the Americas and was second only to New York City as a location for out-of-state and international banks (Burkholz 1980, 45). Regardless of whether they have participated in the new prosperity or been pushed aside by it, members of the non-Latino population have found themselves ethnically transformed, by local definition, into "Anglos."

Latinos have become a strong and active political force as their numbers have grown in various cities. Effective grass-roots organizing has created an important voting bloc in the Sunbelt. In southwest Texas, the political machinery familiar to Chicagoans and New Yorkers of an earlier era reemerged in the 1980s, referred to as *la maquinaria* (Hernandez 1983, 132–135). In the very close 2000 presidential election, Latino votes in the Southwest and Florida were correctly seen as crucial by both major political parties.

The status of Latinos as an urban minority seems to be at a critical juncture. If an increase in numbers and visibility is indeed a key factor in intensifying prejudice and discrimination, then there are two key factors in determining whether the future holds increased assimilation or increased stigmatization for this group. The first is the perceived long-term effectiveness of the illegal alien control laws. The other factor will be the form that the international trade agreement between Canada, Mexico, and the United States eventually takes and the largely unforeseeable consequences of its implementation. If it stems the flow of immigration, legal and illegal, from the South, it will relieve tensions. If it is perceived to do so by causing a large-scale transfer of industrial work to Mexico, that will likely increase prejudice and scapegoating against all Latinos. At any rate, differences in the cross-border standards of living will certainly remain. Given the economic realities of the situation, the future status of Latinos in the United States lies partly in the hands of the poor populations of Mexico, who are separated from the opulent economy to the north by a permanently permeable border, and partly in the hands of those groups and individuals in the United States who, for whatever ideological, economic, or political purposes, find this an exploitable population or issue.

Asian Americans and the Problem of Scapegoating

The Asian population of some urban areas in the United States has grown considerably within the past two decades. In 1965, the restrictions in the immigration laws that had long discriminated against Asians were modified. The limited acceptance of refugees from Southeast Asia beginning in the mid-1970s also contributed to the growth in numbers and visibility. The projected 12.5 million Asian Americans and Pacific Islanders in 2005 will include 61 percent foreign-born, among them considerable numbers of Chinese, Koreans, and Southeast Asians.

The outflow of investment capital from Hong Kong, in anticipation of the incorporation of the territory by China in 1997, had found its way into Chinatowns around the world, and these continue to expand. In the 1980s and 1990s, the Chinatown in lower Manhattan spilled over its historical boundaries, and the upscale transformation of properties and increased costs of living and of doing business have driven many residents to found new Chinese American enclaves elsewhere in the city. Meanwhile, many other groups of newly arrived Asians are transforming the cultures of residential neighborhoods and retail locations. The smuggling of illegal Chinese immigrants became big business for Chinese organized crime. Several incidents involving stranded and detained ships crowded with undocumented passengers bound for the United States brought this flow of illegal immigrants to the attention of the public by the mid-1990s.

Asians were subjected to discrimination, harassment, and brutality in the early days of immigration. Prejudice and discrimination flared again during and after World War II. Anti-Asian sentiments arose again, briefly, with the arrival of the Southeast Asians following the end of the U.S. military actions in Vietnam. In 1975, the *New York Times* (May 2, 1975, 17) reported the results of a national poll in which 54 percent of the respondents said that those fleeing what had been South Vietnam should not be permitted to enter the United States. The typical respondent was concerned that the refugees would become a welfare burden and would place further pressure on an already stressed employment market. Yet the hostility to the acceptance of refugees seldom exploded into overt conflict because official government policy moved to defuse the potential problem. Refugees were scattered in family-size units throughout the country. This policy was designed to prevent Southeast Asians from becoming a conspicuous minority in any one location. Efforts were made to find sponsors to help settle, house, train, and employ or find employment for new arrivals in order to make their transition as smooth and unobtrusive as possible. Especially in smaller communities, the policy of refugee diffusion caused many to experience bitter loneliness. On the whole, however, economic adjustment was rapid. Within two years, 94.5 percent of employable refugees were employed. The public position adopted by the AFL-CIO was that these jobs were the ones rejected by other segments of the population (Wain 1981, 188–189). In fact, Southeast Asians have successfully competed at a wide range of occupational and income levels, although many had to accept employment, especially initially, that was neither commensurate with their training nor comparable to the positions they held before dislocation.

Korean immigrants to the United States have been arriving quietly, and when possible have preferred self-employment in typically small-scale enterprise in the big city. New York City's Broadway between 31st and 23rd Streets became one of several American "Koreatowns" in the late 1970s, and featured a concentration of Korean restaurants and other businesses that catered to both the Korean and general populations (Kim 1981, 103–104, 108–112). Korean grocers and shopkeepers have become a familiar fixture in most large cities, especially in areas with minority concentrations. Their economic niche is that of the recently arrived entrepreneur, the small family business in the poorer neighborhoods.

Resentment against Asians began to increase in the United States during the 1980s. To Americans in general, Asians provided a focus, however displaced or illogical, for resentment over the eroding status of the United States in the world economy and for what that eroding status meant in the loss of jobs and national pride. Foreign competition became an offhanded explanation for deindustrialization, and Asians became a target of resentment against foreign competitors. This is the classic process of scapegoating, blaming society's problems on a group that can be easily identified and victimized. As the incidence of violence against people of color and immigrants in New York City increased, the city's Human Rights Commissioner said, "I sense that immigrants are being scapegoated for a lot of our problems. A certain kind of xenophobic bigotry has come out of the closet" (*New York Times*, December 11, 1992, A18). All identifiable immigrant groups came in for attack in the most recent wave of U.S. nativism, but Asians were especially targeted for scapegoating due to the success of the economies of Japan, Taiwan, and South Korea.

Japanese Americans have achieved the greatest social mobility and economic assimilation of all Asian Americans. Yet they are particularly wary of an increase in anti-Asian sentiment, due to the success of the Japanese economy and its direct competition with the U.S. economy. There is a tendency among Japanese Americans to attempt to maintain a low profile and not to appear to be directly connected with Japan-based firms. Japanese Americans took offense at the too frequent racist statements made by Japan's public officials, fearing that these statements and any worsening tensions over trade policy would make them a particular target of anti-Asian resentment and acts of violence (*Far Eastern Economic Review*, November 22, 1990, 36).

The plight of Korean immigrants is particularly notable because while they are subjected to anti-Asian prejudice by the white majority, they are also disdained by minority groups in the neighborhoods where they do business, particularly in black neighborhoods. The tension between African Americans and Korean Americans is conditioned by the economic role that Koreans typically play in poor communities and also based on cultural misunderstandings that may grow into open conflict because of a particular incident or set of local incidents. A series of slights, daily angry confrontations over rigid business policies or, more dramatically, a shooting of a young person during a robbery attempt, have all brought black and Korean groups into open conflict in New York, Philadelphia, Chicago, and, most notably, South Central Los Angeles. During the riots in Los Angeles in 1992 following the trial of the officers implicated in the Rodney King beating, Korean businesses were the primary targets of looting and arson. A year later, as the federal rights trial of the four officers implicated in the beating was drawing to a close, Korean business owners were arming themselves and vowing to save their businesses should there be a repeat of the civil disorders. There was not.

In poor neighborhoods, blacks are resentful of Korean retailers, saying that they overcharge, are rude, take over black businesses, and take dollars away from black communities. They charge that Korean merchants give little in return and that they fail to hire local people to work in their shops. Koreans respond that blacks misinterpret their politely reserved demeanor, that they buy only properties that are for sale, and that they operate at such low profit margins that they must operate with family members. However, it is reportedly accurate that at least some Korean business owners harbor negative stereotypes toward blacks. In turn, some blacks base their resentment on the mistaken belief that Koreans have somehow been given special assistance by the government in order to purchase their shops at the cost of would-be black business owners (Jo 1992, 399–400). Evidence contradicts this belief: A comparison of metropolitan areas shows a positive correlation between the number of shops owned by immigrants and the number owned by blacks in the same areas (Muller 1993, 192).

The misunderstandings and resentments are deep and will be difficult to resolve. The Korean merchants of Chicago hired their own mediator to improve relationships between the merchants and the communities in which they operate. The mediator, a black woman, reported that before she identified herself and her mission, she encountered in Korean shops the kinds of policies and demeanors that black customers complain about (*New York Times*, June 2, 1993, A7).

Asian Americans offer an example of the dynamism and complexity of ethnic group and minority group statuses. Asian Americans are culturally and geographically diverse in origin, but in the United States there are developing tendencies toward a pan-Asian identity. The tendency is reinforced in part by the prejudices of non-Asians.

Many Chinese, Japanese, Korean, and Vietnamese occupy high status and highly remunerated positions in the United States. Three decades ago, it was possible to write of Asian-American groups almost entirely in terms of their cultural (ethnic) distinctiveness. During the 1980s and 1990s, they came much closer to conforming to the politically defined status of minority groups because their existence became politicized. For these groups, minority status is not so much due to their growing urban presence, though that is a factor, as to events in the wider world that make them a symbol of an American "problem." Asian Americans may find it difficult to influence the outcome of their marginal status between that of cultural identity group and politically stigmatized minority group. The outcome depends primarily on what changes are forthcoming in the economic fortunes of the United States, and how these are perceived to be related to external events, most particularly, to policies and economic fortunes in Asia. As the sporadic episodes of Asian bashing that have taken place to date demonstrate, it will make little difference whether the victim is of Japanese, Thai, Korean, or Vietnamese extraction. To the people who select the victims, all Asians look alike.

To the extent immigrant groups can affect their status, Asians face the classic no-win dilemma of the urban immigrant. Ordinarily, if the newcomers prosper, their success is regarded with the conviction that it came at the cost of profits, jobs, or taxes to the native-born. If they fail, their failure confirms the suspicion of immigrant inferiority (Cafferty et al. 1983, 70–71).

Native Americans and the City

In the past five decades, the Census Bureau has recorded a dramatic increase in the Native American population, and most of this growth has been within the urban population, which now contains the majority of Native Americans. According to the 1950 census, there were 380,000 Native Americans: Projections by the Census Bureau in the 1990s anticipated a total of 2.4 million in 2000 (actual count of the 2000 Census is not available at this writing). This increase is due largely to changes in enumeration criteria (the Bureau adopted the method of self-identification in 1960) and to a resurgence in interest and pride in Native American identity—involving "ethnic switching" in which people who had not identified themselves as Indians in earlier censuses choose to do so (Gonzales 1998). Whatever the basis of the apparent population explosion—five times more Indians were counted in 1990 than in 1950—it had little impact on the visibility of Native Americans as an ethnic minority. In 2000, self-identified Indians still made up less than one percent of the total population of the United States.

The increase in the *urban* American Indian population is the result of a combination of factors. The Bureau of Indian Affairs adopted a relocation program in 1952 that produced fairly large scale migrations from reservation lands and contributed to increases of Native American populations in such cities as Chicago, Dallas, Denver, Los Angeles, and San Francisco. Underdevelopment of economic opportunities on tribal or council lands and poor educational and medical services at home made the city relatively attractive for many others and pushed them to migrate. Often the target of migration was an urban area near large Indian lands, but there has also been a general southeasterly nationwide movement of the native population. Washington, D.C., had the highest rate of growth of native peoples during the 1980s, attracting especially those with higher education to government jobs (Shumway and Jackson 1995).

The minority status of Native Americans is well established in their treatment historically. They were subject to conquest, genocide, relocation, containment on isolated reservations, and cultural reprogramming, ostensibly in the interest of assimilating them into Euro-American society—a society that regarded them with negative stereotypes and did not welcome their participation. Unlike other U.S. minorities, their minority status is not reinforced by a highly visible urban presence. Although several large cities (including Chicago, Los Angeles, San Francisco, New York, and Phoenix) have substantial Native American populations, the proportion is so small relative to the total U.S. urban population that, as an urban minority, they receive little notice. The largest number of Native Americans in any city live in Los Angeles, but they still make up less than one percent of the region's population. The highest proportion live in Oklahoma City, where Indians make up 4.8 percent of the population. Native Americans remain subject to stereotype and discrimination, but in contrast to other high-visibility urban minorities, their urban presence has done little to directly enhance their minority status in the eyes of non-Indians. It has, however, modified their ethnic culture and consciousness, and urban-based efforts to find an effective political voice have contributed importantly to these changes.

In the early 1970s, there was a resurgent interest among urban Native Americans in their ethnic roots. This produced the National Indian Youth Council (NIYC) and the American Indian Movement (AIM) and a growing interaction between urban and reservation residents. The political goals of AIM included raising ethnic consciousness and pride, and the forging of a common identity among all Native Americans in Indian culture. The activities and goals of this *urban-based movement*, to the extent that they have created a *pan-Indian identity*, have been interpreted as undermining authentic native cultures (Svenson 1980). In this view, to be authentically Indian (Native American) means to have remained Sioux, Apache, Hopi, Navajo, and so on. The idea of a single Native American culture has no basis in tradition; instead, it grew out of the perceived necessity to mobilize all Native Americans into a single movement in order to make them a national political force. In this case, and from this perspective, to the extent that *urban* ethnicity becomes the basis of identity for Native Americans, it will replace traditional, autonomous identities among the various indigenous ethnic groups. However, it has also been argued that cultural identity, in the form of ethnicity, is ever-evolving, not static. As we have noted earlier in the chapter, ethnicity is often a multilayered set of group affinities, not a choice of either-or. The "new Indians" that emerged out of the urban political arena and affected the views of Native American culture that had evolved on the reservation had both a *supratribal* and a traditional tribal identity. "Indian" identity did not simply replace tribal identification, but interacted with it to promote emergent cultural forms on the reservation that were in part a product of the urban experience. "A number of researchers report that the Indian pride and rights movement of the 1960s and 1970s led to renewed interest in tribal history and sparked tribal activism that was often led by reservation returnees from urban activist experiences" (Nagle and Snipp 1993, 220).

Urban experience, however, has also led to tensions between the urban migrant and reservation-based populations. Those living in cities may still participate in council affairs, and these younger, more traveled members have often become impatient with reservation leadership's reluctance to confront more aggressively the United States Bureau of Indian Affairs. Urban tribal members are at times seeking different policies than rural members; urbanites have sought the extension of programs and benefits to cover non-reservation populations, while rural members have sought long-term reservation development (Officer [1971] 1984, 61–62).

Other conflicts of identity and purpose emerge as natives reside for generations away from tribal lands. The rate of intermarriage between Native Americans and non-Native Americans is much higher in the city than in homelands. This has produced generations of *mixed-bloods*, a term of prejudice among many Native Americans who disapprove of intermarriage. When the adult children of these marriages become interested in seeking their ethnic roots, their lack of native physical characteristics and cultural knowledge makes their acceptance as tribal members problematic, and this is true in both rural and urban Native American communities whose members are suspicious of "wannabes" and usurpers (Krouse 1999). There is more at stake than simple gatekeeping here, more than simple prejudice against absorbing "outsiders." A number of government programs have been set aside to partially compensate Native Americans for their losses as the United States absorbed their lands and resources, and to assist native peoples in overcoming generations of imposed isolation and exclusion. People who have identified themselves as Native Americans all their lives and who have lived with the consequences of minority status regard the motives of newcomers with suspicion (Gonzales 1998). Also, some reservation-based native peoples have amassed substantial wealth through gambling casinos and, to varying extents, other private enterprises in which tribal members claim a share. In such situations, long-lost members who find a new interest and can lay claim to a native identity based on having a native grandmother or great grandfather may be regarded with some doubt. What it means to establish oneself as a Native American—moreover to be recognized as such by insiders and outsiders, so long after the era of conquest, displacement, and the subsequent pressures for cultural assimilation—is to engage in a process of contested identity. This is especially so for urban Native Americans.

Earlier in this chapter, we discussed the manner in which European immigrants who came to the cities of the United States had to renegotiate their cultural heritage to suit their new circumstances. Native Americans are currently making those same adjustments. A few examples may illustrate the process. The city of Phoenix exemplifies some of the complexity hidden in the phrase "Native American community." Many native cultures are represented in the metropolitan area: Navajo, Pima, Apache, Hopi, O'Odaham, and others. Traditionally, native identities in the area were based on these separate groupings. Over time, however, some have subordinated their traditional tribal-based affiliations in favor of associating themselves with the more sophisticated, politically powerful, and urban-based pan-tribal council, which has received philanthropic and federal support. Since the mid-twentieth century, existing native ethnic divisions have been cross-cut by an economic division as some individuals and families became upwardly mobile and joined the middle class while the majority remained blue collar and working class. The relationship between native and non-native communities is, on the surface, contradictory. The native subcultural presence imparts some of the city's distinctive character. Native culture has been an important tourist attraction, with Indian-themed crafts shops and galleries catering primarily to the tourist trade, but native peoples remain the subject of negative stereotyping by the white population (Liebow 1989, 68–70). As is the case with immigrant groups, the dominant culture finds idealized and mythologized elements of exotics more agreeable than their personal presence.

The image conveyed here is that of the typical U.S. ethnic process, involving cultural adaptation to the immediate environment: In this case, specific tribal affiliations interact with a pan-tribal identity that is a product of the urban environment. Some groups, such as the Navajo, may be able to hold themselves apart from the tribal melt-down because they have the large numbers—what Fischer (1975) referred to as the *critical mass* (Chapter 4)—to maintain a distinctive and separate identity. But, while the process is hardly complete for any of the tribes represented in the Phoenix area (Liebow 1989, 90–91), the ethnic identity known as "Indian" or "Native American" emerges despite resistance, as have the "Asian American" or "Latino" categorizations, which also subsume a diversity of cultural origins.

The members of some native cultures in the Americas have all but lost direct contact with the past and provide examples of the power of the urban environment to give rise to highly modified or novel ethnic experiences. One example of this comes from Chile, in South America, and another from New England. Urbanization threatens the practices and beliefs of the Mapuche Indians of Chile. Almost half the population was living in cities by the late nineties, their communal lands had been divided and privatized by the national government in 1979, and that same decree declared that the Mapuche no longer existed. The remnants of their culture are undervalued by the nation, and most are content to be known by Spanish rather than Indian names, in order to avoid the lower status of anything associated with being Indian. However, some Mapuches in cities and rural areas had the feeling expressed by one that "something lacked inside of us." Those who were interested founded formal organizations to keep their culture alive by holding workshops and classes on Mapuche culture, and they go to great lengths to observe traditional ceremonies that need to be modified in order to work in urban areas (Orellana-Rojas 1998). What will emerge from these efforts in time? Will it be a sustained Mapuche traditional culture? Or a culture that is as much a novel product of the urban environment?

A similar but in many ways more complete attempt to eradicate a culture was visited upon the Narragansett Indians who lived along a section of the New England coast in the path of development of the earliest European towns. This group's territories were among the first to be engulfed by urban settlement. The state of Rhode Island in 1880 officially "detribalized" what little remained of the surviving community and sold off its few remaining holdings, just about 100 years before the same thing happened to the Mapuche. But by the 1930s, a half century after their official demise, descendants of mixed Indian, African, and European ancestry began an effort to revive the Narragansett's memory of their native heritage. Since then, the organization has held annual celebrations and meetings. As members consult museums and historical sources to aid them in reconstructing a picture of the past, "the modern Pow Wow is becoming more markedly ethnic. Indian dances, either self-invented or adapted from those performed by other groups, Indian clothing such as Plains area headdresses and beadwork, and names specifically introduced for this occasion, replaced the square dancing, conventional clothing and mainly English names of earlier years" (Simmons 1981, 46–48).

The Mapuche and Narragansett offer us parallel examples of groups struggling to assert native cultural identities in an urban world far removed from the environments that originally gave rise to their societies. Especially in the case of the Narragansetts, the cultural content of the heritage they present to themselves and the world is as much a deliberate invention as it is a historical recollection. It is full of errors of memory and odd borrowed pieces. Is it ethnicity at all? In fact, the participants act like the members of any other urban ethnic group, trying to establish a sense of where they have come from and what that means for who they are. The only ones who can really answer such questions of meaning are the ones involved in the experience. As Gordon (1964, 23–24) taught us, ethnicity is not about cultural content; the urban context is bound to modify that. Rather, ethnicity is "a shared feeling of peoplehood."

A Conclusion: The Recruitment of Labor and the Creation of Minorities

As economic conditions change, the status of large categories of urban immigrants changes as well. During periods in which growth and prosperity bring about labor demand, industry welcomes—often actively recruits—workers from poorer regions or countries. Here the motives of industry and the preference of the existing labor force are fundamentally opposed. Immigrants are readily perceived as cheap replacement labor for native-born workers, or as a scab force of potential strike-breakers—a way in which immigrant labor has often been used. In either event, the new immigrants are typically left largely on their own to bear the wrath of the angry majority. To make matters worse, rapid industrial expansion is seldom accompanied by the construction of adequate, inexpensive housing for the growing labor force. All of these factors lead to tensions and often open conflict between the new and old workers. Even where tensions are managed during periods of growth and labor expansion, ensuing periods of economic recession and unemployment exacerbate animosities. Immigrant workers are blamed for unrest, for unemployment itself, and for the burden that their disproportionately unemployed numbers place on taxpayers. The reactionary impulses bred by hard times invite all to blame the one most easily despised and least capable of self-defense, the victim, the newcomer.

Such conclusions flow readily enough from the historical experience of certain groups of urban immigrants in the United States—most recently, African Americans, Latinos and Asians. An examination of the immigrant labor history of European countries in the past 50 years invites similar conclusions.

France, Germany, and Britain are among those Western European nations that have been liberal importers of foreign labor. In France, workers from North and West Africa and the poorer countries of Southern Europe were recruited for work in the secondary labor market (unskilled and unstable employment) that was avoided by native workers. The end of the brief era of midcentury prosperity and industrial expansion found French slums dominated by the foreign-born, and riots against Arab and African aliens occurred (Cross 1983, 223). Beginning in 1955, West Germany recruited two million workers from North Africa, Southern Europe, and Turkey to keep up with its labor demands. By the mid-1970s, as the period of economic demand was weakening in Germany as elsewhere, conflict among foreigners and native workers took place over jobs, inexpensive housing, and access to public services (Reimann and Reimann 1979, 66, 80). In the case of Great Britain, the influx of subjects and former subjects of the empire began also in the 1950s, a period of economic growth; but this was also a period of severe, continuing urban housing shortages. These combined conditions led quickly to confrontations between newcomers and natives. As elsewhere, conservative politicians exploited the fear of foreigners and fanned resentments (Studlar 1979, 89–91).

In the 1970s, increasing recognition throughout the major European labor-importing countries of the "problem" nature of the immigrant population was heightened by the fact that there were substantial concentrations of immigrants in certain cities or regions of host countries (Rogers 1985, 14). The economic uncertainty of the 1980s saw a continuation of conflicts that had emerged in the 1970s in Europe, with the lines drawn between the estimated 12 million immigrants and Europeans whose governments and major industrial interests had failed to consider realistically the long-range consequences of the large numbers of immigrant workers who would be attracted by recruitment programs. Their parents may have been regarded as visitors of uncertain duration in the countries where they settled, expected to return "home" at some point, but the new generation emerged as a European minority.

The 1990s were a period of reaction in Europe, as right-wing extremists and hate groups attacked foreigners and as far-right political voices railing against foreign labor drove the political center to the right. In part, the reactionary movement received impetus from the large numbers of asylum seekers and political refugees, people dislodged from their home countries by political and economic changes that have swept through the Eastern European nations. By 1993 Germany had absorbed 5.2 million foreigners, France 3.6 million, and England 1.8 million. Governments began to bribe the foreign-born with payments to return to their countries of origin.

In the mid-1990s, there were many well-publicized attacks on immigrants in European nations, including house-burnings in Germany. West Germany had welcomed "guest workers" since the rebuilding boom eras, beginning in the 1950s: "No one complained about too many foreigners in 1955" (Light 1996, 61). With the reunification in 1989 and the surplus of cheap East German labor, however, the German government in May 1993 ended its open-borders policy and severely restricted further immigration. In the same month, the French Parliament also placed severe restrictions on immigration, especially from non-European nations. Light (1996) reminded us that immigration policy, whether in Europe or the United States, represents a balancing act. Governments are willing to risk the potential public dissatisfaction over the admission of immigrants who don't conform physically or culturally to the popular nationalist image of itself. In periods of prosperity, when it is easier to argue that admitting cheap foreign labor is a relative advantage to citizens who can take better jobs, the racial issue is dormant. But in periods of economic downturn, when competition between citizens and immigrants is more graphic, the racial issue surfaces among the general population, and leaders must follow or be replaced. The movement to have English declared the official language of the United States, Proposition 187 in California, and alarming right-wing political movements in Europe and the United States are all indications that the lesson of overcoming the fear of changes wrought by immigration is a lesson that must be relearned by every generation. The question for the future—a future where communication and economic integration on a global level will render national borders all but obsolete—is whether the inevitable increase in the mixing of populations will produce a greater or lesser degree of mutual tolerance between peoples of different cultures.

6

PATTERNS AND CONSEQUENCES OF URBANIZATION IN POOR COUNTRIES

The most dramatic story of urbanization today is unfolding in the least urbanized regions of the world. These have the greatest potential for sustained urban growth. Within the last four decades, the urban populations of Africa and Asia have mushroomed, and those of Latin American countries have continued the dramatic growth begun decades earlier. In these areas, urban populations sprawl outward, engulfing surrounding towns and countryside, and the skylines of city centers are transformed by the vertical glass and steel structures of the international style of architecture. By the end of the twentieth century, a substantial majority of the world's largest urban agglomerations (those with populations of over 5 million) were located outside the more industrialized nations. In 1975, there were 21 urban areas with more than 5 million people, and already 11 of them were located in poorer countries. In 1975, there were 5 cities worldwide with 10 million or more people, and 3 of them were located in poorer countries. By 2000, there were 19, and 16 were in the less developed poorer nations. In 2015, there will probably be 23, with all of the newcomers in the less developed nations (United Nations Population Division 1999, 8).

Images of the "Third World" City

Cities throughout the world share certain characteristics in common, yet striking differences are apparent between the cities of the more developed and less developed nations. In every large city, there is an obvious division between the conditions of the wealthiest and poorest people, but nowhere is the contrast between wealth and poverty more dramatically evident than in the cities of the world's poorer nations. This chapter will focus on the major social, political, and economic issues that attend rapid urban growth in poor countries. It also will attempt to convey something of the experience of life in these cities. One terminological difficulty needs to be mentioned at the outset and then set aside rather than resolved: The terms *poor countries* or *less developed nations* are used for nations with widely differing levels of wealth, population size, and global influence. Examples include Haiti, which in 1995 had 7 million people and a gross national product (GNP)—the value of all goods and services produced—equivalent to $250 per person; Mexico, with 89 million people and a GNP of $3,320 per person; and India, an emerging world power, with 929 million people, but a GNP per person of only $320. Until the last decade of the twentieth century, the conventional term for pulling such diversified nations into a single category was the *Third World*. The term had a political connotation that implied that these countries often stood together in their shared interest in opposition to the First World (the wealthy capitalist industrialized powers) and were of strategic importance in the global contention between the First World and the Second World nations (the centrally planned or socialist countries). With the decline of the Second World in the post-Soviet Union era, as China came to play an important role within the capitalist global economy, the Third World terminology lost a lot of its meaning. It is used in this text in juxtaposition with other terms that are equally ineffective for capturing the socioeconomic and political diversity of the regions we use it to describe. The compelling reason for continuing to treat these diverse nations as a unit is that the urban issues they confront—and the urban conditions under which so many millions live their lives—bear important similarities, especially when contrasted with prevailing conditions within the cities of richer nations.

In the cities of poor nations, there *are* large pockets of affluence in the neighborhoods where the families of business and government professionals live. Their wealth is clearly reflected in the size of their homes. Their grounds are manicured by individuals selected from a pool of underemployed labor, and their security is provided by public and private guards. The poor live in slums and shantytowns. The latter are constructed of cardboard, tin, plastic, or any other cast-off material that will serve to cover a section of a roof or wall. The houses of the poor, on the edge of the city, ring the city's modern center and the residential districts of the more affluent.

Early in the morning, the poor can be seen leaving their makeshift shelters to travel in their tens and hundreds of thousands toward the city center, markets, comfortable neighborhoods, and industrial sites, where they will toil to produce a subsistence income or continue the long search for work in the hope of finding a way to subsist. Many make the daily journey on foot, crowding the dusty or muddy paths that flank the roads and highways, which carry the autos of better placed citizens to offices and other business establishments. At dusk the pathways leading back to the slums and distant squatter settlements will be clogged again. It is dangerous to be abroad after dark in many Third World cities, even for the poor.

Although it is true that the less developed nations of the world currently contain two-thirds of the world's population plus the most rapidly growing urban populations and giant cities, the majority of people who read this text will probably never set foot in a Third World city. Most of this chapter will be taken up with a political and economic analysis of Third World urbanization. We begin with a description of Mexico City; Bangkok, Thailand; and Lagos, Nigeria, in

Parts of cities in poor countries look like cities anywhere. Aga Khan walk in Nairobi differs only in detail from similar scenes of cities in the southern United States or Europe. Those visitors who venture beyond the central business districts, however, are quickly reminded of the differences.

order to make the analysis that follows more tangible. No description, especially a brief one, can adequately convey an image of the economic, political, and social energies of the streets, markets, and neighborhoods. The serious student of the city has no alternative but to visit the cities of the poor nations in order to begin to appreciate them.

Mexico City

Because it is one of the three largest urban complexes in the world, Mexico City contains many of the problems of Third World cities in exaggerated proportion. It has serious and perhaps ultimately unmanageable environmental problems; it has an international, and perhaps deserved, reputation as a wild city; and it provides an enormous stage for a rich, colorful social and street life.

> *It is one of the poorest cities in the world; over half the population is un- or underemployed. Street vendors hawking black-market Levis and fake Rolexes, pirate videos and cassettes, baby clothes, underwear and leather jackets crowd virtually every major thoroughfare. Mexico City is also one of the most polluted*

*cities in the world. . . . During the winter months, a zinc-colored pall hangs over
the city like the sky in a Hollywood rendition of a post-nuclear world. (Martinez
1995, 35)*

Mexico City has roughly 18 million people, about the same number as Bombay (Mumbai) or São Paulo. Estimates of Mexico City's population vary depending on which districts are included or excluded. Also, the rapidly growing portion of the population that lives in makeshift dwellings in unofficial neighborhoods without fixed street names or addresses has to be estimated rather than counted.

*The apparently haphazard stacking of houses on hillsides in the cities of poorer countries
may betray the squatter origins of a neighborhood. Over time, squatter housing is structurally upgraded by the resident "owners," and more or less permanent title to the property
is eventually established.*

In addition to the air pollution, which regularly exceeds the international guideline for safety, there is another serious environmental problem. This is the problem of subsidence: Mexico City is sinking. The city gets much of its water from underground wells, and between 1940 and 1985 the growing need for water pumped from hundreds of wells under the city caused portions of the downtown area to sink by over 20 feet. Water is pumped out twice as fast as the natural rate of replacement. The city's water problems include treating and disposing of wastewater, and keeping sewage and drinking water separated. Subsidence and increasing water demand, in the absence of serious conservation and monumental engineering efforts, will compound the problem in the near future (Sletto 1995). Environmentalists have commented that, "Judging from the state of both air and water resources . . . one can conclude that the megalopolis of Mexico City is highly unsustainable in its present condition" (Ezcurra and Mazari-Hiriart 1996).

Politics are dramatic. On October 2, 1996, a federal police commander who was investigating drug traffickers was assassinated upon arrival in the city: His taxi was sprayed by automatic weapon fire as he left the airport (*New York Times*, October 3, 1996). Judges, lawyers, and political candidates have been murdered in recent years by factions opposed to their positions or policies. In January 1997, street sweepers were in the 97th day of a hunger strike when police forcibly broke up the strikers' demonstration and campsite, ostensibly for the strikers' own good. The official reaction was likely conditioned by the fact that there had been more than 3,000 protest marches on behalf of various causes in the city during the previous year (*New York Times*, January 20, 1997). Crime is a fairly serious problem. In a newspaper poll of 200 residents in 1996, 88 percent reported they or a family member had been victims of crime in the previous 12 months (Goldman 1996). Whatever sampling bias might have been involved, the high rate of victimization reflected in the survey reinforces the general impression that crime is an important component of the range of informal economic activities by which the poor manage to get by. Police tactics in handling suspects, while not as violent as in some large cities, like Kingston, Jamaica, or São Paulo, Brazil, do not meet professional standards (Chevigny 1996). It remains to be seen whether the change in national government as the result of the loss of the Institutional Revolutionary Party (PRI) in the 2000 Presidential election will be sufficient to reduce routine political corruption, alter the tradition of the often violent resolution of political differences, and begin to address the environmental and social problems that face Mexico City.

The vacillations of the national economy, as Mexico settles uneasily into its place in the international economic order, have affected unevenly the economic fortunes of the population of *la capital*. In 1994 the national currency (the peso) was devalued, and in the following year standard measures of national economic growth registered a 7 percent decline. In 1996 the economy rebounded, and by 1997 Mexico was enjoying a general recovery with rapidly increasing stock market averages and some concern that the peso had become too strong against the currencies of other nations—a condition that would make Mexican exports and labor more expensive relative to the international competition. At the end of the twentieth century, Mexico's economy was robust, growing at a rate of 7.8 percent in the first half of 2000. Since Mexico signed the North American Free Trade Agreement (NAFTA) in 1994 with Canada and the United States, exports more than doubled to $135.9 billion in 1999. But the economic recovery did little to improve the conditions of the Mexican poor. The official government position is that 40 million of Mexico's 100 million people were poor in 1998, 26 million of them living in extreme poverty. Critics of these figures say that a more correct estimate is that nearly three-quarters of the population, 72 million Mexicans, live in poverty. The poorest 40 percent of Mexicans received only 12.5 percent of the income earned in the country in 1998—2 percent less than the same segment of the population earned a decade earlier. The richest 10 percent of Mexican households lived on an average income of $6,900 a month in 1998, while the poorest 10 percent of the households got by on an average of $158 a month (Reuters, August 30, 2000, "Rich Get Richer, Poor Get Poorer in Mexico"). This means that Mexico's poor are not the poorest in the world, but at these levels, poverty can be life threatening, especially among urban populations who must bear the higher costs of living. In 1997, it was estimated that one-fifth of Mexican families were too poor to provide adequate food for their children (*New York Times*, August 12, 1997).

Most of the international attention that Mexico City receives focuses on its considerable problems—problems magnified by its standing as one of the three largest cities in the world. What is it like to live in such a place? Opinions vary, but there are those who think that the quality of life is good, and many work to improve conditions and the image of the city. Tepito is a *barrio* in the center of the city—a self-aware "neighborhood" of 120,000 people (Estera 1995). The area is perceived as a slum by officials, and every mayor of the city in succession has threatened to eliminate it. Yet, despite its reputation at midcentury as the worst place in the entire city to live, it has gradually become a thriving community as the result of a determined effort on the part of the people who live and work there. Now, a variety of shops produce and sell a wide range of consumer goods at bargain prices. Local efforts to build a reputation of legitimacy and to rebuild the community have included gaining the assistance of architects who created a rehabilitation plan that won a first-place prize in a worldwide UNESCO competition.

Tepito's successful redevelopment attracted affluent patrons to its shops and markets, but these patrons drew pickpockets whose activities threatened the fragile retail economy of the area. Tepitans established a security system: When a pickpocket was detected, he was seized, his head was shaved, and his shoes were confiscated. Sent running through the barrio in this condition, he would be recognized by others and beaten as he ran. Common thieves are often harshly treated by crowds in Third World cities. In Tepito, residents claim vigilante justice has had the effect of eliminating pickpockets.

Tepito has hundreds of small trade and block associations, and mutual credit societies abound. The area embodies a way of life that goes beyond economic activities, and "Tepito's history and practices have circulated over the entire city. A thousand Tepitos have been born and reborn." The author of the statement concluded that these Tepitos make living in Mexico City clearly superior to life in New York, Tokyo, or Paris (Estera 1995, 68–69). Others agree. Martinez (1995) believed that life in Mexico City compares favorably in many ways to that in Los

Angeles. Characterizing Los Angeles as a place in which people feel isolated and alienated from one another, a place where a sense of community is lacking and races and classes are deliberately separated, Martinez portrayed Mexico City's social and street life as rich, colorful, and inviting to all social classes who are more mingled in activities as well as residence than are the residents of Los Angeles.

Mexico City draws our attention as the gigantic center of a nation of nearly 100 million people. But another important story of urban growth is taking place far from the city, on Mexico's northern border with the United States. In the long run, this northern development may cause a serious erosion of the potential for continued industrial growth and employment opportunities in the central region around Mexico City itself. Migrants from many parts of Mexico have flocked north to such rapidly growing cities as Nogales and Tijuana, on the border; Monterrey, a city of 1.1 million located 120 miles south of Texas; and booming border towns such as Reynosa, near McAllen, Texas, which in August 2000 was drawing up to 300 newcomers a day to work in factories assembling products for export. Under the *maquiladora* plan, companies from the United States build assembly plants in northern Mexico under special tariff agreements. The North American Free Trade Agreement allows U.S. firms to take advantage of Mexico's lower labor costs. The assembly operations of major U.S. companies stand side-by-side with manufacturing operations from all over the world representing the best known consumer brands. Workers move north from regions with fewer employment opportunities and lower wages. The city of Monterrey has prominent employers, such as Johnson & Johnson, Honeywell, and Whirlpool, and in addition the growing city offers employment to migrants as waiters, maids, and construction workers. Unemployment is low, and employers aggressively compete for workers. The Zepeda family moved there from Chiapas, in the South. The husband traded his $32 a week job in Chiapas for a $54 dollar a week construction job in Monterrey. Like other migrants, the Zepedas found everything in the North more expensive, and the increased income only afforded the entire family of four a single room. But they had applied for government-built housing and were happy overall with their move (The Associated Press, August 27, 2000, "Job-Hungry Mexicans Go North").

Mexico competes for international industrial investments with other world regions that have labor surpluses. In contrast to most Third World nations, the economies of a few Asian countries have grown remarkably during the last decade. Those most usually cited are Hong Kong, Singapore, South Korea, and Taiwan. Thailand is a more recent addition to the short list of rapidly growing Third World economies. The region around the capital city, Bangkok, has experienced perhaps the most dramatic economic revolution of all in the past two decades. In fact, the Bangkok region has often been regarded as something of a separate entity from Thailand as a whole, both by international investors and government administrators.

Bangkok

In the mid-1990s rapidly-growing Bangkok, with 7 million people, was 35 times larger than the next largest city in Thailand. The city gained a dual reputation for its accommodating nature as a place for business interests and for its sex industry, which exploits the poverty of young Thai women and the appetites of tourists and business travelers. Bangkok has proven an irresistible target for investors, and its growth has been prodigious. Thai exports, led by computer parts, consumer electronics, and toys, increased at a rate of 29 percent annually from the mid-1980s through 1990, and the economy overall grew at a rate of 8 to 13 percent between 1987 and 1995, which was one of the most rapid growth rates in the world. The elimination of export taxes attracted foreign investors and manufacturers from all over the world (Robinson et al. 1991, 10).

But, in 1997, Thailand and other economies in Southeast Asia experienced a financial crisis that sent shock waves throughout the global economy. Changes in banking policy helped the country's large banks, but undermined the competitiveness of its smaller finance and security companies, and multiple failures in these institutions led to a withdrawal of vital foreign capital. The booming economy had led to speculative overbuilding on a massive scale, and builders could not sell their properties or repay their loans, aggravating the problems of lending institutions in general. Corruption and cronyism also contributed to Thailand's economic difficulties. At the same time, rising labors costs relative to the country's regional neighbors, like Vietnam, threatened to make it a less attractive place for foreign industries to invest (Leightner 1999). Yet, foreign manufacturers located in Thailand actually profited from the country's hardships. When national currencies are devalued, there is a trade-off between local purchasing power and the potential for increasing sales of exports—because the value of the currency of foreign consumers goes up relative to the devalued currency. Also, foreign manufacturers who store their wealth in sounder and more stable currencies (such as dollars, marks, or pounds), but who pay workers in local currencies, benefit from the decline in the value of the local currency (they don't adjust wages with respect to shifting exchange rates). When Thailand's currency, the *baht*, fell in value from 25 to the U.S. dollar to 56 to the dollar, worldwide sales of electronic exports remained stable or improved, and profitability actually increased for foreign firms that could take advantage of the situation (Van Yoder 1999).

The accommodating atmosphere of Bangkok has to date been maintained by a laissez-faire government policy toward urban development. The city grew in the absence of planning, lacking even zoning laws: Industrial, commercial, and residential projects developed side-by-side in a helter-skelter fashion. Within this spatial disarray, the wealth of corporate investors is displayed conspicuously in the buildings they have erected to show off the up-to-date character of their companies. Office towers mimic architectural elements of gothic cathedrals and Roman temples. Condominium developments contain miniature Tudor mansions and rococo villas. One hundred Thai firms joined the competition to create buildings that would leave a memorable impression for their corporate customers, if not lasting aesthetic value. A confusing competition exists among Thai architectural firms to create an authentic Thai style of architecture. One of the most popular firms created a looming structure for the Bank of Asia in the form of a giant robot; another adapted abstract principles borrowed from European cubism to create a building in the form of a human figure sitting at a computer. One critic wrote that the overall effect has "turned fashion into caricature, and given Bangkok the look of a Hollywood film lot" (Scott 1989, 40).

Amidst these structural fantasies, vehicular traffic crawls at 4 miles per hour along major thoroughfares. A new highway system has had little impact on Bangkok's notorious, ever-increasing congestion. The number of vehicles competing for space on city thoroughfares increases annually at a prodigious rate. Traffic, which in the mid-1980s already included 400,000 registered motorcycles (a world record for a single city), creates a noise level that is a health hazard. (It is the local fashion to install a resonator on the exhaust system to enhance the engine's roar.) A survey of traffic police found that 60 percent had suffered some hearing loss; also, more and more traffic control officers were reporting that they experienced weakness and trouble breathing due to the pollution created by auto emissions (*Far Eastern Economic Review,* November 29, 1990, 52–53; Xoomsai 1987, 12).

In addition, hundreds of manufacturing companies that have gone into operation since the 1980s contribute to Bangkok's air quality problems. By 2000, the government had undertaken pollution control measures and was hiring international consulting firms to develop further pollution control programs. The prospect for success was unclear. According to one U.S. firm that received a $7.7 million contract from the Thai government to work with the 500 companies in the one industrial district of Samut Parkarn, emphasis was to be placed on *voluntary* adoption of new, less environmentally damaging technologies (Harrigan 2000).

During its period of rapid growth, it may be unfair to hold Bangkok to standards of orderly development and environmental responsibility that cities in Western nations have also failed to live up to, especially during periods of revolutionary growth. If the conditions that attend the growth of Thailand's premier city are the price to pay for raising the living standards of the mass of its population, then the costs of growth might be understood as the kind of trade-off that must be expected on the frontiers of urbanization.

But the bargain is not so simple. By official estimates, based on restrictive definitions, 25 percent of the people of Bangkok live in slums. These are again the makeshift shelters of the poor, in this case built on stilts above stagnant pools of pollution and mosquito marshes, which are prone to flooding. Susanne Thorbek spent six months living in one of these slums while researching the lives of the women she writes about in her book, *Voices From the City* (1987). The slum was built on the edge of the harbor, and parts of it were at the time targeted for removal by the Port Authority. Thorbek's description is vivid:

> The houses are varied: some are good, built of teak, raised on stilts above the muddy ground; others are just small huts thrown together with odd bits of wood and sacking. There are large puddles and small ponds along the road, and tall coarse grass is growing between them. Rubbish lies everywhere . . . sometimes a pile of scrap metal which the Port Authority or one of the factories in the harbor area have thrown out.
>
> People, mostly women and children, are standing or sitting in the ponds washing plastic . . . a little further down the road a herd of the nearby slaughterhouse's cows are grazing. A good, solid, well-kept walkway leads up to my house. It was

built the last time the people were forced to move. . . . There is also a short-cut. Here the walkways are just built from single planks; several are broken and in some places supports have collapsed. When you go along the walkways it is like going through people's living rooms. Most of the houses are open out toward the walkways and groups of women, with an occasional man and many children, sit talking. (38)

Most of the women who lived in the slum had worked in the export factories at some time. Thorbek's subjects resented the typical conditions of factory work. Their supervisors were authoritarian; they were watched constantly and not allowed to talk with each other; and they often had to pay a deposit on the industrial machinery at their workstation in case they damaged it. If they were let go before the end of the sixth-month trial employment period, they lost the damage deposit. There was no accident insurance. At the time of her study (the late 1970s or early 1980s), child labor laws and legislated maternity provisions were widely disregarded (Thorbek 1987, 52–58).

The effectiveness of legislation and enforcement procedures for protecting Thai industrial workers remain in question. In May 1993, a factory that manufactured dolls for export burned to the ground in Bangkok. More than 200 people were killed and over 500 injured. Statements by government officials indicated that the factory had ignored warnings to improve safety, while company officials responded that they were in full compliance with existing government building and safety codes. Most of the dead and injured were young women (*New York Times,* May 12, 1993, 2).

BOX 6-1   Working Conditions in Poor Countries

Since 1996, when a company associated with television talk-show host Kathy Lee Gifford was accused of labor violations in Honduras, the term *sweatshop* reemerged as part of the popular vocabulary in North America. People have become generally aware that some of the familiar brand name items that they have in their homes and on their person, purchased from high-priced retail outlets and discount chains alike, are tainted by the inhumane and exploitative conditions under which they were produced. Some are produced in the United States and other economically advanced nations, but systematic forces of global profit-seeking drive manufacturers to seek the absolute lowest paid laborers in the world, and these, of course, are found in the greatest abundance in the poorest countries. There, foreign capital, in the form of industrial investments, joins forces with national governments to insure that the conditions

of labor that drew foreign investment in the first place do not change sufficiently to drive it away.

Barbie dolls and Disney Productions cartoon characters are produced at plants in Bangkok. Thousands of young women work in the labor-intensive production process of sorting, sewing, and assembling the toys under what are reportedly health-threatening conditions. Common ailments relating to working with and around hazardous materials in the hot and dusty plant atmosphere include hair loss and respiratory problems. Workers, in 1997, were earning $4 or $5 a day, from which they had to purchase uniforms, scissors, and optional protective masks. The medical doctor who headed Thailand's National Institute of Occupational and Environmental Medicine was removed from her job when she raised serious concerns about occupational hazards. She was reportedly told that her investigation

Continued

BOX 6-1 *Continued*

of large international investors was potentially damaging to her country and to its workers. The workers themselves, young women in their teens and twenties, are fearful of speaking out about health concerns because they believe they will lose their jobs, or worse. While their pay is meager, they are using part of it to support parents who remain in the areas from which the young women have migrated and to keep younger siblings in school (Foek 1997).

Capital is often described as "hyper mobile" in today's global marketplace: It can be moved quickly in response to information about opportunities for profit maximization. Wherever manufacturing operations require a high degree of hand labor, the wage of industrial workers is a key factor in the production process. In industries where investment in buildings is a relatively small part of the overall cost of production, where construction costs are subsidized by welcoming governments, or where lower labor costs elsewhere mean that the cost of moving will quickly be made up in savings on wages, the response of manufacturing firms has been described as a race to the bottom, a race to where the world's lowest labor costs are located. When workers in the Barbie doll plant in Bangkok were making $4 to $5 a day, workers in Vietnam were receiving $2 a day from a manufacturer subcontracted to produce Nike running shoes. The asset of such poor countries in the global marketplace is the poverty of their workers. Governments are mindful of the competition for foreign capital and hostile to the formation of labor organizations that would undermine the country's position in the world by improving workers' conditions. In 1997, Haitian T-shirt stitchers earned 36 cents an hour; workers who stitched soccer balls in Jalandhar, India, made 35 cents per ball. It doesn't take much to move these kinds of operations to another country with even lower wages. A 1997 Canadian labor policy survey of 98 companies with manufacturing operations or subcontractors in poor countries received a less than 50 percent response rate (despite repeated callbacks). Only six respond-

ing companies (Apple Canada, Hudson's Bay Company, Cambior, Inc., Pratt and Whitney, Hydro-Quebec, and Ontario Hydro) had ethical codes that permitted monitoring by noncompany observers (*Canada and the World Backgrounder,* December, 1997, 25–27).

The fact that sweatshop conditions and wages are created by the globalizing economy—a remote and uncontrolled "given" force in the world—leads some to conclude that this is a natural order that cannot be productively tinkered with. Kathy Lee Gifford, who became a national spokesperson on behalf of sweatshop workers everywhere, and Clinton administration Labor Secretary Robert Reich were criticized for their opposition to low wages in poor countries. David R. Henderson, writing in *Fortune Magazine* (October 28, 1996), argued that efforts to prevent North American companies from hiring local workers at prevailing wages in poor countries is damaging to the workers and their families. "Take the 31 cents an hour some 13-year-old Honduran girls allegedly earn at 70-hour-a-week jobs. Assuming a 50-week year, that works out to over $1,000 a year. This sounds absurdly low to Americans, but not when you consider that Honduras's GDP per person in 1994 was the equivalent of about $600." It follows from this logic that when you buy a T-shirt, sneakers, or toy manufactured by poor workers, you are helping the workers who made the product.

This is an interesting proposition. If we take it a step further, should we support local labor movements and unionization aimed at increasing wages and improving conditions in places like Bangkok, or do we take the side of governments that these are dangerously unsettling movements that are likely to have locally disastrous consequences? If globalization really holds the promise of a better life for poor workers, how long should we be willing to wait before the promise materializes? More to the point, how long can poor people working in hazardous surroundings afford to wait?

Bangkok illustrates many of the ironies of the Third World city. Under market arrangements, some suffer, struggle, and fail in order for the overall process of expansion and accumulation to succeed. There will be work as long as wages remain low, yet wealth builds an opulent city full of excess around the working poor. Growth promises to continue as long as there are no controls on the shape that the market provides, yet the city threatens to choke on its own success.

Lagos

Lagos, Nigeria provides a somewhat extreme example of the kind of out-of-control urban growth that has characterized urbanization in poor African nations. This is the former capital city of a nation of 117 million people; divided between the Muslim North and Christian South and comprised of over 250 ethnic groups, it has been plagued by threats of secession and civil war, and has enjoyed only a decade of nonmilitary rule since independence from Britain in 1960. The country is rich in oil but the annual income per capita is only $380. Nigeria's government was cited as the "most corrupt" in a survey of 54 governments by the German-based organization Transparency International. A 1991 audit revealed that $18 billion in oil income had vanished without a trace (Morris 1998). It is not surprising that in a nation characterized by corruption that buoys up traditions of interethnic hostility and mistrust, there is a serious dispute over whether the oil revenues should be controlled by the central government or by the peoples of the delta region where the oil is produced (Ejobowah 2000). The move of the national capital from Lagos, located on the coast, to the more central location of Abuja, dampened neither ethnic hostility nor the growth of Lagos.

In the mid-1970s, Lagos had a population of about 2.5 million. A 1991 census recorded a population of 5.6 million, a figure generally considered by experts to represent at most half of the city's inhabitants. While projections are always risky, the United Nations has estimated that the population of Lagos will reach 20 million by 2010 (Jacot 1999), making it one of the largest cities in the world. Given current conditions, the prospect is daunting. Historically, the heart of Lagos was located on an island, which initially concentrated but failed to limit its growth. By 1990, the city had sprawled onto the mainland, rapidly spreading along the coast and inland. The city region includes much swampland and a series of islands linked by congested bridges, and is administered by 20 separate local governments. The 200 poor residential areas scattered along the periphery of the city are without sewers or paved roads. The residences of the wealthy are concentrated on two islands, which are fortified for protection (Jacot 1999). Overbuilding and the relocation of the federal government to Abuja left many modern office structures vacant, and these have continued to lose commercial tenants—both foreign interests divesting their Nigerian operations and domestic companies finding it difficult to support the high rents. Many of the most imposing structures on Lagos's major thoroughfares are half empty and in a state of disrepair (Salami 1999). Lagos has gained a reputation as one of the world's most dangerous cities. Police corruption is generally acknowledged to be rampant. Various law enforcement operations within the city have been militarized, and citizens hire organizations to protect their homes and businesses (Babalola and Adepoju 2000).

Yet people come to Lagos, hundreds of thousands of migrants each year, and they survive there. Half of the city's residents are estimated to be dependent on the informal or underground economy (discussed further later in this chapter) to provide untaxed and unregulated goods and services. In the early 1960s, Marris (1961, 129–131) found that street sellers in Lagos depended on maintaining networks of regular clients in order for their businesses to survive. Thirty years later, Peil (1991, 94–95) described how important informal self-employment was in giving people in poor neighborhoods a livelihood that allowed minimal subsistence. In one poor district of the city, one-fourth of the men and three-fourths of the women were self-employed street traders. All social classes created a demand for prepared foods sold in the marketplaces, door-to-door, and even on the grounds of the local police college where the illegality of the traders (they lack proper licenses) was overlooked. As the city sprawls outward, new arrivals with little cash, in addition to providing their own work, create their own housing out of inexpensive or found materials.

The government policy toward street traders and unauthorized spontaneous housing development has been inconsistent. Periodically, squatter's dwellings are destroyed and informal markets razed, especially when their locations are considered problematic. In 1990, an informal housing district called Maroko was destroyed by the government. The community, which housed an estimated 300,000 people, was located in a low-lying area along the coast. It was visible from Victoria Island, the original heart of Lagos, which has become one of the protected havens of the affluent. People reportedly were killed in the demolition of the eyesore, and many now live in "new Maroko," some distance down the coast, on a site sanctioned by government. In April 1999, Ikosi Market, which reportedly employed 12,000, was destroyed by government forces. The government considered it a firetrap and magnet for criminals. The marketers, who fought back until police reinforcements arrived, estimated that several dozen of their number had been killed and a quarter of the market structures were destroyed (Otchet 1999).

Yet the market was open for business in the following days. The resilience and knack for survival of Lagosins have been noted by observers (Peil 1991, Otchet 1999). In cities like Lagos, for the poorest of the inhabitants, there is no option but to do what one has to each day to get by, which means taking advantage of every informal opportunity and the vast black market tradition of the city. It often means somehow making something from nothing. A man earns $65 a month hauling garbage away for private households and another $55 from salvaging what is reusable. Children fill buckets with water during a downpour and offer to wash the mud from the feet of passersby for a few cents. A man pays $6 to a tanker driver to fill his 100-gallon drum and resells the water by the bucketful (Otchet 1999). At a construction site, wheelbarrows placed under an awning are rented out by the night as sheltered sleeping places. And "area boys"—loose gangs of unemployed young men—look for any opportunity to cash in on a chance to rob, shake down, and extort as one kind of adaptation to a desperate situation where law is ineffective. Because people *can* survive, and because there is a chance to tap into the nation's wealth that is concentrated in Lagos—65 percent of Nigeria's GNP is concentrated there—people will continue to come. In 2010 or 2015, if trends hold, we will be describing a Lagos of 20 million people, perhaps twice its present size. What are the prospects that conditions will have improved for the people living there? What can the local or national government do to improve the situation? These are difficult questions.

These descriptions of Third World cities convey some of the dramatic variety and contradictions that these cities represent. What we need are some conceptual tools for making sense of these images. We turn now to an analysis that provides us with some structural ways to consider urbanization in poor countries.

Migration and Population Growth

Table 6-1 presents population data from selected countries in each of the major underdeveloped regions. These countries have been selected because they represent the substantial differences that exist within the major regions in overall population size, as well as in the level and rate of urbanization. The two right-hand columns indicate how rapidly the urban portion of the national populations increased between 1965 and 1980 and between 1980 and 1998. While the number of years in the two periods are not perfectly equivalent (the latter period is longer by three years), the proportional increase clearly slowed for about half the countries in the 1980 to 1998 period. However, except for Latin America, where urbanization levels have reached or exceeded levels in many European nations, poor countries continue to add rapidly to their urban population at rapid and even accelerating rates. Even where the rate of increase is slowing (for example, Nigeria, Bangladesh, Mexico), larger urban and national population bases in the latter period may mean that more people were added to the cities between 1980 and 1998 than in the earlier 15 years.

Urban population growth is the result of both the natural increase of urban populations (higher birthrates than death rates) and the migration from rural areas. Even though migration contributes a little less than half to the growing numbers in most regions, the characteristics of the migrant population cause it to have an especially significant impact on urban growth. First, the majority of migrants are young adults in the peak reproductive age groups, which increases their potential contribution to urban growth (Todaro [1979] 1984, 16). Second, the migrants arrive as ready participants for the urban labor force; consequently, their arrival places immediate demands on the employment market (Gugler 1986). As a result of sustained migration, a rather small proportion of the adult population was actually born in a Third World city.

The great majority of rural-urban migrants have moved to the cities for economic reasons. Although noneconomic factors may precipitate an individual's decision to migrate, it is the overall imbalance of life chances between rural and urban areas that favors the city and provides the general momentum for movement to urban areas. The relative attractiveness of cities is due to two factors. First, the economic growth strategies of governments during the 1950s and 1960s

TABLE 6-1   Population, Urbanization Levels, and Percent Changes
for Selected Countries

	Total Population in Millions 1998	Percent Living in Urban Areas			Percent Increase in Level of Urbanization	
		1965	1980	1998	1965–1980	1980–1998
Africa						
Kenya	29	9	16	31	78	94
Mali	11	13	19	29	46	53
Nigeria	121	17	27	42	59	55
Ghana	18	26	31	37	19	19
Ivory Coast	14	23	35	45	52	29
Zambia	10	23	40	39	74	−3
Asia						
Bangladesh	126	6	14	23	133	64
Thailand	61	13	17	21	31	24
China	1,239	18	20	31	11	35
Indonesia	204	16	22	39	38	77
India	980	19	23	28	21	22
Pakistan	132	24	28	36	17	29
Malaysia	22	26	42	56	62	33
Philippines	75	32	38	57	19	50
Latin America						
Guatemala	11	34	37	39	9	5
El Salvador	6	32	39	46	8	10
Bolivia	8	40	46	61	15	33
Mexico	96	55	66	74	20	12
Brazil	166	50	66	80	32	21
Chile	15	72	81	85	13	5
Argentina	36	76	83	89	9	7
Venezuela	23	70	79	86	13	9

Source: World Bank 2000, 230–231, World Development Indicators, *www.worldbank.org/data/wdi2000/pdfs/tab3_10.pdf*, 150–154.

featured industrial modernization and metropolitan expansion (Todaro [1979] 1984, 8). Second, the city is more attractive because of the growth of rural populations and the changes in the structure of agriculture (the growing problem of landlessness among rural populations) that, in the most extreme cases, make migration imperative. The decision for most, however, is a matter of weighing the costs and benefits of rural and urban life. Though many face hardship and few prosper, most migrant urbanites are convinced that they have improved their condition (Gugler 1986).

Generally, individual decisions to migrate result in an improvement of personal living standards, but the aggregate effect of millions of such decisions is reflected in high urbanization rates, urban unemployment, and crowding. Growth has created massive unemployment and underemployment, congestion and uncontrolled patterns of settlement, aggravated housing shortages, and an inability on the part of governments to provide adequate services. These conditions have generated both concern and sharp disagreement over the question of whether galloping urbanization in underdeveloped countries is beneficial or detrimental to economic growth and the welfare of the populations involved.

Modernization and Political Economy

Those who study Third World urbanization are divided over the fundamental issue of how to explain the cause of the persistent state of underdevelopment of the poor nations' economies and how to remedy the problem. Analyses proceed from the assumptions of two opposed paradigms, the *modernization* approach and the *political economy* approach. Urbanization plays an important part in both schemes. In the modernization view, urbanization accelerates the diffusion of technological innovation and more efficient social arrangements. According to the diametrically opposed arguments of the political economists, growing cities symptomize the inequality and parasitic domination that characterize the underdevelopment process. It is important to understand the reasoning involved in each approach, and since writers often do not explicitly acknowledge the assumptions upon which their reasoning is based, it is useful to be able to recognize which frame of analysis is being employed.

Modernization

The roots of the modernization school lie deep within classical sociology. What we are considering is not a particular theory, but a paradigm, a general framework of understanding that includes certain widely shared assumptions about how social change proceeds. This framework, reaching back to the work of Tönnies and Durkheim, sees modernization as a progression from simpler to more complex and interdependent forms of association. Change comes about as a society shakes loose from "traditional" technologies and archaic social and economic arrangements. Tradition and modernity are thus seen as polar opposites; as one emerges, the other subsides. In this view, change takes place at different rates in different societies, but eventually all societies will undergo such a transformation, converging toward a similar end point. In contrast to traditional society, which embodies the opposite conditions, modernization involves movement toward an industrial market economy that is characterized by continuous economic growth, the proliferation of bureaucracy, high rates of literacy and formal education, a reduction in inequality, lowered birth and death rates, a decline of religious influence, meritocracy, democratic political tendency, and urbanization.

In its application to Third World societies, the modernization approach is presented as a formula for economic development. The problem of underdevelopment is seen as stemming from entrenched tradition and a failure to adopt modern values, methods, and economic and social arrangements. "Development is conceptualized as gradual, qualitative passage from less to more differentiated social forms" (Portes 1976, 63).

Although those who operate within the modernization framework often express concern about rapid urbanization rates, they find offsetting advantages in
urban growth. For example, migration to the city is seen as an important source of
positive change. "Employment in modern jobs in urban settings connects rural-
urban migration to economic expansion and modernization, linking modernity to
geographic mobility. Development, occupational change and migration appear
strongly interrelated, particularly when employment is expanding in modern sectors within large cities, drawing rural labor surpluses" (Goldscheider 1983, 237).
Cities are the points from which productive innovation emanates. Accordingly, it
is suggested that "if the world city system is considered as a hierarchical diffusion
mechanism," and if we assume that the larger the city, the greater the rate of technology transfer from abroad, then, according to this view, the largest city may still
be too small in many African countries (Richardson 1984, 135).

Cities are thus seen to be the engines of modernization (World Bank 2000,
125–138). They both embody the complex economic relationships that are prescribed for a truly modern society and act as points of innovation and diffusion for
change. Rapid urbanization may involve social and economic dislocations (crowding, unemployment), but these are simply inevitable, temporary by-products of the
progress that they symptomize. Rational economic competition may appear to
treat the loser roughly in the short term, but in the end all will profit from the economic growth and the overall expansion of economic opportunities. It is a familiar
invocation.

Political Economy

The political economy perspective on urbanization involves a critical interpretation of common patterns of market-induced economic change, focuses on the dislocations and abuses that it sees in the concentration of wealth and power, and
sees these conditions as permanent rather than temporary characteristics of prevalent patterns of change. Once again, we are not considering a particular theory but
a set of assumptions about the causes of underdevelopment and the role of urbanization. In this approach, emphasis is placed on the historical, as well as the
present, relationships between rich and poor countries that are enmeshed in a
common global economic system. Underdevelopment is understood as the consequence of the ability of rich and industrialized economies to dominate poorer and
less powerful territories. In the past, the political structure of domination involved
the formal apparatus of colonialism. Powerful countries have since learned that
their economic interests could be served with less trouble and obligation simply
by dictating terms of trade to former colonies that have remained economically
and technologically dependent. The condition is referred to alternatively as *neocolonialism* or *dependency.*

It is understood that this external structure of underdevelopment is articulated within poor nations by patterns of urbanization that still reflect the political and spatial arrangements of the colonial past. Urban centers are the collection and transhipment points for raw materials destined for the world market. In the hinterland, the labor that produces materials for export receives a small fraction of the market value of its product. Within the domestic economy, the greatest share of the value produced by rural economic activity is realized as profit in the largest urban centers. Cities are the centers of wealth, the home of the elite, and the seats of government. In this light, they stand in an exploitative relationship to the remainder of the nation. This feature of underdevelopment is aptly termed *internal colonialism:* "a process that produces certain intranational forms of patterned socioeconomic inequality directly traceable to the exploitative practices through which national and international institutions are linked in the interest of surplus extraction and capital accumulation" (Walton 1975, 34–35).

In a relatively early formulation, Frank (1967, 8–12) linked together the internal and external structures of underdevelopment, seeing the condition as the result of a chainlike series of exploitative relationships. In these relationships, powerful world centers, metropoles, dominated the economic, political, and social life of intermediate satellites, the urban centers of the underdeveloped countries themselves. These intermediate satellites, in turn, extracted economic surpluses from smaller, subordinate centers, and so on down the chain. The weight of the entire system ultimately rested on the rural producer.

Although the rigidity of Frank's interpretation has been criticized, his basic thesis, that the relationship between the metropolis and hinterland is parasitic, continues to provide the cornerstone upon which political economy's analysis of urbanization is built. That analysis has increasingly focused on the question of how patterns of urbanization reflect the conflict between social classes as opposed to the more abstract idea of conflict between urban and rural places.

The political economy paradigm is linked historically to and shares certain similarities with the Marxian tradition's analysis of imperialism. These similarities include a distrust of market (capitalist) forces for producing for the general good and an emphasis on the primary importance of external relationships between rich and poor countries in perpetuating the impoverishment of Third World economies. However, the perspective has become so widely employed and ideologically diffused since the 1970s that any formal link to Marxist analysis is often indiscernible.

The conceptual division of the world's nations into two tiers, the colonial powers and the former colonies, the core and the periphery, implies a rigid system in which wealthy nations are bound to succeed and poor nations bound to fail economically. The implicit rigidity of the model cannot account for the dramatic growth of such places as Taiwan and South Korea. Wallerstein's (1979, 1980) *world system theory* corrected the stagnant bias of the dichotomous model by dividing the nations of the world into three tiers: the core, the *semi-periphery,* and the periphery. The semi-periphery includes states that have managed some upward (or downward) mobility within the past few centuries. Wallerstein's interpretation remains within the political economy approach. He saw the relationships between rich (core) and poor (periphery) countries as essentially exploitive, with poor nations remaining in a dependent role. However, he found that the long view of history reveals that the international economic system makes adjustments that affect those particularly weak nations within the core and those particularly well placed economies on the periphery, causing some of these to move into the second tier, the semi-periphery. In the present phase of world economic change, the internationalization of the labor market has allowed some Third World economies to move into the semi-periphery.

Urbanization and Spatial Inequalities

According to political economists, patterns of urban growth that have been set in place in the colonial past have serious consequences for the prospects and direction of economic change in the future. For example, it has been argued that in the case of West Africa, uncontrolled urbanization that builds upon the urban spatial patterns of the colonial past, responding strictly to the demands of an export-oriented economy and its politically powerful agents, enlarges three serious dimensions of inequality. First, it increases the imbalance in life chances between urban and rural sectors of the economy by concentrating scarce public investment resources in the cities; as a result, the conditions of the already better-off urbanites are enhanced at the cost of ruralites. Second, typical patterns of public investment mean that capital cities, among all of the urban areas, receive a disproportionate share of attention. Finally, within cities, the market-directed patterns of urbanization accentuate the disparities in wealth between the masses and a tiny elite (Gugler and Flanagan 1976). The growth of cities, the construction of elegant office, apartment, and government complexes, and even the growth of universities and medical centers in the capital cities cannot be interpreted as promising the diffusion of "modernization." Instead, they symbolize the ability of greedy, powerful, urban-based political forces to control a nation's wealth. Wherever growth or investment is observed, these questions must be asked: Who will it benefit? Whose interests are served?

This issue of urban investment serves to separate clearly the respective modernization and political economy understandings of the problem of underdevelopment. Political economy distinguishes between economic growth and economic development. Economic *growth* may mean that very few will benefit from concentrated economic activity. At a minimum, *development* refers to broad participation as indicated by the improvement of the general material conditions of a population. The distinction is based on the observation that national economies often expand, while the condition of much of their population remains unchanged or even deteriorates. Economic growth does not ensure development in this view. Modernization, on the other hand, takes the notion of diffusion as its central assumption. To speak of growth is to talk about development. Urban and rural interests are ultimately one and the same, since all share in the prospect of a common future. The paradigm demands the following conclusions regarding urban investments, offered in this case by a senior World Bank economist:

> *The fact that certain public investments are made in urban areas does not necessarily mean that they are primarily or exclusively made in support of the urban*

economy. Investments in urban port facilities, warehousing, marketing facilities, and transport terminals may be crucial ingredients for a strategy of accelerated rural development. It would thus be overly simplistic to aggregate all public expenditures in urban areas and compare this with aggregate public expenditures in rural areas and to conclude that the former are made in support of urban development and the latter in support of rural development. (Linn 1982, 631)

So long as the more efficient collection, transhipment, and export of raw materials are assumed to benefit rural populations, this reasoning is inescapable.

The antithesis of this view holds that these urban investments, especially since they are in transport and export facilities, enhance the dominant position of the city and improve its ability to exploit its position. For example, Third World agriculture is linked to the international marketplace through the cities, and it has been argued that this integration has brought about changes in agriculture that have produced negative consequences for many small agricultural producers. Such innovations as the mechanization of agricultural production and even the increased yields of staple grains associated with the Green Revolution in India have not distributed their benefits equally among rural populations. Critics argue that world-market-induced agricultural change systematically favors the large landholder over the small landholder, increases the free-floating, landless rural labor force by promoting the elimination of smaller farmers, and reduces the demand for rural labor. This means that some unknown, but perhaps increasing, proportion of the Third World's rural-urban migrants are displaced rural farmers and laborers without urban employment skills. There is considerable skepticism regarding the modernization assumption that this displaced labor will be absorbed by the demand for an industrial workforce.

Industrialization and Employment
There is ambiguity about the relationship among four key factors—urbanization, industrialization, employment, and economic development—in Third World economies. Modernization theorists anticipated that industrialization would accompany urban growth and provide employment for the growing population of urban workers. The affluence of these workers and the growing efficiency of agriculture were to generate and sustain economic takeoff. That has happened in very few areas. In the first place, due to the low income of large segments of the population, domestic consumer markets are quite small in most Third World countries, and the lack of demand means that there is little in the way of a base on which to develop a domestically oriented manufacturing industry. As we have noted, the export manufacturing boom of the 1980s was concentrated in only a few countries. Most nations simply experienced very limited industrialization.

Where industrialization has occurred, it has at times meant few new jobs for the army of workers who crowd hopefully into the cities. Critics have pointed out that imported modern industrial technology requires fewer workers, and it may have the undesirable consequence of displacing workers in traditional industries. Yet, there are those few countries where the most recent phase of rapid urban growth appears to be driven by industrialization and the need for new urban workers. The current picture thereby provides a basis for continued debate between the political economists and the modernization theorists.

There are two general patterns of industrial growth in Third World cities. First, in contrast to the experience of countries that enjoyed their greatest urbanization during the Industrial Revolution, the rate of industrialization measured in terms of the creation of new manufacturing jobs in Third World cities has lagged far behind the rate of urbanization. Additionally, for the most part, industrial growth that took place after World War II used the imported technology of late industrialization. This technology is capital-intensive rather than labor-intensive—that is, the technology is designed to *reduce* the role of labor. "Transposing this capital-intensive technology wholesale to poor countries means a heavy drain on scarce capital . . . and employment for only a few from a large and rapidly growing, low-productivity labor-force" (Gilbert and Gugler 1992, 88). Efforts to develop appropriate technologies that would more effectively employ people faced several obstacles. There were not a lot of surviving labor-intensive technologies in advanced industrial nations to adapt to new applications in poor countries; national elites wanted the industries located in their cities to appear up-to-date; the largest employers typically offered higher wages and therefore had this incentive for limiting the size of their labor force; finally, much of the industrial investment comes from foreigners who are familiar with and prefer the methods of advanced technologies (Gilbert and Gugler 1992, 88–89). Capital-intensive technologies at best produce only modest demands for industrial labor and have the potential to *reduce* the demand for labor by driving previously existing, smaller scale, more labor-intensive competitors out of business, while inducing others to mechanize in order to remain competitive.

There is a second pattern of industrial growth, however, in which modernization theorists find strong support for their view of development. One of the leading features of economic globalization is the direct international competition among manufacturing companies that has led to vigorous efforts to lower labor and other production costs by moving assembly operations to parts of the world where cheap labor is readily available. Growing pools of that kind of labor can, of course, be found in the expanding populations of the cities of poor countries. Especially during the last three decades of the twentieth century, geographically mobile manufacturing operations have shifted increasingly to the cities of poorer countries, creating dynamic export manufacturing zones in northern Mexico, South Korea, the Bangkok region, and, within the last ten years, even poorer countries like Vietnam, driven by the same forces of international competition. Modernization theory has become a very powerful vision of world progress.

Writers for the World Bank, in the Bank's 1999/2000 *World Development Report*, expressed the modernization view of economic development in the boldest, most unqualified terms and tied development directly to rapid urbanization: "Globalization promotes economic growth which is the driving force behind urbanization" (125). Economic concentration in cities is a natural phenomenon: "Healthy, dynamic cities are an integral part of economic growth. . . . As countries develop, cities account for an ever-increasing share of national income" (126). In this view, the natural and universal pattern of growth spreads benefits to all segments of the population: "As industrialization proceeds, manufacturing activities begin to move to smaller cities outside the capital. This shift occurs because congestion costs increase and because, to some extent, the benefits of agglomeration [concentrated economic activity] decrease as production standardizes in mature plants" (129). What should be the role of government in attempting to control or direct economic growth? "The unhappy record of past government efforts to prevent rural-urban migration or to steer urban growth to particular locations leads to a straightforward conclusion: Governments are not skilled in determining where households or firms should locate. National governments can perform a more useful function by working to provide an environment conducive to economic growth regardless of location" (131). The position of the World Bank is that, in the fluid environment of the international economy, there is little scope for meddling with market forces and that modernization is not a theory, but a pragmatic description of reality.

The introduction to this chapter described the nature of the economic growth that accompanies the labor-intensive export manufactures. It creates wealth and urban growth. But the type of economic growth produced exemplifies the distinction that political economists make between economic growth and economic development. That is, questions remain about how much the production of wealth has improved the life chances of the majority of the workers, including those who participate directly, and whether elements of the population who live beyond the immediate metropolitan area where the growth is occurring will benefit. Some nations, not all, are targeted for investment by internationally mobile capital. In those economies, the typically modest middle class of skilled workers and lower-level managers is expanding within the major cities. However, political economists emphasize that large numbers of poor people—in city and countryside—remain, and for many of them conditions are worsening as their numbers grow, rather than improving. Their cheap labor and agricultural products subsidize the standard of living of the more affluent segments of the urban population. By holding down the price of agricultural products and manufactured exports, their poverty can also be seen to subsidize the living costs of consumers of imported goods throughout the world. It remains an act of faith, an expression of ideology, and no more than a hypothesis expressed by some economists that all nations and all peoples will, in time, find a place in the dynamic sectors of the international economy.

During the 1970s and 1980s, the critical political economy approach established itself as the ascendant paradigm in the study of development. Today, the modernization perspective appears to have won the day, led by the voices of most world political leaders, funding institutions, and powerful entrepreneurial interests.

Dissent is largely voiced by political economists and among workers and their representatives in deindustrializing nations. The skepticism of the latter group, of course, is induced by the prospect of a declining personal standard of living once their industrial jobs are gone. The other side of industrial decline in one part of the world is the expansion of industry in another, however, and a modest number of economies, foremost among them the People's Republic of China, have enjoyed high rates of economic growth in recent decades. Socialist China struggles ideologically with its present status as the greatest modern success story of capitalist expansion. Modernization theory, in its present form, points to the sweeping worldwide ascendancy of the belief that any nation that turns its back on full participation in the world market economy will be left behind by its potential benefits. Modernization theory today transcends its former role as a way to interpret the potential for development of Third World economies: Today, it is indiscernible from the popular and official description of the internationalizing marketplace that sees the world as a single economy in which all parties have a stake in the same future. The collapse of socialism is seen as a vindication of the theme—always a part of the modernization view—that provides wealthy nations and multinational corporations with an ideological justification for their interventions in the Third World, casting them in a benevolent role in their dealings with poor countries.

In a world swept by internal unrest and impacted by an international market that finds new uses for those pockets of poor people who have languished, underutilized, the argument between modernization and dependency theorists may seem an overly formalized debate among old ideological warriors. But we can only leave the debate behind once we have all agreed that international capitalism produces positive results for all of those in the world whom it touches, and that those it neglects will benefit in due time. For our purposes, as students of the city and its relation to issues of inequality, the same questions remain. What is the balance of risks, penalties, and benefits for local populations of market-led growth patterns? To what extent is participation in economic change generally available to all members of a nation's population? To what extent are benefits concentrated? Are entire regions and ethnic groups excluded? And, what are the long-term effects of such exclusion? Will exclusion lead to dissent and secessionist insurgency by those in distant and neglected regions who feel left out? Will it lead to more or less permanent revolution and state repressions of such movements?

In parts of Asia and perhaps Latin America, exported industrialization has led to the development of the term *Newly Industrialized Countries (NICs)*. But this has so far created a new economic division among Third World nations, because Africa contained by the mid-1990s no NICs or even near-NICs (Shaw 1995, 8). The kind of evidence that has so far been brought to bear in the debate between modernization theorists and political economists allows for broad interpretation. Support can be found for either thesis in the available aggregate measures on urbanization and economic development rates. Such aggregate measures have prompted some to suggest that it may be necessary to employ both perspectives to fully understand the relationship between patterns of urbanization and economic development (Bradshaw 1987). Smith and London (1990) concluded their comparative analysis of a limited number of gross indicators of urbanization and underdevelopment with the observation that the evidence weighs more heavily in favor of political economy than modernization. They admitted, however, that at the present stage of investigation what is needed is case studies of individual states and that such case studies continue to be informed by both paradigms.

Resolution of the debate over whether market-led forces will ultimately provide for a convergence toward a future of generalized affluence, or a new phase of underdevelopment and exaggerated inequalities, will surely be supplied some time in the future by the long view of history. Case studies may show how international forces of economic change are modified by local histories and circumstances to produce particular patterns of urban growth, employment, and well-being (So 1990, 267). The conditions need to be understood on a city-by-city, if not neighborhood-by-neighborhood, basis. In the following section, we continue to consider some prominent structural features of Third World urbanization and how these are understood from the modernization and political economy perspectives.

The Challenges of Urban Growth

Certain common features of urbanization in poor countries warrant particular attention. In this section, we will examine urban *primacy*, the widespread phenomenon of urban *squatter settlement*, and the development of the *informal sector* of the urban economy. Each of these is the product of uneven economic growth (that is, when the more rapid growth of some areas results in a substantial disparity in life chances between regions) and especially of the concentration of wealth in the larger cities. Populations are disproportionately drawn to the metropolis by the greater opportunity it is perceived to hold; urban populations are left to provide their own shelter on wages too meager and in numbers too great to be matched by the legal housing supply, and many are forced (while others can choose) to employ themselves in street trades, legal and otherwise, due to the failure of prevailing economic patterns to produce a sufficient labor demand. Taken together, the manifest pressures of very rapid population growth have been called *overurbanization.* The term means that migration and natural increase supply greater numbers of people than the urban economy, services, and resources can absorb. Overurbanization means that there are many more people than can be employed and that the overflow of population spills into the slums and illegal housing settlements. The problems of overurbanization tend to be most acute in the largest cities. Together, these issues raise the question of the appropriate scope and direction for urban planning and policy.

Primacy

The *primate city* concept was developed to describe a situation whereby one city has grown to several times the size of any other city within that country. Primate city patterns contrast with national urban systems that conform more to the *rank-size rule*, which is assumed to mark more "mature" or "balanced" systems. The rank-size rule predicts that the largest city will be roughly twice the size of the second largest, three times the size of the third largest, and so on. A primate city is thereby considered to be overgrown. The most outstanding examples of primate systems occur in the Third World. In 1980, Mexico City was six times larger than the next largest city, Guadalajara; Dakar, Senegal, was nearly seven times larger than second-ranked Thiès; and the greater Buenos Aires area in Argentina was twelve and a half times larger than the Rosario urban agglomeration (United Nations 1983, Table 8). The primate tendency is especially common in smaller nations. For example, the populations of Caribbean capitals are several times those of their second-largest cities, with Port-au-Prince, Haiti (nine times the size of Cap Haitien), and Kingston, Jamaica (twelve times the size of Montego Bay), providing the most extreme examples (Cross 1979, 78). For a long time, the most pronounced example of primacy, greater Bangkok, was by 1980 more than forty times larger than the next largest city in Thailand (Wyatt 1984, Table 2). In the mid-1990s, although Bangkok had continued to grow, so had other Thai cities, and the capital was by then only twenty-one times larger than the second city.

In addition to size, primacy means that a city dominates a nation functionally: The city is the political, economic, social, and cultural center of the country. With some notable exceptions, primate cities tend to serve as a nation's major port, usually a function preserved from the days of colonialism when these cities occupied central locations in a colonial trade system. Often the structure of the colonial economy is reflected in the pattern of the transportation networks currently in place. These radiate outward from the major centers and channel materials bound for export through them. The dominant position of these colonial administrative centers was strengthened with the arrival of independence, as they became national centers of government. As a symbol of independence and national pride, the capital remains an inviting target for both migrants and investment capital. Growth generates growth.

The economic consequences of urban primacy must, of course, be seen differently from the perspectives of modernization and political economy. Primacy promotes the avowed goals of modernization.

> The statistical association between increasing primacy and faster economic growth is well known. . . . Perhaps more importantly, high levels of primacy may be critical in certain historical states of economic development. If the world city system is considered as a hierarchical diffusion mechanism, the larger the primate city the higher the rate of technology transfer and innovation adoption from abroad. On this argument, many primate cities, especially in Africa, are too small. (Richardson 1984, 134–135)

If cities generate positive change, then it follows that primate cities are simply bigger generators.

On the other hand, if it is true that benefits to urban interests come only at the cost of rural populations and if cities in the Third World are parasitic, then primate cities are simply the greatest parasites. They concentrate economic activity, public investment, services, amenities, and political power in a narrowly circumscribed location, most typically a geographically eccentric one. Since the benefits of growth are concentrated in this way, primacy is the graphic antithesis of true development. Populations in peripheral and remote areas are exploited and neglected in equal measure to their distance from the capital/chief port/economic hub and their relative lack of strategic political economic importance.

In the minds of its affluent inhabitants, the capital can come to stand for the nation, and all the territory beyond may be seen as a backward, often embarrassing, and at times politically troublesome hinterland. In a sense, Bangkok, Buenos Aires, and Dakar are arrogant tyrants who demand the lion's share of the benefits of the national economy; as the centers of government, they make up the rules to suit themselves and demand the loyalty, or at least the obedience, of the remainder of the population. In another sense, the cities cannot be parasitic, and they cannot exploit, because the cities *themselves* do not act (London 1980, 22). The *city* does not maintain nor does it enjoy its preeminent position. Patterns of privilege are maintained by people, social classes, and political and economic interests, who enjoy the benefits of the status quo, and by their political agents. In this view, the conditions that may have led to the inception of primate city patterns are kept in place by those who stand to benefit from them. As the primate city grows in size, the economic and political interests concentrated there grow in their capacity to exert their will over the rest of the country.

Comparative research suggests that urban primacy in poorer countries may have stabilized in the period between 1970 and 1980. The analysis, which draws on the world system perspective of political economy, makes the argument that the period between 1970 and 1980 was marked by a growth in export manufacture in some areas of the Third World, and that this type of industrialization does not require primate city location, but can operate efficiently in smaller cities and towns (Lyman 1992). The interpretation can also be seen as accommodating to the modernization perspective, whose proponents would find a correlation between export manufacturing and the diffusion of urban growth quite consistent with its worldview.

Squatter Settlement

Those who occupy land without legal title to it are called *squatters*. In many Third World cities, they comprise the most rapidly growing segment of the population. Most have no choice but to shelter themselves as cheaply as they can. They do not have the resources to purchase land legally. Rental property available to the poor, where landlords hold reasonably secure title to the land, is generally in limited supply, overcrowded, decaying, and located in neighborhoods with the worst reputations for crime. In addition to those who are squatters by necessity, some who could afford to do otherwise choose to pursue this risky strategy in order to minimize costs and, with the money saved by not renting or purchasing land, obtain the maximum benefit from their housing investment. The strategy is risky because both colonial and postindependence governments, whose lands are typically targeted for takeover by squatters, have often pursued violent eviction policies, involving the destruction of property and brutal attacks on residents. Since many squatters have no alternative means of housing themselves, illegal settlements

Squatter settlements are a ubiquitous feature of Third World cities. This favelas is on the very edge of São Paulo, Brazil, one of the three cities currently vying for the distinction of being the largest in the world.

have persisted, and the squatter movement has become a ubiquitous feature of the Third World city.

The question of whether the occupation of a lot or a house is legal or illegal is often a difficult one, and the issue may become more complicated over time. In addition to illegally occupied space, an even larger portion of residential land is in legal limbo in some sub-Saharan African cities. Some of the land may be granted according to custom; deeds may or may not be registered; or some construction, service provision, or other business may take place outside of labor, commercial, and tax regulation (Cooper 1983, 31). In the past, patently illegal appropriation of property has been less widespread in Africa than in Latin America, because those wanting to set up their own housing in African cities were able to acquire land from local chiefs in the area. Many "squatters" in suburban Kinshasa believe they have obtained legal title to their residences in this way; however, there is no official acknowledgement of their tenure. Many illegal residents of Lusaka and Nairobi may not know that the property they rent does not belong to their "landlord" (O'Connor 1983, 185–186). In Kingston, Jamaica, people living in makeshift housing may or may not be squatters. Some of them are legal tenants of "rent yards," properties divided and rented to those who construct their own housing from whatever materials they can manage (Cross 1979, 86).

There is considerable variation among illegal squatter settlements with respect to the construction standards of the housing and the economic condition of inhabitants. Within Latin America, conditions range from the desperate squalor of the most-crowded *favelas* of Rio de Janeiro and São Paulo to the solid houses of the older *barriadas* of Lima. At the upper end of the scale, squatter housing is indistinguishable from modest middle-class legitimate housing. At the lower end, conditions can equal those of the worst crowded urban slums in the same cities.

One of the most remarkable features of squatter settlements is the speed with which an area is invaded and settled by its inhabitants. In Mexico, squatter settlements have gained the designation *pueblas paracaidistas* because it appears that a whole new town of people has parachuted from the sky, literally overnight, to cover a formerly unoccupied tract of land near the city. Such simultaneous incursions are no accident; invasions are carefully planned, often a long time in advance. Castells (1982, 274), who is inclined to interpret squatting as an expression of class struggle and solidarity, reported that new invasions of squatters are assisted by those who have already settled elsewhere as the result of similar mass takeovers. The objective is to undermine the possibility of effective countermeasures by the government. In 1976, in Monterrey, Mexico, squatters successfully took over good land close to a municipal park, avoiding retaliation by timing their occupation to coincide with an electoral visit by President Lopez Portillo. As Mangin reported, the squatters of Lima undertook even more formal and elaborate strategies:

> *The enterprise generally took the form of a quasi-military campaign. . . . For the projected barriada community the leaders recruited married couples under 30 with children; single adults were usually excluded (and still are from most barriadas). Lawyers or near-lawyers among the recruited group searched land titles to find a site that was owned, or at least could be said to be owned, by some public agency, preferably the national government. The organizers then visited the place at night and marked out the lots assigned to the members for homes and locations for streets, schools, churches, clinics and other facilities.*
>
> *After all the plans had been made in the utmost secrecy to avoid alerting the police, the organizers appealed confidentially to some prominent political or religious figure to support the invasion when it took place; they also alerted a friendly newspaper, so that any violent police reaction would be fully reported. On the appointed day the people recruited for the invasion, usually numbering in the hundreds and sometimes more than 1,000, rushed to the barriada site in taxis, trucks, buses and even on delivery cycles. On arriving, the families immediately began to put up shelters made of matting on their assigned lots. (Mangin 1967, 23)*

With time, the housing in these settlements of Lima was upgraded, with cement and brick construction gradually replacing the makeshift huts of the invaders. The organizers of the original movement became the leaders of named *barriada* associations (for example, "Fathers of the Families of Mariscal Castilla," "Defenders of Mirones," "House Owners of Santa Clara de Bella Luz"), which performed such functions of government as the regulation of conflicts over lot ownership. Eventually, the authority of the association would give way as the city recognized and provided services for the squatter settlement, and came to regulate it as part of the metropolitan community (Mangin 1973, 318–319). Castells (1982, 256) argued that in this way speculators used the poor as an advance guard to open up new areas of the city for development and to force new portions of land onto the real estate market.

The description in Box 6-2 provides good insight into some of the practical problems of regulating squatter development.

BOX 6-2   A Squatter Settlement in Tamada, Thailand

A large slum and squatter settlement has developed on government land in the northern section of town during the past three years. This land belongs to a central government unit, not the municipality—a fact few local residents know. Nearby residents complain about the unsanitary and dilapidated slum conditions as well as the seemingly suspicious nature of many slum dwellers; they fear the spread of disease, fire, crime, and prostitution into their neighborhood.

The central government unit refuses to take responsibility for its land. It had plans to build an office building and housing compound there, but since the arrival of the squatters, the officials prefer not to force the people off; this would probably create a political incident having unfavorable public relations consequences for the unit. Instead, the central officials publicly sympathize with the squatters; privately they blame the municipality for failing to regulate this land.

Since the municipality lacks authority to regulate land use and enforce housing codes, it can do little except send officials from the health section and fire brigade to inspect and take preventive measures in the slum and squatter settlement. In addition, the police are uncooperative because they fail to enforce local sanitation codes. Publicly, the police sympathize with the squatters and claim they lack the necessary manpower to enforce local ordinances. Privately, however, the police prefer avoiding this

area because they fear the local toughs and because some police officers have a vested interest in keeping the houses of prostitution operating. Hence, the police acquiesce to the slum conditions and shift responsibility by blaming the municipality for allowing these conditions to develop.

The slum continues to grow as more squatters move into the area. Moreover, slum residents are particularly pleased with the extension of municipal health and sanitation services into their area. They were recently informed that the municipal schools would also accept their children. A few local politicians were especially helpful in that they promised to increase services to the slum area—if residents registered to vote. The slum and squatter dwellers pay no taxes, they receive free services, and they anticipate more services in the future.

Nearby residents continue to complain about the slum and squatter area and the inequitable distribution of benefits. For them, the municipality is more concerned with promoting the slum next door than with improving their immediate neighborhood. Consequently, the problem of the slum and squatter settlement is not solved. It becomes complicated as no more decisions are made. Municipal officials decide to wait rather than further antagonize the protesting taxpayers and voters. They continue to blame both the central unit and the police for this problem. (Krannich 1982, 327–328)

This brief description reveals the division of interests that exists and the complexities of the political strategies at work. Research that has proceeded from within the modernization paradigm has portrayed squatters as politically unsophisticated and disengaged. This is because modernization theses anticipate the orderly diffusion of modes of political participation characteristic of Western society. Leeds and Leeds (1976, 199–201) are critical of the ethnocentric bias that this approach represents. In their study of the political behavior of squatters in Brazil, Chile, and Peru, they observe that such an approach implies that Anglo-American forms of political organization and expression are more rational and politically mature, and, according to a "unilinear evolutionary principle," urban proletariats will learn the appropriate behaviors as development proceeds. In contrast, they cite one researcher's observation that in Rio "the *favela* resident who says he can do something to influence the government is not more efficacious, more modern, or more competent a citizen, but simply more deceived by the rhetoric of government—less in touch with reality. It is a tribute to the *favela* residents' common sense that this group is in the minority" (Perlman 1971, 383). On the other hand, it may be pointed out that this resident had already engaged in a most effective collective political strategy in the successful invasion and takeover of government lands. The investigation of political activism has to range beyond questions of party membership and voting behavior. The reality of Third World politics is that there is often little to choose between at this level. In Monterrey, Mexico, a different type of political consciousness was evidenced by squatter resistance to the legalization of their property claims. They believed that legalization would undermine the solidarity of their urban movement by allowing the government to put pressure on individual property owners to fall into line (Castells 1982, 275–276).

The political significance of the squatter movement is that it represents an initial, minimal, and deliberate rejection of the authority of the state. Squatters remain less than a revolutionary force, but perhaps this is because government policy involves acquiescence and accommodation rather than confrontation with the concentrated numbers that have moved outside the law to gain a foothold in the city.

Comparisons of Inner-City Slums and Peripheral Squatter Settlements

While squatters represent a rapidly growing element of the urban population, poor people and others of limited means who seek housing in Third World cities do have another option. They may pay rent for their shelter. Earlier studies done in the 1960s and 1970s commented favorably on the opportunities created for the inhabitants of growing squatter settlements, at the same time that concern was expressed over the fate of those who clung to decaying, slum rental-housing in the inner-city areas. Shantytowns were interpreted as drawing to them more enterprising families and individuals who were prepared to seize the chance to establish a claim to urban permanence and mobility, at the same time participating in a popular movement with political overtones. By contrast, the central slums drew the poorest of the poor—the unemployed and unskilled, the vagabond, the alcoholic, and the delinquent. There was no incentive for occupants to upgrade the rental housing of the central slums, and there was little about these areas that engendered positive identification or commitment. How different from the mushrooming squatter settlements on the periphery, which embodied committed habitation and which offered informal economic opportunities and political participation.

Eckstein (1990), in a study of residential areas in Mexico City, criticized what she called the conventional approach that contrasts positive features of the squatter "settlements of hope" with the negative factors of the inner-city "slums of despair," at least as the generalization applies to Latin America. She argued that the economic crisis faced by Third World economies like that of Mexico during the 1980s, where staggering international debt caused national governments to cut back on expenditures for social services, created favorable consequences for the residents of centrally located slums. At the same time, conditions created disadvantages for squatters located in isolated settlements at the edge of the city. In addition, a natural maturation process in the peripheral squatter settlements undermined the basis for solidarity and political organization in those areas.

While the cost of living rose during the 1980s and the real wages of the poor declined, local economic activity in the inner-city area that Eckstein studied intensified. (The research site is similar to "Tepito," described at the beginning of the chapter, and they may be one in the same.) Due to its central location and its reputation for offering hard-to-come-by, novel, and contraband goods, the location offered a good living to residents who tapped into the popularity of the local market in one way or another. While the quality of housing remained generally poor, rent control laws were partially effective, keeping the average cost of housing reasonable. The earthquake that hit the city in 1985 galvanized neighborhood associations into broader political units that successfully persuaded the government to rebuild destroyed portions of the area with relatively low-cost model housing.

Meanwhile the debt-ridden state neglected social services that it was once prepared to provide to squatter settlements. Eckstein emphasized the liabilities that have attended the maturation of squatter settlements in Mexico City. Population growth has generated crowding in these areas as the children of homeowners marry and have children. They stay to minimize expenses and avoid the inconvenience of newer squatter settlements more distant from the city center. Second, many owners have erected multifamily rental units on their property. This has led to the economic "downgrading" of squatter settlements, as tenants are reputed to be poorer than homeowners. At the same time, changes in land tenure laws that allow for the sale of squatter properties have caused a dramatic inflation in land and housing prices in these settlements, and led to a division in residents between the poor and the middle class. It is only the latter who can afford to purchase houses and sites in established squatter areas where the market establishes prices for shelter.

The stratification of the population of former squatter areas, between the poor home owner, the transient tenant, and the middle class, obviously compromises the basis for political solidarity and collective action to the extent that common residence is crosscut by ownership and class issues. Finally, the residents of the peripherally located settlements are at a disadvantage in contrast to the centrally located slum dwellers for establishing the kinds of informal businesses that we turn our attention to in the next section. Eckstein provided a provocative case study which, as she pointed out, needs to be further tested for its applicability to other countries in Latin America and in other world regions.

The Informal Sector

Just as large numbers of urbanites have to invent their own solution to the problem of housing, many have to be self-dependent in establishing a livelihood as well. Although the urban population of the Third World has experienced massive growth since the middle of the twentieth century, open unemployment rates reportedly increased relatively little in the same time. This is because of the increase in self-employment in the informal sector of the economy, which has served as a safety valve by absorbing the overflow labor supply generated by migration to the cities (Sethuraman 1981, 188–200).

Although migration is the primary factor in creating the surplus urban labor supply and forcing larger numbers to turn to self-employment, it would be a mistake to conclude that self-employed trades and services are made up primarily of rural-urban migrants. This was clearly not the case, for example, in Surabaya, Indonesia, where survey evidence revealed that recent migrants were not disproportionately represented in the tertiary (service) or self-employment sectors (McCutcheon 1983, 98). Peattie (1975, 113–118) made a distinction between "easy-entry" street trades in Bogotá and those more difficult to get started. Anyone could set up a stand and sell a few vegetables in a less profitable location in one of the poor *barrios* of the city. However, making a viable living involves a substantial capital outlay for a site highly trafficked by the more affluent, as well as for licenses and stock. In addition, for those trades where access to commodities is controlled by those already established, newspaper vending, for example, there are syndicates and other controls that restrict entry by new competitors. Peil (1981, 85, 111), who reported data for a number of West African cities, found no exclusionary strategies among self-employed craftspeople, but she agreed that newly arrived migrants lacked the capital to enter small-scale trading without some sponsorship. Although most self-employed persons believed that there was already too much competition, they still commonly employed apprentices. In this way, they provided themselves with inexpensive help for the short term, and in the long term, they provided young people with training and entry points to their crowded urban trades.

The proportion of the workforce occupied in the informal sector of nine different Third World cities was found to be fairly consistent, at between 40 and 50 percent. For example, it was estimated that 30 percent of the total income in the Lima area was generated within the informal sector. In the Lima region in 1976, the informal sector yielded a value of about U.S. $400 million, compared to the total value of about U.S. $1,340 million for all economic activity (Sethuraman 1981, 193). The net profit realized by each self-employed worker varied considerably with the size and relative success of the enterprise. In Djakarta, the average yield was about U.S. $1.50 per day. Twenty percent earned less than U.S. $.50 a day from their activities, and only one-third earned near the equivalent of U.S. $2.00 or more (Moir 1981, 116). While the majority struggled at the level of subsistence, there were a few at the top of a very wide range of earnings with conspicuously high incomes. A few lottery ticket vendors in Bogotá drove their own cars (Peattie 1975, 115), and the most well-to-do among Peil's (1981, 109) West African respondents was an electrician who reported his previous year's income at £5,000. Peil observed that the government-regulated minimum wage in West African countries meant that the regulated sector employees would earn more than the least successful of the self-employed, but that the regulated wages had a relatively low upper limit. Craftspeople working on their own in printing and building trades could do better than the well-paid wage earner. Whatever the level of skill and earnings, it was a common observation that the self-employed enjoyed the freedom and control their occupations gave them (Moir 1981, 120; Peil 1981, 88, 111).

Eckstein (1990, 172) described a carefully coordinated strategy employed by vendors in a centrally located barrio in Mexico City. The objective was to expand the amount of area devoted to market space in the congested central area of one of the world's largest cities. The strategy, which progressively captured more and more street areas from vehicular traffic, was reminiscent of planned residential invasions. Local residents were in a superior position to learn through rumor when and where the market was expected to spill over its existing boundaries into a new street. The colonization involved weeks of preparation, during which hopeful vendors paid dues to an organizer who negotiated with government for the rights to the targeted space. During the duration of these negotiations, people squatted without attempting any commercial activity on the site they expected to occupy. The dues paid to the organizer were within the means of all but the poorest families. The investment was in time and patience. The return was in the right to the occupied site once market activities began in the area. Eckstein reported that the rights to such properties, once established, traded for as much as $5,000 in the mid-1980s.

One general principle that appears to hold all across the informal sectors of the Third World is that occupations and income are stratified by gender. As a rule, women traders face formal cultural restrictions or are handicapped by a lack of capital, less formal education, and responsibilities for children; they are found in the less lucrative trades, such as selling vegetables or prepared foods (Nelson 1988, in the case of Nairobi, Kenya). Their precarious economic arrangements make them susceptible to illegal activities, especially prostitution. While there are exceptions, such as the accounts of wealthy trading women in West African cities (Granmaison 1969), self-employed women in Third World cities operate closest to the margins of survival, operate the smallest and least lucrative enterprises, and earn the lowest incomes. As elsewhere in the world, the situation is made more desperate where they have sole or primary responsibility for the support of their children.

There is a higher proportion of female-headed households in Latin America, the Caribbean, and sub-Saharan Africa, in contrast to Asia and the Near East. Enumerations from the early 1980s showed, for example, that 45 percent of households in both Botswana and Barbados were headed by women. Cuba, Venezuela, and Honduras had between 22 percent and 28 percent; Bangladesh, South Korea, and Indonesia had between 14 percent and 17 percent. The comparable figure for the United States was 31 percent at the time (Buvunić and Gupta 1997, 261).

A disproportionate number of households headed by women in Third World countries are poor for the same reasons that female-headed households are poor in other parts of the world. Women have less access to employment and trading resources than do their male counterparts. And as elsewhere, children in households headed by women are directly affected by the lower earning capacity of women. Data from Brazil show that poor households rely much more heavily on the earnings of children, and in São Paulo and Porto Alegre, school attendance rates are lower for children in female-headed households. In these households, the rates decline particularly dramatically as children grow older. Predictably, the labor force participation rate is higher for children in households headed by women. The lower earning power of women, especially self-employed women, has begun to draw the policy attention of development aid agencies; programs dedicated particularly to the needs of children in households headed by women, especially those programs devoted to keeping children in school, are currently considered to hold promise (Barros et al. 1997).

Indications are that women, whose enterprises are more marginal than those of men, may be more vulnerable to displacement by formal sector competitors. In the markets of the rapidly growing city of Huaraz, Peru, women outnumber male traders, but their enterprises—selling vegetables, grain, fish, and household items—are smaller than those of men. While some women traders have always been employees rather than independent traders, this pattern has become more widespread as increasing numbers of women are in the employ of individuals or stores for whom they sell for wages or commissions. While the significance of this pattern may suit modernization theory, the autonomy that women street traders value is undercut; the enterprises that employ women traders who are not self-employed will be operated by men (Babb 1990).

The informal sector provides enough room to get by, but few will get ahead. Migration continues because even the poorest conditions of urban survival most often represent a material improvement over life in the rural areas. The optimism of the agents and theoreticians of the modernization doctrine notwithstanding, Third World governments in increasing numbers have concluded that urbanization, in its most typical forms, has created serious problems that require the attention of planners and policymakers.

Globalization and the Urban Policy Dilemma

Patterns of economic change and urban growth in Third World countries have for the most part reflected their economic and political ties to the rest of the world. This has been true under conditions of colonialism and neocolonialism. It will remain true in the future as regional and local economies find their way in the continually restructuring international division of labor. Those observers of the emerging international order—of globalization—who point to its promise, are really modernization theorists in the sense that they believe there is a convergence of interests of all world peoples around a single marketplace. It would follow from this view that there is little point any longer in distinguishing between the First World and Third World. In the new world economy, national borders do not exist as real boundaries to trade and investment, except as holdovers from a previous age. The future is seen as a seamless web of opportunities. Large concentrations of poor people, for example, are now seen as an asset, transmuted by their poverty into a competitive labor force on the international labor market. In that market, today's underpaid workers will eventually become tomorrow's consumers, whose demand for processed and manufactured goods spurs further development. This is classical modernization theory.

The vision of the new *global modernization theorists* is not so much new as it is refocused and reinvigorated by a resurgent belief virtually everywhere in the world in market solutions to the problem of gross international inequality. Belief in the ability of the free workings of the market to transform underdevelopment into development—the same belief that has produced frustration for so many years in so many places, that has fostered regional neglect and hardship—is rejuvenated. A single rational system combining all of the world's assets into a unified market gives everyone a place on the same playing field. The hope is that this unity will make a key difference between the failures of the past and the promise of the future. Critics believe, however, that such hopes remain acts of faith and a basis for skepticism. They ask, What has really changed?

For example, in Latin America, only Mexico and Brazil have managed to develop significant advanced manufacturing sectors with a diversity of skills and technologies. These two countries produce the majority of manufacturing exports for all of Latin America, thus reflecting growing inequality in the region. Modernization theorists are encouraged by these developments and would tend to envision Mexico and Brazil leading the way to the convergent future for the rest of the continent and the Caribbean. Seen in a different light, Mexico and Brazil represent some of the greatest problems of market-led economic growth, featuring cities choking on their own growth, the same old patterns of neglect of populations in remote regions and the consequent chronic threat of insurgency from the people who experience this neglect. There is actually little indication that neighboring nations are on the road to diversifying and self-sustaining economic growth. For the most part, the long-standing pattern whereby goods are designed and marketed in wealthy nations like the United States and assembled or processed in poorer nations, remains in place. Part of this division of labor means that the nations where goods are produced remain on the periphery, distant from and subordinate to centers of product design, marketing, and control. The limited benefits from this international arrangement for areas of the world where assembly takes place are in the form of the modest wages earned by workers who have jobs only so long as they are willing to work for so little. Poor national economies are locked into competition to offer transnational corporations the lowest wages, employing tactics like devaluing the national currency on the international market to enhance their workers' competitiveness—to earn less rather than to buy more in that market. National policies today are being further liberalized to allow foreign capital and transnationals to operate more freely. Women take 80 percent of the jobs in export-processing zones and are paid between 20 percent and 50 percent less than men working in the same localities (Gereffi and Hempel 1996). Political economists and others skeptical of the message that the new world order offers the promise of significant change over the old post-colonial order are not likely to be convinced by these patterns that the problems of underdevelopment are somehow different today. Modernization theorists are prone to point to the economic growth of Asian economies like Taiwan and South Korea over the past quarter century as examples of what can happen when nations decide to accept the free and unrestricted operation of the marketplace. But the Third World represents, as we have said, a diversity of economic situations, and what the future holds for areas that historically have gained far less than they have given in their peripheral role in the world economy remains to be seen. Africa contains no newly industrialized countries nor even near-newly industrialized countries. Shaw (1995) suggested that many of its nations are best described as Fourth or Fifth World states, in terms of the lack of promise for their participation in a global economic revolution and in terms of their remoteness from any generalized prosperity.

In pursuing social policies directed at the softening of stark regional inequalities, Third World nations today are at a critical juncture. Urban planning—the desire to control urban growth and redistribute economic opportunities in a more balanced rural and urban pattern—requires a courageous act of will. A strong urban policy is a statement that a government is not altogether willing to trust market forces that concentrate populations and resources in order to produce the optimum rate and direction of urbanization. The decision to control or divert patterns of urban growth may appear to interested outsiders as a symptom of a meddlesome orientation of a particular regime toward issues of social welfare—a caution to those contemplating an investment gamble in a poor country.

The fact is that by 1990 the vast majority of nations had implemented some policy to stem urban growth. However, Table 6-2 shows that the number of nations that had actually developed policies to control urban growth was less than the number whose officials had expressed some level of concern in the consequences of uncontrolled growth. The policies of those governments that would like to modify migration and urbanization trends tend to be modest due to lack of resources. And, the task of discouraging urban migration is a formidable one, involving as it does balancing the life chances available in cities with those offered by rural areas. As Todaro put it,

> *The ultimate solution to urban development problems lies, paradoxically, in rural development. . . . Policies designed to create more urban jobs or expanded social services can only serve to exacerbate the problem. As long as economic opportunities in rural areas remain bleak, every attempt to respond to the mounting*

TABLE 6-2   Government Perceptions and Policies Regarding
Migration and Urban Growth

	Number of Governments Concerned about Migration		
	Minor Change Desired	Major Change Desired	Total Number of Countries
Less Developed Countries	39	74	131
Least Developed Countries	12	25	41

	Governments with Policies to Control Migration					
	Accelerate Trend	Decelerate Trend	Reverse Trend	Maintain Trend	No Intervention	Total Number of Countries
Less Developed Countries	5	56	38	4	28	131
Least Developed Countries	3	15	10	0	13	41

Source: United Nations 1992b, 164, 167.

> *social dilemma of the city by providing greater opportunities in the urban area will call forth an even greater urban-rural migration. (Todaro [1979] 1984, 17, 20)*

Globalization underlines the policy choices facing national government planning agents. In the global marketplace, the old question reemerges as to whether national governments should act to regulate the inequalities associated with patterns of market-led growth—runaway rates of urbanization, urban primacy, the further peripheralization of remote regions. Should national resources instead be invested in making leading regions, the largest cities, national capitals, and ports, and the universities, hospitals, and shopping districts located in them more attractive? Modernization theorists have been arguing for decades not to interfere with patterns of growth, including urbanization, that are natural to the operation of the market (Berry 1973, 77; Linn, 1982, 635; O'Connor 1983, 319; World Bank 2000, 130). Will governments be inclined to continue to pursue control policies in the present climate, which recasts the arena of competition for growth initiatives as occurring not so much between rural and urban populations *within* nations as *between* nations, all competing for international investment and tourism? In this light, showcase investment in the capital and largest cities is seen as the formula for success and for further neglect and inequality within nations. Remote and neglected populations have shown varying amounts of patience with being left out of the national plan, with waiting for the natural workings of the global market to notice and incorporate them in its unfolding scheme. Some of these will make their impatience heard through militant and inconvenient protests in the capital, like some of the 3,000 protests that took place in Mexico City in 1995, or through secessionist strategies at home, like the guerrilla movement in Mexico's remote and economically neglected southern Guerrero state. The difficulty of developing national policies that temper the urge to serve further growth with measures to balance the distribution of opportunities has become greater within the new visibilities and sensitivities of the global arena.

Comparative Urban Studies

A vast body of social research on Third World urbanization does not focus explicitly on the issue of underdevelopment (although underdevelopment and the attendant patterns of inequality can be shown to underlie each of the social forms that we consider here). This research is concerned, instead, with changes in the organization of social life and experience brought on by urbanization. We will focus on three aspects of change: kinship, community, and ethnicity. These provide interesting contrasts, as well as parallels, with the experiences of urbanizing populations in Western countries. In seeking such parallels, it is necessary to bear in mind Janet Abu-Lughod's (1975, 13–16) admonition that comparative urbanologists have tended to be too quick in recognizing common patterns. This means that they are often willing to gloss over significant differences between the West and the Third World and to ignore the different historical circumstances that have generated superficially similar results. Most importantly, she criticized the bias that observers bring to such comparisons; modernization theorists assume that change means evolution toward some common, "modern" form, most closely approximated at present by Western urbanization.

Abu-Lughod's point is fundamental for urban sociology. It raises the question, at least implicitly, of whether the city as a social form exerts an independent causal effect on other forms of social organization and on behavior. From the insights provided by the perspective of political economy, we have already seen that the historical factors that gave rise to the city in Western industrialized countries and in the Third World were very different—aside from the fact that cities have been bound together in the same world economy. It seems that if an awareness of the different historical circumstances is taken as a starting point and if modernization notions of convergence are avoided, cautious comparison—including a readiness to recognize parallels where they exist—may be permitted. Urban sociology has failed to profit sufficiently from comparative studies that systematically incorporate Third World evidence. Any effort to establish general principles of urban sociology that neglects Third World examples runs the risk of becoming obsolete once such comparative studies are established: Worse, it reinforces the ethnocentric tendency to treat Third World examples as exotic exceptions to prematurely established principles. As the discussion in the following chapters will suggest further, it is quite possible to see cities themselves as merely the spatial expressions of more fundamental economic and political patterns. However, these concentrated arenas of heterogeneous human activity have the capacity, as social arenas, to modify experience and the organization of social life.

Urbanization and Kinship

As was pointed out in Chapter 4, the results of a number of urban kinship studies have drawn into question the historical assumption that Western urbanization meant the end of traditional kinship systems. Research has also demonstrated that kinship systems are a powerful resource throughout the Third World for poor people struggling to make the most of their circumstances under the uncertain conditions of rapid change.

A common function of kinship systems in poor countries is the concerted effort to bring migrants to the city. Todaro ([1979] 1984, 17) described the widespread pattern whereby rural parents' ultimate goal for their children is that they eventually land an urban white-collar job. In addition to marking their children's success, such a position would represent long-term security for parents who fully expect to be looked after by their socially mobile offspring in the future. These parents resist vocational training for their children in skills that have applications in a rural setting.

Beyond providing sponsorship for the education of potential rural-urban migrants, kin support the actual migration to and settlement in the city. In Africa "kinship ties generally provide the migrant with an initial base in town; . . . it is doubtful if so many people would migrate to African towns if they could not rely on kinsmen to provide them with board and lodging until they find a job and a house" (O'Connor 1983, 76). Although the barriada associations of Lima often restricted households to nuclear family members in the beginning, after a while many residents were allowed to accommodate relatives who had come directly from the provinces, as the barriada became a direct target of new rural-urban migrants (Mangin 1973, 318). In New Zealand, Polynesian migrants were commonly taken by a relative from place to place in seeking a job: The veteran urbanite eased the transition for those with a poorer command of English (Graves and Graves 1980, 202).

Initial settlement is only the first of the obstacles rural-urban migrants must face. Day-to-day existence holds many potential crises for the majority of urbanites of very modest means and those who live at or near subsistence. Illness, injury, unemployment, or some other financial trouble present serious and not uncommon crises in the absence of formal systems of compensation or social security. One may rely on friends in such times of need, but it is kin upon whom the responsibility ultimately falls in most cultures. Kin may not always be pleased to receive requests for financial help or accommodation, and relationships may become strained and contact among family members full of friction; but there is an overall rationale to kin ties that holds the system together, especially for the poor. Banck presented the following account from Brazil, which addresses the various dimensions of kinship and demonstrates conclusively that what may appear as a one-sided sacrifice at one moment makes good sense in the long run to all involved.

> *They are both 50 years old and they have been married for 26 years. . . . They are childless. . . . The main reason for coming to the town was to help with the education of a niece, one of their godchildren. They both got jobs and their earnings*

made it possible for the girl to become a primary school teacher. Then they went back to their family in the interior, but four years ago they returned to [the city] in order to help with the education of two of their nephews. . . .

The woman sometimes worries about the future, when both she and her husband will be old. . . . "Sometimes at night I lay awake worrying about it all.". . . "Well, there will always be someone who will help us.". . .

This household's sole reason for existing is education. It will be dissolved once this goal is attained. . . . a strategic coalition in an almost pure form. (Banck 1980, 236–237)

Banck (1980, 239–240) was careful to point out that the way kinship operates in Brazil does not represent a survival of a cultural tradition, nor is it a matter of harmonious reciprocations within tight-knit consensus groups. Instead, kinship typically works as a bitter, squabbling, jealous adaptation to the "harshness of the societal transformation" taking place in countries like Brazil. Similarly, Graves and Graves (1980, 213) cautioned that "urban kin relations can . . . be viewed not as the persistence, modification, or diminution of an earlier cultural form, but as part of an active, ongoing adaptation that individuals are making to their changing world." This means that the key variable in understanding the operation of kinship in urbanization is economic, not cultural. The forms that kinship takes are determined not by past patterns but by the exigencies of the present. Thus, in Brazil it is only the better-off who can afford to interpret the nuclear-family household as an independent unit, who can say, "No, really, you have to do it on your own" (Banck 1980, 238). The poor know that is not possible.

Among modernization theorists, extended kinship is most often viewed as parasitic. They argue that potential entrepreneurs are held back because their expanded fortunes would simply lead to expanded demands by a widening pool of clamoring kin who would absorb the potential investment in unproductive consumption. Such interpretations consider only the obligations of the successful businessperson and fail to consider the pooling of family resources that was likely to have contributed initially to the individual's success. Furthermore, "the member who accepts the demands that the extended family makes on him as legitimate and who derives satisfaction from the contribution he can make to the extended family's well-being has every reason to make a maximum effort" (Gugler and Flanagan 1978, 130).

Evidence of the potential advantages of extended family in urban business ventures in Ludhiana, India, demonstrates that extended kinship can provide a pool of labor, capital, and resources—including "connections" with the right people for obtaining licenses, permits, and materials. Firms operated on a nuclear-family basis suffer by comparison. The author of the study concluded that in addition to serving as an effective structure for survival in environments of scarcity, the extended family was also effective in marshaling resources for mutual advancement (Tangri 1982, 201–203).

Widespread migration patterns, in which some members of extended families have gone to the city while others remain at home, have served to tie rural and urban areas together in what may be seen, from one vantage point, as a complementary arrangement. In tropical Africa, the city provides income to ambitious and able-bodied migrants, while their rural area of origin promises them a secure refuge in subsistence agriculture upon retirement or in the event that urban political or economic conditions become unmanageable. Rural areas provide a source of workers, although often in overabundance, for urban labor needs, while these workers provide a source of income for kin in rural areas through the common practice of remitting a portion of their urban incomes.

The question of determining the *net* impact of this kinship system on development is interesting but impossible to resolve. On the one hand, families working in concert have the capacity to provide a far greater supply of urbanites than would be the case were individuals left to make their own way to the city. In this way, kinship contributes to the momentum of urbanization. On the other hand, the kinship system works to soften the inequity of concentrated wealth by redistributing urban incomes to rural areas, as urban migrant workers share a portion of their earnings with those who helped sponsor their migration.

A Marxist analysis sees the same system in a different light. It finds complementarity only from the perspective of those in whose interest it is to minimize labor costs. In this view, the urban-based capitalist labor market exploits the precapitalist rural arrangement that floods the cities with new workers (that reproduces required labor) at no cost to their eventual employers. In the city, competition among job seekers keeps labor costs down. In addition, labor is expected to survive unemployment by its own devices (and it does), and wages are kept low by the fiction that only small urban family units or individuals are dependent on the worker's wage.

Thus, at the individual or familial level of analysis, extended kinship may be viewed as a mechanism of mobility and an asset. A societal level of analysis may emphasize the negative impact of extended kinship, focusing on its capacity to accelerate urbanization rates. Finally, an analysis focusing on the relationship of workers to the production process may emphasize the self-exploitive features of extended kinship and its negative consequences for labor. At none of these levels of interpretation are the interests of the kinship unit and the wider society assumed to coincide.

Communities and Networks

The poorer, more run-down sections of cities give outsiders the impression that social life in these areas must be disorganized and predatory. This is at least as mistaken a view in Lagos or Lima as it is in Boston or Chicago. Indeed, we have already seen, in addition to the cohesion provided by kinship, the well-organized social structure of squatter developments in Mexico and Peru. Certainly these areas, bristling with a self-conscious determination to survive, qualify as urban defended neighborhoods. In poor areas, where so many are dependent on a steady clientele for their informal trading activities, the community develops a face-to-face quality and level of mutual recognition among inhabitants that belies the large numbers involved. In the apparent jumble of housing and subdivision of dwelling spaces, which make servicing by authorities or utility agencies difficult or impossible, intricate and complex arrangements are worked out among residents (for the sale and metering of electricity, for example, where multiple households tap the line of a single utility customer). Just as few can afford to neglect their kin, only the very well situated can ignore their neighbors.

As our discussion in Chapter 4 indicated, it is necessary to liberate the concept of community from the confines of the neighborhood and substitute the imagery of the social network. The social network concept has been applied profitably to sub-Saharan African urbanization for three decades. The idea that people's social lives are lived simultaneously in different arenas of contact is especially applicable to the case of African rural-urban migrants. Although they may be away from their village of origin for their entire working life, with only occasional return visits, they typically remain involved in the social affairs of their "home place." Yet on a day-to-day basis, they are cut off from contact with those at home.

Epstein's (1969, 111) distinction between an individual's *effective* and *extended* network has been useful for understanding the social context of life in such situations. Boswell (1969, 287–296) pointed out that those individuals with whom a person spends most of the time (effective network) may not be the same individuals a person will depend on in a time of personal crisis (extended network). At such times, long-dormant ties may be revived as individuals call on those who share claims of obligation, such as kin, or other special categories of relationship from the past, such as schoolmates from home.

Most recently, a leading authority on urban-rural social ties, Josef Gugler (forthcoming), reassessed and reaffirmed the continued importance of these relationships, especially in Africa, where most of the urban adult population are migrants from rural areas. He pointed out that it is helpful to deconstruct (to articulate) the multiple dimensions that provide the incentive for urban migrants to remain engaged in their community of origin. Rewards for remaining engaged include access to farmland, a site and cheap labor for house-building, cheap labor to be employed in a sweatshop, a supply of goods to be traded at the urban end, a political constituency for office-seekers, refuge in case of political persecution or civil war, prestige and admiration, cultural grounding, and an important basis for identity. Most migrants are obliged to remain engaged because they have parents and other relatives, perhaps spouses and children, living in their birth community. In Gugler's classic phraseology, urban migrants live in a "dual system."

That a migrant's home place remains an important sphere of involvement is attested to by the large number of "home improvement" (village development) associations in West African cities. Most migrants not only have family still living in their village of origin, but also visit frequently and expect to retire there (Gugler and Flanagan 1978, 64–70). During the 1960s, 5 million pounds, or about 10 percent of all the incomes earned in the city of Accra, Ghana, was reported to flow annually out of the city, most finding its way into rural Ghana (Caldwell 1967, 143). Aronson (1970, 289–290) concluded that in the amount of money, energy, and advocacy invested by urbanites in their rural home areas, the Ijebu Yoruba of Nigeria "do far more in self-help than the Nigerian government can hope to do for many more years to come in the way of social and economic development." McGee (1982, 62–63) was more equivocal regarding the balance of benefits to rural Asia: "At one level there is little doubt that the remittance of income earned in urban areas allows people in rural areas to maintain a level of life which might otherwise deteriorate substantially. But on the other hand these linkages also offer the possibility of access to elements of the capitalist mode of production, as for instance in the creation of new needs (e.g., tin roofs) which mop up the earnings." However, it seems that such urban-initiated home improvement projects, such as the construction of schools or clinics or the supply of pure water or electricity, have clearly provided a net benefit to rural recipients. In any event, such projects leave little doubt that the issue of community identification and involvement for migrant urbanites is not confined to the city. Also, city styles and tastes reach far into the countryside of every Third World country, carried by migrant daughters and sons.

Urbanization and Ethnicity

Many Third World cities, particularly those of Africa and South Asia, recruit their migrants from culturally diverse regions. As a consequence, the urbanization experienced by these populations includes an ethnic dimension. It has been suggested, at least with reference to Africa and the United States, that similarities in urban ethnicity invite cautious comparative analysis (Hannerz 1974). Very little of this has been forthcoming, however. Perhaps this is due to the unfortunate entanglement of the social sciences in the language of colonialism, which obscures the fact that researchers are examining very similar processes when they study urban intergroup dynamics in more- and less-developed countries. Group identity, which is described as ethnicity in the geographic context of Europe or the United States, is still too often labeled "tribalism" in poorer nations. Two examples of ethnic solidarity, one from sub-Saharan Africa and the other from Indonesia, will serve as reminders of the importance of the urbanization of culturally diverse groups in creating the conditions under which group identities emerge.

In sub-Saharan Africa, rural-urban migration fosters identification with expanded cultural and linguistic groups. Initially, a migrant feels that he or she belongs only to the people of the village that is left behind. Once confronted with the cultural variety of the urban population, the individual is apt to recognize a common ethnic membership with co-lingual groups from other villages as well. As happened in the case of European immigrants to the United States, the sense of peoplehood is expanded by urban contact with diverse populations. Similar to the European immigrants, African urban migrants find ethnicity to be a useful political and economic strategy that requires an adaptation, rather than the simple preservation, of custom.

The most complete illustration of the pragmatic adaptation of ethnicity remains Cohen's (1969) study of Hausa settlers in the predominantly Yoruba city of Ibadan in southwestern Nigeria. Hausa merchants monopolized the important long-distance trade in cattle and kola nuts between Ibadan and their native territory in the northern part of the country. When they felt that their trade monopoly was being threatened by other groups, they reasserted their control by reaffirming their identity as a distinct and socially separate people. This reaffirmation included the adoption of cultural elements that had not been traditional components of Hausa practice, wherever such components served to reenforce the quest for a clearly distinct group identity. One especially effective adoption involved the exchange of the long-standing Islamic association that the Hausas shared with other groups in Ibadan for membership in a particularly strict and exclusive Islamic sect. This meant that Hausa men would be drawn together regularly in group prayer where worship would become an expression of ethnic solidarity and exclusiveness. Hausa trade was based largely on credit among dealers, took place outside the formal apparatus of banking and other trade service institutions, and depended on reputation and trust among distant clients. Given the common interest that all traders shared in maintaining control of the trade within their ethnic group, it is logical that the measure of a man's trustworthiness would come to be judged by the degree of Hausaness that he demonstrated. Just as the renewed ethnicity supported trade, the conditions of trade reenforced ethnic expression.

Over 300 ethnoreligious groups are scattered throughout the island nation of Indonesia, and inevitably members of these groups encounter each other as migrants to the major cities. In his urban research on two main islands, Sumatra and Java, Bruner (1974) found that ethnic identity affected all aspects of social life—residence, educational and occupational opportunity, religion, friendship, and political patterns. In Indonesia, there are cross-cutting territorial and ethnic divisions. In the northern part of Sumatra (North Sumatra), all other groups are opposed to the large and successful Chinese population. Yet, the population of Sumatra (including the Chinese), taken as a whole, generally resent the Javanese domination of Indonesia, a domination symbolized by the location of the capital, Djakarta, on the island of Java. Bruner focused his attention on the dynamic ethnicity of the Batak, whose sense of peoplehood interacted with their urban locations and political situation. In the city of Medan in their home region of Sumatra, there were many Batak. In the more distant city of Bandung on Java, there were proportionately fewer Batak residents. In Medan, there were exclusive ethnic neighborhood associations, and their members were plentiful enough that individuals could choose to enclose themselves socially within the cultural group. In Bandung, there were neighborhood associations, but due to a lack of "critical mass," they were not restricted to single ethnic groups, and there was a tendency toward the assimilation of Batak migrants into the locally dominant culture. On Sumatra, the Batak distinguished among themselves, preferring to dissociate into Mandailing Batak and Toba Batak identities. In Bandung, the Javanese failed to perceive the relevance of such a distinction and lumped the groups together as Batak. During periods of heightened political tensions among the various ethnic groups in Indonesia, the Batak members themselves saw the advantages of all urban Batak uniting. At least temporarily during these periods, the members emphasized their common ancestry and became one people. Bruner observed that the relevant unit of analysis in understanding these patterns of ethnicity was the urban arena, and that the practice of identifying oneself differently depending on social context was universal.

Both of these studies show, as was pointed out in Chapter 4, that cities provide conditions appropriate to the development of ethnic identification. In the poorer nations of the world, the city has become an arena for working out regional differences. The city is the locus in which these interests confront each other in a struggle for the limited resources of both the urban sector and the economy as a whole. It is in this light that we can see the interesting parallels, as well as the fundamental difference, that exist between urban ethnicity in the Third World and the ethnic processes that resulted from immigration to the cities of the United States. In the latter, immigrants used group solidarity as a tool in their competition for economic position and power in an alien land. The same issues and strategies divide the urbanizing populations of the Third World today. But the similarity between the two cases ends here. In the nineteenth and early twentieth centuries, immigrants to the United States arrived in a country whose national identity was relatively intact and jealously guarded. Third World ethnic identities often rival and at times overpower still-emerging national identities. When ethnics are migrants rather than immigrants, their homeland and the alien urban environment both lie within the borders of a single nation. Where migrant groups express exclusive identities and interests against one another and where they support rival political leaders who appeal to ethnic loyalties, the implications are more serious than in the transitional age of ethnic politics in the United States. Wherever nationalist sentiment is still problematic, still struggling to emerge or to crystallize, there is the chance that ethnic or regional identification could, in the extreme case, lead to separatist tendencies. In the more newly independent nations, the creation of a national sense of peoplehood depends in large part upon a popular perception of the government's evenhanded treatment of every region and cultural grouping. Only if we assume that it is desirable for populations to acquiesce to the patterns of regional neglect that typify underdevelopment can we conclude that strong and enduring ethnic and regional loyalties are the true problem.

7

URBAN GROWTH AND TRANSITIONS IN THE UNITED STATES

At the start of the twenty-first century, the cities of the United States continue to undergo fundamental economic and demographic transformations that are rooted in their individual and collective histories. In the past two decades or so, the decline in the fortunes of many cities has given rise to urgent discussions about "the urban problem." Analyses of the shifts in economic activity that have brought about current urban conditions typically focus on changes associated with the post–World War II era. It is easy to conclude that the early histories of contemporary U.S. cities have little to offer an analysis of the current conditions of the urban United States.

It is impossible to fully understand contemporary urban patterns and prospects, however, without examining the history of urbanization that has created over the past two centuries a dynamic, nationwide network of metropolitan economies. The size, situation, and economic conditions of cities today are linked to their origins, their relationship to regional neighbors, and their place in a continuously refocusing national and international economy. Current changes need to be understood as an articulation or revision of earlier arrangements.

The most striking feature of the urbanization of the United States is that in every period of development and in each newly emerging urban region, urban growth was spurred by an open competition among urban promoters interested in achieving regional domination for their city. The competition stemmed from the recognition that a city's economic prosperity was tied to the relative importance that could be achieved for the city within the developing national system of intermetropolitan dominance and subordination. Local urban boosterism was more a matter of self-interest than of civic passion, for it was understood that having the world believe that one's city or town was the premier settlement in the region (hence, *the* place to do business) could help to make it so. For the entrepreneur and property owner, who would benefit from the subsequent growth, the rewards would be more tangible than symbolic. "More people" translated simply into "more customers" as well as higher property values.

Today, it is still appropriate to focus on the competition between cities within the United States as they vie with each other to attract auto assembly plants, promote themselves as the high-tech research and development site of the future, or wrangle for their share of government programs. The difference between past eras and the present is that now municipal governments are involved in global competition for investments and jobs. The terms and outcomes of the new competition will reshape the urban landscape here, as they will in Europe, China, Japan, and elsewhere. For now, we focus on the historical forces that produced the U.S. urban landscape.

Urban Growth before the Twentieth Century

The urbanization of the United States followed the same east-to-west pattern as the opening and settlement of new land. It involved three distinct phases, which are shown in Table 7-1. In 1790, the date of the earliest census and the first phase

TABLE 7-1   Urban Population Growth, 1790–1880

	1790	1850	1880
Percentage of urban population in United States[a]	5.1%	15.3%	45.7%
East			
New York	33,131	515,547	1,164,673
(Brooklyn)		(138,882)	(599,495)
Philadelphia	44,096	121,376	847,170
Boston	18,320	136,881	362,839
Baltimore	13,503	169,054	332,313
New Orleans	—	116,375	216,090
Charleston	16,359	42,985	49,984
Midwest			
Chicago	—	29,963	503,185
St. Louis	—	77,860	350,518
Cincinnati	—	115,435	255,139
Cleveland	—	17,034	160,146
Detroit	—	21,019	116,340
Milwaukee	—	20,061	115,587
West			
San Francisco	—	34,776	233,959
Los Angeles	—	1,610	11,183
Seattle	—	—	3,533
Denver	—	—	35,629
Omaha	—	—	30,518
Dallas	—	—	10,358
Houston	—	2,396	16,513
Birmingham	—	—	3,086

Source: Adapted from Still 1974, 79, 210–211.
[a]U.S. Bureau of the Census 1982, 1–49.

of growth, the settlement pattern was dominated by the major eastern and southern ports, cities that already had long histories. A second phase of urbanization got under way largely between 1820 and 1850 and scattered rapidly growing cities throughout the central Midwest. By 1880, the third phase, urban growth had pushed past the Rockies to the West Coast, although the gold rush had given San Francisco a head start by midcentury.

During the colonial era, U.S. cities served the same function as colonial cities anywhere. They were commercial ports where goods, gathered from the productive hinterlands, were collected for shipment overseas, in exchange for imports from elsewhere in the expanding world economy.

> *Even farmers in distant villages were brought into the commercial world of the Atlantic economy through a series of complex interchanges. Country storekeepers concluded dozens if not hundreds of small trades with local farmers in order to accumulate sufficient inventory which, in turn, could be exchanged with a town merchant in places such as Salem, Massachusetts, New London or Hartford, Connecticut, or Lancaster, Pennsylvania, for supplies of "West Indian" goods (sugar, molasses, rum, or spices) or English commodities. (Klebanow, Jonas, and Leonard 1977, 16–17)*

Early Promoters

In the late 1600s, competition was already underway among promoters and city builders to attract population and commercial investors. Box 7-1 is from the pamphlet *A Further Account of the Province of Pennsylvania* that William Penn published

---

BOX 7-1   Philadelphia: The Orderly Colonial City

From . . . a Year within a few Weeks the Town advanced from fourscore to Three hundred and fifty seven Houses; divers of them large, well built, with good Cellars, three stories, and some with balconies. . . . There is also a fair Key [quay] of about three hundred foot square . . . to which a ship of five hundred Tuns may lay her broadside. . . . We have also a Ropewalk . . . and cordage for shipping already spun at it.

. . . There inhabits most sorts of useful Tradesmen, as Carpenters, Joyners, Bricklayers, Masons, Plasterers, Plumers, Smiths, Glasiers, Taylers, Shoe-makers, Butchers, Bakers, Brewers, Glovers, Tanners, Felmongers, Wheelwrights, Millrights, Shiprights, Boatrights, Ropemakers, Saylmakers, Blockmakers, Turners, etc. . . .

. . . The hour for Work and Meals to Labourers are fixt, and known by Ring of Bell. . . . After nine at night the Officers go the Rounds, and no Person, without very good cause, suffered to be at any Publick House that is not a Lodger.

. . . Some Vessels have been here Built, and many Boats; and by that means a ready Conveniency for Passage of People and Goods. . . . Divers Brickerys going on, many Cellars already Ston'd or Brick'd and some Brick Houses going up. . . . The Town is well furnish'd with convenient Mills. . . . The improvement of the place is best measur'd by the advance of Value upon every man's Lot. . . . The worst Lot in the Town, without any Improvement upon it, is worth four times more than it was when it was lay'd out, and the best forty. (As reprinted in Still 1974, 15–17)

in England in 1685 to promote his new town, Philadelphia. Note the emphasis on order and the good prospects of return on investments.

Philadelphia fulfilled Penn's promise and by 1790 had grown to over forty-four thousand in population, larger than its rival New York and more than double the size of Boston or Baltimore. Like many of the New World cities (for example, Charleston, Hartford, New Haven, and Providence), Philadelphia was laid out in a variation of the gridiron or checkerboard pattern of right-angle streets and avenues for the sake of order and efficiency. Apart from the additional designation of a few open places as public parks or commons, there was little more to the planning of cities in these early times than the laying out of streets. Land use in early colonial New England towns was closely governed from the start, as were all aspects of life, but by the 1760s or the 1770s, land regulation of any kind was under attack in New England because it was believed to pose a potential hindrance to trade and economic activity (Klebanow, Jonas, and Leonard 1977, 30). The grid plan, on the other hand, served commercial interests well. It lent itself to the ready transfer of property ownership and use by offering standardized lot sizes and shapes that could be converted from one use to another with a minimum of resistance. "It accommodated a distinctly modern attitude toward city building that considered nothing permanently fixed but the individual parcels of real estate. These lots enjoyed a life of their own, unrelated to any more general schemes of ordering the cityscape" (Barth 1980, 30). Urban merchants were vigilant in their opposition to government interference in trade. In the 1760s, the merchant classes led the early resistance to restrictive colonial policies. The rank and file of the urban-based movement may have consisted largely of urban workers and sailors (the latter comprised the largest occupational group in the colonial seaport cities), but it was instigated and led by angry men of wealth and position.

The Race for Regional Domination

During the revolutionary war, most cities experienced a drastic drop in population. With independence, however, the competition for trade and population resumed, and within a few decades, New York emerged as the leading port and most populous city in the United States. It achieved this position by adopting policies congenial to commerce, through innovations in shipping and by virtue of having become the leading hub of finance. After 1817, New York permitted British manufacturers to consign goods directly to auctioneers in the city, eliminating British exporting and American importing agents, and thus ensuring merchants in other cities of the lowest wholesale prices. In the same year, New York ship lines began regularly scheduled transatlantic service (packet service), which offered merchants an attractive predictability and dependability in that they would now know by advance scheduling when ships would sail. By the 1820s, New York also began to emerge as the financial capital of the hemisphere, doing extensive business throughout the United States and extending its influence into the nations of Latin America as they gained their independence (Glaab and Brown 1983, 38). In 1825, New York's hegemony was consolidated again with the completion of the Erie Canal system. In the expanding United States, a city's fortunes were dependent on the extent and wealth of its hinterlands. The Erie Canal opened new land for commercial development along its entire length and greatly enlarged New York City's access to vast new territories by forging an "overland" route to the Great Lakes network of waterways. The canal cut transportation costs to a fraction of their former levels. In addition, it set off a flurry of canal building among New York's rivals that lasted until the mid-1850s (Warner 1972, 67–68).

The period from 1820 to 1870 marked the era of most rapid urban expansion. The proportion of the total population of the United States living in cities grew from just over 7 to over 25 percent. To appreciate the hidden significance of these numbers, it is necessary to keep in mind that the total population of the country expanded from 9.6 to 39.8 million during this period. The number of people in urban areas increased from just under 700,000 in 1820 to just under 10 million in 1870 (Klebanow et al. 1977, 41). The changing geographic distribution of the urban population was as impressive as the numbers involved, as urbanization spread westward across the continent. During this period, cities with 25,000 or more people grew from a string of a few such centers along the East Coast to an urban system comprised of fifty-one cities of that size (Warner 1972, 70–71). It was a period in which the canal system that had just emerged was made practically obsolete by the growth of the railroads. The railroad had its most vital impact in the West and Midwest, but the significance of this new transportation technology was quickly recognized everywhere. In the following excerpt from a letter to the mayor of New York City, the president of the New York and Albany Railroad urged that action was once again required for New York to maintain its hegemony over its East Coast rivals.

> The announcement of the completion of a railroad from Boston to Albany demands the attention of the people of this city; . . . this new avenue of trade and travel, with such inducements as are offered for its use, must make . . . serious inroads upon the trade and commerce hitherto enjoyed by this city.
>
> This new avenue also opens a continuous line of railroad (nearly completed) from Boston, through Albany and Troy, to Buffalo. It branches off, in the New England States, by a web of well constructed railroads, carrying the products of the western country direct to every eastern seaport; inviting the producers of our own State, as well as the hardy sons of Michigan and Ohio, by an uninterrupted channel, to markets beyond the borders of this State—open at all seasons, and therefore offering unquestioned advantages during many months of the year, while our water course and canals are fast bound by ice.
>
> The facilities of rapid transportation, the ready market for interchange of commodities, in winter or summer; the establishment of steam packets with England, and probably with France, are advantages held out by Boston—a proof of her wealth, and highly honorable to her character for enterprize; at the same time an example is held up to us, and a warning given, that if we omit to improve that natural advantage we so eminently enjoy, we must revert to the position of deriving supplies from Boston and elsewhere, instead of being the great center of trade and commerce of the Union. (As reprinted in Still 1974, 81–82)

It would be difficult to overstate the impact of the railroads on the urbaniza-tion and economic integration of the United States. They opened new land for de-velopment. The routes taken by their main long-distance lines determined whether a town would grow into a city—by being drawn in a central way into the expanding national economy—or remain a locally oriented outpost. Rail lines allowed and encouraged specialization and national economic integration both for growing smaller cities and for agricultural regions. Warner (1972, 88–89) of-fered the following examples: "Albany concentrated on shirts, nearby Troy on collars; Bridgeport on corsets, brass, and machine tools; New Bedford and Fall River on cotton textiles; Elizabeth, New Jersey, on electrical machinery; Chester, Pennsylvania, on iron and steel; Allentown, Pennsylvania, on silk goods . . . etc." Similarly, the railroads provided for the efficient distribution of regionally specialized agriculture: oranges from Florida, lettuce from California, strawber-ries from Louisiana, lumber from Idaho. As urbanization spread from coast to coast and cities grew in every region, a national economy began to crystallize. Urbanization was an extension and physical expression of the voracious appetite of the growing economy.

The Midwest

City building in the Midwest amounted to a competition among towns to make the most of their locations on important water routes. River sites, like those at Pittsburgh and Cincinnati on the Ohio River, developed where natural obstacles interrupted navigation. Upriver ports, like St. Louis, benefited from the introduc-tion of steamboats, which turned rivers into two-way transportation routes. Where river currents had previously limited the direction in which heavy cargo could travel, steam provided a powerful means of carrying goods and people up-stream. After the mid-1800s, the leadership of the river cities in the Midwest was challenged by the rapid growth of the Great Lakes cities of Cleveland, Milwaukee, Detroit, and especially Chicago. Chicago grew from a population of less than five thousand people in 1830 to a half million in 1880—by which time it displaced St. Louis as the Midwest's most populous city. Ten years later, more than a million people lived there.

Chicago's growth may be accounted for by a number of geographic and tech-nological features that tended to reenforce its position as a regional magnet for population and economic activity. Warner (1972, 100–101) observed that "Chicago owed its importance to its situation at a point where cheap long-distance water transportation met the more expensive land transport. Even more significant was the fact that at the very moment the inventions in farm machinery, the perfect-ing of the railroad, and the unmistakable westward flow of the American popu-lation made the occupation of the Midwest profitable, Chicago rose to service this giant hinterland." Like the other major Midwestern cities, Chicago quickly added manufacturing to its function as a regional trade center. As Warner (1972, 101) pointed out, Chicago soon made "every item needed to run a railroad or start a farm, to build a town, to furnish a home, or to clothe a family." In 1856, its posi-tion in the national economy had been anchored by its crossroads location on 10 trunk-line railroads.

The first transcontinental railroad was completed in 1869, and by 1885, there were four. The futures of cities that could attract such a line were assured, while places like Parksville, Missouri, and Auraria, Kansas, became historical footnotes, significant for their failed efforts to attract a major route (Miller 1973, 29). Entrepreneurs in Kansas City, a modest town struggling for regional leadership in the 1860s with such modest neighbors as Leavenworth and St. Joseph, financed construction of the first bridge across the Missouri River and attracted a leg of the transcontinental Union Pacific line. In this way, Kansas City's dominance over the territory was established. Civic leaders in the city of Denver, to which gold mining had given the initial impetus for growth, similarly engaged in a vigorous campaign of railroad-building in order to tie into the transcontinental system (Glaab and Brown 1983, 118–120). Omaha, which was already an important trading town on the Missouri River by the time the railroads reached it in the late 1860s, developed rapidly into a city on the transcontinental route.

The West

On the West Coast, San Francisco established itself as "the city" of the Pacific region. By 1880, its importance as a port supported the development of a wealthy and sophisticated population, which ranked ninth in size among U.S. cities. Los Angeles expanded more gradually in the nineteenth century, despite the vigorous efforts of promoters who attracted competitive rail lines to the city and who laid out and sold land to speculators in over one hundred "paper" new towns in Los Angeles County from 1884 to 1888. Although most of the speculative plans fell through as the land market in the area folded in 1889 and the city lost a third of its population, the rail lines and attractive climate set the stage for the spectacular growth that would begin a decade or so later. By 1910, Los Angeles's population was well over three hundred thousand.

Along the northern coast, Seattle's business interests held off the challenge of rival Tacoma (touted by promoters as having a potential greater than that of Chicago and New York), as Seattle became a key northwestern terminus for transcontinental rail lines (Glaab and Brown 1983, 122–128).

The cities of the South were slow to emerge in the 1800s. Houston was one of a few Gulf port towns that had begun to grow into cities by the latter decades of the century. Dallas remained a relatively small settlement until the railroads arrived in the 1880s. Birmingham, Alabama, pronounced by its promoters as the "magic city" of the South upon its establishment as an industrial center in 1871, also grew quite slowly until after the turn of the century.

By the 1890s, most of today's major cities were in place, even though, owing to the small size of many of them, it would have been difficult to project their relative importance a hundred years into the future.

Nineteenth Century Arenas of Wealth and Poverty

The cities of the nineteenth century were part of a process of economic expansion that produced a powerful national economy and enormous individual fortunes. In the 1850s, big-city merchants competed with one another as each built palatial dry goods stores, celebrated in tourist's guides as "places to see." In Boston, it was Jordan Marsh; in Philadelphia, Wanamaker and Brown; and in 1859 in New York, Lord and Taylor opened the doors of a five-story, white marble emporium that was described as being "more like an Italian palace than a place for the sale of broadcloth" (Still 1974, 148). After the 1880s and the architectural innovations of steel frame construction and the elevator, such temples of commerce were joined by the skyscraper. By the end of the century, New York could boast more than half a dozen buildings over three hundred feet tall and many more nearly that height. Standing together, these buildings embodied the wealth-generating capacity of the economy, and U.S. cities took on their reputation as arenas in which the actors were obsessed with the making of money. Visitors to New York described the "mad race for wealth"; an Italian visitor to the city in 1882 labeled it "la Mecca del dollaro" (Still 1956, 206–207).

Just as the urbanization of the United States produced great wealth, it also produced poverty and hardship in the cities. The conditions of the poor, especially with regard to housing, had been a social concern in the older urban centers since the beginning of the period of rapid urban expansion in 1820. As urbanization proceeded, popular concern for quality housing for the poor was overwhelmed by the sheer demand for housing and the readiness of private interests to take advantage of the desperate situation poor people found themselves in. The inadequate, partitioned space provided by landlords was often subdivided by the tenants themselves in order to meet their rents, which were due in advance (Barth 1980, 44). Immigrants added increasingly to the demand for cheap living space as the century wore on. As the following commentary from the 1850s observes, the fact that even the poorest, in adequate numbers, could constitute a profitable market, was not lost on enterprising property owners.

> It was soon perceived by astute owners or agents of property, that a greater percentage of profit would be realized by the conversion of houses and blocks into barracks, and dividing their space into the smallest portions capable of containing human life within four walls. . . . Entire blocks of buildings, worn out in other service, were let in hundreds of sub-divided apartments, and rates of rent were established, as well as seasons and modes of payment, which while affording the wretched tenantry some sort of shelter within their scanty means, secured at the same time prompt payment of weekly dues, and an aggregate of profit from the whole barracks (risks and losses taken into account) of twice or thrice the amount which a legitimate lease of the building to one occupant would bring, if granted for business purposes at the usual rate of real estate interest. (State of New York [1857] 1963, 270)

In New York, affordable housing for the poor included cramped rented space in cellars, attics, and shacks put up on the back lots of existing housing. These forms of accommodation were replaced in time by four- and five-story tenements that could house about 20 families, exclusive of boarders. The profitability, and ostensibly the healthfulness, of these structures was improved upon after 1879 by the "dumbbell" design. These six-story structures were so called because of an indentation 2½ feet deep that ran for 50 feet along each side of the building, suggesting a dumbbell shape when built alongside a similar structure. They were designed to provide space for about 300 people but accommodated many more because the poor families who lived in them took in boarders and relatives. The prizewinning design was much applauded at the time for its improved provision of light, ventilation (every room had a window), and toilet facilities (every story had two toilets) (Jackson 1984, 325). In fact, the buildings created congested neighborhoods with their high population densities, and the deep air shafts between each building provided little daylight or air and were quickly recognized as convenient dump sites by tenants.

Cities remained unhealthy places throughout the century, becoming more so with time, especially for the poor. Death rates were higher and life expectancies shorter than for rural populations. Epidemics of contagious diseases, such as yellow fever and cholera, were recurrent; dysentery, malaria, and tuberculosis were regular threats as well. The streets of the city, both paved and unpaved, were used by residents as common dumps for all types of refuse. Heavy horse traffic added manure to the litter. Streets were cleared only irregularly. After midcentury, growing U.S. cities found it increasingly difficult to supply their populations with clean water and to adequately manage sewage problems. The first professional, nonvolunteer fire fighters were not introduced until midcentury, and the number of major conflagrations that consumed large tracts of urban real estate in various cities attested to the fact that their resources and methods remained inadequate through the turn of the century.

The Walking City

What remains to be added to this picture of nineteenth century cities is a description of their spatial arrangement or land use patterns. The U.S. city of 1820 to 1870 was not quite a "disorganized hodgepodge" of businesses and residences, but there was a remarkable mix of property use within local areas. Commercial houses tended to center around transport nodes, like dock facilities; but in the blocks beyond, one might find sugar refineries and slaughterhouses side by side with banking and insurance firms (Warner 1972, 82). Sam Warner (1962, 15–16) referred to the "discipline" imposed on the spatial configuration of the "walking city"—a city where all but the most affluent depended on their own leg power to get around. He noted that in 1850 the "walking city" of Boston was a densely settled area within a two-mile radius of city hall. In order for the whole city to retain a unity of focus and function, he reckoned that access by foot to any point within an hour or less was necessary. On the other hand, Hawley (1981, 86–88) emphasized the "cellular" operating structure of the nineteenth-century walking city. The fact that most people worked long hours and had to travel their daily rounds quickly and efficiently afterwards meant that "the urban agglomeration was a congeries of more or less self-contained districts or quarters, each with its own industries and shops and other institutions. Within each district there was no clear separation of rich and poor. Employers and employees, if they did not share a place of residence, lived side by side." Although some general patterns of spatial separation had emerged by 1870, such as the exclusive residential enclaves of Beacon Hill in Boston, Chestnut Street in Philadelphia, and Washington Square in Manhattan, the mixing of groups, classes, and functions remained a distinctive characteristic of the nineteenth century city. Warner considered that there may have been some virtue attached to this pattern:

> *If the criterion of urbanity is the mixing of classes and ethnic groups, in some cases including a mixture of blacks and whites, along with dense living and crowded streets and the omnipresence of all manner of businesses near the houses in every quarter, then the cities of the United States in the years between 1820 and 1870 marked the zenith of our national urbanity. (Warner 1972, 84)*

Early Public Transportation and the First Suburbs

Changes in transportation technology transformed the shape of the cities and their patterns of land use. More efficient means of moving people about meant that urban patterns were no longer controlled fundamentally by walking distances. The tendency for skyscrapers, introduced before the turn of the century, to concentrate in one area of the city fixed the central business district; this was the specialized, high land-value area that tended to focus on white-collar employment, attracted certain types of retail stores, and, therefore, caused traffic to converge. Residential densities in these areas declined as housing of most types proved less able to support the high costs of central location. The urban radius of settlement was increased by transportation technologies that allowed people to commute between more distant residences and places of work.

The omnibus, horse drawn and capable of carrying a dozen passengers, was introduced in Paris in 1819 and reached New York in the late 1820s. The larger and more efficient horse-drawn streetcar, first employed in New York in 1832 and adopted in the 1850s and 1860s by Boston, Philadelphia, Baltimore, St. Louis, Cincinnati, and San Francisco, ran more quickly between points on its own tracks. It was still too expensive for the average worker to use as a daily conveyance. Further improvements in transportation were represented by cable cars, the use of elevated rails that ran above the congested streets, and electric streetcars and trolleys. Subways appeared just before the turn of the century, with Boston leading the way in 1898. The net effect of these improvements was to allow residents who could afford it the chance to move yet farther from the business district, making "the daily commute part of their urban existence" (Barth 1980, 53–56). Certainly, many people rode. In the 1860s New York's principal street rails were already carrying 45 million passengers annually, and Boston's, 6.5 million (Still 1974, 86). Nevertheless, in 1899 the *average* commuting distance was still only about a quarter of a mile in the country's largest city, New York (Pred 1966, 209). This suggests that for many the cellular pattern described by Hawley still characterized the urban experience at the turn of the century.

Those who migrated to the periphery in the late nineteenth century—away from the congestion, grime, and smoke of the increasingly industrialized cities—

were among the earliest, although not the first, American "suburbanites." A new type of community had, in fact, emerged earlier, around midcentury, which gave new meaning to the term *suburb*. Binford (1985, 1ff.) noted that after the 1850s, suburbs had become the location of communities that housed many city workers. These had the nature of small towns, communities in themselves, but were "influenced by an urban economy and inhabited by urbane citizens."

The number of urbanites who joined in the migration to the suburbs increased gradually from midcentury "until by the 1890s it had attained the proportions of a mass movement" (Warner 1962, 22). The city's residential radius increased dramatically by the end of the century, but the pattern of urban extension retained a certain discipline reminiscent of the old walking city. Rather than sprawling thinly in every direction, the population extended from the densely built center of the city in narrow fingers or spokes of settlement, leaving green undeveloped space in between. Although rail lines freed the affluent from the center of the city, commuters had to remain within walking distance of the transportation spokes. Uncontrolled urban sprawl would wait until the following century.

By the end of the 1800s, the urban network of the United States was clearly outlined. Between roughly 1840 and 1880, the Northeast urban industrial region had established its dominant position. In this region, the command centers of the national economy were located, as well as the cities that led the others in innovation (Miller 1973, 39). As industrial growth came to play an increasingly important role in the national economy, intercity rivalries focused on efforts to attract new manufacturing plants. Some manufacturing had been a feature of the urban economies since the colonial period. By the late nineteenth century, it had become the most vital element. In 1899, Detroit's twenty carriage and wagon shops—the forerunners of the automobile industry—employed 318 of the city's 38,000 workers. By 1916, the auto industry in Detroit employed 120,000 (Glazer 1965, 51, 79).

The Expanding Metropolis: Through World War II

The 1900s were the urban century for the United States. The urban proportion of the population continued to grow rapidly during the early part of the century. As Table 7-2 shows, according to the 1920 census, there were for the first time more

TABLE 7-2   Urban Population Growth, 1900–1950

	Total Population	Number Urban	Percent Urban
1900	76,212,168	30,214,832	39.6
1910	92,228,496	42,064,001	45.6
1920	106,021,537	54,253,282	51.2
1930	123,202,624	69,160,599	56.1
1940	132,164,569	74,705,338	56.5
1950	151,325,798	90,128,194	59.6

Source: U.S. Bureau of the Census 1982, 1–49.

than 100 million people living in the United States, of which the majority (51.2 percent) were urban. By 1950, nearly 60 percent of the population, or just over 90 million people, were classified as urban. Table 7-3 indicates how much the cities whose growth we traced in Table 7-1 had grown by 1940. What the figures alone cannot show is that as the country was becoming more urbanized, the urban population, and the cities themselves, were undergoing a fundamental transformation.

The Growing Edge

One of the most significant changes had been underway since the beginning of the twentieth century. Every subsequent census showed that the population of the metropolitan areas *outside* the central cities was increasing at a more rapid rate than the population of the central city. As the century progressed, it became increasingly evident that the densely concentrated cities of the 1800s, whose industries, stores, offices, and residences were crowded together, had been a temporary arrangement. The earlier pattern was attributable to the fact that the limitations of transportation and the needs of industry and commerce made the condensed arrangement the most workable. After 1920, however, the automobile age would see these cities "come apart."

During the 1920s, there was already substantial suburban development around several large cities, such as Atlanta, Cleveland, Milwaukee, and Buffalo (McKelvey 1968, 42). Together with this early suburban growth, the unprecedented growth rates of warm-climate cities, such as Miami (234 percent) and Los Angeles (133 percent), over the course of the 1920s hinted at major shifts in the future of urban growth patterns.

The 1920s also marked a change in the source of new urban populations. The decades of southern and eastern European migration had hardened biases against the foreign-born. World War I had stifled the immigration flow, which caused it to build up through postponed emigrations and additional dislocations in Europe; thus, when immigration resumed, it was with a renewed intensity. In 1921 alone there were 805,000 new arrivals. A mounting xenophobia helped to bring about

TABLE 7-3   Size of Selected Cities in 1940 by Region

East	Size	Midwest	Size	West	Size
New York	7,454,995	Chicago	4,825,527	Los Angeles	2,916,403
Philadelphia	3,199,637	Detroit	2,377,329	San Francisco	1,461,804
Boston	2,177,621	St. Louis	1,432,088	Seattle	504,980
Baltimore	1,083,300	Cleveland	1,267,270	Houston	528,961
New Orleans	552,244	Milwaukee	766,885	Dallas	398,564
Charleston	121,105	Cincinnati	787,044	Birmingham	459,930
				Denver	407,768
				Omaha	325,153

Source: U.S. Bureau of the Census 1952, 166–168.

the implementation of a strict immigration policy in the following year. Labor re-cruiters had already turned to southern blacks as a replacement for the sharply curtailed supply of immigrant European labor during the war years. This marked the beginning of the era of the Great Migration from the rural South to the urban North, which was described in Chapter 5. It would have a pervasive impact on the social structure of the urban United States in the decades to come.

The 1920s also witnessed changes in agriculture that accelerated migration to the cities from the rural areas. Table 7-4 shows that farm population declined from nearly 32 million in 1920 (the first census that separately enumerated farm popu-lation) to just over 4.5 million in 1990. This represents a corresponding decline from 30 to 1.8 percent in the proportion of the national population living on farms. Actually, this decline in farm population represented a much more substantial loss of rural population than the numbers suggested: The reduction of farm families led directly to a reduction in the number of people employed in sales and services in rural areas.

The mechanization of agriculture, especially the introduction of the tractor, began to have an impact on farming in the 1920s. The adoption of mechanized methods expanded rapidly just prior to and during World War II. As farmers turned to machinery, the larger capital investment that the machinery required meant that individual farmers had to acquire more acreage and become bigger op-erators. This meant fewer farm families. It also meant that young people would have greater difficulty getting started in farming due to the higher investment costs; as a result, more would leave rural areas. Higher efficiency meant less need for hired labor, and this change also reduced the number of tenant farmers. Over-all, this represented a substantial decline in the agricultural population. This de-cline was bound to affect the volume of trade done by local businesses in small rural towns and service centers where livelihoods were dependent on these pop-ulations. The situation was made worse for nonfarm, but agriculturally depen-dent businesses and occupations by the automobile and improved roads that ended the relative isolation of these communities. Improved transportation meant that rural businesses no longer had the monopoly on local trade on which they

TABLE 7-4   U.S. Farm Population, 1920–1990

Year	Total Farm Population
1920	31,974,000
1930	30,529,000
1940	30,547,000
1950	23,048,000
1960	15,635,000
1970	9,712,000
1980	7,241,000
1990	4,591,000

Source: U.S. Department of Agriculture 1981, 35; 1991, 363.

had been dependent (Field and Dimit [1970] 1978, 308–309). Many of the smaller population centers that depended on local trade declined or vanished altogether.

Metropolitanization

The early decades of the twentieth century marked the metropolitanization of the urban arena in the United States. The developments in transportation and communication meant that the effective population of a particular urban area included not only those who lived and worked in the central city or whose lives were circumscribed daily by the political boundaries of a particular municipality, but all those whose residential and economic situations were dictated by the presence of a large city. The city, together with its satellites and suburbs, comprised a metropolitan community or region. As Popenoe (1985, 95) pointed out, this is more an economic unity than a political or a social one. Hawley (1981, 151) differentiated between a metropolitan community and a metropolitan region. The zone of daily interaction and communication with the center comprises the metropolitan community. Zones of lesser frequency make up the region. The major point is that the urban arena has enlarged dramatically, and that, in contrast to nineteenth century populations, any accounting of urbanization at this point has to distinguish between inner-city or core populations and outer-city, suburban, and fringe populations.

Together, these metropolitan areas represented the mainstream of the national economy. A U.S. government study reported that by the end of the 1920s, the country's 96 major metropolitan areas, with a combined population of 38 million urbanites and 17 million suburbanites, contained 45 percent of the total population. The 155 U.S. counties (of the over 3,000 total) that contained the larger cities held 74 percent of all industrial wage earners, 81 percent of all salaried employees, and 65 percent of all industrial establishments, as well as accounted for 80 percent of the value added by manufacturing. The report also reflected many of the concerns of the time regarding the conditions of the cities. In particular, it noted that "an overemphasis on individualistic enterprise and speculation, in the face of unparalleled growth and expansion," along with the lack of effective regulatory controls, was the cause of some of the more acute problems the cities were facing. Among its concerns, the study listed traffic congestion, "the herding of the low-income groups into dark, poorly ventilated dwellings, the contagion of blight near the heart of the city, . . . undue concentration of land values, inequitable apportionment of local tax burdens, and inadequate public services" (Urbanism Committee of the National Resources Committee [1937] 1963, 452, 455). Planners and administrators would remain occupied with these issues until the present time.

Remaking the Cities: Transportation, Government Policy, and the Wheels and Wings of Industry

As we have seen, suburban development predated the automobile. Streetcar companies pursued two policies that encouraged suburban settlement. They ran their lines well beyond the built-up areas of the city, into the green and inviting open spaces beyond. Also, they maintained the five-cent fare and a policy of unlimited transfers, which made travel to and from these more remote places economical, not only for daily business commuters but for their families as well. Population grew in new developments along and at convenient points between transportation arteries, and the growth of existing villages within commuting distance of the city was also encouraged (Jackson 1985, 119). By 1900, industries in Chicago that were pressed for space began to locate outside the more built-up areas of the city, and by 1910 Chicago's Outer Belt Line Railroad, circling 35 miles from the Loop, stimulated the growth of the satellites of Waukegan, Elgin, Aurora, Joliet, Chicago Heights, and Gary (Miller 1973, 137). By that date, the suburban trend was already a threat to central city business in the older cities of the Midwest and the East. Scott remarked that businesspeople had only to look to the popularity of the automobile, as measured by its sales, to gauge the momentum of the trend.

> *[The automobile] released a man from dependence on the crowded transportation system . . . it enabled him to live on the edge of the city, where larks sang in the fields and wildflowers bloomed in the spring; it invited him to explore the rural lanes and quiet valleys on Sundays. It gave him more power for his personal enjoyment than the ordinary man had commanded in any previous age. (Scott 1969, 185–186)*

Not every sufficiently affluent urbanite would be beguiled by such imagery, but millions were.

The Automobile Age

In 1908, when there were 24 companies in the United States producing low-priced cars, Henry Ford introduced his Model T. In 1914, he introduced the moving assembly line, which featured a highly rationalized and integrated assembly process. An even larger plant with even more simplified worker operations was opened in 1919. Essentially, the same car that had cost $950 in 1910 could be owned for $290 by 1924. Moreover, wages were rising during the twenties; consequently, more people could own cars (Jackson 1985, 159–175). In the 10 years from 1905 to 1915, the number of registered automobiles increased from eight thousand to 2.3 million. By 1925 there were 17.5 million; by 1930, 23 million. The production of automobiles and auto-related manufactures provided an especially important impetus to urban growth after 1910. Cities that experienced the greatest growth from 1910 to 1920 were those that built cars (where Detroit led the way), those that made auto parts (as was the case in Akron and Youngstown), or those that produced fuels (for example, Los Angeles, Dallas, and Houston). Chicago, Milwaukee, and Buffalo grew from the manufacture of iron and steel, an industry closely tied to the production of automobiles (McKelvey 1969, 78).

Americans may have been enjoying the new freedom provided by the automobile, but there was a paradox in this apparent liberation: They were becoming dependent.

The enormity of the shift was apparent by 1941, when the Bureau of public roads surveyed commutation patterns. It found that 2,100 communities, with populations ranging from 2,500 to 50,000 did not have public transportation systems of any kind and were completely dependent upon the private automobile for personal travel. Such a situation would have been inconceivable twenty-five years earlier. (Jackson 1985, 189)

In order for the full potential of the automobile as a device for shaping the pattern of human settlement to be realized, streets and highways had to be improved. In 1921, only 13 percent of the roads outside of cities were paved. The first federal highways act, passed in 1916 in response to popular and business demands for improved roadways, directed every state to establish a state highway department to plan routes, supervise construction, and maintain roads that federal funds would help to build. A series of related provisions during the early to mid-1920s created the familiar, numbered "U.S." route system that served as the framework of interstate transportation until the superhighway system was built in the 1960s (Warner 1972, 38).

The growing highway system meant that trucking enjoyed an increasing advantage over railroads for hauling freight. The expanding network of good roadways meant that shipping by truck could provide a greater flexibility in routing and scheduling, especially for relatively short distances where shipping by train proved a cumbersome alternative. Since the open highway, not the central city or the railroad's freight yard, was of primary importance in determining the location of firms that were highly dependent on trucking, this change in transportation contributed in the long run to the decentralization of industry.

Of course, the greatest impact that the motor vehicle would have on the shape of the city was provided by the automobile. The physical area covered by the city had always been limited by travel distances. Before the widespread ownership of cars and the improvement of roads, a radius of sixty minutes from the city center seldom covered more than six miles, limiting the area of cities to perhaps one hundred square miles. With the improvements in transportation, the area of the radius was increased to about twenty-five miles, which meant that the city's effective population now resided in a "zone of accessibility" amounting to just under two thousand square miles (Hawley 1981, 148).

As the margins of city after city sprawled outward, the people, economic interests, and government bodies of the United States were making some important decisions about the future of transportation and the shape that cities would take. The people were using public transportation less, especially the electric streetcar. The number of electric streetcars in the country peaked in 1917, as did total ridership in 1923 (Jackson 1985, 171). The number of people using public transportation continued to decline during the depression years of the 1930s, just as motor vehicle registration continued to increase. When public transportation looked to government for support, as it often did in the early decades of this century, it was turned down. It was refused subsidy because, unlike the wholly subsidized highway system, it was considered a private investment rather than a public good.

When the companies took their case to the public, as they did in Detroit and Los Angeles, their appeals for financing through taxes were rejected. The position of streetcar companies was made worse in many cities by the refusal of the municipalities in which they operated to allow them to raise their fares above a nickel (Jackson 1985, 170).

There is strong evidence, at least for many of the major cities, that the erosion of the public transportation system did not come about solely because of the preference for personal transportation or taxpayer or government shortsightedness. A report of the results of a U.S. Senate subcommittee investigation shows that the major auto interests, unwilling to trust the replacement of public transport by autos to market demand alone, worked systematically to dismantle the public ground transportation system. The report suggested that the auto market had become saturated by the mid-twenties. The document focused especially on the efforts of General Motors to stimulate sales by reducing the attractiveness of public transportation.

GM was reportedly committed to replacing rail travel with bus travel, and then buses with private cars. In 1925 the company bought the then largest manufacturers of buses and in the following year assisted in the formation of the intercity Greyhound bus service. In 1932 it began to purchase intercity electric railways and local street rail systems for the purpose of replacing them with bus operations. In 1936 it expanded this operation, aided by investment funding supplied by Standard Oil of California, Firestone, and two other companies that were suppliers of bus-related products. Through the establishment of a holding company, local electric rail companies were purchased, converted to bus lines, and then resold to local investors who would agree to continue to use GM-manufactured replacement vehicles. Due to the higher costs of operating the less efficient, noisy diesel vehicles on congested streets that were shared with all other forms of traffic, it was not surprising that the bus companies did not turn out to be viable enterprises. The "bus ultimately contributed to the collapse of several hundred public transit systems and to the diversion of several hundreds of thousands of patrons to automobiles." This had been the plan. By 1949 GM could be linked to the replacement of more than one hundred electric transportation systems in 45 cities, and in that year the company was convicted by a federal jury in Chicago of criminal conspiracy. The court imposed a sanction of $5,000 on the company and a fine of $1 on its Treasurer for having played a key role in the scheme (Snell 1974).

It would be difficult to overstate the degree to which motor vehicles altered the cities and urban life. The parking lot and traffic light became ubiquitous features of the cityscape. In 1925 the attraction of the open road accounted for 24,000 deaths and 600,000 injuries due to traffic accidents. Younger cities and those that grew rapidly after 1920 took their sprawling shapes from the automobility of their growing populations. The suburban growth around older cities was often even more remarkable. Between 1920 and 1930, the suburbs of the 96 largest urban areas grew twice as fast as the inner cities. Some suburbs, like Grosse Pointe outside Detroit and Elmwood Park near Chicago, grew at several times the city rates. A *National Geographic* feature, published in 1923, that focused on the new suburban phenomenon, already counted distant Long Branch and Morristown, New Jersey, and Stamford, Greenwich, and New Canaan, Connecticut, as New York suburbs (Jackson 1985, 176).

In 1925 Harlan Douglas struggled to define the nature of the emerging urban fringe in his book *The Suburban Trend:*

> *Out toward the fringes and margins of cities comes a region where they begin to be less themselves than they are at the center, a place where the city looks countryward. No sharp boundary line defines it; there is rather a gradual tapering off from the urban type of civilization toward the rural type. It is the city thinned out.*
>
> *Confronted with the expanding cities the adjacent country also begins to look cityward. The result is not, however, a compromise of equals. The original movement was, and the major movement is the city's. The suburb is a footnote to urban civilization affecting the near-by country-side. . . . The brand of the city is stamped upon it. It straddles the arbitrary line which statistics draw between the urban and rural spheres; but in reality it is the push of the city outward. . . . It is the city trying to escape the consequences of being a city while still remaining a city. (Douglas 1925, 3–4)*

Besides describing the suburbs, Douglas (1925, 216–219) expressed concerns about their social impact; he wasn't the last one to do so. Among his concerns was the prospect that suburbanites who worked in cities would experience a divided loyalty, lead a bifocal existence. Living in one environment and working in a different one would mean that people would be torn between the two, unable to devote more than half their will or half their heart to either. From this point in its history onward, the suburb would become a favorite target of critics and social commentators.

The Great Depression and Urban Conditions

The stock market crash and the Great Depression that began in 1929 interrupted the rapid expansion of the suburbs. Although they continued to grow at greater rates than the central cities through the 1930s, the construction of residential housing was off dramatically, by 95 percent from 1928 to 1933 (Jackson 1985, 187). Millions were unemployed, and cities had neither the social programs nor the financial means to deal with the scope of the problem. Their revenues contracted along with the private sector of the economy. In New York City, 1 million people were without work; in Chicago, 660,000. Unemployment in Toledo and Akron in the early thirties was running over 50 percent of the workforce. In Detroit, government leaders hoped at the outset of the depression in 1929 that the number of families on relief would not exceed 3,500. By 1930, 12,500 families were dependent on city welfare, and in 1931 there were almost ten times that many. At its worst point, in 1933, one-third of the city's workforce was unemployed (Glazer 1965, 97–99). In cities throughout the country, municipal tax bases declined along with urban land values, as the numbers of tax delinquencies grew (Miller 1973, 160). Every large city had a "Hooverville," a shantytown that housed the otherwise homeless. These settlements were so called in honor of the president, who favored dealing with the economic problems that beset the country through policies that would extend aid to businesses, thus stimulating the economy.

The early 1930s marked an intensification of a long-term, growing awareness and concern in the country regarding the conditions of the urban poor, in general, and the conditions of urban housing for lower-income people, in particular. These concerns received focus and expression in Edith Elmer Wood's *Recent Trends in American Housing,* published in 1931. By her estimation, there were 9 million housing units that needed to be replaced at the time at an estimated cost of $40 billion. At the end of 1931, Hoover convened the National Conference on Home Building and Home Ownership, but his instructions were to keep the federal government out of "the housing business" (Scott 1969, 283–284). Characteristic of his administration's approach was the week set aside in October of 1931 when cities were to conduct a community chest drive to raise funds to help themselves (Miller 1973, 160).

The cities did not receive substantial help from the federal government until 1937 when Congress finally passed the United States Housing Act of 1937, a policy consistent with the spirit of Roosevelt's New Deal programs. The act, which was opposed by real estate, construction, and some financial interests, and supported by mayors, social workers, the NAACP, and some business interests, provided subsidy for low-income housing development. Very importantly, it contained a commitment to the ideal of providing "decent, safe and sanitary dwellings for families of low income," and it created the United States Housing Authority. Low-income families were defined as those who could not "afford to pay enough to cause private enterprise in their locality . . . to build an adequate supply of decent, safe, and sanitary dwellings for their use." According to its provisions, the federal government could loan up to 90 percent of the total cost of a project at low-interest rates for a period of up to 60 years, making the undertaking of such projects, especially during the depression, attractive and viable. There was also a provision for rent subsidies. The $800 million provided for the program did not go far. During the next four years, only 21,600 units were built, and an additional 168,000 subsidized; the need, however, was for between 8 and 10 million units (Scott 1969, 328–330). Still, the federal government had entered the housing business, an area in which European governments had long provided services.

World War II and the Altered Course of Urban Growth

As the United States geared up for war production in the early 1940s, many of the problems and dislocations of the depression remained unresolved in the cities. Although industries were gradually converting to the production of weapons and other war materials prior to direct U.S. involvement in the war, the sudden entry of the United States into the conflict had a convulsive effect in urban areas. The housing stock was aging and in poor repair and, for lower-income groups, in short supply. Industry had not fully recovered from the depression, and many people remained unemployed, underemployed, or employed in positions that they found unsatisfactory. Large numbers in the agricultural population had been marginalized. The war meant expanded industrialization and more urban growth, but these would take place in new and often wholly unexpected locations.

A number of cities grew substantially during World War II as a result of orders placed with local industries by the War Production Board, which was interested in achieving the maximum utilization of all regional labor pools. The larger cities of Norfolk, Miami, Phoenix, and San Diego grew between 72 and 92 percent during the war, largely as a result of the war industry. Smaller cities that achieved spectacular growth for the same reason included San Bernardino, Lubbock, and Albuquerque (McKelvey 1968, 122–123). Within four months of the initiation of the U.S. defense program, the combined contracts of San Diego's four aircraft industries amounted to more than twice the total assessed value of the city. As the city struggled to accommodate the 15,000 to 30,000 newcomers attracted by industrial expansion between the months of April and October of 1940, the Army, the Navy, and aircraft companies announced that another 45,000 new migrants would be seeking housing in the next eight months, while an additional 16,000 would be accommodated in military barracks and camps (Scott 1969, 373–374).

San Diego's experience was repeated in a number of other cities. During the war, Philadelphia absorbed an additional 150,000 industrial workers; Pittsburgh 30,000. Tacoma had 10,000 new building and shipyard workers. Louisville had 40,000 new workers; Indianapolis 20,000; and Wichita 15,000. In the 18 months after the raid on Pearl Harbor, 350,000 migrated to Detroit. Los Angeles, where the reorganization and growth of aircraft industries had been underway during the thirties, played a major role in producing aircraft during the war. Between 1940 and 1944, its population grew by 780,000. A special 1947 census revealed that one-third of the population of Los Angeles had not lived there in 1940 (Clark 1983, 283–284).

Under conditions of rapid growth, people were often forced to live in whatever shelter they could find or build in the housing-short cities. At Gadsden, Alabama, newly arrived steelworkers set up house in garages, barns, old store buildings, and shacks with dirt floors. At Abilene and Mineral Wells, Texas, men paid three dollars a day to rent cots in tar-paper shacks with no sanitary facilities. In Jacksonville, Florida, some made shelters of palmetto leaves spread over wooden frames. Clearly, the circumstances were exceptional, but the war merely intensified the housing shortages that had been characteristic of U.S. cities.

Many of the newcomers came from rural areas. Nearly 1.3 million had left the farm and migrated to war production areas by the fall of 1941, just a year and a half after the start of the defense program. However, many more than this were migrants from other urban areas (Scott 1969, 386–388), relocated by employment opportunities brought by the war. The migrants included large numbers of poor blacks from the rural South. The black population of Detroit doubled during the forties, from 149,000 in 1940 to 300,000 in 1950, and represented a proportional growth of 9 to 16 percent of the population. The number of blacks in Los Angeles grew from 64,000 to 171,000, or from 4 to almost 9 percent of the city's population.

The sorting and reconcentration of populations in crowded, decrepit urban centers and the combination of economic boom and political neglect produced a legacy of tension and disorder that would be punctuated in many cities, including Detroit and Los Angeles, by conflict and riot in the coming decades.

The Continuation of Urban Trends Since World War II: Patterns of Growth in Decline

The beginning of the war was marked by an increase in marriage rates that was soon followed by an increase in birthrates—the so-called "good-bye babies" born to couples about to be separated. After the war, marriage and birthrates continued to rise. In 1947, 6 million families were "doubling up" with relatives and friends due to housing and apartment shortages. Another 500,000 lived in Quonset huts or other temporary shelters (Jackson 1985, 232). These conditions indicated that major changes in the nation's urban structure could be expected.

The Federal Government's Role in Suburbanization

In 1944, Veterans Administration mortgage loans had been added to the other loans available through the Federal Housing Administration, and, together, these government guarantees helped to fuel an unprecedented growth in the housing industry. Housing starts, which had numbered only 114,000 in 1944, were at 937,000 in 1947, and 1,692,000 in 1950 (Jackson 1985, 233). After a brief stumble, the postwar economy was stable and strong. Millions of urban apartment dwellers, with new families and a modest degree of affluence and security, took to the suburbs.

From 1950 to 1970, population densities in the largest central cities (cities with a population of a million or more) declined by about 10 percent, while the densities of smaller central cities declined by about 35 percent. Between 1950 and 1960, the number of people who lived *in* metropolitan areas but *outside* of central cities increased at a rate five times that of the central city populations; from 1960 to 1970, the increase was about four times as fast (Zimmer 1975, 26).

In addition to population, the cities lost businesses in the period after the war. The central business district, which had once been at the center of all major urban activities, declined in importance as automobiles continued to replace public transportation. Whereas it had served as the hub of a managed public transport system, traffic management schemes for private transportation generally included efforts to orient traffic away from the downtown. While cities of all sizes tended to suffer from a decrease in retail trade, the decline was sharpest in cities from 250,000 to 500,000 in population. Between 1950 and 1967, cities in that size range lost two-fifths of their retailers, while cities above that size range averaged a loss of about one-fourth. Moreover, the decline in the *share* of the total sales for metropolitan areas that was claimed by central city establishments was much greater (Zimmer 1975, 55–63).

Besides the encouragement the federal government provided through its mortgage and underwriting schemes (FHA and VA loans), it provided further impetus to urban decentralization through its highway building programs. The 1956 Federal-Aid Highway Act set aside $100 billion over a period of 13 years for the revision and expansion of the interstate highway system: The new system was designed to link most major cities with superhighways. Coupled with vigorous local road building and improvement projects, the effect was to expand the suburban commuter radius of cities. As Popenoe (1985, 95) pointed out, the effective size of a metropolitan community (discussed earlier in this chapter) was limited by the daily journey to work. Typically, that distance did not exceed one hour's driving time (one way). Calculated in this way, it was easy to see that as roads improved, more distant points of destination were accessible within a given driving time. In effect, the radius of the metropolitan community expanded. In Providence, Rhode Island, between 1955 and 1965, the ten-minute travel zone from the city center increased by about 2 miles; the twenty-minute zone grew from 7 to 14 miles; and the forty-minute zone grew from 18 to 25 miles (Zimmer 1975, 29–30). In Los Angeles, between 1953 and 1962, freeway construction expanded the area within half an hour's drive of downtown from 261 square miles to 705 square miles (Clark 1983, 273). Inexpensive gasoline and oversized and overpowered automobiles, which somehow combined the comfort of living room furniture with instrument panels and exterior designs suitable to the awkward dawning of the aerospace age, further softened the time/distance friction between home and work.

In 1950, the U.S. Census Bureau attempted to accommodate the expanded urban form—the metropolitan community—by instituting a new unit of measurement. In that census year, the bureau began to enumerate metropolitan populations by employing the Standard Metropolitan Statistical Area (SMSA) as a unit of measure. The term was simplified to Metropolitan Statistical Area in 1990. This measure counts all cities or closely clustered cities with a population of 50,000 or more, and adds to this the population of the surrounding county or counties shown by commuting patterns and other economic measures to be integrated with the urban core. Since the measure was standardized for all such cities and surrounding counties, MSAs sometimes contain farms and even unsettled tracts. But the measure does recognize the fact that the populations of suburbs are a functionally integrated part of any urban core. After a thorough review for the 2000 census, the measure was found to be still useful and was retained as the basic method for counting metro populations.

The Selling of the Suburbs

The building and selling of the suburbs was a remarkable achievement in and of itself. Although people were being transformed during the 1950s from a predominantly blue-collar to a white-collar workforce and were increasingly encouraged to think of themselves as middle rather than working class, the new prosperity was modest. If they were to buy suburban housing in large numbers, it wouldn't be the expensive, prewar variety that had been limited largely to the upper middle class. In every large city, however, a number of builders found innovative ways to lower construction costs in order to capture a share of the new market. None competed more successfully than Abraham Levitt and Sons.

Before the war, the Levitts operated their construction company on a modest scale on Long Island, their most ambitious project having been one 200-unit development in 1934. During the war, they mass-produced housing for the federal government. In 1946, they began to plan their first large-scale housing development, called Levittown, on Long Island. It would eventually consist of 17,400 housing units in a single development, and house some 82,000 residents. The company kept the cost of the housing units low (the units sold for $7,990) by standardizing the components that went into each house, precutting and prefabricating parts wherever feasible, and by dividing the production process into 27 separate operations, each one performed in sequence by a specialized crew. In effect, the Levitts had done to the construction of housing what Henry Ford had done to the building of automobiles. The Levitts' "Model T" was a uniform, Cape Cod style house, built on a concrete slab, with only the lower of the one and a half stories completed. Designed "not to stir the imagination, but to provide the best shelter at the least price," these developments, consisting of repetitious units of housing, row upon row, on 60-by-100-foot cookie-cutter lots, soon drew the attention of critics. But the huge project was such a popular success that it was repeated near Philadelphia, Pennsylvania, and in Willingboro, New Jersey (Jackson 1985, 234–238). These subdivisions simply represent the most massive examples among the hundreds of suburban subdivisions that emerged in the 1950s and thereafter in response to the clamor for this most tangible of all the components of the American Dream.

Just as massive urbanization had given rise to concerns about the social consequences of the new and unfamiliar settlement pattern in the previous century, suburbanization raised similar questions in the minds of many in the fifties. It was suspected that suburbs would prove to be the great cultural and political leveler, that they would, among other things, present a compulsory obligation to neighbor, destroy individualism, and create a monotonous homogeneity. Alternatively, the suburbs have been portrayed as lacking in the kind of sociability generated by socially heterogeneous urban neighborhoods (Jacobs 1961; Sennett 1970).

It remains unclear to what extent and in what ways middle-class suburbanites differ from their urban counterparts. It has been argued, especially with regard to the more negative characterizations, that supportive evidence is lacking (Donaldson 1969). Berger (1960) suggested that myths about suburbia persisted despite the lack of supporting, and even in the face of contrary, evidence because they were myths we loved to hate. His point was that, given the lack of a clear image or theme with which to symbolize "American culture," we seized on the image of the suburb, most easily pictured in all of its negative stereotypes, to fill the void. It is the American's image of America.

At another level, there can be little question of the harmful impact of metropolitan suburban growth. That those living outside central cities continue to

BOX 7-2   The Migration to the Suburbs

Radio journalist Ray Suarez wrote about some of the sociological consequences of suburbanization in *The Old Neighborhood: What We Lost in the Great Suburban Migration* (1999). One consequence, explicit in his title, was the loss of the old neighborhoods—cells of inner-city sociability and identity, places that made life in the industrial city livable, places especially attractive once they were left behind and when embellished by nostalgic memories. He said that reminiscence "takes on a rhythm of ritual and truth" when repeated often enough by former residents of the old neighborhood: "We *never* had to lock our doors. Everybody knew everybody. We weren't afraid" (12). But sometime after midcentury, people were afraid, especially as their children reached their teen years, and even urban die-hards left for the suburbs as schools and services declined and neighborhoods became browner and blacker. White middle-class families left as the image of white America was dissolving and the city proper came to symbolize the diversity of the nation's population. It would be difficult to overstate the significance of the physical separation by class and race that was entailed in the movement to the suburbs. The myth that all Americans were "in it together" became insupportable. "When we no longer lived and worked in proximity to one another, we no longer knew the same things. Once we no longer knew the same things, we no longer had a need for cultural cohesion. Once we no longer had cultural cohesion, it was easier and easier to draw circles of concern more narrowly around one's own doorstep" (15).

Richard Sennet (1970) believed that middle-class residential suburbs actually were a way of sustaining the myth of cultural uniformity—the cultural uniformity of those who lived in the suburbs. In his version, people who fled

the cities were able to preserve their prejudices and protect themselves from the complicated business of learning more deeply about both themselves and those who were culturally different; they escaped the demanding task of learning to deal with people as individuals, learning that real people in real situations resisted easy categorization according to class, race, and subculture. The sociological significance of the racially and socioeconomically homogeneous suburb is that it is a protected haven for the preservation of ignorance. In his provocative interpretation, Sennet portrayed suburbanites as having entered a perpetual intellectual adolescence, an arrested know-it-all state of social development, in which prejudice and misconceptions about other people will seldom be tested by the actual experience of face-to-face contact. There is an added tendency to retreat further into the private world of home and family, with only superficial contact with neighbors in middle-class suburbs. This sustains the idea that all suburban families are just about the same and intensifies a kind of abstracted commitment to an image of local community. So, in a sense, the suburbs preserve the idea described by Suarez, that "we're all in this together," meaning all suburbanites who fit an idealized profile, with circles of concern drawn "more narrowly around one's own doorstep." Both writers agreed that the old neighborhoods of the inner city provided richer opportunity for meaningful interaction than the suburban housing tracts that later came to symbolize the typical American residential setting. But it is interesting that Suarez portrayed the image of the old urban community as mythological, in part, while Sennet found the notion of community in the suburb where people have little contact with each other a pure myth.

commute to work or use the central city for other purposes can be seen as suburban exploitation of the city. This is because suburban populations tend to rely on urban services, at least part of the time; but because they reside in a different municipality and pay taxes where they have their residence, they are using urban services without paying for them. This means that those who reside in the central city must pay proportionally more for urban services. Studies have shown, in fact, that the proportion of the metropolitan population living outside the central city is directly related to the per capita costs of providing urban services. This is because the cost of providing services to nonresidents when they are in town increases the cost of running the city; this then appears as a higher per capita cost (Zimmer 1975, 76).

The Blurring of the Suburbs

The alterations that suburbs are currently undergoing demand a change in their popular image and in the ways they are seen to relate to old central city areas. It must be conceded that, from the beginning, suburbs have defied meaningful generalization. The term simply refers to an area immediately adjacent to a city, extending outward beyond that point. As such, *suburb* has referred to residential clusters and corridors, small satellite towns and villages, industrial expansions, and even cities subordinate to a greater central influence, like those in the New York metropolitan area. For the discussion of suburbs to be at all meaningful, a distinction must be made between the affluent residential suburb, the one that provides the foundation to our erroneous but indelible imagery, and all other types. However, after we have made this distinction and decided to focus strictly on the residential form, we may find that today even the residential suburbs are changing in ways that offer new challenges to the usefulness of the concept.

By 1973, Masotti described a growing heterogeneity of residential suburbs. Except for members of the "marginal underclass," suburbs were becoming more heterogeneous by class, race, ethnicity, marital status, and life cycle stage. While single-unit dwellings continued to predominate, increased housing costs were providing a market for multiunit construction. These multiunits were attractive to many childless households. Thus, suburbia was no longer exclusively a family place.

Masotti observed that a more fundamental transition was taking place; the suburb was becoming less an urban fringe and more an independent "neocity." Post–World War II commuting patterns increasingly reflected a decentralization of manufacturing, service industries, commerce, and retail trade. Many older suburbs were successful in maintaining their exclusively residential quality through increased property taxes and zoning restrictions; but newer suburbs, along with some older ones, worked to attract industries, office complexes, or major shopping centers. This has reduced suburb-to-center-city commuting and increased intersuburban commuting. Moreover, many of those living in the central city, especially skilled and semiskilled workers, began to commute to work in the suburbs. The suburbs were thus becoming more independent of the central areas or, as Masotti (1973, 15–17) put it, less suburban and more urban.

Meltzer (1984) observed a similar trend. He emphasized the interdependence of the various suburban and formerly central urban locations and argued that the metropolitan concept, which implied domination of a system by its center, be dropped in favor of "metroplex." He allowed that the old central city could retain some of its exclusive functions, especially as an administrative and commercial

The North American suburb can take many forms. This is the familiar classic version.

location; but he reasoned that the specialization, as well as the growing complexity, of those sites originally developed as suburbs would make them central or equally important in other ways. The urban form, transformed over the course of the century into a metropolitan community, was transformed again into a network of more or less equal urban nodes.

Meltzer's metroplex description applies better to some cities than others, and at the turn of the century, it is still not clear whether it describes a common future for all cities in the United States. Certainly, when a city attains this form, the complexity of the question of where one lives carries us far beyond the experience of the suburbanites of the mid-twenties, whose supposedly confused loyalties troubled Harlan Douglas. Consider the case, related by Jackson (1985, 265), of one resident of the "centerless city" of Orange County, California (southeast of Los Angeles): "I live in Garden Grove, work in Irvine, shop in Santa Ana, go to the dentist in Anaheim, my husband works in Long Beach, and I used to be the President of the League of Women Voters in Fullerton." Jackson doesn't say whether the woman found the variety troubling or attractive.

Edge City

The journalist Joel Garreau (1991) argued that every U.S. city experiencing growth in the last decades of the twentieth century was growing in the manner of Los Angeles, with multiple urban cores. He called these growing conurbations

Edge city is the place for motor vehicles. Outside the shopping mall, office building, or residential subdivision, the pedestrian is a deviant.

"edge cities" because, in his view, they represent a new frontier of urban growth, a mass emigration of not only people but also function away from old urban centers. The new urban fringes perform the traditional functions of the city. Among the more than 200 of these places that Garreau identified are the Route 128 and Massachusetts Turnpike corridors outside Boston, the Schaumburg area west of Chicago's O'Hare International Airport, the Perimeter Area north of Atlanta, and, of course, sections of Orange County.

Garreau identified the minimal qualifying features of an edge city as five million square feet of leasable office space (more, for example, than there is in downtown Memphis); 600,000 square feet of leasable retail space (the equivalent of a "fair-sized" mall); more jobs than bedrooms; the local perception that it is a more or less self-contained, mixed use area; and it needs to have taken on its present dimensions rather rapidly, within the past few decades. Taken together, the edge cities are presently the most important feature of North American urban space, and they are changing the character of urban life. Two-thirds of the office facilities in the United States are located in edge cities, and most of the buildings that house them have been built within the past two decades. The commuting pattern that sends commuters around rather than in and out of the metropolitan region's center has become a reality in these places. Edge cities rarely have a governing body, nor do their dimensions respond to official municipal boundaries. More of the residents of these areas live outside the city proper than within it.

Garreau described the experiential quality of the edge city, appealing to what he believed is a common set of references that resonate with most Americans: One typically arrives via a super highway, is deposited into a sea of bumper-to-bumper traffic, passes along a landscape of alternating lawns and parking facilities, place-marked by office developments. The rapidly transforming nature of the area is highlighted by multiple detours around the rising dust of heavy construction sites that seem to be among the few enduring features of edge city. Signs mark the locations of corporations that apparently have been "named for Klingon warriors." Once the stranger who is familiar with such places locates the shopping mall, the "Dante-esque vision brings a physical shiver to the spine and a not altogether ironic murmur of recognition to the lips: 'Ah! Home!'" (7).

Garreau attributed the creation of the edge city world to popular taste. In his view, this world is a collective spatial representation of how North Americans think they want to arrange their lives—until they are confronted with the aggregated consequences of so many making similar suburban (the term is in jeopardy of a total loss of meaning here) choices. But his analysis makes it clear that to the extent popular taste is responsible for the endlessly sprawling built environment, it is led and manipulated by those who engineer and build these new urban spaces for profit. Garreau pointed out that the elements of developed space that are found in edge city must be understood with reference to the developer's worldview (see Box 7-3). Developers are close students of human nature, and they are developing their own pragmatic pseudo-science. The emerging discipline has no interest in how humans should operate, only in the question of how they will operate: Being able to anticipate consumer behavior translates into profit (117).

BOX 7-3   Talking the Talk of Real Estate Developers

Most revealing is the hard-edge language speculators and developers use. The insider's code reveals, through metaphor and implication, a mind-set that is one-dimensional and bottom-line in its orientation. Physical space is a "blank" until it is developed. The aesthetic dimension of space and form is leveled by a bitingly utilitarian frame of reference: Open landscapes are in need of "animation" through the use of flagpoles or "active water features" (e.g., fountains) or "plop art" (large abstract sculpture). Alternately, a "beautiful building" is one that is fully leased. Language is emptied of meaning in application to market goals: A "community" is anything the promoter says it is, from the businesses gathered into an industrial park to those collected in a shopping mall. "Negative-absorption" refers to a development where more tenants are moving out than moving in. Gadgets and innovations designed to attract the attention of clients and provide a rationale for higher rents are referred to as "ooh-ahs" (the sound the client is supposed to make), while upscale shops receive the more widely recognized designation, "chi-chi, frou-frou." "Class-B space" is where the "grunts" or "wage-slaves" will work. Difficult situations in which developers find themselves hemmed in by circumstances that threaten the profitability of the project are referred to in metaphors that depict attacks by Mexicans or American Indian tribes. The competent developer will have left a "back door" to escape through (Garreau 1991, 443–451).

It is important to keep in mind that the rapid expansion of urban space called forth negative popular and intellectual reactions in the first decades of this century, the "anti-urbanism" that was discussed in earlier chapters. That earlier urban growth was also produced by speculators and developers seeking profits, no less than is the case for the newly created urban spaces of today. As we consider the new sprawling urban annexes, some of us may find ourselves in the position of making nostalgic comparisons between the old, preferred urban form and the new, alien one. But as students of social science, we have to remind ourselves that a large part of our job is to discover and explain the authenticity that these new forms represent as an urban way of life. In increasing numbers, people live in these places; they are the setting for certain types of urban experience; and we can be sure that they suit the tastes and lifestyle of many who live there.

The Rise of the Sunbelt and the Crisis of the Industrial City

In recent decades there have been a number of shifts in urbanization that reflect nationwide and even international economic trends. Many of these represent a continuation or acceleration of more long-term trends, the cumulative effects of which have spelled crisis for long-established industrial centers. What the outcome will be in the longer term for the southern and southwestern cities, which have experienced the most recent rapid growth rates, is open to question.

Delineated in various ways, the Sunbelt is generally considered to include that part of the country situated below a line running along the northern borders of North Carolina, Tennessee, Arkansas, Oklahoma, New Mexico, and Arizona, and incorporating Las Vegas and Southern California. Alternate schemes include Denver, all of California, and even all of the West Coast. These inclusions test the "Sunbelt" designation but combine urban regions that share the feature of having recently experienced population increases and economic expansion at rates higher than the national averages. These increases and expansions have occurred while cities in other regions, particularly the Northeast and North Central areas, collectively designated as the Frostbelt or Snowbelt (and, in part, the Rustbelt), were stagnant or declining.

These older northern industrial centers were actually experiencing an acceleration of trends that had begun much earlier in the century. The proportion of U.S. workers employed in manufacturing peaked in 1920, then declined slightly from 30.8 to 28.9 percent by the end of that decade. Even in predominantly industrial cities like Detroit and Pittsburgh, by the 1920s the largest gains in employment were being made in the trade, clerical, and professional categories. Among the seven large U.S. cities that had more than 50 percent of the labor force in manufacturing in 1920, only Akron maintained that proportion a decade later, and by then its rate of growth was the second lowest in that group (McKelvey 1968, 33–34).

After the industrial resurgence of wartime, the national economy began a gradual deindustrialization, as the proportion of service jobs steadily increased against the numbers employed in manufacturing. As the economy expanded, the number of workers employed in wholesale and retail trade, transportation, and teaching, as well as those employed as counselors, caretakers of people and property, installers, repairers, gardeners, and the like, increased at a much faster rate than the number of industrial workers. The trend toward service employment continues. Of the 19 million jobs added between 1970 and 1980, 90 percent were in the service sector. The U.S. Bureau of Labor Statistics projects that almost all of the 23 million jobs expected to be created between 1990 and 2005 will be in the service-producing sector (Carey and Franklin 1991, 45).

As the relative availability of manufacturing jobs decreased, the location of these opportunities for employment also changed. As we have seen, industry had joined the suburban trend. From 1963 to 1977, the total number of manufacturing jobs in the central cities of the 25 largest metropolitan areas dropped by 700,000, while their suburbs added about 1.1 million (Logan and Golden 1986, 430). What was more serious for the populations of the older industrial regions was that such employment opportunities were moving out of their metropolitan areas altogether. From 1958 to 1972, the more established industrial cities of the North lost between 14 and 18 percent of their manufacturing jobs, while the cities of the Sunbelt increased theirs between 60 and 100 percent (Checkoway and Patton 1985, 6). New York city was an especially big loser. From 1947 to 1976, the city lost half its factory jobs, which dropped from a peak of 1.2 million to 543,000 (Danielson and Doig 1982, 54).

Even though new jobs were opening up in northern central cities at the same time that manufacturing jobs were shrinking in number, northern cities still lost people to the Sunbelt. Between 1970 and 1980, a decade of rapid growth for the southern and southwestern cities, St. Louis lost 27.2 percent of its population; Cleveland 23.6 percent; Detroit 20.5 percent; and Cincinnati 15 percent. Except for Cincinnati, each of these cities also experienced a net population loss from their total metropolitan area (Checkoway and Patton 1985, 3). Meanwhile, Phoenix grew by 35.8 percent, its MSA by 56 percent; the city of Houston by 29.4 percent, its MSA by 46.4 percent; and the city of San Diego by 25.7 percent, its MSA by 37.1 percent (Rice and Bernard 1983, Table 1-3). Again, the case of New York provides an upscaled version. After the war, New York began losing core population: Between 1950 and 1980, Manhattan lost 532,000 or 27 percent; Brooklyn 282,000 or 19.4 percent. Until the 1980 census, gains in the outer population rings of the metropolitan region were sufficient to offset the losses of the inner areas (core and inner ring). However, the net deficit between the numbers lost and those added from 1970 to 1980 showed a loss in regional population for the first time. The loss was nearly half a million, or about 5 percent of the population (Danielson and Doig 1982, 51, 64–65).

The Nature of the Sunbelt Advantage

The shift of population and economic activity to the South was the result of certain economic advantages offered by the region and of government policies. The inherent economic attractiveness of the Sunbelt stemmed from the relative advantages the region offered to businesses seeking to expand profitability by reducing the costs of operation. The South offered lower land, labor, and energy costs, as well as lower taxes. In addition, federal government policy, from military spending to highway programs, had bestowed disproportionate benefits on the cities of the southern rim. The location of energy reserves and the continued attraction of warm climates also played a role. Cities in Texas, Oklahoma, and Louisiana prospered after World War II as the result of gas and oil exploitation; the climate in Arizona and Florida invited the development of retirement havens; and many of the newer cities, as well as the more colorful older cities, benefited from tourism. Meanwhile, the decline of industrial employment and central city populations in older northern cities, which had been built around central industrial cores, tended to accentuate the growing contrast between the declining and the developing regions of the country.

The United States' heavy industrial complex, geared to maximum production during World War II, came through the war fully intact, even though the industrial capacity of the rest of the world was devastated. It needed only the market incentive to retool for peacetime. In the early 1950s, the industries of the United States produced more than 50 percent of the world's steel. The U.S. steel producers, however, failed to innovate to keep pace with changes evolving elsewhere in manufacturing technology. The productive capacity of overseas competitors naturally expanded as their economies rebuilt and prospered, and by the late seventies, the U.S. share of international steel production had fallen to 16 percent. By that time, cheaper foreign steel had, in fact, brought about the implementation of trade measures to shelter steel produced in the United States from import competition. By the mid-1980s, U.S. steel companies were struggling to reorganize into diversified holdings that would include scaled-down steel production operations. The problems of the steel industry were rooted in the international marketplace and, therefore, not readily amenable to domestic policy solutions. Steel was heavily dependent on the U.S. auto industry, which shared 44 percent of its market with imported cars by 1985. In addition, an increasing proportion of the components of U.S. cars are manufactured overseas. In December 1992, General Motors announced intentions to phase out seven parts-manufacturing plants, which had employed 18,000 people around the United States. The company reportedly found it was unable to compete with foreign factories and non-union plants within the United States. Along with other plant closings, which had been announced earlier by the corporation, this brought the total number of jobs that would be eliminated by one company to 80,000 (*New York Times*, December 4, 1992).

But the elimination of factory workers was not due solely to the replacement of U.S. workers by overseas workers. As U.S. industry adopted more efficient, cost-cutting technologies that had largely been developed elsewhere, the innovations in production meant that fewer workers would be required, even as production levels increased. Between 1982 and 1986, the volume of manufactured goods increased by 23 percent, which meant that the proportion of the GNP represented by manufacturing remained constant within the expanding economy. What had changed is that large numbers of former production workers, many of whom had held union jobs with good pay and benefits, found themselves in service occupations, often with poor pay and reduced employee benefits. A 1984 survey of workers who had lost their jobs due to displacement between 1979 and 1983 found that one-fourth were unemployed. A similar study, conducted in 1990 of workers displaced between 1985 and 1989, found that 14 percent were unemployed. Displaced workers in the latter half of the 1980s were finding work more readily than those displaced in the first half of the decade, but still showing higher than average unemployment rates. About half of those displaced from manufacturing jobs between 1985 and 1989 were earning less than before (29 percent suffered earning cuts of 20 percent or more), and 23 percent of those who previously received health insurance coverage were not covered by any plan (a higher percentage of blacks and Latinos had lost coverage) (Herz 1991, 6–9).

The overall changes in manufacturing employment help explain the decline of the old northern industrial cities. But what of the rise of the South? For the most part, the increase in employment in the South seems due primarily to the creation of new jobs, rather than the relocation of jobs pirated from northern states. In fact, the number of business closings in the Sunbelt and the Frostbelt are about equal. The difference is that the opening of new positions in the South was much more frequent (Rice and Bernard 1983, 17).

The South has self-consciously courted and accommodated the wishes of business. City governments have eased restrictions, such as those stemming from environmental concerns, and states have seen to it that industry remains in a strong bargaining position relative to labor. Perhaps the reputed subcultural heritage of the region may have caused the rate of unionization to be lower than in the North, but all of the states except New Mexico, Oklahoma, and California have "right-to-work" laws (Rice and Bernard 1983, 16). In the late seventies, the labor force of one such state, Texas, had only a 13 percent union membership rate, compared to a rate of 28 percent for the country as a whole. At the time, the Houston Chamber of Commerce boasted that Houston had "the nation's best business climate" (Kaplan 1983, 198).

The remarkable growth and momentum that the Sunbelt achieved would not have occurred without vigorous assistance from the federal government. Recall that during World War II government policy called for the distribution of defense industries that would take advantage of all sizable population centers. This meant that cities in the relatively less-industrialized South would receive large plants, which, in turn, attracted dramatic increases in industrial populations. At the end of the war, the end of military production threatened traumatic upheaval and dislocation in the Sunbelt. In Los Angeles, at the peak of war production, 280,000 had been employed in the aircraft industry. In 1946, that number dropped abruptly to 55,000. The crisis that had been created by peace and the idling of the great war apparatus was relieved by the Korean and Cold Wars, and by 1955 aircraft industry employment was at 275,000. By 1967, 350,000 were employed by the aerospace industry in Los Angeles. The city, with its vast military, industrial, technological, and educational complex, was a jewel in the crown of the "Space Crescent" (perhaps a more descriptive label than "Sunbelt," since it lacks the climatic assumptions). This designation refers to a linked network of cities fanning across the continent from Cape Canaveral, Florida, through the Southwest and up the Pacific Coast to Seattle. It is a region where, broadly speaking, traditionally conservative political values had by the 1980s been crystallized by a concentration of aerospace and defense-dependent industries (Clark 1983, 284–285).

By 1979, the Sunbelt states were receiving 78 percent of the defense payroll and 58 percent of all major government contracts. A number of programs that were designed to be equally beneficial to all states have proven especially so to the Sunbelt. For example, the federal highway assistance programs came at a time when Sunbelt cities were growing most rapidly, and helped shape the largely suburban quality of their growth. Highway systems also consolidated the position of regional leaders, like Atlanta and Dallas, by funneling people and products to them. Federal programs designed to redevelop urban areas were put to good use by cities like Tampa and New Orleans that were interested in creating impressive downtown centers, helping to symbolize the region's new vitality (Rice and Bernard 1983, 15–16).

Federal funding disparities between northern and southern regions have invited analyses that emphasize the exploitative nature of regional relationships. It has been pointed out that between 1975 and 1979 Snowbelt states sent Washington, D.C., $165 billion more in taxes than they received, while the Sunbelt received $112 billion more than it sent (Macdonald 1984, 24). In that era, declining Snowbelt cities and struggling northern states could be seen as subsidizing the growth of the South and Southwest. Recent reductions in the North/South disparity in the amounts that states sent to and received from Washington don't alter the historical fact: It is reasonable to assert that economically declining northern states helped pay for the economic growth of the South. The regional division has not escaped the attention of those who look after territorial interests.

In fact, the long tradition of conscious interurban and interregional rivalry, which has characterized so much of the urban development of the United States, today pits North against South. In addition to active chambers of commerce that promote individual cities, regional interests marshalled their forces to present a common front in opposition. The Southern Growth Policies Board supplied "southern policy makers with statistical information and other reports about how economic development can best be promoted and how states of the region can best profit from federal policy." The northern response included the formation of a congressional caucus called the Northeast-Midwest Economic Advancement Coalition, founded in order to help redirect federal funds northward. The success of the coalition led southern and western congressional delegates to respond with one of their own (Rice and Bernard 1983, 13–14). The position of northern interests was not made easier by recent census counts: Due to the redistribution of population, the Sunbelt gained significantly in representation each decennial year since 1980, with eleven new members to the House of Representatives in 2000, and the Snowbelt lost seventeen.

Sunbelt Liabilities

For all of its promise, and despite the favoritism shown it by Washington, the potential for growth in the Sunbelt is not unlimited. In many areas of the region, urbanization would appear to be a self-limiting process. The natural ecology of a number of states is delicate and poorly suited to the demands that large concentrations of population place upon it. Florida is a low peninsula of alternating sandy soils and low-lying swampy areas, without the capacity for storing the large volumes of fresh water required by urban populations and industries. Water is an even more serious problem in the Southwest. Industries and suburban lawns in arid zones demonstrate what can be done through determined hydraulic engineering. But these projects draw contested water supplies from distant locations. The Colorado River symbolizes the Southwest's chronic water shortage problem. It supplies much of the water requirements of the region and is contested along its length by seven states, several Indian nations, and Mexico (Macdonald 1984, 37).

The seriousness of the problem is reflected by the World Commission on Water for the 21st Century's citation of the Colorado River as one of the world's most serious river water supply problems, along with Egypt's Nile and China's Yellow River (Rice 2000, 18). Although projections indicate that the rapidly growing populations dependent on the Colorado may be 30 to 50 years from the point of acute crisis (Phillips 2000, 23), California has been warned by the U.S. Department of the Interior to curb its demands or face reduced allocation. California and other states have initiated extraordinary plans to store and conserve river water, including lining with cement the All American Canal, which carries Colorado River water through the Arizona Desert in order to prevent loss through natural seepage (Dessoff 2000). In the long run, there are only so many extraordinary options available, and as the ecological limits of the region become increasingly evident and inconvenient, we can only assume population growth will be slowed.

All forms of environmental pollution have become increasingly serious in the Sunbelt. Relocation to Phoenix had long been a standard prescription for people suffering from serious respiratory problems. By the 1980s, however, the rapid growth of that city's population had created air pollution levels that caused area doctors and the president of the Arizona Lung Association to warn people who needed to breathe clean air to stay away from the area. Data from the Environmental Protection Agency showed that Phoenix had the most violations of acceptable carbon monoxide levels of any city, surprisingly placing it ahead of chronically troubled Los Angeles in second place and Denver in third place. The carbon monoxide levels in Arizona led the federal government to threaten to withhold highway funds. In New Mexico, the EPA withheld antipollution funds due to Albuquerque's resistance to the implementation of an auto emissions control program despite the poor air quality in that city. In Texas, rapid urban growth outstripped the capacity of sewage treatment programs, which led to the occasional dumping of raw sewage into the waterways. Arkansas, Louisiana, and Oklahoma have been plagued by neglected chemical waste dumps (Associated Press Report, July 31, 1986).

Just as many of the larger urban centers in the North remained surprisingly dependent on one or a few industries, and were therefore sensitive to fluctuations in demand, some southern and southwestern metropolises have also remained narrowly dependent and vulnerable. Houston benefited greatly from the staggering oil price increases after 1973. The Houston area had nearly one-fourth of the oil refining and over one-half of the petrochemical manufacturing capacity of the country. It produced over two-thirds of the *world's* oil industry tools (Kaplan 1983, 198). When oil prices fluctuate, the cities most dependent on oil are bound to be affected most acutely. In the wake of the unexpected price declines of 1986, Houston's growth and its building boom ground to a halt. Newly constructed office complexes stood largely unoccupied, unemployment was above 9 percent—more than two points above the national average—and the opulent symbol of oil industry prosperity and Texas flamboyance, the Shamrock Hilton Hotel, closed down. By the late 1980s, Denver had come to symbolize the hollowness of metropolitan economies tied too closely to the international oil trade. In 1989, a large proportion of Denver's downtown commercial real estate was empty and for sale.

Sunbelt cities have been vulnerable to a common tendency that occurs whenever rapid growth generates the possibility for earning spectacular profits from investment. Such profitability is reserved for those willing to act fast—by anticipating rather than responding to expanding market demand—and it promises returns proportionate to investments—the bigger the better. Speculation remains profitable so long as demand can absorb the units, whatever their nature, at the rates investors are induced to produce them. Here the self-limiting tendency is that, at some point, production is bound to run ahead of demand. It often happens that saturation occurs just as the point of greatest investor activity is reached. A boom-and-bust mechanism similar to this has operated in the Florida housing market.

Florida has been a popular East Coast retirement and vacation destination for decades. Since the 1960s and 1970s, the state has also shared the industrial expansion experienced by other areas of the Sunbelt. The steadily growing population created a housing demand that offered the potential of substantial profits for large development firms. The combined capacity of these firms to build new luxury residences, mass-produced tract homes, and condominiums has periodically resulted in oversupply. Speculation led to overbuilding in the mid-1970s and again in the early 1980s (Macdonald 1984, 53–54). During the 1990s, the population of Florida continued its long-term growth trend, increasing by an estimated 16.8 percent during the decade. The buoyant U.S. economy was reflected here as elsewhere in a demand for larger and fancier housing. The industry response to the demand for more upscale units in Florida and other Sunbelt states was described in the following terms in the trade publication *Professional Builder* (1998, 72). Referring to several residential building projects, the authors wrote, "These projects exemplify some of the hottest trends in new housing today: European design; value engineering; neotraditionalism and nostalgia; timeless, distinctive detailing; high-density infill; small homes that live big; courtyard plans that play off outdoor living areas; high-end attached product; and multiple flex options for move-ups." American consumers were dreaming bigger, builders were providing bigger versions of the American Dream. At the end of the 1990s, smart money knew that the Florida housing market was one place to be. An upscale waterfront condominium development (units sold from a half million to 1.2 million dollars) in Jacksonville

Beach nearly sold out before construction got underway (*Florida Times-Union*, December 18, 2000), the median sale price of homes in most areas continued its upward trend through late 2000, and brand new communities like Seaview and the Disney Company's fanciful "neotraditional" community of Celebration, Florida (just outside of Orlando), were created out of capital and thin air. At this writing, with new home starts proceeding at a lively pace, analysts were only beginning to raise questions about whether or when the 2001 economic slowdown would impact the demand for residential luxury, whether and to what degree the problem of oversupply would reemerge.

Generalized Patterns of Growth and Decline

Although it is appropriate to contrast the North and South in terms of decline and growth as we have done here, it is also necessary to emphasize the differences that exist among the cities within each region and to recognize certain similarities between the two regions. There are certainly vital northern cities with vigorous economies that naturally tend to escape mention in any discussion of urban crisis and decline. The Twin Cities of Minneapolis/St. Paul provide an outstanding example. Likewise, discussions that focus on the "New South" tend to overlook the fact that we are not talking about new cities, but existing cities that are being made over by recent changes.

Before the South was the Sunbelt, it was a region of slow urban growth, but of urban growth nevertheless. By World War II, this growth had produced established urban cores. The dramatic growth that has occurred since the war is really an expansion around the older centers. Once again, as was the case with northern suburbanization and metropolitanization, we are talking about the growth and differentiation of urban regions. The processes are not precisely the same for both North and South, since the latter featured more substantial regional economic and population growth rates as decentralization took place. Yet certain similarities raise the questions of whether all of the cities of the United States are going through the same long-term process, and whether the outcome of that process will produce stronger or weaker urban economies. The questions may be answered both yes and no.

For example, Noyelle and Stanback (1983, 222–223) read the economic transformation of U.S. cities not in terms of the rise of one region and the decline of another, but in terms of a common transition that cities in all regions undergo. As the central role and central location of manufacturing has become obsolete, central cities have become the locus of specialized, high-level service concentration, and especially of corporate headquarters. In this view, it is not the North/South division that gives the country's urban system its structure, but the development of an urban hierarchy consisting of multiple tiers of dominant and subordinate positions. Writing in the early 1980s, Noyelle and Stanback placed the greater New York, Chicago, Los Angeles, and San Francisco metropolitan areas at the top of the urban hierarchy, the largest cities with the most diversified economies. Below these the next tier of important regional centers included Philadelphia, Boston,

Dallas, and New Orleans. Next came subregional centers with less diversified economies such as Akron, Detroit, Rochester, and San Jose. The bottom tier was occupied by economies with singular production themes (San Diego, Buffalo, Youngstown) and residential or resort centers (such as Nassau and Suffolk Counties [in New York], or Anaheim, Orlando, and Las Vegas). The important point is that Noyelle and Stanback presented this hierarchy as a dynamic system, in which the position occupied by a city can shift over time. These authors predicted that a city's economic diversity rather than its Sunbelt or northern location is the best indicator of a successful future (Noyelle and Stanback 1983, 223–227).

During the 1970s and 1980s, some Sunbelt cities fell on hard times. By the end of the 1980s, many southern cities seemed to have reached the end of a cycle of growth. Because of their dependence on a collapsing domestic oil industry, the formerly prospering states of Colorado, Oklahoma, Louisiana, and Texas were gathered together by major lending institutions under the acronym "COLT," a code word for highly risky investment, and development projects in these states were routinely rejected by wary lenders (*National Real Estate Investor*, September 1992, 92). Yet, measured in terms of investment activity and population change, Sunbelt urban growth overall outpaced that of northern regions throughout the 1980s, although variations within regions demanded more careful and more qualified generalized comparisons between regions. Twenty-eight of the 30 most rapidly growing metropolises between 1980 and 1990 were in the Sunbelt, and the population growth in some of these was remarkable. For example, the population of the Las Vegas area grew by 60 percent (see Box 7-4), while Orlando's population increased by 53 percent. Some large metro regions, like Phoenix, San Diego, Dallas, and Atlanta, continued their growth at rates above 30 percent for the 10-year period. Of the 75 largest metropolises nationwide, only 7 lost population, including those centered on the old, heavy-manufacturing cities of Cleveland, Detroit, and Pittsburgh. The New Orleans metro region was the only one located in the Sunbelt to lose population. Regional growth occurred at very modest rates around most of the old urban centers of the North, and some of the larger inner-cities showed some growth. Boston and New York defied the Northeast's established trend of inner-city population decline and had modest increases in population. At the same time, the *inner-city* populations of Atlanta, Denver, and New Orleans in the Sunbelt declined between 1980 and 1990 (Slater and Hall, 1992, 11, 20).

The decline of urban-based manufacturing continues, and it is occurring in the Sunbelt as well as in old urban centers in the North. Industrial workers are still being displaced from their jobs by plant shutdowns and reduced production. National survey data continue to show that large numbers of manufacturing workers are being displaced each year. However, the decline of manufacturing has eliminated more than production jobs; since the late 1980s, the ranks of the unemployed have come to include former engineers and executive managers whose positions were eliminated as companies closed their manufacturing divisions or shrunk their management staff in order to keep profits at a level that would satisfy shareholders.

BOX 7-4   At Home in Las Vegas

Las Vegas may be the near-perfect example of the "fantasy city" (Hannigan 1998), but by 1997 it was also simply "home" to well over a million people. Matthew Jaffe (1998) sketched the following portrait. Las Vegas is a boomtown that has discovered the formula for sustained prosperity and growth. It mixes permanent Mardi Gras for visitors with everyday living for residents. The city has nine of the world's ten largest hotels. More than 26 percent of its residents work in the tourist industry, serving 30 million visitors each year. It is a city where continuous building and rebuilding rapidly revise the urban landscape, where little remains the same for long, and where once-distant points of desert quickly become new residential subdivisions. Nearly 15,000 new residential units were built in the first half of 1997 in Las Vegas's Clark County.

What is it like to live in a metropolitan area calculated to make fantasy the permanent reality, where hotels attempt to "authentically" mimic other times and places, where a housing development company gives away as part of a promotional campaign a full-sized replica of Homer Simpson's cartoon house in a subdivision where real people will be living? According to Jaffe's local informants, newcomers are surprised to discover just how much they enjoy living in the city. One compares it to Detroit in that city's heyday, a place where blue-collar workers and their bosses could afford to enjoy themselves. Another booster likened it to New York in its time, another city that grew so boldly and quickly that it never had time to look back.

Perhaps Las Vegas will replace Los Angeles as the image we think of when we picture the quintessential U.S. city, as Los Angeles replaced New York and Chicago. In its forever unfolding newness, it represents a permanently renewable frontier of urban experience. And it represents a kind of success; it makes money effortlessly. It is a place to which 30 million pilgrims journey every year at considerable personal expense to leave significant offerings at opulent temples in an atmosphere designed to help them escape their everyday lives, an atmosphere sustained by the efforts of more than a million residents living their everyday lives.

After the lessons of the 1980s that showed how vulnerable local investment conditions were to worldwide economic fluctuations (the rise and fall of oil prices, in that case), a hypersensitivity developed among Sunbelt real estate investors and lenders to the question of just where and how to invest. Despite the often spectacular failures of development projects due to building more office space than was locally demanded, overall a general optimism remained regarding the wisdom of investing in development, especially of commercial properties, in Sunbelt cities. The buoyant spirit of entrepreneurship was reinforced by real estate investment professionals, who had something optimistic to say about virtually every city in the golden crescent. A new paradigm for understanding profitable investment had emerged by the early 1990s: There was a more or less rapid cycling natural rhythm to investment opportunity in southern cities. Profitability was a matter of timing: The question was *when*, not whether opportunity would present itself with regard to a particular city.

In various issues in the early years of the decade, the trade journal *National Real Estate Investor* reviewed the prospects of struggling boomtowns and found that they were either recovered, recovering, or on the verge of beginning recovery. The "A List" of metropolitan investment prospects still included Dallas, Houston, Denver, Portland, Washington, D.C., Atlanta, Columbia, S.C., Charlotte, N.C., and Seattle (Valuation Network, Inc. 1993, 3). According to the inevitable-recovery paradigm, the oil-price-shift victims—Dallas, Denver, and Houston—were currently good prospects for commercial investment because their devastated economies had been the first to bottom out, and it followed that they would be the first to recover. The fact that local commercial real estate markets were suffering from an office space glut—28 million square feet in the case of Dallas—meant that bargain rentals were beckoning businesses once again, and this suggested demand for further building at some time in the proximate future. Atlanta's commercial building growth rate had slowed during the early 1990s, but it was thought that the attention the city would garner from the 1996 Summer Olympics would correct the trend (*National Real Estate Investor,* May 1993). In the early 1990s, one piece of bad Sunbelt news was that Seattle's remarkable decade of growth had peaked for the moment, and the word was that new investors might find it difficult to recoup their investments in the short term (*National Real Estate Investor,* June 1992).

By the end of the twentieth century, we have learned that predicting the economic performance of individual cities in a globalizing economy is as difficult as ever. In that context, regional differences within nations seem to decrease in importance, even more so than the shrinking importance of international boundaries. Sunbelt/Snowbelt distinctions within the United States seem already to be historical references. The debate that appears more relevant is whether deindustrializing trends nationwide will lead to increasing un- and underemployment rates in all regions. As more of the manufactured goods consumed in the United States are produced outside the country, manufacturing jobs within the United States, as a proportion of the total number of jobs, are likely to continue to decline. For decades, the creation of new employment showed a concentration in the service sector. The question today is whether the trade-off between manufacturing jobs and service employment will represent a net decline in living standards for the lower tiers of workers and an inability in the aggregate purchasing power of consumers to sustain sufficient economic expansion.

Many of the questions raised by economic internationalization remain to be answered, but there are suggestions that it is having a homogenizing effect regarding earlier regional divisions. Electronic data processing and communication technologies are creating growth opportunities in widely divergent locations—from well-established centers in California and Texas to recently established locales in North Carolina and downtown Manhattan. A *Fortune* magazine feature article in 1996 (November 11) named 15 cities as the best places in which to live, work, and operate a business. While some measures were frivolous, including the price of items thought to be coveted by an upscale readership (for example, the price of a loaf of French bread or a martini), the index also included average level of education, median household income, and the rental rates for a square foot of office space. The list of the 15 best cities included more older and northern cities than Sunbelt growth-era cities: Boston, Philadelphia, Minneapolis, Raleigh-Durham, St. Louis, Cincinnati, Washington, D.C., Baltimore, and Milwaukee—along with Denver, Dallas-Fort Worth, Atlanta, and Nashville. Seattle topped the list.

By the mid-1990s, Seattle had recovered its momentum and its reputation as a growing city on the leading edge of economic and technical change, and was once again primed to provide an example of how quickly local conditions can change. The city's good fortune at the end of the twentieth century was buoyed by its place in the international Pacific Rim economy, its central place in the dynamic Cascadia region, and its nodal position in the booming information technology sector of the national economy. In midyear 2000, new office buildings were fully leased before completion and office vacancy rates hovered around a very low 2 percent (*Wall Street Journal,* July 5, 2000). City government policy urged companies to locate within the downtown area, population grew rapidly during the 1990s, housing costs shot up, and low-income housing units decreased by half. One in four residential renters were paying between 45 percent and 50 percent of their monthly income on housing, and poor and minority populations were being squeezed out of the city by housing costs. But projections were for robust growth in the high tech sector, and unemployment remained low through October 2000 (*Interactive Week,* October 30, 2000). For growing numbers of skilled workers with the right training, life was good. When the effects of the severe decline of the information technology market hit the local economy that year, 2.8 million feet of new office space were under construction in Seattle (*Wall Street Journal,* July 5, 2000). By the end of the third quarter of the year, high-tech firms had quickly abandoned millions of square feet of office space in major cities around the country, and Seattle's vacancy rate more than doubled (*Wall Street Journal,* July 3, 2001). Questions about the immediate future of the city—tied to questions about the immediate future of the information technology industry that had led and sustained the prosperity of the mid- to late-1990s—were immediately raised.

Clearly, the configuration of the urban system of any nation, and the shape of an individual city within that system, is only a temporary arrangement—a matter of catching a complex, evolving structure at one point in time. As the reshuffling of urban populations takes place among regions, the shape of the city and the opportunities for employment within it shift as well. As opportunities shift, available jobs and the people who need them don't always end up in the same place. No invisible hand coordinates economic strategies and social needs. Investment decisions are made with respect to the welfare of investors and shareholders, not laborers. There is no reason to believe that the international forces presently reshaping the urban system and the cities themselves will be any more sensitive than past forces to the needs of people with modest job skills and limited educational attainment. In fact, such workers undoubtedly will find it more difficult to find secure employment in a world in which the demand for labor at all levels shifts so rapidly. It is important to remember as we discuss the shifting fortunes of cities that we are really speaking figuratively. Cities are merely the focal points of human activity, and as such do not experience economic changes; people do. In every era of economic growth that we have examined in this chapter, urban change has produced empires for some and hardship for others, even within the same urban space. We can expect the same, as the vector of change becomes the international corporation doing what it can, or what it must, to remain profitable in the world economy.

8

ECOLOGY AND CAPITALISM
Globalization and Locality

Chapter 7 described changes in the shape and functions of cities in the United States during the course of the nineteenth and twentieth centuries. The account was largely descriptive. In this chapter, we tie urban structural changes to theoretical frameworks that attempt to identify and explain in a systematic fashion the nature of the forces that modify urban environments. There is disagreement here, and theoretical disagreements in the social sciences are serious and difficult to resolve. This is because theoretical differences often reflect opposite assumptions about whose interests are served by prevailing political and economic arrangements and whether some remote set of factors, or the people themselves, are responsible for the hardships they face. These are precisely the differences that divide theories about urban structures and futures. They have to do with fairness and social justice, on the one hand, and the capacity of individuals and governments to control the effects of global forces on local conditions, on the other. In part, the arguments are over whether market forces can be trusted to produce the maximum benefits for the greatest number. In part, the disagreements are about how much we are in control of our own fates.

First, we will consider the efforts of classical *urban ecology*, or *human ecology*, which bases its analysis of how cities grow and change on the joint influences of the market and technology to produce a rational and predictable urban form. Next, we will examine the *political economy* perspective—and in particular its Marxist influence—which emphasizes the destructive, socially divisive, and wasteful effects of market operations on the urban environment and on the lives of people who live there. The differences that separate ecologists and political economists are very similar to those that separate modernization and political economy theorists in Chapter 6. We then will consider the need to expand the framework of spatial analysis beyond the metropolis or even the region, in order to understand the changes affecting cities: This reflects an emerging recognition among social scientists and policymakers that the appropriate frame of analysis for understanding local conditions is the globe. This realization has serious implications for the subdiscipline that has until now been called "urban sociology," a designation somewhat narrower in scope than the analytic task at hand. Finally, we will bring people back into the picture, with a critical examination of the argument presented by some contemporary theorists that it is a mistake to ignore the capacity of people acting locally to affect their own futures. To the extent that the fate of localities is not determined wholly by distant forces, we must attend to analysis of local distinctions that lead to differences in the impact of global factors. Explaining these differences is the work of a sociology of locality, and at least in this sense urban sociology has important work to do.

Urban Ecology and Urban Political Economy

As the early twentieth-century cities were taking and changing shape, some urban sociologists began to devote a large share of their work to an understanding of the morphology of cities. They developed predictive models in an attempt to identify a general pattern by which cities grew and changed. These early efforts resulted in the development of a subdiscipline of urban sociology known as urban ecology. Rooted in the traditions of the Chicago school of urban sociology (discussed in Chapter 3), this approach has sought to uncover systematic relationships among the various types of land uses commonly found in urban areas. In its most current expression, ecologists have begun to focus on the relationships among cities *within* national urban systems.

In recent years, political economists, whose arguments are often derived from Marxist analysis, have offered alternative interpretations of the patterns of urban spatial development under capitalism. These interpretations have emerged as fundamental criticisms of the urban ecological models. In its most Marxian form, the alternative scheme sees the city as the spatial expression of market forces and capital accumulation, as well as an arena of conflicting class interests that pits the demands of efficient and convenient market operation against the needs of labor. Recent urban political economy explores the rise and fall of urban regions as these changes are tied to economic trends.

Both the ecologists and the political economists see the city as an arena in which competition between different interests determines the overall territorial pattern. Where the two are likely to differ fundamentally is in the interpretation of the underlying significance of the conflict and its outcome. Both approaches are increasingly drawn toward expanding geographic units of analysis.

Urban Ecology

The study of the social effects of the urban arena is, in the broadest sense of the term, the study of *urban ecology,* or as some refer to it, human ecology. *Human ecology* may be considered the study of people-environment relationships. Therefore, the idea that the city, as a physical *environment,* exerts an effect on human behavior and relationships is at base an ecological idea. In this sense, Wirth's analysis of the impact of the size and density (and the consequential heterogeneity) of urban populations is an ecological analysis. However, the term *urban ecology* can also be understood in a somewhat more restricted sense, having to do with the process and patterns by which the spatial features of urban areas emerge, the ways in which the various population and functional elements in the city arrange themselves over its limited surface. In that sense, urban ecology is the study of the distribution of and relationships among populations, services, industries, and open space in the urban arena.

The ecological orientation is tied to Robert Park's interpretation of the forces that order urban space. His frame of analysis was introduced in Chapter 3. According to Park, populations tend to break down urban space into "natural areas." The inspiration for this approach comes directly from natural science.

Some thirty years ago Professor Eugenius Warming, of Copenhagen, published a little volume entitled Plant Communities (Plantesamfund). Warming's observations called attention to the fact that different species of plants tend to form permanent groups, which he called communities. Plant communities . . . come into existence gradually, pass through certain characteristic changes, and are eventually broken up and succeeded by other communities of a very different sort. These observations later became the point of departure for a series of investigations which have since become familiar under the title "Ecology." . . .

Within the limits of every natural area the distribution of population tends to assume definite and typical patterns. Every local group exhibits a more or less definite constellation of the individual units that compose it. The form which this constellation takes, the position, in other words, of every individual in the community with reference to every other, so far as it can be described in general terms, constitutes what Durkheim called the morphological aspect of society. . . .

Local communities may be compared with reference to the areas which they occupy and with reference to the relative density of population distribution within those areas. Communities are not, however, mere population aggregates. Cities, particularly great cities, where the selection and segregation of the population has gone farthest, display certain morphological characteristics which are not found in smaller population aggregates. (Park 1926, 3–4)

In this passage, taken from Park's address to the American Sociological Society in 1925, the influential sociologist repeated his observation that the spatial organization of the city followed a natural order. Before the same forum, R. D. McKenzie (1926, 172–181) cataloged the major features of the ecological framework, which included the following:

Tendencies toward area specialization and the segregation of dissimilar populations

The centralization of services and activities that were most specialized or most in demand, along with the decentralization of nonspecialized services like grocery and drug stores

Population concentration as the result of concentrated patterns of commercial and industrial growth, along with tendencies toward dispersion as motor and electric transport grew in importance in contrast to steam locomotion (a formerly centralizing transportation technology)

Invasion and succession—the processes whereby one segment of the urban population took possession of a specific urban territory from another

A great part of the attraction of early ecology was the idea that natural laws could be borrowed or adapted from the natural sciences, thereby providing the basis for predicting the distribution of urban land uses. The most notable and well-known effort to develop a comprehensive description of the forces that shaped the urban environment was Burgess's (1925) *concentric zone hypothesis*. Based largely on the familiar case of Chicago, Burgess's model of urban structure was founded on the view that various elements of a heterogeneous and economically complex urban society actively competed for favorable locations within the city. The model assumed steady urban growth and the desirability of central location for commercial and financial interests. As the number of wealthy and powerful institutions competing for desirable central locations increased, this growth at the urban center meant a continuous outward process of the invasion and succession of businesses and different population segments across a series of existing, spatially specialized zones that encircled the center. Together, these concentric zones comprised the total area of the city (Figure 8-1).

Burgess identified five major urban zones. The commercial heart and center of the city was Zone I, occupied by department stores, banks, office buildings, and expensive specialty stores that could afford to share the rental costs of this most desirable commercial location. The outer portion of this zone was occupied by commercial and industrial enterprises that were less dependent upon the most centralized location and less able to pay the highest ground rents, and perhaps required more space (e.g., warehouses).

Zone II was the zone in transition. This was the old residential area surrounding the commercial core, containing the oldest housing in the poorest state of repair in the city. The area was continually being invaded at its margins by the outward growth of the central business district. It housed the poorest populations of the city, including the most recent immigrants as well as minorities. These populations were forced to share their residential areas with criminals, prostitutes, and other undesirable company, all of whom used the common territory as a locus of operation. In the competition for urban space, the poor did not have the means to choose to live elsewhere.

Zone III was the zone of workingmen's homes. It was characterized by a predominance of two-family dwelling units and represented the upward mobility of its working-class residents who had managed to leave behind the deterioration of Zone II. Zone IV consisted of better residences, including residential hotels and better-quality apartments. Single-family dwellings in this area tended to be situated on large lots, reflective of the ability of their owners to support such residential investment. Zone V was the commuter zone where, for those willing to bear the inconvenience of distant, peripheral location, the already growing suburban population was able to satisfy its desire for home ownership.

Based on the example of one large city, Burgess's land-use hypothesis raised questions about the adaptability of the model to other cities. Subsequent efforts to discover consistent features in the physical arrangement of the urban environment

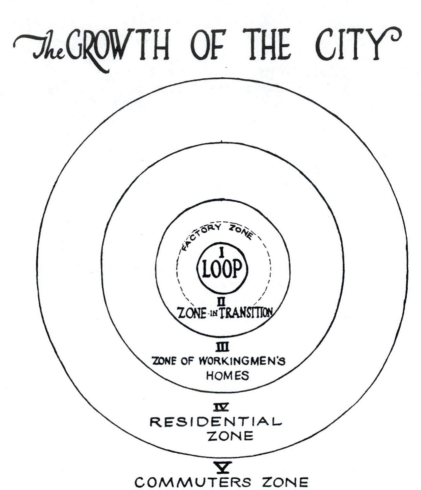

FIGURE 8-1   Concentric Zone Hypothesis—This is the quaint drawing that
appeared in Burgess's original essay. It is one of the most
famous diagrams in all of sociology.

Source: Ernest W. Burgess. 1925, 51. "The Growth of the City: An Introduction to a Research Project."
In *The City,* edited by Robert E. Park and Ernest W. Burgess, 47–62. Chicago: The University of
Chicago Press. © 1925, 1967 by The University of Chicago. All rights reserved.

came to emphasize the complexity of the factors that shape cities. Consequently,
the Burgess model came to be regarded as an oversimplification. Homer Hoyt
(1939) studied changes in residential patterns in 142 cities for the years 1900, 1915,
and 1936. By largely restricting his attention to housing costs and looking at the
changes that had taken place over time, Hoyt found that homogeneous areas of residence tended to grow outward from center toward periphery in wedge-shaped
sectors, rather than in alternating rings as Burgess had thought (Figure 8-2). In

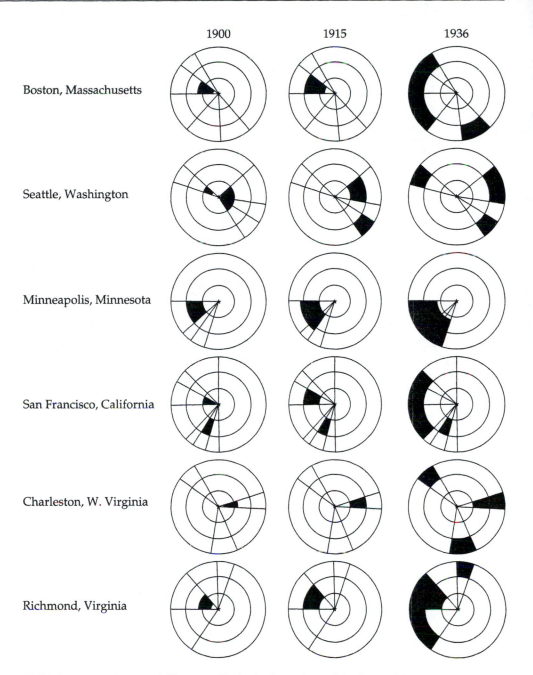

FIGURE 8-2   Sectoral Theory: Shifts in Location of Fashionable Residential Areas in Six U.S. Cities, 1900–1936

Source: Homer Hoyt. 1939, 113. *The Structure and Growth of Residential Neighborhoods in American Cities.* Washington, D.C.: Federal Housing Administration.
Note: Fashionable residential areas indicated by solid black.

Hoyt's *sectoral theory*, housing of a particular type and value followed definite paths, typically along communication corridors. Variations in topography also had a pronounced effect on residential patterning, with better residences generally occupying higher land. The attractiveness of adjacent and nearby land use also exerted a significant influence on the development of areas, with good transportation routes, access to shopping and business districts, and the residential location of community leaders offering attractions to the more affluent.

Hoyt's work began to suggest a problem for the early ecologists' hopes for developing a general model of urban land use. It suggested that the variety of influences to which the physical patterning of cities was subject would defy reduction to a single generalizable description. Harris and Ullman (1945) would also show that the tendencies toward metropolitanization would make generalization more difficult.

As indicated in Chapter 7, the shape of U.S. cities had already begun to change dramatically over the course of the first four decades of the twentieth century, producing a more decentralized urban pattern. Harris and Ullman described a much different city in 1945 than the one on which Burgess had based his model. Many rapidly growing cities were annexing or incorporating formerly outlying and independent townships, previously self-centered communities in their own right. No simple concentric zone or sectoral hypothesis could be applied to such amalgamations of population. Although Harris and Ullman believed that a single major business district could still be identified for most cities, the new urban form that they diagrammed had more the quality of a patchwork than of a centralized design (Figure 8-3).

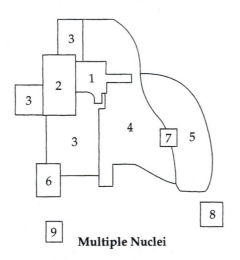

District
1. Central Business District
2. Wholesale Light Manufacturing
3. Low-class Residential
4. Medium-class Residential
5. High-class Residential
6. Heavy Manufacturing
7. Outlying Business District
8. Residential Suburb
9. Industrial Suburb

Multiple Nuclei

FIGURE 8-3   Multiple Nuclei Model

Source: Reprinted from "The Nature of Cities" by Chauncy D. Harris and Edward L. Ullman in volume no. 242 of *The Annals of the American Academy of Political and Social Science* © 1945, by the American Academy of Political and Social Science.

According to this scheme, called the *multiple nuclei model,* patterns of growth and change still followed the general ecological principles identified by Burgess. The location of particular activities was still determined by their need for certain facilities, such as a central business district's requirement of transportation routes. Similar activities tended to profit from proximate location, as in the case of the entertainment district. Other activities were mutually repellent, for instance, residences and certain types of industry. Finally, the cost of location remained a major factor in deciding whether access to the most desirable sites was feasible for a given enterprise or social class. The main difference between this model and earlier formulations was that there were multiple nuclei that attracted and repelled newcomers in the broadened urban arena. Each area was formed in consideration of multiple adjoining areas. As the city grew and changed over time, new districts became attractive. For example, outlying areas attracted heavy industry from increasingly congested inner-city locations, which were most attractive in the era of centralized transportation routes when the city was smaller and relatively compact; with highway access, the inner-city locations lost favor to outlying sites. As a result, heavy industry was likely to emerge in two or more locations, perhaps far removed from one another. Similarly, metropolitan growth generated multiple business districts, as those of existing towns on the periphery were incorporated into the sprawling ecology of the growing metropolitan centers, and new business districts emerged to serve populations some distance from existing centers. Likewise, different grades of housing, various types of commercial activities, and so on emerged not in one but in multiple locations.

Harris and Ullman's model was "conceived as a further move away from the massive generalization and toward reality" (Carter 1972, 175). But where did it leave the effort of urban ecologists to anticipate the distribution of population, open space, services, industry, and commerce within a particular urban arena? Harris and Ullman's work did not suggest any uniform patterning of land uses among cities, and with respect to any given city, locational decisions were ad hoc and based on the existing distribution of land uses. All that could be said was that the future of a given space would be determined by the future uses of those spaces nearby, and the manner in which the space was connected to or cut off from other areas of the city. That is, the predictability of the pattern of urban space seemed to be limited.

Evaluating the Classical Ecological Schemes

Despite the frustrations encountered in the attempts to develop an ecological model of the city, urban ecologists continue to probe urban environments for principles of organization. The search for a general, predictive model has failed for a number of reasons. For one, ecological models were based on the premise that economic competition for space would ultimately determine the use to which an area is put. They did not take account of the capacity of government to influence patterns through planning. Moreover, they failed to consider the potential role of sentiment, such as favoring the preservation of historic sites or open areas.

With regard to criticisms of specific ecological schemes, it is interesting to note that most critics have taken aim at Burgess's early model, bypassing its later revisions. To the extent that the concentric growth model appeared accurate or useful, it was conceded to have been so with respect to those rapidly growing cities of the Midwest that had large immigrant populations at or just after the turn of the century. The greatest problem with the model was its limited generalizability. Schnore and Winsborough (1972) studied the residential location of different status groups (status measured by education) in 184 cities in the United States and found that the concentric hypothesis, which predicted that lower-status residents would be concentrated nearest the city center, was borne out in only about half of the cases.

Hawley (1981, 98–101) noted that the Burgess hypothesis works better as a formulation of growth processes than as a generalized description of spatial patterns of cities. Most of the critics focused on the spatial description, however, and pointed out that there was considerable heterogeneity within the proposed zones. Hawley believed that the argument as to whether a zonal or sectoral description works best results from a too literal interpretation of the zonal hypothesis—which Burgess intended only as an ideal typical description. With respect to the specific criticism that crosscutting transportation routes tend to draw cities into star-shaped rather than circular patterns, Hawley responded that if distance is measured in time and cost of travel rather than in lineal units, the "distortions" in the concentric pattern caused by transportation routes could be accommodated. He suggested that the concentric pattern be considered a descriptive formulation, a useful first approximation. It may be added that if we look for trends in land-use patterns that can be generalized from city to city—without looking for particular shapes or designs—ecology can remain a useful orienting framework. Box 8-1 makes this point with regard to current residential trends that are repeated in many cities at the same time.

The test of any theoretical model comes in cross-cultural application. In a review of the international literature on urban ecology, London and Flanagan (1976) tested the hypothesis (Hawley 1981, 315; Schnore 1972, 21) that cities everywhere were converging toward a common configuration, described by the Burgess model and approximated most closely by cities in the Western industrialized nations. As had previous studies, this study focused on the residential location of different social statuses among the urban population. Examination of the comparative evidence revealed that, despite pronounced variations in the ecological patterns across and within world regions, there did appear to be some emerging similarities of residential patterns. However, it could not be assumed that cities everywhere were coming to conform to the Burgess model or any other existing model. The diversity of historical eras (e.g., of mercantile, colonial, or industrial-capitalist origins) that gave rise to contemporary urban centers around the world has left its distinctive mark on the shapes and internal physical arrangements of cities. These cities have been altered by economic growth, prosperity (or the lack of it), and the transportation and communication technologies that prevailed during the formative era, as well as the deliberate efforts of government to control

BOX 8-1   Re-Invasion and Succession Downtown

For urban ecologists, the city is less a map than a dynamic, animated arena of shifting land uses. It is also a mosaic of *natural* processes and natural areas, where residents and businesses gravitate to certain areas in a shifting process of invasion and succession, exemplified most clearly in Burgess's concentric zone theory. But Burgess was describing the process as he witnessed it in Chicago in the 1920s. In that era, the endlessly expanding central business district was the engine that drove changing land-use patterns, rippling outward from the middle of the city, where the wealthiest corporations and other businesses were best able to meet the high land costs. How has the pattern changed at the turn of the century, when most commercial growth is located on the periphery of urban areas, when the city form has sprawled into the metropolitan region, and the urban center has become a less desirable location for many businesses?

Ellen Perlman (1998), focusing on the city of Memphis, provided a brief and useful overview of the contemporary version of invasion and succession, which is taking place in cities of various sizes with different kinds of downtown histories. In this pattern, residential use is replacing business use in the old centers of such cities as Philadelphia, Dayton, Denver, Tulsa, Baltimore, Dallas, Atlanta, and Richmond, Virginia, in addition to Memphis. The simultaneous nature of the change is important because it supports the classical ecologists' contention that shifting patterns of land use are a natural phenomenon, representing general *cultural preferences* and tendencies within the population, as they are expressed under particular *historical circumstances*. In this case, the cultural preference is that of affluent professionals and others without young children who are attracted to central urban locations because they are bored with the suburbs. The historical circumstances that allow the residential invasion of commercial properties include the fact that central location is no longer as attractive to commercial interests as it once was—the commercial buildings built decades ago in central locations are not suitable for current business needs. Many of these properties are physically sound; can be economically converted to residential use as lofts, apartments, and condominiums; and are aesthetically attractive to consumers looking for funky alternative living space. In Memphis, the buildings renovated by private interests for residential use include the 1913 Hotel Grand that had been ruined by fire in the riots that followed Martin Luther King's assassination in 1968, a warehouse, an old National Biscuit Company distribution site, the Goyoso Hotel, and the Memphis Cotton Exchange, which was converted into 202 apartment units. The scale of the invasion is modest but significant, with an estimated 1,000 new residents moving to pricey, renovated (and some newly built) downtown properties each year.

The re-invasion of the central city may reflect a "natural" convergence of preferences for a segment of the affluent population, but the movement is avidly supported by the efforts of local government, which recognizes the importance of attracting to the downtown a resident population with a substantial disposable income. The movement is also supported by developers and realtors who enthusiastically support the arrival of well-heeled newcomers. The invasion does have a downside. Often referred to as "gentrification," critics are concerned about the impact of the combined activity of government, businesses, and the new renters and buyers on the cost of housing in the inner city. The consequences for the poor and those with modest incomes are discussed in the section of Chapter 10 that deals with gentrification.

or otherwise shape urban growth. These varied factors will continue to provide substantial resistance to the development of a worldwide convergence of urban land-use patterns.

Postwar Modifications in the Methods and Scope of Urban Ecology

As a consequence of the general perception that the classical ecological models were overly simplistic, urban ecologists refined the methodology with which they approached the complexity of the urban environment. A widely employed technique, referred to as *social area analysis,* was developed by Shevky and Williams (1949) and later formalized by Shevky and Bell (1955). Shevky, Williams, and Bell identified three fundamental features according to which urban populations could be identified and differentiated: economic status, family status, and ethnic classification. They observed that these characteristics were found in identifiable configurations that set the various areas of the city apart from one another. These clusters were identified as "social areas" by the researchers, who argued that the areas were also popularly perceived as distinguishable by their residents and others; that is, that they had a popular subjective reality independent of that which was discovered by the research.

The method attracted a number of analyses of various urban areas in the United States and elsewhere. Although some researchers found the original variables of social area analysis limited, computer technology, employing a statistical technique called factor analysis, expanded the number of variables that could be easily considered. In *factorial ecology* any number of social variables may enter the equation to determine which variables among them are found clustered together in different areas of the city. The clusters are then identified—that is, labeled—on the basis of the quality they seem to measure. For example, an area shown to be distinguished from the surrounding areas by a high concentration of young adults, single people, or married couples without children, with relatively high educations, high incomes, and short average residency would suggest a distinct and identifiable district. After such an area was indicated by the data, an appropriate descriptive label would be selected and applied.

A major appeal of these techniques is that they can be readily applied to periodically available census data, and in this way detailed changes in the spatial configuration of urban land-use patterns may be revealed. The research is readily replicable, and invites cross-cultural application in cases where the appropriate data exist. It is not surprising that area-analysis methods gained wide appeal among researchers. However, social area analysis and the closely related factorial ecology have been broadly criticized as theoretically weak approaches. Whereas the older and, admittedly, overly simplistic schemes failed to describe too much regarding existing patterns, the new methods were seen as describing much while explaining little. Moreover, Burgess's goal was to anticipate and predict development, whereas social area analysis and factorial ecology are largely silent with regard to projection.

Recent Concept Developments

Two recent developments in urban ecology are particularly noteworthy. The first involves harnessing principles of structural functionalist theory to the spatial analysis of society. The second involves the efforts of some ecologists to articulate the dynamics of the interrelationships that exist among cities.

Functionalist Urban Ecology

This theoretical trend has been associated primarily with the work of the eminent urban ecologist, Amos Hawley. Under his influence, understanding of the basic forces that shape the patterns of human settlement has shifted from an emphasis on competition for space to a concern with interdependence, systemness, and equilibrium (Hawley 1986). His thesis borrows heavily from the social model of Talcott Parsons's (1951) functionalism.

Functionalism is partially rooted in Durkheim's analysis of the organization of society (Chapter 3), especially his assumption of organic solidarity. It lays heavy emphasis on the functional integration of the major specialized structures (institutions) of society. As societies evolve, they become more complex and their major components accommodate one another, both in their form and the way they work; advanced societies are characterized by a functionally integrated set of institutions. Parsons's model of society (or the *social system*) emphasizes a tendency toward balance or equilibrium among the various components of the system and consensus among its human participants. The earmarks of a modern society are a continued trend toward interdependence, complexity, balance, and consensus.

Although he tried to distance his assumptions from some of the features of Parsons's classical functionalism, Hawley's (1986, 29 ff.) efforts to formalize his theoretical ecology clearly retained a close affinity to Parsons's vision of the social system. Hawley's emphasis is on spatial organization, and cities are the most complex and orderly expression of society's spatial dimension. The units of society are linked together in interdependence "with reference to the ways they can be useful to one another."

The spatial expression of such a system is derived from the fact that the interdependencies that make it up are constrained and shaped by time and space. All activity is time-consuming, so we should expect that units will organize themselves efficiently in space with regard to their mutual and respective needs and routines. One important way that system efficiency is secured is by the spatial concentration of units engaged in interrelated functions. "Thus human settlement is all but universally nucleated. The city is the preeminent example of interunit accessibility heightened by concentration." Given the tendency toward complementarity and efficiency, any disruption introduced into the system will be followed by a readjustment toward a state of system balance or equilibrium.

Hawley (1986, 45) offered the "steady-state" equilibrium model as a helpful abstraction, and warned that we should avoid confusing models with descriptions of reality. It remains to be seen how useful urban ecologists will find such an abstraction for giving their research direction or in interpreting their findings.

It has often been stated, with regard to Parsons's classical functionalist theory, that theories cast at such a level of abstraction offer little practical guidance for empirical research.

Interurban Ecology

In another development in this branch of urban sociology, ecologists shifted their focus away from the description of individual settlements and toward the relationships among cities (F. D. Wilson 1984, 283–288). Urban ecologists became concerned with interurban linkages within national systems of cities. Within a national urban system (the analysis can also be applied to international systems), cities are linked together in a hierarchical division of labor according to the financial, commercial, and political institutions that they house. This division allows the largest metropolitan areas to exert powerful influences over areas lower on the chain. Patterns of domination are subject to modification over time, because existing arrangements are vulnerable to changes in transportation, communication, and the ability of major economic decision-making/power-wielding units to change locations within the urban system. In more concrete terms, this means that a city's position in the hierarchy of power relations may be modified by the decision of a major corporation to relocate its home office or major manufacturing facility. Another cause of realignment could be locational decisions for major transportation routes (recall the impact of the railroads, which were discussed in Chapter 7).

This more recent interurban emphasis in urban ecology reflects the recognition that the most powerful organizations in contemporary society are multilocational and that the cities which house, for example, a corporation's various units are subject to that company's intraorganizational influences.

> *In fact, these units are the major source of intermetropolitan, interurban, and intraurban interdependencies. These linkages stem from the existence of a division of labor within such organizations and across corporations, firms, and governmental units. They involve the flow of various services, as well as decision-making information, control information, and coordination information, between the headquarters and other organizational units. (F. D. Wilson 1984)*

In this broader perspective, ecologists are interested in the dominance that some urban places exercise over others. The most influential cities tend to feature high concentrations of wholesale facilities, which are the locus of corporate decision making and which control capital flows, credit, employment, and the dissemination of information. This emphasis in human ecology appears to hold promise for the development of greater insight into contemporary settlement patterns. It is, however, a major step away from the more familiar ecological approaches, a step in the direction of political economy.

Urban ecology remains a very influential paradigm within urban sociology (Flanagan 1993, 62–68). Many among the current generation of urban sociologists, and their teachers, were trained to think in social ecological terms. The functionalist assumption that the spatial arrangement (the nature of settlement patterns) of all societies will conform to a common, most efficient design strongly affects comparative research on European and North American cities. And one can easily find the old debates between Burgess and Hoyt echoed in contemporary descriptions of cities, debates about whether newly discovered patterns of urban land use in this city or that conform more to the circular or wedge-shaped model.

Political Economy and Urban Sociology

The basic premise of classical and functionalist ecology is that the economic competition for urban space produces a spatial order that is efficient in a natural and universal sense. To extend the implications of this view slightly, the assumption is that all or most of those who share the city share common economic interests, and that an emerging urban design that benefits one group benefits all others.

It is possible, however, to begin with the opposite set of assumptions and to come to a very different conclusion regarding the question of who benefits from patterns of growth and change, which are shaped by the marketplace and the ability of those with the greatest wealth to have their way. If we begin with the idea of scarcity of resources, that is, the idea that there are not enough of the generally coveted goods and benefits that society produces for everyone to get as much as they want, then we can look upon the outcome of competition in which wealthy individuals and institutions prevail in a different light. Many social scientists start from the premise that conflict between groups with unequal resources represents the underlying reality of the social order, not harmony and common interest. Some have focused on the urban arena as one of the key settings where the battle for resources is carried out.

Political economy is the study of how political decision-making and social policy articulates with the economic interests of different social classes, intervenes in competition with the effect of advantaging or disadvantaging the differing and often opposed goals of particular groups of actors. What kinds of divisions are we talking about? Do wage earners and employers have the same interests? Are there ways in which the policies of government might benefit one at the cost of the other? The same questions might be asked with regard to the propertied and the propertyless, the affluent and the poor, members of minority and members of majority groups, established residents and more recent immigrants, men and women. With specific regard to urban populations, we may raise questions about whose neighborhoods are torn down to build new highways; whose interests are served by the decision to build highways rather than to support mass transit through subsidizing its costs of operation; the pursuit of policies that promote the hiring of disadvantaged people for public jobs, or the prohibition of such policies; the taxing of corporations in order to support city-run day care centers, or the offer of tax incentives to corporations to keep local plants open—leaving the city with less in the way of revenues for social programs. Such decisions differentially affect the ability of people to compete for benefits and opportunities; they help some and hinder others. These are policy or political decisions that affect the ability of different groups to be more or less successful in the competition for their share of society's scarce goods.

Beginning in the late 1960s, a growing number of critical theorists turned their attention to cities and to the signs of social unrest that were most evident there. In 1968, a series of student and worker riots occurred in Paris, which were interpreted officially as *urban* uprisings. In Britain, declining employment in major industrial cities and housing shortages led to questions about the economic processes that determined the allocation and utilization of urban space. A series of urban riots in the United States during the decade, the economic decline of central cities, and the loss of urban industrial jobs also attracted the attention of critical urban analysts.

The questions that were raised by contemporary political economists were consistent with those raised by Marx a century earlier, and categories of analysis that focused on capital accumulation and class conflict came to the fore of emerging theories about cities and conflict. Although Marx himself did not focus on cities in his examination of capitalism (he did believe that they were important to the development of revolutionary class consciousness), the mode of critical inquiry developed during the 1970s by urban theorists was strongly influenced by his ideas. This new Marxist perspective was particularly critical of traditional urban sociology, of the ecologists, and of those who worked in the urbanism tradition because nothing in that body of work had anticipated the urban uprisings. At the core of the classical traditions was a distraction, according to the Marxist view, a "fetishism of space," meaning that the classical schemes mistakenly saw in urban space an independent or ultimate causal factor. According to the Marxist perspective, the ultimate causal factors in any society are its economic arrangements. What Park, Burgess, Wirth, and others in the ecological school and the urban tradition should have focused on was *how a particular set of urban structures and effects were produced by capitalism.* Capitalism created particular forms of land use and the massive cities that instilled feelings of alienation and anomie. The urban environment itself was an effect—a product of a capitalist industrial revolution and its aftermath—rather than a cause. The analysis of space, as having a reality in and of itself, was a conceptual dead end. And now that cities were declining as economic centers, and were routinely beset by class and racial tensions and disturbances, the point was clearer than ever, according to the Marxist view. The key to understanding urban problems was to focus on economic conditions rather than some mysterious property of size, density, or ecology.

The distinction being made here is not so subtle or academic as it may at first appear. In terms of social action, cities or ecologies are not real agents that create social conditions or social change in the same sense that individual capitalists, corporations, or collective movements based on class interests are. In this view, it makes no sense to speak in terms of the suburbs versus the cities, or of the competition between Chicago and St. Louis. These are

> *fundamental distortions of reality. Two points on the earth's inanimate surface cannot have opposing interests. History is made only when groups of people have*

interests opposed to those of other groups of people. The city is considered appropriately as a mere reflection of the larger economic and social fabric. . . . In analyzing any urban problem and, therefore, in analyzing any mode of production, class relations are paramount. (Sawers 1984, 4–7)

The new mode of analysis was given much of its impetus by the work of Manuel Castells, first with the publication of and then with the English language translation of his *The Urban Question* ([1972] 1977). Castells is critical of the idea that a given ecological context (the city) can give rise to a specific system of social relations (urban culture, or urbanism). He attributes the development of this perspective to the German school of urban sociology, "from Tönnies to Spengler, by way of Simmel," which we reviewed in Chapter 3. These ideas were developed further in Chicago by Park and his student Wirth, whom Castells credits with the most serious attempt within the conventional urban studies paradigm to establish a distinct subject matter and field of study specific to urban sociology (Castells [1972] 1977, 75–77). However, Wirth's effort failed, in his view, because the assumptions of the paradigm on which it was based were fatally flawed.

For Castells, the problem with the argument that the urban environment produces a particular effect on culture is that those conditions described as a consequence of urban environment are, in fact, produced by capitalist industrialization. The fragmentation of roles, the predominance of secondary relationships, and accentuated individualization are not produced by urban life but by the industrial system under capitalism (Castells [1972] 1977, 81). What had been recognized as "urban life" was itself produced by economic forces. What had been seen as a cause of behavior and experience was in itself merely a consequence of a more fundamental set of causes. To miss this point and to treat the urban environment as an independent variable with consequences for experience, behavior, and organization is to engage in an exercise in "bourgeois ideology." This is because any science not built upon a clear appreciation of class antagonisms will stand in the way of the recognition of the fundamental conflict at the heart of capitalist society.

In the decade following the appearance of Castells's work in English, many Marxist analyses were applied usefully to such issues as urban industrial decline, the Sunbelt phenomenon, uneven economic development, metropolitanization, and other trends. These various efforts can be broken down into two areas of emphasis: those that were primarily concerned with capital accumulation and those that focused more on class conflict (Gottdiener 1985, 72–73). Looking at these separately helps us to see what it means to apply Marxist analysis to urban space.

Capital Accumulation
We need to begin by acknowledging that separating capital accumulation and class struggle as we do here is somewhat artificial since, as David Harvey (1985a, 1) reminded us, they are very much interwoven aspects of the same system of production and distribution, capitalism. In that portion of his work devoted primarily to the issue of accumulation, he wrote that "the urban process," whatever else it may entail, "implies the creation of a material physical infrastructure for production, circulation, exchange, and consumption." The *built environment* is produced by the

accumulation and organization of capital. That is, it takes time for capital to complete its circulation from money back to money plus profit. The urban environment was built, and is continuously destroyed and rebuilt, for the sake of creating a more efficient arena for circulation. Buildings and machinery that are destroyed in the process may still be perfectly useful, but they are not optimally efficient for current purposes; consequently, they are discarded before their time in a process of "creative destruction" that is continually accelerating.

> We look at the material solidity of a building, a canal, a highway, and behind it we see always the insecurity that lurks within the circulation process of capital, which always asks: how much more time in this relative space? The rush of human beings across space is now matched by an accelerating pace of change in the production of landscapes across which they rush. Processes as diverse as suburbanization, deindustrialization and restructuring, gentrification and urban renewal, through the total reorganization of the spatial structure of the urban hierarchy, are part and parcel of a continuous reshaping of geographical landscapes to match the quest to accelerate turnover time. The destruction of familiar places and secure places . . . provokes many an anguished cry. (Harvey 1985b, 28)

Harvey argued that the capital for investment in the built environment is produced by capitalism's chronic overaccumulation, the failure of direct competition among commodity producers to fully absorb investment resources. That is, under normal conditions, more saleable commodities are produced by capitalism than can be consumed. Investment in the kind of fixed capital that the built environment represents, such as homes or offices, is less attractive from a profit motive standpoint than is the production of saleable commodities. However, such investment provides a temporary solution (heavily subsidized by state guarantees and dependent upon the availability of credit) to capitalism's chronic overaccumulation problem. Harvey observed that just such a potential overaccumulation dilemma faced the United States after World War II. From this perspective, rapid suburban development may be interpreted as a strategic market response that simultaneously created a mass-market investment opportunity for surplus capital and an outlet for the pent-up demand for individual home ownership. In this view, private ownership of housing provides a mechanism of social stabilization, which was employed in the United States both during the unsettled 1930s as a means of generating social stability among the more affluent elements of the workforce and again in the urban confrontations of the 1960s when the suburbs were opened to promote home ownership for lower-income and minority families (Harvey 1985a, 28–29).

Class Conflict

Sawers's (1984) urban analysis focuses primarily on class conflict. The division between those who receive their income from property and those who receive their income in the form of wages is fundamental and unalterable. Owners have no choice under capitalism but to do whatever is in their power to realize profits to be reinvested as capital. As a class, they must try to organize society, and more particularly, urban space, to enhance profit maximization. Workers are primarily interested in an organization of space that enhances their interests as consumers. In this way, the fundamental conflict between capital and labor extends beyond the division of society into wages and profits. Capital and labor are also in conflict over the manner in which space in the urban arena is to be used. This conflict is manifest in battles over rent control, traffic safety, health issues, land use, and other divisions of interest that are basically thinly disguised forms of class struggle (Sawers 1984, 6–9).

In the current phase of the evolution of capitalism, the globe is enmeshed in a single capitalist system of producers, markets, and labor reserves. The decline of the older industrial cities of the United States must be understood in this perspective. In fact, every urban era and the condition of any society's cities can be understood only with reference to their particular histories. The crisis of the older industrial cities is simply a result of the fact that when confronted with cheaper labor reserves, industrialists will usually vote with their feet (Sawers 1984, 7–10). In their introduction to the first edition of *Marxism and the Metropolis*, Tabb and Sawers wrote of the significance, in the context of class struggle, of the flight of industry from the urban centers where it had emerged:

The city, in this case Chicago, is in a constant state of demolition and reconstruction. According to Marxist theory, useful buildings are destroyed before their time in the quest to make urban space more profitable.

General Motors, General Electric, and all the other generals whose corporate headquarters impressively rise above our large cities were once small companies with a few employees. But because they are able to plow the surplus back into the firm, they could steadily hire more workers and grow larger. Their machines were produced by past generations of workers, and are in this basic sense the embodiment of workers, of "dead labor."

Living labor confronts the power of these corporate giants. . . . When workers demand higher wages and better working conditions, and the corporate power refuses, relying on its size, financial and political strength, and most of all on its ability to deny the workers a means of living, it has appropriated this strength from the sweat and blood of past workers. When a company moves from a city to a place where it can find labor that will work for less, it takes the productive capacity built by its workers away from them—creating unemployment, eroding the tax base, leading ultimately to the urban crisis. (Tabb and Sawers 1978, 9)

Chapter 7 provided an overview of the urban history of the United States. Box 8-2 briefly reexamines that history employing Marxist categories of analysis.

Evaluating the Contributions of the Marxist Approach

Western sociological thought may be classified according to various schemes, the simplest of which is to divide it between the mainstream and Marxist traditions. As the labels imply, there will be those theories that fall within a single core of the more widely accepted frameworks of thought and a separate body of ideas, Marxism, that stands outside this tradition. That this classification holds for urban sociology is underlined by the fact that, for the most part, it has been possible up to this point to discuss what has been done in the name of urban sociology with minimal reference to Marx. Principles of Marxism are not easily synthesized with mainstream assumptions. Also, given that Marxist theory both attacks the legitimacy and questions the viability of capitalism, it has been perceived as a set of arguments based primarily on ideological rather than scientific assumptions. Put simply, in this view Marxism is not a science but a political position, and from within the mainstream, its practitioners are perceived as less than legitimate. This, in fact, is the same way that many Marxists tend to view the main body of mainstream or "bourgeois" sociology.

The incompatibility of mainstream and Marxist traditions in urban sociology stems from the basic differences in the assumptions of the two approaches. The early ecologists understood that urban land-use patterns were the result of competition (facilitated or constrained by transportation and communication technology) among various elements of the urban population. Marxists argue that urban patterns, like all areas of social relations in society, are the result of the basic economic process of capital accumulation, profit-taking strategies, and various particularly urban manifestations of the class struggle.

During the 1970s and through the early part of the following decade, the Marxist perspective appeared to provide a useful alternative to the urban culture and community studies approaches—approaches that had failed to predict or explain the urban disturbances of the 1960s. However, the popularity of radical crit-

---

BOX 8-2   U.S. Urban History from a Marxist Perspective

David Gordon (1984) interpreted U.S. urban history from the perspective of Marxism. He identified three distinct eras of capitalist development, each associated with a particular kind of city.

1. In the Colonial and Post Colonial City, merchant capitalists made profits from the sale of commodities not produced by themselves or others in their employ. Merchant interests that were located in one city struggled for regional and national dominance over those in other cities. The wealth of the owner class grew throughout this period, dating through the mid-1880s, in contrast to the general poverty of many of their fellow citizens.

2. The second era emerged between 1850 and 1870, and was characterized by the emergence of the Industrial City. During this period, the wealth of capital accumulation was increasingly invested in manufacturing. The efficiency of the factory production system was perfected through (1) the deskilling of craft work into standardized production processes that could be staffed with semi-skilled labor and (2) the relocation of factories among reserve armies of the unemployed, which had the effect of extending a strong element of discipline over the labor force. In this second stage, segregated working-class housing districts emerged, closely associated with factory locations. The dense concentrations of labor were increasingly restive by the 1880s. During this period, worker resentment and industrial disputes grew in reaction to the acceleration of the work process, an acceleration that was demanded by manufacturers who were locked in competition with one another. Conditions were right for creating the kind of class consciousness and

worker actions that Marx had predicted. Gordon argued that labor unrest was, in fact, a powerful enough force to contribute to the demise of the Industrial City and the rise of the Corporate City in the period between 1898 and 1920.

3. The Corporate City sprawled into the metropolitan region, not in response to innovations in transportation technology, but as the result of intensifying activism, which had sprung up in the concentrated working-class districts of the earlier Industrial City. Gordon offered the examples of Hammond and Gary, Indiana, two outposts of industrial development beyond the urban fringe of the Chicago area. These were developed in response to what Chicago industrialists of the era identified as a "hotbed of trades unionism" as they complained about "all these controversies and strikes we have here." The emergence of a resistant class consciousness was a concern of the times. The Corporate City featured an intensification and expansion of the central business district. The dispersion of the manufacturing operations, in response to labor activism, freed the new corporate giants to locate their executive and administrative offices convenient to those of other corporations, banks, law offices, and advertising firms and marketing agencies. The image of the massive corporate headquarters dominating the skyline of the major metropolitan centers describes the cities that we became familiar with over the course of the twentieth century. The question of what shape the market will demand of the city of the global future remains open, from a Marxist or any perspective.

---

icism was short-lived. The generally more conservative mood of the 1980s, both within universities and in general, placed the radical analyses of social issues further outside the framework of legitimate scholarly discussion. The collapse of many socialist experiments at the end of the decade considerably weakened serious consideration of models alternative to capitalism.

It has always been the case in the United States that the pursuit of Marxist avenues of analysis is perceived as more than a theoretical option. The idea that, if one pursues an avenue of reasoning opened first by Marxist principles, then one is doing Marxist analysis, is politically off-putting to many. The question of whether one is a Marxist if one finds Marxist analysis plausible can generate serious problems of professional identity and intellectual legitimacy in conventional academic circles. Also, both the ecological and the Marxist approaches have been criticized as overly structural and deterministic. They are unable to explain why different groups, neighborhoods, or cities adapt to the same set of conditions in different ways and produce different outcomes.

Many of those who had engaged in Marxist analysis retreated to what were argued to be less polarized and more productive avenues of interpretation. In one of the most notable examples, Castells shifted his analysis from class conflict to a more generic study of urban-based social movements (Castells 1983). By the early 1980s, many critical writers ceased referring to themselves or what they did as "Marxist," and the political economy approach became a catchall category for a variety of work that emphasized the idea that social arrangements were based fundamentally on conflict among various categories of social actors with different levels of access to power. Some who considered their work political economy operated within Marxist assumptions, while the work of others bore little relationship to Marxism. Readers have been left somewhat on their own, without the encumbrance of weighty labels, to take what they find most useful and leave what they cannot use from the literature that focuses on economic and political inequality. There was a recognition, among many analysts, that ideologically orthodox interpretations of events had to give way to sound analyses of urban problems. Tabb and Sawers (1984, v), in the second edition of their *Marxism and the Metropolis*, placed primary emphasis on "explaining the urban reality around us, rather than defending a particular school of thought. We, like many other progressive scholars in this country [the United States], have become much less concerned about whether we are really Marxist than whether we are really right." On the other side, some urban ecologists have asked how the critical issues raised by political economists might be incorporated in their work. Hawley (1984) commented that those working within the divergent approaches of ecology and political economy might learn from each other. He suggested that the two were actually complementary approaches, since each focuses in its efforts on economic, social, and spatial factors that the other tends to neglect.

The Rationalization of Space and the Emergence of Regional and Global Perspectives

When urban sociology first began to emerge as a distinctive concern in the work of the classical theorists of general sociology, the city was portrayed as an integral feature of the wider society. Weber observed that cities existed within economic fields that extended beyond their individual borders and control. Durkheim's *The Division of Labor in Society* was not devoted to the study of cities, but societies. Cities appeared only as points of concentrated settlement in which the division was most elaborated, points that tended to specialize among themselves and that became increasingly interdependent in societies characterized by an increasing degree of functional interdependence. Despite the emphasis on societal integration in these early works, there has been a strong tendency among the urban sociologists who followed to divide societies into urban and nonurban elements, studying the former with little regard for the latter. And although there has been considerable discussion about the need to conceptually reintegrate society, supported by a general recognition that the settled environment has undergone modifications that render old ways of thinking about cities obsolete, we have continued to employ the old labels and categories.

> *Pick any textbook in urban sociology, for example, and you will be told about the "city" as the form of urban settlement, about "urbanization" as involving the concentration of people within bounded areas, and about the "differences" between the "urban way of life" and its "suburban" or "rural" counterpart. Despite the obsolete nature of these concepts, they remain the central focus of urban textbooks even though most Americans have been living in polynucleated metropolitan areas outside the central city since the 1970s. (Gottdiener 1985, 5)*

The issue here involves more than the words that are chosen to describe different-sized settlements and different positions on the map. In the older ways of thinking about space, "urban" and "rural" represented different extremes, opposite conditions of social life. It was the effort to distinguish urban culture—to describe urbanism as a distinct way of life—that reinforced the popular habit of thinking about country and city life as opposites. In the current consideration of economic structures—of globalization of economies and of culture—we are drawn to emphasize the connectedness among all the places in the world, to see the way that all points large and small are part of the same world system. This economic and social integration of space is best expressed as *rationalization*, the unification of the economic value of different elements of population and other resources into a single strategic market system. The well-worn conventional terms *rural* and *urban* will doubtless survive alongside new and often awkward forms of expression. But they can no longer be understood to refer to opposite conditions, independent subject matters, and, least of all, independent arenas of action.

Sociology has just begun to develop a subdisciplinary perspective of appropriate scope that is able to transcend the old subdisciplinary boundaries and to address much broader categories of spatial analysis. In the past two decades, we have learned to consider, in quick succession, regional or national space and then global space in order to understand the changing fortunes of particular cities. Here we consider some of the issues in the emergence of the regional and the global perspectives, and how these broader perspectives relate to traditional urban studies. At the end of the chapter, we focus on the question of the continued relevance of urban sociology as a distinct and worthwhile division of social science.

Regional Studies

In the 1970s, demographers in the United States were taken by surprise by a significant change in population trends. During that decade, for the first time, the population of nonmetropolitan areas grew more rapidly (in proportionate terms) than metropolitan populations. This amounted to a reversal of the long-standing, steady pattern of increasing urbanization. At the same time, the continuation of a somewhat longer term trend also helped to draw the attention of analysts away from cities toward distant and smaller population points. Manufacturers continued to move their assembly and processing operations out of larger metropolitan areas to smaller towns with lower labor and other production costs. It appears for the present that the deconcentration of population during the 1970s was a temporary phenomenon. However, the decentralization of manufacturing continues. Both redistribution patterns remain significant because both can be read as indicators of the potential for continued decentralization in the coming century.

Nonmetropolitan Growth

For about a decade during the 1970s, a majority (79 percent) of the nonmetropolitan counties (those without a city of 50,000 or more people) gained population (Brown and Beale 1981). The importance of the increase was not in the numbers involved, but in the fact that the long-term trend of more rapid urban than nonurban growth had been reversed. Social scientists began to talk about a "population turnaround" and "reverse migration" patterns, and attempted to analyze the causes and long-term consequences of nonmetropolitan growth. However, the 1990 census confirmed that the direction of migration had switched back again during the 1980s, and the long-term pattern of population concentration in and around the cities had resumed (Figure 8-4).

Even though the period of reversed migration is over, at least for now, the questions raised about the dynamics and impact of nonmetropolitan population movements continue to interest urban sociologists. This interest has to do with the recognition of the connectedness of changes in the largest and smallest population centers. The issue of the widening impact of the metropolitan center on increasingly remote areas was shown to be an important feature of small-town life long before the spurt of growth in the 1970s (Vidich and Bensman [1958] 1968; Warren [1963] 1972).

A major share of the study of nonmetropolitan patterns has been undertaken by *rural* researchers and has been discussed most often in journals devoted to *rural* sociology. As migrant streams between nonmetropolitan and metropolitan areas have reversed and rereversed themselves, the process reinforces the logic that these areas are components of a single system consisting of relative costs and opportunities and should be studied as such by a single body of information-sharing scholars. This seems reasonable, since people who are deciding between metropolitan and nonmetropolitan living apparently employ this kind of comparative framework. The same is true of large, urban-based real estate speculators and developers and metro-based corporations considering relocation of their manufacturing or clerical divisions. Locational decision-makers large and small operate within an expanded field of action that incorporates central and remote locations.

Gottdiener (1985), who found political economy a more useful frame of analysis than urban ecology, emphasized the need to treat space as a continuous field of

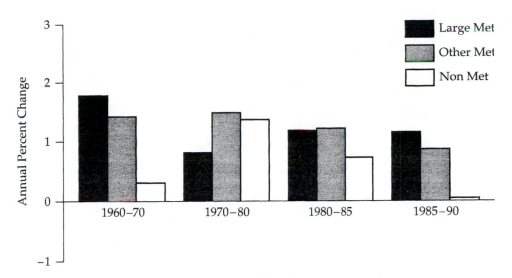

FIGURE 8-4   Patterns of Metropolitan and Nonmetropolitan
Population Growth

Source: William H. Frey. 1993, 3–58. "People in Places: Demographic Trends in Urban America." In
Rediscovering Urban America: Perspectives on the 1980s, edited by Jack Sommer and Donald A. Hicks.
Washington, D.C.: U.S. Department of Housing and Urban Development.

action, considering, for example, that developers and real estate speculators can
strike at will within a tract of wilderness as easily as they can within the heart of
the metropolis. Modern transportation and communication technologies, in the
service of the investment calculus, lend a seamlessness to physical space. Local
economic and political events, whether in the city or an outlying area, are shaped
by regional, national, and international conditions. For this reason, urban sociology and rural sociology confront a basic difficulty as independent exercises in
analysis. Their fields of vision and frames of reference are artificially cut off.

The idea that a regional frame of analysis is important for understanding local conditions is not altogether new. The recognition that communities, especially
smaller communities, have increasingly been subject to the influence of larger and
more remote political and economic forces is, in part, an offshoot of the community studies tradition in sociology. Many studies of smaller towns have emphasized the importance of external influences, but none more explicitly than Vidich
and Bensman's ([1958] 1968) *Small Town In Mass Society.*

Vidich and Bensman's work remains a valuable source of insight into how external economic and political influences systematically transform a small center
into a dependent and passive recipient of plans, prices, and cultural influences
that originated elsewhere. Their selection of "mass society" as the force of change
reflected one of the prevailing theoretical themes of the 1950s when their work
was carried out in New York State. It represented a variation on the same mainstream conflict perspective that characterized Wirth's "urbanism" model. The

depiction of the small town of "Springdale" showed the erosion of its economic base, even as the number of middle-class commuters who lived there was increasing to the point that they were becoming a potentially powerful political force in the limited range of issues left to the locality's decision.

Another older argument for regional analysis was rooted in functionalist or systems theory, Warren's *The Community in America* ([1963] 1972). He distinguished between "horizontal ties," the relationships among the various organizations within a community, and "vertical ties," the linkages between the various community-based organizations and their affiliates, branches, or headquarters located elsewhere. The horizontal ties collectively represented the degree of internal systemness or integration within a local community, and the vertical ties indicated the degree to which the community was linked to external systems. Warren argued that a "great change" had occurred in the organization of the community, whereby the degree of external linkage had increased dramatically. He recognized that communities were not what was linked, but their specialized organizational units. Also, the nature of these external linkages was different from local or intracommunity relationships among institutions. For instance, external linkages between chain store and regional headquarters, branch plant and national office, and school and state education department were enacted or deliberate and bureaucratically structured. Thus, they provided more direct and efficient channels of communication and command than did the informal, "crescive" ties between different organizations located in the same community. The implication, of course, was that communities of all sizes had been infiltrated by mechanisms of manipulation from outside and had lost whatever degree of autonomy they may have had. Although Warren's functionalist assumptions caused him to seek (and find) some indications that localities were moving to formally structured local relations and thus struggling to restore some balance or "equilibrium" between internal and external systems, the main point of his analysis was clearly the "great change" that regionalized spatial organization.

A striking feature of nonmetropolitan demographic and economic trends is their responsiveness to wider economic conditions. The period of unusual population growth in nonmetropolitan communities during the 1970s coincides with a decade when nonfarm occupations in small towns increased rapidly. Between 1962 and 1978, 56 percent of the increase in the 1.8 million manufacturing jobs created in the United States was found in nonmetropolitan areas (Bunce 1982, 169). But by the end of the decade, a nationwide recession brought a sharp reversal to remote counties accompanied by a loss of 600,000 jobs between 1979 and 1982. This marked the end of the period of more rapid population growth in those areas. During the remainder of the 1980s, nonmetropolitan employment grew at very modest rates, hampered by the higher value of the U.S. dollar measured against foreign currencies. This made labor in foreign countries, especially Third World countries, cheaper to employ, and it made the U.S. rural work force less of a bargain then it had been in the 1970s. It also made prices of goods produced in the United States more expensive and less competitive on the world market, and the nonmetropolitan sector of the economy is especially dependent on exports. During the 1980s, "stories abounded about manufacturers closing rural plants and contracting for overseas production" (Hady and Ross 1990, 2).

Part of the logic of the market system is that employers are drawn to rural areas by their depressed economies, low taxes and land costs, weak regulatory restrictions, and desperate-to-work and non-unionized labor forces. Wage labor in smaller remote communities earns the lowest average wages of any settlement type, and wages rise with each and every increment in settlement size (Beeson and Groshen 1991). Rural income levels also vary by region, and the rural workforce in the South has historically been among the poorest. It is not surprising, therefore, that many of the employment gains during the 1970s came in the South, where almost a million new manufacturing positions were created in nonmetropolitan locations. Many of those positions were in industries characterized by seasonal work and low profit margins (Haren and Holling 1979, 38).

The low wages, land costs, and tax structures characteristic of rural areas must be sufficiently attractive to industry to overcome the number of disincentives that rural locations offer. These disincentives include restricted opportunities for contact with other producers or auxiliary industries and services, insignificant local markets, loss of the advantages that would be offered by the clustering of competitors, the cost of training a relatively unskilled labor force, bad connections with long-distance traffic, the possibility that some members of the local community may be hostile to the proposed change, and the lack of cultural and educational facilities (Hansen 1970, 232). It is worth noting that most of these obstacles are sensitive to improvements in transportation and communication.

Developments in the World Wide Web, satellite communications, fiber optics, e-mail, and facsimile (fax) machines in principle allow for the more remote location of workforces employed in routine data processing and customer service operations. Testa (1992, 23–25) warned that the prospect for rural sitings of such jobs tended to be oversold, and that increased opportunities for employment stemming from new technologies are offset, in rural areas as elsewhere, by the labor-saving nature of technological innovation. Innovations not withstanding, certain aspects of marketing, communications, and finance operations are subject to the same needs for face-to-face meetings and contacts that make nonmetropolitan locations inconvenient for other industries. Any new positions that may be created in nonmetro areas will be "back office" or lower order jobs with lower pay. They may suffer the same transitory nature that characterizes other forms of rural employment.

State and local governments have been vigorous in their efforts to foster development in economically stagnant out-of-the-way places. States have instituted thousands of *enterprise zones* nationwide to help stimulate depressed local economies and to create more jobs. The programs are designed to lure businesses into these depressed areas through the granting of tax credits and subsidies (the enterprise zone concept is discussed more fully in Chapter 10). While most people automatically associate the enterprise zone strategy with urban areas, in 1990 almost half of all state enterprise zones were in nonmetro areas. Fragmentary evidence suggests that nonmetropolitan enterprise zones may be more effective than urban zones in creating or saving manufacturing jobs (Robinson and Reeder 1991, 30, 34).

The governments of virtually all of the small towns in the United States have for some time been locked in competition with one another to attract industry and employment opportunities. Local governments are preoccupied with overcoming the negative features that they fear would discourage industry from locating in their area. They willingly provide additional incentives to those offered by the low-wage and low-tax character of their town. "Smokestack chasing" has become a major activity for local governments, which may offer to acquire and prepare industrial sites, extend access roads, provide utility connections, perhaps underwrite some of the costs of construction, reduce tax rates or grant outright tax holidays, and absorb whatever additional costs must be borne for the provision of police, fire protection, sewer construction, and roadway maintenance. In addition to any state or federal assistance, these costs must be borne in part through the sale of bonds or through local taxes (Summers et al. 1976, 73, 93).

In these ways, small-town municipal governments become partners in the risks of private enterprise by gambling that their investments will pay off in net gains for the community. It is difficult to calculate costs and benefits in such cases, since even the strictly economic costs often defy measurement, and costs and benefits tend to be absorbed by different segments of the population. The obvious costs are the initial ones, indicated above, that governments (and through them, taxpayers) agree to undertake in order to enhance the attractiveness of their location for incoming industry. Other costs are more difficult to anticipate. In many areas, such as southern California, nonmetropolitan growth poses a particular threat to the environment (Goodenough 1992). Expanding industrial activity and any attendant population growth will soon uncover any existing shortcomings in local environmental and land use planning codes. Once the relationship between the municipality and the industry is established, it is difficult to bring pressures to bear that will correct the situation.

> *Small communities . . . are ill equipped to finance pollution abatement facilities. Industries that locate in nonmetro cities or towns typically transform these into one-company towns along with the local powerlessness that this implies; citizens or community officials are unlikely to take local environmental actions that would cause their principal employer to seek another location. (Buttel 1981, 682–683)*

Industries vary in the degree of geographic mobility they enjoy. For some, it is easy to move on quickly with little cost to a new area, while others undertake a greater level of investment in a locality. Generally the less footloose make the better and more responsible corporate citizen, which can be expected to support local environmental regulations so far as doing so is consistent with the relative productive advantage of their location (Gappert 1995).

Some of the long-term costs of population and industrial growth that are incurred by local communities are difficult to see and may not immediately manifest themselves. An increase in the average household income leads to an increase in the cost of living as prices of housing and services are adjusted to meet demand. Low- and fixed-income people share the costs of development, although not all share in its benefits. Some members of the local community will therefore find themselves in a worse relative position as a result of local population and economic growth (Summers and Lang [1976] 1978, 412–413). At the end of the decade of rapid growth, studies by the department of Housing and Urban Development (HUD) came to the same conclusion. In some communities increased economic activity or people moving in from areas with higher wages and costs of living drove up housing costs, making it difficult for long-time residents to find affordable housing. Even the improvement in the local employment picture that is expected to result from relocating industry does not always materialize. Sometimes the new jobs do not go to local people, who may lack the skills required, and workers with those skills may be willing to commute from distant locations. Some workers at the new facility are likely to be continuing employees who transfer residence along with a relocating or branching industry. However, some evidence suggests that a high proportion of the jobs created with enterprise zone support do go to local residents (Robinson and Reeder 1991, 34).

New employment possibilities may cause members of the local population who were formerly not actively seeking work to join the workforce. In rural areas, light manufacturing industries featuring low-skill positions and low wages tend to increase the participation of women in the workforce. Nonwhites are underrepresented in nonmetropolitan industry (Summers and Lang [1976] 1978, Summers et al. 1976). Expanding opportunities (Freudenburg 1982) may not produce the hoped for effect of preventing young people from migrating from their home community (Freudenberg 1982; Seyfrit 1986). In fact, the influx of population can produce an increase in local unemployment.

Of course, the critical emphasis in this evaluation of the impact of growth in outlying areas is simply to indicate that this kind of change carries certain costs, and that the assumed benefits are open to question. There is also evidence that the majority of the people living in or migrating to these areas approve of and benefit from the kinds of changes that are taking place. Baldassare (1981a, 1981b) rejected in the strongest terms what he referred to as "the dominant theme" in evaluating the impact of growth on smaller settlements. He saw no evidence that population growth has a disorganizing effect on local communities. Research dating from the period of rapid population growth remained largely pro-growth. Long-term residents do not resent the increase in population in "their" towns (Fliegel 1980, 110; Voss and Fuguitt 1979, 210–212). Residents of faster growing nonmetropolitan communities have expressed a higher level of satisfaction with public services and with the availability of leisure activities (Baldassare 1981b, 133–134). Some research has revealed that both migrants and native residents, by large margins, favor attracting more industry, attracting tourism, developing their business districts, and attracting new residents (Fliegel 1980, 116). The West Coast may be an exception here. Between 1986 and 1987 over 50 referenda to control local growth were placed on ballots in California towns, and over 70 percent of those were passed (Goodenough 1992, 130). Finally, evidence suggests that while only a minority of jobs in new industry go to local residents who were living in poverty, the local poor who are successful in competing for these jobs are obviously better off than they were previously (Till 1981, 216–220).

It is not surprising that the majority of those living in small towns, given the century-long pattern of steady out-migration, would tend to view positively the prospects of a reversal of the long-term decline of the local population, services, and opportunity for employment. The promise is that more neighbors, friends, and offspring will have a better chance to stay close to home, and that residents will be able to share increased prosperity and improved services. Enough serious questions have been raised, however, to cast some doubt on the issue of the aggregate benefits of nonmetropolitan growth, despite positive attitude survey findings. Some of the kinds of costs, like municipal investments that do not pay off in the long term or harmful environmental consequences, which often take decades to reveal themselves, cannot be measured by social surveys. If low-income people are hurt by increases in the cost of living that accompany growth, this will not show up in interviews with factory workers or questionnaires distributed to local populations. Most members of the local, low-income population will not be employed in the new factory jobs, and poorer people tend not to respond to surveys in those instances where sampling techniques are adequately designed to locate them.

Beyond these concerns, there is the fact that nonmetropolitan economic growth is most often instigated by extralocal conditions and orchestrated by nonlocal actors. Dependence on any one industry in small towns creates a particular vulnerability. Given the dynamics of the international marketplace and labor supply, it is likely that the conditions that make a particular location a rational choice at one point in time will change. Once established, the decision to remain in a nonmetropolitan location must be remade repeatedly by decision makers remote from the local concerns of the dependent population. This vulnerability must be considered in any calculation of the costs of industry-related nonmetropolitan growth.

The broadening of the perspective of urban sociology—from metropolitan to regional and national levels of analysis—has been a necessary step, but only a step, in approaching an understanding of how local conditions are shaped by forces operating on a larger scale. Regional and national conditioning factors are themselves ultimately conditioned by shifts in the global political and economic arena. There have been few periods in human history when the connection between global shifts and local conditions have been more dramatic, and the impact has never been more immediate.

The world has become a single market system, a seamless web of producers, financial resources, labor, and consumer demand, unified by communication and transport technology, and divided only according to enormous disparities in the wealth and living conditions of the people who inhabit its various regions. Even economic inequality contributes to the world's objective integration. The market's addiction to seeking out the poorest populations as laborers, populations whose low wages lower the costs of production and the cost of the product, thereby subsidizes the living standards of everyone else in the world who uses what they produce—in agriculture, manufacturing, and services.

International commerce, international finance, international law, and the identification and coordination of global resources and markets are the utilitarian art forms that characterize the present age. The global economy represents a new kind of arena, an arena of action that is spatial only in the most comprehensive sense, that defies any consideration of space smaller than the globe itself. This is the space in which business is done, in which fortunes are made, and play in this global arena is not restricted to huge multinational companies. Consider the case of the 28-employee computer design company "in" California. The financing for the company was raised internationally; its components were engineered and produced in Japan and were assembled and distributed to the world marketplace from Taiwan and Singapore. The spirit of the international marketplace is summed up by one of the new global managers: "We plan to manufacture in any country in the world where there is an advantage—to make things in Thailand where the cost is low, or Germany because the market is big, to do R&D in Boston" (Reich 1995, 164–165).

Governments in every region have recognized the need to accommodate to the importance of international trade, the value of which has increased 70 times since 1950. Regional trade agreements are a direct response to this inspiring reality. With the ratification of the Treaty on the European Union, Europe has taken a major step in the direction of becoming a single economy, with a single currency and 350 million consumers. In North America, Canada, Mexico, and the United States have responded to the realities of the international economy with the North American Free Trade Agreement (NAFTA), which lowers trade barriers among these nations with a combined population of 375 million. Beyond NAFTA, there is at least the prospect of a hemispheric agreement among nearly all of the Americas, including most Latin American and Caribbean nations, thus creating a common market that would stretch from the Arctic Circle to Cape Horn. Across the Pacific, six Asian nations with 325 million people have created a special trading unit (the Association of Southeast Asian Nations, or ASEAN) with agreements to lower trade barriers (Fry 1995, 22–23). In Africa, similar joint undertakings are being planned.

It is not only national leaderships that recognize the need to plan for a future of much closer global coordination. Most U.S. states and Canadian provinces have permanent offices in foreign countries, the sole purpose of which is to attract trade. Most U.S. governors and Canadian provincial officials lead delegations on annual overseas pilgrimages designed to promote their products and entice investment. Periodic missions to other countries by U.S. mayors are sponsored by the National League of Cities and the U.S. Conference of Mayors. These efforts of local government officials reflect the fact that the United States is the leading host nation in the world for foreign investment, that five million U.S. citizens work for foreign-owned companies, and therefore "the lives of local constituents are being increasingly affected by actions that occur and decisions that are rendered outside the boundaries of their own nation state" (Fry 1995, 25).

So the "smokestack chasing" spectacle of small towns competing for new industries, prisons, landfills, or anything else that would create employment in nonmetropolitan regions in the United States is now repeated on a global scale by municipalities of every size. In the new era, the efforts of city officials are directed not only at interurban competition, but also at coordination among leaders from different cities to make their entire region more attractive. One of the most striking features in this regard is the coordination of efforts between city governments in different countries. North America provides some examples, but there are also many instances of cross-border municipal coordination in Europe as well. The North American setting seems to indicate that cross-border development works best between nations and cities that are roughly economic equals. "Cascadia" is the Pacific coastal area that extends from Alaska southward through British Columbia to Oregon; it is a region united by vital common development interests that overshadow its straddling an international border. The region's economic and urban focus is the Vancouver-Seattle-Portland corridor. The businesses in the port cities on either side of the Canada/U.S. border have traditionally been and remain competitors, but there is a growing appreciation among all parties, especially planners and government officials, that the entire area comprises a single transportation and trade corridor on the northern reaches of the export-import-oriented international Pacific Rim economy. Urban officials have come to recognize the mutual advantages, in terms of growth potential, of increasing the attractiveness of the entire region. The development of the Vancouver-Seattle-Portland corridor is being monitored and managed jointly by local and regional cooperative government initiatives devoted to *sustainable urbanization*, which means that attention is paid to ways that the region's tendency for economic and population growth can be managed to maintain the attractive natural resources that contribute to the enviable quality of life enjoyed by many residents (Artibise 1995).

The activities and perspective, especially, of the Vancouver and Seattle governments exemplify what has come to be called "intermestic" government. The term combines the traditionally separate spheres of policy making that are undertaken by national governments: "international" and "domestic" policy. However, here the concerns are combined with reference to strategies now undertaken by city governments themselves, to promote domestic or local economic well-being by taking an active and promotional role in international affairs. Now cities address policy issues that were formerly the exclusive domain of national governments, as urban officials forge relationships and agreements with international partners, and vigorously lobby national policy-making bodies to develop foreign policy legislation and agreements consistent with regional interests. The internationalist orientation of municipal governments is evidenced in specialized trade negotiations, official international ties among foreign cities that have grown out of local peace movements, and the establishment and the development of many "sister city" linkages—where two cities in different countries proclaim a special relationship with each other. Some of these relationships have developed into locally sponsored foreign aid programs for poorer sisters (Cohn and Smith 1995).

However, it has also been noted that where cross-border regions do not begin from a position of mutual strength—where there is more pronounced cross-border economic inequality—the globalization process can accentuate disadvantageous symptoms of underdevelopment in the poorer region. In Mexico, free trade agreements with the United States have fostered geographically imbalanced growth patterns generally criticized by political economists as being ultimately inconsistent with economic development (Chapter 6). Mexico's northern border with the United States has experienced spectacular industrial and population growth in the past two decades due to the influx of assembly plants from the United States and elsewhere in the world. These manufacturing plants along the border, the *maquiladoras,* are located "centrally" with regard to the global economy, adjacent to the enormously important U.S. markets. But in Mexico City, centrally located within Mexico itself, yet hundreds of miles from the U.S. border, the number of jobs has declined with the northward shift in industrialization. Meanwhile, in the southern extremes of Mexico, frustration and guerrilla warfare have developed, in part a reflection of the lack of economic activity there and the local perception of being left out of national economic growth initiatives (Heirnaux 1995, 119–122). In this light, Mexico presents an example of the classical problem of imbalanced, market-led economic growth, which, in countries with large numbers of poorer people, can be a politically destabilizing liability.

In sum, globalization describes a future that is not as clear as many would hope and raises questions about what role various regions, governments, and individuals will play, how they will participate, who will benefit, and whose fortunes will decline. Despite the energy with which public bodies and private interests prepare for that future, the efforts are generated as much by a sense of uncertainty about the economic future as they are by an enthusiastic conviction that all will be well. Above all, there is a sense of inevitability, that the proximate future will be ruled by the logic of a single marketplace that is in no one's power to control.

Urban Sociology and Structural Determinism

A portion of this chapter has been concerned with delineating the differences that set apart the functionalist roots of urban ecology and the Marxist roots of critical urban theory. There is, however, one fundamental similarity between functionalist ecology and urban Marxism. Contemporary critics point out that both suffer from a simplified structural determinism. What this means is that each theory claims that structural requirements move social change unfailingly in a particular direction and that a particular outcome is inevitable. Ecologists sought the logic of spatial organization in natural forces that were produced by the urban environment itself—the competition engendered by the value of centrally located real estate—resulting in an overall efficiency and harmony of land-use patterns. Marxists found the answer to the question of expanding metropolitan environments in class conflict and the need to disperse industrial populations. Even in Marx's hope for the development of a revolutionary class consciousness and the overthrow of capitalism, consciousness and revolution were the inevitable results of nineteenth century urban working conditions and the relationship between wages and profit.

Revolutionary ideas were the inevitable intermediate consequences rather than causes in themselves. In a structurally determinist scheme, human action is dictated by the social conditions that surround the action. Similarly, critics of functionalism have pointed out that the functionalists don't need to talk about human action at all. The social system acts. We simply assume that humans are in there somewhere, staffing the required statuses and providing the energy that allows society to move steadily and eternally in the direction of equilibrium—the balance among institutional forms, accompanied by improvements in living conditions and consensus among all citizens. Both the classical Marxist and functionalist schemes are deterministic because they point to a limited set of factors that produce an inevitable result.

Determinism is generally regarded in the sciences as weak theory because it reduces complex reality. It oversimplifies. If society really operated so simply, the predictive abilities of the social sciences would be far greater. As it is, we are often surprised by outcomes—by human actions—and this would seem to be at least as true in urban sociology as in other branches of science concerned with human behavior. How is it that several cities faced with the same set of conditions—the same set of social requirements (for the functionalist) or the same declining fortunes with respect to international capitalism (for the Marxists)—will show widely varying consequences in terms of growth or decline? Why do some old inner-city neighborhoods continue to decline while others remain stable and still others reverse their formerly declining fortunes with improving conditions and new people moving in?

Two possibilities might explain why local changes are not more predictable. The first is that they occur by chance, randomly. This would indicate that society is a disordered environment, which makes predictive social science impossible. The second possibility is that patterns of change vary among local areas because people are not really so helpless and passive as determinist theories make them appear. That is, localities and cities change along different lines because local populations are effective agents in responding to social forces—to threats and to opportunities. They are able to change the changes that confront them.

Is Globalization Another Determinist Theory?

"Globalization" is fundamentally a label applied in a descriptive manner to the internationalization of the market economy and its various social and cultural consequences. As a description, it is theoretically and ideologically neutral and can be incorporated equally in service to a Marxist, functionalist, or any other macrological (large-scale) theoretical perspective. In a critical political economy, globalization can be understood to describe the final stages of capitalism, the period when every inch and every inhabitant of the globe, to the extent that they are useful elements that can be exploited for profit, have become incorporated into the world marketplace. Castells (1985b) is among those who observe that the new international capitalism has placed a relative handful of large transnational corporations above the control of national governments; it has given them a new power to be exercised in pursuit of profit. Within classical Marxism, there has always been the question of whether capitalism could survive its ultimate success. Is it a system that can survive a state of no growth, no further expansion? Will it collapse? Globalization as an idea, as a purely descriptive interpretation, is silent on such questions; it is neutral ideologically.

Most of the world, especially its journalists, policymakers, and leading entrepreneurs, are poor Marxists—better functionalists, although they are not likely to think explicitly in terms of the theoretical frameworks that order their habits of thought. The idea of globalization has been captured by those who see in the future a more perfect world with a single economy based on market principles. Therefore, in practice, globalization represents an apparently worldwide capitulation to the notion that there is no alternative to the rational organization of international resources by market factors, that it is folly to resist the influences of the crystallizing international marketplace, that this represents the logical and inevitable future that is ultimately beneficial to all consumers, and all workers. A single world marketplace, it is believed, ultimately lowers prices, creates work, raises wages, and increases standards of living everywhere. In an editorial commenting on the allegedly misguided rioting of strikers in South Korea, France, and Argentina—where events and government decisions had heightened concerns over job security—*The Economist* (January 18, 1997, 16) counseled that governments must work harder to get their citizens to understand "that open economies and flexible labor markets are net creators of wealth and jobs." With reference to the deindustrialization pattern that has afflicted the labor market in the United States and other countries, the essay points out that workers need to be educated to appreciate that many good new jobs have been created, that it is a mistake to dwell on the image of the deadbeat "McJob" replacements for lost industrial work. The editorial appeals to the workers of the world and all interested others for "Perspective, please—and consent." Consent, and trust, that the economic reorganization now sweeping the globe is about to deliver, finally, that which has always been the inevitable outcome of market democracy, the best of all probable worlds, the greatest good for the largest number at any given moment, a dynamic system in which economic displacement is short term and adjustment always yields long-term improvement.

The argument should sound familiar. It is the functionalist argument recast on a global scale. It also represents the modernization perspective, discussed in Chapter 6 in application to underdeveloped economies, as it is here applied to the global system. Two important conceptual points need to be recognized: First, to the extent that we accept this popular interpretation of globalization, we are coming very close to embracing the most conservative traditions of social and economic thought with regard to the beneficence of capitalism as a force for human good. Second, there *is* a strong element of *determinism* imbedded in the idea that a single, remote force is shaping all societies, pointing toward an inevitable set of progressive and universally positive outcomes, converging toward similar futures for all cultures. Note that globalization does not have to be interpreted this way, but arguments to the contrary do not represent the prevailing doctrine today.

We must continue to insist that the term be used in a descriptive and ideologically neutral manner. The global perspective on change, to the extent that it remains a descriptive proposition, permits us to circumvent the ideological debates and avoid the trap of determinism. It admits to the possibility of the effectiveness of local efforts directed at self-determination, without predicting whether particular local efforts will or will not be effective. As such, it is in step with new developments in urban sociology in recent years. The new perspective draws our attention back to cities and to the efforts of local leadership to balance the effects of global forces with human action—to local efforts to direct change.

Human Agency and Urban Change

Just as it is undeniable that the global economy is a powerful force affecting local conditions, it is also true that conditions vary considerably between localities. This is a troublesome feature of reality with regard to sweeping theories of change: General theory is not capable of explaining or predicting variations among similar communities precisely because general theory describes typical or average outcomes. Then it must be that in localities, where the same external forces have resulted in different consequences (some places more favorable, some less favorable), that local actors have employed different strategies to manage these changes. That is, it must be that local people are capable of altering the impact of external forces.

As we have seen, sociology and other social sciences have been faulted for developing theories that dictate human action, and some thinkers have been involved for the past two decades in "deconstructing" social theory in a way that acknowledges people's greater freedom to choose and to act. Many find this a more attractive and humanizing way to portray the conditions of our existence.

Especially influential has been the work of Anthony Giddens (1981, 1984, 1985). He argued that it was a mistake from the beginning for social science to attempt to adapt the model of the natural sciences—sciences that deal with processes and materials that produce unvarying results under similar circumstances over a number of experimental trials. The subjects of the social sciences are human beings, and one key difference is that they are aware of the forces of change that confront them and their communities. They are also aware that they have choices about how to react to the remote and powerful forces that we have been discussing, and they mobilize resources, including the ideas provided by the relevant social sciences, in order to redirect change in a way that suits them. What this means for urban sociology is this: If we want to understand how particular urban regions, cities, and neighborhoods change, then we have to depend less on theory and more on local histories, resources, and the imagination of local leadership. The deliberate effort of human beings, thinking and acting, alone or together, is called *agency*.

Giddens's approach, called *structuration theory*, helped to shift the research agenda in sociology during the 1980s and 1990s. There has been a general call to place more emphasis on discovering the sources of local differences and to mistrust theories that are unable to account for these variations in local outcomes.

This newer emphasis on agency and local history repeats a pattern that has occurred before in urban sociology, as the field has vacillated between an emphasis on theory and empirical research (Flanagan 1994). From time to time, there has appeared a consensus that abstract theories are leading in the wrong direction (the community studies correction to the errors of the urbanism thesis reviewed in Chapter 3) or that unstructured empirical research is producing fragmented and theoretically uninteresting facts (for example, the factorial ecology approach in this chapter). Throughout the last two decades, growing attention has been devoted to local factors, especially the power of local political and business elites to influence change.

The work of Logan and Molotch (Molotch 1976; Logan and Molotch 1987) is especially influential in the growing body of material describing "growth elites." Logan and Molotch argued that every city contains a number of influential actors who are eager to promote their own interests. While elites themselves may be divided into different factions—for example, those interested in promoting heavy manufacturing may hurt the prospects of others who promote tourism or residential real estate development—elites share in common a pro-growth mentality and constitute a local "growth machine." Whether depicted as working together or locked in competition over the direction of growth, the outcome is predicted to be the same: This group is an effective lobby that will insure that local resources will be expended on projects that enhance the relative attractiveness of the city or metro region (Logan, Whaley, and Crowder 1997).

The question is, How effective are local efforts in the face of the kinds of global economic restructuring we have described? There remains today a tentative belief in the potential effectiveness of local action in the competition for the attention of international investors. The formula generally involves an all-out cooperative effort on the part of government and private enterprise. In addition to attempting to retain or attract manufacturing, generally considered the jewel of development strategies because of the employment benefits historically associated with it, local developers recognize that urban economic strategies need to be diversified to make the most of research facilities; service trades; and commodification of cultural, leisure, and informational activities as well as to capitalize on any touristic attractions an area may have or be able to develop (Proulx 1995, 172). With specific regard to technological research, development, and manufacturing firms, it is wise to try to develop a certain number of complementary enterprises and support systems, and to develop among them a sense of the need for the coordination of efforts in order to create the kind of flexible responses to product and service provision demanded by client vendors and consumer markets. What this means is that modernizing industrial districts, such as Baden-Wurttenberg in Germany and Silicon Valley in California, foster the appropriate regional technological culture as well as a local political force that is in step with the shifting demands of today's markets and is likely to be readily served by benevolent local political leaderships desperate to sustain or improve the local economy (Indergaard 1997). The effectiveness of local political support is enhanced by government units with broad geographical jurisdictions: This prevents any lingering inclinations toward local municipal competition that might stifle regional development, enhances the capacity of a single government body to coordinate the economic assets of a larger region, and is a more effective representation in the international arena. Canadian governing bodies tend to fit this qualification more than those in U.S. metro areas (Kresl 1995), but as we have seen in the example of Cascadia, cities in separate jurisdictions can cooperate even when located in different countries.

Those who urge local action and formulate strategies are mindful that local efforts to control the future are limited and may be canceled out by such external constraints as the withdrawal of federal programs or the "perverse leverage of corporations in a threatened industrial order" (Indergaard 1997, 678). Even John Logan (Logan, Whaley, and Crowder 1997), who worked with Molotch on expanding the local-elite "growth machine" thesis, is forced, on the basis of a survey of empirical research efforts stimulated by that thesis, to conclude that "after two decades of research, we are still unsure whether growth machines make a difference to urban development" (624). There is very limited indication that cities that competed vigorously for economic growth were more successful in attracting investors and new firms, but the study was not able to show a significant improvement in employment. They qualify even that evidence by pointing out that the direction of causality between promotion and growth is in question: Faster growing local economies may attract growth promoters. This is similar to the pattern related by Kresl (1995, 64; Heenan, 1977) regarding the competitive edge of Coral Gables (Florida) over the larger Miami area in luring Latin American investments in the 1970s. A number of Miami's senior development advisors fled the city government for what they thought was the more progressive development atmosphere of Coral Gables, in a pattern where growth begot promotion. Logan's (Logan et al. 1997) second qualification regarding the effectiveness of growth elites is that promotion may only work in larger areas, since no evidence indicates smaller places that work hard to promote growth are more successful in attracting it than their less active counterparts. Logan and others propose that cities probably should be divided into two tiers with reference to this issue: The objective situation facing some places that lack advantages to offer investors is that they are not likely to be winners in the zero sum game of attracting growth. So, one category is reserved for attractive places with momentum on their side, and "at the other extreme, [are] cities unlikely to succeed, for which policy choices are largely symbolic or—when they divert public funds—pork-barrel allocations to favored insiders" (623).

There is one very important consequence of the pro-growth mentality that local elites stir up—a feature until recently neglected by elite theory, also unthought of in the current political atmosphere that single-mindedly subscribes to the equilibreal model, which portrays economic growth as serving the interests of all concerned. This is the social cost of placing foremost on the political agenda expenditures directed at attracting investors. Infrastructural investments designed to make a local area look ripe for development that is likely never to occur means that funds that might have been expended elsewhere are no longer available. To the extent that the growth machine dominates the political agenda, public school and crime protection budgets may be left wanting. Logan, Whaley, and Crowder (1997, 626) concluded that new research needs to be directed at

> *a distinctive set of outcomes other than those directly related to growth. These include the intensification of inequalities within cities, and the preemption of political space by privileged minorities. In cities dominated by progrowth regimes, do deeper gaps develop between rich and poor neighborhoods? Is there more intense racial segregation? Are there greater disparities in police and fire protection between residential and commercial districts? Is there less local support for social welfare expenditures relative to infrastructure development?*

These are the issues to which we turn our attention in the next chapter, as we discuss poverty, power, and crime. As we once again narrow our focus to the problems that occur *in* cities, it is worthwhile to keep in mind that these patterns have their roots in political and economic issues that are located in the global sphere of shifting and uncertain fortunes. Remember the global dimension of our narrower focus, our "urban" sociology.

9

POVERTY, POWER, AND CRIME

Cities offer dramatic contrasts in wealth and poverty. This has been a feature of urban settlement since the time of the first cities, and is accentuated today in both rich and poor countries in the size, concentration, and physical separation of impoverished segments from the rest of the urban population. It is often the case that we do not find the poorest of a country's population in its largest cities (because they live in neglected rural areas), but the segregation and concentration of large numbers of the poor, by economic and political means, make poverty more highly visible in urban areas. This chapter focuses on the conditions of life of the most systematically disadvantaged segments of the urban population in the United States.

The Features of Urban Poverty in the United States

The latter half of the 1990s saw a significant decrease in poverty levels in the United States. Between 1995 and 1999, the total number of poor people in the United States dropped from over 36 million to just over 32 million, from nearly 14 percent of the population to 11.8 percent. Still, given the numbers of people who remain in poverty, poverty remains a serious problem in this wealthy nation; it casts a shadow over the future of millions of children whose chances for full participation in the economy may be blocked no matter what level of prosperity is granted to others. Table 9-1 presents an overview of poverty in the United States in 1999. In that year, the more than 32 million poor fell below a designated "poverty line," set at an income of $16,895 for a family of four in 1999 (and adjusted for family size). Many critics regard the poverty criteria to be quite conservative and believe the measure should be set 25 percent higher. If this had been done in 1999, the poverty threshold would have been set at $21,119, and more than 44 million people in the United States would have been below the poverty line—nearly 16 percent of the population.

While most of those counted as poor are white, African Americans and Latinos are disproportionately represented among the poor. In all groups, children and young people bear a disproportionate share of the burden. This is especially true for black and Latino children: 33 percent of African Americans under the age of

TABLE 9-1   Number and Proportion of the Population below the Poverty Level—
by Race, Hispanic Origin, Age[c], and Region, 1999

| | Number (000s) below Poverty Level | | | | Percent below Poverty Level | | | |
	All Races[a]	White	Black	Hispanic[b] Origin	All Races	White	Black	Hispanic[b] Origin
All ages	32,258	21,922	8,360	7,439	11.8	9.82	23.6	22.8
Under 18	12,109	7,568	3,579	3,506	16.9	13.5	33.1	30.3
18–24 years	4,603	3,125	1,165	941	17.3	14.8	29.3	23.8
65 or older	3,167	2,409	626	358	9.7	8.3	22.7	20.4
Northeast	5,678	3,764	1,590	1,204	10.9	8.7	24.3	26.2
Midwest	6,210	4,112	1,793	423	9.8	7.5	26.4	16.3
South	12,538	7,679	4,468	2,454	13.1	10.4	23.2	22.3
West	7,833	6,398	508	3,389	12.6	12.2	18.3	23.2

Source: Dalaker and Proctor, 2000. Tables A and 5, pp. vi, 28–30.
[a]Includes other racial categories not shown separately.
[b]"Hispanic Origin" is the term chosen by the Bureau of the Census for Latinos. Hispanics may be of any race.
[c]Selected ages shown; does not add up to total.

18 lived in poverty in 1999, as did 30 percent of the under 18 Latino population. The 65 and older generation no longer represents an especially disadvantaged category, as it did until recent decades. Poverty is distributed generously throughout the four regional divisions of the United States and is everywhere higher for members of minorities.

Table 9-2 shows the distribution of the poor among metropolitan, central city, and nonmetropolitan locations, and the numbers and proportion of these divisions of the population that fell below the poverty line in 1999. Given the greater proportion of the U.S. population living in cities, it is not surprising that both metropolitan areas as a whole and the central cities within them (a subset of the metropolitan population) contain more poor people than nonmetropolitan areas. Note, however, that when we contrast metropolitan and nonmetropolitan populations we find that a somewhat greater proportion of people living in nonmetropolitan areas is poor. This contrast held for all three racial and ethnic categories through the early 1990s. However, the highest concentration of poverty overall is found within central cities: 16.4 percent of central city populations are poor, in contrast to a 11.2 percent poverty level for metropolitan populations in general, and 14.3 percent of the nonmetropolitan population.

Poverty within central cities is concentrated in so-called "poverty areas." These are census tracts where at least 20 percent of the population is poor according to official measures. More than half of the central city poor lived in these tracts where the poverty rate reached 38.4 percent of poverty area populations in 1990. Within metropolitan areas, minorities, and therefore minority poverty, tend to be more highly concentrated in designated poverty areas within the inner city. While

TABLE 9-2   Poor in Metropolitan Areas, Central Cities,
             and Nonmetropolitan Locations, 1999

	Total Number of Residents	Number below Official Poverty Line	Percent below Poverty Line for this Category
USA	271,059,000	32,258,000	11.8
Metropolitan Areas	221,348,000	24,816,000	11.2
Central Cities	80,761,000	13,123,000	16.4
Outside Metropolitan Areas	52,145,000	7,442,000	14.3

Source: Dalaker and Proctor, 2000. Table 2, pp. 7–10.

14 percent of all whites lived in central city poverty areas in 1990, 40 percent of American blacks lived in these census tracts (Devine and Wright 1993, 89–90). It may be said, therefore, that the problem of concentrated urban poverty is especially serious for minority populations whose numbers are concentrated in the central cities of the largest metropolitan areas. This is one of the features of poverty in the United States to which we pay special attention in the discussion that follows.

Poverty is a problem of vast proportions in the United States, affecting more than 32 million people. It is not a wholly urban phenomenon. Yet, it is useful to analyze urban poverty alone because, as it occurs in U.S. cities, poverty is closely related to the nature of contemporary urban experience and the structure of opportunity in cities. In order to be understood fully, poverty must be considered in connection with the economic and political system that distributes opportunities and rewards, as well as in connection with race and ethnic group membership, age, and gender.

Explaining Poverty

The recognition of poverty as a serious social problem has come slowly and reluctantly in the modern era, despite its widespread nature. Certainly there was a general awareness that serious deprivation existed during the Great Depression of the 1930s. The nation found it more difficult to think seriously about poverty in the 1950s, a period of general growth and improving conditions for the working and middle classes. The prosperous mood of the decade of the white collar and the expanding suburb admitted to few problems outside of "the bomb" and the cold war. Michael Harrington's book, *The Other America*, injected a stiff jolt of reality at the end of the decade, however. Harrington's message was that the poor existed in the millions and that their existence became only too apparent if one took the trouble to look for them. The poor were not gone, but simply hidden away, out of sight from the rest of the population.

The question for the scholars and the policymakers was, Why did poverty persist in the affluent society? The chorus of responses that emerged has created a debate where, because there is so much at stake, there is little prospect of an amicable resolution. The point of contention that lies at the heart of the issue is, To what extent are the poor responsible for their poverty and to what extent are they locked into their condition by forces beyond their control? Once again, the division in responses is familiar: The debate is between a cultural and a structural interpretation of poverty. A strict culturalist asks, "What is wrong with the poor?" A structuralist asks, "What is wrong with the distribution of opportunities and rewards in society?"

The questions themselves determine the kinds of answers that will be found to address the problems associated with poverty. If the opportunity structure—the social mechanisms for getting an education and a good job—is assumed to work fairly and well, but the attitudes and behavior of the poor are obstacles to a better life, then minimal programs can be directed at helping poor people redeem themselves, mostly for the benefit of their innocent and neglected children and for the purpose of keeping all family members out of jail where they will only create additional tax burdens for the rest of us. Alternatively, an approach to poverty that emphasizes the way economic changes eliminate the need for blue-collar workers, the lingering consequences of racism for poor minorities, or the way wealth is highly concentrated is essentially a critique of the fundamental nature of the existing social and economic order. As such, it can be taken as a call for sweeping increases in the role of the state for the care of the dislocated and the poor. Such social theories, which question the legitimacy of the basic features of society, are difficult to incorporate into social policy. Certainly, proposals to study the ways that cultural and structural factors interact to produce the problems associated with poverty are a good idea. In practice, however, such approaches end up focusing on how to change the habits of the poor rather than on the built-in disadvantages imposed by structure and global change and, therefore, do not represent a comprehensive alternative.

The "Culture of Poverty" and Its Critics

Oscar Lewis, to whom the formal development of the "culture of poverty" thesis is attributed, was not a strict culturalist. He began with the assumption that poverty tended to be a feature of a highly stratified, competitive economic system that included high rates of unemployment and underemployment for unskilled labor, low wages, and a failure to provide for social, political, and economic integration. He noted also that it was the poorest members of society who suffered the greatest dislocation and hardship during periods of change (Lewis 1966a, 21; Lewis 1966b, xliii–xlv). These are features of the contemporary urban arena that are emphasized by those who cite *structural* elements in explaining the persistence of poverty in the midst of affluence. However, Lewis parted company with the structuralists at this point. He held that the cultural adaptations of the poor to economic disappointment and defeat, which were a response initially to the broader features of the economy, became a system of values and attitudes that poor people passed on to their children—a *culture of poverty*. In this way, even if opportunities improved around them, the poor would not be able to take advantage of them because poverty had become a way of life. It would be a way of life for their children as well, because by the time children were six or seven years old, they would have internalized the values and philosophies of the permanently poor. Thus, poverty was a vicious behavioral cycle, based on subcultural adaptations and passed on from parents to children; that is, each generation was trained (socialized) to be poor by the previous one.

The empirical basis of Lewis's work was provided largely by the urban slums of Mexico and Puerto Rico. His conceptual argument, however, has been traced to the Chicago tradition in urban sociology and the work of Robert Park. It is based on Park's argument that natural areas generate their own moral order, like that of the slum: Once emerged, the social orders characteristic of these areas become self-generating and self-perpetuating. From such an assumption, it is a logical step to the culture of poverty argument (Waxman 1983, 48–49). Lewis identified some 70 interrelated psychological and social characteristics of the poor. These characteristics worked to perpetuate poverty. Among the most essential were the following:

A strongly fatalistic belief (They left their future to chance or to fate.)

Weak ego development (incapacity for self-control)

Strong present-time orientation (They lived for the moment.)

Little ability to defer gratification or plan for the future

Preoccupation with *machismo*

Knowledge only of one's own neighborhood and one's own way of life

Lack of class consciousness (They failed to appreciate the economic forces that generated their position in society.)

In addition, the poor failed to value childhood as a protected and prolonged stage of development. Initiation into sexual activity occurred early in life, and the family structure was characterized by the central place and authoritarian rule of the mother and by bitter sibling rivalry for limited material and emotional resources (Lewis 1966a, 23).

Lewis's thesis was given its most widely known urban application by Edward Banfield ([1968] 1974). The publication and revision of his *The Unheavenly City* gave rise to a great deal of controversy. The tone of the following excerpt should suggest why those who believed poverty to be a quality of the poor themselves were appreciative of the book's thesis, and why those who felt the fault lay with the structure of society were inspired in their criticism.

Each class culture implies—indeed, more or less requires—a certain sort of physical environment. It follows that a city (or district within a city) which suits one culture very well is likely to suit another very poorly or not at all. . . . The lower class individual lives in the slum, which, to a greater or lesser extent is an expression of his tastes and style of life. . . . The subcultural norms and values of the slum are reflected in poor sanitation and health practices, deviant behavior, and often a real lack of interest in formal education. With some exceptions, there is little general desire to engage in personal or community efforts for self-improvement. . . .

In the slum one can beat one's children, lie drunk in the gutter, or go to jail without attracting any special notice; these are things that most of the neighbors themselves have done and that they consider quite normal. (Banfield [1968] 1974, 69, 72)

Like Lewis, Banfield distinguished between people who were poor—a broader category of persons of disadvantaged economic circumstance—and the lower-class poor—a subset of the poor who comprised a cultural category of persons possessing the traits he had described. Although Banfield, like Lewis, acknowledged that what he identified as lower-class culture had more remote or "ultimate" causes, the immediate and practical cause of an individual's or a family's poverty were ways of thinking and behaving which, if they were not built into the personality, were at least a set of more or less deeply ingrained habits.

What bothered the critics, above anything else, were the policy implications of Banfield's (and Lewis's) position. Since poverty is, in this sense, internally caused—carried around inside of people—improving the circumstances of the poor is unlikely to have any appreciable impact on their behavior, at least not in the short term. "In principle, it is possible to eliminate the poverty (material lack) of such a family, but only at great expense, since the capacity of the radically improvident to waste money is almost unlimited" (Banfield [1968] 1974, 143).

For Lewis's part, it is generally forgotten that his motivation was to develop a sympathetic understanding of the poor. He argued that any analysis that attempted to understand poverty as the outcome of strictly cultural factors was bound to fail. He was concerned that middle-class persons, including social scientists, were prone to focus on the negative aspects of this subculture and would fail to recognize the practical utility of this adaptation, of "the readiness to exploit the pleasures of the moment for people with few resources and little hope." He believed that if such an adaptation were not possible, "the poor could hardly carry on." Yet, although he recognized the importance of wider social, economic, and political conditions in providing a foundation for his culture of poverty, his focus was, after all, on the habits of the poor. He believed that these habits were primarily to blame for what he saw as their sadness and suffering, the emptiness of their lives, and their inability to understand or avail themselves of whatever opportunities might exist. In his own words, "Indeed, poverty of culture is one of the traits of the culture of poverty" (Lewis 1966a, 25; Lewis 1966b, xliii–xliv).

Critics of the culture of poverty thesis surfaced almost immediately, arguing that the interpretation distorted reality, prejudiced understanding, and encouraged the formulation of policies that would perpetuate the disadvantages associated with poverty. In 1968, Charles Valentine published a detailed criticism of the culture of poverty approach, arguing that in its most extreme form it represented "little more than a middle class intellectual rationale for blaming poverty on the poor and avoiding recognition of the need for radical change in our society" (1968, 144). These concerns were echoed by William Ryan (1971) in his book, *Blaming the Victim*. Ryan noted that blaming the victim had become the generic excuse for the shortcomings of a society that had failed to provide adequately for all of its members. He observed that this approach to understanding the poverty of individuals and families had much in common with the literature on the Third World that explained the lack of economic development and technological progress in terms of some aspect of national culture or character, such as a lack of achievement motivation (Ryan 1971, 6). The culture of poverty approach to understanding the place of poor people within societies is the counterpart of the modernization approach, reviewed in Chapter 6, to understanding why some countries are poorer than others.

The most serious concern for the critics of the culture of poverty is the kind of policy making for which its assumptions have provided the basis. That is, the "war on poverty" programs were developed to attack the vicious cycle of poverty, to save the poor from themselves. In Ryan's words,

> *There is a terrifying sameness in the programs that arise from this kind of analysis. In education, we have programs of "compensatory" education to build up the attitudes and skills of the ghetto child, rather than structural changes in the schools. In race relations, we have social engineers who think up ways of "strengthening" the Negro family, rather than methods of eradicating racism. In health care, we develop new programs to provide health care information (to correct the supposed ignorance of the poor) and to reach out and discover cases of untreated illness and disability (to compensate for their supposed unwillingness to seek treatment). Meanwhile, the gross inequities of our medical care delivery systems are left completely unchanged. (Ryan 1971, 7–8)*

The critics argue that the antipoverty programs undertaken in the mid-sixties as part of the War on Poverty were based largely on culture of poverty assumptions and were more misguided and less effective than they might have been. Those programs were based on the idea that poverty was a product of people's habits; the programs, therefore, failed to address economic and political processes beyond the control of individuals.

The Structure of Poverty
A survey of people below the poverty line in the United States would reveal that they are in that position for a variety of reasons. Among those reasons are certain categories of explanation that affect large numbers of individuals. There are former industrial workers whose plants have closed, people who are not working and who have not worked for a long time, or people who are working, but at wages that do not allow them to rise above formal poverty status. There are those living in regions that formerly hosted more robust economic activity, such as mining or agriculture, but where the area's productivity has been played out or the product has simply become uncompetitive, and now there is no work. There are those who continue to bear the burdens of prejudice and discrimination in their

past and present forms. There are other victims of social and economic change who have been pushed out of the mainstream and onto the margins of the economic process.

All of the people in these categories have one thing in common: What they have done to become poor is far less important in determining the size of the poverty population than changes in the structure of the economy. What kinds of cultural or attitudinal adjustment they make to cope with poverty is, in this light, simply not interesting or important in understanding the dimensions of the problem of poverty.

The argument is that poverty is built into society, that it is *structural*, rather than cultural, in origin. There are those who argue that poverty comes about in the form of dislocations that result from periodic adjustments in the focus of the economy, while others see the poor as a built-in, permanent, and normal feature of the distribution of rewards. In either view, the general argument is that poverty is not something that the poor do to themselves, nor is it something that they individually can do much about.

Both cultural and structural arguments can be applied to either urban or rural locations. Analysts who approach poverty from a culture of poverty perspective have applied their analysis to relatively isolated populations as well as to urban neighborhoods. Structural arguments can be applied to declining mining towns, depopulating farming regions, or cities abandoned by industry. From a structural point of view, it is important to attend to the historical characteristics of a particular locality in order to explain poverty there.

A number of structural elements combine to affect the rates of poverty in cities in the United States. One of the major factors is the restructuring of metropolitan economies and shifts in the kinds of jobs that are available in the changing U.S. economy. These shifts in employment structure include the loss of inner-city manufacturing jobs to the suburbs, redistribution of industry away from the older industrial cities toward the southern and western regions of the country, employers seeking cheaper labor in overseas markets, and changes in the occupational structure brought about by technology. One other glaring structural feature of stratification in the United States is the disproportionate number of the poor who are people of color. Furthermore, the trend over the past two decades or more has been toward the concentration of the inner-city minority poor within large inner-city districts where high proportions of them are crowded together, intensifying their isolation and the effects of poverty. However, as we will see, the seemingly logical argument that ties together the persistence of disproportionate levels of minority poverty with their relative isolation from industrial jobs must be qualified. There remains room for culture of poverty theorists and structural exclusion theorists to continue to disagree.

Chapter 7 described the seriousness of the loss of industrial jobs in central city areas. By 1977, the central city locations of the largest metropolitan areas had already lost 700,000 of the manufacturing jobs they had in 1963, while the suburbs picked up 1.1 million (Logan and Golden 1986, 430). The displacement of workers whose jobs are eliminated has become a serious economic issue in all industrialized nations. The Bureau of Labor Statistics reported that nationwide 4.2 million U.S. workers who had worked at their present job for three or more years were displaced between January 1993 and December 1995, a number just slightly below the number that had been displaced between January 1991 and December 1993. Thirty percent of workers who had lost industrial jobs were still unemployed after two months; many others had settled for part-time jobs, and of those who had found new full-time positions, 30 percent suffered a reduction of 20 percent or more in their earnings. Women were less likely to be reemployed than men, and some of them had dropped out of the labor market altogether. Also, older workers and people of color were somewhat less likely to have found new employment at the time of the survey in February 1996 (U.S. Bureau of Labor Statistics 1996).

The loss of industrial jobs is serious in small towns, where the local economy may be heavily dependent on one major employer, but the aggregate loss of many large and small industries also has had devastating effects on metropolitan economies. The losses mean that some central city populations are physically distanced from the kinds of employment that provided a living and economic stability to the waves of immigrant poor who had come to these cities to seek work in earlier times. The distance between inner-city residence and suburban employment is not trivial to the poor, and the distance increases as metropolitan mass transportation systems are withdrawn. When these jobs are exported to other nations, the isolation of workers from industrial work moves beyond the question of adequate transportation systems.

Local jobs in the inner city tend to be in the service sector, and it is in this sector that most new inner-city jobs are being created—just as in the national economy as a whole. Some service jobs, like fast food employment or office cleaning, do not demand much skill or training and are poorly paid. Other service sector jobs, like medicine or technical consultation, are well-paid, but demand skills and training. To the extent that city centers have become centers of finance, marketing, and corporate management, they offer the image of an odd economic environment in which a *dual employment structure* exists: That is, workers are recruited for jobs at the top and bottom of the wage system. As a general rule, white-collar positions commanding attractive salaries are not available to the urban poor today, just as they were unavailable to poor immigrants at the turn of the century.

Life in large cities is expensive. Rent on a modest apartment can easily cost well over $1,000 a month. Expensive urban space and expensive workers who earn high wages are naturally matched to one another. Service workers with on-the-job training, and non-unionized, unskilled industrial workers who are able to get by on the low wages that employers must pay in order to remain competitive in the international marketplace, are anachronistic—out of place—in the economic environment of the great commercial and financial centers. In these places, people without special skills are among the working poor, others have dropped out of the labor market, and yet others have become part of the frantic hustle of working several jobs, shifts, and angles (some inside and some outside the law). This last category are chronically deprived of sleep and leisure in order to maintain some semblance of the material conditions associated with the American Dream. Cities include many people whose labor is simply of marginal utility and therefore has low exchange value in a period of rapid change. In this light, how surprising is it that we find serious poverty in the city along with serious levels of crime and frustration?

Patterns of Metropolitan Segregation

It has become evident that residential segregation plays a large role in contributing to the greater poverty of minorities, primarily African Americans and Latinos. Patterns of segregation have been slow to change in the course of the last quarter century. Taeuber and Taeuber (1965) devised a segregation (or dissimilarity) index to measure the degree of racial segregation in the 207 largest cities in the United States. Using decennial census data for 1940 through 1960, they employed their index of dissimilarity on a block-by-block basis to indicate any disproportionate concentrations of minorities. A score of 100 for a particular city reflected a perfectly segregated population; a score of 0 indicated perfect integration, where each block housed blacks and whites in proportion to their numbers in the urban population. In 1960, the mean for the 207 cities was 86.7, indicating a high degree of racial segregation as the norm. On a city-by-city basis, scores ranged from a low of 60.4 for San Jose to a high of 98.1 for Fort Lauderdale. Segregation scores tended to be lower in the South. This was considered to be a lingering reflection of the traditional residential location of black hired help close to their white employers' housing. Today, this is reflected in a superficial pattern of integration.

Van Valey, Roof, and Wilcox (1977) traced the pattern of urban segregation from 1960 to 1970. When the comparison was limited to those 137 cities for which data were available in 1960, virtually no change occurred in the ten-year period: These cities, which had an index of 75.4 in 1960, had an index of 75.1 in 1970. Those cities that had the greatest degree of segregation in 1960 remained among the most highly segregated in 1970. In the original sample 70 MSAs, or just over half, had experienced some increase in the degree of segregation.

Taeuber (1983) found that segregation continued at high levels between 1970 and 1980. Analysis of block data for the 28 cities with black populations of more than 100,000 revealed a range of scores from a low of 59 for Oakland to a high of 92 for Chicago. Overall, the segregation index for the 28 cities declined slightly, from 87 in 1970 to 81 in 1980. Taeuber noted that even assuming a steady rate of reduction similar to that which occurred in the ten-year period, cities would remain highly segregated for decades to come.

Jargowski (1993) attempted to measure the ghettoization of the African American population. He identified urban ghettos on the basis of poverty rates (those with rates 40 percent or higher qualified). By his measure, poor blacks had become increasingly isolated over the course of the 1980s, and half of the African American poor in metropolitan areas lived in ghettos. All told, about six million African Americans, or one in six, lived in ghettos in 1990, a 36 percent higher proportion than in 1980. There were differences by region: The metropolitan areas of the Midwest and Southwest saw a dramatic increase in ghettoization during the decade, which more than offset declines in the Northeast and Southeast.

African American Suburbs

The population movement that has had the greatest impact on residential segregation in the second half of the twentieth century has been the suburbanization of the white metropolitan population. It produced a pattern in which African American and other minority populations were concentrated in inner cities ringed by largely white, middle-class suburbs. Within the suburbs themselves, the African American population grew from a bare 3 percent at the end of World War I to only 4.2 percent by 1960. During the 1950s, there was some movement of blacks to older residential areas outside of central cities, and during the 1960s civil rights legislation generated a modest increase in black movement to formerly all-white areas outside of central cities. This movement was largely to older areas of housing and those closer to existing ghettoized suburbs; but because of the "civil rights climate" and the "specter of civil unrest," there was some opening of noncentral city housing to black residence (Stahura 1986, 132–135). Altogether, the black suburban population increased during the 1960s by 728,000, which, due to the relatively small number of suburban blacks in 1960, represented a gain of 28.3 percent. Their numbers expanded again between 1970 and 1977 by 1,163,000, or 34 percent. A survey of 1,773 suburbs in 55 metropolitan areas revealed a continued increase in the proportion of minority suburban growth between 1980 and 1990. Against the combined proportion of Asians, blacks, and Latinos, the majority of all suburbs were still more than 85 percent white: 64 percent of suburbs compared to 76 percent in 1980. In fact, almost a third of all suburbs were more than 95 percent white in 1990. By contrast, a small but growing number of suburbs had more minority than majority residents (Phelan and Schneider 1996, 662–663).

Minority experiences in the suburb vary. Asian Americans tend to be fairly well integrated in predominantly white suburbs (Massey and Denton 1987). The same is true for some Latino groups, but there may be a trend toward increasing segregation over time (Logan and Alba 1993). In general, analysts agree that African American suburbs share many features with poorer central city locations. These include more pronounced segregation (compared to other minorities); lower income; poorer quality, older housing; higher taxes; and strained municipal finances (Stearns and Logan 1986; Phelan and Schneider 1996). The movement of blacks to suburbs is largely movement to suburbs that are already home to large numbers of African Americans, to locations from which whites are moving away. The pattern is described as one of "invasion and succession" in the classical ecological sense. "Suburbs with large black populations, in particular affluent ones, become identified as places presenting a new and expanded set of housing opportunities for blacks and other nonwhites who are locating to suburbia [where] housing options may be restricted by a dual housing market and other forms of discrimination" (Phelan and Schneider 1996, 667).

In large metropolitan areas, it doesn't take much for a particular residential tract to become identified in the minds of whites as undergoing a change to a predominantly nonwhite location. The key criterion that white residents use in deciding if the racial balance has tipped may be whether or not whites continue to move into the neighborhood. If some white out-movers are not replaced by white in-movers when property changes hands, the general white exodus is soon underway (Lake 1981, 241–242). The pattern is particularly pronounced where the minority is African American. A more general factor associated with the degree of suburban segregation within an urban region is the size of the minority population in that region. In regions with particularly large minority populations, there is a higher degree of segregation: Here, "whites use segregation to preserve their social position in the face of a threatening—that is, large—minority advance" (Logan, Alba, and Leung 1996, 875). In regions where there are large representations of Asians or Latinos, whites will be sensitive to residential concentrations of those categories and will move from suburbs where they are located in number. This is true for affluent suburbs in the Los Angeles area, where whites leave when Latinos are perceived to reach a critical mass. However, whites of more modest means are moving into Latino/multiethnic Los Angeles neighborhoods in search of affordable housing, but not into black suburbs (Phelan and Schneider 1996, 668–669).

Biracial residential patterns tend to be unstable in suburbs. The case of Saint Louis is in many ways typical of the pattern of black suburbanization. Most has occurred through the extension of a black residential corridor stretching northwest from the city. Although some racial mixing took place in some broad northwestern sectors, the sectors remained segregated internally, and there was some indication at the time they were studied that they were in transition toward more homogeneous black settlement (Farley 1983, 150–156).

Clearly, when we speak of white suburbanization and black suburbanization, we indicate different processes with distinct consequences for those involved, movements resulting in different types of suburban settlements. Black suburbs have, in addition to their generally poorer residents, such distinguishing characteristics as narrower tax bases, higher property tax rates, and a higher level of commitment to expenditures on social programs (Schneider and Logan 1982, 768–769; Phelan and Schneider 1996). Of course, all of these features are interrelated. The continued segregation of whites and blacks into discrete communities in the suburbs means that suburbanizing blacks encounter conditions in their suburbs similar to those they attempted to leave behind in the central cities. Also, suburban blacks continue to be separated from the superior tax resources of more affluent white communities; at the same time, black communities continue to bear a disproportionate share of the burden of caring for the poor.

Race and Urban Poverty: Ecology, Culture, and the Mismatch Debate

In 1970, Gunnar Myrdal proposed the recognition of a special category of human beings, *the permanent underclass.* He was concerned with a strata of the world population, the urban and rural poor of the Third World, people who had neither the skills nor a chance for education that would allow them to become profitably integrated into the world economy. These were superfluous people whom the international economy had permanently left behind. There was nothing for them to do. From the foregoing discussion of the structural roots of poverty, it is probably evident how the term came to be applied to the urban poor of the United States.

The *underclass* had become a widely used term and its existence a controversial issue by the late 1980s. For one thing, it is a potentially radical critique of the world and national market systems, strongly implying that some segment of society is systematically excluded from a reasonable share of the economic benefits produced and distributed by that economy. On the other side of the debate, conservative political interests appropriated the term to refer to those they believed to be locked in the culture of poverty. Given the perfectly opposed manner in which the term came to be used—meaning both that the very poor were permanently displaced by remote forces *and* that they were the cause of their own misery—its continued usefulness was challenged. Some argued that only those who had deliberately withdrawn from the formal economy should be counted among the permanent poor (Auletta 1982, 27–30). Others reserved the label for those who had become dependent on welfare payments. Still others wanted to include those who have been employed for most of their adult lives, but who have not been able to rise above poverty (Glasgow 1980, 9), an interpretation more consistent with Myrdal's original interpretation. Given the operational disagreements, it is not surprising that estimates of the size of this segment of the poor in the United States ranged between 2 and 18 million people—hardly a useful estimate. Ultimately, the term came to focus attention on the minority poor of inner-city black ghettos and Latino *barrios*.

Two decades ago, William Wilson (1978) contributed considerable insight to the concept of the underclass, but the title of his book, *The Declining Significance of Race*, provoked a controversy that obscured his potential contribution. He was making the point that the large-scale decline of stable and reasonably well-paid work for people with only basic skills and training had produced a threat to the well-being of a broad cross-section of people trying to enter or remain in the working class. Part of his argument was that the restructuring of the economy, especially the loss of industrial work in the central cities, was affecting members of all races who were dependent on these opportunities to make a decent life for themselves and their families. Like Myrdal, he was saying that a large segment of the population was becoming permanently excluded from the economy, permanently obsolete, members of a permanent underclass. Again, this is a radical critique of the capitalist economic system's capacity to provide reasonable opportunities for all members of society.

However, Wilson's thesis offered a potential tool to conservative political interests. It contained two elements that invited abuse by the opponents of Civil Rights legislation (especially opponents of affirmative action policies) and of social welfare programs. First, the emphasis in the title of the book implied that racism was no longer as serious a problem as it had been in the past. In fact, Wilson did argue that the relative disadvantage faced by blacks was a matter of historical circumstance. Blacks were disproportionately represented in the growing underclass because they were relatively recent arrivals to the industrial cities. True, they had been discriminated against in jobs, education, and housing in the past, but in the post–Civil Rights era, their problems were not a matter of deliberate discrimination based on prejudice, but were the result of the structural and color-blind elimination of urban employment prospects due to increased international competition and technological changes in manufacturing. Wilson also emphasized that there had been black social mobility in recent decades and that the African American population of the United States was now highly stratified. Hence, the significance of race in determining the distribution of disadvantage had declined. Second, conservative political elements in society found comfort in Wilson's pointed critique of liberalism, especially of liberal social scientists' reputed reluctance to be more critical of the pathology of lower-class black culture in the inner cities. Liberals, he said, were afraid to be critical of the dysfunctional habits of poor blacks because they didn't want to be accused by their colleagues of blaming the victim. He argued that the culture of the inner-city poor was debilitating and undermined the potential for mobility, and that it needed to share an appropriate measure of the blame for the lack of social mobility from the ghetto.

Critics found a number of problems with Wilson's thesis that are still important to emphasize more than two decades later, in part because Wilson is an important figure in social science, and in part because there is lingering confusion surrounding the work. Critics were quick to comment on the unfortunate implications of Wilson's book, one remarking caustically that the title *(The Declining Significance of Race)* represents "calculated, evocative packaging and promotion— or in marketing lingo, *hype*" (Edwards 1979, 98). Another wrote "it unwittingly risks adding unsubstantiated support to the dominant ideological myth . . . that racial problems were basically solved during the 1960s" (Pettigrew 1980, 116). It was acknowledged that Wilson had opposed this interpretation of his work, but once the implication had been invited by a leading black social scientist, opponents of assistance to minorities were quick to exploit it.

At the beginning of the twenty-first century, it is too easy to see in everyday experience and news accounts that racism remains an important structural feature of the distribution of opportunity and of poverty in the United States. A more helpful way to make Wilson's distinction between historical and contemporary effects is to differentiate between overt racism and institutional racism. Overt racism may be explicit or subtle. The law has made it more difficult to discriminate and to seem to be discriminating. Overt racism has to do with the willingness and ability of employers and others to discriminate openly against members of minority groups.

Subtle racism or discrimination involves unfair practices accompanied by an attempt to hide the intent from the victim and any other interested parties. Employers, realtors, and rental agents have devised various practices to circumvent fair housing and employment laws without seeming to do so. The following passage demonstrates what may have been a crude and inept attempt to conceal discrimination. Although one can never be sure, several such encounters in an individual's experience would suggest the obvious conclusion. The account also offers insights into how expectations of discrimination, combined with the structural disadvantages of urban poverty, deeply discourage young people who are attempting to find work. This concise but vivid picture is presented by Regina Eugene, a teenage resident of Louisville:

> *Employment is a joke for most people and it's also a joke for me. I'm growing up in a poverty stricken area. It's hard trying to find a job. Day in and day out I'm looking in the want ads. Usually you got to be 18 years old. Most of the time, the job is in some community that I've never heard of. Every time something turns up that I'm qualified for, it's way out of my district. Once I went to a Wendy's because they had an ad in the paper. When I got there I was told there weren't any more applications in the store and to come back tomorrow. The next day I came back and I was told the ten positions had been filled. Then I asked the man was he prejudiced. He looked at me stunned. I walked out. Finding a job is a bitch in our democratic society. Our system was designed so that everyone can develop to his or her potential, but we can't develop to our potentials because we can't get what we need. (Williams and Kornblum 1985, 33)*

Institutional racism is at least as serious a cause of poverty among minorities as are conscious, contemporary expressions of prejudice and discrimination, and it is especially important for understanding urban poverty. Institutional racism refers to the pattern where disadvantages are built into the political and economic structure of society, and where these disadvantages have become so ingrained that they persist independently of fluctuations in prejudice and expressions of racism. Institutional racism is responsible for the disadvantages experienced by urban minorities today to the extent that those disadvantages are the lingering result of laws and practices that historically limited their full political and economic participation. Institutional racism perpetuates the conditions associated with the status of the newly arrived immigrant, preserving the position of minorities as a neglected pool of cheap labor with no choice but to usefully absorb the substandard housing and other leftover and inferior products of wider society.

This is where William Wilson's analysis fits most usefully—the part of his argument that states that historically blacks were excluded from full participation in an industrial economy, that this exclusion lasted until that economy began to deindustrialize. Now economic change rather than overt racism reinforces the disproportionate burden of poverty and the attendant challenges faced by poor African Americans. In 1975, 27 percent of blacks, 25 percent of Latinos, and 8 percent of whites fell below the official poverty line. In 1995, the respective figures were 26 percent, 27 percent, and 9 percent. There had been virtually no change in the distribution of poverty. It must be noted that this static pattern of disproportionate representation is not inconsistent with Wilson's argument that the significance of race was declining during the last quarter of the twentieth century in the United States. The figures also reflect the misleading nature of the observation.

The Continuing Significance of Race

Wilson (1987) is among those who have stressed the role of the neighborhood in perpetuating poverty, especially in minority areas of large cities. The interpretation combines structural and cultural factors and argues that a systematic deterioration of opportunity and hope creates an environment in which hopelessness becomes an institutionalized attitude.

This is an ecological interpretation because the residential neighborhood is assumed to be causally linked to the perpetuation of poverty. It is argued that, historically, minority areas of the city (i.e., African American areas) were once integrated in terms of social class. They included black professionals, middle-class, and working-class families as well as the poor. The integration of residential neighborhoods outside all-black ghettos provided sufficient geographic mobility that those who could afford to do so moved away. This left behind areas that were not only homogeneously black, but homogeneously poor, as well. At the same time, the decline in attractive industrial employment opportunities, especially in the inner city, undermined the position of the remaining working class. These structural transitions created "a new urban reality," which stripped the traditional African American communities of role models, community leaders, and positive cultural influences in general. What young people growing up in such communities learn are lessons in living that are not conducive to social mobility.

Considerable research has addressed the changing class and employment structure of inner-city minority residential areas, specifically with regard to the concentration of poverty. Unfortunately, researchers are limited largely to using census tract type divisions in comparing different residential areas. The comparisons suffer from the lack of precision one might hope for, since these divisions are generally not drawn for the purpose of identifying homogeneous residential populations, and the references we encounter here to "neighborhood" or "community" deserve to be regarded with suspicion. Nevertheless, the pattern they investigate is clearly evident, though gross levels of measurement insure that debate over cause and effect will persist.

The poorest neighborhoods in the inner city, those identified as having 40 percent or higher poverty rates, are referred to as "extreme poverty neighborhoods." The percentage of all central city poor living in these tracts increased from 16.5 percent in 1970, to 22.5 percent in 1980, and then to 28.2 percent in 1990. In the 100 largest metropolitan areas, 41.6 percent of all African Americans living in central cities lived in extreme poverty neighborhoods in 1990 (Kasarda 1993; Coulton et al. 1996). This intensification in the location of urban poverty is consonant with Wilson's observation on the importance of the exodus of nonpoor urban minorities from inner-city locations. Logically, their out-migration would leave these areas poorer on average. Massey and others (Massey and Eggers 1990; Massey and Denton 1993) express another view of black inner-city isolation: They argue that it is due to segregation, rooted historically in clear and deliberate efforts to exclude African Americans from white neighborhoods. These historical patterns are reinforced today by whites, the majority of whom may accept the principle of open access to housing, but most of whom "still feel uncomfortable in any neighborhood that contains more than a few black residents." These are whites who vote with their feet when that threshold is reached (Massy and Denton 1993, 11). This is a pattern we saw supported in suburban minority/majority housing trends. Goering and others (1997) showed that even public housing projects perpetuate the pattern of segregation, with predominantly black projects located in the poorest neighborhoods while the projects with substantial numbers of white tenants are located in neighborhoods with substantially lower poverty rates. Massey and Denton argued that racism, manifest as residential segregation, is intensified during each serious downturn in the economy, deepening the residential and cultural isolation of the African American poor. They distinguished between African American and Latino residential experiences. Most categories of Latino origin, except Puerto Ricans, are more residentially integrated than blacks. Betancur argued to the contrary, that the apparent Latino integration may be a transitional pattern, whereby they temporarily succeed whites and other ethnics in deteriorating neighborhoods. As the area becomes identified as a Latino enclave, members of the dominant group exit, a process followed shortly by increased immigration of African Americans and the gradual exit of Latinos. In this light, we can see that any snapshot of Latino residential patterns is bound to show a higher level of integration because it will include these continually transitioning areas, but the integration reflected will be ephemeral and hide an underlying racism. Out-moving Latinos will be moving to new transitioning areas, which whites are fleeing. To emphasize the distinctiveness in Latino and black residential patterns is to miss the more important similarities of their experiences as dominated groups (Betancur 1996). Latino minorities historically and presently have been recruited to do the heavy, dirty, and exploitatively remunerated work at the convenience of the host society, then dismissed in periods when there was nothing useful for them to do. As in the case of blacks, Latino minorities are subject to exclusionary processes based on origin and their perceived racial otherness. They are well represented within categories of the poor, including the structurally excluded underclass.

The mechanism of minority isolation surely combines some element of externally imposed involuntary segregation as well as some voluntary out-migration of more affluent minorities. The question remains, To what extent are the members of minorities who remain concentrated in poor neighborhoods disadvantaged by their isolation? The remainder of the discussion in this chapter focuses primarily on impoverished black Americans whose experience has received the most empirical attention.

One area to consider is education. Data compiled by the U.S. Department of Education (1996), which compare urban, suburban, and rural school districts, show that the racial imbalance between urban and other school districts increased between 1980 and 1990, along with the poverty rates of students in urban schools. Concerns about student safety, weapons in the school, and student pregnancy were much greater among urban than other school teachers. Jencks and Mayer (1990) reviewed a number of studies comparing the performance of minority students in racially mixed and racially homogeneous urban residential tracts. The size and nature of the geographic units that were compared varied, but some studies compared students from different zip codes—once again, not the most refined measure.

The general hypothesis, that African American students from economically and racially mixed neighborhoods would show higher levels of achievement, received some support. Jencks and Mayer (1990, 173–178) warned that their findings are more tentative than conclusive, but speculated that better data might further support these tentative indications: Having more affluent classmates would appear to encourage students from poor backgrounds to learn more effectively in elementary school and to complete high school. Neighborhood composition has no apparent effect on whether or not poor minority students will attend college. Coming from a less-poor neighborhood correlates with lower rates of teenage pregnancy. Economically mixed neighborhoods are actually associated with a higher incidence of criminal activity for poor black youth, but also with higher levels of legitimate earnings later in life. Jenks and Mayer concluded by lamenting the lack of time-series data that would allow more certainty about these patterns. Quantitative correlational data leave open the question of whether mobility or the lack of mobility of poor, black, inner-city residents is caused by neighborhood cultures or by the national and international restructuring of employment opportunities and wages.

By far, the majority of the studies of the effects of minority social and economic isolation focus on the question of structural unemployment and its connection to poverty. In its initial form, what has come to be known as "the mismatch theory" stated that the increasing distance between jobs located on the metropolitan periphery and minorities located at the economically decaying center would produce structural unemployment and higher levels of poverty (Kain 1968). The intuitive logic of the observation seems beyond debate, but research has forced a modification of the thesis.

Many prominent studies (for example, Ellwood 1986; Jargowsky and Bane 1990; Jargowsky 1996; Jencks and Mayer 1990) have called into question the mismatch hypothesis that higher rates of black employment result from the sheer absence of opportunities in local inner-city areas. There is something going on with regard to the impact of metropolitan economic restructuring and the reduction of certain kinds of jobs for inner-city residents, but evidence indicates that the problem is not simply the lack of any type of opportunity. For example, Jargowsky and Bane (1990) pointed out that although Boston lost manufacturing employment at rates similar to those of other northern cities between 1970 and 1985, poverty rates in the centrally located ghettos decreased for a time during this period. Similarly, Cohn and Fossett (1996) found that the higher unemployment rates of African Americans in Boston and Houston could not be explained on the basis of distance between residence and jobs in these two dissimilar metro areas. In these cities, "blacks are physically near more jobs than whites are. This finding holds despite analysis being restricted to consider only entry-level, blue collar jobs and allowances being made for group differences in search and commuting capabilities" (557).

This would seem to settle the debate about the impact of deindustrialization once and for all, except for findings that clearly associate black poverty rates and the loss of manufacturing due to restructuring. Galster, Mincy, and Tobin (1997) found that nationwide, between 1980 and 1990, the greatest levels of black poverty were generally associated with census tracts that had lost the greatest number of manufacturing jobs, and that "each increment of restructuring was significantly associated with poverty growth" (797).

Jargowsky (1996) systematically reconsidered the evidence regarding the connection of minority poverty rates and ecological patterns of employment opportunity, and suggested that minority poverty rates in especially impoverished urban areas may be associated with the kinds of jobs that are being lost in these areas and the profiles of certain local residents who are most likely to be adversely affected. Building on the finding that industrial decline probably has a disproportionate effect on young residents with less education (Bound and Holzer 1993), Jargowsky (1996, 144) concluded "though the exact mechanisms are somewhat murky, structural changes in the economy have worked to disadvantage those with lower levels of education and job skills . . . Because of the poor quality of inner-city schools and the correlation between socioeconomic background and educational attainment, the decline in demand for low-skill labor has had a disproportionate impact on inner-city minorities, particularly young men." He added that finding a job that pays decent wages is particularly difficult. This seems to be the crucial point. Although it is difficult—given the gross levels of measurement, sometimes partial (city-by-city) data, and somewhat contradictory evidence—to determine just how much the availability of all types of jobs is associated with urban poverty, evidence does seem to point to the lack of availability of certain kinds of work as a major factor. For example, Jargowsky and Bane's (1990) finding that the greatest correlation between the loss of manufacturing work and poverty was in the North, where a higher proportion of the lost manufacturing jobs would have been union jobs, lends indirect support to the idea that it is the loss of higher level opportunities for workers with modest training that may be the crucial factor. Galster and others (1997, 800) made the point more directly:

> *Besides affecting the number of jobs, economic restructuring has affected several features of employment. . . . The net effects of these changes have been a decline in high-wage but low-skill manufacturing jobs and a growth in both low- and high-wage service sector jobs. Although high-wage service sector jobs have increased, these generally have skill requirements that low-skilled workers cannot meet.*

Today, analysts increasingly lean toward explanations of inner-city minority poverty that emphasize either a loss in well-paid jobs, if not a reduction in the absolute availability of employment (Jargowsky 1996; Galster et al. 1997), or a combination of factors that include discrimination in hiring and compensation levels (Cohn and Fossett 1996, 572). The simple mismatch/job-loss thesis seems to need work. At the date of writing, the issue has not been resolved, and it probably will not be clarified for another decade. Empirical evidence, however, often has an interesting way of throwing open another round of debate. This might yet be the result of a study of one-hundred neighborhoods in Ohio central cities. The study did not focus on industrial jobs, but on "residentiary businesses"—largely customer-oriented enterprises, such as retail trades. The study is interesting because it found a relationship between poverty rates and the decisions by entrepreneurs to leave a particular area. One striking finding was that a poverty level of 10 percent of local residents—a very modest poverty rate—was associated with the departure of some retailers and service trades, such as furniture and furnishings stores, realtors, and medical offices. An additional 10 percent increase in poverty levels was associated with the departure of significantly more businesses. It was found that at a poverty level of 20 percent, the local economy was effectively "ghettoized." The loss of banks, private medical offices, supermarkets, beauty shops, video rental stores, and other businesses is not only inconvenient, but also represents a deterioration in the range of employment opportunities (Bingham and Zhang 1997, 787–794). Implicit in this study is the idea that poverty itself drives out work opportunities, a reversal in direction for the usual job-loss and poverty-concentration hypothesis.

The discussion to this point leaves open the question of the relative influence of local ghetto or barrio culture on the behaviors and consequent poverty levels of local populations. If African Americans and Latinos have higher levels of unemployment, but the problem is not due to the lack of jobs they have access to, then what is left to explain the differences in unemployment and labor force disaffiliation than the negative attitudes of minorities toward work, reflecting the self-perpetuating effect of lives lived in neighborhoods without positive role models, in a neighborhood-wide culture of poverty. Macro or structural theorists can respond with reference to the correlation between restructuring and poverty rates. Jargowsky (1996, 144) drew the following conclusion:

> *Taken together, the macrostructural explanations of neighborhood poverty— which hold that ghettos and barrios are the result of larger, metropolitan level processes—can explain about four-fifths of the variance in ghetto poverty. Although the importance of these metropolitan processes does not preclude a role for the cultural values of ghetto residents, it does suggest that such factors play a secondary role, at best.*

Urban Households Headed by Women

Another major dimension in the profile of urban poverty involves households where a woman is the sole adult provider, a pattern widely discussed as the "feminization of poverty" in the 1980s. Table 9-3 indicates how the number of families

TABLE 9-3   Households Headed by Women with Children under 18 Years Old, 1980–1999

	All Races			White			Black			Hispanic		
	1980	1990	1999	1980	1990	1999	1980	1990	1999	1979*	1990	1999
Number of households headed by women	6,299	7,707	8,736	3,995	4,786	5,500	2,171	2,698	2,892	502	921	1,353
As percent of all household family units** that race/year	10.4%	11.6%	12.6%	7.5%	8.4%	9.4%	34.4%	36.1%	35.8%	16.6%	18.5%	20.4%
Number of female-headed households in poverty	2,703	3,767	3,634	1,433	1,814	1,980	1,217	1,513	1,333	288	536	630
Percent of female-headed households in poverty	42.9%	47.1%	41.5%	35.9%	37.9%	35.6%	56.0%	56.1%	46.1%	57.3%	58.2%	46.6%

Source: Dalaker and Proctor, 2000. Table B-3, pp. B-14 to B-19.
*Figures for Hispanic category from 1980 are not available; data from 1979 are used.
**With children under 18.

in the United States that were maintained by women grew between 1980 and 1999. The growth in this segment of the population reflects the increased number of divorced and separated women, and the number of never-married women who had children (it includes teenagers in charge of their own households). The table reveals that a majority of female household heads are white, but disproportionate numbers are African American and Latino. While the numbers of families run by women continued to increase over the 19-year period, the proportion of such households in the Latino population is considerably higher than that in the total population, and the proportion of African American households run by women is highest of all, and leveled out at nearly three times the national rate.

A disproportionate number of single-parent households headed by women are poor, and this translates into high rates of poverty for children. Table 9-4 shows that children in two-parent families have a better chance of escaping poverty, and this characteristic holds across racial groups. African American children experience the highest rate of single-parenting, and African American and Latino children in single-woman households run the greatest risk of poverty. Table 9-5 indicates that most single mothers work, and most of those hold full-time, year-round employment. Others work part of the year or part-time. A substantial number of mothers with young children do not work, and the proportion of nonworking women

TABLE 9-4 Percent of Children under the Age of Six Living in Poverty:
Race and Type of Household, 1999

White	14.6%
Married Couple	9.0%
Female Householder	44.4%
Black	36.6%
Married Couple	10.0%
Female Householder	59.0%
Hispanic	30.6%
Married Couple	24.0%
Female Householder	54.6%

Source: Dalaker and Proctor, 2000. Table 2, pp. 3–5.

TABLE 9-5 Comparing Married Couple- and Female-Headed Households[a]:
Work Experience, Race, and Poverty, 1999

	Worked Year-Round Full-Time		Worked, but Not Year-Round, Not Full-Time		Did Not Work during Year	
	Number (millions)	Percent below Poverty	Number (millions)	Percent below Poverty	Number (millions)	Percent below Poverty
Married Couples (Husband's Work Experience)	22.0	3.2%	2.9	17.9%	1.1	35.6%
Female-Headed Households (Householder's Work Experience)						
White	2.8	8.7%	1.7	48.2%	.8	70.7%
Black	1.4	18.6%	.9	68.3%	.5	81.5%
Hispanic	.6	19.3%	.4	61.4%	3	75.5%

Source: Dalaker and Proctor, 2000. Table 3, pp. 18–21.
[a]Households with children under 18.

householders is higher for black and Latino groups. Compared to the national average for married couple households (top row), every working/nonworking category of women-headed households suffers higher rates of poverty. Also not surprisingly, the highest rates of poverty for young children are in families where the mother does not work, and this pattern is accentuated for minorities.

Although households headed by women make up a distinct numerical minority of the population overall, by the mid-1980s they had come to contain about half of all people in poverty. Employing Michael Harrington's well-known term of reference for the poor, Pearce (1983, 70) wrote that "the 'other America' is a changing neighborhood: Men are moving out; women and children are moving in."

Women are burdened by cultural and legal conventions that force them to assume primary responsibility for the raising of children. Only 5 percent of never-married mothers receive any form of financial support from the fathers of their children. The disadvantages that women share go beyond family structure to social structure. In addition to the fact that single women often bear all or most of the cost of raising children, women face well-known structural barriers to full participation in the workforce. If they are able to work out childcare arrangements, they are still confronted with occupational segregation into a relatively narrow range of low-paying occupations collectively referred to as "pink-collar" work. It could be argued that this form of wage discrimination is especially critical for unskilled or semiskilled working-class occupations, not because wage discrimination doesn't occur at all employment levels, but because at the lower reaches of the pay scale, it more often means the difference between a living wage and poverty for a head-of-household and the dependents in that household. In the past decade, gender discrimination has proven to be as tenacious a problem as race discrimination. Women continue to earn less than that earned by men in comparable positions of skill and responsibility. This is part of the structure that conditions women's place in society. Federal and local job-training programs have helped little in changing the situation because they continue to prepare poor women for low-paying jobs, such as clerical work or food service.

The welfare reform measure of 1996, the Personal Responsibility and Work Opportunity Reconciliation Act, has been an experiment in the capacity of the market to absorb additional workers. For those experiencing mandatory entry into the labor force, largely women heads-of-household, it is a no-choice challenge to overcome many of the same structural barriers to working and maintaining a family that have been in place all along, and many of these women face additional personal challenges. The welfare reform measure, which was designed to move welfare recipients off welfare rolls and into self-support through work, led critics to forecast disasters in the form of massive numbers of destitute families with children being turned out into the streets. Others were concerned that the jobs with which this new workforce was to support itself would not materialize. Alternatively, there was concern that women who were being forced to find work at any wage level would take jobs from existing workers once employers recognized the potential labor bargain the new workers represented. The roughly 4 million new job seekers represented additional displacement pressures for people making six or seven dollars an hour (*New York Times,* April 1, 1997).

We can assume that, to some degree, all of these forecasts were correct, but the question is, How serious have the negative effects been and for what number of people—when compared to the benefits? The big picture of the human consequences of welfare revision has been difficult to assess because the impact is still unfolding. The economic prosperity of the late 1990s led to a shortage of entry-level service and other low-wage workers at the very time when former welfare recipients hit the labor market. The impact of terminating welfare support has been different for rural and urban populations, as well as varying from city to city, due to differences in local support programs for women making the transition and differences in the availability of jobs. The emerging evidence on the impact of revised welfare policy is broad and complex enough to fuel endless debate. Conservatives who have long favored cutting the welfare rolls through mandatory work requirements point to substantial reductions in those rolls since the legislation took effect. Critics, on the other hand, counter that people who were poor and living on government payments are now among the working poor; they are people who have jobs but insufficient earnings to raise themselves and their children out of poverty (Haskins and Primus 2000). This does not represent unaltered circumstances for the affected families. Critics point to some evidence that the condition of poverty for some children who remain poor has deepened, and that children of mothers forced to find work have been put at risk because the poor do not have the means to make adequate childcare arrangements.

The loss of government supports may indeed be having a more serious impact in rural than in urban areas. Rural employment opportunities are not being produced at the same rate as metropolitan ones. Also, rural transportation issues—for instance, access to an automobile—are critical for those who have to travel miles to get to the nearest work site. In general, it is not surprising that some portion of women welfare recipients face serious barriers to employment, personal obstacles that explain why they were receiving welfare payments to begin with: These may include lack of a high school degree, little work experience, poor work skills or work habits, a personal history of discouragement due to perceived discrimination, lack of access to a car, a diagnosis of mental disorder, substance dependence, health problems on the part of the recipient and her children, and the debilitating effects of domestic abuse. The combination of such barriers is serious. Women who faced a greater number of them had more difficulty finding and keeping a job. In a comparison of women with children who were still receiving welfare versus those who had managed to find work, more than half of the welfare-reliant mothers had no car or driver's license, compared with a fifth of those working; and a fourth of continuing welfare recipients met the criteria for at least one psychiatric disorder, compared with a tenth of workers. Other personal barriers presented obstacles of similar magnitude (Danziger 2000).

National thinking about poverty, which might well be centered on the issue of gender, is instead clouded by the issue of race. One of the cultural or emotional consequences of the concentration of minority poverty in the inner city, a question most often raised regarding the mind-set and behavior of poor people themselves, needs to be addressed with regard to its impact on the majority group's attitudes toward poverty. That is, the visibility of concentrated *minority* poor—the social disorder and deviance attributed to them—causes society to forget that most poor people are non-Latino whites. In this way, the problem of poverty becomes associated in the popular mind with race. If blacks, and most visibly urban blacks, remain seriously disadvantaged, then what are they doing to keep themselves in that condition?

This perspective has never been far below the surface in thinking about race and ghetto poverty, and it has remained a strong undercurrent in journalistic analysis, in the popular mind, and among some sociologists. It is reflective of the themes in a number of controversial but influential works, from Moynihan's *The Negro Family* in 1965 through Wilson's *The Declining Significance of Race* in 1978. As Wilhelm (1986a, 209) summed it up, the thesis runs "Blacks are in a mess, and while they may have gotten that way because of racial oppression by Whites, nonetheless, today, racial factors no longer matter since it is a specific quality of life among Blacks, family disintegration, that they themselves bring about that explains economic deterioration for at least the past 3 decades." He observed that, according to the deteriorating family thesis, a person enters poverty either because someone has failed to enter marriage or because someone has left a marriage. The facts of the feminization of poverty become posited as a cause of poverty in this way, providing a variation on the well-worn culture of poverty thesis. By focusing on the deficiencies of the family, analysts and policymakers are deflected from confronting directly and critically the difficult issues of racism and the damaging effects of the dynamics of capitalism (Wilhelm 1986b, 140). The argument that the problem is a matter of personal or subcultural maladaptation reflects the implicit assumption that "the free enterprise system [is] an open market, and that failure to enter it or to fully exploit it [is] due to personal inability, not market constraints" (Glasgow 1980, 73).

The revised welfare policy reflects this view of the causes of poverty. Whether the work requirement represents the simple and final solution to the centuries-old question of what is a nation's responsibility to its poor may have to await a less prosperous time, when there is a surplus of workers rather than a surplus of entry-level, low-skill, low-wage jobs. In such a period, when the conventional wisdom regarding the causes of poverty will have absorbed the lesson that the solution involves cutting through the culture of poverty, it may be difficult to reverse course and move to a more lenient system of broad-based public supports. It may be that we are on the threshold of a new economic future where scarcity and significant rates of unemployment are features of a permanently bygone era. It is in such a utopian time that work requirements for the poor, even with their serious shortcomings, are bound to cause the least harm.

The Dual-City Hypothesis

Some have sought to summarize the dynamics of poverty that are presently emerging in terms of "separate societies," one for the affluent who are part of the process of change, the other for those who are being left behind by economic, demographic, and technological shifts in the economy. For urban areas, the change is described by the dual-city hypothesis, the spirit of which was captured by a former deputy mayor of New York, Robert F. Wagner, Jr., when he observed that "My sense is that increasingly American cities are becoming two cities—a city of people who are making it, and a city of people who are not making it" (Wilhelm 1986a, 203).

In their book, *Separate Societies,* Goldsmith and Blakely (1992) repeated that bleak (for Americans) but commonplace observation, "The American Century is over." According to these authors, the optimistic view that the future would hold improving conditions for all citizens has been undone by the economic changes already cited here, and it has been replaced by the realistic expectation that some will be left behind by these changes. Goldsmith and Blakely believed that the consequences are especially dire for the very poor of the inner cities. Cities have acquired a dual income structure, have become *dual cities.* The upper level is represented by the ascending (at least during the 1980s) salaries and perquisites of the managers, lawyers, accountants, and financial consultants who work in the global headquarters of the major corporations whose towers occupy the costly real estate in the central business districts of the largest cities. This upper tier also includes those who provide professional services for the corporations or their highest officers and their families. The bottom tier supplies the cleaners, servants, delivery workers, and other low-paid service workers, and those with casual or no employment, the underclass. The larger the city, the greater the disparity between the incomes at the very highest and lowest income levels (Goldsmith and Blakely 1992, 107–108; Garofalo and Fogarty 1979).

On the other hand, Castells and Mollenkopf (1991) found it necessary to modify substantially the dual-city hypothesis in application to the largest city in the United States, New York. They stated that the two-strata model is so seriously out of line with the complex class structure of New York that it is misleading. On the surface, it is possible to identify the top-most and bottom-most strata of the population in terms of the dual-city model. While the city lost more than half of its manufacturing jobs and experienced an increase in its poverty rolls during the 1980s, it also experienced a boom in real estate values and the construction of office towers. Yet, the city consists of many more layers of employment and wealth than can be represented by the two most distant strata. In between, there are the largely clerical labor force, the internally stratified public sector workforce, the remaining manufacturing jobs, a highly divided service sector including self-employed entrepreneurs, and many other variations. The image of a dual city may be useful as a political slogan to draw attention to a real problem in the division of wealth and the plight of the excluded and struggling bottom layer, but it is weakened by the fact that it overlooks much of the reality that is there for critics of the concept to point out.

Nevertheless, Castells and Mollenkopf conceded that, despite its failure as a literal description, the dual-city model is useful in conceptualizing systematic changes that create increasingly difficult conditions for minority youth seeking work, while the same changes provide the basis for lucrative salaries and benefits for top executives. The dual-city concept is also useful for distinguishing between the city as a center of concentrated corporate power and individual wealth and the city as a desperate environment for poor people in search of shelter and jobs, and for distinguishing between the city as an arena of privilege for a white, male, executive elite and a place where everyone else outside the upper-most stratum hustles to make ends meet. There is more complexity to urban stratification than implied by the dual-city hypothesis; yet the metaphor has an intuitive appeal and therefore will likely persist.

The Correlates of Urban Poverty: Powerlessness, Crime, and Victimization

For those who must endure it, poverty in the city means more than having a lower income and more limited life chances than the affluent. It also means that political access and the kinds of leverages required to implement change by influencing the institutional political processes are restricted. In addition, it means a greater proximity and vulnerability to crime, both in the greater likelihood of becoming a victim and the greater risk of becoming actively engaged in committing crimes.

Powerlessness

The relative power of different groups in society is determined by differences in their access to the important decision-making processes and, assuming a given level of access, their willingness to participate. That is, a group of individuals may be said to be powerful if they have the ability to make policy decisions or are in a position to influence those who will make such decisions. How much power do the urban poor have? The answer depends on how much influence they can exert on the decisions that affect the distribution of resources and rewards in their cities. There are two ways to respond to the question. One is to consider the sizable gains that minority groups have made in the control of local urban government. The second is to ask to what extent local government is an effective unit for dealing with the problems of the cities and their poor residents.

Since the end of large-scale European immigration, the political history of the urban poor has indicated, up until recent decades, low levels of participation in the electoral process. Since the sixties, participation in local electoral politics has been on the rise among the minority poor, along with the more effective organization and mobilization of the minority vote. Several major cities, including Atlanta, Cleveland, Chicago, Detroit, and Philadelphia have elected black mayors; and minority populations have gained much wider representation at all levels of government, especially those having important urban constituencies. These political victories are important and represent practical as well as symbolic progress. Yet they also contain an obvious and bitter irony. As minorities gain control of local government, the areas governed no longer contain the resources that allow them to be maintained and operated as viable units. When local urban black leadership looks to wider, largely nonurban upstate, downstate, or federal political bodies for help, the response is often not helpful.

> *The terms for securing wider support for survival and uplift are set in large measure by the caste segregation that still divides us. In Michigan, for example, Mayor Coleman Young, state representatives Sanders and Vaughan, and school*

board president Golightly have been informed by the white majority in the state, successive national administrations, and a one-vote majority on the Supreme Court that they may seek solutions to the problems of racial ghettoization only from within the resulting area of black containment. Some increased state and federal aid will sometimes be forthcoming to ease the most immediate burdens of being confined within a central city that has lost and continues to lose much employment, business, tax base, and private capital to neighboring white suburbs; but any political logrolling by black interests will be limited to whites finally ceding local control of blacks-only ghettos to blacks. This limitation on the terms of political debate harks back to the years immediately preceding Brown [v. Board of Education] *when many whites offered to put resources, and sometimes even black control, into woefully underfunded blacks-only schools as the price to maintain Jim Crow. (Dimond 1985, 401–402)*

Newton (1975) observed that the fragmentation of the urban political arena is a general pattern, occurring throughout the large metropolitan areas of the United States, which has affected the ability of the poor to participate meaningfully in the political process. He pointed out that the 227 existing SMSAs in 1967 had 20,703 different units of government. In 1960, there were approximately four times as many government units in the St. Louis SMSA as there were nations in the world.

Newton framed his argument in terms of a criticism of *political pluralism.* For decades, pluralist and elitist theorists have been locked in a debate over just how democratic the political process is in the United States. Pluralist theory is anchored in research conducted in the 1950s in New Haven, Connecticut, that focused on the decision-making process in a number of key issues that were of concern to local government: urban renewal, public education policy, and political nominations. The published research results, most notably those of Robert Dahl (1961), supported the pluralist contention that the decision-making process involved a division of labor among top decision makers and that important policy was not decided by a few powerful individuals. Instead, decision making was carried out by different actors with particular expertise in each of the three areas of concern. Other important pluralist assumptions supported by Dahl were that various kinds of resources were available to different citizens for influencing officials and that "virtually no one, and certainly no group of more than a few individuals, [was] entirely lacking in some influence resources" (Dahl 1961, 228).

An important feature of pluralist theory is that officials are accessible to public influence and are vulnerable to public disapproval, since they lead only so long as they have the support of voters and taxpayers. Their policy making must reflect the desires of the electorate, or they will be dismissed by the public.

The opposed thesis, that power is wielded by a relatively small and largely inaccessible elite, was developed most fully by C. Wright Mills (1956) in his work *The Power Elite;* but his interest was in political control exercised at the national rather than the local level. Analyses of metropolitan elites take their lead from Floyd Hunter's (1953) study of Regional City (Atlanta). Other works, such as

Robert and Helen Lynd's (1937) Middletown (Muncie, Indiana) study, also reflected that the control of local politics might rest in the hands of a small, powerful group (in the Lynd study it was the "X" family of industrialists who owned or had contributed to every major institution in the city).

Whereas pluralist research tends to focus on the formal decision-making process involving the duly elected and appointed political leadership, the researching of local political elites has employed the "reputational method" of establishing the effective power holders within a community, whether or not these individuals are political officeholders. In the Atlanta study, Hunter submitted a list of names of potential elites to 14 persons whom he believed were knowledgeable about the local power structure and asked each to select 10 people who could be considered prominent and generally accepted leaders in the city. From their responses, he derived a shorter list of 40 names of local leaders, interviewed each of these in turn, and again asked for the names of 10 others who were thought to be widely acceptable for leadership roles in the community. He found that 12 names emerged repeatedly as an elite core of power holders within the broader 40-name group. Consistent with the elite theory's contention that cities tend to be operated by a handful of powerful individuals who might not be a part of the official city administration, none of the 12 names and only 4 of the 40 names were part of the formal government.

The debate over whether the democratic pluralist description or the power-behind-the-scenes elitist description best fits the actual decision-making process of urban areas has continued to generate study and restudy. A large part of the difficulty is thought to stem from the use of the different methods employed by the two sides in establishing who the leaders are. Elitist studies that tend to be based primarily on the reputational method have been criticized because they report only what people believe to be the case, rather than study the actual exercise of power. On the other hand, pluralists have been criticized for focusing too exclusively on the formal decision-making process of government and ignoring the influence of corporate, financial, and nongovernmental leadership.

Newton's (1975) contribution to this debate was not so much to support the power elite interpretation as to show that if the pluralist assumptions about popular access to the decision-making process had ever held, they did no longer in the metropolitanized, fragmented urban arena. He dismissed the pluralist view that the fragmentation of the urban political arena had improved the ability of each voice to be heard by providing a smaller, more accessible forum for the expression of individual political views. Instead, he pointed out that the division of the city into discrete political units had cut off the poor politically, in addition to isolating them economically. Now, with the poor relegated largely to the inner city and the few isolated enclaves outside of it, the poor and the affluent jurisdictions confronted each other in an adversarial fashion. The situation was antithetical to the pluralist model in which groups with disparate resources and interests competed within the same political arena. The economic resources of the metropolis and the economic problems of the metropolis were separated spatially from one another. From the point of view of the poor, frag-mented government was nongovernment; while for the affluent, concerned with guarding their tax dollars, such nongovernment was good government.

To the extent that the political fragmentation of the metropolitan community represents a division between races, it continues to be reflective of the pattern iden-tified as *internal colonialism.* In 1969, Blauner observed that it had already become "almost fashionable to analyze American racial conflict . . . in terms of the colonial analogy" (Blauner 1969). The analysis is based on the argument that the origins of race relations both in the United States and in European colonialism are rooted in the same expansionist traditions of world domination and the subordination of non-Western peoples. Blacks remain a colonized people in the United States be-cause their circumstances began similarly to those populations in conventional colonial situations, with forced entry and involuntary cultural transformation. To-day, their condition continues to be determined and administered largely by out-siders. The major manifestation of colonial status is the powerlessness of the peo-ple of the ghetto. In making his case, Blauner relied upon the succinct and powerful language of Kenneth Clark (1964, 10–11): "Ghettoes are the consequence of the imposition of external power and the institutionalization of powerlessness. In this respect they are in fact social, political, educational, and above all—economic col-onies. Those confined within the ghetto walls are subject peoples. They are victims of the greed, cruelty, insensitivity, guilt and fear of their masters." More recently, Feagin (1986) used the internal colonialism concept to characterize both the histor-ical and the continuing situation of blacks in the United States. Historically, he drew a parallel between research showing how immigrants from British colonies to England got the most inferior and marginal jobs and endured the highest levels of unemployment, and U.S. studies that trace how rural blacks from the underde-veloped agricultural regions of the South—analogous to a colonial region—faced similar barriers in northern cities. Consequently, the serious and systematic preju-dice and discrimination that blacks continue to face are colonial legacies.

To the extent that urban governments with their limited resources are in a po-sition to work on behalf of their poorest and most powerless citizens, and are so disposed, they may face constraints, given current economic trends, demanding that a large share of these resources go to support the ventures of large corpora-tions, rather than directly to the poor. It is useful to consider policy making as the outcome of political pressures on urban administrations to serve the needs of their various constituents. Feagin (1983) is one of those who found this conflict to be de-fined most appropriately in terms of class struggle. He observed that the direction of urban development has been determined, at least since the 1940s, by develop-ers, bankers, industrial executives, and their business and political allies who, to-gether, are the chief players in the real-life game of Monopoly. As we have re-peatedly heard from a variety of analysts, cities are built and rebuilt for profit, as witnessed by their major physical features: office towers, shopping centers, in-dustrial parks, convention centers, and suburban developments. The needs of ordinary people, and certainly of the poor, are considered only secondarily.

Today it may be more difficult than ever for even the most compassionate municipal governments to consider the needs of the poor first, as a major priority. Jones and Bachelor (1986, 202–206), who were not completely critical of the ability of major industry to work its will on the urban landscape, observed, "The reality of mobile capital and stationary cities means that businessmen hold a major bargaining chip in dealing with city officials on economic development issues." In a study of three different instances of city government and automotive industry coordination, they found that "in each case, the community effort [to retain industrial plants] is directed at making water run uphill: attracting capital where it would not normally flow. Bluntly put, businesses do not need to control city governments, because they do not need the city." Their study reviewed the cases of Detroit, Flint, and Pontiac, Michigan, three cities that made major financial concessions to auto manufacturers in order to retain employment in their area. In Detroit, the most celebrated of the cases, the city underwrote the massive expenses of relocating a General Motors plant at the same time that police were being cut from the city payroll. Other cities have been forced into similar difficult choices by the mobile capital of free enterprise. Nothing illustrates the point so well as the mobility of professional sports teams (Box 9-1).

BOX 9-1   Big League Sports Extort the Public Purse

Until 1953, except for a few stadiums that had been built by cities attempting to lure the Olympic Games, all professional sports stadiums and arenas had been built with private funds (Siegfried and Zimbalist 2000, 96). In that year, "Using a publicly financed stadium as bait, the otherwise sensible city of Milwaukee enticed the Braves to relocate from Boston . . . and the relationship between communities and sports franchises has suffered ever since" (Sullivan 1998, 55). Just as major corporations can gain financial concessions from urban government by threatening to leave town, the wealthy owners of professional sports teams can threaten to take their marbles and go elsewhere. Their goal is to get the city to use public funds to build them a new stadium. The stakes are high. Barely a generation ago, the state of the art in sports facility construction was the domed stadium, a technological marvel of its age. Times and sports fans' tastes have changed, and these multimillion dollar venues are considered obsolete. Today, the state of the art is the vastly more expensive outdoor stadium with a retractable roof. New stadiums are designed to maximize revenues from luxury suites, club boxes, concessions, catering, advertising space, parking, and

related entertainment-theme activities. The outlay in public funds is considerable. In the 1980s, the average arena cost about $100 million to build. In the 1990s, the cost rose to an average of $200 million. During the 1980s alone, 48 facilities were constructed or received a major renovation (i.e., a renovation costing more than $100 million) (Siegfried and Zimbalist 2000, 97).

Why do financially strapped cities subsidize the professional teams? There are many more cities than professional teams, and owners can play one city's offer against another to gain the maximum concession for relocation or staying where they are. The owners of professional franchises are reluctant to expand the number of teams. That would decrease their leverage in bargaining with cities. Urban governments are motivated by the fact that they can enhance or maintain their city's image as a "big league" town by attracting or retaining footloose owners. Stadiums represent potential tourist revenues, direct employment, spin-off employment, and retail activity near the park or arena, and are a way to keep the downtown (if that is where the facility is located) attractive to metro area residents and visitors who might find no other reason to go there. For reasons

BOX 9-1   *Continued*

both practical and symbolic, owners of professional teams in football, basketball, baseball, and hockey are in a position, similar to that of large industrial employers, to extort major concessions from city governments. In 1998, the Miami Heat of the National Basketball Association declared their home stadium obsolete after only eight years in their custom-built $53 million Miami Arena. They threatened to move to another city if Miami refused to build them a new $165 million arena with public funds. At first the city government capitulated, but was later forced by a public protest to withdraw the offer. The Florida Panthers of the National Hockey League, who shared the Miami Arena, quickly got neighboring Broward County to agree to build a new $212 million facility. Former National Football League commissioner Pete Rozelle once commented that the United States had entered an era of "franchise free agency" (Bernstein 1998).

There is actually a good deal of controversy about the economic yield versus the cost of subsidy for the new facilities. The evidence regarding team benefits appears clear: "Depending on the sport and the circumstance, a new stadium or arena can add anywhere from $10 to $40 million in revenues to a team's coffers." It also appears that the new stadiums may allow "demographically lesser cities (e.g., Memphis, Charlotte, Jacksonville, and Nashville) . . . to compete with larger cities with older stadiums." This means that the new style stadium potentially increases the number of cities in the competition to lure the limited number of teams (Zimbalist 1998). It is not as clear that cities that retain or attract a new or migrant team will benefit materially in a major way. Nevertheless, mayors of cities facing urban decline find the prospect of investing in order to tie a major professional sports franchise to a downtown stadium a risk worth taking. "Because some sports and entertainment complexes such as Jacobs Field and Gund Arena in Cleveland are able to attract more than four million visitors to downtown areas that were essentially avoided for years, more and more mayors justify their investments in sports facilities as an effort to enhance the vitality of urban life" (Rosentraub 1997, 180). Unfortunately, there is a lack of evidence that this urban revitalization strategy produces results. Between 1980 and 1995, central cities with downtown sports facilities experienced more rapid population decline and no better retention rates of finance, insurance, real estate, or retail jobs than cities without centrally located sports facilities. "Sports is clearly important to a substantial number of people. This importance, however, does not make it an engine for development" (Rosentraub 1997, 205–206).

Cities building new stadiums costing $200 million or more face additional outlays for infrastructure and debt service that often double the cost of the project (Zimbalist 1998). This is in the face of evidence that there are limited material benefits to be gained from stadium and arena construction. In most circumstances, sports teams have a small positive economic effect, similar perhaps to the influence of a new department store (Zimbalist 1998). Stadiums appear to be an inefficient way of creating jobs. According to a study by the Congressional Research Service, a new $177 million Baltimore football stadium would create 1,394 jobs at a cost of $127,000 each. Another study estimated that a proposed $1 billion stadium for the New York Yankees would cost $500,000 per job (Bernstein 1998). In purely economic terms, larger stadiums make limited sense.

From the fan's point of view, there is not much to be gained, except that a major league team has come to or stayed in town. "If the goal is to get close to the action, it remains the case that the nature of each sport creates a physical limit to the number of good seats that can be created" (Noll and Zimbalist 1997, 17). The ability of franchise owners to extort public funds from urban governments is an example of how consumers are hurt by oligopoly control of markets. A limited number of wealthy owners and players, and the people who can afford to occupy the limited number of luxury boxes and good seats at the game, benefit disproportionately from the public subsidy of professional sport, while the less well heeled fans will watch the games on TV on the days they are not blacked out and wonder how long before the "home team" gets a better offer from another city.

The case of Detroit and General Motors deserves special attention because of the notoriety it gained. Early in 1980, General Motors approached the city of Detroit to announce its intention to close its old and technically inefficient Cadillac and Fisher Body plants and enquire about the possibility of locating an alternate site for the construction of a three-million-square-foot replacement plant. If the company moved, the city would lose over 6,000 jobs and the prospect of $15 million per year in new property taxes. The potential loss held both practical and symbolic significance for the declining industrial city. Detroit's economic development commission rapidly undertook the search for a new site and settled on an area that was known, due to its ethnic composition, as "Poletown." The site acquired by the city covered more than 460 acres. The city used its eminent domain powers (the right of government to take private property for public use) to take over the property, evict the 3,438 residents, and demolish the 1,176 buildings (including 16 churches, 2 schools, and 1 hospital) that stood on the site. The project involved direct costs to the city of just under $200 million, which it was expected would eventually be recouped in tax revenues if the plan resulted in the retention of General Motors within the city. The company was granted a tax abatement of 50 percent on the new plant, while the city managed to get the company to agree to employ at least 3,000 workers in the more automated production process. The following factors are significant in this case: The expenditures came about as the result of a unilateral decision made by a private industry to abandon its old plants; the company set early deadlines to review the city's progress in locating, acquiring, and preparing an appropriate site, thus giving government little time to consider alternatives; and the city government undertook all of its actions and expenses without any guarantee from the company that it would not, in the end, change its plans (Fasenfest 1986, 109–117).

If, in hard times for the cities, the resources of government can be manipulated in similar fashion by the most powerful economic actors in the urban arena, there would seem to be little that ordinary people can do to assert their will in the struggle for a share of the limited pie. Yet there is a form of power that ordinary people hold, and this is in their numbers. Although the process is more conflictual and does not function as smoothly as the pluralist model of representative democracy would hold, observers have pointed to the potential of urban social movements for bringing policy more in line with the popular will. Whether these movements are conceived of broadly as coalitions of citizens' interest groups (Feagin 1983, 15–16; Castells 1983), or more narrowly in terms of social class (Castells 1985a, 93), they are seen as a potentially effective force for preventing government from neglecting any one group for too long. While Castells expected urban priorities and the patterns of development to regularly express the interests of the dominant class, at the same time they "will also be earmarked by resistance from exploited classes." It is as Piven and Cloward (1977, 36–37, 354–359) showed in their work: When the poor have remained compliant, the government sees little need to intervene in the interest of the redistribution of resources on their behalf. Rather, such intervention has most often been in response to the perceived capacity of the poor to disrupt the operation of the economic order. In marked contrast to the 1960s, the poor of the inner cities were not a major, *felt* political presence through the 1980s.

In 1992, the explosive potential of the inner cities was felt once again as South Central Los Angeles erupted in violence in response to the outcome of the trial of the police officers indicted for beating Rodney King. A chain reaction of destructive anger flickered in the streets of other U.S. cities, and then an uneasy quiet settled in again. Discussion and analysis quickly turned to questions of the authenticity of the anger that had been expressed. To what extent was the destruction and violence an expression of popular sentiment? Was it fueled by the actions of organized gangs who found the vacuum left by retreating law enforcement agents too tempting to resist? And, reflecting the standing debate within academic circles, there was the question of race. Rodney King was black, but many in the uncounted crowds who looted and destroyed property were not. What element did racism play in the anger? What element was accounted for by social class? There was no question that the decline and neglect of inner cities was a key factor, that place, and unemployment, poverty, and frustration fueled the collective expressions of anger.

Crime and Victimization

Coinciding with the improving economic conditions from the mid- to late-1990s, the United States enjoyed a decline in crime rates. The 1998 Crime Index compiled by the FBI indicated that serious offenses reported to police had declined 5 percent from the previous year, following the recent trend, and represented the lowest annual serious crime count since 1985. The rate for the most serious property and violent crimes—known as "index offenses"—was the lowest recorded since 1973 (FBI 1999, 6). Nevertheless, crime remains a serious problem, and the highest rates of serious property and violent crime are associated with urban areas.

The urban poor are disproportionately represented in national crime statistics, both as accused perpetrators and as victims. In general, people in cities are more likely to commit common crimes or be victimized. Table 9-6 reflects one of the clearest and most consistent relationships known to the social sciences—the size of cities as it relates to the incidence of crime. As the population of cities increases, the overall rates of violent and property crimes increase, as does the incidence of each of the individual categories of crime shown in the table. The one significant exception to the rule is the category of areas with less than 10,000 people, which have a higher than expected crime rate. While the reasons for the near-lockstep relationship between crime and city size are poorly understood, there is evidence to deny any simple explanation based on the idea that crime results from a simple frustration-aggression reaction due to conditions of crowding (Freedman 1975). What is clear is that urban crime remains concentrated in a relatively small number of areas within a city, areas characterized by high levels of chronic poverty, unemployment, substandard housing, teenage pregnancy, and drug use. While the economic costs of crime are spread throughout the urban population, its effects are greatest on the poor themselves.

Explanations of why crime rates are higher in the poorer districts within cities once again pit culturalist against structuralist assumptions. James Q. Wilson (1983, 14ff.) has been the leading spokesman for the culturalist position. He argued that

TABLE 9-6   Crime Rates[a] by City Size, 1998

| City Size | Violent Crime | | | | |
	Total	Murder[b]	Forcible Rape	Robbery	Aggravated Assault
250,000 or more	1,218	14.3	51	466	687
100,000–249,999	758	8.6	45	252	457
50,000–99,999	588	5.3	40	177	368
25,000–49,999	454	3.7	32	118	300
10,000–24,999	373	3.3	27	83	259
Less than 10,000	397	3.0	28	59	305

| City Size | Property Crime | | | |
	Total	Burglary	Larceny Theft	Motor Vehicle Theft
250,000 or more	5,840	1,186	3,655	1,000
100,000–249,999	4,867	943	3,016	907
50,000–99,999	4,712	958	3,235	517
25,000–49,999	4,247	842	3,015	390
10,000–24,999	3,913	733	2,893	286
Less than 10,000	4,249	779	3,226	243

Source: Federal Bureau of Investigation 1999. Table 16, 188–189.
[a]Offenses known to the police per 100,000 people.
[b]Includes non-negligent manslaughter.

the economic position of the poor, in and of itself, cannot be used to explain their apparent disproportionate involvement in crime. He pointed to the expansion of programs designed to assist the poor and the young in the 1960s, as well as the greater prosperity of that decade, which together "brought greater plenty to more people" than ever before in the history of the United States. At the same time, "crime soared."

Most recently, Wilson's point of view linking crime to moral rather than material impoverishment has been advanced by Bennett, DiIulio, and Walters (1996). Writing for a popular audience and hoping to sway public opinion and thereby social policy, in much the way Wilson had, Bennett (the former drug czar and secretary of education) and his colleagues proposed a "get tough" policy toward youthful offenders, whom they predicted will become an increasingly ruthless predatory force if authorities don't crack down hard, putting more offenders in prison for longer periods of time.

Bennett and others rely on Wilson's (1983, 16–33) observations that during the 1960s and 1970s crime grew despite public programs and an improving economy. Wilson's point was that the material deprivations that attend poverty are not a direct cause of crime, but that many of the poor had become part of a "lower class" that he defined in terms of its uncivil cultural values and habits.

Retail fortress: In the year following the 1996 urban rioting in which many businesses were destroyed by arson, Walgreens built this pharmacy surrounded by a high chain-link fence in one of St. Petersburg's affected neighborhoods. The fence, with its single strategic access point, caused resentment among local residents as business proceeded as usual.

According to Wilson (1983, 16–33), crime grew not because people were poor, but because many among the poor had become part of a lower class, a category set off by its *cultural* values and habits. The growth of this category has been marked by several factors: the increasing number, among those eligible, who have applied for and received welfare payments; the increasing use of drugs; and the increasing proportion of the poor who are young. This last feature has produced a "critical mass," similar to the concept of the same name developed by Fischer (1975, 1984) that was introduced in Chapter 4. Wilson used the idea to explain how the dominant numbers of young people on the street allowed them to set the moral tone for the conduct of public life. Public life, in turn, is marked by a lack of "community," little concern with standards of public behavior and no respect for property. It represents a breakdown of the informal social controls that normally enforce lawful and respectable behavior. The assumption is that a set of internal control mechanisms govern the behavior of most people: Most of us are unwilling to risk the disapproval of others in our community. Members of the lower class are unconcerned with rules of propriety regarding their behavior and that of others; in addition, they fail to assert any control over their offspring, resulting in a generally disordered and threatening public environment.

Wilson's interpretation of the involvement of the poor in crime is strongly reminiscent of the culture of poverty argument. It has produced strong criticism and provoked a continuation of debate, both about the causes of crime and the degree to which the poor are victims of structured inequality versus their own attitudes and habits. Since, in Wilson's view, engaging in criminal behavior is the result of a lack of commitment on the part of criminals to conventional morality and guidelines of behavior, the only policies that make sense are those that convince potential lawbreakers of stern, swift, and certain punishment by law. That is, in terms of social policy, crime should be dealt with primarily through attention to more stringent formal social controls: aggressive enforcement of laws, speedy trials and sentencing, and appropriately severe punishments. General social programs designed for improving the economic conditions of the poor, while they may have merit in their own right, are simply not effective tools for reducing criminal behavior. This is because, according to the argument, people steeped in a lower-class system of values are still culturally lower class and can be expected to behave accordingly, even if given training and more money.

The controversy over the linkages between poverty or inequality in general and criminal behavior will prove difficult to resolve. Part of the problem involves the ideological question of the degree to which higher than average rates of certain types of criminal behavior represent a moral failing or the limited options of the poor or the economically cut-off. Many researchers are motivated by intuition to find the causal connection, but questions of what to measure and how to interpret findings have left the debate open. Take the example presented by Currie (1985, 144–149) of two Highland Parks in the Midwest. Highland Park, Michigan, is part of the inner city of Detroit. It had a population just under 30,000 in 1983; in that year, one family in three was poor; there were 27 murders, 55 reported rapes, and 796 robberies. Highland Park, Illinois, a community of about the same size, is a lakeside suburb just north of Chicago. In 1983, one family in 67 was poor; in that year, there were no murders, one reported rape, and seven robberies. Clearly, there was a link between living standards and crime here, but what was it? Is poverty itself the key variable? Are people driven by the desperation of their circumstances, by anger and frustration, or by weak moral standards to commit more crime? Of what relative importance is race? Social isolation? The many recent studies of crime and economic circumstance have attempted to address these issues.

Currie found the most convincing causal linkages between *unemployment* and crime. He cited the work of M. Harvey Brenner (1976) who demonstrated a complex relationship between lack of work and criminal involvement. Brenner found an intermediary behavioral connection between unemployment and property and violent crime in drug and alcohol abuse. Unemployment is associated with higher rates of drug use, and the high cost of drug dependency with property crime. Unemployment is also associated with increased alcohol use, and alcohol use is associated with violent crime. Other research from the 1970s failed to find a correlation between imprisonment and prior periods of unemployment (Parker and Horowitz 1986), but that may be because many out-of-work youth and other discouraged poor were not actively seeking work and, therefore, were not counted among the unemployed.

More recent research involving a state-by-state comparison of Uniform Crime Rates and unemployment due to worker displacement did find a connection between unemployment and crime. Once again, we find a mediating factor: in this case, a form of political consciousness. Grant and Martinez (1997) observed that it is important to examine the labor relations histories of local economies in order to understand different rates of criminal activity. They argued that there has been in some areas since the 1940s a well-established "capital-labor accord," a sort of good-faith moral contract between corporations and organized labor, based on a sense of the cooperative working out of differences between labor and capital toward the mutual self-interest of the parties. But the emerging global economy has presented capital with a new set of rules for survival, including the need to lower the costs of production associated with labor through automation or by moving assembly operations overseas, which leads to a sense of abandonment on the part of labor. In this context, attitudes of displaced labor toward the option of engaging in criminal behavior are imbedded in the sense of relative rights and wrongs.

> *We are arguing that how people respond to economic restructuring is partly a function of their imbeddedness in the capital-labor accord, which has defined the terms of work/property relations throughout the post-war period. We thus understand crime to be politically motivated, and, loosely speaking, a collective response, though not necessarily in the extreme sense of being an organized and calculated attempt to bring about revolution. (776)*

However, they were linking at least some criminal reactions to a form of class consciousness important enough to show up in a nationwide study of property crime rates. A city-by-city analysis led Olzak and Shanahan (1996) to conclude that a more overt and collective expression of politically motivated criminal behavior—the urban riot—is also predicted by the local contraction of employment opportunities.

The impact of lack of employment opportunity on crime rates may be compounded by segregation and race. It is likely that the grim employment prospects for young black urban males makes the meaning of unemployment fundamentally different for them than for others and may have a different effect on criminal involvement and crime rates. Inner-city unemployment is more likely to be perceived as permanent by those affected, rendering them more likely to consider illegitimate options (Duster 1987, 306–309).

Research conducted in black, Latino, and white neighborhoods in Brooklyn revealed that the amount of illegal activities they harbored and the length of time that young men remained involved depended largely on the availability of economic opportunities. The black neighborhood, with shrinking numbers of commercial establishments, experienced a higher number of predatory crimes than the other neighborhoods due to the fact that there were few opportunities for targeting commercial properties. The Latino neighborhood contained factories owned and operated by outsiders, which were a favorite target of young burglars. Stolen goods were sold within the neighborhood at discount prices to residents who were ambivalent about the morality of the practice. In neither of these neighborhoods were residents acquiescent with regard to predatory crime that victimized *local* people, and it was highly advisable that young residents pursue any such activities outside their own territory. In the white neighborhood, participation in criminal activity was reportedly lower among young people. Although crime among white youths was economically motivated, it typically ended when young men found jobs through family and neighborhood networks (McGahey 1986, 253–254). It was this last feature that set apart delinquent activities among the three groups—the probability of a satisfactory economic future within the legitimate mainstream.

Somewhat distinct from issues of unemployment, the question of the relationship between *inequality* or *poverty* and crime has also been investigated by researchers (Bursik and Grasmick 1993; Krivo and Peterson 1996; Messner and Tardiff 1986; Martinez 1996; Shihadeh and Flynn 1996; Patterson 1991; Heimer 1997). The research most often attempts to present a balanced treatment of structural and cultural factors that may affect life chances and influence crime. Once again, among the structural influences that have been considered is economic restructuring, which has narrowed employment opportunities for the poor in inner cities. Most writers also point to the geographic mobility of the middle and working class who have left the inner city and the poor behind. This ecological factor, as we have termed it in an earlier section in this chapter, is actually a bridge between cultural and structural interpretations of disadvantage. It focuses on the relative isolation of the urban poor and the emergence of a local culture that is destructive to any hope of social mobility of the inner-city poor. Among the destructive cultural influences associated with crime, the most frequently identified include young single women giving birth, routine family violence, and the adoption of communication and other personal styles that are out of step with mainstream expectations and therefore inhibit upward mobility (Krivo and Peterson 1996; Shihadeh and Flynn 1996; Heimer 1997).

A potential liability of empirical studies that attempt to balance the effects of global structural influences with neighborhood or family influences on behavior is that the remoteness of global factors may provide a built-in tendency to emphasize the locally observable causes. This tendency is evident in Heimer's (1997) account of violent delinquency, perhaps because she dealt with the behavior of young people. She found "structural" factors at best to be poorly defined and chose instead the *differential association theory* of deviance, which attributes criminal behavior to neighborhood and other local (family) influences. This theory has a decidedly local focus, arguing as it does that criminal behavior results from the lessons learned within a deviant subculture and involves the internalization of the attitudes and skills required for becoming a committed, successful lawbreaker. Heimer acknowledged social class as a relevant consideration in understanding violent delinquency, but her discussion of class is almost solely in terms of negative behavioral characteristics attributed to the lower class, especially family violence and the consequent acceptance of violent patterns of behavior in general. This is much different from a consideration of social class that attributes patterns of criminal behavior to feelings of alienation, anger, or other antagonistic perceptions of young people toward wider society. Instead, class is seen as a useful variable because of the different values and behaviors—cultural factors—that are attached to it. Another cultural interpretation of higher rates of violence among young *black* males emphasizes the effects of the wider culture. King (1997) pointed to the violent history of slavery and lynchings, and the influence of images of violence in the media coupled with the message that wider society places a relatively low value on the lives of African American male teenagers and young men. He described these as the relevant cultural rather than subcultural considerations in understanding violence among a particular segment of the inner-city poor.

Some of the studies that attempt to balance structural and cultural explanations also address the issue of race and the increasing segregation and isolation of poor people in black ghettoes. This work generally follows the argument of William Julius Wilson (1978, 1987) (distinguish him from James Q. Wilson, although some similarities will be evident), which warns that once historical and structural factors are taken into account in explaining the plight of people in the ghettoes, social science must be prepared to look critically at the pathologies that arise in these environments—that is, to look at the effects of the local culture. Shihadeh (Shihadeh and Flynn 1996; Shihadeh and Ousey 1996) emphasized the ecology of *social isolation* that is associated with high crime rates in the inner city. Black social isolation refers to the segregation of poor blacks in neighborhoods that are increasingly homogeneous in terms of class as well as race, resulting in a concentration of social disadvantage. Not only are lower-income minority neighborhoods cut off from an adequate supply of entry-level jobs and the information networks that might help people find work, but also the people who live there are surrounded by dysfunctional ghetto adaptations that represent countercultural habits, which place a behavioral barrier between them and employment. What the authors had in mind includes "the cool and aggressive pose of young men, where clothing, hairstyles, facial expressions and gait are all used to shore up an identity of physical toughness," where childbearing is the means to recognition and prestige for unmarried girls, where violence is seen as an acceptable method of resolving grievances. In these neighborhoods, where there is a failure of neighbors to exert control over the behavior of others, the stigma of social and economic failure is removed—even the stigma of having served time in prison is neutralized (Shihadeh and Flynn 1996, 1331–1332). And, given the isolation of these communities in terms of class and race—a pattern of isolation made worse by affluent suburbanization—there are no alternative role models (Shihadeh and Ousey 1996).

While those who make the argument say it is not a culture of poverty interpretation (Shihadeh and Flynn 1996), they point out that ghetto street culture stands convention on its head, that it adopts a set of styles and a logic that are perfectly opposed to the way people who are going to get ahead in the world behave and think. Their findings, based on a comparison of the numbers of major crimes and the degree of segregation in large cities (alternatively, the degree of suburbanization), bear out at least the physical or spatial aspect of the isolation argument. That is, cities with higher levels of black isolation have higher levels of black murder and robbery (Shihadeh and Flynn 1996), and cities with higher levels of suburbanization also have higher black inner-city crime rates (Shihadeh and Ousey 1996). Krivo and Peterson (1996) also articulated the relationship between social class and crime in terms of cultural and behavioral qualities, but argued that the concentration of poverty in not simply poor but *extremely disadvantaged* neighborhoods is the key link to crime, not necessarily racial isolation. Their research, comparing crime and poverty in different neighborhoods in Columbus, Ohio, showed that while gross rates of violence were nearly three times as high in black neighborhoods, the difference between black and white neighborhoods was drastically reduced when the economic status of residents was controlled for (see Shihadeh and Ousey [1996] for contrasting findings). They suggested that the small remaining differences might be explained by the greater concentration of public housing in black neighborhoods, and by the larger and more isolated character of extremely disadvantaged black districts.

To summarize, there is clearly a link between both unemployment and poverty, on the one hand, and violence and street crime, on the other. The degree to which this relationship is directly determined by social status or economic exclusion and the degree to which criminal behavior is mediated by cultural values and habits remain open to question. To show that there is a statistical link between poverty and crime, and then to posit the importance of the moral breakdown of poor neighborhoods as a key to understanding that linkage, may obscure as much as it appears to explain.

It would be foolish to dispute the notion that poor neighborhoods carry within them cultural influences that encourage criminal options. However, this is not the same as saying that we have discovered within the subcultural attributes of poverty the root causes of criminal behavior. We must still explain what has caused these cultural pockets to be so large and widespread in society and to affect the behavior of a greater proportion of some racial groups than others in a society where racial stratification is so clearly established. We need to think more about the potential implications—in a society where white people control the institutions, the news media, and the economy—of saying that part of the reason that poor black people have more problems than white people is that they are developing styles and habits in isolation from whites and others who have become members of the dominant society by virtue of leaving those habits and minority-dominated neighborhoods behind.

If, when we say this, we mean that poor minorities are physically cut off from the opportunity structure—from education and jobs—that is one thing. To say that the institutions and habits of those minorities are the problem is another. One need only consider the debate over *ebonics,* the question of the legitimacy or integrity of distinctively black, inner-city language patterns—patterns rooted in centuries of tradition (Jackson 1997; Smitherman 1997)—to understand the hazard of thinking that cultural adaptations to political and economic realities are the problem. Minority patterns of speech and other forms of self-expression have developed in isolation because people were not only excluded but oppressed, and these oppressed peoples needed coded forms of expression, which became covert idioms of defiance. These codes continue to develop today as systems of communication that make members of the mainstream, the majority, uncomfortable because they are difficult for outsiders to understand. It is only natural, when the outsiders are in the mainstream, for them to demand the abandonment of linguistic traditions that echo defiance, and it is only natural for those within oral traditions that allow them to articulate themselves in an artful, familiar manner to resist. When members of the majority make the standardization of speech a criterion for admission to full social and economic participation, as they have the power to do, their demand lacks an appreciation of the extraordinary sacrifice they are requesting. It may be argued that a *truly balanced* approach to understanding structural and cultural influences on poverty in general, and crime in particular, would begin by recognizing the priority of the structural roots of inequality. Then, cultural adaptations can be appropriately interpreted as what people have done to make their way and to realize their ambitions for limited amounts of comfort, power, and influence.

Today, part of the structural reality of crime is that there is an informal economy operating throughout the world, some of it operating outside the law, much of it within the boundaries of large cities, where it flourishes in poor neighborhoods, shanty towns, and ethnic minority neighborhoods—because these are the places where conditions restrict opportunities for legal employment and entrepreneurship. The illegal sectors of the informal economy include drug traffic, prostitution and other illegal services, extortion, and the full range of the usual street crimes. The strategy of attacking or correcting the subcultures that we encounter in these places, thereby attempting to get at the root causes of crime, is questionable. It is the same as the strategy of building more prisons, which will accommodate a disproportionate number of the poor and other marginalized peoples of any society in which crime is a problem. The link between poverty or economic dislocation and crime has been established. To then pursue interpretations that cause us to consider cultural attributes of the poor and the otherwise disconnected may be a distraction from the main issue. Some would say that such a conclusion involves a value judgment. The conclusion and the anticipated criticism are a reflection of the ideological nature of the debate over the causes of crime.

A number of points should be made in closing our discussion of crime. First, with regard to crime and race, our discussion shifts too easily from a discussion of one to a discussion of the other. This reflects two real features of criminal issues in the United States. Although most crimes are not committed by African Americans, the vast majority of members of this minority feel the same way about crime as do other members of society, and the bulk of criminal episodes are intraracial, the prevailing mind-set has historically identified crime, especially violent crime, as interracial, with black perpetrators and white victims. Also, blacks and Latinos are disproportionately represented among prison populations. Nevertheless, dwelling on the connection between race and crime as we have done here associates, however inadvertently, minorities with negative images. Also, regardless of whether cultural or structural factors are emphasized in discussions of problems associated with minorities, one may come away with an image of a victimized people in desperate circumstances: Either they victimize themselves through dysfunctional subcultures or are helpless in the face of historical or global forces that are pushing them aside. Both images are inaccurate. There is a new emphasis in African American scholarship that stresses the integrity of the culture of working-class African Americans and the strength reflected in the efforts of families and individuals to make a life for themselves under the adverse conditions that have prevailed historically and still prevail today (Goings and Mohl 1996). A discussion of the problems still faced by this minority should take nothing away from this positive emphasis.

To focus on the illegitimate behaviors of the disadvantaged, and especially the behaviors of disadvantaged strata of minorities, causes us to miss two other critical features of crime in the United States. Critics have argued that an overemphasis on the role of the poor in most thinking about crime ignores the more serious kinds of deviance in high places that can result in higher monetary costs and more suffering societywide than what the poor can manage to do to each other and to the rest of us. Since our interest here is urban sociology, however, government and corporate crimes are too tangential to warrant exploration.

A further consequence of focusing on the criminal behavior of the minority poor is to miss the fact that the majority of the victims of inner-city crime are also minorities. This is the intraracial feature of crime and victimization just noted. Minority poor have the highest victimization rates for property and violent crimes. Among a sample of African American men and women aged 65 or older in Atlantic City, New Jersey, 51 percent knew someone who had been victimized within the previous twelve-month period, and 27 percent had themselves been victimized. Not surprisingly, 83 percent of the men and 70 percent of the women (men had somewhat higher victimization rates) were classified as having a "high fear of crime" (Joseph 1997). While the rest of society continues to worry about the dangers that city streets full of poor young minority males pose for them, there appears to be less of a sense of urgency that the greatest danger these young people pose is to each other. Black men are roughly six times as likely to be killed as white men. Whether or not an individual becomes engaged in violence on the inner-city block or in the public housing project is not entirely a matter of personal choice. Here, the day-to-day strategy involves avoiding trouble when possible and confronting it when necessary. Williams and Kornblum's (1985, 74) young subjects told them that it was better to face a fight and lose than to run away. Those who appeared afraid to fight faced intimidation and extortion; in effect, access to public space was denied to them. In such an environment, where there is no opportunity to appeal to the societal forces of law and order, there is an appealing logic to the adage "strength in numbers." The first-person accounts of Sanyika Shakur (1993), Nathan McCall (1994) and others of gang life, criminal involvement, and

BOX 9-2   In the Line of Battle

One of the troubling things about a war far away is that, after the initial shock of the first news of casualties, we become numbed by the continuing reports of dead and wounded. This emotional callousing-over reportedly happens for combatants and for civilians caught in the line of battle, but it is different. People are forever changed by the experience of warfare. Samual Greengard and Charlene Marmer Solomon (1995) spoke to young people in some of the violent neighborhoods of Los Angeles. For the most part, their essay allows those whose lives had been touched by violence to speak for themselves. Here are some of their words. A 14-year-old boy reported that he was watching a little league baseball game with his parents. "All of a sudden, we started hearing these loud noises, like firecrackers, and we all started running because it sounded like they were getting closer. It was two rival gangs shooting at each other. I was really scared. I wanted to stay as close to my family as I could. I saw my mom start running with my sister, and then my dad grabbed us and we all started running. . . . Now, whenever I see on the news or in the paper there are all these incidents where innocent people get killed . . . I see my family running."

An 18-year-old eleventh grade student counts herself lucky because no one in her family has died or been injured as a result of violence. She can't say the same of friends. Some time after her first brush with violence, when a girlfriend standing beside her was wounded in a drive-by shooting, she was at a party when an argument broke out between rival gangs. "The guns came out . . . I ran out of the house. . . . A bunch of us were on the ground . . . I heard a lot of shots, and then a guy I know yells, 'They hit me! They hit me! I don't want to die!' Then I hear an ambulance. But before the ambulance could leave, I heard him say one last time, 'I'm dying, I'm dying.' And then he died. He was 21—he had a little daughter."

Psychologists say that young people exposed to this kind of violence are permanently transformed; they never get over it. One who has worked with young people and families of victims says the result is that "There is a feeling of helplessness and powerlessness that goes along with being a victim of a crime. There's usually a general preoccupation with the event—and that makes it difficult to focus on other things. For kids, there's a profound feeling of vulnerability. They believe nobody can protect them. And when kids are victimized in a significant way, they are no longer able to trust; they see the world as a menacing place. No amount of reassurance can make them feel safe again."

the brutality of the streets are chilling. The families of these young gang members were not at all in total disarray, but the streets of the segregated society in which they lived were the compelling influence in their lives. Children in their preteen years are recruited into a living hell where they will learn to kill and many will be killed, where all are likely to do some prison time once they outgrow the juvenile detention system.

Wider society expresses confusion and distaste regarding the largely intraracial warfare between young men that takes place in the inner city. Wider society insists that order be restored by the police. In the inner city, where armed teenagers police their own neighborhoods, trespassers, other armed teenagers, may be shot on sight. An adversarial stalemate has crystallized between the desperate young men and society. Some scholars argue that some proportion of poor and especially minority prison incarceration rates is due to prejudicial arrest and sentencing procedures. While some room for debate remains, evidence continues to accumulate that courts and especially pretrial decisions are biased against Latino and black defendants (Spohn, Gruhl, and Welch 1987, 181–186). Even the way crimes are classified in the abstract and the length of sentences for particular crimes can have implications for the unequal treatment of minorities. Minnesota law classified possession of three or more grams of crack cocaine as a third-degree felony punishable by up to twenty years of imprisonment: possession of up to ten grams of cocaine powder was a fifth-degree felony punishable by a maximum of five years in prison. Ninety-seven percent of persons arrested for crack were black, while 80 percent arrested for possession of powder were white (Alexander and Gyamerah 1997).

Poor people in the inner city have a different relationship with the official organs of state than do most other Americans. Public hospitals are crowded; emergency rooms are places where an individual can wait for hours to be treated for serious illness or injuries by an overworked staff; and the wait for an ambulance is more life-threatening than in other urban districts. Few poor people have medical insurance. Police are slow to respond to emergency calls; they are perceived as unsympathetic and ineffectual, as antagonistic and dangerous. At a time when there is general concern about security and safety in the public schools, inner-city students are particularly concerned about protection from their fellow students. In the United States, perhaps 100,000 students carry a gun to school each day, according to estimates. A survey of inner-city high schools in four states found 35 percent of males and 11 percent of female students readily admitted that they carried a gun (they weren't specifically asked if they regularly took their gun to school). Over 11 percent of male students and 1.5 percent of female urban high school students in Seattle said they owned a gun, and a third of these reported having shot at someone at least once. Those inner-city students who regularly carry weapons are more likely to be involved in illegal activities, but a significant number reported they carried a weapon to defend themselves (Page and Hammermeister 1997). In recognition of the hazards of attending school, 35 percent of the largest U.S. school districts employ metal detectors. An article in *American School & University* recommends for the purpose of enhancing safety that classroom telephones with quick-dial 911 features be installed (consistent with the recommendation of the U.S. Department of Education and the National School Safety Center), that teachers and other school officers be equipped with wireless phones, and that surveillance cameras be set up inside and outside the schools to monitor activity continuously—in addition to the installation of metal detectors (Day 1999, 54–55). Such an environment may be perceived by inner-city youth as a reminder of the general hazards of their existence and do little to foster a feeling that they are secure for the time being from confrontation with rivals. At any rate, they are likely to know from experience that security measures designed for their protection do not extend beyond the immediate school environment. Part of the structural reality in which poor people live involves the nature of, or lack of, institutional support from various layers and agencies of government. When a segment of the population is neglected or allocated substandard support, that is not a reflection of the values of the neglected poor or minority population itself, but of the values of the wider society in which they live.

A Conclusion: Structure, Culture, and the Poor

The majority of serious academic writers on the subject, including Oscar Lewis himself, acknowledge the structural roots of poverty. At the same time, critics complain that structuralists have been afraid to acknowledge the self-destructiveness of the behavior and values of the poor. What bothers the culturalists, who want to talk about the need to do something about the values and behavior of the poor, is that structuralist interpretations are a dead end in terms of suggesting social policy. Structural interpretations see the causes of poverty in a market economy that is bound, both periodically and in the long term, to exclude many workers because they have become redundant or surplus to the market's demand for labor. In the view of culturalists, structuralist interpretations, which see poverty built into the normal workings of the economy, are a recipe for despair, seeming to offer the poor an invitation to *adopt* a culture of poverty attitude. But, recall that Lewis himself observed that the marginal and expendable position of the poor and working poor is precisely what made a culture of poverty attitude a logical philosophical adaptation for people with tenuous ties to the economy.

It is true that interpretations that focus primarily on the structural roots of poverty do not hold out much hope for the poor. This is because the structuralist interpretation is a *radical* critique of social arrangements. That is, the structural argument says that the arrangement by which the opportunities for work and rewards are organized and distributed under the market system is fundamentally flawed if full participation and employment are assumed to be desirable goals. The way that the market system is currently changing, producing a contraction of opportunities for work and reward for the lower social classes, undermines their already vulnerable position. The despair, perceived helplessness, and anger of the most disadvantaged elements of the population, especially the black urban underclass, make a lot of sense in this view.

If growing urban unemployment and poverty result from remote and inexorable changes in the global economy, there is little scope for effective local policy. Because the power of national and local governments to alter global conditions is dubious, we have seen something of a shift in emphasis from ultimate (structural) causes of poverty to intermediate (cultural) causes of poverty in the most widely read current accounts. These attend to the community, the failure of culture-bearing institutions, and the failure of will within the affected areas. Attention has once again turned to the poor and the question of the degree to which they are responsible for their choices, their behavior, and their condition. The behavior of inner-city poor people is too often unproductive (many drop out of the labor force), apolitical (many fail to engage in the political process), and criminal (many are involved in the use of illicit drugs and mutual victimization).

William Julius Wilson continues to be a strong voice in the analysis of inner-city poverty. In 1987, his widely read book, *The Truly Disadvantaged*, extended his argument that contemporary racism is not the primary cause of inner-city black poverty (12); that the ultimate causes of poverty are deindustrialization and the transformation of employment opportunities (180–181); and that the failure of social science to provide an adequate analysis of inner-city poverty stems from the liberal posture of most of those who study it. Liberal ideals and sympathy for the poor have made social scientists afraid to confront the unpleasant truth that the inner-city poor are caught up in their own tangle of pathology, which is their collective cultural response to hard times (6–15). In all, Wilson shifted the focus of the culture of poverty argument only slightly in his emphasis on the detriment of the homogenization of social class within black inner-city neighborhoods. The view expressed by Wilson, which has since been often repeated and widely accepted, is that the social mobility of some African Americans in the past few decades has left ghetto neighborhoods without hard-working, successful role models and stabilizing influences.

In 1996 Wilson published *When Work Disappears*, the title referring to the familiar "mismatch" theme, reviewed earlier in this chapter—the decline of industrial jobs in the inner-city. In this work, he inched yet closer to an emphasis on structural factors that perpetuate inordinate levels of black urban unemployment. There is also an acknowledgment of the racist motivations and worldview of contemporary white employers who *are* prejudiced and *do* openly and deliberately discriminate against blacks, especially young black men (111 ff). Yet, his fundamental position remains unaltered. That is, the problem faced by poor inner-city African Americans is, in part, a structural one based on class rather than race and, to the extent that race is a continuing factor in black poverty, this stems as much from ghetto culture and values as from discrimination and segregation. In a chapter titled "The Meaning and Significance of Race," Wilson reached the following characteristic conclusion: "In summary, the issue of race in the labor market cannot be reduced to the presence of discrimination." The loss of inner-city blue-collar employment has reduced the availability of jobs for black men, "who grow bitter and resentful in the face of their employment prospects and often manifest or express these feelings in their harsh, often dehumanizing, low-wage work settings." Their antagonism and erratic work histories cause them to be labeled as undesirable workers and provoke employers to prefer immigrants and women. However, local cultural influences within the poor African American community also need to be considered, because these men are "Embedded in ghetto neighborhoods, social networks and households that are not conducive to employment" (Wilson 1996, 144).

There is still "balance" in this view of factors that are external and internal. There is also implicit balance in assessing responsibility for the perpetuation of the problems. That is, once we have accounted for the structural roots of the disproportionate share of the burden of poverty borne by blacks, it appears that they must now shoulder their share of finding a solution by overcoming the more self-defeating subcultural habits of thought and action. At the level of national policy,

Wilson still favored an approach that is not race specific, that addresses the structural problems of the reduction of jobs: The problem is still that *work* is disappearing, not that racism has not.

Another important contemporary voice in the analysis of inner-city poverty is Cornel West. He has seemingly taken Wilson's advice, and has provided to date by far the most sensitive and detailed interpretation of the nature of despair among the black urban underclass. His book, *Race Matters* (1993), quickly became a best-seller, and so his message reached large numbers who are interested in race and poverty. Like Wilson, he recognized that urban poverty is rooted in the decline of industry. He accepted the argument that it is necessary to incorporate both structural and cultural (behavioral) factors in a holistic analysis of black inner-city poverty. Where liberal structuralists are afraid to consider cultural factors, he focused on the *nihilistic* threat to black America that is contained in the "monumental eclipse of hope" (12) that characterizes the most troubled element of the black population. West more emphatically acknowledged the importance of contemporary racism in limiting the roles that blacks are permitted in mainstream society. He is angry, but his tone is conciliatory. His message is essentially spiritual.

According to West, there is a pervasive sense of futility and powerlessness, meaninglessness, and a destructive disposition toward the world and self in inner-city neighborhoods ghettoized along the lines of class as well as race. This is the tragic response of people, especially young people, without resources, who face "the workings of U.S. capitalist society" (16). Not only has the capitalist society wrenched away the jobs that had previously afforded a living to inner-city populations, but also, just as importantly for West, capitalism has laid down the ethos of a cutthroat market economy devoid of "any faith for deliverance or hope for freedom" (16).

In addition to narrowing the goals of ordinary individuals to those of private gain and privatized consumption, the marketplace metaphor has neutralized leadership. In contrast to the vigor of Malcolm X or Martin Luther King, black political leadership has largely become self-serving and timid (38), and black intellectuals quickly learn that the way to secure faculty positions in the most prestigious universities is to offer no more than the gentlest criticisms compatible with conservative worldviews (41). Meanwhile, black youth express their frustration in unprecedented, climbing suicide rates and in callous, cold-hearted violence toward others. "Sadly, the combination of the market way of life, poverty-ridden conditions, black existential *angst,* and the lessening fear of white authorities, has directed most of the anger, rage and despair toward fellow black citizens, especially toward black women who are the most vulnerable in our society and in black communities" (18).

While we must never lose sight of the "structural conditions that shape the sufferings" of poor urban blacks, West's recommendations for improvement are focused on what the people of these communities can (and he believed must) do for themselves. He called for a spiritual uplift, a psychic conversion where self-hatred and hatred of the other are replaced by self-love and an affirmation of black culture. The movement will need to restore within black communities the institutional apparatus necessary for support, since "For the first time there are now no longer viable institutions and structures in black America that can effectively transmit values such as hope, virtue, sacrifice, risk, and putting the needs of others higher or alongside one's own needs" (West 1992, 196). A successful movement would need to revive the former vigor of African American institutions ranging from the mosque and church, the family, and such commonplace gathering points as the barbershop and beauty shop. West called on the black community to develop their own black criteria for self-evaluation. "A love ethic must be at the center of a politics of conversion" (1993, 19).

West provided us with a long-overdue correction to the old culture of poverty argument, and he has done so by updating the culturalist argument while arguing that we must remain cognizant of the structural roots at the base of institutional decay and individual despair. He updated the image of the culture of the inner-city poor by giving prominence to its previously neglected but most dynamic feature, rage. The poor are not simply dispirited; they, especially the young, are angry, and they act on their anger. There is a political component to the culture of the poor. It is not embodied in voter participation but in violence, turned outward against nonblacks and the middle class, but more often turned inward against peers and self, in high homicide rates and climbing suicide rates for young black men.

West sidestepped the question of the structural exclusion of the black underclass, not by ignoring it as the ultimate cause of poverty, but by focusing instead on remedies for correcting tendencies toward reputed self-hatred and, thereby, on the importance of black institutions and courageous black leadership. His recommendations for change are directed not at the ultimate causes of inequality, but on their ultimate consequences, the weakening of black institutions and negative self-image. The rejection of the structuralist interpretation is not based on a rejection of its basic thesis, but a rejection of the imputed powerlessness of individuals and communities to resist its negative consequences. West's message to black America is clearly of the need to continue to struggle to carve out a livelihood and self-regard that is not a simple by-product of racism, neglect, and an economy that relegates many to poor work or no work. The call is to use black institutions, such as churches and mosques, to strengthen self-regard and individual purpose, to resist victimization. Most of all, he calls on individuals to become the agents of their own futures.

West's philosophical idealism (the position that emphasizes the autonomy of ideas) is an important point of reference in current discourse on poverty and race in America. It does not beg the question of the structural roots of poverty; neither does it address the question of whether or how that structure is to be modified. West's recommendations remain in the realm of culture and advice to the victim. There is room for another position in the discussion of the culture of the underclass, a materialist interpretation (material conditions give rise to particular ways of thinking) that appreciates subcultural adaptations on their own political, moral, and aesthetic terms. Tommy Lott's (1992) essay on the political aesthetic of inner-city rap music serves to illustrate the point.

Lott began by accentuating the fact that the present generation of inner-city black youth has been "marooned" by economic change. It is a mockery, in this view, to think that the success of the black middle class can provide any sort of demonstration effect for poor black youth. The idea of the potential benefits of black middle-class role-modeling of economic success perpetuates the myth that the problem of black poverty is the result of the inadequate acculturation of poor blacks. There is, Lott believed, a sophisticated awareness among those left behind that this kind of "bootstrap uplift" philosophy "utilizes token models of success to rationalize the exclusion of the masses of black people" (78–79). He observed that any emphasis on differences between the culture of middle-class blacks and that of poor blacks implies that structural conditions are right for black social mobility for those who know how to take advantage of opportunities. He pointed out that if one takes this view, one has come dangerously close to implying that the dysfunctional nature of the culture of poor inner-city blacks, not the system of distribution, is what limits their escape from the ghetto. Both Wilson and West, in different ways, took the position that the inner-city culture of poor blacks is a problem.

Lott argued that it is a solution, of sorts. The culture of the inner-city ghetto is a political culture, a manifestation of an angry awareness that the political and economic structure of social change has left many people behind, that a disproportionate number of those people are black, and that the present generation of inner-city blacks, in particular, will never have had a chance for participation in mainstream economy and society. What is seen from the outside by members of mainstream society as socially dysfunctional behavior is a natural by-product of life on dangerous inner-city streets where youth invent means of survival in the disordered conditions of their neighborhoods. In the view of this generation, one creates one's own order. Business opportunities take the form of dealing drugs for young and ambitious entrepreneurs. And rap is the communications media channel, the "TV" of the black inner city (Lott 1992, 79).

Rap music provides a counterpoint to the mainstream interpretation built on media images of black lower-class culture. In the mass media, the image of black urban males is employed to signify the dangers of crime, as the case of Willie Horton was used to embody the theme of the black rapist to mobilize fearful voters during a presidential campaign. Rap music strikes back at these images, not by neutralizing them, but by using the stereotypes to capitalize on black and white middle-class fears of the young black male. It is the inner-city black version of the efforts of young performers to confront the fears of the gentry with outrageous images. The space between criminality and the music is narrowed by the fact that rap artists "sample" copyrighted materials and incorporate them into their productions, in the lyrics and profanity—which intensify the message of violence and opposition to law and the police—and in the outlawing of rap from many radio stations. In Lott's words,

Rap culture is the basis of an authentic public sphere that counterposes itself to the dominant alternative from which black urban youth have been excluded.

Middle class social uplift has been exposed by rap artists as inauthentic role modeling. Such role models lack validity among black urban youth, who are fully aware that they face structurally-based urban unemployment. . . . As inhabitants of extreme-poverty neighborhoods many rap artists and their audiences are entrenched in a street-life filled with crime, drugs, and violence. Being criminal-minded and having street values are much more suitable for living in their environment. Without either glorifying or condemning this attitude, I want to draw attention to the sense in which rap music has shown the potential to engender a liberating consciousness in black youth. (1992, 81)

There is no question that black inner-city poverty and victimization are entrenched and unyielding. Whether we consider the position taken by Wilson, West, or Lott, the same radical critique emerges: The source of poverty and all that follows from it is a natural product of economic change, of readjustments in the international and regional marketplace that are bound to have negative effects on some marginally involved segments of the population. Minorities, by definition, fit this description. Both Wilson and West hoped for grass-roots interventions that would modify what they see as the destructive cultural consequences of entrenched poverty. Lott refrained from judgment, instead suggesting ways that the culture is empowering and coherent when judged on its own terms. He challenged middle-class sensibilities that make remote observers prone to judge the "other"; he asked instead that we try to hear and understand, with empathy and without judging, the authentic voices of black inner-city youth commenting from their own perspective on the costs and consequences of poverty. Apart from a needed alternative perspective on what has been viewed overwhelmingly as the pathology of inner-city poverty areas, little guidance is offered here for public policy. Meanwhile, the popular news media raised the question of the link between rap music and violence (*Newsweek* cover story, November 29, 1993), and a 19 year old was sentenced to death in Austin, Texas, convicted of shooting a state trooper. He attributed his actions to the influence of anti-police rap music.

The troubled lives and deaths of rap artists reflected the violence of the streets from which they and their art form emerged, lending the weight of authenticity to their troubling messages. The point here is not that there is something wrong with Lott's interpretation. The point is that a dangerous situation exists in which acts of violence, including those directed at the state, are likely to occur. Rap is part of a defiant language as it continues to evolve. Everywhere it assails the ears of those who might otherwise be a more complacent majority—a majority whose children support the hip-hop industry by spending their middle-class allowances, who carry it into their communities on their car stereos, into the suburban malls, into their homes. This *is* a form of power; it harnesses the marketplace. It is an aggressive and pervasive reminder to people who never have to go there of the desperation and anger that lives in the inner city.

It is easy to get public officials and academics to agree that changes in the international economy and domestic restructuring have presented cities with major problems and that poverty is one of the consequences of these changes. Yet when discussion turns to the question of what policies would be practical to pursue to alleviate urban poverty, the focus reverts to the problem of culture and what poor people can do to help themselves. This is not surprising because if some version of the culture of poverty is the cause of poverty, then remedies take the form of educating or reforming the poor. From a liberal perspective, head-start and job-training programs are an effective way to change attitudes and habits. From a conservative perspective, nothing will work, short of forcing people to go to work, and policy measures should remain minimal. A radical perspective remains focused on the structural roots of the problem, the international economy and domestic restructuring. This focus taxes the imagination with regard to what effective policies might be employed to alleviate poverty, much less eradicate it.

In Chapters 10, we will consider the kinds of policies that the United States has pursued with regard to its cities, and contrast these with the nature of policies carried out in other countries. A key criterion that will be employed to evaluate the various strategies will be that of social justice: the question of which segment of a nation's population is best served by its urban policies. Most particularly, we will be interested in the impact of policy on the urban poor.

10

URBAN POLICY

In this chapter, we deal with urban policy. Archeological evidence clearly shows that deliberate efforts by public authorities to manage and control the urban environment date from the time of the earliest known cities. Since these early times, the complexity of the task of controlling urban growth and change has increased along with changes in technology and the greater size of cities. Urban policymakers and planners confront the objective of maintaining an orderly environment under conditions of constant change while balancing the often conflicting goals of economic development, social justice, and environmental protection (Campbell and Fainstein 1996, 7). Because of the diversity of interests that exist in cities, any decision made by urban planners will be seen as best serving the interests of some while ignoring or minimizing the needs of others. We begin our discussion with the recognition that urban policy making is controversial in terms of how much is desirable as well as what kind.

The Nature of Urban Policy

The chief characteristic of policy making is that it is an attempt to impose a government-initiated *command* structure on an environment that would otherwise be produced by a multitude of private decisions. It represents the authority of government to say "no" to certain kinds of individual choices in the name of protecting the rights and welfare of other citizens. In the case of urban policy, this might involve, for example, restricting private interests from establishing businesses or building certain types of structures incompatible with existing property uses in a particular area (e.g., privately owned residences). In most of the cases that we can imagine, such restrictions would seem to serve the interests of all concerned and impose minimum costs on any party. However, we can also anticipate that policies that restrict the location of certain kinds of industry to areas distant from residential areas, and concentrate them in particular zones where competition for sites bids up the price of land for development, will lead to complaints about government interference with private enterprise.

The tension between government command authority and private interests is immediately evident. In the name of creating order, how far should a system go in restricting private initiative and individual freedoms? The answer to the question always comes as a matter of degree, since all societies impose restrictions on what their citizens may do. This is because there is a general understanding that one individual's choice may contravene another's welfare and rights. It should be apparent that the need for such controls is likely to be felt most keenly in densely built environments that contain large numbers of people and extremes of wealth and deprivation. That is, the urban arena itself intensifies the perception of the need for the imposition of public controls.

The task of overseeing the making and remaking of cities falls jointly to government officials and professionally trained planners. The former provide authority for controlling the urban environment through legislation, while the latter provide through their professional training particular schemes for promoting orderly change. The questions that sociologists and others ask of these agents are, first, whether their plans are sufficiently far-reaching to make a real difference, and second, which segments of the population are best served by their policies.

Different political and economic systems around the world vary widely in the degree to which urban policy is an important, comprehensively treated priority. Having said this, at this juncture in the evolving history of urban planning, we may make a broad generalization. If we picture a continuum of urban policies ranging from the most restrictive government-imposed control structure at one extreme to the most hands-off policy of market-determined urban change at the other, we can place classic socialist nations like the old Soviet Union toward the command end, mid-twentieth century European states toward the middle, and the United States toward the minimal-interference end of the continuum. Next, if we were to animate this arrangement—set the cases arranged along the continuum in motion—we would perceive an interesting, convergent movement. Over the course of the last 50 years, the cases toward the more strictly controlled command end of the continuum and those in the middle would slide along the continuum toward the United States. In the past 20 years, this convergence toward a less restrictive management policy has accelerated. The convergence of thinking is, in large part, generated by the model of globalization that insists that government pursue policies that promote rather than restrict the activity of business. This broad generalization tells us that while it is possible to imagine a more fully controlled urban environment, and while some governments have in the past initiated substantial undertakings to direct change, today's cities are shaped largely by market demands and by governments attempting to accommodate to those demands. This does not mean that governments have abandoned all attempts to control the direction of urban change. However, governments have generally scaled back their efforts to impose controls on the direction and shape of urban change, and where possible have attempted to harness market forces to achieve policy goals at the same time as they redefine policy goals to make them consistent with the interests of private enterprise. This trend in thinking is as true in the People's Republic of China as it is in the United Sates. What the scaling back of

There is a natural tension between public planning authority that seeks to manage the location of different kinds of business and the freedom of private enterprise to locate where it chooses: This McDonald's franchise is at the center of Milan's stately and upscale Galleria shopping mall. Is there a public policy issue here?

urban planning goals means, in less abstract terms, will become clearer in the course of this chapter.

Early Plans: The Grand Scale and the Humane Order

Some see modern city planning as growing out of the twentieth century efforts to deal with problems presented by the nineteenth century cities of the Urban Revolution. The qualities that characterize current approaches to urban policy had their inception in the industrial era. Industrialization and the accompanying population growth and urban concentration renewed the recognition that the physical urban environment demanded some sort of control. There were practical problems of water and air pollution, of health-threatening inadequacies of outmoded sewage systems and crowded and decaying housing, of clogged transportation arteries. While early in the twentieth century, some leading social theorists (the Social Darwinists) argued that any government meddling would be sure to do more harm than good, the conditions of the industrial cities made it abundantly clear that, at least with regard to the urban environment, the general welfare could not be left to private choices. The earliest activities undertaken by public authorities were to expand thoroughfares, provide for public transportation, upgrade sewers and water supplies, and oversee the provision of gas and electricity (Sutcliffe 1981, 5).

While municipal authorities were engaged in the practical and pressing day-to-day problems of keeping the city running, others were inspired by the shortcomings of the urban environment to dream lofty dreams of the perfectibility of the urban form. These were an important few who saw in the conditions of the city both the inequities of the machine age and the potential for creating a more utopian mode of living. Urban designers like Ebenezer Howard, Le Corbusier, and Frank Lloyd Wright thought that any plans to remold the human environment would be useless if the "benevolent humanism that motivated them" resulted in schemes that would merely cover up, rather than alter, the basic inequities that they perceived to be a part of their society (Fishman 1977, 5). While the ideas put forward by the utopian visionaries attracted a large audience, the practical impact of their schemes remained limited. Their visions deserve our attention as hypotheses of what might be if one person were given power of command to implement that person's idea of the ideal urban society.

Ebenezer Howard's vision of the more perfect human habitat provides a good example of just how ambitious the early planners could be in pursuit of their revolutionary social goals of improving life for all members of society. All details of the new society would have to be anticipated and laid out in a way such that every person would have convenient access to all the services and amenities that society had to offer (Box 10-1). Howard was attracted by the potential advancements that great cities like London offered, but repelled by the extremes of wealth and want that they produced. A totally planned and managed environment could provide livelihood and satisfy the other needs of all citizens. A large part of the trouble, he believed, was that town and country had until then been considered the only two possible forms of settlement. In his book, *Garden Cities of Tomorrow*, he proposed to combine the most favorable features of these two more limited forms. He envisioned a setting that combined "all the advantages of the most energetic and active town life with all the beauty and delight of the country" (Howard [1902] 1965, 42–46).

The kernel of his idea—the desirability of maintaining open, green spaces within newly planned towns—found limited implementation in the British towns of Letchworth (founded in 1903) and Welwyn (1920). In the United States in the 1930s, his work also inspired a few experimental "greenbelt cities," largely residential housing tracts that we would perceive as typically "suburban." But aside from the idea that people would benefit from more green space, his utopian social vision was destined to remain no more than an idea. No authority existed in free societies to impose such a total plan on citizens.

The ideas of the French planner, Le Corbusier, suffered the same fate: They drew attention, even from government officials, and the architect/planner was given commissions to carry out limited implementations of the physical aspects of his visions, but his socialist goals went beyond the limited authority of the state. Where Howard was committed to decentralizing the city, Le Corbusier believed that the concentration of population in large skyscrapered cities was the key to efficiency and improved living standards for all. Today, his drawings strike us as unremarkable representations of contemporary, high-rise urban living. But we must remember that he was working on his ideas in the early part of the twentieth century and that he had more in mind than apartment house architecture. For Le Corbusier, the urban problem was that workers, unhappy with their material

---

BOX 10-1   Ebenezer Howard's Garden City

This is a detail from Howard's drawings of his Garden City and its integrated environs. In addition to transportation systems, parks, municipal buildings, and the circular Crystal Palace, note the attention to such details as institutions for practical education and institutions that would segregate populations with special needs from the rest of the population. The glass-enclosed crystal palace we would recognize as a shopping mall, and this would double as a recreational area in inclement weather.

Another feature of the plan is that the size of the Garden City would be limited. If the population grew beyond the target of 32,000, the overflow would pod-off into an identically appointed segment, a sufficient number of segments eventually forming a circle around a central city at the middle of a cluster of satellites. The social reformist element of the plan was that the limited size would permit effective political participation. The spatial engineering would promote efficiency and ensure relatively equal access to amenities for all citizens. The socioeconomic organization of the Garden City would be modestly collectivized and egalitarian (Howard [1902] 1965, 142–143).

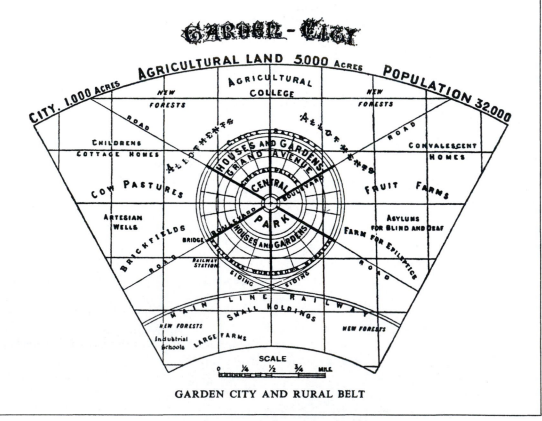

GARDEN CITY AND RURAL BELT

conditions (recall the French sociologist Emile Durkheim's concern with worker "anomie" in Chapter 3), were particularly frustrated with the condition of their housing. Their limited shelter was all too clearly a holdover from an older technological era. Better housing for the whole population played a central part in Le Corbusier's thinking about a new and more equitable social order. But his environmental plans went far beyond housing to the very restructuring of society. The city of the future would necessitate a hierarchical administrative structure that would see to all phases of social and economic life, including the cooking and laundering that was formerly performed within each household. With their staffs of gourmet chefs, housekeeping services, and laundries, Le Corbusier's massive apartment blocks resembled, by his own admission, the ocean liners of his era (Fishman 1977, 192–198).

An important feature of Le Corbusier's ideas was that they were designed to free people from the drudgery of everyday chores: The implications for freeing especially women from household maintenance are significant. And this was no scheme for the laboring class to more fully serve the needs of the rich: All households would receive the benefits of the proposed services. But in practical terms, Le Corbusier believed his plan would necessitate a strict hierarchy of command authority for its implementation since, he believed, the sweeping changes he proposed would have to be imposed from above. The implementation of such changes meant that planners needed both the authority for the acquisition of property and state or privately provided economic resources for their acquisition. When Le Corbusier turned from the drawing board and lecture hall to seek government help in the execution of his plans, he found that the key reality confronting the planner was that the urban landscape was divided into thousands of privately held parcels of property. His quest for the ideal city became a search for government structures that would give him the power of implementation. He was not successful (Fishman 1977, 205–212).

Much can be learned from contemplating the elaborate visions of Howard and LeCorbusier. Their work has been described as naïve utopianism, on the one hand, and inhumanly formalized and rigid, on the other. The considered responses of the early planners are understandable, given the magnitude of the perceived problems and the promise that the new age of abundance might hold if its productive energies were harnessed to a force other than individual self-interest. Such idealism is largely a feature of the past. In the present, elaborate idealizations of coordinated beehived cityscapes are the stuff of science fiction rather than the planning profession. Yet there are individuals who continue to think on a grand scale and in terms of the total plan that will produce a controlled and more efficient human environment. Paolo Soleri works on a small scale and without the support of government. Soleri's vision has taken him to the plateau of central Arizona where he, a small staff, and a shifting band of students and elder volunteers have created Arcosanti, an environment of steel and concrete that is neither an urban landscape nor altogether not an urban space. It is more a campus, growing slowly and organically as a totally planned environment, where those who long for a more enlightened vision of urban possibility can work and exchange ideas and have a sense that they are participating in a rich alternative. The work is funded only by donations, seminars, and the sale of the Cosanti Foundation trademark pottery and bronze-cast bells. Arcosanti is a demonstration project, an experiment in the efficient use of space through unified design. Its projected total population at maturity, between 6,000 and 7,000 people, is not the answer to the problem posed by the modern megacity. Indeed, the present permanent popula-

Visionary planners appear to at least some of their contemporaries as impractical thinkers. Paolo Soleri's Arcosanti (top) is a relatively small-scale experiment to demonstrate how human habitat can be concentrated in a fashion that preserves natural space. It attempts to overcome the kind of suburban development represented by the city of Tucson (bottom) shown sprawling into the desert and mountains. Some believe it is private development, especially in this environment, that is impractical in the long run.

tion of several dozen people, the slow pace of construction, and the lack of economic resources would appear to raise questions of the project's viability. But the staff appears to have an enduring patience.

As much as by Soleri's philosophy, the citizens of Arcosanti are driven by the idea of building an alternative to the wasteful use of space that they see unfolding elsewhere in the United States. The deserts and the mountains of Arizona and other southwestern states, with their delicate arid ecologies, are being consumed with unprecedented efficiency by suburban housing developers. Arcosanti may appear in its small scale not to be an effective answer to market-driven sprawl, but for its many annual visitors, it manages to raise the question of alternative futures, serves as a classroom where people are encouraged to think about the collective impact of our lifestyle, and acts as a reminder that currently we proceed without any vision but the powerful one of individual choice expressed in terms of home ownership.

Today, official organs of government planning address the question of managing the urban environment. Their agenda is different from that of urban visionaries, past and present. Whereas the visionary planners may have erred in assuming that too much was possible through the revision of the urban environment, more recent planning efforts may be criticized as insufficiently bold or visionary.

The Record of Policy in the United States

In the rapidly growing cities of nineteenth century America, bristling with entrepreneurial ambition, there was a sense that growth needed to be controlled and directed as well as encouraged. At the very least, there were practical concerns related to the efficient flow of business: The width and placement of public thoroughfares needed to be determined, and where possible laid out in efficient grid fashion, with all or most streets and avenues intersecting at right angles. Beyond such minimal planning concerns, there was also a sense that people would benefit from open and green areas, something to counteract the "visual squalor without parallel in the industrializing world" that uncontrolled building and public signboard advertising had created in the cities of the United States (Sutcliffe 1981, 92–97). Of the two types of concerns, the practical variety received the most attention from government. The agencies of government in charge of implementation have historically had little power and few resources, so far-reaching or ambitious plans have had little prospect of realization. Symbolic of the limited impact that concerns with overall design have had on U.S. cities is the case of San Francisco. When a substantial portion of the city was destroyed by earthquake and fire in 1906, there was already an officially commissioned plan in hand for renovating the city by reproportioning the size of city blocks and broadening streets. The devastation of the city offered a perfect opportunity to put the plan into effect, but it was scrapped in favor of rebuilding structures where they had stood, in order to get on with business as quickly as possible (Sutcliffe 1981, 88, 102–115).

Urban policy in the United States has been characterized from its inception by two features. The first is that the feasibility of any plan has been judged in terms of its limited scope. Second, worthy plans were those that stabilized property values and enhanced the predictability of the city as a business environment. This is not surprising. It is consistent with the view that circumstances that benefit business benefit all citizens, that within the market system the prosperity of private enterprise is a shared good. The position is reflected in the words of the architects of a proposed plan for the city of Chicago early in the last century: "How are we living? Are we in reality prosperous? Is the city a convenient place for business? Is it a good labor market in the sense that labor is sufficiently comfortable to be efficient and content?" (Burnham and Bennett 1909, 32–33). Planners had to sell their ideas to public administrators. They did this by emphasizing the need to protect capital with minimal interference, with plans that emphasized "partial reform through efficiency techniques that transformed obsolete land uses into more productive values" (Boyer 1983, 70). Plans that found the greatest acceptance were those that were pro-capital: Ideas that were redistributive, that smacked of socialism, faced the greatest resistance. Two examples illustrate the point: zoning and housing.

The most popular and widespread government-imposed restriction of the twentieth century was zoning. Zoning divides the spatial area of a city into districts where certain types of building and land uses are permitted and others are banned. By 1913, for example, cities in some states in the upper Midwest had banned commercial and manufacturing businesses from certain designated residential areas. The strategy was designed to protect property values for homeowners. New York City in 1916 implemented a more detailed zoning ordinance in response to demands by owners of department stores in fashionable Fifth Avenue locations who were concerned about the encroachment of noisy manufacturing establishments. For the homeowner as well as the large investor in real estate, the practical benefits of zoning were evident, and the measure was rapidly and widely adopted by city governments. Zoning represents the approach that protects capital with minimal interference. It remains symbolic of urban planning in its most limited form.

While the protection of private property provides an example of readily acceptable market goals, the question of government responsibility for ensuring an adequate housing supply is just the kind of social welfare goal that has historically drawn criticism and resistance from entrepreneurs and other taxpayers in the United States. As noted in Chapter 7, the Hoover administration resisted demands for a federal housing policy during the depths of the Great Depression, in what proved to be the futile hope that developers and builders would discover a profitable way to provide housing for people with low incomes. Pressure remained on the government to intervene directly in upgrading housing: American policies could be made to appear negligent in contrast to those of European governments that had for decades supplemented the private housing market with government-provided housing; the aging and overcrowded housing stock in U.S. cities made housing conditions a national embarrassment both during the Depression and in the post–World War II years.

Ultimately, the country publicly and legally committed itself to the provision of "decent, safe and sanitary dwellings for families of low income" in the United States Housing Act of 1937. Congress reaffirmed its commitment in the Housing Act of 1949, declaring "that the general welfare and security of the Nation and the health and living standards of its people require housing production and related community development sufficient to remedy the serious housing shortage." The government has never come close to meeting its obligation. In the following section, we review the major components of government housing programs that actually represent over time a retreat from the kind of commitment to the provision of housing contained in the Housing Acts that remain the law of the land. Whereas zoning laws represented minimal interference with market freedom and stabilized investment environments, government housing programs involve a sustained commitment of public funds and creative energies to the massive task of creating millions of wholesome dwellings for the least advantaged cross section of society. While the difference in the success of the two programs may have been predictable, the degree to which the United States has failed to establish an effective housing policy is symbolic of the very limited capacity for urban planning.

Housing Programs in the United States

Historically, the two most ambitious programs related to the provision of housing in the United States were the urban renewal and the public housing programs. While urban renewal was not a housing program per se, it had a significant impact on the existing urban housing supply both through demolition of the existing stock and the planned provision of replacement units. The public housing program represents a limited foray by government into the direct provision of housing for the poor.

Urban Renewal

This program provided federal support for the revitalization of decaying districts of inner cities. Within the renewal site—which would include several city blocks—old buildings, including housing units, were torn down to make way for new structures that integrated businesses and residential units. Each project involved a partnership between federal and local government and private enterprise.

Locally, the renewal process was set in motion by the official designation by local government of slum and blighted areas suitable for renewal. Planning, administration, property acquisition, clearance of existing structures, and site improvement were public costs shared by the federal government (which provided two-thirds of the expenditures for each project) and local government. Improved sites were sold to private developers, with taxpayers absorbing the difference between government expenditures and the resale price.

The partnership between government and industry was, in fact, more extensive. Local renewal projects had to be proposed as a package to the federal government, which provided the bulk of the funding for local renewal. The federal agency evaluated each proposed project in terms of its potential for returning a profit on investment—that is, the commercial viability of the completed plan. The selection of particular sites by local governments was heavily influenced from the outset by developers, lending institutions, and other interested partners for whom the enterprise was an investment gamble, heavily subsidized by government though they were. Since federal requirements specified that local governments and investors would have to make a case for the *economic* viability of a particular package, it is not surprising that the worst, most desperate slums were not selected for renewal due to their poor strategic location and their lack of promise as commercial sites.

Urban renewal soon become one of the most controversial government-sponsored urban programs. In addition to neglecting the worst tracts of inner-city housing, government could condemn and raze decent residential buildings adjacent to a selected site in order to consolidate "buildable packages" or blocks of land (Meltzer 1984, 59–61). The 1949 Housing Act that authorized the demolition of run-down housing also specified that rebuilt areas be primarily residential in character. However, there was no real mechanism that insured that the number of destroyed housing units would be rebuilt, or that low-rent units would be replaced by similarly priced housing. Criticism mounted that urban renewal amounted to removal of the poor and minorities from the inner cities.

Public Housing

For anyone growing up in the cities of the 1950s, reference to "the projects" could mean only one thing: the government-built housing projects that were home to the poorest and most troubled elements of the population. Projects varied a little in their reputation, but generally there was a stigma attached to the address. To outsiders, the projects meant trouble. The 1950s was the decade when the government housing projects were being built, when they were brand new. The conditions and reputation of the projects would get much worse.

Over the course of two decades, government supplemented the private housing supply with apartment blocks, where units were allocated on the basis of need on an equitable first-come, first-served basis, and where rents were low and assessed on a sliding scale according to the family's ability to pay. One other potentially positive feature of the program was that it was massive in scale, and a given project typically provided space for hundreds of needy family units. Yet, all the potential merits of the plan hid liabilities that soon became evident.

The stigma that quickly became attached to living in the projects meant that most families who gravitated to them had no alternative. The effect was to homogenize the residents, insuring that the tenant population would be more or less comprised of those in the lowest income categories. While the projects were intended to be racially integrated and while many initially were, the conditions of life in the projects and the visibility of minority families in large numbers had the usual effect on white residents: It drove them elsewhere, and the projects became vertical ghettos for black and Latino residents. With regard to fairness in eligibility and rents adjusted to income level, the efforts of government agents to make sure that families qualified for residence, and that income was honestly reported, led to intrusive surveillance policies. Housing authorities arrogated sweeping powers of investigation into family finances (requiring regular, detailed documentation of income from renters) and family living arrangements (restricting who might be allowed to sleep in the apartment, an especially difficult provision for complex families and those who were involved in less institutionalized forms of cohabitation). Housing authority agents had the power to spot check and carry on investigations of tenants' domestic circumstances at will. This changed the meaning of "home" for those whose low incomes did not entitle them to privacy.

The greatest criticism of the city projects was focused on what initially may have appeared to be their most commendable feature: their prodigious size. Given the severity of the urban housing shortage in the United States, the housing strategy required a dramatic effort if it was going to result in a conspicuous reduction in the number of families with an acute need for shelter. Therefore, individual projects were very often conceived on a grand scale. The Pruitt-Igoe project in St. Louis, which accepted its first tenants in 1954, consisted of thirty-three 11-story buildings. A total of twenty-seven hundred units were built on this centrally located 57-acre site.

Whatever the size of a particular project, urban land costs demanded that the most efficient use be made of the space that federal dollars would buy. The

Massive public housing projects are most often identifiable on sight. One of the buildings in Chicago's Cabrini Green Housing Project is boarded up and ready for demolition.

emphasis, therefore, was on high-rise apartment blocks. Although many of the building designs for the high-rise housing projects won prizes for the architectural innovations they offered, the high-rise public apartment building became a notorious symbol of the failure of the housing program in the United States.

Some of the failure might be attributed to what were thought to be the necessary spending limits: What types of cosmetic features could be justified in buildings designed to house poor people? The elimination of community gathering areas within buildings or of protective grates around structural hazards could mean the difference between a livable and safe environment for families, especially children, and an environment fraught with dangers, including places where gangs of young people could prey on children and the elderly. The serious problem posed by the typical federal housing projects in the inner cities was becoming evident even as new buildings continued to be constructed. Critics pointed to crime, accidents, and the dehumanizing and isolating features associated with this housing strategy.

The Pruitt-Igoe project in St. Louis stood as the most prominent illustration of the unworkability and short life of the mass housing policy for the poor. Although it may have attracted more than its share of notoriety, due to its short life span and the dramatic and well-publicized manner of its destruction, and although it provides merely one extreme example among many, Pruitt-Igoe is an irresistible symbol of the failure of high-rise public housing. The problems of the safety and security of residents, stemming from structural hazards and crime, emerged almost simultaneously with the opening of the project in 1954. By 1958 occupancy rates had begun to decline. Various infusions of public funds, special programs, concentrated social services, and sociological studies failed to remedy the deterioration, crime rate, and despair of the tenants who fled the unlivable space. Vacancy rates climbed steadily, from 18 percent in 1961 to 65 percent in 1970. Demolition began in 1972 with the dynamiting of three central buildings and was completed in 1976, two years after the last residents had moved out and just twenty-two years after the first had moved in. Critics blamed the failure on the massive scale and high-rise design, the inadequacy and reductions in routine kinds of funding for the maintenance and operation of the project, and society's failure to address the more fundamental problem of the poverty of the tenants (Montgomery 1985, 230–241). All these reasons, and especially the last, would appear to be plausible explanations for the dramatic failure of this attempt to provide shelter for those of modest means.

The task that remains is to explain how a number of older government-sponsored housing projects have continued to provide livable family environments, decade after decade. The answer seems to lie in what the older (and in some cases newer) projects do *not* have in contrast to the high-rise projects. For example, the sites they occupy are less densely populated on a persons-per-acre basis, and the number of families in any given project is smaller. Many of the developments built on a less-ambitious scale are small enough to be tucked away, to become part of existing neighborhoods, rather than to dominate or eradicate the social fabric of these areas. The urban town house, duplex, or apartment building of three or four stories allows parents to watch their children at play outside, and residents are

It is not absolutely necessary to do public housing badly. Single story units distributed in small clusters represent an attractive alternative.

mutually recognizable and more attuned to the presence and behavior of strangers. In addition, the space outside is more inviting, facilitating contact among neighbors.

The Renewed Search for Market Solutions to the Housing Problem

By 1970, government was moving away from the direct provision of housing in favor of paying rent subsidies, enabling low-income households to compete for space in the private housing market. The public housing program was judged ineffective, and a 1973 report by the United States Department of Housing and Urban Development (HUD) flatly stated that the direct effort of government to provide housing had failed: The report endorsed a direct subsidy program for renters. Government did not simply abandon the public housing projects overnight. By 1997, 1.3 million households still lived in government-supplied housing units, while the number receiving rent subsidies was 1.5 million. In city after city, however, the projects were coming down, while Congress year by year debated the future of the direct subsidy program.

Under the subsidy program, renters operate as relatively independent shoppers seeking housing in the privately owned rental market. Under what is known as the Section 8 program, the federal government provides rent vouchers or rental certificates to households that qualify for the program. To qualify, a family's income cannot exceed 50 percent of the prevailing median income in their county or metropolitan area (HUD establishes and periodically adjusts the income criteria for each area). Each family accepted into the program is responsible for finding a suitable rental unit: Suitability is established by formal criteria and by an inspection conducted by a local housing authority acting on HUD's behalf. The family is usually responsible for contributing 30 percent of its adjusted income to the monthly rental, with the balance paid directly to the landlord by the federal agency.

While this program adjusts the income of poor families in a manner that allows them to compete for housing on the open market, it does not adjust the supply of available housing. HUD's budget for rent subsidy is not unlimited, and when all funds budgeted for a local area are allocated, applicants are put on a waiting list. When the wait becomes unreasonably long—and sometimes families who qualify wait for years to become actively enrolled—housing authorities close the list. On the supply side, landlords are not obligated to participate in the program and, once in the program, can withdraw from it. Some tire of meeting government standards and repeated inspections; others grow impatient with the perennial debates in Congress over whether to continue the program or whether to cut the level of funding. Landlords were tempted to drop families on assistance in favor of more affluent renters in the booming urban economies of the late 1990s that increased the open-market costs of housing rentals more rapidly than the rate of inflation. According to HUD secretary Andrew Cuomo's Spring 2000 *State of the Cities* report, 5.4 million families not receiving housing assistance (12.5 million people) were living in substandard housing and/or paying more than 50 percent of their income in rent.

The record of housing policy in the United States is not a record of progress; it is not a record of finding increasingly effective policies built on past experiences. It is a record of experimentation, of reluctant action inconsistent with the lofty ideals of the Housing Acts of the 1930s and 1940s that declared safe and healthy housing a necessity for all citizens. As is the case with U.S. urban policy in general, lawmakers appear dedicated to market solutions over commitments to direct intervention to solve what many consider a "housing crisis" for people with low and moderate incomes. The reluctance of lawmakers to consider adequate shelter a direct responsibility of government is clearly reflected in their withdrawal from the provision of public housing for all but the elderly. It is evident in their decision to subsidize instead the private housing market through rent subsidies, thereby incorporating an element of private enterprise and government partnership into social policy. The acceptability of policy measures that boost market activity is reflected also in the most successful U.S. housing program: the provision of mortgage guarantees and income tax credits that have supported widespread home-ownership in the middle-class suburbs. Government guarantees have the effect of lowering mortgage interest rates, while the large share of homeowners' monthly payments that go to interest and taxes are fully tax deductible: In effect, this is a generous housing subsidy for the middle class and affluent. The strong symbolic appeal of home ownership, which lies at the heart of the American Dream, has not gone untested as a strategy for providing shelter for individuals and families of modest means.

Urban Homesteading and Project Hope

Urban homesteading and *Project HOPE* are two government programs that were designed to provide nonaffluent inner-city populations with a chance to own their own homes. Urban homesteading was first unveiled in the 1960s and refined in the 1970s to bring together housing needs, reduce certain government liabilities, and reaffirm popularly acknowledged American values in one package. Poor people needed housing, and government held a large number of abandoned and dilapidated housing units. By applying a label that conjured up a pioneering imagery, the plan involved transferring ownership and responsibility for improvement of units from government to families for a nominal fee. Purchasers, who were eligible for special improvement loans and mortgage rates, agreed to reside in the property for a given period of time and improve it. They were then free to continue to reside in or sell the improved and marketable housing. It was reasoned that families motivated by this type of opportunity would provide stabilizing influences and good role models in the neighborhoods they occupied (Hughes and Bleakly 1975, 3–4; Varady 1986, 47–49).

A logical extension of the urban homesteading plan was developed in 1992 by a government interested in getting out of the public housing business. In that year, HUD secretary Jack Kemp began implementing the National Affordable Housing Act that had been signed by President George Bush in 1990. Its purpose was to sell public housing to tenants, to condominiumize the still-standing public housing projects. Given the uplifting label of *Project HOPE* (Home-ownership and Opportunity for People Everywhere), Kemp declared that it would "bring the power of private property ownership to thousands of low-income families across America. President Bush and I believe every American family should have the chance to realize the American Dream and upward mobility." By late in 1992, Kemp claimed that 50,000 families had become partners with the federal government in ownership of former public housing apartments or other multiunit vacant or foreclosed properties (HUD News Releases, August 22 and October 2, 1992).

There is considerable controversy as to how well these programs met either the needs of property holders or government. It was difficult for families of modest means to meet the upgrading standards under the urban homesteading plan. Project HOPE had at least the potential virtue of preserving some number of housing units, many of which would otherwise have been abandoned and razed. Taken together, the programs, which were aimed at selling off the least desirable units in the national urban housing stock to the poor, cannot be seen as having a major impact on the needs of the 5.4 million families that were still underhoused in the late 1990s. The reliance on market forces to provide adequate housing for everyone in the economically divided cities of the United States has produced the inevitable: urban landscapes where the haves and have-nots compete for secure shelter, where the affluent wrest upgradeable units from the less affluent, where the battleground for livelihood and shelter drives many concerned property own-ers into fortified residential retreats, and where downward pressures on the re-maining urban housing supply push millions into substandard housing or onto the streets. In the divided cities of the United States, *gentrification* and *gated com-munities* are produced by individuals and families attempting to create order in the absence of effective policy, and homelessness is the predictable outcome of a housing supply no longer augmented by government efforts and the admission by government that it has failed to meet the needs of the millions who live at the margins between shelter and the street.

The Battle for Shelter in Contemporary America

The common observation, by both social scientists and public officials, that the economic expansion that carried the United States into the new century was widening the gulf between the urban affluent and the urban poor is brought into sharp focus in the competition for residential space. People who reside in U.S. cities don't need to be told that they are expensive places in which to live. Mid-town two-bedroom apartment rentals in Manhattan and San Francisco ranged between $1,800 and $3,500 in summer 2000. Using the criteria of the real estate in-dustry, housing should represent no more than 33 percent of a household's ad-justed income. Using that simple formula, a $2,100 rental requires an annual ad-justed income of $75,000: Many household units in New York and San Francisco riding the prosperity of the expanding economy easily qualify. Many do not. Of the latter, many are able to find housing at less than the prevailing rental rate, but this will mean living in neighborhoods and in buildings that compromise health and safety. As the rise in rental rates exceeds the general rate of inflation in major cities, pressures increase for the poor and families of modest means.

Williams and Smith (1986) offered a useful framework for understanding the rising costs of living in major cities: *Manhattanization* is the consequence of the globalizing economy as it impacts major or "global cities" like New York. These are the cities that represent the nerve centers of the global economy, are home to the corporate headquarters of the most powerful enterprises. The incomes and perquisites of rising executives set the ceilings on rent and land values. The val-ues reflected in the real estate section of the *New York Times* are not so much set by local conditions as they are by the wealth that flows through the international economy. As that economy reaches beyond the global cities like London, New York, or Tokyo, prices in other cities, like San Francisco, are adjusted to reflect the degree to which the emerging international capacity to pay has reached them. Ac-cording to Williams and Smith, if corporate headquarters or other important cor-porate administrative offices play an important role in the local employment structure, the population of that city can expect to feel a commensurate increase in the costs associated with living there. Costs will rise as local professionals and businesses that service elite tastes set their fees to reflect the depth of the corpo-rate purse accustomed to paying for the best around the world. Some will benefit from the Manhattanization of the local market for goods and services, and others will experience it as the hardship of costs rising beyond their limited means.

Gentrification

Dating from the mid-1960s, at least, many inner cities have undergone a transformation most commonly referred to as *gentrification*—a term that denotes the return of the middle classes or "gentry" in force into central city residential neighborhoods. The process typically involves the purchase and conversion of entire buildings by owner occupants in areas that may have been run down for decades or generations. Especially popular are townhouses that may be converted from multi- to single-family use in areas where there are a number of similarly attractive potential conversions, perhaps in the Victorian style (Schill and Nathan 1983, 30). Also popular are conversions of factory or warehouse "loft" structures. But gentrification refers to any area that is undergoing a change in population from predominantly lower- to higher-income residents. The process is marked by a conversion in local businesses as well, as commercial enterprises come to reflect the upscale tastes and incomes of the new residents.

In cities where there were alternative accommodations for people of modest means, this trend might be welcomed purely as the spontaneous revitalization of

The battle for space proceeds quietly in this affluent neighborhood, just a block from bustling Halstead Street, in Chicago's Wrigleyville district. Rents here are well beyond the reach of many Chicagoans.

economically depressed inner-city areas. But in a nation where the term *housing crisis* is used to describe the prevalent condition of cities, gentrification has obvious implications for controversy: As the affluent take over housing, what happens to the less affluent who formerly lived there? One related issue involves the question of just how spontaneous a process this has been. Has it been produced by numerous, independent individual choices to carve out an attractive private space in the city, the decision by young professionals to opt for the excitement of urban as opposed to dull suburban living, a decision reinforced perhaps by bargain urban real estate in contrast to more costly suburban alternatives? Certainly, many early urban gentrifiers were motivated by such considerations. But critics point out that once the "trend" had been identified as such, realtors and property speculators quickly saw the opportunity to capitalize, and sold the idea of gentrification to a wider spectrum of prospective buyers. Areas were identified as gentrifying or on the verge of gentrification by realtors and city administrations anxious to promote and accelerate the movement. Where first wave gentrifiers tended to be more adventurous risk takers, latecomers to the movement were more averse to investment risks, more interested in preserving property values, concerned with neighborhood economic homogeneity, and likely to seek official designation of their neighborhood as a protected historical district.

Because of its potential for making a tight housing supply even tighter, gentrification has remained a controversial issue. Central to the controversy is the question of the impact of gentrification on the displacement of the poor from properties they formerly occupied. Some argue that a more important source of the residential displacement of the poor is the practice of abandonment of derelict buildings by slumlords who have extracted all they can from their long-neglected properties. Measuring the relative impact of gentrification and abandonment is difficult. At times, landlords will withhold services (heat, garbage removal) and repairs because they are about to walk off, while others who plan to upgrade their property for more affluent tenants will engage in the same practice to drive out their present lower-rent tenants. One set of estimates for New York City in the mid-1980s put the number of households displaced by abandonment at between 31,000 and 60,000 per year, and the number displaced by gentrification at between 10,000 and 40,000. In 1979, HUD issued a *Displacement Report* that minimized the impact of displacement due to gentrification, but Legates and Hartman (1981, 1986) said that their own estimate of 2.5 million people displaced each year in the United States by gentrification was conservative. The displacees are disproportionately lower class and elderly. Substantial numbers end up moving into accommodations that represent a deterioration in standards and/or where rents are higher (Legates and Hartman 1986, 194–197). Of course, for some of those who are forced to pay higher rents, their new housing and neighborhood represent an improvement (Schill and Nathan 1983, 7). In any event, there is no doubt that gentrification contributes to the reduction of available low-rent units in the central cities where the supply of such housing is already in critically short supply.

The detailed case study of a gentrifying Philadelphia neighborhood by Anderson (1990) sheds some light on the process. The gentrifying area eats inexorably into adjacent poor black neighborhoods already hard hit by the loss of industry. The border area where upward mobility meets economic decline is characterized by resentment, lack of understanding, exploitation, hostility, and fear. The city government is clearly on the side of the upwardly mobile population and is interested in upgrading the area. The young men from the poor neighborhoods take their power in the form of public swagger and intimidation. The tension is underlined by racial differences. Gentrification in this area of Philadelphia is a formula for hostile confrontation as well as change. The battle for shelter and security for poor and affluent people in the city provides a focus for class conflict. Increasing numbers of those who can afford it retreat into fortified residential enclaves.

Gated Communities

The battle between the classes for space and security has produced a particular type of strategic retreat for many of those who can afford to live there: the gated community. The atmosphere of uncertainty and threat is sufficient to have produced private residential garrisons that prevent all but authorized service-worker poor people from entering or passing through.

Gated communities are a type of residential association. There were 50,000 of these in 1950, 150,000 in 1992. They range from condominium associations, whose members pay fees to maintain common property, to the 20,000 walled or gated communities that have become more popular in recent years. As the term suggests, *gated communities* erect gates across access roads; they also limit points of entry; build perimeter walls and fences; and employ private security guards, surveillance cameras, and infrared motion detectors. In the mid-1990s, the St. Andrews complex in Boca Raton, Florida, was spending $1 million a year on helicopter and canine patrols. Perhaps 45 percent of homeowners' associations nationwide display some evidence of this type of security organization (Kennedy 1995).

The number of people who live in gated communities nationwide is nontrivial. Although they have been most popular in California, Florida, and Texas, they are now a feature of most metropolitan areas (some municipalities prohibit them), and some 8 million people live in them. Realtors report that erecting gates and limiting access has become popular enough to raise property values, although leading researchers say there is little evidence to indicate that gated communities contribute either to an increase in neighborliness or, surprisingly, to much of a reduction in crime rates. Gates and fences are likely to prevent entry by motorists or casual potential trespassers, but are probably not a deterrent to serious criminals (Blakely and Snyder 1997a, 1997b).

Critics target a broad range of negative features. The gated and walled community approach to security has been referred to as segregationist, isolationist, anticommunity, and medieval. In the latter sense, builders and developers are feudal lords offering protection from the hordes (McKenzie 1994). By the end of the 1990s, there was sufficient criticism of the gated community that some municipalities and policymakers had begun to impose restrictions on builders. Still, gated communities remained in demand in those metropolitan regions where security was a concern, and builders were happy to respond to home buyers willing and able to underwrite the added expense (Baron 1998). The gated community may be read as a sign of the generalized anxiety that attends inequality and entrenched divisions by class and race within society. They are a symptom not only of the failure of urban policy to create order, but also of the failure of the market to maintain a reasonable distribution of economic opportunity. These systematic failures are most visible within cities because that is where poor and minority populations are concentrated. Under such circumstances, we may expect the most timid or controlling elements of the dominant population to attempt to wall themselves off from the poor. It is an expression of their perception of social reality, of the instability of the social order. It reflects a disparity of life chances that produces an odd juxtaposition of images.

On the outskirts of Johannesburg, South Africa, in the post-apartheid era, we have the gated community of Fourways Gardens, a community that might just as well describe a protected suburban enclave in the metropolitan United States. Armed guards patrol an area surrounded by eight-foot high walls topped with electrified fences. Inside, there are recreational facilities including a golf club and restaurant so that residents need venture out only for business. The white residents of this fortified community are attempting to cope with their fear of crime in the uncertain atmosphere in which the state has declared equality of opportunity but has not been able to deliver (*The Economist*, December 2, 1995).

In a suburb of Baton Rouge, Louisiana, deep in the U.S. South, is a gated community called the Country Club of Louisiana, where houses cost between $300,000 and $3 million. There is a golf and tennis club complex, intended architecturally to re-create the style of a Louisiana plantation. In 1999, Percy Miller caused a stir well covered by the national press when he and four associates moved into the steel-gated community. Miller, proprietor of the top-grossing rap label No Limit Records, had earned $56.5 million in the previous year alone. This made Master P, as he is known in the business, the tenth highest paid entertainer in any medium. The other four new residents were C-Murder, Silkk the Shocker, Mystikal, and Snoop Dogg. All had made their fortunes in hit recordings that celebrated gunfights, misogyny, and the drug trade. They didn't feel welcomed by their neighborhood association, but it is not surprising that they were there. These were people who had made substantial fortunes, who had much to lose, and who had heard the message that there was a struggle going on between the wealthy and the poor in U.S. cities. Without effective urban policy, one has to engage in self-protection: one has to defend oneself.

Losers in the Battle for Space: The Homeless

History may not repeat itself, but the basic political and economic arrangements of society often cause us to question how much we learn from the past. Sweeney (1993, 15) reminded us that in the latter part of the 1800s, given the meager levels of public assistance available at the time "every poor family and some middle class families, too, found themselves one personal or economic crisis away from destitution." Destitution would certainly include homelessness. A hundred years ago, the response to the growing problem of homelessness was to pass various

Tramp Laws that criminalized homelessness but did nothing to relieve the condition or its causes. There are troubling parallels between this time and that.

It is difficult to say just how many homeless people there are in the United States. The homeless may be all too visible as individuals, but for purposes of enumeration, they are an invisible population. So, we are left with estimates, even after the last two censuses that made an effort to count them. And there is the problem of defining the homeless population. Does this population include only those who were homeless last night, or does it include everyone who was without shelter at some time last year? The first method might miss the woman who lives in a cheap hotel until her social security check runs out in the third week of each month and then spends the rest of the month on the street (Peroff 1987, 35–39). Measuring the number of homeless is not just a problem in social science, it is also a political problem. Supporters of austere social policies are interested in minimizing the figure and thereby the need for expenditures to address homelessness. In 1984, during a conservative Republican era, the official government (HUD) estimate was 250,000 to 300,000 homeless nationwide. During the same time, activists who sought to draw attention to the plight of the homeless estimated ten times the government figure, 2 to 3 million. The difference represents different political agendas, and the figures represent the alternate methods of measurement, nightly versus yearly bases. In its 1990 enumeration, the Census Bureau's workers could find only 178,828 people in shelters and 49,793 on the street on a single March night that year. The Urban Institute, dedicated to bringing urban social problems to the attention of the public, reported that 1.8 million people were homeless at some point in 1987 and that the figure had grown to 3.5 million in 1996. But the Institute's estimates of people homeless at any given moment those years, 600,000 in 1987 and 842,000 in 1996, are also much higher than the census figures, which most agree grossly understate the dimensions of the problem.

Clearer than the issue of absolute numbers were indications in the 1990s that the homeless population was growing and changing, even as the national economy and many Americans were experiencing a period of sustained prosperity. The contradiction between growing prosperity and growing homelessness is only apparent rather than real: As the national prosperity continues, rents continue to rise, and more households are squeezed out of the scarce supply of affordable units at the lower end of the private housing market. The mayors of every city and HUD agree on the major cause of homelessness: the crisis in the undersupply of affordable urban housing. No one has devised an effective plan for addressing the problem. In 1995, a U.S. Conference of Mayors Task Force on homelessness reported that requests for emergency shelter were increasing and that more of these requests were coming from families with children. One-fourth of the families requesting aid were turned down (Worsnop 1996). In 1999, the Conference of Mayors reported that requests for food and shelter were growing at increasing rates, and half of the cities studied in that year's report had turned away more than half of the requests for aid because they did not have the resources to provide assistance (Ward 2000a).

Family units comprise a large proportion of the homeless population: an estimated 37 percent. In the 1990s, they were the fastest growing category of the homeless. Many of the families included both parents, but single-parent families headed by women were overrepresented. One study of homeless families found that 81 percent were single-parent units headed by women (Nunez and Fox 1999). Women and children who live on the street, whether in family units headed by women or on their own, are often there due to domestic strife in addition to economic desperation. Many of the women who find themselves homeless are victims of abuse or desertion, and many adolescents on their own and homeless are running from abusive or otherwise insupportable family situations. Both categories are particularly vulnerable.

Women's subordinated social status appears to be a key factor for many women who find themselves without shelter. Women in traditionally dependent domestic roles may be more liable to homelessness (Golden 1992). Domestic violence or childhood abuse is often a part of the story that homeless women tell. A study of 450 homeless women in a New England city revealed that 60 percent had been physically assaulted or sexually molested by age 12 and a majority had suffered attacks by husbands or boyfriends. All told, 90 percent were victims of some form of abuse (Bassuk 1997). And the image of homeless women as elderly "bag ladies" is misguided: In one study, the average homeless woman was 28 years old (Sullivan and Damrosch 1987).

Children and adolescents are another important segment of the homeless population. Preteen-age children are often enumerated as family members, but adolescents are often living on their own, and their numbers are especially difficult to establish because they often drift, stay with friends, habituate places overlooked by enumerators, and are not accepted as clients by some agencies that serve the homeless. Estimates of the number of homeless adolescents range from the hundreds of thousands to three million. They include runaways, escapees from juvenile facilities, and those who are reported as lost or missing by their families. On the street, they are particularly vulnerable and often victimized. One-fourth of young people living on the street reported engaging in "survival sex," the exchange of sex for money, food, or shelter (Greene, Ennett, and Ringwalt 1999). The effects of homelessness are compounded by the developmental stages at which young people confront the uncertainties and stigma of their situation. Homeless students who are enrolled in schools typically change schools frequently and have poor attendance records. They stay away to hide their situation, to avoid the stigma attached to it. Their long-term academic potential declines, and they have problems of social and psychological adjustment, especially difficulties in forming relationships based on mutual trust (Reganick 1997; Vissing and Diament 1997).

Despite general agreement that the inadequate housing supply is the major cause of homelessness, discussions continue about the individual characteristics of members of the homeless that distinguish them from the general population. Chief among these are mental disorder and substance abuse. During the 1970s, the population of state psychiatric institutions nationwide was significantly reduced as part of a plan to treat patients in a more humane and hospitable community environment. Newly developed medications at that time could stabilize behavior

BOX 10-2 Homeless Women

When Elliot Liebow, the author of the widely known study *Tally's Corner* (see reference in Chapter 3), learned he was dying of cancer, he quit his government job and went to work as a volunteer in homeless shelters near Washington, D.C. His habits as an anthropologist inevitably led to note-taking behavior as he worked with homeless women. He compiled these notes into a sensitive and insightful book, *Tell Them Who I Am: The Lives of Homeless Women* (1993), before his death. He was able to convey admirably the women's own perspective, to represent their own voices.

Liebow did not find it useful to distinguish among his subjects in terms of mental illness versus mental health, or in terms of drug use or dependency. Sharing many hours with them, he found mental stability a relative quality, which might show signs of deterioration toward the end of the month when monthly government support payments ran out. He was impressed with the resilience of the women. He commented "one wonders why more homeless people do not kill themselves. How do they manage to slog through day after day, with no end in sight? How, in a world of unremitting grimness, do they manage to laugh, love, enjoy friends, even dance and play the fool?" (25).

Life in public shelters is difficult. Fatigue is a constant condition: At night there is the constant noise of snoring, weeping, women crying out in bad dreams, and the insomnia that comes with the gnawing question, "How did I end up here?" There is boredom: The shelters turn out their residents by day. They walk the streets; they look for someone to talk to. But as one woman put it, the long day is a reminder that you're not needed anywhere, that it doesn't matter what you do because no one cares. Because homeless people are not totally without possessions, there is the problem of where to keep things, especially clothes, priceless mementos of a more stable past, religious items, and important documents. Most carried them around with them, but others rented storage lockers in which they kept a surprisingly large number of personal and household items, stored for a time when things would be better and they would leave the shelters and the street. Health care is a challenge: Commonly prescribed remedies like keeping off your feet, bed rest, or using a vaporizor were out of reach and might well mean simple ailments would become more complicated and serious. Finding a job is made more difficult by the lack of a permanent address and the behavioral and diagnostic stereotypes associated with homelessness.

Liebow's work reminds us that homelessness is not necessarily a permanent condition. Many of his subjects were able to leave the shelter and the street, sometimes obtaining well-paid work, advancing themselves through training, reestablishing normal relationships with relatives, and diminishing their disordered behavioral tendencies or the unconventional thought patterns that had attended their experiences as homeless persons. But the accounts of life after the homeless shelter often include the kinds of crises that give the impression that some of the women are one crisis away from returning to the street. In that way, their present condition parallels that of many women who have not yet experienced homelessness.

and mood swings in more of the profoundly affected individuals, and it was believed that these people could function as outpatients in open environments with the proper degree of supervision from community-based clinics. The first aspect (the release of formerly confined patients) was embraced enthusiastically by public administrators interested in saving money, but the second (establishing and staffing an adequate number of community-based clinics) cost money, and so implementation was delayed or neglected altogether. Many proposed clinics never materialized. Former patients, without adequate supervision, wandered the streets, neglected or bartered their medications, and because of their behavior and at times their appearance, became a highly visible part of the homeless population. They helped inform the public image of the homeless, along with street-dwelling abusers of crack, heroin, alcohol, and other substances. The skid row alcoholic, inhabiting the margins of shelter between the flophouse and the street, has long been an indigenous fixture in the imagery of urban America. Many of the homeless are indistinguishable from the rest of the poor we encounter in the city. So it is the behavior of those who fit the stereotypes that stands out. This results in a distorted profile of homelessness: The profound problems of the long-term or permanent homeless are visible not only to the casual observer, but also are over-represented in studies of the currently homeless. Many more people than those on the street or in shelters at the time of a given study have been homeless recently. Others, to their shock and dismay, will find themselves unable to shelter themselves independently in the future. But studies of street people count and profile only those on the street at the moment: These will always include a disproportionate representation of those whose problems will never allow them to independently leave the street, and this will reinforce and distort the popular understanding of the causes of homelessness as idiosyncratic (Phelan and Link 1999). This is a point worth pondering.

Homeless people are perceived as nuisances in downtown shopping districts. This homeless person stands outside an empty storefront, the only welcoming place on the block.

It is easy to understand how mental illness and addiction become appealing standard-bearers in explanations of why there is homelessness in times of plenty. Yet, while city mayors and others concerned with the analysis of homelessness pay appropriate attention to the personal problems that bring individuals onto the streets, there is an unusual degree of consensus regarding the primary cause. Government officials do not hesitate to refer to it as the housing crisis. Government believes it does not have adequate means to intervene effectively. In December 1999, the President announced the allocation of an additional $900 million to aid the homeless: $750 million was to go to job training and other social services, the remainder to provide food and temporary shelter (Ward 2000a). But there is another side to homeless policy. Since the mid-1990s, city governments have been engaged in efforts to reduce the visibility of homeless people in retail and middle-class residential areas. The nationwide trend drew the critical attention of the popular press as a featured article in *Time* reported 35 municipalities, from Tampa, Florida, to Tucson, Arizona, were "enacting or enforcing punitive anti-vagrancy ordinances, banning everything from loitering on median strips to getting food handouts in public parks" (December 20, 1999, 69). New York's mayor, Rudolph Giuliana, threatened to ban able-bodied homeless adults who did not find employment from receiving city-provided shelter. Chicago "privatized" the sidewalk in front of businesses, making loitering a trespass offense. Police in San Francisco arrested nuns serving hot meals in a downtown public area for not having a permit. *Streetwise*, a Chicago street-peddled publication that advocates for the homeless, regularly reports on the nationwide trend of hostile official efforts to move the homeless out of central areas of cities.

The Tramp Laws of a century ago made the public condition of destitution illegal by severely restricting a poor person's ability to exist in public. Today, urban governments attempt to sweep away the homeless, while government leaders at all levels announce that the cause of the growing problem of homelessness is at root beyond the capacity of homeless individuals or families to resolve: At present, there is no movement toward a solution, and the number of homeless continues to grow. This can be viewed in the wider context of the failure to develop and stick with a comprehensive urban policy in the United States.

The U.S. Failure to Develop a Comprehensive Urban Policy

The development of an effective, overall urban policy is no mean achievement, and no nation has developed a completely effective and enduring national plan to deal with the problems of its cities. Still, the record of the United States stands out as particularly piecemeal, uncoordinated, and inconsistent. The reason for this is that individual metropolitan regions are divided into multiple self-governing units and that urban policy at the national level shifts with each change of government administration.

The United States lacks the government structures and political traditions to effectively contain and shape patterns of urban expansion. From the earliest days of population and economic growth, jealously independent towns and cities have defied the attempts of regional planning commissions and state legislatures to impose a regional coordination of efforts in such areas as fresh water supply and water pollution control, containment of urban and suburban sprawl, transportation, parks, and the coordination and economical provision of public services. Government and businesses in small towns harbored suspicions about being overpowered and exploited if they entered into cooperative schemes with larger and more powerful urban centers. Today, effective planning requires that the territorial unit addressed by planners comprise at least the metropolitan community or region. However, enormous metropolises like Los Angeles or New York have thus far presented insurmountable difficulties in the development of territorially comprehensive plans because the areas involved are divided among so many independent governments. Even in metropolitan areas of modest size, it is not unusual to find a dozen independent townships. Outlying populations of all metro regions are realistically concerned that area-wide cooperation would involve an increase in taxes and represent an increased strain on local services.

Limited Strategies

At the national level in the United States, there have been some limited efforts to develop more comprehensive planning strategies. A model cities program sought to integrate rehabilitative efforts directed at inner-city areas. The New Towns strategy, which hearkened back to the work of Ebenezer Howard, was designed to create new urban environments with limited populations and coordinated services and institutions. Enterprise zones and empowerment zones in recent years have been attempts to jump start economic growth in depressed inner-city areas by providing incentives to induce private businesses to relocate there.

Model Cities

The Model Cities program was designed to concentrate existing federal government assistance programs—in the form of education, training, jobs programs, economic rehabilitation funds, and housing supports—in a few cities. The concentrated benefits were expected to provide demonstration projects that would bring about meaningful change, showing other cities what was possible through coordinated effort. An additional feature of the plan was the incorporation of local community leadership in the planning process. As a result, the plan for a given community would generate grass-roots support among local citizens. Although Model Cities seemed to include all the necessary elements for success, the program contained fatal flaws that emerged in the implementation stage. Whereas the Model Cities plan had been proposed for only a few cities, the legislation that was passed to authorize it increased the number of locations to more than one hundred. This meant that the funding allocated to the program would be spread too thin, defeating the impact of the program in any given location. Coordination between different federal government agencies responsible for administering the plan failed to materialize, and there was conflict between administrators and grass-roots representatives. In 1972, there was a change in philosophy at the national level as Lyndon Johnson's "Great Society" administration gave way to Richard Nixon's efforts to disengage government from direct intervention into the problems of urban minorities and the poor. The Model Cities program was terminated, never really having gotten under way (McFarland 1978, 84–88).

New Towns

An alternative strategy to that of rebuilding old urban districts was to start over and build communities from scratch somewhere else. Such an approach would largely avoid dealing with the tangled problems of the existing ownership rights of established property holders, of what to do with local poor and minority residents while the redevelopment took place, and of what resistance might develop among locals (because, in effect, there were no locals) in response to the implementation of the master plan. The beauty of such an approach has appealed to planners since Howard's time. Three federally sponsored "greenbelt" towns were constructed in the early 1930s: Greenbelt, Maryland; Greenhills, Ohio; and Greendale, Wisconsin. These early U.S. New Towns contained little or no provision for industrial or commercial developments and remained garden suburbs—in the end housing slightly more than 2,100 families among them (Scott 1969, 338–339).

The more recent history of the New Town philosophy in the United States has been dominated by towns that were conceived and built as for-profit enterprises with government subsidy. In the 1960s, Lyndon Johnson suggested that self-contained New Towns become part of the general strategy for ameliorating the problems of the inner city, and between 1968 and 1970, Congress passed legislation granting benefits and guarantees to New Town developers. Usually cited as among the most successful private venture New Towns are Radburn, New Jersey; Reston, Virginia; and Columbia, Maryland. Each of these may be judged success, if success is measured by whether these are pleasant places in which to live for middle-class families. Radburn, a suburb of New York City, never became anything like a self-contained settlement or socially integrated town comprised of different social classes. Reston and Columbia are more recent and more ambitious efforts at designing complete and class-integrated communities—at the planning stage. But because they represented substantial market ventures for their financial backers, which included major oil companies, developers eventually found it necessary to drop such plans as side-by-side housing for different social classes—too risky a concept given the need to attract affluent families.

New Towns have had a very limited impact on the lives of the average city resident and were too slow to provide a return on investment compared to other ventures. This planning strategy was never intended to address the problem of providing livelihood and a place to live for the city's neediest underhoused and underemployed residents. The problems of cities in the United States have been linked rather convincingly to the inability of the market to create either adequate housing or employment for the inner-city poor: It would be surprising if these deficiencies could be remedied simply by allowing private enterprise to choose new sites for urban development.

Enterprise and Empowerment Zones

In recent decades, some version of the enterprise zone concept has played a major role in the approach to urban poverty in the United States. The goal is to match the unemployed urban workforce with newly created jobs by enticing employers into the central city, presenting them with incentives for locating there and hiring the local unemployed. The Heritage Foundation, a conservative think tank dedicated, in its own words, to the "principles of free enterprise, limited government, individual liberty," has taken credit for importing the idea from the United Kingdom where it was first employed. Conservatives who endorsed the idea argued that this approach to economic revitalization would harness the natural potential of private enterprise to do what bureaucratic command structures were unable to do—to generate sustained economic recovery in blighted areas.

Details vary among different states and cities that have adopted the plan, but they are all modeled to some degree on the first U.S. enterprise zone established in Connecticut. There, qualifying employers in the designated areas were granted a 50 percent reduction in state corporate income tax payments for the first ten years, a five-year 80 percent reduction in local property taxes, a grant of $1,000 for each new job created, grants for job training, and special low-interest loans (Hardison 1981, 10–20). By 1992, 35 states and the District of Columbia had enterprise zones: They were located in depressed rural as well as urban areas, and the number of zones varied widely across states. New York State had 19, while Arkansas had 458, making the entire state an enterprise zone. The success of the zones in creating new jobs is difficult to assess. For example, in central Los Angeles the designation of a zone coincided with an increase in small businesses, but because very few of the new businesses took advantage of the support offered by the plan, most of the new business activity cannot be attributed to the program. The record is clearer in the troubled Los Angeles community of Watts: The creation of a zone there had little impact, as there was very little increase in the number of businesses to interpret (Riposa 1996). However, the federal government position, as expressed through the office of Housing and Urban Development, was that by 1992 enterprise zones had saved or created hundreds of thousands of jobs where those jobs were most needed (U.S. Department of Housing and Urban Development 1992, 1, 83).

The Clinton administration embraced the enterprise zone approach to urban economic recovery, changing the title of the program and the targeted districts to "empowerment zones" in 1993. The new program required that localities compete for funding by proposing comprehensive plans that addressed not only the creation of jobs, but also the coordination of social services and education programs. The community proposals that were successful would receive $100 million in social service grants, along with a range of tax reduction incentives. In addition, a system of advisory and specialist resources networked from the cabinet level down to community citizen councils was set up to assist and monitor the achievement of goals that had originated within the community itself. Over five hundred communities applied. Only six received the full support available under the program. About seventy others received some funding (Riposa 1996).

Harlem was one of the winners in the federal funding lottery, receiving $100 million and the full package of tax incentives, to which the state of New York added another $200 million in aid. An article in *Black Enterprise,* however, qualified the benefits of the plan. The latest Harlem renaissance would bring a dozen large retail businesses to the area, including Walt Disney, Rite Aid, Pathmark, and the Gap, as well as a Magic Johnson movie theater and a massive retail-entertainment complex, to be located near the Apollo Theater. Community leaders and small business owners were concerned because a disproportionate share of the benefits of the program would go to the new employers, and they wondered what the impact would be on small existing operations that were just getting by (Smith 1997).

In a society committed to allowing private enterprise to provide the leading edge of change, the enterprise zone and empowerment zone programs appear to be a natural outcome in the evolution of social policy: The older enterprise zone approach, especially, minimizes the role of government command or enacted elements and maximizes the role of the market. It provides government payments and subsidies to businesses to draw them into the economic vacuum of the inner cities. In return, business provides work for the unemployed and poor. Critics have raised questions about the kinds of jobs, the working conditions, and the rate of pay received by those who are employed under the enterprise zone plan. Coldly considered, the inner-city poor in a wealthy nation can be seen as providing a kind of domestic asset within the framework of the global economy. The old enterprise zone schemes of the 1980s made sense within this framework. By combining government subsidies with the lower wages that prevailed in poor districts, the enterprise zone labor force was made competitive with its overseas counterparts in poor nations. The point was not lost on critics of the plan. They charge that employers received government subsidies to create sweatshop environments allowing poor U.S. laborers to become competitive globally through the creation of Third World conditions at home. The criticism is one-sided, but it provides a useful reminder regarding potential worst-case outcomes of profit-driven social policies. In order for the Clinton empowerment zone plan to avoid similar criticisms, it was important that the educational and service components of the program remain central and highly visible features. Any tendency for the self-sustaining element of the program, the profit-incentive element, to run ahead of the social and community-building provisions would need to be avoided. As we have seen, this has in the past proven difficult in the tradition of urban planning in the United States. Elements of planning programs and entire planning philosophies can dissolve with changes in administration.

American social policy as it impacts cities had already undergone a major change in 1996, with potentially devastating impact on the urban poor and underhoused. The Personal Responsibility and Work Opportunity Reconciliation Act of 1996, the "welfare reform" act, limited the period during which poor families with children could receive welfare support to two years. The act was likely to have a disproportionate impact on places where the large number of the poor were concentrated. The intent of the time limit restrictions placed on federal support payments was to reduce government expenditures and to force the able-bodied poor to find work. The reason for the popularity of the measure among lawmakers and tax-payers is self-evident. From the early nineties through the beginning of the new century, unemployment rates were falling and there was a demand for workers. In the conventional wisdom of the era, it was a good time to send unemployed poor people to work. As we have seen in the analysis of poverty in Chapter 9, the feasibility of the change in policy would depend on there being sufficient demand for the right kinds of labor in areas in which poor people were living, and, since the majority of terminated adult welfare recipients were women with children, the availability of affordable or subsidized childcare facilities.

Four years after the restrictions were put in place, the consequences had begun to emerge. The National Conference of State Legislatures summarized the results of several statewide studies that revealed that 50 percent to 70 percent of all adults who left welfare (voluntarily or otherwise) after the more restrictive rules were passed were receiving some income from employment. However, for the subset who waited until their eligibility actually ran out, the proportion of those who had found work was significantly lower. This meant that there were enough families "not working to cause serious concerns. We know very little about the situation of those families, their means of support and the long-term stability of their financial support systems" (Tweedie, Reichert, and O'Connor 1999). The typical hourly wage of former welfare recipients who had found work was between $5.50 and $7.00. Most families experienced economic hardship, but the conference report says that there was little evidence late in 1999 that the changes in eligibility had contributed to homelessness. The director of the National Law Center on Homelessness and Poverty did not agree. While she acknowledged that there was still in March 2000 scanty data available on the impact of welfare restrictions on homeless rates, she based her impression that the restrictions were producing homelessness on reports from those who provide services to the homeless around the country. In their view, the increased numbers of homeless they were seeing were families who had their benefits reduced or who had been eliminated from the rolls (*Policy and Practice of Public Human Services* 2000).

Given the political nature of the question, it may still be some time before sufficiently compelling evidence emerges to effectively challenge the feasibility of current policies that include three major features: what government admits are inadequate levels of support in housing assistance; a lottery whereby cities compete for a few comprehensive empowerment zone grants; a policy of transforming a long-term program in which the poor are entitled to welfare support from the state into a temporary assistance program with fixed limits that require the poor to find work. Since the 1970s, there has been a renewed hostility toward "big government," fueled by political rhetoric that charges that large-scale programs of government assistance do not work. In this view, any policy is suspect if it is not based on individual initiative and the utilization of market mechanisms to achieve socially desirable goals. This policy emphasis does not resolve the long-standing debate over the responsibility of the state for the welfare of the poor versus the responsibility of all adults for their own welfare and that of their children. It does not resolve the debate between the structuralists, who argue that the conditions of poverty and homelessness are produced by remote forces, and the culture of poverty theorists who argue that the causes are in the habits of the poor themselves. Instead of fully engaging both sides of the argument, the position taken by government policymakers presently favors the individual responsibility and bad-habits interpretation. It will take some time, given the prevailing wisdom, to understand that prosperity can have negative consequences for millions in the rising costs that attend it and to recognize that ambitious, consistent social policy has never really characterized the approach to addressing urban problems in the United States.

Urban Policy outside the United States

A selected review of urban policy outside the United States reveals two useful insights. First, in recent history, many nations have engaged in comprehensive urban planning originating at the national level and directed at achieving major social and economic goals. Second, policy around the world has come to resemble that of the United States in recent years, characterized by what is considered to be a pragmatic reluctance to interfere with market forces, a much more limited set of objectives, and a more limited commitment of government resources to urban planning.

Urban Policy in Western Europe

In the twentieth century, urban policymakers in Western Europe shared certain problems in common. Urban growth tended to be concentrated in a particular city or urban region; construction and street patterns were holdovers from the very rapid and often haphazard period of industrialization in the last century; and, after World War II, there was an acute housing shortage in many countries. Governments had a longer history of intervening vigorously with plans to control patterns of growth and in the direct provision of housing. By the mid-twentieth century, most had a national urban plan in place.

In the three cases we consider here, the United Kingdom, France, and the Netherlands, the major planning problem was defined as controlling concentrated urban growth and diverting development to economically declining or stagnant peripheral regions. In England, population growth and economic concentration in and around London was a persistent concern, associated with unmet housing demand, traffic congestion, and unbalanced regional development. In France, growth had been concentrated in the north central region, around Paris, a primate city (concept discussed in Chapter 6) that, like London, historically has been a magnet for industrial, commercial, and population growth. The planning problem was perceived as redirecting growth to other cities. In the Netherlands, the magnet for growth is comprised of a ring of cities surrounding a rich agricultural region in the South. Taken together, the cities, which include Amsterdam, Rotterdam, Utrecht, The Hague, Haarlem, Leiden, Delft, Dordrecht, and Hilversum, make up the ring city, the Randstad. There is no primate city, but rather a primate urban region composed of several large- and medium-sized cities. In this case, the problem was how to control additional Randstad growth while preventing urban sprawl from consuming the rich interior farmlands. As was the case in England and France, there was also the goal of redirecting population and economic growth—in this case toward the underpopulated and economically inert northern reaches of the country.

The strategy for limiting and redirecting growth varied in each of the three cases. In England, an act of Parliament in 1938 confined the development of the city of London and its immediate environs within a coordinated master plan designed to limit expansion and redirect industrial development to depressed regions of the country. The 1938 act decreed that the outward growth of London be halted where it was. A greenbelt—a ring of undeveloped open country and farmland—was permanently set aside to remain free of commercial development of any sort. Further growth in the region would be confined to eight satellite towns located outside the ring and designed to be self-contained residential, commercial, and industrial units that would not promote commuting to work in London.

The London Plan was partially effective. The greenbelt was maintained in principle, the satellite cities attracted population and industrial growth, their shopping districts proved attractive, and overall the new towns with their demand for industrial labor provided a degree of class integration. However, there was little provision for controlling growth in the areas between the new towns, and these areas became the sites of residential and other mixed growth as the new towns themselves were ringed by a maze of speculatively built development. This was soon to become known as "commuter country," and many residents travelled daily from far beyond the greenbelt to their jobs in London (Hall 1984, 39–43).

In France, the greenbelt strategy for controlling the growth of Paris was rejected in favor of a plan that would allow growth outward from the existing margins of the city only in narrow, strictly controlled ribbons or fingers stretching east and west along existing transportation corridors. The plan, administered by a regional planning authority, featured the development of autonomous new towns along the narrow corridors. The advantage over the London greenbelt strategy was that the corridor plan would provide a self-limiting check on regional development by moving new development further and further away from the center. Very quickly, prospective residents and businesses, with no choice but to locate in the increasingly distant peripheral towns, would find it more attractive to locate in a different city where they could be closer to the center.

The Dutch strategy for saving the green heart at the center of the Randstad complex also involved a narrow corridor strategy. A regional planning authority took control of development and took advantage of a division of labor that existed among the various Randstad cities. Plans focused on engineering an effective public transportation system that whisked travelers among cities that specialized in various levels of government, finance, commerce, and industry. The kinds of diversified lighter industrial growth that take place in suburban rings in other countries went to smaller cities like Haarlem, Leiden, and Hilversum. Residential development was tightly restricted to narrow zones within the urbanized ring.

Just as the master plans were taking effect in these countries, the nature of the major urban problem reversed. From the mid-1960s onward, inner-city decline became an increasing concern in Europe, especially in terms of the loss of industrial jobs. Between 1966 and 1976, the London area within the greenbelt lost half a million industrial jobs; by the mid-1980s, Paris lost 300,000 jobs and 500,000 residents; within the Randstad, the leading city—Amsterdam—declined in population between 1965 and 1982 by 155,000, leaving just 700,000 residents (Hall 1984, 25, 36–37; van Weesep 1988, 100). The reasons for decline everywhere were the same: technological and regional restructuring, with old industrial jobs disappearing into more efficient manufacturing techniques and reappearing, transformed, in distant and less expensive manufacturing locales. National urban policies immediately became more accommodating to market trends, less restrictive, and less ambitious in scope.

The conservative Thatcher government in Britain published the *Action for Cities* policy, affirming its commitment to the spirit of "enterprise and resourcefulness," and attempted to lure employers back into central city areas with a program of incentives, vowing to eliminate unnecessary red tape, to help reduce costs, and in general to provide a "welcoming" environment for business (Edwards and Deakin 1992). Consistent with this emphasis, the enterprise zone idea, which originated in England, provided limited results (Pacione 1990, 196–199). Direct expenditures for social programs to relieve the social costs of decline were cut back during the 1980s. A City Challenge program in the 1990s invited municipalities to submit applications for funding for badly needed services and development projects. Under this program, the winners receive shares from a limited pool of funds set aside by the national government; the losers try again the following year. (In 1991, one of the winning bids came from Bethnal Greene, the area studied in the 1950s by Young and Willmott [1957] and discussed in Chapter 3. The now primarily Bangladeshi community received funding for an English-as-a-second-language program). The winner-take-all lottery style policy was under review in the mid-1990s. In France and the Netherlands also, policy was modified to attract or keep business in whatever location suited it. The European Union is a single marketplace, which has broadened the geography of decision making for executives determining where manufacturing, transshipment points, and executive offices will be located. Europe has embraced the reality of the dissolving significance of international boundaries produced by globalization. As a common economic region, it will be a more powerful force in the international economy. A necessary correlate appears to be the loss of the capacity of local governments to regulate change beyond devising policies to welcome private enterprise.

Centrally Planned Economies

It is useful to consider briefly the kinds of policy associated with centrally planned or socialist economies. Despite the political and economic revolutions that have dismantled the USSR and drawn the single other large-scale example of socialism, the People's Republic of China, squarely into the global marketplace, the planning

experiments of the recent past remain useful illustrations of the frustrations of socialist command policy to resist international market forces.

Under the principles of socialism, the spatial distribution of opportunities and
cultural benefits must be considered part of the general pattern of distribution of
social benefits. In line with the principle of eliminating inequalities, attention must
be paid to the location of housing, services, education, employment, shopping,
and green space for recreation. Cities need to be built in such a way that all will
be provided for equally—at least to a reasonable degree. To the extent that social
class, as measured by differences in income and other benefits, is a persistent feature of socialist society—and there is no question but that it exists in every socialist experiment—it is the job of the planner to reduce those inequalities by seeing
first and foremost to the needs of the less highly remunerated. That is, the planner's job is to reduce inequalities consistent with the goals of socialism.

Under the Soviet system, the goals were to limit the size of cities (centers of
privilege in comparison to rural and small-town life) through the use of greenbelts
and totally planned satellite towns; to promote growth in the less populated eastern regions (thereby bringing urban amenities to those areas); to see to the coordination of urban housing, economic development, and the distribution of services according to an overall urban plan; and to make a massive effort to provide
housing, thereby addressing the dire and persistent housing shortage. The plans
were repeatedly frustrated by what may be recognized as market factors associated with demand.

Plans to limit the growth of large cities in the western part of the nation were
obstructed by internal migrations that defied vigorous measures for controlling
domestic population movements. The population grew beyond the greenbelts of
the major cities as migrants employed devious schemes of relocation (Morton
1984, 5). As a result, growth in the eastern regions lagged far behind, and inequalities persisted among those western Soviet cities. The fact that industrial development continued to be heavier in western cities was rationalized by a change
in ideology that said development anywhere benefits all citizens (Badcock 1984,
314–315). Efforts to engineer all aspects of city development failed due to a lack of
coordination among the various government bureaucracies that administered
housing, industrial development, education , and so forth. Different components
of new growth often lagged far behind one another. For example, the construction
of housing and shopping facilities might come long after the higher priority construction of new plants beyond the edge of existing urban development, so that
workers and their families faced hardships of commuting or obtaining necessities.
Finally, the goal of providing all workers with adequate housing was subverted
by the equivalent of Western gentrification, as the social elite made effective
claims to new housing on the basis that their more vital professions made it important that they be located closer to offices or plants where they worked (Szelenyi
1977, 1983). Long before the end of the Soviet system, market forces were at work,
undermining socialist principles.

In the People's Republic of China, the market is also having an enormous impact on the shape of urbanization. The Chinese government is attempting to rein-

vent socialist policy to fit a system where change is driven by the energy of international capitalism. Since the mid-1980s, China's economy has grown at a remarkable rate, averaging 8.3 percent a year between 1985 and 1995 (World Bank 1997, 214). China has repeatedly reaffirmed its commitment to facilitating an economic revolution, if not a political one.

During the revolutionary era, Mao Zedong took a dim view of the contribution of cities and the urban population to the Chinese Revolution. Traditionally, the consumer cities of capitalism and imperialism absorbed and squandered the productivity of peasant labor, and tight controls were placed on the growth of the urban population in the 1950s. During the 1960s and 1970s, millions of Chinese were involuntarily relocated from city to country, and large numbers of the administrative and educated classes were exiled to rural areas for alleged offenses of privilege. By the end of the Mao era, there were 20 million fewer urban Chinese than there were in 1960 (Kirkby 1989).

Beginning in 1979, China undertook a series of economic reforms that led in the 1980s to a full-fledged effort to gain a secure foothold in the expanding world market and to take advantage of the potential China had for becoming a powerful actor in the global economy. Restrictions on population movement to the cities became more relaxed. By the end of the 1900s, the relaxation of migration control restrictions and the active recruitment of urban labor had created a different China from the one Mao had departed. At the same time, the end of the enforced commune system in rural areas revealed a surplus of rural labor at levels of 30 or 40 percent, contributing to a large floating migrant labor population in search of work (Xie and Costa 1991, 321). Many in the surplus rural labor force found their way to the expanding coastal cities where they worked as temporary laborers (Wang and Hu 1999). The immense potential for urban growth in a nation of 1.2 billion people who had been subject to decades of restrictions against relocation has begun to be realized. At midcentury, there were 6 cities with over a million people and 35 with 200,000 or more (Chen 1991, 342–345). By 1993, 18 cities had more than two million, 126 had more than one million (Wang and Hu 1999).

In contrast to Mao's distrust of urban growth, the stance of China's present-day leadership may be termed flexible, though not without misgiving. The policy at present is to encourage growth in several designated cities along the coast, at the same time encouraging investment in the less inherently attractive (to foreign investors) interior and poorer regions. The latter component is more consistent with the redistributive goals of a socialist state, but development in the interior and western regions is markedly lower than along the coast, and poverty rates are significantly higher. Rural populations are generally poorer than urban populations, but China has had some modest success in addressing regional and rural-urban disparities in wealth (Tang 1999). Still, as the world's most prominent remaining socialist adventure, the question remains whether China will be able to reconcile socialist goals with breakaway market-led growth. Planning or command structures are not much in evidence in congested cities where traffic crawls along at a few miles per hour, polluted air and water is the norm, people live in small and intensely crowded housing units, and millionaires and the impoverished struggle to hold their place in the booming marketplace.

The experience of China at the turn of the century underlines the collapse worldwide of major efforts to control urban change. The only policy choice that exists with regard to the world market economy is to figure out a way to find a place in it or be left behind. According to this wisdom, policymakers must accept the desirability of growth, including market-driven urban growth, as a given. This new order holds out the prospect of revolutionary changes in the configuration and the hegemonic order of the cities of the world. It appears that bankers, mobile capital, and private firms of architects will have as much or more than government policymakers to say about the shape of cities and the direction of change in the future. Many are finding the new world order, without vigorous urban policies that soften the impact of the global market, a hard town to live in.

Three Dimensions of Successful Urban Policy

Despite its lowering profile worldwide, it is still possible to envision a set of principles, a set of lessons that emerge out of such a survey of urban planning as we have undertaken in this chapter, that defines effective urban policy. We may want to keep in mind the sweeping visions of Howard, Le Corbusier, and Soleri, and learn also from the failed or modestly successful planning efforts of governments. There seem to be three criteria that may be used to judge the prospect for failure or success of an urban plan.

Scale
A successful urban policy is one that is cast on a broad scale, where national priorities are set in advance, where an overall philosophy of urban development is in place and ongoing. We have reviewed a number of such policies. In every case, policy goals have been modified over time to reflect the changing definition of the urban problem. The existence of a national urban policy has at least provided the context for an orderly assessment of ongoing changes. European nations today, even before a unified Europe matures, have begun to ask questions and organize broad regional consortia to deal with international interurban cooperation in the future. While the nature of these cooperative ventures is still in the process of definition, the important point is the scope of imagination involved here, building on a history where urban policy has been conceptualized as a national priority.

Comprehensiveness
A comprehensive plan channels growth; it does not build a barrier against it. In the past, France and the Netherlands offered examples of comprehensive planning. In order to prevent sprawl, planners sought to channel growth into acceptable urban corridors allowing growth to continue, tapering away from major cities in a self-limiting fashion. Comprehensive planning accommodates to the momentum of trends in popular taste and the designs of popular enterprise by a guarded, permissive shaping of these forces, rather than simply attempting to obstruct

change that is already well under way. Often, the greatest challenge facing policy-makers is reconciling the momentum of popular trends with social goals. In the late 1970s, a presidential commission in the United States reported that the urban policy that made the most sense was to accept the decline of the northern and eastern cities as a fact and to help the population in these declining areas to follow businesses and jobs that were moving to states in the South where cities were growing. A comprehensive plan, however, requires more than simply going with the flow. The cities of the North and East were not being abandoned by the economy; they were undergoing a fundamental change in the type of economic activities that were concentrated there. The challenge of raising the standards of training and education for local populations in former industrial centers remains unmet a generation later.

Social Justice

Any attempt to define this criterion is sure to start an argument. It is, to be sure, based on a value judgment, but appears a necessary consideration in assessing the effectiveness of a particular social policy. It follows the premise that changes that benefit some of the population of a city, region, or nation, may harm others. Similarly, a social policy will probably serve the needs of some more than others. Will the poor of China's central and western regions eventually benefit from the affluence of the booming coastal provinces? How much inequality is too much before a socialist state is no longer socialist? In recent decades, the following questions have been debated as matters of policy: Should Manhattan get a new highway on the West Side? Should the population of San Francisco be capped? Should the Greater London Council with its regional planning authority be scrapped, and the greenbelt be opened to private development? Who will be served best by these proposed changes? The poor don't drive in Manhattan; they aren't likely to move en masse into high-cost San Francisco; nor are they likely to buy villas or condominiums if the greenbelt becomes a suburb. Who will benefit most from any of these measures? The question provides a minor exercise for the sociological imagination. As subjective an issue as social justice is, it is seldom difficult to recognize in context.

11

A UNIFIED PERSPECTIVE FOR URBAN SOCIOLOGY

It is clear from the preceding chapters that urban sociology addresses a broad subject matter. The theme that unifies the various areas of interest into a cohesive subdiscipline within sociology is that all we have spoken of here is related in some systematic manner to the urban arena. That is, the proper subject matter of an urban sociology incorporates the social phenomena created or changed by cities. Urban effects may include the nature of experience (a feeling of powerlessness or freedom, an aversion to strangers, or a tolerance for different kinds of people), influences on behavior (becoming part of a social movement or engaging in a form of deviance), the emergence of different forms of social organization (new political parties or subcultures), or shifts in the focus and objectives of social policy (to balance living conditions between rural and urban areas or to lower the visibility of the homeless). Urban sociology is the study of social phenomena that are of the city. Other things that happen in the city, just as they happen elsewhere, do not interest us in the same systematic way.

We have demonstrated that the urban environment operates as an important sociological variable. That is, the urban environment really does affect the way people feel as well as what they do. Yet several important questions persist with regard to this urban variable: Does the urban environment operate as an *independent* variable, as a basic causal factor, or is it merely an *intervening* variable? Is the city itself a *result* of some prior cause—a manifestation of the political and economic organization of a society, or more appropriately, of *global* political and economic arrangements? When we look at the effects of the urban environment (size, density, and heterogeneity, as they were identified by Wirth), are we identifying *ultimate* causes? Or are the aggregations of people and productive forces that make up the cities merely the way the *international marketplace* organizes itself into dense nodes of activity in order to facilitate business? These are no incidental questions for urban sociologists. The questions raise the issue of whether it makes sense to talk about urban factors at all, or whether we should go to the heart of the matter by studying the international economy instead.

The field of urban sociology has arrived at an important juncture. In order for it to progress, it is necessary to begin to reconcile the fact that it contains two very different sets of interests and approaches. The arguments and issues addressed in the preceding chapters suggest that there are no comfortable labels for identifying the distinct approaches. The labels that seem to do the least violence to the respective orientations are *culturalist* versus *structuralist.*

The culturalist approach is rooted in the tradition of Tönnies, Durkheim, and Wirth, and argues that the urban arena gives rise to a distinctive way of life, identified as urbanism. Individual culturalists have been concerned with formulating particular images of urbanism. The common feature shared by all of the work in this tradition is that the urban environment generates a distinct cultural form. This may be manifest as interpersonal or general social aversion, as in Wirth's classic essay (1938), or in the form of cohesiveness and subcultural richness, as in Fischer's (1975, 1982) point of view. Thus, the city, as a social environment, is capable of creating novel ways of feeling and acting, which can be called subcultural phenomena.

The fact that culturalists also talk about structural variables, such as size and density (Wirth) or critical mass (Fischer), need not be confusing. The culturalists begin with the premise that differences in social organization, such as the size of a given population, will generate differences in the nature of the participants' experience and the manner in which individuals interact. This was the basis of Simmel's observation on how cities affected "mental life" and the insight of Park as he linked urban ecology and behavior. However, the culturalist's interest is focused on the outcome that is produced by structural characteristics of the urban environment. Size and density produce "urbanism," which is the subcultural expression of the experience of life in the urban environment. This is what sets the subject matter of urban sociology apart for the culturalists. The urban arena itself creates the sociological variables in which urban sociologists are interested; that is urbanism as a distinctive way of life.

By the 1960s urban sociology, dominated by the culturalist orientation, was facing something of a crisis. A chorus of criticism raised the complaint that urban sociologists had as yet failed to adequately identify their subject matter. As cities sprawled into metropolitan regions, and the electronic media of "urban" communication and entertainment spread into every village and hamlet, the question became, What is it that urban sociologists study? They had failed to identify the theoretical object of their discipline (Harvey 1973). The culminating theoretical achievement of classical urbanism, Wirth's essay, was in disrepute as an "antiurban" tract. Yet it was the best that the culturalist tradition had managed to produce in terms of a theoretical statement. Fischer's (1975) pro-urban subcultural thesis was still years away.

By the end of the 1960s, there was a growing body of work in urban political economy. Its focus was mainly on the problem of underdevelopment, and it found the most compelling explanation of the cause of underdevelopment in the structural relationship between rich and poor economies. Political economists posited the existence of a global network of economic relationships and opened an important tangential linkage between the study of the international economy and urban sociology. Cities represented intensive nodes of power and economic manipulation, instruments through which the underdevelopment of poor nations was bound to the development of rich nations (Frank 1967). In the rich countries, the urban environment could be properly understood as the physical arena in which world corporations threw their weight around, dictating the rise and fall of local economic fortunes; it was where their executives lived and played, inflating the cost of living and affecting the housing supply for the less affluent of the region. In the view of the political economists, traditional urban sociology was inadequate because its focus was on what cities did, the sociological consequences of the urban arena itself (Castells [1972] 1977). The whole approach was misguided because cities were themselves only a manifestation of political and economic relationships and the urban arena did not give rise to, but only reflected, the workings of the international economy.

From the perspective of political economy, it is appropriate to study the urban arena but only as an intensified spatial manifestation of wider processes. The major fault of the culturalists is that they tend to see the city as a self-contained arena of action; thus, they begin and end their studies in the middle of the full range of operational factors. For the culturalists, the city is the producer of social action. For the political economists, the city is the product of broader economic and political relationships, more to be explained than to explain.

The structuralist approach carries its own set of liabilities. At the heart of much of the work in political economy is a radical critique of the capitalist world system. It is radical in the simple political sense that it questions the fundamental legitimacy, the equity, of the way the international marketplace distributes advantage and disadvantage: The poor countries of the world are held hostage by the wealthy nations; the poor and the working class are the expendable victims of economic change, as international corporations and mobile capital seek to optimize profits in a global arena; and the less affluent elements of populations around the world are systematically squeezed to pay inflated rents, or squeezed out of housing altogether by the inflation of local property values that are responding to extra-local economic trends.

The fact that these arguments have come to make sense to so many social scientists and others does not negate the fact that the observations assail the status quo. In nations that subscribe to the ideology that capitalism is a benevolent force, synonymous with democracy, the arguments of political economists are heresy in polite circles. However, eventually, social criticism, if it has merit, becomes part of the perspective and vocabulary of mainstream social actors—political figures and journalists, for example. "The permanent underclass," "structural displacement," and references to the dual city phenomena in explaining inequality have been picked up, discussed, and reported in general public discourse. The debates borrow concepts from critical works in social science.

Nothing has moved the political economy perspective to the fore so much as the general popular awareness of globalization and the questions it poses for the future. Discussions of the global future underline the uncertainty of how average workers in rich nations will fit into postindustrial economies. These discussions also raise related moral and ethical questions regarding the conditions of Third World and other workers as the competition among geographically mobile corporations to drive down production costs highlights the systematic linkage between workers in different parts of the world. In effect, the tightening structure of economic globalization has moved the questions raised by political economists and the radical critique of market-driven change into the arena of public discussion. Questions currently raised about the future of work and the interests of workers are questions about class interests—and in the tradition of Western discourse, these have been the most radical and disturbing issues for the past two centuries. Still, the prevailing voices in the debate about the future are those that emphasize its promise, the ability of the system of private enterprise to adjust to the changing conditions and to produce benefits for the greatest numbers. In its favor, capitalism has proven its ability to endure through its flexibility and to submerge all alternative systems in its wake. Interested parties may express a concern about the direction in which global change is taking them, but there appears no "living" alternative. Every nation clamors for a place at the same table set by competition and the profit motive.

This is an exciting time for the social scientist, and for the urban sociologist in particular, but the global dimension of change has created a new perspective in which to view the role of cities. The structural emphasis of those analyses that focus on the global economy see the urban arena as only an intervening variable, not a fundamental causal factor, in understanding urban processes and urban lives. This perspective suggests that urban sociology plays a different role in the hierarchy of specialist sociologies at the beginning of the twenty-first century, a status much different from the one held at the beginning of the twentieth century when the sheer dimension of urbanization drew the attention of the leading theoreticians in the field. The new emphasis on the causal role of global economic unification dwarfs even the largest urban arenas and tells us that what happens in cities is ultimately conditioned by worldwide events.

The global perspective, in reality, simply gives the urban sociologist another layer of analysis to consider, another tool for understanding what is observed on the city street. It is a long road from observing the way political and economic forces operate on a global scale to explaining how an elderly woman feels about leaving her Chicago apartment or knowing whether a recent young male migrant to Nairobi feels a stronger attachment to the city or his homeplace. However, it adds to our understanding to trace the feelings of the elderly woman and the young man to trends in the international economic system that manifest in Chicago as unemployment statistics or crime rates and in Kenya as the balance between rural and urban economic opportunities. It could be argued that there are more immediate, yet legitimate sociologies that might be done in either case that would yield worthwhile insights in the experiences and feelings of these two distant individuals. Political economy is a remote theoretical tool, with little to offer in the way of innovative methodological devices to employ in the immediate empirical investigation of the details of these two lives. On the other hand, a traditional study of these people that failed to point to the link between the condition of their lives and the global economic order would be incomplete. In any serious analysis, it is vital to link the immediate and more remote spheres of analysis.

Consequences of the Division in Urban Sociology

To date, the culturalist and structuralist approaches in sociology have most often generated fundamentally different conclusions about the nature or consequences of urban life. Each tradition contains certain background assumptions about the social order that promote dissimilar questions and answers. Table 11-1 attempts to isolate the differences between the culturalist and structuralist approaches. It contrasts their underlying assumptions and their emphases in some basic areas of concern that we dealt with in earlier chapters. Represented here is an affinity among certain major bodies of ideas. The culturalist concepts have two things in common. First, they are part of the mainstream liberal tradition in urban sociology that connects certain current themes and approaches through the Chicago school (Park, Burgess, and Wirth) to the classical theorists (Durkheim, Weber, and Simmel). Secondly, these themes take the urban environment as the main explanatory variable in describing what happens in cities. The city gives rise to distinctive patterns of thought and interaction that represent the leading edge of change in the world. This is true for the industrial city, where the environment

TABLE 11-1   Distinguishing Features of the Culturalist and Structuralist Approaches

	Culturalist Approach	Structuralist Approach
Characteristics of the urban arena	Size and density give rise to distinctive modes of thinking, interaction, and organization.	Cities represent a concentration of political and economic forces and relations that extend around the globe.
Ideology	The urban form is progressive and reflects modernity, advanced organization, and technology.	The urban form is the locus of wealth and privilege, and the product of accumulated capital.
Forces that shape the environment	The emphasis is on ecology and community, local environmental features.	The emphasis is on political economy, an extraterritorial focus.
Development and underdevelopment	In modernization theory the city creates momentum for development through the spread of modern attitudes, technology, and forms of organization.	Political economy argues that cities are parasitic in the Third World and maintains that there is an international imbalance in development.
Stratification	The culture of poverty thesis prevails.	A structured inequality rooted in changes in the world economic system and regional patterns of growth and decline prevail.

may generate alienation or cohesion, depending on the theory in question, and for the Third World, where the city is the vessel that carries new ideas, technology, and modes of organization (bureaucratic processes) to the less-developed countries. Cities contain great wealth and poverty, as well as all social levels in between. Economic competition for optimal location creates a distinctive pattern of land use that includes pockets of poverty where behavior patterns are encouraged that trap poor people in a cycle of poverty, which they pass on to their children.

The structuralist approach makes very different assumptions. The city is an intensified point of economic activity in a world system characterized by an uneven and inequitable distribution of wealth and power. The important organizing principles are not local but worldwide, and the city, rather than fostering sociological differences, simply reflects them. The behavior and relationships that are manifest locally have their origins outside of the urban arena. As cities grow in the Third World, they perpetuate and articulate the unevenness of development. They become the centers for opulence and privilege, while the wealth of these nations is actually produced in rural areas where the laborer gets little return for hard work or enterprise. Third World cities suck the wealth out of the countryside, and, in turn, their commercial interests are dominated by global agents located in the cities of the more-developed nations. At the same time, all segments of the population are not prospering within the cities of the rich nations. As capital accumulates to be invested in property and to pay to executives, it inflates local housing markets and drives the poor into subminimal housing or onto the streets. The city does not make things happen but reflects what is happening on a global scale.

This categorical presentation is intended to denote observable tendencies toward association among certain lines of thought. As is the case with any complex body of ideas, the patterns of association are perhaps not as neat as the table or these summaries might imply. For the culturalists, there is bound to be an outcry from those who identify themselves with the culturalist approach but who deny the validity of the culture of poverty thesis. Also within the culturalist tradition, there are ecologists who are not modernization theorists. On the other hand, there are political economists who from time to time slip into an ecological or modernization framework in their discussions. This may be due to the fact that many of those who focus their work on the city cannot escape the tradition of Weber and Durkheim or Simmel and Park. At the same time, culturalists or ecologists cannot escape the significance of the perspective of political economists (Hawley 1984). Also, in the postmodern era, it became a virtue to remain uncommitted to a particular theory and to select theoretical constructs that best fit the evidence. In this atmosphere, the mixing of elements from different paradigms, or eclecticism, is deliberate.

Toward a Unity of Spatial Sociology

Today urban sociology appears to be at a juncture where one of two courses of conceptual development will occur. In the first, the culturalist and structuralist

perspectives will continue their independent development. Many of those working in one or the other perspective remain dedicated to their tradition. However,
new students of urban sociology are bound to be exposed to both traditions. This
is desirable because each tradition contains valuable insights into the social causes
and consequences of the urban form. The insights provided by one tradition cannot be disregarded in favor of the other. Consequently, it seems likely that, despite
their differences, a combination of the approaches into one overall perspective
will emerge.

Today urban sociology appears to hold promise as an orienting mechanism
for the field of social science. It is the branch of sociology that is concerned with
the organization of space. This is the very issue that presents urban sociology
with its identity crisis: What is the unit of space that an urban sociology studies?
In a way, the crisis is a false one having to do with tradition and labels. The
problem for classical urban sociology is that it has lost to a large extent its traditional subject matter with the transformation of the city into the metropolitan
community, the metropolitan region, megalopolis, and the endless suburbanization of the landscape. Urban political economists have adequately redefined the
scope of territorial analysis, as they address the entire globe. But they hardly seem
to be doing an *urban* sociology. They are as interested in the articulation of the
world system in rural areas as in urban areas. Essentially, there are no more urban
or rural sociologies, as the recognition of the economic linkages among all regions
has erased the rationale for the conventional division of labor between urban and
rural sociologists.

This opens up the possibility of a new paradigm. What has been urban sociology up until now becomes the sociology of spatial relations. Its subject matter is
the local manifestation of global trends. While ethnographers and survey researchers alike may still want to focus their attention on localities in order to understand the sociology of local space, they will need to cast their analysis (theory)
at the level of the international economy to understand what their empirical research is telling them.

As a science develops, it often happens that an emerging paradigm creates a
crisis for and eventually defeats a traditional framework of understanding or view
of the universe (Kuhn 1972). It also happens, however, that the emergence of an alternative system of thought can subsume an existing one, thus creating something
of a division of labor (as between biology and chemistry). Something like the latter
seems to be happening at this juncture in the field of urban sociology. The traditional culturalist paradigm is not on the verge of obsolescence: It remains too productive, for example, in Fischer's (1975) subcultural theory of urbanism. Instead,
the culturalist tradition is in a position to be absorbed, as a sociology of locality
within the global perspective on spatial relations offered by structural sociology or
political economy. The superordination and subordination of the structuralist and
culturalist perspectives within a single paradigm merely recognizes which is the
narrower (culturalist) and which is the broader (structuralist) geographic view. The
broader perspective remains the ultimate analytical framework.

This interpretation of the natural division of labor among urban sociologists is reinforced by the recognition of the primacy of economic globalization as the major force shaping local events. Yet it is easy to see the importance of studying cities (localities) in order to understand the practical impact of global change. As Sassen (1996, 630) put it, the traditional spatial focus of urban sociology remains useful because "a focus on cities and communities allows for a more concrete analysis of globalization, and in that regard we can think of cities and communities as strategic sites for an examination of global processes and major politicoeconomic processes." That is, the study of cities helps in understanding globalization as well as the reverse.

While the social impact of the worldwide *hypermobility* of capital may be most immediately and clearly evident on Wall Street, the consequences are just as real in the South Bronx, East St. Louis, and other noncentral segments of the world system. Sassen pointed to the example of the acute stock market reversal of 1987, which saw widespread attention devoted to the plight of high-income Wall Street professionals, but the consequent impact of the crisis in the unemployment of Dominican office cleaners living in northern Manhattan was just as real in that community. The market boom in the mid- to late-1990s saw the creation of a new line of taxis in Manhattan servicing only the financial district, and the consequent peripheralization of "gypsy" cabs to low-income neighborhoods. In this light, it is reasonable and appropriate to ask how any local change may be traced back to its nonlocal origins. Sassen suggested that there is a connection between expressive criminal tendencies, such as vandalism, skinhead angst, and the anger of rap, on the one hand, and the "sharpened inequality being witnessed in the process of economic globalization," on the other. Her point is that there is a new starkness to inequality that is the product of the global age, a new arrogance of corporate power, and an immediacy in the communication of the message that urban space is the province and property of remote forces. In reaction, the relatively powerless can be expected to use the streets and public spaces to make their claims for recognition and entitlement, to claim "their rights to the city." While the close juxtaposition of affluence and want have a history as old as cities themselves, there is a new clarity in the extremes, "The distance, as seen and lived, between the urban glamor zone and the urban war zone has become enormous. The extreme transparency and high public visibility of this difference is likely to contribute to further brutalization of the conflict" (Sassen 1996, 635). An appreciation of the connection between global processes and local outcomes provides a job description for the urban sociologist.

In offering the thesis that structuralist analysis takes precedence over culturalist observations, we are inviting the criticism that we have joined the ideological as well as the scientific debate that separates the two camps. There are a few points to be made in response. First, it is not possible to work in the field of urban sociology and not be swayed by one set of arguments or another. The tendency of this author to favor the structuralist interpretations should have been evident throughout the text wherever these contrasting perspectives were presented. Logically, the

structuralist paradigm is broad enough to offer a framework within which culturalist observations may be evaluated, while the reverse does not appear to be possible. Finally, while it is true that the structuralist perspective, dominated as it is by
the views of political economy, tends to be fundamentally critical of existing patterns of settlement and international relationships, political economy has come to
embrace a wide range of sociologists whose work covers a broad political spectrum. Theoretically, there is no *a priori* reason that taking a broader geographic view
in the study of the urban arena would not generate a conservative body of work, if
the evidence warranted it. In fact, we have seen that many interpret the emerging
global economy in just this way, as promising a future where a single market un-
hampered by traditional trade barriers will finally fulfill the promise of capitalism.

Having sided with the structuralists, let us hasten to acknowledge the important contribution that a culturalist orientation offers for the understanding of one
aspect of globalization. One of the key features of the culturalist tradition is the
debate that emerged between those who were persuaded by the urbanism thesis
that saw alienation and social isolation as the major consequence of urban living
and those who found "saved" or "liberated" communities in the city (Chapter 4).
Here we may want to recall especially the work of Claude Fischer (1975, 1984)
who argued that patterns of association in the city are not associated so much with
neighborhoods as they are with common interests and that people seek out like-
minded associates with common interests wherever they may reside within a metropolis—thus forming what he referred to as urban subcultures. This is the manner in which urban life becomes especially socially rewarding, because through
sheer mass it provides us with a large number of potential relationships—if we
can find them. You may recall his argument that a "critical mass" of like-minded
friends and acquaintances will deepen group identities and enrich the qualities of
belonging within the group. This is a feature of urban *culture* because—among all
human settlement patterns—it is within the largest cities that individuals have the
best chance to find others with the same interests.

It is time to carry the liberation of community from geographic confines a step
further. Just as the idea of community was carried beyond the boundaries of the
neighborhood, it can now be carried beyond the boundaries of the metropolis—
beyond any spatial referent less than the globe itself. The urban culturalist tradition has given us useful tools that we may extend to conceptualizing patterns and
consequences of association in cyberspace—the most liberated of all spaces harboring human activity and interaction. Here we can find parallels that invite the
use of terms and concepts developed within the urban culturalist tradition.

We might begin by considering how the social isolation school of urbanism—
characterized by Wirth's "urbanism as a way of life" thesis (1938)—can be applied
to the world of electronic sociability. Some critics believe that electronic space
leads to a form of isolation, whereby individuals who are most comfortable in the
solitary and private space before their monitor may withdraw to a world that involves no face-to-face contact. That world incorporates maximum heterogeneity
(exclusive of the world's poorest) and generates heated debates on all topics of
interest. It is a world in which incivility and abuse are buffered by the mutual in-

visibility of participants. It is a world contrived by commercial interests that constantly assail users with insistent advertising, much like the billboarded commercial atmosphere of the urban arena. Some participants may become wary of fully engaging in the conflictual environment of chat rooms and content themselves with casual visits, hanging on the fringe, not wanting to be involved. There are suggestive parallels in this emerging world for isolationist interpretations like Wirth's or Simmel's early twentieth century interpretations of urban life.

But there would seem to be even more potential for those interested in applying various theses growing out of the urban community studies tradition. All of the forms of community characteristic of cities find parallels here: "communities saved" of aging hot-rod enthusiasts, face blocks of recognizable participants who habituate particular server lists and discussion groups (family genealogists), defended communities of those who feel their worldview is threatened by outsiders (various conspiracy theorists and hate groups), and communities of limited liability whose members occupy multilayered cyber communities simultaneously. The critical mass that draws the like-minded together in the great cities is even more characteristic of the Web, where search engines usher those with common interests along paths where they may encounter each other and build deep and enduring subcultures like those described by Fischer. It is here that those seeking information and support for their socially unconventional proclivities or for their scheme to execute the most spectacular violent crime or those whose artistic expression, personal philosophy, and paradigm-defying scientific insight will find and challenge each other. In terms of community, we might say that the World Wide Web is the ultimate city. Or it may be that the great metropolis with its archaic geographic limitations was simply a stage of human social development, a historic way station, a physical spatial construct that was getting us ready for the next phase of human association: the global social dimension.

Whatever way we think about it, it is far too early to conclude that we have moved beyond the spatially limited forms of habitation and association that make up the subject matter of urban sociology. Cyberspace has not replaced physically defined space although it has supplemented it in important, liberating ways. And the conceptual tools developed within the cultural tradition in urban sociology provide useful metaphorical schemes for thinking and talking about the next stage of human existence. As students of urban sociology, we might well welcome the challenge that new forms of association present us, as we wonder what to call the field of social science that combines the study of locality with the study of electronically mediated patterns of association that are space defying.

The Future of Urban Sociology

Social science has been faulted for its tendency to be late in recognizing important new trends and patterns: The criticism is that journalists tend to be on the scene long before the sociologists arrive with their more cumbersome (but, hopefully, more systematic) methodologies. It is not clear how this interpretation squares with the fact that the dean of North American urban sociologists, Robert Park, was first a newspaperman who changed careers when he came to believe that sociology would write the "big story" of the city.

When Park turned his attention to the study of cities early in the twentieth century, it was because he was inspired by the awesome dimensions of the rich and rapidly changing city of Chicago. He believed that this social laboratory—as he saw it—provided a glimpse into an unfolding and uncertain future. Chicago was an overgrown boomtown, a crossroads for rail and shipping facilities that siphoned off the still newly opened, rich natural resources of the vast center of the United States and shipped them east and beyond to the world market.

But as the twentieth century advanced, the capacity of the maturing urban form to inspire awe faded. The sociologists of Park's generation were largely migrants to the city, coming from farm and small town origins. Today's sociologists and their students are themselves the products of the urban world, of urban culture. If Chicago, a city of 2 or 3 million, was inspiring to Park and his colleagues, do Bombay, Mexico City, and Sao Paulo at over 18 million each have the capacity to excite the imagination in the same way today? At the beginning of the twenty-first century, the "big story" of societal change cannot be contained within a city of any size. Instead, what fascinates us—the window through which we attempt to glimpse the future—is the global reach of the international economy and the parallel dimensions of communication technology. Yet, cities still provide us with the one setting where the consequences of globalization are etched most clearly. Here we suggest a few areas in which urban sociology still has the potential to write some of the big stories of the next several decades—by connecting local and global changes: renewed efforts to understand the largest cities, an ecology of the cities and the environment, the association between violence and the city, and the territorial separation of the affluent and the poor.

The largest cities of the world represent a frontier of human experience. By 2000, there were 19 cities of over 10 million people, and 16 of these were in poor countries; by 2015, there will be 23, and 20 will be in poor nations (United Nations Population Division 1999, 8). In terms of their sheer size, these have come to be called "megacities." By virtue of their importance as political centers and nodes in the international economy, they are referred to as "world cities." In his introductory remarks to a 1999 workshop in Washington, D.C. that brought together an international panel of experts to discuss world cities in poor countries, the keynote speaker observed that while social scientists had lavished much attention on the largest cities in wealthy nations, relatively little work had been done on the giant cities of poor nations (Gugler 1999, 2). These cities provide arenas of social action unprecedented in human experience. What they have to tell us about the relationship between wealth and poverty, strategies for survival that operate among gray areas straddling legal and illegal enterprise, emergent forms of association and identity, the burgeoning of informal sectors linked directly to the global economy by pirated violations of patent and copyright laws, new ethnic coalitions, movements for gender equality, and innumerable other areas of organization and experience, has yet to be fully explored. The collective impact of giant cities as sites of industrial production and human concentration affect the rest of the world, and not the least among these is the effect on the environment.

The World Health Organization (WHO) and the United Nations Environmental Program (UNEP) have since 1974 collaborated on a project called the United Nations Environmental Monitoring System. The organization sees as particularly problematic the growth of the 10 million-plus megacities. While pollution controls have generally improved in the largest cities of the industrialized nations, the rapid growth of Third World megacities has meant increasing levels of air pollution and other environmental problems (*Environment* 1994). As the collective population of the largest cities in poor countries continues to grow, its capacity to contaminate will probably continue to outstrip the limited means of governments to exercise effective control, and the impact will not be confined to the "local" environment.

Urban environmental social issues are by no means restricted to poor countries. In recent decades, a recognition has emerged that poor and minority populations in wealthy countries suffer a disproportionate share of the consequences of urban environmental contamination (Bullard 1983, 1994; Bryant and Mohai 1992). Potential environmental hazards (hazardous waste treatment, storage, or disposal facilities—TSDFs) tend to be concentrated in or near poor neighborhoods and communities, and the correlation is even stronger regarding racial minorities (Bullard 1994). The pattern has generated the term *environmental racism*. The close association of minority residence and noxious industry or other unattractive land uses may reflect a combination of a lack of resources on the part of minorities to opt out of such areas, and at least an indifference on the part of authorities to restricting further hazardous use concentration in areas of combined industrial and minority residence (Boone and Modarres 1999). Whatever the process by which it emerges, the bulk of evidence points to a correlation between hazardous sites and poor and minority residential location (Downey 1998; Hird and Reese 1998). The correlation was sufficiently evident that in 1994 the Clinton administration undertook the task of evaluating the problem in order to develop policies addressing "environmental justice."

The connection between cities and the environment appears to offer a natural opportunity for urban ecologists to explore a unifying theme that could link traditional methodologies with analyses of national and international political economy. Globalization, as a new context for thinking about spatial relationships, offers a sufficiently broad framework for thinking about environmental problems and social and economic justice. Critics call for the wealthiest nations to assume a leading role in promoting responsible policies with regard to consumption and manufacturing that will lead to a sustainable natural environment. At the beginning of a new century, we all recognize that the issue of environmental equality addresses the one global system that is truly without borders. Yet, not all nations are willing to sign international agreements that would begin to address the establishment of binding authority to protect the environment. Perhaps the drama and magnitude of the aggregate impact of the great cities in poor countries—with population and pollution growing out of control—and issues of environmental justice in wealthy nations will make the dimensions of the problem and the need for international cooperation inescapable to all elements of a world leadership that already fully understands economic globalization.

Another area of analysis that invites the attention of urban social science is the manner in which various dimensions of armed conflict and violence intersect with the study of cities. Cities are the magnets for varieties of violent expression that go beyond the consistent correlation between violent crime and city size. Urban centers have no monopoly on violence but tend to be arenas in which violence is played out on a large scale—or in calculated efforts to attract the attention of a wider audience. Cities showcase episodes of violence that range from mass killings by individuals expressing idiosyncratic frustrations, to popular protests quelled by police or other armed force, through sectarian warfare, to terrorism. Those who engage in violence as a political strategy understand the value of using the urban arena to advance their cause. Whatever the underlying motive, a relatively small amount of violence played out in the urban arena yields far more press coverage than a more vicious bloodletting in a rural area. Alienated assassins who want to take revenge on society or the world know they can make no stronger statement than by carrying out their vengeance on a crowded commuter train or on the Empire State Building observation tower. There are more reporters and more cameras in the city, and more people around the world will witness and relive the attack. If the goal is a strategically planned act of terror, there is a better chance that the message will be communicated to a greater audience. If we understand that a primary objective of terrorism is communication (Schmid and de Graaf 1982), we immediately see the city as the natural habitat of political violence.

The urban arena is also a natural stage for the show of might for demonstrators and insurgents. Revolutionaries can either preserve their anonymity in the crowd, or they can boldly enhance their fame by taunting authority on its own turf. Governments understand the connection between violence, communication, and the effectiveness of the urban theater, and attempt to control what is communicated. In the past, Ireland and South Africa placed restrictions on news media reporting of political violence. But information is harder to control when it is witnessed firsthand by thousands. Alternatively, at times governments use the urban arena to demonstrate their military force (the potential for state violence) by parading troops, rolling tanks and other armored vehicles through the streets, or using the audible droning of aircraft flying low over capitals and provincial centers as a reminder of who is in charge.

One further connection with global dimensions that exists between political conflict and the city is found in the waves of domestic and international refugees seeking respite from civil and international warfare and political persecution around the world. In 1999, the United Nations High Commission on Refugees estimated that there were 21.5 million international refugees displaced from their national homeland and an additional 30 million internally displaced persons who were forced from their homes but still living within their country of origin. Add to these perhaps 70 million people worldwide who have left their home country to seek work and by legal or illegal means are resident in a foreign country. We may assume that a generous proportion of today's refugees and other immigrants follow the pragmatic historical trend of gravitating to cities where their status of entry is unknown, where foreigners abound, where the informal economy offers opportunities for employment, and where the support and companionship of compatriots is most readily available. International political dislocations and the economic integration of the globe is reintroducing widespread first-generation ethnic diversity to cities in many world regions. The presence of some immigrants is visible, for example, in the unlicensed street hawkers who have arrived from poorer nations and world regions, who move their portable wares and cardboard display tables in and out of the shadows of European and North American cities in a kind of dance with the police and other government agents employed to discourage their presence. The result of the renewed urban diversity offered by economic and political refugees—many of whom are people of color or from regions of the world formerly underrepresented in international migration—includes both the opportunity to enjoy a richer urban social mosaic for those who have the capacity to do so, and the instigation of xenophobic right-wing political reaction for those who do not. The latter find an outlet in foreigner bashing. The way remains open for urban sociologists to develop a sociology of the politics of violence that represent some of the many tangled and less examined strands of globalization.

One final dimension of the urban landscape that calls for more systematic treatment is the impact of the global economy on the local class structure and how this manifests itself in the competition for residential space. As Sassen (1996) observed, urban spaces are among the best vantage points for viewing the impact of the international economy, and this is particularly so regarding the juxtaposition of the expanded affluence of the global economy's primary participants, and those who subsist on or beyond the fringes of the benefits it bestows. Beyond the places where empowerment zones are likely to turn up are the large tracts of "extreme poverty" neighborhoods that we discussed in Chapter 9, where people are especially poor, where legitimate economic opportunities are especially scarce and declining, and where the populations tend to be made up primarily or exclusively of people of color. If we step outside the box of accustomed everyday experience and look at the whole, we will recognize that the dramatic difference in standards of living is dividing urban space into newly segregated patterns that separate the affluent from everyone else. As Zukin (1995) pointed out, symbols of surveillance and safe perimeters abound in the form of special security guards and ever-present electronic video equipment that watches us for our own good. Others have gone further in drawing our attention to the fortified strategic design of safe public spaces that divide the affluent and the poor (Davis 1990), and to the fortified nature of private property and public buildings in even the poorest neighborhoods (Vergarra 1994).

The most telling spatial dimension of the social distance between affluent and poor is in the strategic division of the spaces they occupy. Safe fun spaces are set aside in the themed districts we described in Chapter 1, the fantasy cities that are increasingly evident within renovated or built-from-scratch urban recreational districts. In addition, the deliberate and strategic separation of classes is demonstrated in the peculiar emerging urban residential ecology, the voluntary residential isolation of the affluent in restricted-access communities. Within rich and poor countries today, we find at least some members of the comfortable classes garrisoned in protective residential enclaves and the poor and those of modest means left to work out security arrangements for themselves. It appears that in the future, even in the richest nations, the poor will be required to support themselves or be supported by voluntary charity organizations, the responsibility of the state for the poor and for minorities will be interpreted in a much more limited way, and the glacial movement of economic and political refugees from the poorest to the richest nations will persist. The city of the future will not look like the dreamscape of a visionary architect, a beehived model of efficiency in balance with nature. At least, that is not the urban future that we are currently constructing. The city of the future is being built today in Mexico City, Lagos, and Bombay/Mumbai—and in New York, Tokyo, and London. It will look like today's city—only more sprawling and segregated. Each will be two cities—a city for the affluent and a city for the poor. At a time when the wealthiest appear to have the material means and the accumulated knowledge of over 5,000 years of city building, we appear to lack the will and imagination to engage the notion of social justice in a responsible fashion—one that would produce a future city that would stand as a model of social integration, a celebration of diversity that provides the most attractive dimension of the truly urban form, a celebration of the potential richness of the cultures of the globe meeting in inclusive cityscapes. Instead we have Celebration, Florida, produced by private enterprise.

Celebration offers us something of a diversion: a chance to look at a large chunk of popular culture careening through metropolitan space and to be amused. But its significance is far more serious in terms of what is absent. It is a glimpse into the leading edge of evolving urban social policy, or the lack thereof. It symbolizes the consequence of allowing the market to determine the kind of urban landscape that will be produced by large and powerful businesses responding to consumer tastes and the disposable income of the affluent classes. There is nothing inherently wrong with this experiment, designed to sanitize and mythologize urban space, to provide profits for developers and protect the investments of homebuyers. The problem is that there is little here for the poor and minorities, outside of temporary and service work. The market alone cannot be trusted to provide integrated spaces that bring together the richness of racially and economically diverse populations. There is little in urban policy that demonstrates the exercise of a level of imagination equal to the enormous tasks presented by the needs of the world's nonaffluent urban populations.

In the more-developed and the less-developed economies alike, governments are faced with a difficult situation. How will they deal with urban change? Is there a single criterion by which to gauge their success or failure? One criterion that appears to make sense is *social justice,* how well societies live up to their responsibilities to their poorest and weakest members. We may envision two dimensions for formulating equitable social policy. One dimension is clearly that of social class. In this era of the restructuring of the global economy, what is it that society owes to the poor and the working class who are bearing the costs of economic change? The second dimension that policymakers must consider, one that complicates the dimension of class, is the spatial dimension. What is the economic impact of change on the old urban centers? On those cities that are currently more

BOX 11-1   Celebration, Florida: A Disney Production

In his *Celebration Chronicles,* Andrew Ross (1999) presented an account of Celebration, a theme town conceived of and built by the Disney company in central Florida, where real people live real lives in brand-new antique housing built around a brand-new, old-fashioned town square, with every physical aspect calculated to appear as time-worn as any picture-perfect authentic hometown of 50 or 60 years ago. Originally, there was some thought of giving the town a mythologized history, dating it from pirate days or Sherman's destructive southern campaign, but the idea was scrapped. Instead, the town took on the marketable neotraditional trappings of housing that presents a dated outward appeal combined with interiors that boast all the updated modern conveniences. Actually, home buyers have a choice of six style traditions ranging from Victorian and Greek Revival through the simple but elegant French Farmhouse. Furnished model homes painstakingly suggest appropriate interior decor, but decisions about interior decorating are ultimately left up to the resident families. This is not a minor point, since the appearance of home exteriors is carefully governed by the town Pattern Book, in which "Everything that contributes visually to the public realm is regulated by codes aimed at refining the 'conversation' between buildings and the streetscape" (28–29). In fact, home buyers can be expected to carefully maintain their investments in compliance with the town image, having laid out an average $330,000 as first-wave purchasers in 1997—which bought a much smaller home and lot than it would in other nearby communities. There is rental property, and Ross lived in an apartment on the square. The downtown area around the square has two- and three-story apartment buildings, some built to look like they had been designed as apartment buildings and others to look like old mansions that had been renovated for multiunit rental. But even contrived aged-looking buildings have a brand-new finished look, and the streets are vacuum cleaned early every morning.

The "product," the quality of life in a reinvented and sanitized hometown, was surprisingly disappointing, given the organizational reputation and success of the Disney company. Ross reported that many buyers experienced long delays in taking possession of their homes, the quaint exteriors and modern interiors were architecturally mismatched and awkward, the quality of construction was poor and dissatisfaction widespread—one problem being that skilled construction workers were in short supply in the Orlando metropolitan area where Celebration was being built, and unskilled workers earning low wages were substituted for craftspeople. If you didn't like your house or the community and wanted to move out, you had to wait at least a year to do so in accordance with the anti-speculation agreement each buyer was required to sign. People had to give up other freedoms—Ross's rental agreement prohibited him from introducing any "unsightly vehicle" to Celebration's streets. Social services were wanting, and people had to journey too far outside the community to shop. And the town itself was at odds with the environment: The fact that the town site formerly consisted of swamp and low-lying plains led to drainage problems for some property holders; during one period, encephalitis-bearing mosquitoes drove the population indoors after sunset; and pesky alligators kept reinfesting the artificial lake built within their former natural habitat.

But Ross concluded that Celebration is a worthy experiment undertaken on a grand scale with good intentions, and urged us not to join the ranks of Disney-bashers. True, in order to control the image of the town, the regulations reached into what most of us consider personal matters (such as how many individuals are allowed to sleep in one bedroom). But Celebration represents one experimental alternative to sprawling subdivisions that spread out through the delicate ecologies of Florida and other states.

prosperous? On the peripheral metropolitan regions? In the backcountry? How are the life chances of the inner-city poor tied to those living in remote and long-neglected regions and those living in small declining steel and mining towns? How are the lives of the poor in the cities of the more affluent societies tied to the poor of the Third World? The questions of class and location are tied together. They are questions of national and international responsibility and social justice. They are questions best addressed by an analysis carried out within a sociological framework with a strong spatial orientation, a dynamic and adaptive spatial sociology growing out of the urban sociological tradition.

BIBLIOGRAPHY

Abramson, Harold J. 1973. *Ethnic Diversity in Catholic America.* New York: John Wiley and Sons.

Abu-Lughod, Janet. 1975. "The Legitimacy of Comparisons in Comparative Urban Studies: A Theoretical Position and an Application to North African Cities." *Urban Affairs Quarterly,* 11:13–35.

Adams, Robert McC. 1966. *The Evolution of Urban Society: Early Mesopotamia and Prehistoric Mexico.* Chicago: Aldine.

Alba, Richard D., John R. Logan, and Kyle Crowder. 1997. "White Ethnic Neighborhoods and Assimilation: The Greater New York Region, 1980–90." *Social Forces* 75:883–909.

Alexander, Rudolph, Jr., and Jacquelyn, Gyamerah. 1997. "Differential Punishing of African Americans and Whites Who Possess Drugs: A Just Policy or a Continuation of the Past?" *Journal of Black Studies* 28:97–111.

Allen, Irving Lewis. 1983. *The Language of Ethnic Conflict: Social Organization and Lexical Culture.* New York: Columbia University Press.

America's Top-Rated Cities: A Statistical Handbook. Volume 1: Southern Region. 1999. Lakeville, Conn.: Grey House Publishing.

Anderson, Elijah. 1990. *Streetwise: Race, Class, and Change in an Urban Community.* Chicago: University of Chicago Press.

Anderson, Michael. 1971. *Family Structure in Nineteenth Century Lancashire.* Cambridge, England: Cambridge University Press.

Arensberg, Conrad. 1939. *The Irish Countryman.* New York: Macmillan.

Arensberg, Conrad, and Solon T. Kimball. 1940. *Family and Community in Ireland.* London: Peter Smith.

Argyle, Michael. 1982. "Inter-cultural Communication." In *Cultures in Contact: Studies in Cross-Cultural Interaction,* edited by Stephen Bochner, 61–79. Oxford, England: Pergamon.

Armengaud, Andre. [1970] 1976. "Population in Europe 1700–1914." In *The Industrial Revolution 1700–1914,* edited by Carlo M. Cipolla, 22–76. New York: Harper and Row.

Aronson, Dan R. 1970. "Cultural Stability and Social Change Among the Modern Ijebu Yoruba." Ph.D. Dissertation, University of Chicago.

———. 1979. *The City Is Our Farm: Seven Migrant Ijebu Yoruba Families.* Cambridge, Mass.: Schenkman.

Artibise, Alan F. J. 1995. "Achieving Sustainability in Cascadia: Model of Urban Growth Management in the Vancouver-Seattle-Portland Corridor." In *North American Cities and the Global Economy,* edited by Peter Karl Kresl and Gary Gappert, 221–250. Thousand Oaks, Calif.: Sage.

Auletta, Ken. 1982. *The Underclass.* New York: Vintage.

Babalola, Lanre, and Femi Adepoju. 2000. "OPC Takes Over Policing of Lagos." *Africa News Service.* (August 24).

Babb, Florence E. 1990. "Women's Work: Engendering Economic Anthropology." *Urban Anthropology* 19:277–302.

Badcock, Blair. 1984. *Unfairly Structured Cities.* Oxford, England: Basil Blackwell.

Bagchi, Amiya Kumar. 1982. *The Political Economy of Underdevelopment.* Cambridge, England: Cambridge University Press.

Baldassare, Mark. 1981a. *The Growth Dilemma: Resident's Views and Local Population Change in the United States.* Berkeley: University of California Press.

———. 1981b. "Local Perspectives on Community Growth." In *Nonmetropolitan America in Transition,* edited by Amos H. Hawley and Sara Mills Mazie, 116–143. Chapel Hill, N.C.: University of North Carolina Press.

Banck, Geert A. 1980. "Survival Strategies of Low Income Urban Households in Brazil." *Urban Anthropology* 9:227–242.

Banfield, Edward C. [1968] 1974. *The Unheavenly City Revisited.* Boston: Little, Brown.

Barnes, J. A. 1954. "Class and Committees in a Norwegian Island Parish." *Human Relations* 7:39–58.

———. 1972. *Social Networks.* Addison-Wesley Modular Publications, Number 26. Reading, Mass.: Addison-Wesley.

Baron, Lois M. 1998. "The Great Gate Debate." *Builder* (National Association of Home Builders) (March) 21:92–94.

Barros, Ricardo, Louise Fox, and Rosane Mendonça. 1997. "Female-Headed Households, Poverty, and the Welfare of Children in the Urban Brazil." *Economic Development and Cultural Change* 45: 231–257.

Barth, Gunther. 1980. *City People: The Rise of Modern City Culture in Nineteenth-Century America.* New York: Oxford University Press.

Bassuk, Ellen. 1997. "From Research to Action." *The Women's Review of Books* (February) 14:24–26.

Beck, Roy. 1996. *The Case Against Immigration.* New York: W.W. Norton.

Beeson, Patricia E., and Erica L. Groshen. 1991. "Components of City-Size Wage Differentials, 1973–1988." *Economic Review* (The Federal Reserve Board of Cleveland) 27, No. 4:10–24.

Bennett, William J., John J. DiIulio, and John P. Walters. 1996. *Body Count: Moral Poverty and How to Win America's War Against Crime and Drugs.* New York: Simon and Schuster.

Berger, Bennet M. 1960. *Working Class Suburb* Berkeley, Calif.: University of California Press.

Bergier, J-F. [1971] 1976. "The Industrial Bourgeoisie and the Rise of the Working Class 1700–1914." In *The Industrial Revolution 1700–1914,* Vol. 3, Edited by Carlo M. Cipolla, 397–451. New York: Harper and Row.

Bernstein, Mark F. 1998. "Sports Stadium Boondoggle." *The Public Interest* (Summer) 132:45–57.

Berry, Brian J. L. 1973. *The Human Consequences of Urbanization: Divergent Paths in the Urban Experience of the Twentieth Century.* New York: St. Martins.

Betancur, John J. 1996. "The Settlement Experience of Latinos in Chicago: Segregation, Speculation, and the Ecology Model." *Social Forces* 74:1299–1324.

Binford, Henry C. 1985. *The First Suburbs: Residential Communities on the Boston Periphery 1815–1860.* Chicago: University of Chicago Press.

Bingham, Richard D., and Zhongcai Zhang. 1997. "Poverty and Economic Morphology of Ohio Central-City Neighborhoods." *Urban Affairs Review* 32:766–796.

Blakely, Edward James, and Mary Gail Snyder. 1997a. "Places To Hide." *American Demographics* 19:22–25.

———. 1997b. *Fortress America: Gated Communities in the United States.* Washington, D.C.: Brookings Institution Press.

Blauner, Robert. 1969. "Internal Colonialism and Ghetto Revolt." *Social Problems* 16: 393–408.

Boissevain, Jeremy. 1974. *Friends of Friends: Networks, Manipulations and Coalitions.* New York: St. Martin's Press.

Boissevain, Jeremy, and J. Clyde Mitchell. 1973. *Network Analysis: Studies in Human Interaction.* The Hague: Mouton.

Boone, Christopher G., and Ali Modarres. 1999. "Creating a Toxic Neighborhood in Los Angeles County: A Historical Examination of Environmental Inequality." *Urban Affairs Review* 35:163–187.

Boswell, D. M. 1969. "Personal Crises and the Mobilization of the Social Network." In *Social Networks in Urban Situations: Analyses of Personal Relationships in Central African Towns,* edited by J. Clyde Mitchell, 245–296. Manchester, England: Manchester University Press.

Bott, Elizabeth. [1957] 1971. *Family and Social Network.* London: Tavistock.

Bound, John, and Harry Holzer. 1993. "Industrial Shifts, Skills Levels, and the Labor Market for White and Black Males." *Review of Economics and Statistics* 75:387–396.

Boyer, M. Christine. 1983. *Dreaming the Rational City: The Myth of American City Planning.* Cambridge, Mass.: MIT Press.

Bradshaw, York W. 1987. "Urbanization and Underdevelopment: A Global Study of Urbanization, Global Bias, and Economic Dependency." *American Sociological Review* 52:224–239.

Brandes, Stanley H. 1975. *Migration, Kinship, and Community: Tradition and Transition in a Spanish Village.* New York: Academic Press.

Brenner, M. Harvey. 1976. *Estimating the Social Costs of National Economic Policy.* United States Congress, Joint Economic Committee Print. Washington, D.C.: U.S. Government Printing Office.

Brown, David A., and Calvin L. Beale. 1981. "Diversity in Post-1970 Population Trends." In *Nonmetropolitan America in Transition,* edited by Amos H. Hawley and Sara Mills Mazie, 27–71. Chapel Hill, N.C.: University of North Carolina Press.

Bruner, Edward M. 1974. "The Expression of Ethnicity in Indonesia." In *Urban Ethnicity,* edited by Abner Cohen, 251–280. London: Tavistock.

Bryant, B., and P. Mohai (eds). 1992. *Race and the Incidence of Environmental Hazards: A Time for Discourse.* Boulder: Westview Press.

Bullard, Robert D. 1983. "Solid Waste Sites and the Black Houston Community." *Sociological Inquiry* 53:273–288.

————. 1994. "Overcoming Racism in Environmental Decision Making." *Environment* (May) 36:10–44.

Bunce, Michael. 1982. *Rural Settlement in an Urban World*. New York: St. Martins.

Burgess, Ernest W. 1925. "The Growth of the City: An Introduction to a Research Project." In *The City*, edited by Robert E. Park and Ernest W. Burgess, 47–62. Chicago: University of Chicago Press.

Burkhardt, Jacob. 1985. *The Architecture of the Italian Renaissance*, introduced and edited by Peter Murray, translated by James Palmes. Chicago: University of Chicago Press.

Burkholz, Herbert. 1980. "The Latinization of Miami." *The New York Times Magazine* (September 21):44–47.

Burnham, Daniel H., and Edward H. Bennett. 1909. *The Plan of Chicago*. Chicago: The Commercial Club.

Bursik, Robert J., Jr., and Harold G. Grasmick. 1993. "Economic Deprivation and Neighborhood Crime Rates." *Law and Society Review* 27:263–283.

Bustamante, Jorge A. 1980. "Immigrants from Mexico: The Silent Invasion Issue." In *Sourcebook on the New Migration: Implications for the United States and the International Community*, edited by Roy Simon Bryce-Laporte, 139–144. New Brunswick, N.J.: Transaction Books.

Buttel, Frederick H. 1981. "Environmental Quality and Protection." In *Nonmetropolitan America in Transition*, edited by Amos H. Hawley and Sara Mills Mazie, 668–703. Chapel Hill, N.C.: University of North Carolina Press.

Buvinic, Mayra, and Geeta Rao Gupta. 1997. "Female-Headed Households and Female-Maintained Families: Are They Worth Targeting to Reduce Poverty in Developing Countries?" *Economic Development and Cultural Change* 45:259–279.

Cafferty, Pastora San Juan, Barry R. Chiswick, Andrew M. Greeley, and Teresa A. Sullivan. 1983. *The Dilemma of American Immigration: Beyond the Golden Door*. New Brunswick, N.J.: Transaction Books.

Caldwell, John C. 1965. "Extended Family Obligations and Education: A Study of an Aspect of Demographic Transition Amongst Ghanaian University Students." *Population Studies*, 19:183–199.

————. 1967. "Migration and Urbanization." In *A Survey of Contemporary Ghana*. Vol. 2, *Some Aspects of Social Structure*, edited by Walter Birmingham, I. Neustadt, and E. N. Omaboe, 111–146. London: Allen and Unwin.

————. 1968. *Population Growth and Family Change in Africa: The New Urban Elite in Ghana*. Canberra, Australia: Australian National University Press.

Campbell, Scott, and Susan Fainstein. 1996. "Introduction: The Structure and Debates in Planning Theory." In *Readings in Planning Theory*, edited by Scott Campbell and Susan Fainstein, 1–14. Cambridge, Mass.: Blackwell.

Canada and the World Backgrounder. 1997. "Sweatshop Economics." (December) 63:25–27.

Caplow, Theodore, Howard M. Bahr, Bruce A. Chadwick, Reuben Hill, and Margaret Holmes Williamson. 1982. *Middletown Families: Fifty Years of Change and Continuity*. New York: Bantam.

Caraley, Demetrios. 1992. "Washington Abandons the Cities." *Political Science Quarterly* 107:1–30.

Carey, Max L., and James C. Franklin. 1991. "Industry Output and Job Growth Continues Slow into Next Century." *Monthly Labor Review* (November) 115:45–63.

Carter, Harold. 1972. *The Study of Urban Geography*. London: Edward Arnold.

Castells, Manuel. [1972] 1977. *The Urban Question*. London: Edward Arnold. Originally published as *La Question Urbaine* (Paris).

————. 1982. "Squatters and Politics in Latin America: A Comparative Analysis of Urban Social Movements in Chile, Peru and Mexico." In *Towards a Political Economy of Urbanization in Third World Countries*, edited by Helen I. Safa, 249–282. New Delhi: Oxford University Press.

————. 1983. *The City and the Grassroots*. Berkeley, Calif.: University of California Press.

————. 1985a. "Urbanization and Social Change: The New Frontier." In *The Challenge of Social Change*, edited by Orlando Fals Borda, 93–106. Beverly Hills, Calif.: Sage.

————. 1985b. "High Technology, Economic Restructuring, and the Urban-Regional Process in the United States." In *High Technology, Space, and Society*, edited by Manuel Castells, 11–40. *Urban Affairs Quarterly Reviews*, Vol. 28. Beverly Hills, Calif.: Sage.

Castells, Manuel, and John Hull Mollenkopf. 1991. "Conclusion: Is New York a Dual City?" In *Dual City: Restructuring New York*. Edited by John Hull Mollenkopf and Manuel Castells, 399–418. New York: Russell Sage Foundation.

Chandler, Tertius. 1987. *Four Thousand Years of Urban Growth: An Historical Census*. Lewiston, N.Y.: St. David's University Press.

Chandler, Tertius, and Gerald Fox. 1974. *3000 Years of Urban Growth*. New York: Academic Press.

Charyn, Jerome. 1987. "The Rough Adventure of the Street." *Dissent* (Fall) :624–626.

Checkoway, Barry, and Carl V. Patton. 1985. "The Metropolitan Midwestern Perspective." In *The Metropolitan Midwest: Policy, Problems, and Prospects for Change*, edited by Barry Checkoway and Carl V. Patton, 1–28. Urbana, Ill.: University of Illinois Press.

Chen, Xiangming. 1991. "China's City Hierarchy, Urban Policy and Spatial Development in the 1980s." *Urban Studies* 28:341–367.

Cheng Te-k'un. 1982. *Studies in Chinese Archeology.* Hong Kong: Chinese University Press.

Chevigny, Paul. 1996. "Law and Order? Policing in Mexico City and Kingston, Jamaica." *NACLA Report on the Americas.* (September–October) 30: 24–31.

Childe, V. Gordon. 1951. *Man Makes Himself.* New York: The New American Library.

———. 1957. "Civilization, Cities, and Towns." *Antiquity* (March):210–213.

Clark, David L. 1983. "Improbable Los Angeles." In *Sunbelt Cities: Politics and Growth Since World War II,* edited by Richard M. Bernard and Bradley R. Rice, 268–308. Austin, Tex.: University of Texas Press.

Clark, Kenneth. 1964. *Youth in the Ghetto.* New York: Haryou Associates.

Cohen, Abner. 1969. *Custom and Politics in Urban Africa: A Study of Hausa Migrants in Yoruba Towns.* Berkeley: University of California Press.

———. 1974. "The Lesson of Ethnicity." In *Urban Ethnicity,* edited by Abner Cohen, ix–xxiv. London: Tavistock.

———. 1981. "Variables in Ethnicity." In *Ethnic Change,* edited by Charles F. Keyes, 306–331. Seattle, Wash.: University of Washington Press.

Cohn, Samuel, and Mark Fossett. 1996. "What Spatial Mismatch? The Proximity of Blacks to Employment in Boston and Houston." *Social Forces* 75:557–572.

Cohn, Theodore H., and Patrick J. Smith. 1995. "Developing Global Cities in the Pacific Northwest: The Cases of Vancouver and Seattle." In *North American Cities and the Global Economy,* edited by Peter Karl Kresl and Gary Gappert, 251–285. Thousand Oaks, Calif.: Sage.

Collett, Peter. 1982. "Meetings and Misunderstandings." In *Cultures in Contact: Studies in Cross-Cultural Interaction,* edited by Stephen Bochner, 81–89. Oxford, England: Pergamon.

Cone, Annabella. 1996. "Misplaced Desire: The Female Urban Experience in Colette and Rohmer." *Literature Film Quarterly* 24:423–431.

Conot, Robert. 1974. *American Odyssey.* New York: William Morrow.

Cooper, Frederick. 1983. "Urban Space, Industrial Time, and Wage Labor in Africa." In *Struggle for the City: Migrant Labor, Capital, and the State in Urban Africa,* edited by Frederick Cooper, 7–50. Beverly Hills, Calif.: Sage.

Cornell, Stephen. 2000. "Discovered Identities and American Indian Supratribalism." In *We Are a People: Narrative and Multiplicity in Constructing Ethnic Identity,* edited by Paul Spickard and W. Jeffry Burroughs, 98–123. Philadelphia: Temple University Press.

Coulton, Claudia A., Julian Chow, Edward C. Wang, and Marilyn Su. 1996. "Geographic Concentration of Affluence and Poverty in 100 Metropolitan Areas, 1990." *Urban Affairs Review* 32:186–216.

Cramer, Mark. 1995. *Funky Towns USA: The Best Alternative, Eclectic, Irreverent, and Visionary Places.* Annapolis, Md.: TBS Publications.

Crampton, Norman. 1995. *The 100 Best Small Towns in America.* New York: Macmillan.

Craven, P., and Barry Wellman. 1973. "The Network City." *Social Inquiry* 43:57–88.

Cross, Gary S. 1983. *Immigrant Workers in Industrial France: The Making of a New Laboring Class.* Philadelphia: Temple University Press.

Cross, Malcolm. 1979. *Urbanization and Urban Growth in the Caribbean: An Essay on Social Change in Dependent Societies.* London: Cambridge University Press.

Currie, Elliott. 1985. *Confronting Crime: An American Challenge.* New York: Pantheon.

Curry, Leonard P. 1981. *The Free Black in Urban America, 1800–1850: The Shadow of the Dream.* Chicago: The University of Chicago Press.

Dahl, Robert A. 1961. *Who Governs? Democracy and Power in an American City.* New Haven, Conn.: Yale University Press.

Dahya, Badr. 1974. "The Nature of Pakistani Ethnicity in Industrial Cities in Britain." In *Urban Ethnicity,* edited by Abner Cohen, 77–118. London: Tavistock.

Dalaker, Joseph, and Mary Naifeh. 1998. *Poverty in the United States: 1997.* Current Population Reports. Washington, D.C.: Government Printing Office.

Dalaker, Joseph, and Bernadette D. Proctor. 2000. *Poverty in the United States, 1999.* Current Population Reports, Series P60-210. U.S. Bureau of the Census, Washington, D.C.: U.S. Government Printing Office.

Danielson, Michael N., and Jameson W. Doig. 1982. *New York: The Politics of Urban Regional Development.* Berkeley, Calif.: University of California Press.

Danziger, Sheldon. 2000. "Approaching the Limit: What Have We Learned from Welfare Reform?" Paper presented at a Conference on Rural Dimensions of Welfare Reform, sponsored by the Joint Center for Poverty Research, Northwestern University/University of Chicago, May 2000 (Revised July 2000). http//:www.jcpr.org/wp/Wprofile.cfm?ID-203.

Davies, Hunter. 1999. "Beaten up in the toilets at Wembley—for being a fan." *New Statesman* (November 1) 128:62.

Davis, Donald F., and Barbara Lorenzowski. 1998. "A Platform for Gender Tensions: Women Working and Riding on Canadian Public Transit in the 1940s." *Canadian Historical Review* 79:431–466.

Davis, Kingsley. 1955. "The Origin and Growth of Urbanization in the World." *American Journal of Sociology* 60:429–437.

———. 1969. *World Urbanization 1950–1970.* Vol. 1, *Basic Data for Cities, Countries, and Regions.* Berkeley, Calif.: University of California Press.

Davis, Mike. 1990. *City of Quartz.* London: Verso.

Day, C. William. 1999. "Technology's role in security." *American School & University* 72:54–55.

Dear, Michael J., and Jennifer R. Wolch. 1987. *Landscapes of Despair: From Deinstitutionalization to Homelessness.* Princeton, N.J.: Princeton University Press.

DeMarco, William M. 1981. *Ethnics and Enclaves: Boston's Italian North End.* Ann Arbor, Mich.: University Microfilms International Press.

Dessoff, Alan. 2000. "Plans Address California Water Needs." *Water, Environment, and Technology* (September) 12:32–34.

Devine, Joel A., and James D. Wright. 1993. *The Greatest of Evils: Urban Poverty and the American Underclass.* New York: Aldine De Gruyter.

DeVise, Pierre. 1976. "The Suburbanization of Jobs and Minority Employment." *Economic Geography* 52:348–362.

Dills, Lanie, and Lynn West. 1995. *Great Gay and Lesbian Places to Live: "The Official Guide."* Memphis, Tenn.: Lanie Dills.

Dimond, Paul R. 1985. *Beyond Busing: Inside the Challenge to Urban Segregation.* Ann Arbor, Mich.: University of Michigan Press.

Dinnerston, Leonard, Roger L. Nichols, and David M. Raimers. 1979. *Natives and Strangers: Ethnic Groups and the Building of America.* New York: Oxford University Press.

Doctorow, E. L. 1982. "Introduction." In *Sister Carrie,* by Theodore Dreiser, v–xi. New York: Bantam Books, [1900] 1982.

Dolan, Jay P. 1975. *The Immigrant Church: New York's Irish and German Catholics, 1815–1865.* Baltimore: Johns Hopkins University Press.

Donaldson, Scott. 1969. *The Suburban Myth.* New York: Columbia University Press.

Douglas, Harlan Paul. 1925. *The Suburban Trend.* New York: The Century Company.

Downey, L. 1998. "Environmental Injustice: Is Race or Income a Better Predictor?" *Social Science Quarterly* 79:766–778.

Dreiser, Theodore. 1913. *A Traveler at Forty.* New York: The Century Company.

Durkheim, Emile. [1893] 1933. *The Division of Labor in Society.* Translated by George Simpson. Glencoe, Ill.: The Free Press.

Duster, Troy. 1987. "Crime, Youth Unemployment, and the Black Urban Underclass." *Crime and Delinquency* 33:300–316.

Eames, Edwin, and Judith Granich Goode. 1977. *Anthropology of the City: An Introduction to Urban Anthropology.* Englewood Cliffs, N.J.: Prentice-Hall.

Eckstein, Susan. 1990. "Urbanization Revisited: Inner-City Slum of Hope and Squatter Settlement of Despair." *World Development* 18:165–181.

Economist, The. 1995. ". . . to Jo'burg." (December 2) 337:37–39.

Economist, The. 1997. "Global Economy, Local Mayhem?" Editorial. (January 18) 342:16–17.

Edmonson, Brad. 1997. "The Newest New Yorkers." *American Demographics* (July) 19:16–17.

Edwards, Harry. 1979. "Camouflaging the Color Line: A Critique." In *Caste and Class Controversy,* edited by Charles Vert Willie, 98–103. Bayside, N.Y.: General Hall.

Edwards, John, and Nicholas Deakin. 1992. "Privatism and Partnership in Urban Regeneration." *Public Administration* 70:359–368.

Ehrenhalt, Alan. 1999. "Pleasure and guilt on Michigan Avenue." *Governing* (July) 12:7.

Ejobowah, John Boye. 2000. "Who Owns the Oil? The Politics of Ethnicity in the Niger Delta of Nigeria." *Africa Today* (Winter) 47:28–47.

Ellis, John Tracy. [1956] 1969. *American Catholicism.* 2nd ed. Chicago: University of Chicago Press.

Ellwood, David T. 1986. "The Spatial Mismatch Hypothesis: Are There Jobs Missing in the Ghetto." In *The Black Youth Employment Crisis,* edited by Richard B. Freeman and Harry J. Holder. Chicago: University of Chicago.

Elvin, Mark. 1978. "Chinese Cities Since the Sung Dynasty." In *Towns in Societies: Essays in Economic History and Historical Sociology,* edited by Philip Abrams and E. A. Wrigley, 79–89. Cambridge, England: Cambridge University Press.

Engels, Fredrick. [1936] 1970. "Early Slum Conditions: Manchester in 1844." In *Slums and Urbanization,* edited by A. R. Desai and S. Devadas Pillai, 24–33. Bombay: Popular Parakashan. (Reprinted from Frederick Engels. 1936. *The Condition of the Working-Class in England in 1844.* Translated by Florence Kelley Wischnewetzky. London: Unwin Hyman).

Environment. 1994. "Air Pollution in the World's Megacities." (March) 36:4–37.

Espenshade, Thomas J. 1990. "Undocumented Migration to the United States: Evidence from a Repeated Trials Model." In *Undocumented Migration to the United States: IRCA and the Experience of the 1980s,* edited by Frank D. Bean, Barry Edmonston, and Jeffrey S. Passel, 159–182. Santa Monica, Calif.: Rand Corporation.

Estera, Gustavo. 1995. "What Tepito Can Teach Us." *Utne Reader* (May–June) 69:68–69.

Ewen, Stuart. 1976. *Captains of Consciousness: Advertising and the Social Roots of the Consumer Culture.* New York: McGraw–Hill.

Ezcurra, Exequiel, and Marisa Mazari-Hiriart. 1996. "Are Mega-cities Viable? A Cautionary Tale From Mexico City." *Environment* (January–February) 38:6–26.

Fainstein, Susan S. 1991. "Promoting Economic Development: Urban Planning in the United States and Great Britain." *Journal of the American Planning Association* 57, No. 1:22–23.

Faris, Robert E. L. 1967. *Chicago Sociology: 1920–1932.* San Francisco: Chandler.

Farley, John E. 1983. "Metropolitan Housing Segregation in 1980: The St. Louis Case." *Urban Affairs Quarterly* 18:347–359.

Fasenfest, David. 1986. "The Community, Politics, and Urban Redevelopment: Poletown, Detroit, and General Motors." *Urban Affairs Quarterly* 22:101–123.

Feagin, Joe R. 1983. *The Urban Real Estate Game: Playing Monopoly with Real Money.* Englewood Cliffs, N.J.: Prentice-Hall.

———. 1986. "Slavery Unwilling to Die: The Background of Racial Oppression in the 1980s." *Journal of Black Studies* 17:173–200.

Feder, Ernest. 1976. "How Agribusiness Operates in Underdeveloped Agricultures: Harvard Business School Myths and Reality." *Development and Change* 7:413–443.

Federal Bureau of Investigation. 1992. *Crime in the United States 1991: Uniform Crime Reports.* Washington, D.C.: U.S. Government Printing Office.

Federal Bureau of Investigation. 1999. *Crime in the United States: Uniform Crime Reports.* Washington, D.C.: U.S. Government Printing Office.

Ferraro, Kenneth F. 1996. "Women's Fear of Victimization: Shadow of Sexual Assault?" *Social Forces* 75:667–691.

Field, Donald R., and Robert M. Dimit. [1970] 1978. "Population Change in South Dakota Small Towns and Cities, 1949–1960." In *Change in Rural America: Causes, Consequences, and Alternatives,* edited by Richard A. Rodefeld et al., 305–311. St. Louis: C. V. Mosby.

Firebaugh, Glenn. 1979. "Structural Determinants of Urbanization in Asia and Latin America." *American Sociological Review* 44: 199–215.

Fischer, Claude S. 1975. "Toward a Subcultural Theory of Urbanism." *American Journal of Sociology* 80:1319–1341.

———. 1982. *To Dwell Among Friends: Personal Networks in Town and City.* Chicago: University of Chicago Press.

———. 1984. *The Urban Experience.* 2nd ed. New York: Harcourt Brace Jovanovich.

———. 1995. "The Subcultural Theory of Urbanism: A Twentieth-Year Assessment." *American Journal of Sociology* 101:543–577.

Fisher, Helen S. (Editor). 1994. *Gale City and Metro Rankings Reporter.* New York: Gale Research International.

Fishman, Robert. 1977. *Urban Utopias of the Twentieth Century: Ebenezer Howard, Frank Lloyd Wright, and Le Corbusier.* New York: Basic Books.

Flanagan, William G. 1978. "The Extended Family as an Agent of Social Change: Family Process, Urbanization, and Economic Development." Paper presented at the Ninth World Congress of Sociology, Uppsala, Sweden.

———. 1993. *Contemporary Urban Sociology.* New York: Cambridge University Press.

———. 1994. "The Structural Roots of Action and the Question of Convergence." In *Research in Urban Sociology: Volume 3,* edited by Ray Hutchison. Greenwich, Conn.: JAI Press.

Fliegel, Frederick C. 1980. "Implications of the New Migration for Economic Growth and Development." In *Rebirth of Rural America: Rural Migration in the Midwest,* edited by Andrew J. Sofranko and James D. Williams, 109–120. Ames, Iowa: Iowa State University Press.

Foek, Anton. 1997. "Sweatshop Barbie: Exploitation of Third World Labor." *The Humanist* (January/February) 57:9–13.

Frank, Andre Gunder. 1967. *Capitalism and Underdevelopment in Latin America: Historical Studies of Chile and Brazil.* New York: Monthly Review Press.

Franke, Richard W., and Barbara H. Chasin. 1980. *Seeds of Famine: Ecological Destruction and the Development Dilemma in the West African Sahel.* Totowa, N.J.: Allanheld, Osmun.

Frankenberg, Ronald. 1966. *Communities in Britain: Social Life in Town and Country.* Baltimore: Penguin.

Freedman, Jonathan L. 1975. *Crowding and Behavior.* New York: Viking Press.

Freudenburg, William R. 1982. "The Impacts of Rapid Growth on the Social and Personal Well-Being of Local Community Residents." In *Coping with Rapid Growth in Rural Communities,* edited by Bruce A. Weber and Robert E. Howell, 137–170. Boulder, Colo.: Westview Press.

———. 1992. "Addictive Economies: Extractive Industries and Vulnerable Localities in a Changing World Economy." *Rural Sociology* 57: 305–332.

Frey, William H. 1987. "Migration and Depopulation of the Metropolis: Regional Restructuring or

Rural Renaissance?" *American Sociological Review* 52:240–257.

———. 1993. "People in Places: Demographic Trends in Urban America." In *Rediscovering Urban America: Perspectives on the 1980s*, edited by Jack Sommer and Donald A. Hicks, 3-1 to 3-106. Washington, D.C.: U.S. Department of Housing and Urban Development.

Frey, William H., and William P. O'Hare. 1993. "Viven Los Suburbios!" *American Demographics* 15, No. 4:30–37.

Fried, Marc. 1963. "Grieving for a Lost Home." In *The Urban Condition: People and Policy in the Metropolis*, edited by Leonard J. Duhl, 151–171. New York: Basic Books.

Fry, Earl H. 1995. "North American Municipalities and Their Involvement in the Global Economy." In *North American Cities and the Global Economy*, edited by Peter Karl Kresl and Gary Gappert, 21–44. Thousand Oaks, Calif.: Sage.

Fuguitt, Glenn V. 1985. "The Nonmetropolitan Population Turnaround." *Annual Review of Sociology* 11:259–280.

Galster, George, Ronald Mincy, and Mitchell Tobin. 1997. "The Disparate Racial Neighborhood Impacts of Metropolitan Economic Restructuring." *Urban Affairs Review* 32:797–824.

Gans, Herbert J. 1962. "Urbanism and Suburbanism as Ways of Life: A Re-evaluation of Definitions." In *Human Behavior and Social Processes: An Interactionist Approach*, edited by Arnold M. Rose, 625–648. Boston: Houghton Mifflin.

———. [1962] 1982. *The Urban Villagers: Group and Class in the Life of Italian Americans*. Updated and Expanded Edition. New York: The Free Press.

———. 1973. *More Equality*. New York: Pantheon.

———. 1982. "Political Straddling." *Society*. (March/April):16–19.

———. 1992. "Second-Generation Decline: Scenarios for the Economic and Ethnic Futures of the Post-1965 American Immigrants." *Racial and Ethnic Studies* 15:173–192.

Gappert, Gary. 1995. "Conclusion and Epilogue: The Future of Cities and Their Policies in the Global Economy." In *North American Cities and the Global Economy*, edited by Peter Karl Kresl and Gary Gappert, 286–302. Thousand Oaks, Calif.: Sage.

Gardner, Carol Brooks. 1995. *Passing By: Gender and Public Harassment*. Berkeley, Calif.: University of California Press.

Garofalo, Gaspar, and Michael S. Fogarty. 1979. "Urban Income Distribution: The Urban Hierarchy-Inequality Hypothesis." *Review of Economics and Statistics* 61:381–388.

Garreau, Joel. 1991. *Edge City: Life on the New Frontier*. New York: Doubleday.

Gelfant, Blanche Housman. 1954. *The American City Novel*. Norman, Okla.: University of Oklahoma Press.

George, M. Dorothy. 1931. *England in Transition: Life and Work in the Eighteenth Century*. London: Routledge and Sons.

Gereffi, Gary, and Lynn Hempel. 1996. "Latin America in the Global Economy: Running Faster to Stay in Place." *NACLA Report on the Americas* (January–February) 29:18–27.

Giddens, Anthony. 1981. *A Contemporary Critique of Historical Materialism*. Vol. 1, *Power, Poverty and the State*. London: Macmillan.

———. 1984. *The Constitution of Society: Outline of the Theory of Structuration*. Cambridge, England: Polity.

———. 1985. *The Nation State and Violence*. Vol. 2, *A Contemporary Critique of Historical Materialism*. Berkeley, Calif.: University of California Press.

Gilbert, Alan G. 1980. "Planning for Urban Primacy and Large Cities in Latin America: A Critique of the Literature." *Comparative Urban Research* 8:105–116.

Gilbert, Alan G., and Josef Gugler. 1992. *Cities, Poverty, and Development: Urbanization in the Third World*. 2nd ed. Oxford, England: Oxford University Press.

Giovagnoli, Melissa. 1997. *50 Fabulous Places to Raise Your Family*, 2nd ed. Franklin Lakes, N.J.: Career Press.

Glaab, Charles N., and A. Theodore Brown. 1983. *A History of Urban America*, 3rd ed. New York: Macmillan.

Glasgow, Douglas G. 1980. *The Black Underclass: Poverty, Unemployment, and Entrapment of Ghetto Youth*. San Francisco: Jossey-Bass.

Glazer, Sidney. 1965. *Detroit: A Study in Development*. New York: Bookman Associates.

Goffman, Erving. 1971. *Relations in Public*. New York: Basic Books.

Goings, Kenneth W., and Raymond A. Mohl. 1996. "Toward a New African American History." In *The New African American History*, edited by Kenneth W. Goings and Raymond A. Mohl, 1–16. Thousand Oaks, Calif.: Sage.

Golden, Stephanie. 1992. *The Women Outside*. Berkeley, Calif.: University of California Press.

Goldman, David P. 1996. "Under the Volcano." *Forbes* (October 21) 158:94–97.

Goldscheider, Calvin. 1983. "The Adjustments of Migrants in Large Cities of Less Developed Countries: Some Comparative Observations." In *Urban Migrants in Developing Nations: Patterns and Problems of Adjustment*, edited by Calvin Goldscheider, 233–253. Boulder, Colo.: Westview.

Goldsmith, William W., and Edward J. Blakely. 1992. *Separate Societies: Poverty and Inequality in U.S. Cities.* Philadelphia: Temple University Press.

Gonzales, Angela. 1998. "The (RE-) articulation of American Indian Identity: Maintaining Boundaries and Regulating Access to Ethnically Tied Resources." *American Indian Culture and Research Journal* 22:199–225.

Gonzalez, Nancie L. 1975. "Migratory Patterns to a Small Dominican City and to New York." In *Migration and Urbanization: Models and Adaptation Strategies,* edited by Brian M. Dutoit and Helen I. Safa, 209–223. The Hague: Mouton.

Goodenough, Richard. 1992. "The Nature and Implications of Recent Population Growth in California." *Geography* 77:123–133.

Gordon, David M. 1984. "Capitalist Development and the History of American Cities." In *Marxism and the Metropolis: New Perspectives in Urban Political Economy,* edited by William K. Tabb and Larry Sawers, 21–53. New York: Oxford University Press.

Gordon, Milton M. 1964. *Assimilation in American Life: The Role of Race, Religion, and National Origins.* New York: Oxford University Press.

Gottdiener, Mark. 1985. *The Social Production of Urban Space.* Austin, Tex.: University of Texas Press.

Gottdiener, Mark, and Joe R. Feagin. 1988. "The Paradigm Shift in Urban Sociology." *Urban Affairs Quarterly* 24:163–187.

Gottlieb, Benjamin H. 1981. "Social Networks and Social Support in Community Mental Health." In *Social Networks and Social Support,* edited by Benjamin H. Gottlieb, 11–39. Beverly Hills, Calif.: Sage.

Granmaison, Collete Le Cour. 1969. "Activités Économiques des Femmes Dakaroises." *Africa* 39:138–151.

Grant, Don Sherman, II, and Ramiro Martinez, Jr. 1997. "Crime and the Restructuring of the U.S. Economy: A Reconsideration of the Class Linkages." *Social Forces* 75:769–799.

Gras, Norman Scott Brian. 1922. *An Introduction to Economic History.* New York and London: Harper and Brothers.

Grasmuck, Sherri, and Ramon Grosfoguel. 1997. "Geopolitics, Economic Niches, and Gendered Social Capital Among Recent Caribbean Immigrants in New York City." *Sociological Perspectives* 40:339–363.

Graves, Theodore D., and Nancy B. Graves. 1980. "Kinship Ties and the Preferred Adaptive Strategies of Urban Migrants." In *The Versatility of Kinship,* edited by Linda S. Cordell and Stephen Beckerman, 195–217. New York: Academic Press.

Greene, Jody M., Susan T. Ennett, and Christopher L. Ringwalt. 1999. "Prevalence and Correlates of Survival Sex Among Runaway and Homeless Youth." *American Journal of Public Health* 89:1406–1409.

Greenfield, Sidney M. 1961. "Industrialization and the Family in Sociological Theory." *American Journal of Sociology* 67:312–322.

Greengard, Samuel, and Charlene Marmer Solomon. 1995. "Growing-Up Scared." *Los Angeles* 40:50–61.

Gugler, Josef. 1986. "Internal Migration in the Third World." In *Population Geography: Progress and Prospect,* edited by Michael Pacione, 194–223. London: Croom Helm.

———. 1999. "Introduction." *Proceedings of the Workshop on World Cities in Poor Countries.* Washington, D.C.: The Committee on Population of the National Research, National Academy of Sciences and the National Research Council.

———. N.d. "The Son of a Hawk Does Not Remain Abroad." Unpublished paper. University of Connecticut.

Gugler, Josef, and William G. Flanagan. 1976. "On the Political Economy of Urbanization in the Third World: The Case of West Africa." *International Journal of Urban and Regional Research* 1:272–292.

———. 1978. *Urbanization and Social Change in West Africa.* Cambridge, England: Cambridge University Press.

Gwynne, S. C. 1999. "So What's the Rap on the New Neighbor?" *Time* (August 30) 154:6.

Hady, Thomas F., and Peggy J. Ross. 1990. *An Update: The Diverse Social and Economic Structures of Nonmetropolitan America.* Rockville, Md.: U.S. Department of Agriculture, Economic Research Services.

Hall, Peter. 1984. *The World Cities,* 3rd ed. New York: St. Martin's Press.

Hall, Sir Peter. 1998. *Cities in Civilization.* New York: Random House.

Hallman, Howard W. 1984. *Neighborhoods: Their Place in Urban Life.* Beverly Hills, Calif.: Sage.

Hamill, Pete. [1972] 1977. "Notes on the New Irish: A Guide for the Goyim." In *Pride and Protest: Ethnic Roots in America,* edited by Jay Schulman, Aubrey Shatter, and Rosalie Ehrlich, 290–299. New York: Dell.

Hammond, Mason. 1972. *The City in the Ancient World.* Cambridge, Mass.: Harvard University Press.

Handlin, Oscar. [1951] 1973. *The Uprooted.* Boston: Little, Brown.

Hannerz, Ulf. 1969. *Soulside: Inquiries into Ghetto Culture and Community.* New York: Columbia University Press.

———. 1974. "Ethnicity and Opportunity in Urban America." In *Urban Ethnicity,* edited by Abner Cohen, 37–76. London: Tavistock Publications.

Hannigan, John, 1998. *Fantasy City: Pleasure and Profit in the Postmodern Metropolis.* New York: Routledge.

Hansen, Niles M. 1970. *Rural Poverty and the Urban Crisis: A Strategy for Regional Development.* Bloomington, Ind.: Indiana University Press.

Hardison, David. 1981. *From Ideology to Incrementalism: The Concept of Urban Enterprise Zones in Great Britain and the United States.* Princeton, N.J.: Princeton Urban and Regional Research Center.

Haren, Claude C., and Ronald W. Holling. 1979. "Industrial Development in Nonmetropolitan America: A Locational Perspective." In *Nonmetropolitan Industrialization,* edited by Richard E. Lonsdale and H. L. Seyler, 13–45. Washington, D.C.: V.H. Winston and Sons.

Hareven, Tamara K. 1976. "Modernization and Family History: Perspectives on Social Change." *Signs: Journal of Women in Culture and Society* 2:190–206.

———. 1978. "The Dynamics of Kin in an Industrial Community." In *Turning Points: Historical and Sociological Essays on the Family,* edited by John Demos and Sarane Spence Boocock, 151–182. Chicago: University of Chicago Press.

Hareven, Tamara K., and Randolph Langenbach. 1978. *Amoskeag: Life and Work in an American Factory City.* New York: Pantheon.

Harrigan, Kate. 2000. "Pollution Prevention Gains Footing in Thailand." *Pollution Engineering* (March) 32:12–13.

Harrington, Michael. 1962. *The Other America.* New York: Macmillan.

Harris, Chauncy D., and Edward L. Ullman. 1945. "The Nature of Cities." *Annals* 242:7–17.

Harvey, David. 1973. *Social Justice and the City.* London: Edward Arnold.

———. 1978. "On Planning the Ideology of Planning." In *Planning Theory in the 1980s: A Search for Future Directions,* edited by Robert W. Burchell and George Sternlieb, 213–233. New Brunswick, N.J.: Rutgers University Center for Urban Policy Research.

———. 1985a. *The Urbanization of Capital: Studies in the History and Theory of Capitalist Urbanization.* Baltimore: Johns Hopkins University Press.

———. 1985b. *Consciousness and the Urban Experience: Studies in the History and Theory of Capitalist Urbanization.* Baltimore: Johns Hopkins University Press.

Haskins, Ron, and Wendell Primus. 2000. "Point-Counterpoint: Perspectives on Welfare Reform and Children." *Poverty Research News.* Joint Center for Poverty Research. (July-August) 4:3–5.

Hawley, Amos H. 1981. *Urban Sociology: An Ecological Approach.* 2nd ed. New York: John Wiley and Sons.

———. 1984. "Human Ecological and Marxian Theories." *American Journal of Sociology* 89:904–917.

———. 1986. *Human Ecology: A Theoretical Essay.* Chicago: University of Chicago Press.

Heenan, D. 1977. "Global Cities of Tomorrow." *Harvard Business Review* 55:79–92.

Heimer, Karen. 1997. "Socioeconomic Status, Subcultural Definitions, and Violent Delinquency." *Social Forces* 75:799–833.

Heirnaux, Daniel. 1995. "Globalizing Economies and Cities: A View from Mexico." In *North American Cities and the Global Economy,* edited by Peter Karl Kresl and Gary Gappert, 112–131. Thousand Oaks, Calif.: Sage.

Henderson, David R. 1996. "The Case for Sweatshops." *Fortune* (October 28) 134:48.

Hernandez, Jose Amaro. 1983. *Mutual Aid for Survival: The Case of the Mexican American.* Malabur, Fla.: Robert E. Krieger.

Herz, Diane E. 1991. "Worker Displacement Still Common in the Late 1980s." *Monthly Labor Review* (May) 115:3–9.

Hicks, Donald A. 1982. "Urban Strengths/Urban Weaknesses." *Society* (March/April):11–16.

Higgins, Michael James, and Tanya Leigh Coen. 1992. *Oigame! Oigame! Struggle and Social Change in a Nicaraguan Urban Community.* Boulder, Colo.: Westview.

Hine, Darlene Clark. 1996. "Black Migration to the Urban Midwest: The Gender Dimension, 1915–1945." In *The New African American Urban History,* edited by Kenneth W. Goings and Raymond A. Mohl, 240–265. Thousand Oaks, Calif.: Sage.

Hird, J. A., and M. Reese. 1998. "The Distribution of Environmental Quality: An Empirical Analysis." *Social Science Quarterly* 79:693–716.

Hirsch, Arnold R. 1983. "New Orleans: Sunbelt in the Swamp." In *Sunbelt Cities: Politics and Growth Since World War II,* Richard M. Bernard and Bradley R. Rice, 100–137. Austin, Tex.: University of Texas Press.

Hirsch, Barton J. 1981. "Social Networks and the Coping Process." In *Social Networks and Social Support,* edited by Benjamin H. Gottlieb, 149–170. Beverly Hills, Calif.: Sage.

Howard, Ebenezer. [1902] 1965. *Garden Cities of Tomorrow.* Cambridge, Mass.: MIT Press.

Hoyt, Homer. 1939. *The Structure and Growth of Residential Neighborhoods in American Cities.* Washington, D.C.: Federal Housing Administration.

Huang, Ray. 1988. *China: A Macro History.* London: M. E. Sharpe.

Hughes, Everett Cherrington. 1952. "Preface." In *Human Communities: The City and Human Ecology,* by Robert Ezra Park. Glencoe, Ill.: The Free Press.

Hughes, James W., and Kenneth Bleakly, Jr. 1975. *Urban Homesteading.* New Brunswick, N.J.: Rutgers University Press.

Hunter, Albert J., and Gerald D. Suttles. 1972. "The Expanding Community of Limited Liability." In *The Social Construction of Communities,* edited by Gerald D. Suttles, 44–81. Chicago: The University of Chicago Press.

Hunter, Floyd. 1953. *Community Power Structure.* Chapel Hill, N.C.: University of North Carolina Press.

Indergaard, Michael. 1997. "Community-Based Restructuring? Institution Building in the Industrial Midwest." *Urban Affairs Review* 32:662–682.

Iorizzo, Luciano J., and Salvatore Mondello. 1980. *The Italian Americans: Revised Edition.* Boston: Twayne.

Jackson, Jacqueline Johnson. 1997. "On Oakland's Ebonics: Some Say Gibberish, Some Say Slang, Some Say Dis Den Dat, Me Say Dem Dumb, It Be Mother Tongue." *The Black Scholar* 27(1):18–25.

Jackson, Kenneth T. 1984. "The Capital of Capitalism: The New York Metropolitan Region, 1890–1940." In *Metropolis 1890–1940,* edited by Anthony Sutcliffe, 319–353. London: University of Chicago Press.

———. 1985. *Crabgrass Frontier: The Suburbanization of the United States.* New York: Oxford University Press.

Jacobs, Jane. 1961. *The Death and Life of Great American Cities.* New York: Vintage.

Jacot, Martine. 1999. "The Big City or Bust: Surviving the South's Urban Revolution." *UNESCO Courier* (June) 06:17–36.

Jaffe, A. J., Ruth M. Cullen, and Thomas D. Boswell. 1980. *The Changing Demography of Spanish Americans.* New York: Academic Press.

Jaffe, Matthew. 1998. "Living Las Vegas." *Sunset* (February) 200:70–71.

James, Franklin J., Betty L. McCummings, and Eileen Tynan. 1984. *Minorities in the Sunbelt.* New Brunswick, N.J.: Rutgers University Press.

Jargowsky, Paul A. 1994. "Ghetto Poverty Among Blacks in the 1980s." *Journal of Policy Analysis and Management* 13:288–311.

———. 1996. *Poverty and Place: Ghettos, Barrios, and the American City.* New York: Russell Sage Foundation.

Jargowsky, Paul A., and Mary Jo Bane. 1990. "Ghetto Poverty: Basic Questions." In *Inner-City Poverty in the United States,* edited by Laurence E. Lynn, Jr. and Michael G. H. McGeary, 16–67. Washington, D.C.: National Academy Press.

Jencks, Christopher, and Susan E. Mayer. 1990. "The Social Consequences of Growing Up in a Poor Neighborhood." In *Inner-City Poverty in the United States,* edited by Laurence E. Lynn, Jr. and Michael G. H. McGeary, 111–186. National Research Council, Committee on National Urban Policy. Washington, D.C.: National Academy Press.

Jo, Moon H. 1992. "Korean Merchants in the Black Community: Prejudice Among the Victims of Prejudice." *Ethnic and Racial Studies* 15:395–411.

Johnson, Daniel M., and Rex R. Campbell. 1981. *Black Migration in America: A Social Demographic History.* Durham, N.C.: Duke University Press.

Jones, Bryan D., and Lynn W. Bachelor, with Carter Wilson. 1986. *The Sustaining Hand: Community Leadership and Corporate Power.* Lawrence, Kans.: University Press of Kansas.

Joseph, Janice. 1997. "Fear of Crime Among the Black Elderly." *Journal of Black Studies* 27:698–717.

Kadushin, Charles. 1982. "Social Density and Mental Health." In *Social Structure and Network Analysis,* edited by Peter V. Marsden and Nan Lin, 147–158. Beverly Hills, Calif.: Sage.

Kain, J. F. 1968. "Housing Segregation, Negro Employment, and Metropolitan Decentralization." *Quarterly Journal of Economics* 82:175–197.

Kapferer, Bruce. 1972. *Strategy and Transaction in an African Factory.* Manchester, England: Manchester University Press.

Kaplan, Barry J. 1983. "Houston: The Golden Buckle of the Sunbelt." In *Sunbelt Cities: Politics and Growth Since World War II,* edited by Richard M. Bernard and Bradley R. Rice, 196–212. Austin: University of Texas Press.

Kasarda, John. 1993. "Inner-City Poverty and Economic Access." In *Rediscovering Urban America: Perspectives on the 1980s,* edited by Jack Sommer and Donald A. Hicks. Washington, D.C.: Office of Housing Policy Research (HUD).

Kasinitz, Philip. 1992. *Caribbean New York: Black Immigrants and the Politics of Race.* Ithaca, N.Y.: Cornell University Press.

Kemper, Robert V. 1975. "Social Factors in Migration: The Case of Tzintzuntzenos in Mexico City." In *Migration and Urbanization: Models and Adaptive Strategies,* edited by Brian M. Dutoit and Helen I. Safa, 225–244. The Hague: Mouton.

Kennedy, David J. 1995. "Residential Associations as State Actors: Regulating the Impact of Gated Communities on Non-Members." *Yale Law Journal* 105:761–793.

Kenoyer, Jonathan Mark. 1998. *Ancient Cities of the Indus Valley Civilization.* Oxford: Oxford University Press.

Kim, Illsoo. 1981. *New Urban Immigrants: The Korean Community in New York.* Princeton, N.J.: Princeton University Press.

King, Anthony O. 1997. "Understanding Violence Among Young African American Males: An

Afrocentric Perspective." *Journal of Black Studies* 28(2):79–96.

Kipling, Rudyard. [1913] 1968. "How I Struck Chicago, and How Chicago Struck Me." In *The American City: A Sourcebook of Urban Imagery*, edited by Anslem L. Strauss, 41–48. Chicago: Aldine.

Kirkby, Richard. 1989. "Urbanization, Urban Change and the Strategy for Settlement Growth." *Geography* 74:351–353.

Klebanow, Diana, Franklin L. Jonas, and Ira M. Leonard. 1977. *Urban Legacy: The Story of America's Cities*. New York: Mentor.

Kolack, Shirley. 1980. "Lowell, An Immigrant City: The Old and the New." In *Sourcebook on the New Immigration: Implications for the United States and the International Community*, edited by Roy Simon Bryce-Laporte, 339–346. New Brunswick, N.J.: Transaction Books.

Krannich, Ronald L. 1982. "Governing Urban Thailand: Coping with Policies and Administrative Politics." *Urban Affairs Quarterly* 17:319–341.

Kraut, Alan M. 1982. *The Huddled Masses: The Immigrant in American Society, 1880–1921*. Arlington Heights, Ill.: Harlan Davidson.

Kresl, Peter Karl. 1995. "The Determinants of Urban Competitiveness: A Survey." In *North American Cities and the Global Economy*, edited by Peter Karl Kresl and Gary Gappert, 45–68. Thousand Oaks, Calif.: Sage.

Krivo, Lauren J., and Ruth D. Peterson. 1996. "Extremely Disadvantaged Neighborhoods and Urban Crime." *Social Forces* 75:619–650.

Krouse, Susan Applegate. 1999. "Kinship and Identity: Mixed Bloods in Urban Indian Communities." *American Indian Culture and Research Journal* 23:73–89.

Kuhn, Thomas J. 1972. *The Structure of Scientific Revolution*. Chicago: University of Chicago Press.

Kusmer, Kenneth. 1996. "African Americans in the City Since World War II." In *The New African American Urban History*, edited by Kenneth W. Goings and Raymond A. Mohl, 320–368. Thousand Oaks, Calif.: Sage.

Lachman, M. Leanne, and Deborah L. Brett. 1997. "The Immigration Factor." *Mortgage Banker* (July) 57:68–73.

Lake, Robert W. 1981. *The New Suburbanites: Race and Housing in the Suburbs*. New Brunswick, N.J.: Rutgers University Press.

———. 1990. "Urban Fortunes: The Political Economy of Place: A Commentary." *Urban Geography* 11:179–184.

Laumann, Edward O. 1973. *Bonds of Pluralism: The Form and Substance of Urban Social Networks*. New York: John Wiley and Sons.

Le Corbusier. 1925. *L'art Décoratif d'Aujourd'hui*. Paris: n.p.

———. 1930. *Deuvre Complète 1910–1929*. Zurich: n.p.

Ledebur, Larry C. 1982. "Fluctuating Fortunes." *Society* (March/April):20–22.

Leeds, Anthony, and Elizabeth Leeds. 1976. "Accounting for Behavioral Differences: Three Political Systems and the Responses of Squatters in Brazil, Peru, and Chile." In *The City in Comparative Perspective: Cross-National Research and New Directions in Theory*, edited by John Walton and Louis H. Masotti, 193–248. New York: Sage.

Legates, Richard T., and Charles Hartman. 1981. "Displacement." *Clearing House Review* 15:207–249.

———. 1986. "The Anatomy of Displacement in the United States." In *Gentrification of the City*, edited by Neil Smith and Peter Williams, 178–200. Boston: Allen and Unwin.

Lehan, Richard. 1998. *The City in Literature: An Intellectual and Cultural History*. Berkeley: University of California Press.

Leightner, Jonathan E. 1999. "Globalization and Thailand's Financial Crisis." *Journal of Economic Issues* 33:367–373.

Levine, Hillel, and Lawrence Harmon. 1992. *The Death of an American Jewish Community: A Tragedy of Good Intentions*. New York: The Free Press.

Lewis, Carolyn. 1981. "The Beasts in the Jungle." *Newsweek*. January 19:8.

Lewis, Oscar. 1966a. "The Culture of Poverty." *The Scientific American* 215 (4):19–25.

———. 1966b. *La Vida: A Puerto Rican Family in the Culture of Poverty*. New York: Random House.

Leyden, Liz. 1999. "Little Italy Shrinks; Flavor Lingers." *Washington Post*. (September 13, 1999):A 3.

Lieberson, Stanley. 1980. *A Piece of the Pie: Blacks and White Immigrants Since 1880*. Berkeley, Calif.: University of California Press.

Liebow, Edward B. 1989. "Category of Community? Measuring Urban Indian Social Cohesion with Network Sampling." *Journal of Ethnic Studies* 16:67–100.

Liebow, Elliott. 1967. *Tally's Corner*. Boston: Little, Brown.

———. 1993. *Tell Them Who I Am: The Lives of Homeless Women*. New York: The Free Press.

Light, Ivan. 1996. "Nationalism and Anti-Immigrant Movements." *Society*. (January/February) 33: 58–63.

Linn, Johanne F. 1982. "The Costs of Urbanization in Developing Countries." *Economic Development and Cultural Change* 30:625–648.

Littlejohn-Blake, Sheila M., and Carol Anderson Darling. 1993. "Understanding the Strengths of African American Families." *Journal of Black Studies* 23:460–471.

Litvak-King, Jaime. 1985. *Ancient Mexico: An Overview*. Albuquerque, N.M.: University of New Mexico Press.

Litwak, Eugene. 1960a. "Occupational Mobility and Extended Family Cohesion." *American Sociological Review* 25:9–21.

———. 1960b. "Geographical Mobility and Extended Family Cohesion." *American Sociological Review* 25:385–394.

Litwak, Eugene, and Ivan Szelenyi. 1969. "Primary Group Structures and Their Functions: Kin, Neighbors and Friends." *American Sociological Review* 34:465–481.

Lofland, Lyn H. 1985. *A World of Strangers: Order and Action in Public Space.* Prospect Heights, Ill.: Waveland Press.

———. 1998. *The Public Realm: Exploring The City's Quintessential Social Territory.* New York: Aldine De Gruyter.

Logan, John R., and Reid M. Golden. 1986. "Suburbs and Satellites: Two Decades of Change." *American Sociological Review* 51:430–437.

Logan, John R., and Richard D. Alba. 1993. "Locational Returns to Human Capital: Minority Access to Suburban Community Resources." *Demography* 30:243–268.

Logan, John R., and Harvey L. Molotch. 1987. *Urban Fortunes: The Political Economy of Place.* Berkeley, Calif.: University of California Press.

Logan, John R., Richard D. Alba, and Shu-yin Leung. 1996. "Minority Access to White Suburbs: A Multiregional Comparison." *Social Forces* 74:851–881.

Logan, John, Rachel Bridges Whaley, and Kyle Crowder. 1997. "The Character and Consequences of Growth Regimes: An Assessment of 20 Years of Research." *Urban Affairs Review* 32:603–630.

London, Bruce. 1980. *Metropolis and Nation in Thailand: The Political Economy of Uneven Development.* Boulder, Colo.: Westview.

———. 1987. "Structural Determinants of Third World Urban Change: An Ecological and Political Economic Analysis." *American Sociological Review* 52:28–43.

London, Bruce, and William G. Flanagan. 1976. "Comparative Urban Ecology: A Summary of the Field." In *The City in Comparative Perspective: Cross-National Research and New Directions in Theory,* edited by John Walton and Louis H. Masotti, 41–66. Beverly Hills, Calif.: Sage.

London, Bruce, Donald S. Bradley, and James R. Hudson. 1980. "Approaches to Inner City Revitalization." *Urban Affairs Quarterly* 15:373–380.

Long, Norton E. 1958. "The Local Community as an Ecology of Games." *American Journal of Sociology* 64:251–261.

Lopata, Helena Znaniecki. 1976. *Polish Americans: Status Competition in an Ethnic Community.* Englewood Cliffs, N.J.: Prentice-Hall.

Lott, Tommy. 1992. "Marooned in America: Black Urban Youth Culture and Social Pathology." In *The Underclass Question,* edited by Bill E. Lawson, 71–89. Philadelphia: Temple University Press.

Lukes, Steven. 1972. *Emile Durkheim His Life and Work: A Historical and Critical Study.* New York: Harper and Row.

Lyman, Brad. 1992. "Urban Primacy and World-System Position." *Urban Affairs Quarterly,* 28:22–37.

Lynch, Kevin. 1960. *The Image of the City.* Cambridge, Mass.: MIT Press.

Lynd, Robert S., and Helen M. Lynd. 1937. *Middletown in Transition: A Study in Cultural Conflicts.* New York: Harcourt Brace.

Macdonald, Michael C. D. 1984. *America's Cities: A Report on the Myth of Urban Renaissance.* New York: Simon and Schuster.

Maharidge, Dale. 1996. *The Coming White Minority: California's Eruptions and America's Future.* New York: Random House.

Maine, Henry James Sumner. [1861] 1917. *Ancient Law.* London: E. P. Dutton.

Malcolmson, Robert W. 1973. *Popular Recreations in English Society 1700–1850.* Cambridge, England: Cambridge University Press.

Mangin, William. 1967. "Squatter Settlements." *Scientific American* (October):21–29.

———. 1973. "Sociological, Cultural, and Political Characteristics of Some Urban Migrants in Peru." In *Urban Anthropology: Cross-Cultural Studies of Urbanization,* edited by Aidan Southall, 315–350. Oxford, England: Oxford University Press.

Marris, Peter. 1961. *Family and Social Change in an African City: A Study of Rehousing in Lagos.* London: Routledge and Kegan Paul.

Marsella, Anthony J. 1998. "Urbanization, Mental Health, and Social Deviancy: A Review of Issues and Research." *American Psychologist* 53:624–634.

Marsella, Anthony J., Abraham Wandersman, and Dorothy W. Cantor. 1998. "Psychology and Urban Initiatives: Professional and Scientific Opportunities and Challenges." *American Psychologist* 53:621–623.

Martindale, Don, ed. 1958. "Prefatory Remarks: The Theory of the City." In *The City,* by Max Weber, translated and edited by Don Martindale and Gertrude Neuwirth. Glencoe, Ill.: The Free Press.

Martines, Lauro. 1979. *Power and Imagination: City-States in Renaissance Italy.* New York: Alfred A. Knopf.

Martinez, Ramiro, Jr. 1996. "Latinos and Lethal Violence: The Impact of Poverty and Inequality." *Social Problems* 43:131–145.

Martinez, Ruben. 1995. "Meet the Future in the Past." *NACLA Report on the Americas* (January–February) 28:35–38.

Masotti, Louis H. 1973. "Prologue: Suburbia Reconsidered—Myth and Counter-Myth." In *The Urbanization of the Suburbs*, Vol. 7, *Urban Affairs Annual Reviews*, edited by Louis H. Masotti and Jeffrey K. Hadden, 15–22. Beverly Hills, Calif.: Sage.

Massey, Douglas S., and Nancy Denton. 1987. "Trends in the Residential Segregation of Blacks, Hispanics, and Asians." *American Sociological Review* 52:802–825.

Massey, Douglas S., and Nancy A. Denton. 1993. *American Apartheid: Segregation and the Making of the Underclass.* Cambridge, Mass.: Harvard University Press.

Massey, Douglas S., and Mitchell Eggers. 1990. "The Ecology of Inequality: Minorities and the Concentration of Poverty, 1970–1980." *American Journal of Sociology* 95:1153–1188.

McCall, Nathan. 1994. *Makes Me Wanna Holler: A Young Black Man in America.* New York: Random House.

McCutcheon, Laurie. 1983. "The Adjustment of Migrants to Surabaya, Indonesia." In *Urban Migrants in Developing Nations: Patterns and Problems of Adjustment*, edited by Calvin Goldscheider, 95–136. Boulder, Colo.: Westview.

McFarland, M. Carter. 1978. *Federal Government and Urban Problems: HUD: Successes, Failures, and the Future of Our Cities.* Boulder, Colo.: Westview.

McGahey, Richard M. 1986. "Economic Conditions, Neighborhood Organization, and Urban Crime." In *Communities and Crime*, edited by Albert J. Reiss and Michael Tonry, 231–270. Chicago: University of Chicago Press.

McGee, T. G. 1982. "Labour Mobility in Fragmented Labour Markets, the Role of Circulatory Migration in Rural-Urban Relations in Asia." In *Toward a Political Economy of Urbanization in Third World Countries*, edited by Helen I. Safa, 47–66. New Delhi: Oxford University Press.

McKelvey, Blake. 1968. *The Emergence of Metropolitan America 1915–1966.* New Brunswick, N.J.: Rutgers University Press.

———. 1969. *The City in American History.* London: George Allen and Unwin.

McKenzie, Evan. 1994. *Privatopia: Homeowner Associations and the Rise of Residential Private Government.* New Haven: Yale University Press.

McKenzie, R. D. 1926. "The Scope of Urban Ecology." In *The Urban Community: Selected Papers from the Proceedings of The American Sociological Society, 1925*, edited by Ernest W. Burgess, 167–182. Chicago: University of Chicago Press.

McNairn, Barbara. 1980. *The Method and Theory of V. Gordon Childe.* Edinburgh: Edinburgh University Press.

McRoberts, Kenneth. 1980. "The Rise of a Quebecois Identity." In *The Mobilization of Collective Identity: Comparative Perspectives*, edited by Jeffrey A. Ross and Ann Baker Cotrell, 225–255. Lanham, Md.: University Press of America.

Meggers, Betty. 1975. "The Transpacific Origins of Mesoamerican Civilizations: A Preliminary Review of the Evidence and Its Theoretical Implication." *American Anthropologist* 77:1–23.

Meltzer, Jack. 1984. *Metropolis to Metroplex: The Social and Spatial Planning of Cities.* Baltimore: Johns Hopkins University Press.

Menon, Shanti. 1998. "Indus Valley, Inc." *Discover* (December) 19:67–71.

Messner, Steven F., and Kenneth Tardiff. 1986. "Economic Inequality and Levels of Homicide: An Analysis of Urban Neighborhoods." *Criminology* 24:297–317.

Mieczkowski, Thomas. 1986. "Geeking Up and Throwing Down: Heroin Street Life in Detroit." *Criminology* 24:245–266.

Miller, Zane L. 1973. *The Urbanization of Modern America: A Brief History.* New York: Harcourt Brace Jovanovich.

Millon, Rene. [1967] 1973. "Teotihuacan." In *Cities: Their Origin, Growth, and Human Impact*, edited by Kingsley Davis, 82–92. San Francisco: W. H. Freeman.

Mills, C. Wright. 1956. *The Power Elite.* New York: Oxford University Press.

———. 1962. *The Marxists.* New York: Dell.

Minchinton, Walter. [1973] 1976. "Patterns of Demand 1700–1914." In *The Industrial Revolution 1700–1914*, edited by Carlo M. Cipolla, 77–186. New York: Harper and Row.

Mitchell, J. Clyde, ed. 1969. *Social Networks in Urban Situations: Analysis of Personal Relationships in Central African Towns.* Manchester, England: Manchester University Press.

Model, Susanne. 1997. "An Occupational Tale of Two Cities: Minorities in London and New York." *Demography* 34:539–550.

Model, Suzanne, and David Ladipo. 1996. "Context and Opportunity: Minorities in London and New York." *Social Forces* 75:485–510.

Moir, Hazel. 1981. "Occupational Mobility in the Informal Sector in Jakarta." In *The Urban Informal Sector in Developing, Countries: Employment, Poverty and Environment*, edited by S. V. Sethuraman, 109–120. Geneva: International Labor Office.

Molotch, H. 1976. "The City as a Growth Machine: Toward a Political Economy of Place." *American Journal of Sociology* 82:309–330.

Montgomery, Roger. 1985. "Pruitt-Igoe: Policy Failure or Societal Symptom." In *The Metropolitan Midwest: Policy Problems and Prospects for Future Change,* edited by Barry Checkoway and Carl V. Patton, 229–243. Chicago: University of Illinois Press.

Moock, Janet Lewinger. 1973. "Pragmatism and the Primary School: The Case of a Non-rural Village." *Africa* 43:302–316.

Morris, Nomi. 1998. "Suspicion and Fury." *Maclean's* (July 20) 111:18–19.

Mort, Jo-Ann. 1996. "Immigrant Dreams: Sweatshop Workers Speak." *Dissent* 43 (Fall):85–87.

Morton, Henry W. 1984. "The Contemporary Soviet City." In *The Contemporary Soviet City,* edited by Henry Morton and Robert C. Stuart, 3–24. Armonk, N.Y.: M. E. Sharpe.

Moscow, Warren. 1971. *The Last of the Big-Time Bosses: The Life and Times of Carmine DeSapio and the Rise and Fall of Tammany Hall.* New York: Stein and Day.

Mucha, Janusz. 1993. "An Outsider's View of American Culture." In *Distant Mirrors: America as a Foreign Culture,* edited by Philip R. DeVita and James D. Armstrong, 21–28. Belmont, Calif.: Wadsworth.

Muller, Thomas. 1993. *Immigrants and the American City.* New York: New York University Press.

Mumford, Lewis. 1961. *The City in History: Its Origins, Its Transformations, and Its Prospects.* New York: Harcourt, Brace and World.

Musson, A. E. 1978. *The Growth of British Industry.* New York: Holmes and Meier.

Myrdal, Gunnar. 1970. *The Challenge of World Poverty: A World Anti-poverty Program in Outline.* New York: Pantheon.

Nagle, Joane, and C. Matthew Snipp. 1993. "Ethnic Reorganization: American Indian Social, Economic, Political, and Cultural Strategies for Survival." *Ethnic and Racial Studies* 16:203–235.

Nelli, Humbert S. 1970. *Italians in Chicago, 1880–1930: A Study in Ethnic Mobility.* New York: Oxford University Press.

Nelson, Nici. 1988. "How Women Get By: The Sexual Division of Labor in a Nairobi Squatter Settlement." In *The Urbanization of the Third World,* edited by Josef Gugler, 183–203. Oxford, England: Oxford University Press.

Newburger, Harriet. 1984. *Recent Evidence on Discrimination in Housing.* United States Department of Housing and Urban Development. Washington, D.C.: U.S. Government Printing Office.

Newton, Kenneth. 1975. "American Urban Politics: Social Class, Political Structure, and Public Goods." *Urban Affairs Quarterly* 11:243–264.

Nientied, Peter M., and Jan van der Linden. 1985. "Approaches to Low-income Housing in the Third World: Some Comments." *International Journal of Urban and Regional Research* 9:311–329.

Noll, Roger G., and Andrew Zimbalist. 1997. "Build the Stadium: Create the Jobs." In *Sports, Jobs, and Taxes: The Economic Impact of Sports Teams and Stadiums,* edited by Roger G. Knoll and Andrew Zimbalist, 1–54. Washington, D.C.: Brookings Institution Press.

Noyelle, Thierry, and Thomas N. Stanback, Jr. 1983. *The Economic Transformation of American Cities.* Totowa, N.J.: Rowman and Allanheld.

Nuñez, Ralph, and Cybelle Fox. 1999. "A Snapshot of Family Homelessness Across America." *Political Science Quarterly* 114:289–307.

Nyerere, Julius K. 1968. *Ujamaa: Essays on Socialism.* London: Oxford University Press.

Obermiller, Phillip J. 1981. "The Question of Appalachian Ethnicity." In *The Invisible Minority: Urban Appalachians,* edited by William W. Philliber and Clyde B. McCoy, 9–19. Lexington, Ky.: University Press of Kentucky.

O'Connor, Anthony. 1983. *The African City.* New York: Africana Publishing.

Officer, James E. [1971] 1984. "The American Indian and Federal Policy." In *The American Indian in Urban Society,* edited by Jack O. Waddell and O. Michael Watson, 8–65. Boston: University Press of America.

Ohmae, Kenichi. 1995. "Preface." In *The Evolving Global Economy: Making Sense of the New World Order,* edited by Kenichi Ohmae, *xiii–xviii.* Boston: Harvard Business School.

Oldenberg, Ray. 1989. *The Great Good Place: Cafés, Coffee Shops, Community Centers, Beauty Parlors, General Stores, Bars, Hangouts and How They Get You Through the Day.* New York: Paragon House.

Olzak, Susan, and Suzanne Shanahan. 1996. "Deprivation and Race Riots: An Extension of Spilerman's Analysis." *Social Forces* 74:931–962.

Oppong, Christine. 1974. *Marriage Among a Matrilineal Elite: A Family Study of Ghanaian Senior Civil Servants.* London: Cambridge University Press.

Orellana-Rojas, Cecilia. 1998. "Mapuche: People of the Land." *Native Peoples* (October) 11:74–77.

Otchet, Amy. 1999. "Lagos: Survival of the Determined." *UNESCO Courier* (June) 06:17–22.

Owen, John B. 1975. *The Eighteenth Century, 1714–1815.* Totowa, N.J.: Rowan and Littlefield.

Pacione, Michael. 1990. "What About People? A Critical Analysis of Urban Policy in the United Kingdom." *Geography* 75:193–202.

Padfield, Harland. 1980. "The Expendable Rural Community and the Denial of Powerlessness." In *The Dying Community,* edited by Harland Padfield and Art Gallaher, 159–185. Albuquerque, N.M.: University of New Mexico Press.

Page, Randy M., and Jon Hammermeister. 1997. "Weapon-carrying and Youth Violence." *Adolescence* 32:505–513.

Park, Robert E. 1915. "The City: Suggestions for the Investigation of Human Behavior in the City." *American Journal of Sociology* 20:577–612.

———. 1926. "The Urban Community as a Spatial Pattern and a Moral Order." In *The Urban Community: Selected Proceedings of the American Sociological Society, 1925*, edited by Ernest W. Burgess, 3–20. Chicago: University of Chicago Press.

———. [1929] 1952. "Sociology, Community, and Society." In *Human Communities: The City and Human Ecology*, edited by Robert Ezra Park, 178–209. Glencoe, Ill.: The Free Press.

Parker, Robert Nash, and Allan V. Horwitz. 1986. "Unemployment, Crime, and Imprisonment: A Panel Approach." *Criminology* 24:251–273.

Parsons, Talcott. [1949] 1959. "The Social Structure of the Family." In *The Family: Its Function and Destiny*, edited by Ruth Nanda Anshen, 241–274. New York: Harper and Brothers.

———. 1951. *The Social System*. Glencoe, Ill.: The Free Press.

———. 1955. "The American Family: Its Relations to Personality and Social Structure." In *Family Socialization and Interaction Process*, edited by Talcott Parsons and R. F. Bales, 3–21. Glencoe, Ill.: The Free Press.

Patterson, E. Britt. 1991. "Poverty, Income Inequality, and Neighborhood Crime Rates." *Criminology* 29:755–776.

Patterson, Orlando. 1977. *Ethnic Chauvinism: The Reactionary Impulse*. New York: Stein and Day.

Pearce, Diana M. 1983. "The Feminization of Ghetto Poverty." *Society* 72 (November/December):70–74.

Peattie, Lisa R. 1975. "'Tertiarization' and Urban Poverty in Latin America." In *Urbanization and Inequality: The Political Economy of Urban and Rural Development in Latin America*, edited by Wayne A. Cornelius and Felicity M. Trueblood, 109–123. Beverly Hills, Calif.: Sage.

Peil, Margaret. 1981. *Cities and Suburbs: Urban Life in West Africa*. New York: Africana Publishing.

———. 1991. *Lagos: The City Is the People*. Boston: G. K. Hall.

Perlman, J. 1971. *The Fate of Migrants in Rios Favelas: The Myth of Marginality*. Ph.D. dissertation, Massachusetts Institute of Technology.

Peroff, Kathleen. 1987. "Who Are the Homeless and How Many Are There?" In *The Homeless in Contemporary Society*, edited by Richard D. Bingham et al., 33–45. Beverly Hills, Calif.: Sage.

Perry, David C., and Alfred J. Watkins. [1978] 1979. "People, Profit, and the Rise of the Sunbelt City." In *The Urban Scene: Myths and Realities*, edited by Joe R. Feagin, 139–166. New York: Random House. (Reprinted from David C. Perry and Alfred J. Watkins (eds.). 1978. *Urban Affairs Annual Review*, Vol. 14. Beverly Hills, Calif.: Sage.)

Pettigrew, Thomas F. 1980. "The Changing—Not Declining—Significance of Race." *Contemporary Sociology* 9:19–21.

Pfeiffer, John E. 1977. *The Emergence of Society: A Prehistory of the Establishment*. New York: McGraw-Hill.

Phelan Jo C., and Bruce G. Link. 1999. "Who Are the Homeless? Reconsidering the Stability and Composition of the Homeless Population." *American Journal of Public Health* 115:1334–1338.

Phelan, Thomas J., and Mark Schneider. 1996. "Race, Ethnicity, and Class in American Suburbs." *Urban Affairs Quarterly* 31:659–680.

Philliber, William W. 1981. *Appalachian Migrants in Urban America: Cultural Conflict or Ethnic Group Formation?* New York: Praeger.

Phillips, Andrew. 2000. "Quenching the Southwest's Thirst." *Maclean's* (March) 113:23.

Philpott, Stuart B. 1968. "Remittance Obligations, Social Networks, and Choice Among Monsterration Migrants in Britain." *Man* 3:465–476.

Phythian-Adams, Charles. 1979. *Desolation of a City: Coventry and the Urban Crisis of the Late Middle Ages*. Cambridge, England: Cambridge University Press.

Pike, William E. 2000. "Leaving the City Behind." *The American Enterprise* (March) 11:47.

Policy and Practice of Public Human Services. 2000. "A Conversation with Maria Foscarinis." *Policy and Practice of Public Human Services* 58:37–41.

Piven, Frances Fox, and Richard A. Cloward. 1977. *Poor People's Movements: Why They Succeed, How They Fail*. New York: Pantheon.

Plesur, Milton. 1982. *Jewish Life in TwentiethCentury America: Challenge and Accommodation*. Chicago: Nelson-Hall.

Pollock, Griselda. 1988. *Vision and Difference: Femininity, Feminism, and the Histories of Art*. New York: Routledge.

Popenoe, David. 1985. *Private Pleasure, Public Pain: American Metropolitan Community Life in Comparative Perspective*. New Brunswick, N.J.: Transaction Books.

Portes, Alejandro. 1976. "On the Sociology of National Development: Theories and Issues." *American Journal of Sociology* 82:55–85.

Pred, Allen R. 1966. *The Spatial Dynamics of Urban Industrial-Growth: 1800-1914*. Cambridge, Mass.: The MIT Press.

Professional Builder. 1998. "Sunbelt: Still the Trendsetter." *Professional Builder* (June) 63:72–97.

Proulx, Pierre-Paul. 1995. "Determinants of the Growth and Decline of Cities in North America." In *North American Cities and the Global Economy: Challenges and Opportunities,* edited by Peter Karl Kresl and Gary Gappert, 171–184. Thousand Oaks, Calif.: Sage.

Razin, Eran, and Ivan Light. 1998. "Ethnic Entrepreneurs in America's Largest Metropolitan Areas." *Urban Affairs Review* 33:332–360.

Reganick, Karol A. 1997. "Prognosis for Homeless Children and Adolescents." *Childhood Education* (Spring) 73:133–136.

Reich, Robert B. 1995. "Who is Them?" In *The Evolving Global Economy: Making Sense of the New World Order,* edited by Kenichi Ohmae, 161–182. Boston: Harvard Business School.

Reimann, Horst, and Helga Reimann. 1979. "Federal Republic of Germany." In *International Labor Migration in Europe,* edited by Ronald E. Krane, 63–87. New York: Praeger.

Rice, Bradley R., and Richard M. Bernard. 1983. "Introduction." In *Sunbelt Cities: Politics and Growth Since World War II,* edited by Richard M. Bernard and Bradley R. Rice, 1–30. Austin, Tex.: University of Texas Press.

Rice, Jennifer. 2000. "Water Crisis Looms." *Water, Environment, and Technology* (March) 12:18.

Richardson, Harry W. 1984. "National Urban Development Strategies in Developing Countries." In *Urban Development in the Third World,* edited by Pradip K. Ghosh, 122–148. Westport, Conn.: Greenwood.

Richter, Kerry. 1985. "Nonmetropolitan Growth in the Late 1970s: The End of the Turnaround?" *Demography* 22:245–263.

Ringheim, Karin. 1993. "Investigating the Structural Determinants of Homelessness: The Case of Houston." *Urban Affairs Quarterly* 28:617–640.

Riposa, Gerry. 1996. "From Enterprise Zones to Empowerment Zones: The Community Context of Urban Economic Development." *The American Behavioral Scientist* 39:536–552.

Robinson, David, Yangho Byeon, Ranjit Teja, and Wanda Tseng. 1991. *Thailand: Adjusting to Success: Current Policy Issues.* Washington, D.C.: International Monetary Fund.

Robinson, Kenneth L., and Richard J. Reeder. 1991. "State Enterprise Zones in Nonmetro Areas: Are They Working?" *Rural Development Perspectives* (U.S. Department of Agriculture) June/September 1991.

Rogers, Rosemarie. 1985. "Post-World War II European Labor Immigration: An Introduction to the Issues." In *Guests Come to Stay: The Effects of European Labor Migration on Sending and Receiving Countries,* edited by Rosemarie Rogers, 1–28. Boulder, Colo.: Westview.

Rorig, Fritz. [1955] 1967. *The Medieval Town.* Berkeley, Calif.: University of California Press.

Rose, Peter I. 1969. *The Ghetto and Beyond: Essays on Jewish Life in America.* New York: Random House.

Rosentraub, Mark. 1997. "Stadiums and Urban Space." In *Sports, Jobs, and Taxes: The Economic Impact of Sports Teams and Stadiums,* edited by Roger G. Knoll and Andrew Zimbalist, 178–207. Washington, D.C.: Brookings Institution Press.

Ross, Andrew. 1999. *The Celebration Chronicles: Life, Liberty, and the Pursuit of Property Value in Disney's New Town.* New York: Ballantine Books.

Ross, Christopher O. 1987. "Organizational Dimensions of Metropolitan Dominance: Prominence in the Network of Corporate Control,1955–1975." *American Sociological Review* 52:258–267.

Ross, Jeffrey A. 1980. "The Mobilization of Collective Identity: An Analytical Overview." In *The Mobilization of Collective Identity: Comparative Perspectives,* edited by Jeffrey D. Ross and Ann Baker Cottrell, 1–30. Lanham, Md.: University Press of America.

Ryan, Mary P. 1990. *Women in Public: Between Banners and Ballots, 1825–1880.* Baltimore: Johns Hopkins University Press.

Ryan, William. 1971. *Blaming the Victim.* New York: Vintage.

Sabloff, Jeremy A. 1989. *The Cities of Ancient Mexico: Reconstructing a Lost World.* N.p.: Thames and Hudson.

Sagarra, Eda. 1977. *A Social History of Germany 1648–1914.* New York: Holmes and Meier.

Salami, Semiu. 1999. "Business Void Everywhere." *The News* (Lagos) (June 14), as cited in *Africa News Service* (June 15).

Sanders, William T., and David Webster. 1988. "The Mesoamerican Urban Tradition." *American Anthropologist* 90:521–546.

Sassen, Saskia. 1996. "Cities and Communities in the Global Economy: Rethinking Our Concepts." *American Behavioral Scientist* 39:629–640.

Sawers, Larry. 1984. "New Perspectives on the Urban Political Economy." In *Marxism and the Metropolis: New Perspectives in Urban Political Economy,* edited by William K. Tabb and Larry Sawers, 3–17. New York: Oxford University Press.

Schermerhorn, R. A. 1978. "Preface to the Phoenix Edition." In *Comparative Ethnic Relations: A Framework for Theory and Research.* Chicago: University of Chicago Press.

Schill, Michael H., and Richard P. Nathan, with Harrichand Persaud. 1983. *Revitalizing America's Cities: Neighborhood Reinvestment and Displacement.* Albany, N.Y.: State University of New York Press.

Schmid, Alex P., and Janny de Graaf. 1982. *Violence as Communication: Insurgent Terrorism and the Western News Media.* Beverly Hills, Calif.: Sage.

Schneider, Mark, and John R. Logan. 1982. "Suburban Racial Segregation and Black Access to Local Public Resources." *Social Science Quarterly* 63:762–770.

Schnore, Leo F. 1972. *Class and Race in Cities and Suburbs.* Chicago: Markham.

Schnore, Leo F., and Hal H. Winsborough. 1972. "Functional Classification and the Residential Location of Social Classes." In *City Classification Handbook,* edited by Brian J. L. Berry, 124–151. New York: Wiley-Interscience.

Schwirian, Kent P. 1977. "Internal Structure of the Metropolis." In *Contemporary Topics in Urban Sociology,* edited by Kent P. Schwirian et al., 152–215. Morristown, N.J.: General Learning Press.

Scott, Margaret. 1989. "Shape of Things to Come." *Far Eastern Economic Review* (May 11) 144:40–41.

Scott, Mel. 1969. *American City Planning Since 1890.* Berkeley, Calif.: University of California Press.

Sennett, Richard. 1970. *The Uses of Disorder: Personal Identity and City Life.* New York: Random House.

———. 1977. *The Fall of Public Man.* New York: Alfred Knopf.

Sethuraman, S. V. 1981. "Summary and Conclusions: Implications for Policy and Action." In *The Urban Informal Sector in Developing Countries: Employment, Poverty and Environment,* edited by S. V. Sethuraman, 188–208. Geneva: International Labor Office.

Seyfrit, Carole L. 1986. "Migration Intentions of Rural Youth: Testing an Assumed Benefit of Rapid Growth." *Rural Sociology* 51:199–211.

Shakur, Sanyika. 1993. *Monster: The Autobiography of an L.A. Gang Member.* New York: Monthly Review Press.

Shaw, Timothy M. 1995. "Africa in the Global Political Economy at the End of the Millennium: What Implications for Politics and Policies?" *Africa Today* (Fourth Quarter) 42:7–30.

Shen, J., and N. A. Spence. 1996. "Modeling Urban-Rural Population Growth in China." *Environment and Planning* 28:1417–1444.

Sheppard, Francis. 1971. *London 1808–1870: The Infernal Wen.* Berkeley and Los Angeles: University of California Press.

Shevky, Eshref, and Wendell Bell. 1955. *Social Area Analysis: Theory, Illustrative Application and Computational Procedures.* Westport, Conn.: Greenwood.

Shevky, Eshref, and Marilyn Williams. 1949. *The Social Area of Los Angeles: Analysis and Typology.* Berkeley, Calif.: University of California Press.

Shihadeh Edward S., and Nicole Flynn. 1996. "Segregation and Crime: The Effect of Black Social Isolation on the Rates of Black Urban Violence." *Social Forces* 74:1325–1352.

Shihadeh Edward S., and Graham C. Ousey. 1996. "Metropolitan Expansion and Black Social Dislocation: The Link Between Suburbanization and Center-City Crime." *Social Forces* 75:649–666.

Shumway, J. Matthew, and Richard H. Jackson. 1995. "Native American Population Patterns." *The Geographical Review* 85:185–201.

Siegfried, John and Andrew Zimbalist. 2000. "The Economics of Sports Facilities and Their Communities." *Journal of Economic Perspectives* (Summer) 14:95–113.

Simmel, Georg. [1905] 1950. "The Metropolis and Mental Life." In *The Sociology of Georg Simmel,* edited by Kurt H. Wolff, 409–424. New York: The Free Press.

Simmons, William S. 1981. "Narragansett Indians: Identity Persistence." In *Hidden Minorities: The Persistence of Ethnicity in American Life,* edited by Joan H. Rollins, 35–52. Washington, D.C.: University Press of America.

Sjoberg, Gideon. 1960. *The Preindustrial City: Past and Present.* New York: The Free Press.

———. [1965] 1973. "The Origin and Evolution of Cities." In *Cities: Their Origin, Growth, and Human Impact,* edited by Kingsley Davis, 19–27. San Francisco: W. H. Freeman.

Skardal, Dorothy Burton. 1974. *The Divided Heart: Scandinavian Immigrant Experience Through Literary Sources.* Lincoln, Neb.: University of Nebraska Press.

Slater, Courtenay M., and George E. Hall. 1992. *1992 County and City Extra: Annual Metro, City, and County Data Book.* Lanham, Md.: Bernan.

Sletto, Bjorn. 1995. "That Sinking Feeling." *Geographical Magazine* (July) 67:24–27.

Smith, David A., and Bruce London. 1990. "Convergence in World Urbanization? A Quantitative Assessment." *Urban Affairs Quarterly* 25:574–590.

Smith, Eric L. 1997. "Harlem Renaissance—Take Two: After Years of Neglect, Will Empowerment Zones Allow Harlem to Thrive Once Again?" *Black Enterprise* (February) 27(7):23–25.

Smith, Michael E. 1989. "Cities, Towns, and Urbanisms: Comment on Sanders and Webster." *American Anthropologist* 91:454–460.

Smitherman, Geneva. 1997. "Black Language and the Education of Children: One Mo Once." *The Black Scholar* 27(1):28–35.

Snell, Bradford C. 1974. *American Ground Transport.* Committee Print of the Subcommittee on Antitrust and Monopoly of the Committee on the Judiciary, U.S. Senate, February 26.

So, Alvin Y. 1990. *Social Change and Development: Modernization, Dependency, and World System Theories.* Newbury Park, Calif.: Sage.

Spener, David, and Frank D. Bean. 1999. "Self-Employment Concentration and Earnings among Mexican Immigrants." *Social Forces* 77:1021–1047.

Spengler, Oswald. [1922] 1928. *The Decline of The West.* Vol. 2. New York: Alfred A. Knopf.

———. 1932. *Man and Technics.* New York: Alfred A. Knopf.

Spohn, Cassia, John Gruhl, and Susan Welch. 1987. "The Impact of Ethnicity and Gender of Defendants on the Decision to Reject or Dismiss Felony Charges." *Criminology* 25:175–191.

Stack, Carol. 1974. *All Our Kin.* New York: Harper and Row.

Stahura, John M. 1986. "Suburban Development, Black Suburbanization, and the Civil Rights Movement Since World War II." *American Sociological Review* 51:131–144.

Stansell, Christine. 1986. *City of Women: Sex and Class in New York, 1789 to 1860.* New York: Alfred A. Knopf.

State of New York. [1857] 1963. "The Slums of New York." Excerpted from the "Report of the Select Committee Appointed to Examine Into the Condition of Tenant Houses in New York and Brooklyn." In *The American City: A Documentary History,* edited by Charles N. Glaab, 260–278. Homewood, Ill.: Dorsey.

Stearns, Linda Brewster, and John R. Logan. 1986. "The Racial Structuring of the Housing Market and Segregation in Suburban Areas." *Social Forces* 65:28–42.

Steffens, Lincoln. 1904. *The Shame of the Cities.* Cambridge, Mass.: McClure, Phillips.

Stein, Howard F., and Robert F. Hill. 1977. *The Ethnic Imperative: Examining the New White Ethnic Movement.* University Park, Pa.: Pennsylvania State University Press.

Steinberg, Stephen. 1981. *The Ethnic Myth: Race, Ethnicity, and Class in America.* New York: Atheneum.

Steiner, Stan. 1974. *The Islands: The Worlds of the Puerto Ricans.* New York: Harper and Row.

Still, Bayrd. 1956. *Mirror for Gotham: New York as Seen by Contemporaries from Dutch Days to the Present.* New York: New York University Press.

———. 1974. *Urban America: A History with Documents.* Boston: Little, Brown.

Stretton, Hugh. 1978. *Urban Planning in Rich and Poor Countries.* Oxford, England: Oxford University Press.

Strong, Josiah. [1885] 1968. "Perils—the City." In *The American City: A Sourcebook of Urban Imagery,* edited by Anselm L. Strauss, 127–134. Chicago: Aldine.

Studlar, Donley T. 1979. "Labor Importing: The United Kingdom." In *International Labor Migration in Europe,* edited by Ronald E. Krane, 88–117. New York: Praeger.

Suarez, Ray. 1999. *The Old Neighborhood: What We Lost in the Great Suburban Migration: 1966–1999.* New York: The Free Press.

Sullivan, Neil J. 1998. "Major league baseball and American cities: a strategy for playing the stadium game." *Policy Studies Review* (Spring) 15:55–64.

Sullivan, Patricia A., and Shirley P. Damrosch. 1987. "Homeless Women and Children." In *The Homeless in Contemporary Society,* edited by Richard D. Bingham et al., 82–98. Beverly Hills, Calif.: Sage.

Summers, Gene F., Sharon D. Evans, Frank Clemente, E. M. Beck, and Jon Minkoff. 1976. *Industrial Invasion of Nonmetropolitan America: A Quarter Century of Experience.* New York: Praeger.

Summers, Gene F., and Jean M. Lang. [1976] 1978. "Bringing Jobs to People: Does It Pay?" In *Change in Rural America,* edited by Richard D. Rodefeld, Jan Flora, Donal Voth, Isao Fujimoto, and Jim Converse, 410–416. St. Louis: C. V. Mosby. (Reprinted from *Small Town.* Ellensberg, Wash.: Small Town Institute.)

Suro, Roberto. 1999. "Crossing the High-Tech Divide." *American Demographics* (July) 21:54–60.

Sutcliffe, Anthony. 1981. *Toward the Planned City: Germany, Britain, the United States, and France.* New York: St. Martin's Press.

Suttles, Gerald D. 1968. *The Social Order of the Slum: Ethnicity and Territory in the Inner City.* Chicago: University of Chicago Press.

———. 1972. *The Social Construction of Communities.* Chicago: University of Chicago Press.

Svensson, Frances. 1980. "Ethnicity Versus Communalism: The American Indian Movement and the Politics of Survival." In *The Mobilization of Collective Identity: Comparative Perspectives,* edited by Jeffrey A. Ross and Ann Baker Cottrell, 65–78. Lanham, Md.: University Press of America.

Swartz, Marc J., ed. 1969. *Local-Level Politics: Social and Cultural Perspectives.* London: London University Press.

Sweeney, Richard. 1993. *Out of Place: Homeless in America.* New York: Harper Collins.

Szelenyi, Ivan. 1983. *Urban Inequalities Under State Socialism.* London: Oxford University Press.

———. 1977. "Urban Sociology and Community Studies in Eastern Europe." *Comparative Urban Research* 4:11–20.

Szelenyi, Ivan. 1996. "Cities Under Socialism—And After." In *Cities After Socialism: Urban and Regional Change and Conflict in Post-Socialist Societies,* edited by Gregory Andrusz, Michael Harloe, and Ivan Szelenyi, 286–317. Cambridge, Mass.: Blackwell.

Tabb, William K., and Larry Sawers. 1978. "Editors' Introduction," In *Marxism and the Metropolis: New Perspectives in Urban Political Economy,* edited by William K. Tabb and Larry Sawers. New York: Oxford University Press.

———. 1984. *Marxism and the Metropolis: New Perspectives in Urban Political Economy.* 2nd ed. New York: Oxford University Press.

Taeuber, Karl E. 1983. "Racial Residential Segregation, 28 Cities, 1970–1980." Working Paper 83–12, Center for Demography and Ecology, University of Wisconsin, Madison.

Taeuber, Karl E., and Alma F. Taeuber. 1965. *Negroes in Cities: Residential Segregation and Neighborhood Change.* Chicago: Aldine.

Tang, Kwong-leung. 1999. "Social Development in China: Progress and Problems." *Journal of Contemporary Asia* 29:95–108.

Tangri, Shanti S. 1982. "Family Structure and Industrial Entrepreneurship in India: The Evolution of a Field Study." In *Towards a Political Economy of Urbanization in Third World Countries,* edited by Helen I. Safa, 188–207. New Delhi: Oxford University Press.

Testa, William A. 1992. "Producer Services: Trends and Prospects for the Seventh District." *Economic Perspectives* (Federal Reserve Board of Chicago), Vol. 16, No. 3:19–28.

Thorbek Susanne. 1987. *Voices From the City—Women of Bangkok.* London: Zed Books.

Till, Thomas E. 1981. "Manufacturing Industry: Trends and Impact." In *Nonmetropolitan America in Transition,* edited by Amos H. Hawley and Sara Mills Mazie, 194–230. Chapel Hill, N.C.: University of North Carolina Press.

Todaro, Michael P. [1979] 1984. "Urbanization in Developing Nations: Trends, Prospects, and Policies." In *Urban Development in the Third World,* edited by Pradip K. Ghosh, 7–26. Westport, Conn.: Greenwood.

Tönnies, Ferdinand. [1887] 1940. *Fundamental Concepts of Sociology (Gemeinschaft und Gesellschaft).* Translated by Charles P. Loomis. New York: American Book Company.

Trench, Sylvia, and Sallie Jones. 1995. "Planning for Women's Safety in Cities." *Women and Environments* (Spring) 14(2):12–14.

Tsai, Frank Wen-Hui. 1980. "Diversity and Conflict Between Old and New Chinese Immigrants in the United States." In *Sourcebook on the New Immigration: Implications for the United States and the International Community,* edited by Roy Simon Bryce-Laporte, 327–337. New Brunswick, N.J.: Transaction Books.

Turner, John F. C. 1982. "Issues in Self-help and Self-managed Housing." In *Self-help Housing: A Critique,* edited by Peter M. Ward, 99–113. New York: Mansell.

Tweedie, Jack, Dana Reichert, and Matthew O'Connor. 1999. "Tracking Recipients after They Leave Welfare." Children and Families Program, National Conference of State Legislatures, Welfare Reform Home Page: Human Services and Welfare. INFO@NCSL.ORG.

Tweeten, Luther, and George L. Brinkman. 1976. *Micropolitan Development: Theory and Practice of Greater Rural Economic Development.* Ames, Iowa: Iowa State University Press.

Udovitch, A. L. 1977. "A Tale of Two Cities: Commercial Relations Between Cairo and Alexandria During the Second Half of the Eleventh Century." In *The Medieval City,* edited by H. A. Miskimin, David Herlihy, and A. L. Udovitch, 143–162. New Haven, Conn.: Yale University Press.

United Nations. 1980. *Patterns of Urban and Rural Population Growth.* New York: Unipub.

United Nations. 1983. *Demographic Yearbook, 1981.* New York: Department of International Economics and Social Affairs.

United Nations. 1988. *World Demographic Estimates and Projections, 1950–2025.* New York: United Nations.

United Nations. 1992a. *Demographic Yearbook, 1991.* New York: United Nations.

United Nations. 1992b. *World Population Monitoring: Population Studies 126.* New York: United Nations.

United Nations. 1997a. *Demographic Yearbook 1995.* New York: United Nations.

United Nations. 1997b. *World Demographic Trends.* Commission on Population and Development, Thirtieth Session, February 1997. Population Information Network, Gopher Website of the United Nations Population Division.

United Nations Population Division. 1999. *World Urbanization Prospects: The 1999 Revision.* (undp.org/popin/wdtrends/urbanization.pdf).

U.S. Bureau of the Census. 1952. *Census of the Population, 1950, Number of Inhabitants.* Washington, D.C.: U.S. Government Printing Office.

U.S. Bureau of the Census. 1981. *Summary: General Social and Economic Characteristics.* Washington, D.C.: U.S. Government Printing Office.

U.S. Bureau of the Census. 1982. *1980 Census of the Population.* Vol. 1. *Characteristics of the Population.* Washington, D.C.: U.S. Government Printing Office.

U.S. Bureau of the Census. 1984. *Statistical Abstract of the United States 1985.* Washington, D.C.: U.S. Government Printing Office.

U.S. Bureau of the Census. 1986. *Statistical Abstract of the United States 1987.* Washington, D.C.: U.S. Government Printing Office.

U.S. Bureau of the Census. 1992a. *Statistical Abstract of the United States 1992.* Washington, D.C.: U.S. Government Printing Office.

U.S. Bureau of the Census. 1992b. *Poverty in the United States: 1991.* Washington, D.C.: U.S. Government Printing Office.

U.S. Bureau of the Census. 1993. *Population and Housing Characteristics for Census Tracts and Block Numbering Areas.* Washington, D.C.: U.S. Bureau of the Census.

U.S. Bureau of the Census. 1996. *Statistical Abstract of the United States 1996.* Washington, D.C.: Bureau of the Census.

U.S. Bureau of Labor Statistics. 1996. *Worker Displacement During the Mid-1990s (Based on Revised Estimates).* http://www.bls.census.gov/cps/pub/disp_htm. Washington, D.C.: U.S. Bureau of Labor Statistics.

U.S. Department of Agriculture. 1981. *A Time to Choose: Summary Report on the Structure of Agriculture.* Washington, D.C.: U.S. Government Printing Office.

U.S. Department of Agriculture. 1984. *Chartbook of Nonmetro-Metro Trends.* Washington, D.C.: Economic Research Service.

U.S. Department of Agriculture. 1991. *Agricultural Statistics, 1991.* Washington, D.C.: U.S. Government Printing Office.

U.S. Department of Commerce. 1986. *Statistical Abstract of the United States, 1987.* Washington, D.C.: U.S. Government Printing Office.

U.S. Department of Commerce. 1996. *Poverty in the United States: 1995.* Washington, D.C.: Bureau of the Census.

U.S. Department of Education. 1996. *Urban Schools: The Challenge of Location and Poverty.* Washington, D.C.: U.S. Government Printing Office.

U.S. Department of Housing and Urban Development. 1979a. *Displacement Report.* Washington, D.C.: U.S. Government Printing Office.

U.S. Department of Housing and Urban Development. 1979b. *How Well Are We Housed? Hispanics.* Washington, D.C.: U.S. Government Printing Office.

U.S. Department of Housing and Urban Development. 1979c. *Developmental Needs of Small Cities.* Washington, D.C.: U.S. Government Printing Office.

U.S. Department of Housing and Urban Development. 1992. *State Enterprise Zone Update: Summaries of the State Enterprise Zone Programs.* Washington, D.C.: U.S. Department of Housing and Urban Development.

U.S. Department of Labor. 1991. *Geographic Profile of Employment and Unemployment, 1990.* Washington, D.C.: U.S. Government Printing Office.

U.S. Department of Labor. 1992. "Employment Growth in Largest Metropolitan Areas, 1991." *News* (Release) (June 12):1–3.

Urbanism Committee of the National Resources Committee. 1937. *Our Cities: Their Role in the National Economy.* As reprinted in Charles N.

Glaab. 1963. *The American City: A Documentary History.* Homewood, Ill.: Dorsey.

Valentine, Charles A. 1968. *Culture and Poverty: Critique and Counterproposals.* Chicago: University of Chicago Press.

Valuation Network, Inc. 1993. *Viewpoint 1993: Real Estate Value Trends.* Special Information Supplement to *National Real Estate Investor* (March) Vol. 15, No. 3.

Van Valey, Thomas L., Wade Clark Roof, and Jerome E. Wilcox. 1977. "Trends in Residential Segregation: 1960–1970." *American Journal of Sociology* 82:826–844.

van Weesep, Jan. 1988. "Regional and Urban Development in the Netherlands: The Retreat of Government." *Geography* 73:97–104.

Van Yoder, Steven. 1999. "Buoyant Despite the Baht: Thailand's Economic Meltdown was Bad News for Locals, but for Electronics Exporters There Was an Upside." *Electronic Business* (July) 25:42.

Varady, David P. 1986. *Neighborhood Upgrading: A Realistic Assessment.* Albany, N.Y.: State University of New York Press.

Vergarra, Camillo Jose. 1994. "Our Fortified Ghettos." *The Nation* (January 31) 258:121–124.

Vidich, Arthur J., and Joseph Bensman. [1958] 1968. *Small Town in Mass Society: Class, Power, and Religion in a Rural Community.* Princeton, N.J.: Princeton University Press.

Villani, John. 1998. *The 100 Best Small Art Towns in America,* 3rd ed. Santa Fe: John Muir Publications.

Vissing, Yvonne M., and Joseph Diament. 1997. "Housing Distress Among Homeless Students." *Social Work* 42:31–42.

Voss, Paul R., and Glenn Fuguitt. 1979. *Turnaround Migration in the Upper Great Lakes Region.* Madison, Wisc.: University of Wisconsin Press.

Wain, Barry. 1981. *The Refused: The Agony of the Indochina Refugees.* New York: Simon and Schuster.

Wallerstein, Immanuel. 1979. *The Capitalist World Economy.* New York: Cambridge University Press.

———. 1980. *The Modern World System II: Mercantilism and the Consolidation of the European World Economy, 1600–1750.* New York: Academic Press.

Walton, John. 1975. "Internal Colonialism: Problems of Definition and Measurement." In *Urbanization and Inequality: The Political Economy of Urban and Rural Development in Latin America. Latin American Urban Research,* Vol. 5, edited by Wayne A. Cornelius and Felicity M. Trueblood, 29–50. Beverly Hills, Calif.: Sage.

———. 1979. "Urban Political Economy: A New Paradigm." *Comparative Urban Research* 7:5–17.

Wang, Gabe T., and Xiaobo Hu. 1999. "Small Town Development and Rural Urbanization in China." *Journal of Contemporary Asia* 29:76–94.

Ward, Janet. 2000a. "Mayors Want Homelessness Back on National Agenda." *American City and Country* (February) 115:4.

———. 2000b. "Rebel with a Cause." (April) *American City and Country* 115:20–31.

Warner, Sam Bass, Jr. 1962. *Streetcar Suburbs: The Process of Growth in Boston, 1870–1900.* Cambridge, Mass.: Harvard University Press.

———. 1972. *The Urban Wilderness: A History of the America City.* New York: Harper and Row.

Warren, Roland L. [1963] 1972. *The Community in America,* 2nd ed. Chicago: Rand McNally.

Warren, Stacy. 1994. "Disneyfication of the Metropolis: Popular Resistance in Seattle." *Journal of Urban Affairs* 16:89–107.

Waxman, Chaim I. 1983. *The Stigma of Poverty: A Critique of Poverty Theories and Policy,* 2nd ed. New York: Pergamon.

Weber, Adna F. [1899] 1965. *The Growth of Cities in the Nineteenth Century: A Study in Statistics.* Ithaca, N.Y.: Cornell University Press.

Weber, Max. [1905] 1958. "The City." In *The City,* translated and edited by Don Martindale and Gertrud Neuwirth, 63–89. Glencoe, Ill.: The Free Press.

Weimer, David R. 1966. *The City as Metaphor.* New York: Random House.

Weinhold, Robert S. 1997. *Rating Guide to Environmentally Healthy Metro Areas.* Durango, Colo.: Animas Press.

Wellman, Barry, and Barry Leighton. 1979. "Networks, Neighborhoods, and Communities: Approaches to the Study of the Community Question." *Urban Affairs Quarterly* 14:363–390.

Wenke, Robert J. 1980. *Patterns in Prehistory: Mankind's First Three Million Years.* New York: Oxford University Press.

West, Cornel. 1992. "Philosophy and the Urban Underclass." In *The Underclass Question,* edited by Bill E. Lawson, 191–201. Philadelphia: Temple University Press.

———. 1993. *Race Matters.* Boston: Beacon.

White, Morton, and Lucia White. 1962. *The Intellectual Versus the City.* Cambridge, Mass.: Harvard University and M.I.T. Presses.

Whyte, William Foote. 1943. *Street Corner Society.* Chicago: University of Chicago Press.

Whyte, William H. 1988. *City: Rediscover the Center.* New York: Doubleday.

Wilcox, Brian L. 1981. "Social Support in Adjusting to Marital Disruption." In *Social Networks and Social Support,* edited by Benjamin H. Gottlieb, 97–115. Beverly Hills, Calif.: Sage.

Wildman, Sarah. 2000. "A Day at the National Mall." *The New Republic* (May 15) 222:14.

Wilhelm, Sidney M. 1986a. "The Economic Demise of Blacks in America: Prelude to Genocide?" *Journal of Black Studies* 17:201–254.

———. 1986b. "Introduction: The Economic State of Black America." *Journal of Black Studies* 17: 139–147.

Wilkening, E. A., Joao Bosco Pinto, and Jose Pastore. 1968. "Role of the Extended Family in Migration and Adaptation in Brazil." *Journal of Marriage and the Family* 30:689–695.

Williams, Jack F. 1983. "Cities of East Asia." In *Cities of the World: World Regional Urban Development,* edited by Stanley D. Brunn and Jack F. Williams, 409–450. New York: Harper and Row.

Williams, Jason. 1999. "Football Fans Rumble on Daily Web Sites." *Fourth Estate* (September 29) 132:9.

Williams, Peter, and Neil Smith. 1986. "From `Renaissance' to Restructuring: The Dynamics of Contemporary Urban Development." In *Gentrification of the City,* edited by Neil Smith and Peter Williams, 204–224. Boston: Allen and Unwin.

Williams, Terry M., and William Kornblum. 1985. *Growing Up Poor.* Lexington, Mass.: Lexington Books.

Wilson, Elizabeth. 1991. *The Sphinx in the City.* Berkeley: University of California Press.

Wilson, Franklin D. 1984. "Urban Ecology: Urbanization and Systems of Cities." *Annual Review of Sociology* 10:283–307.

Wilson, James Q. 1983. *Thinking About Crime.* Revised Edition. New York: Vintage.

Wilson, William Julius. 1978. *The Declining Significance of Race: Blacks and Changing American Institutions.* Chicago: University of Chicago Press.

———. 1983. "Inner-City Dislocations." *Society* 21:80–86.

———. 1984. "The Urban Underclass." In *Minority Report: What Has Happened to Blacks, Hispanics, American Indians and Other Minorities in the Eighties,* edited by Leslie W. Dunbar, 75–117. New York: Pantheon.

———. 1987. *The Truly Disadvantaged: The Inner City, The Underclass, and Public Policy.* Chicago: University of Chicago Press.

———. 1996. *When Work Disappears: The World of the New Urban Poor.* New York: Alfred A. Knopf.

Winsberg, Morton D. 1983. "Changing Distribution of the Black Population: Florida Cities, 1970–1980." *Urban Affairs Quarterly* 18:361–370.

Wirth, Louis. 1928. *The Ghetto.* Chicago: University of Chicago Press.

———. 1938. "Urbanism as a Way of Life." *American Journal of Sociology* 40:1–24.

———. 1945. "The Problem of Minority Groups." In *The Science of Man in the World Crisis,* edited by Ralph Linton, 347–372. New York: Columbia University Press.

Woodrow, Karen, and Jeffrey S. Passel. 1990. "Post-IRCA Undocumented Immigration to the United States: An Assessment Based on the June 1988 CPS." In *Undocumented Migration to the United States: IRCA and the Experience of the 1980s,* edited by Frank D. Bean, Barry Edmonston, and Jeffrey S. Passel, 33–76. Santa Monica, Calif.: Rand Corporation.

World Bank. 1984. *World Development Report 1984.* New York: Oxford University Press.

World Bank. 1992. *World Development Report 1992: Development and the Environment.* New York: Oxford University Press.

World Bank. 1993. *World Development Report 1993.* New York: Oxford University Press.

World Bank. 1997. *World Development Report 1997: The State in a Changing World.* New York: Oxford University Press.

World Bank. 2000. *World Development Report 1999/2000: Entering the 21st Century.* New York: Oxford University Press.

Worsnop, Richard L. 1996. "Helping the Homeless: Will Cuts in Welfare Spending Cause Hardships?" *C.Q. Researcher* 6:75–92.

Wyatt, David K. 1984. *Thailand: A Short History.* New Haven, Conn.: Yale University Press.

Xie, Yichun, and Frank J. Costa. 1991. "The Impact of Economic Reforms on the Urban Economy of the People's Republic of China." *The Professional Geographer* 43:318–335.

Xoomsai, Tawanchai N. 1987. *Bangkok, Thailand: The Quality of Life and Environment in a Primate City.* Working Paper No. 48, Joint Centre on Modern Asia. Toronto: University of Toronto/York University.

Young, Iris Marion. 1990. *Justice and the Politics of Difference.* Princeton, N.J.: Princeton University Press.

Young, Michael, and Peter Willmott. 1957. *Family and Kinship in East London.* Baltimore: Penguin.

Zimbalist, Andrew. 1998. "The economics of stadiums, teams and cities." *Policy Studies Review* (Spring) 15:17–29.

Zimmer, Basil G. 1975. "The Urban Centrifugal Drift." In *Metropolitan America in Contemporary Perspective,* edited by Amos H. Hawley and Vincent P. Rock, 23–91. New York: John Wiley and Sons.

Zukin, Sharon. 1995. *The Cultures of Cities.* Cambridge, Mass.: Blackwell.

Zunz, Oliver. 1982. *The Changing Face of Inequality: Urbanization, Industrial Development, and Immigrants in Detroit, 1880–1920.* Chicago: University of Chicago Press.

NAME INDEX

SUBJECT INDEX